Sheiley Pope 981-09

W9-ALX-603
ork University

POETRY AND PROSE
OF
ALEXANDER POPE

RIVERSIDE EDITIONS

RIVERSIDE EDITIONS

UNDER THE GENERAL EDITORSHIP OF

Gordon N. Ray

Poetry and Prose

of

ALEXANDER POPE

SELECTED WITH AN INTRODUCTION AND NOTES BY

AUBREY WILLIAMS

University of Florida

HOUGHTON MIFFLIN COMPANY · BOSTON

NEW YORK · ATLANTA · GENEVA, ILL. · DALLAS · PALO ALTO

COPYRIGHT © 1969 BY AUBREY WILLIAMS

All rights reserved. No part of this work may be reproduced or transmitted in any form or by any means, electronic or mechanical, including photocopying and recording, or by any information storage or retrieval system, without permission in writing from the publisher.

PRINTED IN THE U.S.A.

ISBN: 0-395-05156-8

TO
Michael, Christopher, Katharine,
Mary Margaret, Rachel,
and Donald

CONTENTS

INTRODUCTION

I. Pope's Life

Alexander Pope, the child of Roman Catholic parents, was born in London on May 21, 1688, a year fateful to all Englishmen, but especially so to English Catholics. The nation, stirred to a pitch of resentment by the fatuous and bigoted policies of a Catholic king, James II, in the month after Pope's birth invited William of Orange to enter England for the purpose of restoring free elections to Parliament and ensuring a Protestant succession to the throne. William, a stern and able Dutch prince who had married James's eldest daughter Mary, made a peaceable invasion of the south of England in November, and a few weeks later James, completely unnerved by the rush and press of events, abandoned his kingdom and fled to France. On December 18 William entered London, and two months later he and Mary, who had been raised a Protestant, accepted the crown as joint rulers of England. With the "Glorious Revolution" of 1688 thus accomplished, repressive measures against Roman Catholics were soon enacted: Catholics could not openly practice their religion, could not live within ten miles of London, could not hold public office, could not take degrees at public schools or universities, could not purchase land.

Such measures were not always strictly enforced, but nevertheless Pope grew up at a time when Catholics, even the most patriotic and loyal to the crown, were widely regarded as playing an alien and subversive role in the national life. He grew up, indeed, in the very shadow of the London Monument, which a few years before his birth had been erected in memory of the Great Fire of 1666 and which bore an inscription accusing Catholics of setting London ablaze in a plot against Protestantism and English liberty. The deep personal indignation roused in Pope by such mistrustful regard of all Catholics, loyal and disloyal alike, rises again and again in his poetry, and nowhere more scornfully than in his allusion to that very site "Where London's column, pointing at the skies/ Like a tall bully, lifts the head, and lyes."

The revolutionary, though relatively bloodless, upheavals of 1688, when "mighty William's thundring Arm prevail'd," led the poet's father, a moderately well-to-do cloth merchant, to retire from business. For a time he maintained his family within the environs of London, but then, around 1700, he moved them outside the ten-mile limit to a small property of 14 acres at Binfield, in Windsor Forest. During this period his son, barred as he was by his religion from normal schooling, received an education, of sorts: his Aunt Elizabeth early taught him to read, and from his father he learned what he later considered "The better Art to know the good from bad." When he was eight he was sent for a time to a school near Winchester, but there he was so cruelly whipped for a satire against his master that his father brought him home. After this experience his education was on the whole informal, yet also astonishingly good, and largely of his own devising: at about twelve he taught himself Greek and Latin, and at about fifteen he went up to London alone to learn French and Italian. Given only sporadic tutoring throughout most of his youth, and that mainly by various priests at home, he seemed in later life the equal in learning of men educated at Oxford and Cambridge.

As a child Pope was of a "particularly sweet temper," with a face that was "round, plump, pretty, and of a fresh complexion." But at the age of twelve, having survived a wound in his throat given by a wild cow that beat him down and trampled over him, he was taken with the illness, probably a tubercular infection, which in four years time utterly changed his form and ruined his constitution, so that for the rest of his life he would seem to "have the headache four days in the week, and to be as sick as a breeding woman the other three." When he was barely twenty his friend William Wycherley, the dramatist, felt compelled to hope that his "great, Vigorous, and active Mind" would not be able to wear out and destroy his "little, tender, and crazy Carcass," and even at full maturity he was described by the painter Sir Joshua Reynolds as standing only "about four feet six high, very hump-backed and deformed":

> He had a very large and very fine eye, and a long handsome nose; his mouth had those peculiar marks which are always found in the mouths of crooked persons, and the muscles which run across the cheeks were so strongly marked as to appear like small cords.

In his youth Pope himself often doubted that the "scurvy tenement" of his body would "last long above ground," but then he would go on: "I care not, I'm only a lodger." And towards the end of his life he seems to condense in a mere four lines a lifetime of fortitude in the face of great and crippling personal deformity:

> What is't to me (a Passenger God wot)
> Whether my Vessel be first-rate or not?
> The Ship it self may make a better figure,
> But I that sail, am neither less nor bigger.

Remarkably precocious as a child, Pope by the age of twelve had written a kind of play, mainly a collection of speeches from the *Iliad.*

and soon after this he wrote four books of an epic poem which he later described as being "Milton's style in one part, and Cowley's in another; here the style of Spenser imitated, and there of Statius; here Homer and Virgil, and there Ovid and Claudian." Such precocity, associated as it was with a winning and even "maddish way" of manner, inevitably attracted attention in the small community of families around Binfield: as one visitor remarked after being in Pope's company when he was about fourteen, "Igad, that young fellow will either be a madman or make a very great poet." Attention and favor of a very special kind certainly came early from the most distinguished of Pope's neighbors, Sir William Trumbull, a retired Secretary of State. With Sir William, Pope spent long hours discussing the classics while riding on horseback through Windsor Forest, and from this same elderly friend he first received the suggestion that he write a poem on the Forest and also undertake a full-scale translation of Homer. Through Sir William, moreover, Pope probably met Wycherley, who in turn may have introduced him to the playwright William Congreve and to William Walsh, a minor poet and critic. In any event, on April 20, 1706, when Pope was yet seventeen, he received this note from Jacob Tonson, the foremost publisher of the day:

> Sir, — I have lately seen a pastoral of yours in mr. Walsh's & mr. Congreves hands, which is extremely fine & is generally approv'd of by the best Judges in poetry. I Remember I have formerly seen you at my shop & am sorry I did not Improve my Acquaintance with you. If you design your Poem for the Press no person shall be more Carefull in the printing of it, nor no one can give a greater Incouragement to it; than Sir Your Most Obedient Humble Servant.

Tonson eventually published the four poems of the *Pastorals* in 1709, and the years intervening were spent by Pope in gathering, from writers both ancient and modern, the critical learning soon to be so flashingly displayed in *An Essay on Criticism.* In 1707 Sir William Trumbull wrote to his nephew: "our little Poet . . . is gone a dreadful long Journey into Worcestershire, to Mr. Walsh, from whence I never expect to see the poor Creature return: He look'd, & really was no more than a shaddow. . . . If ever I see him again, he will come full-freighted with new Criticisms." Two months later the nephew replied from London that he had met Pope by accident near Temple Bar: "The little man wou'd walk with me from thence to the farther end of St. James's Park, and all that way he plied me with Criticisms and Scraps of Poetry."

An Essay on Criticism appeared in 1711, and shortly thereafter Joseph Addison, in *The Spectator,* No. 253, called it "a Master-piece in its Kind." But Addison also deplored some "strokes" of satire Pope had administered to John Dennis, a leading critic of the time who was famous for his irascibility and who had recently written a very bad play called *Appius and Virginia*. In his poem Pope had slighted Dennis twice, once in the guise of a bigoted critic named Appius, who

> reddens at each Word you speak,
> And *stares, Tremendous!* with a *threatning Eye,*
> Like some *fierce Tyrant* in *Old Tapestry!*

Dennis's immediate and wrathful reaction to these lines was an extravagant thirty-page pamphlet entitled *Reflections Critical and Satyrical, upon a late Rhapsody, call'd, An Essay upon Criticism,* in which Pope's poem is found to be utterly despicable and his mind and body even more so: Pope is declared to be as "venomous" and "stupid" and "impotent" as "a hunch-back'd Toad," a libeller of "Protestant Kings," a "squat, short Gentleman" shaped like "the very Bow of the God of Love," stamped with the "outward Form" of "downright Monkey." And Dennis went on: "had he been born of *Græcian* Parents, and his Father by consequence had by Law had the absolute Disposal of him, his Life had been no longer than that of one of his Poems, the Life of half a day."

To so gross and savage an onset Pope, then twenty-three, made no answer. Instead he retired to the rural community around Binfield, there to find solace in correspondence with an older Catholic friend, John Caryll, and there to be diverted by "Two of the finest faces in the Universe," those of two young sisters, Martha and Teresa Blount, granddaughters of a Catholic neighbor. From such friends as these, moreover, he now received the inspiration for his next poems, one a peerless achievement. For Martha Blount, who was to be his lifelong friend and who later was thought by some to be his mistress, he wrote the poetical epistle *To Miss Blount, With the Works of Voiture*. Much more important, he was at this time told by Caryll of a quarrel between two families, the Fermors and the Petres: the young Lord Petre had clipped a lock from Miss Arabella Fermor's hair, and Caryll asked Pope to write a poem about the incident that would laugh the families together again. Pope's response was an incomparable poem in the mock-epic mode, *The Rape of the Lock,* at first published in two cantos in 1712, and then expanded to five cantos in 1714.

During the early years of his career most, though not all, of Pope's friends were adherents of the Tory rather than of the Whig party, but even so he tried, for a time at least, to remain personally neutral in political affairs. And though his Roman Catholic heritage must in any case have disposed him to the more traditional and conservative principles of the Tory cause, he was at this time drawn back to London and there confirmed, by various circumstances, in a set of lifelong friendships and allegiances. For one thing he found himself an object of growing envy and hostility among a group of Whig writers Addison had gathered about himself at Button's Coffee-house. For another, he now formed intimate friendships with the most distinguished writers and statesmen of the Tory government then in power under Queen Anne, the monarch who in 1702 had succeeded William III to the throne and who represented the end of the Stuart line in England. These new friends included Jonathan Swift, the government's ablest literary polemicist; Dr. John Arbuthnot, Queen Anne's learned and facetious personal physician; Robert Harley, Earl of Oxford, the Lord Treasurer and, in effect, the prime minister; and Henry St. John, Viscount Bolingbroke, the Secretary of State. Pope and these men, along with the poets John Gay and the Rev. Thomas Parnell, were soon united in an elaborate scheme to satirize pedantry and false taste in the various branches of every art and science, and from their meetings to this purpose there developed the famed Scriblerus Club, named after a fictive blockhead and pedant to whom they had given the name of Martinus Scriblerus. Formal meetings of the group spanned less than six months, yet its members, individually or collectively, were to create some of the shrewdest satires in English, including *Gulliver's Travels, Peri Bathous,* and *Memoirs of Martinus Scriblerus.* With the death of Queen Anne in August of 1714, this convivial assembly of necessity dissolved, and the advent of a Whig ministry under George I, first of the English Hanoverians, forever precluded a reunion: Swift and Parnell retreated to Ireland; Harley, suspected of favoring the cause of the Stuart line as represented in exile by the son of James II, was imprisoned in the Tower on charges of high treason; Bolingbroke, also charged with high treason, fled to France.

Pope retreated also, again to the country world about Binfield, there to begin work on his translation of the *Iliad.* By now his reputation was such that when his proposals for the translation were announced many of the most eminent persons of the day subscribed to it immediately. And when the first volume appeared in 1715 it not only established his position as the greatest poet of the age, but also brought him the beginnings of the fortune that would make him the first English poet to prosper solely from the public sale of his work and also would enable him to write with indifference to the systems of aristocratic and political patronage which hitherto had governed most literary endeavor. He would never need a noble patron's purse of gold or a governmental sinecure, for now, "thanks to Homer," he could "live and thrive,/ Indebted to no Prince or Peer alive." His triumph at this time was much the sweeter, furthermore, because the public also agreed that his translation far surpassed a rival effort by Thomas Tickell, a protégé of Addison. And because Addison had jealously instigated Tickell's translation in a deliberate effort to undermine Pope's growing reputation as the first poet of his age, Pope at this time composed the scornful lines on Atticus (i.e., Addison) that were to appear so many years later in the *Epistle to Dr. Arbuthnot.*

The remaining five volumes of the *Iliad* appeared in almost annual succession over the next five-year period, up to 1720, and the deep sense of tedium and confinement Pope felt in the task of translating the twenty-four books of the poem emerges clearly in a confession he made long afterwards to his friend Joseph Spence: "What terrible moments does one feel, after one has engaged for a large work! — In the beginning of my translating the Iliad, I wished anybody would hang me, a hundred times. — It sat so heavily on my mind at first, that I often used to dream of it, and do sometimes still." And to this Spence added: "He used to dream that he was engaged in a long journey, puzzled which way to take; and full of fears that he should never get to the end of it."

In 1716 a great surge of anti-Catholic feeling swept England, caused mainly by an uprising in Scotland on the part of Jacobites (supporters of the exiled line of James II). Fear of additional oppressive taxation induced many Catholics to sell their land, and the Popes disposed of their place at Binfield. They settled at Chiswick, on the Thames nearer London, and during 1717 the poet published the first collected edition of his poems, including, among other new pieces, *Eloisa to Abelard,* a poem in which the opposing claims of sacred and profane love were disputed, and ultimately reconciled, in a vivid and often voluptuous style. This year was also saddened, however, by the death of Pope's father, who from the poet's earliest childhood had encouraged and overseen his verses and whom he felt "even more obliged to as a friend, than as a father." Pope wrote to John Gay that "he died easily, without a groan, or the sickness of two minutes; in a word, as silently and peacefully as he lived," and years later, in his *Epistle to Dr. Arbuthnot,* he closed a warm eulogy of his father in precisely such terms:

> His Life, tho' long, to sickness past unknown,
> His Death was instant, and without a groan.
> Oh grant me thus to live, and thus to die!
> Who sprung from Kings shall know less joy than I.

A year after his father's death Pope leased at Twickenham the villa which henceforth was to be his home, about twelve miles from London. Of two stories, the villa faced the Thames, but it was separated from its back five acres by the London Road. To join the two parts of his small estate Pope tunneled a passageway beneath the highway, commenting the while that "What we cannot *overcome,* we must *undergo.*" This subterranean avenue became his famous grotto, its walls furnished with glittering stones and glass and shell gathered or sent from all parts of England, its roof "stellifyed" with Bristol stone, its floor paved with simple pebble and marble. The grotto, he hoped, would be the "best Imitation of Nature" he ever made, and at one time he proposed for it a sentence from Scripture: "Oh come, and see the Works of the Lord!" Eventually the grotto became his "Scene for contemplation," his "Spiritual Retreat" from what he increasingly considered to be the "corrupt and corruptible world within the Vortex of the Court and City" of nearby London. At "Twitnam," in his "Grotto of Friendship and Liberty," attended by those he regarded as his "best" companions, "Chiefs, out of War, and Statesmen, out of Place," he came to his own home truth: "one's chief business is to be really at home."

From his father Pope had inherited a profound love of gardening, and at Twickenham he was soon as happy and busy "in three inches of Gardening, as any man can be in threescore acres" — like "the fellow that spent his life in cutting the twelve apostles in one cherry-stone." In "a bitt of ground that would have been but a plate of salad to Nebuchadnezzar, the first day he was turn'd to graze," he had, he said, "a Theatre, an Arcade, a Bowling green, and what not?" The skill and taste he exhibited in so small a compass soon brought him fame as a landscapist, and by his assistance to noble friends in the shaping of their much more vast and magnificent estates he was soon in the forefront of those who were shifting the emphasis in English landscape gardening from the excessively formal to the irregular and picturesque. In addition, as his letters and poems clearly show, gardening became for Pope emblematic of larger human values and aspirations. From London, "the Land of Perdition," he could retire to the green and serene world of his garden, to "an innocent Employment, and the same that God appointed for his First Man." Gardening was "near a-kin to Philosophy," for, as Cicero has said, *Agricultura proxima sapientiae* (agriculture is next to wisdom). His "passion for a rural life," moreover, led him to believe that "a true relish of the beauties of nature is the most easy preparation and gentlest transition to an enjoyment of those of heaven; as on the contrary a true town life of hurry, confusion, noise, slander, and dissension, is a sort of apprenticeship to hell and its furies." This passion, and his lifelong devotion to his plants and shrubs and flowers, received their best return and commemoration some twenty years after his death, in a line composed by a poet confined in a hospital for the insane: "For Flowers can see, and Pope's Carnations knew him."

Absorbed in his garden and his grotto and his friends, the years between 1720 and 1725 were relatively tranquil for Pope, yet he was at this time busy with a number of projects, some of which were to cause him later turmoil and distress. Part of his time was spent editing the works of two deceased friends, Thomas Parnell and the Duke of Buckinghamshire, tasks that appeared innocent enough at the moment: in his own words, he seemed to have "become, by due gradation of dulness, from a poet a translator, and from a translator, a mere editor." Even so, when the two volumes of Buckingham's works were published in 1723, the government almost immediately seized them as containing passages sympathetic to Jacobitism. The prohibition against the volumes was later lifted, but for a time at least Pope felt himself under suspicion of disaffection to the government. More important for the future, however, were two other developments of these years: his agreement to edit the works of Shakespeare, and his decision to translate the *Odyssey* with the covert collaboration of two minor poets, Elijah Fenton and William Broome.

The edition of Shakespeare, in six volumes, appeared in 1725, and in the very next year Lewis Theobald, an attorney turned poet and scholar, brought out a work entitled *Shakespeare Restored: or, a Specimen of the many Errors, as well Committed, as Unamended, by Mr. Pope in his late Edition of this Poet.* Theobald's exposure of Pope's deficiencies as an editor came hard upon other criticism of his Shakespeare in the weekly journals, and there is no doubt that Pope felt deeply injured by the attacks. He had worked hard, though in unscholarly fashion, on his edition, and much of Theobald's criticism of his labors was both trivial and pedantic, yet his reputation as an editor was now thoroughly smudged. And to add to his sense of harassment he also found himself attacked at this time for misleading the public about the circumstances in which the *Odyssey* was translated and published. Apparently there had been from the start a plan to let the public know eventually that Fenton and Broome were his collaborators in the translation, but for a while at least Pope seemed engaged in a scheme to take credit for the whole.

During the first decade of his literary career, from 1709 to 1719, Pope had written little that could be called personal satire. There were, of course, the few lines on Dennis in *An Essay on Criticism,* the mockery directed at Ambrose Philips's pastorals in *Guardian* No. 40, the equivocal portrait of Addison (not published till much later), and a few witty small poems of no consequence. Even during the next decade, from 1719 to 1728, he was too preoccupied with editing, translating, gardening, and building to answer the multitude of largely gratuitous attacks on his "Father, Mother, Body, Soul, and Muse":

> Full ten year slander'd, did he once reply?
> Three thousand Suns went down on *Welsted*'s Lye.

But it was not to be expected that he would be content merely to cultivate his own garden forever. He had been called by one "an open and mortal *Enemy* to his *Country*" and a "*Popish* Rhymster, bred up with a *Contempt* of the *Sacred Writings*," while others had termed him a mere versifier who had dared to translate Homer without Greek and who had furthermore tricked and swindled the subscribers to the *Odyssey*. Among other names he had been called "an A. P. E.," both for his deformity and for "the initial letter of his christian name, and the initial and final letters of his surname." He had been publicly depicted as a "lurking, way-laying *Coward*" and a "base and foul Pretender to Candour," one whom "God and nature" had "mark'd for want of common *honesty*," and as one who "hired out his *Name* to Booksellers." And so, after two decades of silence in the face of attacks which seemed to grow ever more numerous and slanderous and personal, he at last began to meditate a poem which would not only cast down his enemies in humiliation and dismay but which would also appear, in its larger design, as a defense of civilization itself against all those who in their various ways, public or private, would cheapen or destroy it.

This poem, the *Dunciad*, was worked into shape during long visits by Swift at Twickenham in 1726 and 1727. Then in May of 1728 the first version appeared, in three books and with Lewis Theobald (always presented as "Tibbald" by Pope) crowned as monarch of all duncery and unreason. Though the poem was published anonymously, there was yet no doubt as to the author, and if a contemporary account is to be trusted, the reaction among those whom Pope had made illustrious for their dulness was immediate and violent — and highly gratifying:

> On the Day the Book was first vended, a Crowd of Authors besieg'd the Shop; Entreaties, Advices, Threats of Law, and Battery, nay Cries of Treason were all employ'd, to hinder the coming out of the *Dunciad:* On the other side, the Booksellers and Hawkers made as great Efforts to procure it.

Contrary to his hopes, the *Dunciad* did not rid Pope of his enemies and detractors, but for a period at least it did make their attacks on him seem both feeble and desperate.

If the *Dunciad* threw at least a segment of London's populace into uproar and outrage, a few years later Pope, by an elaborate stratagem, managed to unite the entire town, including the dunces, in warm panegyric of another anonymous poem, *An Essay on Man*. The stratagem itself developed from the biased public reception given in 1731 to the *Epistle to Burlington,* a poem which, among other things, was a satire on the vanity and false taste displayed by any number of the nobility in their houses and estates, but which the dunces and others, by carefully nurtured rumor and gossip, tried to turn into a deliberate lampoon against the estate and person of one particular nobleman, the Duke of Chandos. The campaign against Pope and his poem was completely spiteful and calumnious, but those responsible for it succeeded in their aim of embarrassing the poet by making him seem ungrateful and rancorous towards a man from whom he had received favors and who was, moreover, a good friend of the very Earl of Burlington to whom his poem was addressed.

Evidence of "so great malignity" towards his work made Pope resolve to be doubly cautious in the publication of *An Essay on Man,* a poem which even more than the *Epistle to Burlington* was open, as later events were to prove, to misinterpretation. Accordingly, in early 1733 he published, by his regular bookseller, two poems which bore his name on their title pages: the *Epistle to Bathurst* in January, and the *First Satire of the Second Book of Horace* in February. Having thus established himself publicly as preoccupied with works such as these, he then in late February sent forth, anonymously and by a bookseller not previously associated with his work, the first part of *An Essay on Man.* Over the next few weeks the second and third parts of the poem were likewise published, and according to one story Pope, who had become noted for the exactness of his rhymes, to throw the public off even further went so far as to insert the following bad rhyme in the first edition of the second part:

> A *Cheat!* a *Whore!* who starts not at the Name,
> In all the Inns of Court, or Drury Lane?

All these maneuvers were designed to get an impartial hearing for a poem that could be suspected, by perverse or malicious minds, of harboring unorthodox religious views, and as it turned out, the maneuvers were completely, even amazingly, successful. Not only was the general public enthusiastic in acclaiming what it judged a sublime and noble work of genius, but even Pope's enemies the dunces were hoodwinked into hailing the poem as a great achievement by an unknown writer whose work was "above all commendation." In later editions of the *Dunciad* Pope reprinted, among other "testimonies" to himself, certain of the choicer praises his enemies had thus, all unconsciously, heaped upon his head.

An Essay on Man was conceived originally as both a "general map of man" and as an "Introduction" to a larger poetic design which would embrace the Moral Essays (i.e., the *Epistles to Several Persons*) as well as other poems that were meditated but never actually written. In this larger design the *Essay on Man* was to be the first of four "books," the other three of which were to include poems on such themes as "Knowledge and its limits," "Government, both ecclesiastical and civil," and "Morality, in eight or nine of the most concerning branches of it; four of which would have been the two extremes to each of the Cardinal Virtues." Over the years, however, this original and grandiose scheme was first modified in various ways, then narrowed, and finally abandoned, perhaps because Pope found it beyond his powers, perhaps because he simply wearied of it, perhaps because by now he had discovered, in the "imitation" of Horace and John Donne, a more congenial and pliant poetic mode.

Translation and paraphrase of the satires of Horace, with application of his words to the English scene, had been essayed long before the 1730's, but Pope at this time brought to such attempts a new brilliance and a new and more significant dimension. Falling somewhere between translation and original creation, his Imitations seem to be poems in their own right and to have their own autonomy, yet at the same time they enable him to attack the vices and follies of his own age, and of all ages, with the implication that he is simply a new defender of moral and social values defended by Horace long before. Appropriately enough, furthermore, it is in these poems that the villa and five acres leased by Pope at Twickenham, just outside the reach of London's din, most seem to vie with Horace's ancient villa and farm, in the Sabine hills some thirty miles from Rome, as a setting emblematic of the good and simple life. At Twickenham, among his friends, there was to be found, along with food and drink, "The Feast of Reason and the Flow of Soul." There was to be found "the Virtue and the Art/ To live on little with a chearful heart," and there too, in the passageway he had tunneled under the London Road, the noise and the bustle and the very traffic of the world itself could be subdued, for a time at least, to a mere soothing murmur:

> Know, all the distant Din that World can keep
> Rolls o'er my *Grotto,* and but sooths my Sleep.

But though he could retreat for a time to the privacy and asylum of his garden and grotto, Pope was too much a man of the world to withdraw completely from that world. Very early in his career he had observed that the "life of a Wit is a warfare upon earth," and the truth of his own aphorism was brought home to him once again, in 1733 and 1734, when he found himself embroiled in a "paper war" with two aristocratic and somewhat disreputable members of court society, Lady Mary Wortley Montagu, the clever and accomplished wife of a rich and stolid man of business, and Lord John Hervey, a trusted though profligate adviser to Queen Caroline. Deeply infatuated with Lady Mary at the time he wrote *Eloisa to Abelard* (where he seems in the closing lines to lament her absence from England), Pope gradually and for quite obscure reasons became estranged from her, and by 1728 he felt antagonistic enough to name her in an oblique and disparaging couplet in the *Dunciad*. After the outbreak of public hostilities in the early 1730's, when he felt she had collaboated or conspired with Lord Hervey to libel and abuse him in two poetical pamphlets, Lady Mary appears frequently in Pope's verse, most often as a lewd, avaricious, and slovenly poetess called Sappho. The weak and effeminate Lord Hervey, sometimes called Lord Fanny or Fannius by Pope, received a more harsh, as well as a most artful, retaliation for his defamatory attacks in the poet's next important poem, the *Epistle to Dr. Arbuthnot;* there, in the person of Sporus, a name Pope derived from the youthful homosexual taken in marriage by the Emperor Nero, Hervey is given fictional magnitude as the very type of lubricious evil.

The events of these years suggested to Pope the need for a poem that would serve as an apologia or defense of his life and writings, and accordingly he wrote to his old friend, Dr. Arbuthnot, then in his last illness: "I determine to addresss to you one of my Epistles, written by piece-meal many years, & which I have now made haste to put together; wherein the Question is stated, what were, & are, my Motives of writing, the Objections to them, & my answers." Published in January, 1735, only two months before the death of the friend who had helped him through the "long disease" of his life, the *Epistle to Dr. Arbuthnot* also stands as Pope's most personal "Bill of Complaint" against

> The Tale reviv'd, the Lye so oft o'erthrown;
> Th' imputed Trash, and Dulness not his own;
> The Morals blacken'd when the Writings scape;
> The libel'd Person, and the pictur'd Shape;
> Abuse on all he lov'd, or lov'd him, spread,
> A Friend in Exile, or a Father, dead.

The poem asserts, furthermore, Pope's conviction that "General Satire in Times of General Vice has no force, and is no Punishment." To

Arbuthnot, who had urged him to be more careful and less personal in his satire, he wrote privately: "To reform and not to chastise, I am afraid is impossible, and the best Precepts, as well as the best Laws, would prove of small use, if there were no Examples to inforce them. To attack Vices in the abstract, without touching Persons, may be safe fighting indeed, but it is fighting with Shadows. General propositions are obscure, misty, and uncertain, compar'd with plain, full, and home examples: Precepts only apply to our Reason, which in most men is but weak: Examples are pictures, and strike the Senses, nay raise the Passions, and call in those (the strongest and most general of all motives) to the aid of reformation."

In the *Dunciad* and in the years before 1735 Pope had frequently derided the courts and administrations of England's first two George's, but on the whole he had attempted to stay clear of direct political engagement. As the 1730's wore on, however, he became intimate with a group of younger politicians, both Whig and Tory, who were united in their opposition to the government of Sir Robert Walpole, the Whig prime minister who, except for a relatively brief interval, had been in power ever since 1715. Styling themselves "Patriots," the group had as its leader Frederick, the Prince of Wales, now completely alienated from his father George II, and included such men as George Lyttleton, William Pitt, and William Pulteney, all prominent Whigs, and Sir William Wyndham, a leading Tory. The degree and importance of Pope's intimacy with these men, as well as their esteem for him as a man of really remarkable moral force, is indicated by the urgings they gave him to be with the Prince as much as possible in order to preserve in him that love of virtue and liberty and the public good by which alone they felt England could be saved from total corruption and ruin. If the country was to be saved from the "Fashion of Knavery" which had almost destroyed all honor and honesty, Lyttleton wrote to Pope, then the Prince should "hear every day from the Man of this Age, who is the Greatest Dispenser of Fame, and will be best heard by Posterity." And if the Prince wished to immortalize himself, added Lyttleton, "the only way he can take, is to deserve a place by his conduct in *some writings*, where he will never be admitted only for his Rank." Once again, as he had been some twenty years earlier in the gatherings of the Scriblerus Club, Pope was near the center of the nation's political life.

Greater participation in political affairs is reflected at this time in the Imitations of Horace, most brazenly and yet cunningly in the *First Epistle of the Second Book* ("To Augustus"). Pope knew well that "too much praise turns irony," and in 1737, when the king had seemed especially neglectful of English interests in order to be on the continent in his native Hanover and in the arms of his German mistress, the poet's praise of George Augustus of England in terms appropriate only to a Caesar Augustus of Rome produced an irony that was devastating, and as impudent as it was unassailable. The very next year, moreover, Pope issued the first of the two poetical "Dialogues" which came to be known as the *Epilogue to the Satires.* Originally called *One Thousand Seven Hundred and Thirty Eight,* the dialogues expatiated freely and corrosively over the moral and political corruptions in England of that year. Pope may have planned one such poem annually, but if so the idea was abandoned, perhaps because of the passage, in 1737, of the Licensing Act, a measure designed to suppress criticism on the stage of Walpole's administration. Certainly some fear of repressive action is voiced in the opening lines of "Dialogue II":

> *Fr.* Tis all a Libel — *Paxton* (Sir) will say.
> *P.* Not yet, my Friend! to-morrow 'faith it may;
> And for that very cause I print to day.

After the two "Dialogues" of 1738 Pope published no further poems in the Horatian manner. Samuel Johnson believed he was pressed into silence by the government, but he may have merely grown weary and disillusioned with political struggle, particularly after he came to suspect certain of his "Patriot" friends of motives more mean and self-interested than patriotic. His public reasons for discontinuing such poems he presented in a final note to "Dialogue II":

> This was the last poem of the kind printed by our author, with a resolution to publish no more; but to enter thus, in the most plain and solemn manner he could, a sort of PROTEST against that insuperable corruption and depravity of manners, which he had been so unhappy as to live to see. Could he have hoped to have amended any, he had continued those attacks; but bad men were grown so shameless and so powerful, that Ridicule was become as unsafe as it was ineffectual. The Poem raised him, as he knew it would, some enemies; but he had reason to be satisfied with the approbation of good men, and the testimony of his own conscience.

In the more private pages of his correspondence with friends, a similarly spent and pessimistic cast of mind is occasionally discovered, and in such letters, as so often before in his life and as in so many of his poems, his personal wars and struggles are given a dramatic configuration and significance much beyond the merely personal and private. In such letters he figures as Virtue's "poor Trumpeter," or as one able only to "Skirmish, and maintain a flying Fight with Vice," whose "Forces augment, and will drive me off the Stage, before I shall see the Effects complete, either of Divine Providence or Vengeance: for sure we can be quite Saved only by the One, or punished by the other: The Condition of Morality is so desperate, as to be above all Human Hands."

As the 1730's drew to a close, Pope was startled by an abrupt assault on his work from a new and entirely unexpected quarter. A Swiss theologian, J. P. de Crousaz, in 1737 and again in 1738, suddenly and violently attacked the *Essay on Man*, declaring the poem inconsistent in its parts and at odds with orthodox Christian doctrines. Crousaz's charges, based on an utterly lame and inadequate French translation of the *Essay*, were largely perverse and unwarranted, but they caused Pope much anxiety of spirit. His relief was considerable, therefore, when the Rev. William Warburton, an Anglican clergyman of a bold and contentious disposition, quite on his own initiative gave a vigorous rebuttal to Crousaz's allegations in a series of public letters. Pope promptly sought the friendship of so resolute a champion, and henceforth Warburton served as his closest literary adviser and became his literary executor after his death.

Pope's life was now nearing its end, but nevertheless he prepared once more to draw "the whole polite world," as well as some not so polite, upon himself with the publication of a new and fourth book of the *Dunciad*. This new book, published separately in 1742, greatly expanded the satire of the original three-book version of the poem, and in it Pope fell upon an "Army of Virtuos', Medalists, Ciceronis, Royal Society-men, Schools, Universities, even Florists, Free Thinkers, and Free masons." In the next year, moreover, all four books were revised and published together, and a new hero installed: in this version Colley Cibber, the actor and playwright and buffoon whom George II had appointed poet laureate of England, replaced Lewis Theobald as the personage most fit to preside over duncery and dulness.

The last year or so of Pope's life was spent mainly in preparing, with Warburton's help, a definitive edition of his works. In late 1743 he began to suffer increasingly from asthma and dropsy, and by the early months of 1744 his condition had become serious. In February, out of fear of a Jacobite invasion from France, the proclamation forbidding Catholics to come within ten miles of London was revived, and so Pope, the frail "papist" whose genius and writings had by now given definition to the very age in which he lived, felt obliged to remain at Twickenham except for brief visits to the famed Dr. William Cheselden at Chelsea Hospital. In April and May he grew steadily weaker, and felt himself dying, as he said, "of a Hundred good Symptoms." Towards the end he received the last sacraments from a priest of the Benedictine order, and then, on Wednesday, May 30, in his fifty-sixth year, he died, "about the Middle of the Night, without a Pang, or a Convulsion, unperceived of those that watched him, who imagined he was only in a sounder Sleep than ordinary."

II. Pope's Poetry

Pope's poetry can move us deeply because it so often stirs us to a sense of the innate precariousness of all things. The uncertainty of riches, the decay of beauty, and the crash of worlds, these are the prevailing themes and subjects of his poems. Abrupt and unceremonious death shatters the beauty of a pheasant:

> See! from the Brake the whirring Pheasant springs,
> And mounts exulting on triumphant Wings;
> Short is his Joy! he feels the fiery Wound,
> Flutters in Blood, and panting beats the Ground.
> Ah! what avail his glossie, varying Dyes,
> His Purple Crest, and Scarlet-circled Eyes,
> The vivid Green his shining Plumes unfold;
> His painted Wings, and Breast that flames with Gold?

Worldly goods are ephemeral, coming and going in a day:

> Estates have wings, and hang in Fortune's pow'r
> Loose on the point of ev'ry wav'ring Hour.

In one early poem, *The Rape of the Lock,* a young girl's beauty and virginity are likened to a frail China jar teetering on the edge of destruction: "Who can say," Pope asked in a letter, "that Glass is frail, when it is not half so perishable as human Beauty, or Glory?" And in a much later poem, the *Dunciad,* civilization and the world itself seem to totter and plunge into chaos and darkness.

So sharp and abiding a sense of the "transitory nature of all human delights" came to Pope in part from everyday experience with his own frail and crazy carcass: "In truth, the constant fear of being in Extremity, on every little Cold I catch, or upon any Heat by Motion, makes Life uncomfortable and precarious." But an even wider sense of the precariousness of all things came to him from the vivid and quite orthodox belief, still very much current in his time, that the universe itself was delicately poised on the edge of nothingness. For in spite of the growing number of persons who tended to view the universe as something created once and for all, a great clockwork mechanism made to run of itself, there still were many who believed that God not only had called the universe out of nothing and into being by an initial act of creation, but also that He *sustained* and *preserved* it at every moment in its existence by a continuing and unflagging exertion of His divine will. The universe, in this view, existed in a state of radical and perilous contingency, "so that without His continuall working, all would return to nothing." Furthermore, as if this fundamental contingency of all existence were not itself precarious enough, against the "continuall working" of God there was ranged the sin of man, and sin by its very nature was considered to be an effort to "invert the world, and counter-work its Cause." As John Donne had put it earlier in the century of Pope's birth:

> Wee seeme ambitious, Gods whole worke t'undoe;
> Of nothing he made us, and we strive too,
> To bring our selves to nothing backe.

The same endeavors and consequences of sin had been strikingly allegorized by Milton in Book II of *Paradise Lost,* a poem even closer to Pope's own time, in Satan's promise to return all of creation to the original sway of Chaos and Old Night in exchange for their help on his journey to earth. The mythic possibilities of so grand and cosmic a reversion of all things are then exploited by Pope in his turn: in the *Dunciad* the earth seems to swarm with a multitude of fools and knaves who strive to blot out order and light and to undo God's whole work. The success of their endeavors to dismantle civilization and raze a world is recorded in the poem's final couplets:

> Lo! thy dread Empire, CHAOS! is restor'd;
> Light dies before thy uncreating word:
> Thy hand, great Anarch! lets the curtain fall;
> And Universal Darkness buries All.

Awareness of the way all life and the creation itself are balanced so precariously on the verge of being has certain consequences. One certainly is a heightened sensitivity to all the losses — of love, beauty, friends, talents, life itself — that daily occur, and which Pope set down so hauntingly in these lines:

> Years foll'wing Years, steal something ev'ry day,
> At last they steal us from our selves away;
> In one our Frolicks, one Amusements end,
> In one a Mistress drops, in one a Friend:
> This subtle Thief of Life, this paltry Time,
> What will it leave me, if it snatch my Rhime?
> If ev'ry Wheel of that unweary'd Mill
> That turn'd ten thousand Verses, now stands still.

Another consequence of such awarness, however, is likely to be the development of a certain fortitude of spirit, and a special deportment, in the face of loss. As Pope remarked in an early letter, "a diffidence in our earthly state" makes us "think of fortifying our selves within, when there is so little dependence upon our out-works." The quite deliberate cultivation of a spirit and manner with which to face life's losses and vicissitudes is, in fact, a notable characteristic of Pope's time, so much so that, quite apart from such arts as those of poetry and painting, there were developed those other very special "arts" of living and of dying. In Pope's own work the concept of an "art of living" is strong and pervasive, and as often as not given both force and particularity by a vocabulary drawn from poetry or drama. In these lines, for example, a particular style and mode of life is given definition by the commonplace terminology of contemporary dramatic criticism:

> Let the strict Life of graver Mortals be
> A long, exact, and serious Comedy,
> In ev'ry Scene some Moral let it teach,
> And, if it can, at once both Please and Preach:
> Let mine, an innocent gay Farce appear,
> And more Diverting still than Regular,
> Have Humour, Wit, a native Ease and Grace;
> Tho' not too strictly bound to Time and Place:
> Cricks in Wit, or Life, are hard to please,
> Few write to those, and none can live to these.

In another set of verses, a growth in age and wisdom recommends, even to poets, an art surpassing that of poetry, one in which the soul itself is tuned to grace and serenity:

> There is a time when Poets will grow dull:
> I'll e'en leave Verses to the Boys at school:
> To Rules of Poetry no more confin'd,
> I learn to smooth and harmonize my Mind,
> Teach ev'ry Thought within its bounds to roll,
> And keep the equal Measure of the Soul.

The deliberate contrivance of an "Art of Contentment," or of a manner designed to view "this dreadful All without a fear," may seem at first a forced and merely artificial undertaking, yet life cultivated in such a way was not necessarily stately, stiff, and staring, nor was it often lacking in actual depth and warmth of feeling. The emphasis, in fact, both in life and in poetry, was on an artfulness that concealed the art, a reflection of an ancient aphorism, *ars est celare artem* — the real art is to hide the art. In life the endeavor was to create an air of "native Ease and Grace," a style that would seem natural and artless. In poetry the endeavor was to create an art which "Works *without Show*" and which is "*It self unseen,* but in th' *Effects,* remains." As

Pope himself observed of the principle as it applied to his own verses, "I correct daily, and make them seem less corrected, that is, more easy, more fluent, more natural."

Mere ease, mere fluency, were not of course considered ends in themselves. Pope believed that "a good Poet will adapt the very Sounds, as well as Words, to the Things he treats of," so that "there is (if one may express it so) a Style of Sound." As this statement clearly suggests, such a "Style of Sound" served no merely ornamental purposes, but rather seemed "an Eccho to the Sense," as in this passage describing the belly of a glutton:

> The stomach (cram'd from ev'ry dish,
> A Tomb of boil'd, *and* roast, *and* flesh, *and* fish,
> Where Bile, *and* wind, *and* phlegm, *and* acid jar,
> *And* all the Man is one intestine war). . . .

The seven "and's" italicized in this passage, in their sound and their spacing, suggest the repetitive movements of a mouth in mastication and suggest also a prolonged act of cramming in, and so sound and measure and sense seem joined in indissoluble poetic union. And here, furthermore, as so often in Pope's work, a passage will be found to have its reserves and reticences, its further ranges of meaning. Thus in these lines the four body secretions of bile, wind, phlegm, and acid (reminders of the four "humours" traditionally thought to govern the health and temperament of the individual man) specifically recall the four elements (earth, air, water, and fire) of which the universe itself was thought to be composed. The intestine jar of these "humours" suggests clearly that the "little world" (the microcosm) of man has become warring and chaotic as a consequence of sin, here typified by gluttony. The wide Renaissance belief that the microcosm of man offers an analogy to the larger universe, the macrocosm, is recollected, and so is the traditional Christian view that every individual act of sin is in some mysterious way a wilful attempt, again like that of Satan in *Paradise Lost,* to reduce the creation to its original darkness and discord.

In addition to its reticences of meaning, Pope's poetry has also its reticences of feeling, yet such reticence scarcely implies that either the meaning or the feeling is less than deep and powerful. In his personal and private life he much preferred, Pope said, the "Qualities of the Heart to those of the Head," and he also considered "One good-natured action or one charitable intention" to be "of more merit than all the rhyming, jingling faculties in the world": the eternal felicity of Heaven itself, he wrote, is not attainable "by the strongest endeavours of the Wit, but may be gain'd by the sincere intentions of the Heart only." In the realm of art, and particularly that of dramatic poetry, he judged "the most material part" to be "the moving the Passions," and added that "if a Writer does not move them, there is no art to teach him." When, moreover, he registered in verse his own definition of a "Poet" (as distinct from a mere "Man of Rymes"), he used the vehement, even fervid, language of these lines:

> Let me for once presume t'instruct the times,
> To know the Poet from the Man of Rymes:
> 'Tis He, who gives my breast a thousand pains,
> Can make me feel each Passion that he feigns,
> Inrage, compose, with more than magic Art,
> With Pity, and with Terror, tear my heart;
> And snatch me, o'er the earth, or thro' the air,
> To Thebes, to Athens, when he will, and where.

The lines are as emphatic as they are eloquent, and their stress is overwhelmingly on an art that is magical and passional in its effect.

The poet who drew so finely the "thousand pains" of a forsaken mistress in *Eloisa to Abelard*, and who in *The Rape of the Lock* mourned with such delicate mockery and pathos a young woman's loss of innocence, unquestionably had deep and sensitive feelings of his own. Yet art is ultimately fictive, the passions represented in it "feigned" (as the passage above also insists) and not necessarily the frank outpourings of a poet's most intense and personal feeling. And so even in Pope's most driving satires, where the poet so often and so wrathfully seems to rise in his own person to man civilization's last outposts of truth and freedom, the historical character and personality of the actual Pope must not be confused with the quite fictive and imaginary "Pope" who speaks in the poems. The man who answered a charge of pride and arrogance with this couplet,

> Yes, I am proud; I must be proud to see
> Men not afraid of God, afraid of me,

undoubtedly was capable of a deep and implacable personal arrogance, yet in these lines arrogance has been raised to a fiercely virtuous and even heroic dimension. All art requires distortion or exaggeration or suppression of the actual in favor of the fictive and dramatic, and the art of Pope, even when that art seems most intensely personal or documentary, is no exception. Equally important, moreover, Pope was writing in a tradition of classical rhetoric which greatly encouraged the use of various *personae*, or fictive representations of self, in art.

The word *persona* means, at its most literal, something through (*per*) which one speaks (*sona*, i.e., sounds), and originally it was the term for the masks worn by ancient actors and for the parts or characters they played. The masks worn by Pope in his satires are various, and may be described in different ways. Sometimes he takes the *persona* of a "plain good man," forced by his own conscience and sensibility to speak out against the villainy he discovers all about him:

> Ask you what Provocation I have had?
> The strong Antipathy of Good to Bad.
> When Truth or Virtue an Affront endures,
> Th' Affront is mine, my Friend, and should be yours.

Or he may assume the role of a naïf, or perhaps that of a court fool, as in these scorchingly ironic lines addressed to King George II, noted as much for his neglect of poets as for his neglect of English national interests:

> My Liege! why Writers little claim your thought,
> I guess; and, with their leave, will tell the fault:
> We Poets are (upon a Poet's word)
> Of all mankind, the creatures most absurd:
> The season, when to come, and when to go,
> To sing, or cease to sing, we never know;
> And if we will recite nine hours in ten,
> You lose your patience, just like other men.
> Then too we hurt our selves, when to defend
> A single verse, we quarrel with a friend;
> Repeat unask'd; lament, the Wit's too fine
> For vulgar eyes, and point out ev'ry line.
> But most, when straining with too weak a wing,
> We needs will write Epistles to the King;
> And from the moment we oblige the town,
> Expect a Place, or Pension from the Crown;
> Or dubb'd Historians by express command,
> T'enroll your triumphs o'er the seas and land;
> Be call'd to Court, to plan some work divine,
> As once for Louis, Boileau and Racine.

At other times his voice rings with the zeal of the impassioned "public defender," even perhaps with an inspired Old Testament zeal, as in these lines addressed to his own poetic lance of satire:

> O sacred Weapon! left for Truth's defence,
> Sole Dread of Folly, Vice, and Insolence!
> To all but Heav'n-directed hands deny'd,
> The Muse may give thee, but the Gods must guide.
> Rev'rent I touch thee! but with honest zeal;
> To rowze the Watchmen of the Publick Weal.

The fictive dimensions given by Pope to his own personality have a parallel in the dimensions he gives to all the quite positive historical materials which so pervade his work. More than any other English poet, Pope grounds his themes and meanings in real event and historical personage, and even the scenes and geography of his poetry were in the main both actual and contemporary. Yet the City of London or his own villa at Twickenham become in his imagination and art much more than flat and factual realities. The "City," as a center of trade and finance capitalism and abode of the "Money-headed and Money-hearted Citizen," becomes symbolic of all the most materialistic motives and values in man, a place where "money upon money increases, copulates, and multiplies, and guineas beget guineas in *saecula saeculorum*":

> There, London's voice: "Get Mony, Mony still!
> And then let Virtue follow, if she will."

A bare twelve miles away, on the other hand, there existed the retreat which became, both in his personal life and in his poetry, emblematic of the simple virtues and traditional pieties. There, outside the "Great World" and the "Great Ones" in it, the self could be catechized into its own therapy:

> Soon as I enter at my Country door,
> My Mind resumes the thread it dropt before;
> Thoughts, which at Hyde-Park-Corner I forgot,
> Meet and rejoin me, in the pensive Grott.
> There all alone, and Compliments apart,
> I ask these sober questions of my Heart.

In the privacy of a grotto, as in an interior privacy of soul, a close interrogation of self may teach a man to "possess all in possessing himself."

Pope's poetry, then, is not a mere reflection of the biographical or historical circumstances which so often occasioned its creation: the heroic "Pope" of the satires (brave, honest, noble) and the "Sporus" of the *Epistle to Dr. Arbuthnot* (nasty, vicious, hermaphroditic) do not stand in any kind of one-to-one relationship with the historical personalities that stand behind them. Each such personality has in some way become a fictive entity or type, the one of virtue, the other of vice. At the same time, it is useless to deny, or even to deplore, the fact that so much of Pope's poetry does originate from historical event (even *The Rape of the Lock* was inspired by the clipping of a most historical curl) or from a contemporary situation (the *Dunciad* grew out of Pope's very real anger at a host of hack writers who really lived at one time or another). Yet even the high degree of historicity in Pope's work, unless it is single-mindedly and narrowly pursued, is not really disadvantageous, for the way in which his poetry touches or verges upon history serves in some sense as a unique surety for the relevance of his art to actual life. Conversely, one of his great talents as a poet is his ability to give the materials of place and time a significance that is placeless and timeless.

The historical origins of much of Pope's poetry suggest another dimension of his work: he is at all times both a social and a moral poet. In part, at least, the subjects of his satires are the talk of the town: "Who sins with whom," or "What Strumpet Places sells for Life,/ What 'Squire his Lands, what Citizen his Wife." Such subjects, fashioned from the perennial failings and vices of men and women, imply by their very nature a most intense concern with the moral and social foundations of the human community, and imply also the satirist's right to judge and denounce conduct that would weaken those foundations. And though the warfare between Pope and the more knavish and foolish segments of his society is ultimately structured in decidedly fictive terms, the very topicality and historicity of his materials tends to affirm that the war is actual and that the enemy not only really exists but can be identified and held responsible for his actions.

Pope drew the ethical and social orientations for his art both from traditional Christian morals and doctrine and from the highly stylized images of ancient Greece and Rome that haunted the minds of his age. Thus a poem like *Eloisa to Abelard* finds its climax and its resolution in terms of the idea that divine grace may reorder and complete the most passionate physical yearnings, while the dark and dirty world of the *Dunciad* is created in a point-by-point inversion of the entire Christian scheme of things. *The Rape of the Lock*, suffused though it is with Miltonic memories of temptation and fall, nevertheless has its moral meaning most clearly opened when the speech of Clarissa is set against that of Sarpedon in Book XII of the *Iliad*, while the *First Epistle of the Second Book* ("To Augustus") defines a degenerate monarchal government by placing the inadequacies and ineptitudes of King George II (christened George Augustus) against the imperial pattern established by Caesar Augustus.

Within the very broad and pervasive Christian and classical contexts of his work there are certain very specific and traditional schemes and figures of thought used by Pope to order and structure the arguments of his poems. One such, displayed most precisely in *An Essay on Man*, is the very traditional concept of a great chain or ladder of beings, a vast scale of creatures stretching from God to man, and from man to the very bottom of matter:

> See, thro' this air, this ocean, and this earth,
> All matter quick, and bursting into birth.
> Above, how high progressive life may go!

> Around, how wide! how deep extend below!
> Vast chain of being, which from God began,
> Natures aethereal, human, angel, man,
> Beast, bird, fish, insect! what no eye can see,
> No glass can reach! from Infinite to thee,
> From thee to Nothing!

Placed in the middle and crucial position on the ladder, man combined in his mixed state the physical and sensual nature of the beasts below him and the spiritual and intelligential nature of the angels above him. He was not to try, through pride in his reason, to rise above his station, nor was he to fall below it by surrender to sheer animal appetite. In so critical and so paradoxical a station man seemed often to swing between polarities of doubt,

> In doubt to deem himself a God, or Beast,
> In doubt his Mind or Body to prefer,

and also often seemed to be, at one and the same time,

> Sole judge of Truth, in endless Error hurl'd:
> The glory, jest, and riddle of the world!

The embrace of disparate elements in the nature of man had its counterpart in the larger world, which on all sides seemed to exhibit, in its nature, the ancient concept of *concordia discors,* or harmonization of opposites. The very landscape in *Windsor-Forest,* for example, displays this harmonization of differences:

> Here Hills and Vales, the Woodland and the Plain,
> Here Earth and Water seem to strive again,
> Not *Chaos*-like together crush'd and bruis'd,
> But as the World, harmoniously confus'd:
> Where Order in Variety we see,
> And where, tho' all things differ, all agree.

A salutary variousness could be discovered, ideally at least, in all reaches of nature and human experience: in art, where "*Wit and Judgment* often are at strife,/ Tho' meant each other's Aid, like *Man* and *Wife*"; in society and politics, where "jarring int'rests of themselves create/ Th' according music of a well-mix'd State"; in human passions, "whose well accorded strife/ Gives all the strength and colour of our life"; and in the very cosmos itself, where "All Nature's diff'rence keeps all Nature's peace."

Working in and through all the oppositions to be found in man and in nature there was of course the Divine Power who existed both in and beyond all things, the Christian God in whom all things live and move and have their being, the God who

> Warms in the sun, refreshes in the breeze,
> Glows in the stars, and blossoms in the trees,
> Lives thro' all life, extends thro' all extent,
> Spreads undivided, operates unspent,
> Breathes in our soul, informs our mortal part,
> As full, as perfect, in a hair as heart;
> As full, as perfect, in vile Man that mourns,
> As the rapt Seraph that adores and burns;
> To him no high, no low, no great, no small;
> He fills, he bounds, connects, and equals all.

Clasped in a divine embrace, the natural order of the universe and also the moral and social orders of man seemed to be sustained and guarded by a Providential governance. Under such a government different and conflicting passions and interests were permitted to different men, yet such utter variousness as existed was in the end disposed to the good of all. The avarice and parsimony of one man appeared offset, in this view, by the lavish prodigality of another, and to the question of "what makes one keep, and one bestow," Pope replies that it is the same Power

> who bids the Ocean ebb and flow,
> Bids seed-time, harvest, equal course maintain,
> Thro' reconcil'd extremes of drought and rain,
> Builds Life on Death, on Change Duration founds,
> And gives th' eternal wheels to know their rounds.

Enclosed and guarded though the universe might be within such a Providential order, the individual Christian, and particularly the Christian satirist, could not permit himself the least respite from the daily and unending war between the forces of good and evil. Pope might wish himself in the country, "to contemplate the wonders of God in the firmament, rather than the madness of men on the earth," yet he was continually drawn back to the battleground, "tugg'd back to the world and its regards." The mills of Providence might grind exceeding small, yet they also ground slowly at times, and in any event the individual man was still called to a resolute defence of the good against all the powers of darkness, no matter what their guise or station in life. The sharp dramatization of this moral combat to which every man is called gives to most of Pope's work its fundamental shape and character, and in the context of this moral combat he can write, without the least hint of self-consciousness, such lines as these:

> Yes, the last Pen for Freedom let me draw,
> When Truth stands trembling on the edge of Law:
> Here, Last of *Britons!* let your Names be read;

> Are none, none living? let me praise the Dead,
> And for that Cause which made your Fathers shine,
> Fall, by the Votes of their degen'rate Line!

The posture of defiance in such a passage is certainly extravagant, yet the lines breathe a fierce exaltation in the mission of the poet who is touched "with the Flame that breaks from Virtue's Shrine," and who is therefore bound, in all endeavors and at all costs, to the pursuit and guardianship of the truth that sets men free. To Pope, indeed, the pursuit of poetry and the pursuit of truth were one and the same activity, an identification he makes almost by-the-way in such lines as that where he speaks of his fatigues "in search of Truth, or search of Rhyme." And, in the end, such pursuit brought its own reward, and justified some of Pope's own last best words:

> Truth guards the Poet, sanctifies the line,
> And makes Immortal, Verse as mean as mine.

Too often the measure of Pope is taken from the few pieces of his work that are anthologized over and over. This is unfortunate, for usually it means that the shrewd and mellow and moving works of his later life are disregarded and misprized. Such early and brilliant poems as *The Rape of the Lock* and *Eloisa to Abelard* cannot of themselves sufficiently represent the true genius and achievements of Alexander Pope. As he himself said, "my works will in one respect be like the works of Nature, much more to be liked and understood when consider'd in the relation they bear with each other, than when ignorantly look'd upon one by one; and often, those parts which attract most at first sight, will appear to be not the most, but the least considerable."

ACKNOWLEDGMENTS

The texts of the poems in this volume are those established in The Twickenham Edition of the Poems of Alexander Pope, and they are reproduced here by kind permission of Methuen & Co. Ltd., of London, and the Yale University Press. The prose texts are those of the first editions (the text of ΠΕΡΙ ΒΑΘΟΥΣ incorporates a few passages Pope added after the first edition). The notes signed "P" are Pope's own; the ones signed "W" are those of his literary executor and editor, the Rev. William Warburton. For help in preparing the typescript I wish to make grateful acknowledgment to Mr. Robert Kalmey, Mr. John David Walker, Mr. James N. Palmer, and Miss Gail Compton. For courteous and untiring aid in all sorts of ways, I wish to thank Mr. Ray Jones of the University of Florida Library. For helpful criticism of the introduction I wish to thank Professor J. B. Pickard and his wife, Suzanne, Professor Francis C. Haber, and Professor Robert Gallagher. For his steady and untiring efforts in the reading and correcting of proofs, I wish to thank my graduate assistant, Mr. Michael J. Conlon.

POETRY AND PROSE
OF
ALEXANDER POPE

PASTORALS

WITH A

Discourse on *Pastoral*

WRITTEN IN THE YEAR 1704

Rura mihi & rigui placeant in vallibus amnes,
Flumina amem, sylvasque, inglorius!

VIRG.

A DISCOURSE
ON PASTORAL POETRY[1]

THERE are not, I believe, a greater number of any sort of verses than of those which are called Pastorals, nor a smaller, than of those which are truly so. It therefore seems necessary to give some account of this kind of Poem, and it is my design to comprize in this short paper the substance of those numerous dissertations the Criticks have made on the subject, without omitting any of their rules in my own favour. You will also find some points reconciled, about which they seem to differ, and a few remarks which I think have escaped their observation.

The original of Poetry is ascribed to that age which succeeded the creation of the world: And as the keeping of flocks seems to have been the first employment of mankind, the most ancient sort of poetry was

A DISCOURSE ON PASTORAL: Pope's *Pastorals* were first published in 1709, but the *Discourse on Pastoral Poetry,* which introduces them here, was not published until 1717. If the *Discourse* was written in 1704, as Pope maintained, the poet was then 16 years old. There is certainly some evidence to support a belief that both the *Discourse* and the *Pastorals* were composed in the years from 1704 to 1707.

The epigraph is from Virgil's *Georgics,* II 485–6: "Let the fields and running streams in the vales please me; unknown to fame, let me love the rivers and the woods."

[1] *Written at sixteen years of age.* P.

probably pastoral. 'Tis natural to imagine, that the leisure of those ancient shepherds admitting and inviting some diversion, none was so proper to that solitary and sedentary life as singing; and that in their songs they took occasion to celebrate their own felicity. From hence a Poem was invented, and afterwards improv'd to a perfect image of that happy time; which by giving us an esteem for the virtues of a former age, might recommend them to the present. And since the life of shepherds was attended with more tranquillity than any other rural employment, the Poets chose to introduce their Persons, from whom it receiv'd the name of Pastoral.

A Pastoral is an imitation of the action of a shepherd, or one considered under that character. The form of this imitation is dramatic, or narrative, or mix'd of both; the fable[2] simple, the manners not too polite nor too rustic: The thoughts are plain, yet admit a little quickness and passion, but that short and flowing: The expression humble, yet as pure as the language will afford; neat, but not florid; easy, and yet lively. In short, the fable, manners, thoughts, and expressions, are full of the greatest simplicity in nature.

The complete character of this poem consists in simplicity, brevity, and delicacy; the two first of which render an ecologue natural, and the last delightful.

If we would copy Nature,[3] it may be useful to take this Idea along with us, that pastoral is an image of what they call the Golden age. So that we are not to describe our shepherds as shepherds at this day really are, but as they may be conceiv'd then to have been; when the best of men follow'd the employment. To carry this resemblance yet farther, it would not be amiss to give these shepherds some skill in astronomy, as far as it may be useful to that sort of life. And an Air of piety to the Gods should shine thro' the Poem, which so visibly appears in all the works of antiquity: And it ought to preserve some relish of the old way of writing; the connections should be loose, the narrations and descriptions short, and the periods concise. Yet it is not sufficient that the sentences only be brief, the whole Eclogue should be so too. For we cannot suppose Poetry in those days to have been the business of men, but their recreation at vacant hours.

But with a respect to the present age, nothing more conduces to make these composures[4] natural, than when some Knowledge in rural affairs is discover'd. This may be made to appear rather done by chance than on design, and sometimes is best shewn by inference; lest by too much study to seem natural, we destroy that easy simplicity from whence arises the delight. For what is inviting in this sort of poetry proceeds not so much from the Idea of that business, as of the tranquillity of a country life.

2 **fable:** plot or design.
3 **copy Nature:** see *Essay on Criticism*, ll. 68*ff.*
4 **composures:** compositions.

We must therefore use some illusion to render a Pastoral delightful; and this consists in exposing the best side only of a shepherd's life, and in concealing its miseries. Nor is it enough to introduce shepherds discoursing together in a natural way; but a regard must be had to the subject; that it contain some particular beauty in itself, and that it be different in every Eclogue. Besides, in each of them a design'd scene or prospect is to be presented to our view, which should likewise have its variety. This Variety is obtain'd in a great degree by frequent comparisons, drawn from the most agreeable objects of the country; by interrogations to things inanimate; by beautiful digressions, but those short; sometimes by insisting a little on circumstances; and lastly by elegant turns[5] on the words, which render the numbers extremely sweet and pleasing. As for the numbers themselves, tho' they are properly of the heroic measure, they should be the smoothest, the most easy and flowing imaginable.

It is by rules like these that we ought to judge of Pastoral. And since the instructions given for any art are to be deriv'd as that art is in perfection, they must of necessity be deriv'd from those in whom it is acknowledg'd so to be. 'Tis therefore from the practice of *Theocritus* and *Virgil*, (the only undisputed authors of Pastoral) that the Criticks have drawn the foregoing notions concerning it.

Theocritus excells all others in nature and simplicity. The subjects of his *Idyllia* are purely pastoral, but he is not so exact in his persons, having introduced Reapers and fishermen as well as shepherds. He is apt to be too long in his descriptions, of which that of the Cup in the first pastoral is a remarkable instance. In the manners he seems a little defective, for his swains are sometimes abusive and immodest, and perhaps too much inclining to rusticity; for instance, in his fourth and fifth *Idyllia*. But 'tis enough that all others learn'd their excellencies from him, and that his Dialect alone has a secret charm in it which no other could ever attain.

Virgil who copies *Theocritus*, refines upon his original: and in all points where Judgment is principally concerned, he is much superior to his master. Tho' some of his subjects are not pastoral in themselves, but only seem to be such; they have a wonderful variety in them which the *Greek* was a stranger to. He exceeds him in regularity and brevity, and falls short of him in nothing but simplicity and propriety of style; the first of which perhaps was the fault of his age, and the last of his language.

Among the moderns, their success has been greatest who have most endeavour'd to make these ancients their pattern. The most considerable Genius appears in the famous *Tasso*, and our *Spenser*. *Tasso* in his *Aminta* has as far excell'd all the Pastoral writers, as in his *Gierusalemme* he has outdone the Epic Poets of his country. But as this piece seems to have been the original of a new sort of poem, the

5 **turns:** reiterations of the same word, sometimes with a different meaning.

Pastoral Comedy, in *Italy*, it cannot so well be consider'd as a copy of the ancients. *Spenser's Calender*, in Mr. *Dryden*'s opinion, is the most complete work of this kind which any Nation has produc'd ever since the time of *Virgil*. Not but that he may be thought imperfect in some few points. His Eclogues are somewhat too long, if we compare them with the ancients. He is sometimes too allegorical, and treats of matters of religion in a pastoral style as *Mantuan*[6] had done before him. He has employ'd the Lyric measure, which is contrary to the practice of the old Poets. His Stanza is not still the same, nor always well chosen. This last may be the reason his expression is sometimes not concise enough: for the Tetrastic has oblig'd him to extend his sense to the length of the four lines, which would have been more closely confin'd in the Couplet.

In the manners, thoughts, and characters, he comes near to *Theocritus* himself; tho' notwithstanding all the care he has taken, he is certainly inferior in his Dialect: For the *Doric* had its beauty and propriety in the time of *Theocritus;* it was used in part of *Greece*, and frequent in the mouths of many of the greatest persons; whereas the old *English* and country phrases of *Spenser* were either entirely obsolete, or spoken only by people of the lowest condition. As there is a difference between simplicity and rusticity, so the expression of simple thoughts should be plain, but not clownish.[7] The addition he has made of a Calendar to his Eclogues is very beautiful: since by this, besides the general moral of innocence and simplicity, which is common to other authors of pastoral, he has one peculiar to himself; he compares human Life to the several Seasons, and at once exposes to his readers a view of the great and little worlds,[8] in their various changes and aspects. Yet the scrupulous division of his Pastorals into Months, has oblig'd him either to repeat the same description, in other words, for three months together; or when it was exhausted before, entirely to omit it: whence it comes to pass that some of his Eclogues (as the sixth, eighth, and tenth for example) have nothing but their Titles to distinguish them. The reason is evident, because the year has not that variety in it to furnish every month with a particular description, as it may every season.

Of the following Eclogues I shall only say, that these four comprehend all the subjects which the Critics upon *Theocritus* and *Virgil* will allow to be fit for pastoral: That they have as much variety of description, in respect of the several seasons, as *Spenser*'s: That in order to add to this variety, the several times of the day are observ'd, the rural employments in each season or time of day, and the rural scenes or

---

6 **Mantuan:** Baptista Mantuanus (1448–1516), the "Christian Virgil," wrote Latin eclogues which enjoyed great popularity during the Renaissance.

7 **clownish:** boorish.

8 **great and little worlds:** the little world (microcosm) of man was considered as an epitome of the great world (macrocosm) exterior to him.

places proper to such employments; not without some regard to the several ages of man, and the different passions proper to each age.

But after all, if they have any merit, it is to be attributed to some good old Authors, whose works as I had leisure to study, so I hope I have not wanted care to imitate.

SPRING

The First Pastoral

OR

DAMON

To Sir William Trumbull

Fɪʀsᴛ in these Fields I try the Sylvan Strains,
Nor blush to sport on *Windsor*'s blissful Plains:
Fair *Thames* flow gently from thy sacred Spring,
While on thy Banks *Sicilian* Muses sing;
Let Vernal Airs thro' trembling Osiers play,   5
And *Albion*'s Cliffs resound the Rural Lay.
    You, that too Wise for Pride, too Good for Pow'r,
Enjoy the Glory to be Great no more,
And carrying with you all the World can boast,
To all the World Illustriously are lost!   10
O let my Muse her slender Reed inspire,
'Till in your Native Shades You tune the Lyre:
So when the Nightingale to Rest removes,
The Thrush may chant to the forsaken Groves,
But, charm'd to Silence, listens while She sings,   15
And all th'Aerial Audience clap their Wings.
    Soon as the Flocks shook off the nightly Dews,
Two Swains, whom Love kept wakeful, and the Muse,
Pour'd o'er the whitening Vale their fleecy Care,
Fresh as the Morn, and as the Season fair: 20
The Dawn now blushing on the Mountain's Side,
Thus *Daphnis* spoke, and *Strephon* thus reply'd.

sᴘʀɪɴɢ: These Pastorals were written at the age of sixteen. . . . Notwithstanding
the early time of their production, the Author esteem'd these as the most correct
in the versification, and musical in the numbers, of all his works. The reason for
his labouring them into so much softness, was, doubtless, that this sort of poetry
derives almost its whole beauty from a natural ease of thought and smoothness
of verse. . . . In a Letter of his to Mr. [William] Walsh about this time [Oct. 22,
1706], we find an enumeration of several Niceties in Versification, which perhaps have never been strictly observ'd in any English poem, except in these
Pastorals. P.
    4. Sicilian Muses: Theocritus, the first writer of pastoral, was Sicilian.
    5. Osiers: willows.
    6. Albion: ancient name for England.
    7–10. Sir W. *Trumbull* [1639–1716] was born in *Windsor* Forest, to which he
retreated after he had resign'd the post of Secretary of State to King *William*
III. P.   Sir William befriended the young Pope and served as a kind of
tutor to him.
    11. inspire: breathe into.
    17. The Scene of this Pastoral a Vally, the Time the Morning. P.

DAPHNIS

Hear how the Birds, on ev'ry bloomy Spray,
With joyous Musick wake the dawning Day!
Why sit we mute, when early Linnets sing,   25
When warbling *Philomel* salutes the Spring?
Why sit we sad, when *Phosphor* shines so clear,
And lavish Nature paints the Purple Year?

STREPHON

Sing then, and *Damon* shall attend the Strain,
While yon slow Oxen turn the furrow'd Plain.   30
Here the bright Crocus and blue Vi'let glow;
Here Western Winds on breathing Roses blow.
I'll stake yon' Lamb that near the Fountain plays,
And from the Brink his dancing Shade surveys.

DAPHNIS

And I this Bowl, where wanton Ivy twines,   35
And swelling Clusters bend the curling Vines:
Four Figures rising from the Work appear,
The various Seasons of the rowling Year;
And what is That, which binds the Radiant Sky,
Where twelve fair Signs in beauteous Order lye?   40

DAMON

Then sing by turns, by turns the Muses sing,
Now Hawthorns blossom, now the Daisies spring,
Now Leaves the Trees, and Flow'rs adorn the Ground;
Begin, the Vales shall ev'ry Note rebound.

STREPHON

Inspire me *Phœbus*, in my *Delia*'s Praise,   45
With *Waller*'s Strains, or *Granville*'s moving Lays!
A Milk-white Bull shall at your Altars stand,
That threats a Fight, and spurns the rising Sand.

DAPHNIS

O Love! for *Sylvia* let me gain the Prize,
And make my Tongue victorious as her Eyes;   50
No Lambs or Sheep for Victims I'll impart,
Thy Victim, Love, shall be the Shepherd's Heart.

26. Philomel: the nightingale.
27. Phosphor: the morning star.
28. Purple: in the Latin sense of brilliant or highly-colored in general.
37. rising: carved in relief.
40. twelve fair Signs: the Zodiac.
46. Granville: *George Granville*, afterwards Lord *Lansdown*, known for his Poems, most of which he compos'd very young, and propos'd *Waller* as his model. P.   For Granville, see first note to *Windsor-Forest*. For Edmund Waller, see *Essay on Criticism*, l. 361*n*.
48. spurns: kicks.

STREPHON

Me gentle *Delia* beckons from the Plain,
Then hid in Shades, eludes her eager Swain;
But feigns a Laugh, to see me search around,   55
And by that Laugh the willing Fair is found.

DAPHNIS

The sprightly *Sylvia* trips along the Green,
She runs, but hopes she does not run unseen,
While a kind Glance at her Pursuer flies,
How much at variance are her Feet and Eyes!   60

STREPHON

O'er Golden Sands let rich *Pactolus* flow,
And Trees weep Amber on the Banks of *Po;*
Blest *Thames*'s Shores the brightest Beauties yield,
Feed here my Lambs, I'll seek no distant Field.

DAPHNIS

Celestial *Venus* haunts *Idalia*'s Groves,   65
Diana Cynthus, Ceres Hybla loves;
If *Windsor*-Shades delight the matchless Maid,
Cynthus and *Hybla* yield to *Windsor*-Shade.

STREPHON

All Nature mourns, the Skies relent in Show'rs,
Hush'd are the Birds, and clos'd the drooping Flow'rs;   70
If *Delia* smile, the Flow'rs begin to spring,
The Skies brighten, and the Birds to sing.

DAPHNIS

All Nature laughs, the Groves are fresh and fair,
The Sun's mild Lustre warms the vital Air;
If *Sylvia* smiles, new Glories gild the Shore,   75
And vanquish'd Nature seems to charm no more.

STREPHON

In Spring the Fields, in Autumn Hills I love,
At Morn the Plains, at Noon the shady Grove;
But *Delia* always; absent from her Sight,
Nor Plains at Morn, nor Groves at Noon delight.   80

61. Pactolus: a river, fabled for its gold, in Asia Minor.
62. Phaethon, having been hurled from his father's chariot of the sun, supposedly fell on the banks of the Po. There his sisters were transformed into poplars weeping tears of amber.
65. Idalia: a town in Cyprus consecrated to Aphrodite, the "Celestial Venus."
66. Cynthus: Mt. Cynthus, thought to be Diana's birthplace.   **Hybla:** a mountain in Sicily, famous for thyme and honey.
69. relent: dissolve.

DAPHNIS
Sylvia's like Autumn ripe, yet mild as *May*,
More bright than Noon, yet fresh as early Day,
Ev'n Spring displeases, when she shines not here,
But blest with her, 'tis Spring throughout the Year.

STREPHON
Say, *Daphnis*, say, in what glad Soil appears   85
A wondrous *Tree* that Sacred *Monarchs* bears?
Tell me but this, and I'll disclaim the Prize,
And give the Conquest to thy *Sylvia*'s Eyes.

DAPHNIS
Nay tell me first, in what more happy Fields
The *Thistle* springs, to which the *Lilly* yields?   90
And then a nobler Prize I will resign,
For *Sylvia*, charming *Sylvia* shall be thine.

DAMON
Cease to contend, for (*Daphnis*) I decree
The Bowl to *Strephon*, and the Lamb to thee:
Blest Swains, whose Nymphs in ev'ry Grace excell;   95
Blest Nymphs, whose Swains those Graces sing so well!
Now rise, and haste to yonder Woodbine Bow'rs,
A soft Retreat from sudden vernal Show'rs;
The Turf with rural Dainties shall be Crown'd,
While opening Blooms diffuse their Sweets around.   100
For see! the gath'ring Flocks to Shelter tend,
And from the *Pleiads* fruitful Show'rs descend.

85–6. An Allusion to the Royal Oak, in which *Charles* the second had been hid from the pursuit after the battle of *Worcester*.   P.
90. Alludes to the Device of the *Scots* Monarchs, the *Thistle*, worn by Queen *Anne;* and to the Arms of *France*, the *Fleur de Lys*.   P.
102. Pleiads: mythical daughters of Atlas, transformed into stars, and associated with spring rains.

SUMMER

The Second Pastoral

OR

ALEXIS

To Dr. Garth

A SHEPHERD's Boy (he seeks no better Name)
  Led forth his Flocks along the silver *Thame*,
  Where dancing Sun-beams on the Waters play'd,
And verdant Alders form'd a quiv'ring Shade.
Soft as he mourn'd, the Streams forgot to flow,   5
The Flocks around a dumb Compassion show,
The *Naiads* wept in ev'ry Watry Bow'r,
And *Jove* consented in a silent Show'r.

 Accept, O *Garth*, the Muse's early Lays,
That adds this Wreath of Ivy to thy Bays;   10
Hear what from Love unpractis'd Hearts endure,
From Love, the sole Disease thou canst not cure!

 Ye shady Beeches, and ye cooling Streams,
Defence from *Phœbus*', not from *Cupid*'s Beams;
To you I mourn; nor to the Deaf I sing,   15
The Woods shall answer, and their Echo ring.
The Hills and Rocks attend my doleful Lay,
Why art thou prouder and more hard than they?
The bleating Sheep with my Complaints agree,
They parch'd with Heat, and I inflam'd by thee.   20
The sultry *Sirius* burns the thirsty Plains,
While in thy Heart Eternal Winter reigns.

 Where stray ye Muses, in what Lawn or Grove,
While your *Alexis* pines in hopeless Love?
In those fair Fields where Sacred *Isis* glides,   25
Or else where *Cam* his winding Vales divides?
As in the Crystal Spring I view my Face,
Fresh rising Blushes paint the watry Glass;

SUMMER: The Scene of this Pastoral by the River's side; suitable to the heat of
the season; the Time, Noon. P.
 8. consented: sympathized.
 9. Dr. *Samuel Garth* [1661–1719], Author of the *Dispensary*, was one of the
first friends of the author, whose acquaintance with him began at fourteen or
fifteen. Their friendship continu'd from the year 1703, to 1718, which was that
of his death. P. See *Essay on Criticism*, ll. 108–11n.
 16. A line out of *Spenser's Epithalamion*. P.
 21. Sirius: the Dog-star, associated with summer heat and maladies.
 25. Isis: name given to the Thames about Oxford.
 26. Cam: the river at Cambridge.

But since those Graces please thy Eyes no more,
I shun the Fountains which I sought before. 30
Once I was skill'd in ev'ry Herb that grew,
And ev'ry Plant that drinks the Morning Dew;
Ah wretched Shepherd, what avails thy Art,
To cure thy Lambs, but not to heal thy Heart!
 Let other Swains attend the Rural Care, 35
Feed fairer Flocks, or richer Fleeces share;
But nigh yon' Mountain let me tune my Lays,
Embrace my Love, and bind my Brows with Bays.
That Flute is mine which *Colin's* tuneful Breath
Inspir'd when living, and bequeath'd in Death; 40
He said; *Alexis,* take this Pipe, the same
That taught the Groves my *Rosalinda's* Name —
But now the Reeds shall hang on yonder Tree,
For ever silent, since despis'd by thee.
O were I made by some transforming Pow'r, 45
The Captive Bird that sings within thy Bow'r!
Then might my Voice thy list'ning Ears employ,
And I those Kisses he receives, enjoy.
 And yet my Numbers please the rural Throng,
Rough *Satyrs* dance, and *Pan* applauds the Song: 50
The Nymphs forsaking ev'ry Cave and Spring,
Their early Fruit, and milk-white Turtles bring;
Each am'rous Nymph prefers her Gifts in vain,
On you their Gifts are all bestow'd again!
For you the Swains the fairest Flow'rs design, 55
And in one Garland all their Beauties join;
Accept the Wreath which You deserve alone,
In whom all Beauties are compriz'd in One.
 See what Delights in Sylvan Scenes appear!
Descending Gods have found *Elysium* here. 60
In Woods bright *Venus* with *Adonis* stray'd,
And chast *Diana* haunts the Forest Shade.
Come lovely Nymph, and bless the silent Hours,
When Swains from Sheering seek their nightly Bow'rs;
When weary Reapers quit the sultry Field, 65
And crown'd with Corn, their Thanks to *Ceres* yield.
This harmless Grove no lurking Viper hides,
But in my Breast the Serpent Love abides.
Here Bees from Blossoms sip the rosie Dew,
But your *Alexis* knows no Sweets but you. 70

36. share: shear.
39. Colin: The name taken by *Spenser* in his Eclogues, where his mistress is celebrated under that of *Rosalinda.* P.
41. Alexis: suggests Pope himself as Spenser's poetical heir.
52. Turtles: turtledoves.
56. join: pronounced to rhyme with *line* in Pope's time.
60. Elysium: the classical paradise.

Oh deign to visit our forsaken Seats,
The mossie Fountains, and the Green Retreats!
Where-e'er you walk, cool Gales shall fan the Glade,
Trees, where you sit, shall crowd into a Shade,
Where-e'er you tread, the blushing Flow'rs shall rise,   75
And all things flourish where you turn your Eyes.
Oh! how I long with you to pass my Days,
Invoke the Muses, and resound your Praise;
Your Praise the Birds shall chant in ev'ry Grove,
And Winds shall waft it to the Pow'rs above.   80
But wou'd you sing, and rival *Orpheus'* Strain,
The wondring Forests soon shou'd dance again,
The moving Mountains hear the pow'rful Call,
And headlong Streams hang list'ning in their Fall!
     But see, the Shepherds shun the Noon-day Heat,   85
The lowing Herds to murm'ring Brooks retreat,
To closer Shades the panting Flocks remove,
Ye Gods! and is there no Relief for Love?
But soon the Sun with milder Rays descends
To the cool Ocean, where his Journey ends;   90
On me Love's fiercer Flames for ever prey,
By Night he scorches, as he burns by Day.

81. Orpheus: the mythical poet and musician whose lyre could charm beasts and make trees and rocks to dance.

AUTUMN
The Third Pastoral
OR
HYLAS AND ÆGON

To Mr. Wycherley

Beneath the Shade a spreading Beech displays,
  Hylas and *Ægon* sung their Rural Lays;
  This mourn'd a faithless, that an absent Love,
And *Delia's* Name and *Doris* fill'd the Grove.
Ye *Mantuan* Nymphs, your sacred Succour bring;   5
Hylas and *Ægon's* Rural Lays I sing.
  Thou, whom the Nine with *Plautus'* Wit inspire,
The Art of *Terence,* and *Menander's* Fire;
Whose Sense instructs us, and whose Humour charms,
Whose Judgment sways us, and whose Spirit warms!   10
Oh, skill'd in Nature! see the Hearts of Swains,
Their artless Passions, and their tender Pains.
  Now setting *Phœbus* shone serenely bright,
And fleecy Clouds were streak'd with Purple Light;
When tuneful *Hylas* with melodious Moan   15
Taught Rocks to weep, and made the *Mountains* groan.
Go gentle Gales, and bear my Sighs away!
To *Delia's* Ear the tender Notes convey!
As some sad Turtle his lost Love deplores,
And with deep Murmurs fills the sounding Shores;   20
Thus, far from *Delia,* to the Winds I mourn,
Alike unheard, unpity'd, and forlorn.
  Go gentle Gales, and bear my Sighs along!
For her, the feather'd Quires neglect their Song;
For her, the Lymes their pleasing Shades deny;   25
For her, the Lillies hang their heads and dye.

Autumn: This Pastoral consists of two parts, like the 8th of *Virgil:* The Scene, a Hill; the Time, at Sun-set. P.
  5. Mantuan: Mantua was Virgil's birthplace.
  7. Thou: Mr. [William] Wycherley, a famous Author of Comedies; of which the most celebrated were the *Plain-Dealer* and *Country-Wife.* He was a writer of infinite spirit, satire, and wit. The only objection made to him was that he had too much. However he was followed in the same way by Mr. Congreve; tho' with a little more correctness. P.
  7–8. Plautus (c. 250–184 B.C.) and Terence (c. 190–159 B.C.) were celebrated writers of Roman comedy; Menander (c. 343–291 B.C.) was an admired writer of Greek comedy.
  11. Nature: here probably means *human nature.*
  19. Turtle: *turtur,* Latin for turtledove, suggests the bird's monotonous call.
  24. Quires: choirs.

Ye Flow'rs that droop, forsaken by the Spring,
Ye Birds, that left by Summer, cease to sing,
Ye Trees that fade when Autumn-Heats remove,
Say, is not Absence Death to those who love?   30
   Go gentle Gales, and bear my Sighs away!
Curs'd be the Fields that cause my *Delia*'s Stay:
Fade ev'ry Blossom, wither ev'ry Tree,
Dye ev'ry Flow'r, and perish All, but She.
What have I said? — where-e'er my *Delia* flies,   35
Let Spring attend, and sudden Flow'rs arise;
Let opening Roses knotted Oaks adorn,
And liquid Amber drop from ev'ry Thorn.
   Go gentle Gales, and bear my Sighs along!
The Birds shall cease to tune their Ev'ning Song,   40
The Winds to breathe, the waving Woods to move,
And Streams to murmur, e'er I cease to love.
Not bubling Fountains to the thirsty Swain,
Not balmy Sleep to Lab'rers faint with Pain,
Not Show'rs to Larks, or Sunshine to the Bee,   45
Are half so charming as thy Sight to me.
   Go gentle Gales, and bear my Sighs away!
Come, *Delia*, come; ah why this long Delay?
Thro' Rocks and Caves the Name of *Delia* sounds,
Delia, each Cave and ecchoing Rock rebounds.   50
Ye Pow'rs, what pleasing Frensie sooths my Mind!
Do Lovers dream, or is my *Delia* kind?
She comes, my *Delia* comes! — Now cease my Lay,
And cease ye Gales to bear my Sighs away!
    Next *Ægon* sung, while *Windsor* Groves admir'd;   55
Rehearse, ye Muses, what your selves inspir'd.
    Resound ye Hills, resound my mournful Strain!
Of perjur'd *Doris*, dying I complain:
Here where the *Mountains* less'ning as they rise,
Lose the low Vales, and steal into the Skies.   60
While lab'ring Oxen, spent with Toil and Heat,
In their loose Traces from the Field retreat;
While curling Smokes from Village-Tops are seen,
And the fleet Shades glide o'er the dusky Green.
    Resound ye Hills, resound my mournful Lay!   65
Beneath yòn Poplar oft we past the Day:
Oft on the Rind I carv'd her Am'rous Vows,
While She with Garlands hung the bending Boughs:
The Garlands fade, the Vows are worn away;
So dies her Love, and so my Hopes decay.   70
    Resound ye Hills, resound my mournful Strain!
Now bright *Arcturus* glads the teeming Grain,

44. Pain: toil.
   72. Arcturus: a giant star thought to bring rain when it rose with the sun, in September.

Now Golden Fruits on loaded Branches shine,
And grateful Clusters swell with floods of Wine;
Now blushing Berries paint the yellow Grove;   75
Just Gods! shall all things yield Returns but Love?
    Resound ye Hills, resound my mournful Lay!
The Shepherds cry, "Thy Flocks are left a Prey —"
Ah! what avails it me, the Flocks to keep,
Who lost my Heart while I preserv'd my Sheep.   80
Pan came, and ask'd, what Magick caus'd my Smart,
Or what *Ill Eyes* malignant Glances dart?
What Eyes but hers, alas, have Pow'r to move!
And is there Magick but what dwells in Love?
    Resound ye Hills, resound my mournful Strains!   85
I'll fly from Shepherds, Flocks, and flow'ry Plains. —
From Shepherds, Flocks, and Plains, I may remove,
Forsake Mankind, and all the World — but Love!
I know thee Love! on foreign Mountains bred,
Wolves gave thee suck, and savage Tygers fed.   90
Thou wert from *Ætna's* burning Entrails torn,
Got by fierce Whirlwinds, and in Thunder born!
    Resound ye Hills, resound my mournful Lay!
Farewell ye Woods! adieu the Light of Day!
One Leap from yonder Cliff shall end my Pains.   95
No more ye Hills, no more resound my Strains!
    Thus sung the Shepherds till th'Approach of Night,
The Skies yet blushing with departing Light,
When falling Dews with Spangles deck'd the Glade,
And the low Sun had lengthen'd ev'ry Shade.   100

WINTER
The Fourth Pastoral
OR
DAPHNE

To the Memory of Mrs. Tempest

LYCIDAS

THYRSIS, the Musick of that murm'ring Spring
Is not so mournful as the Strains you sing,
Nor Rivers winding thro' the Vales below,
So sweetly warble, or so smoothly flow.
Now sleeping Flocks on their soft Fleeces lye,   5
The Moon, serene in Glory, mounts the Sky,
While silent Birds forget their tuneful Lays,
Oh sing of *Daphne's* Fate, and *Daphne's* Praise!

THYRSIS

Behold the *Groves* that shine with silver Frost,
Their Beauty wither'd, and their Verdure lost.   10
Here shall I try the sweet *Alexis'* Strain,
That call'd the list'ning *Dryads* to the Plain?
Thames heard the Numbers as he flow'd along,
And bade his Willows learn the moving Song.

LYCIDAS

So may kind Rains their vital Moisture yield,   15
And swell the future Harvest of the Field!
Begin; this Charge the dying *Daphne* gave,
And said; "Ye Shepherds, sing around my Grave!"
Sing, while beside the shaded Tomb I mourn,
And with fresh Bays her Rural Shrine adorn.   20

WINTER: **Mrs. Tempest:** This Lady was of an ancient family in Yorkshire, and particularly admired by the Author's friend Mr. [William] *Walsh*, who having celebrated her in a Pastoral Elegy, desired his friend to do the same, as appears from one of his Letters, dated Sept. 9, 1706. "Your last Eclogue being on the same subject with mine on Mrs. Tempest's death, I should take it very kindly in you to give it a little turn as if it were to the memory of the same lady." Her death having happened on the night of the great storm in 1703, gave a propriety to this eclogue, which in its general turn alludes to it. The Scene of the Pastoral lies in a grove, the Time at midnight. P.

For Pope's friend William Walsh, see *Essay on Criticism*, l. 729n.

11. Alexis' Strain: Pope alludes to *The Mourning Muse of Alexis*, a pastoral poem by William Congreve which had lamented the death, in 1694, of Queen Mary.

12. Dryads: wood nymphs.

14. Willows: symbolic of grief.

THYRSIS

Ye gentle *Muses* leave your Crystal Spring,
Let *Nymphs* and *Sylvans* Cypress Garlands bring;
Ye weeping *Loves,* the Stream with Myrtles hide,
And break your Bows, as when *Adonis* dy'd;
And with your Golden Darts, now useless grown,   25
Inscribe a Verse on this relenting Stone:
"Let Nature change, let Heav'n and Earth deplore,
"Fair *Daphne*'s dead, and Love is now no more!"
   'Tis done, and Nature's various Charms decay;
See gloomy Clouds obscure the chearful Day!   30
Now hung with Pearls the dropping Trees appear,
Their faded Honours scatter'd on her Bier.
See, where on Earth the flow'ry Glories lye,
With her they flourish'd, and with her they dye.
Ah what avail the Beauties Nature wore?   35
Fair *Daphne*'s dead, and Beauty is no more!
   For her, the Flocks refuse their verdant Food,
The thirsty Heifers shun the gliding Flood.
The silver Swans her hapless Fate bemoan,
In Notes more sad than when they sing their own.   40
In hollow Caves sweet *Echo* silent lies,
Silent, or only to her Name replies,
Her Name with Pleasure once she taught the Shore,
Now *Daphne*'s dead, and Pleasure is no more!
   No grateful Dews descend from Ev'ning Skies,   45
Nor Morning Odours from the Flow'rs arise.
No rich Perfumes refresh the fruitful Field,
Nor fragrant Herbs their native Incense yield.
The balmy *Zephyrs,* silent since her Death,
Lament the Ceasing of a sweeter Breath.   50
Th'industrious Bees neglect their Golden Store;
Fair *Daphne*'s dead, and Sweetness is no more!
   No more the mounting Larks, while *Daphne* sings,
Shall list'ning in mid Air suspend their Wings;
No more the Birds shall imitate her Lays,   55
Or hush'd with Wonder, hearken from the Sprays:
No more the Streams their Murmurs shall forbear,
A sweeter Musick than their own to hear,
But tell the Reeds, and tell the vocal Shore,
Fair *Daphne*'s dead, and Musick is no more!   60
   Her Fate is whisper'd by the gentle Breeze,
And told in Sighs to all the trembling Trees;

22. **Sylvans:** forest deities.   **Cypress:** emblematic of grief.
23. **Myrtles:** emblematic of love.
26. **relenting:** melting.
32. **Honours:** foliage.
42. **her Name:** Daphne.

The trembling Trees, in ev'ry Plain and Wood,
Her Fate remurmur to the silver Flood;
The silver Flood, so lately calm, appears   65
Swell'd with new Passion, and o'erflows with Tears;
The Winds and Trees and Floods her Death deplore,
Daphne, our Grief! our Glory now no more!
   But see! where *Daphne* wondring mounts on high,
Above the Clouds, above the Starry Sky.   70
Eternal Beauties grace the shining Scene,
Fields ever fresh, and Groves for ever green!
There, while You rest in *Amaranthine* Bow'rs,
Or from those Meads select unfading Flow'rs,
Behold us kindly who your Name implore,   75
Daphne, our Goddess, and our Grief no more!

LYCIDAS

   How all things listen, while thy Muse complains!
Such Silence waits on *Philomela*'s Strains,
In some still Ev'ning, when the whisp'ring Breeze
Pants on the Leaves, and dies upon the Trees.   80
To thee, bright Goddess, oft a Lamb shall bleed,
If teeming Ewes encrease my fleecy Breed.
While Plants their Shade, or Flow'rs their Odours give,
Thy Name, thy Honour, and thy Praise shall live!

THYRSIS

   But see, *Orion* sheds unwholesome Dews,   85
Arise, the Pines a noxious Shade diffuse;
Sharp *Boreas* blows, and Nature feels Decay,
Time conquers All, and We must Time obey.
Adieu ye *Vales,* ye *Mountains, Streams* and *Groves,*
Adieu ye Shepherd's rural *Lays* and *Loves,*   90
Adieu my Flocks, farewell ye *Sylvan* Crew,
Daphne farewell, and all the World adieu!

73. **Amaranthine:** the amaranth flower was thought not to fade.
78. **Philomela:** the nightingale.
85. **Orion:** the rising and setting of the constellation Orion was thought to bring storm and rain.
89*ff.* These four last lines allude to the several *Subjects* of the four Pastorals, and to the several *Scenes* of them, particularized before in each.   P.

THE

EPISODE OF SARPEDON

TRANSLATED FROM THE
Twelfth and *Sixteenth* Books

OF

HOMER's ILIADS

THE ARGUMENT

Sarpedon, *the Son of* Jupiter, *commanded the* Lycians *who came to the Aid of* Troy. *In the first Battel when* Diomed *had put the* Trojans *to flight, he incourag'd* Hector *to rally, and signaliz'd himself by the Death of* Tlepolemus. *Afterwards when the* Greeks *had rais'd a Fortification to cover their Fleet, which the* Trojans *endeavour'd to overthrow, this Prince was the Occasion of effecting it. He incites* Glaucus *to second him in this Action by an admirable Speech, which has been render'd in English by* Sir John Denham; *after whom the Translator had not the Vanity to attempt it for any other reason, than that the Episode must have been very imperfect without so Noble a part of it.*

THUS *Hector*, great in Arms, contends in vain
  To fix the Fortune of the fatal Plain,
  Nor *Troy* cou'd conquer, nor the *Greeks* wou'd yield,
'Till bold *Sarpedon* rush'd into the Field;
For Mighty *Jove* inspir'd with Martial Flame   5
His God-like Son, and urg'd him on to Fame.
In Arms he shines, conspicuous from afar,
And bears aloft his ample Shield in Air,
Within whose Orb the thick Bull-hides were roll'd,
Pondrous with Brass, and bound with ductile Gold;   10
And while two pointed Jav'lins arm his Hands,

EPISODE OF SARPEDON: This episode from the *Iliad* was the first of Pope's translations from the classics to be published (in 1709, when it appeared with the *Pastorals* in the same miscellany volume). For the episode, which was later incorporated into his full translation of the *Iliad*, Pope received three guineas.
  6. **God-like Son:** Sarpedon was son of Zeus and Laodamia.

Majestick moves along, and leads his *Lycian* Bands.
　So prest with Hunger, from the Mountain's Brow,
Descends a Lion on the Flocks below;
So stalks the Lordly Savage o'er the Plain,　　　　　　　15
In sullen Majesty, and stern Disdain:
In vain loud Mastives bay him from afar,
And Shepherds gaul him with an Iron War;
Regardless, furious, he pursues his way;
He foams, he roars, he rends the panting Prey.　　　　20
　Resolv'd alike, Divine *Sarpedon* glows
With gen'rous Rage, that drives him on the Foes.
He views the Tow'rs, and meditates their Fall;
To sure Destruction dooms the *Grecian* Wall;
Then casting on his Friend an ardent Look,　　　　　25
Fir'd with the Thirst of Glory, thus he spoke.
　Why boast we, *Glaucus,* our extended Reign,
Where *Xanthus'* Streams enrich the *Lycian* Plain?
Our num'rous Herds that range each fruitful Field,
And Hills where Vines their Purple Harvest yield?　　30
Our foaming Bowls with gen'rous *Nectar* crown'd,
Our Feasts enhanc'd with Musick's sprightly Sound?
Why on those Shores are we with Joy survey'd,
Admir'd as Heroes, and as Gods obey'd?
Unless great Acts superior Merit prove,　　　　　　35
And Vindicate the bounteous Pow'rs above:
'Tis ours, the Dignity They give, to grace;
The first in Valour, as the first in Place:
That while with wondring Eyes our Martial Bands
Behold our Deeds transcending our Commands,　　40
Such, they may cry, deserve the Sov'reign State,
Whom those that Envy dare not Imitate!
Cou'd all our Care elude the greedy Grave,
Which claims no less the Fearful than the Brave,
For Lust of Fame I shou'd not vainly dare　　　　　45
In fighting Fields, nor urge thy Soul to War.
But since, alas, ignoble Age must come,
Disease, and Death's inexorable Doom;
The Life which others pay, let Us bestow,
And give to Fame what we to Nature owe;　　　　　50
Brave, tho' we fall; and honour'd, if we live;
Or let us Glory gain, or Glory give!
　He said, his Words the list'ning Chief inspire
With equal Warmth, and rouze the Warrior's Fire;

---

12. **Lycian:** the Lycians were allies of the Trojans.
18. **Iron War:** i.e., the weapons of war.
22. **gen'rous:** noble, courageous.
23. **meditates:** plans.
27–52. Compare Clarissa's speech in *The Rape of the Lock,* V 9–34.

The Troops pursue their Leaders with Delight,   55
Rush to the Foe, and claim the promis'd Fight.
Menestheus from on high the Storm beheld,
Threat'ning the Fort, and black'ning in the Field;
Around the Walls he gaz'd, to view from far
What Aid appear'd t'avert th'approaching War,   60
And saw where *Teucer* with th'*Ajaces* stood,
Insatiate of the Fight, and prodigal of Blood.
In vain he calls, the Din of Helms and Shields
Rings to the Skies, and ecchoes thro' the Fields,
The Gates resound, the Brazen Hinges fly,   65
While each is bent to conquer or to die.
Then thus to *Thoos;* — Hence with speed (he said)
And urge the bold *Ajaces* to our Aid;
Their Strength united best may help to bear
The bloody Labours of the doubtful War: 70
Hither the *Lycian* Princes bend their Course,
The best and bravest of the *Trojan* Force.
But if too fiercely, there, the Foes contend,
Let *Telamon* at least our Tow'rs defend,
And *Teucer* haste, with his unerring Bow,   75
To share the Danger, and repel the Foe.
    Swift as the Word, the Herald speeds along
The lofty Ramparts, through the Warlike Throng,
And finds the Heroes, bath'd in Sweat and Gore,
Oppos'd in Combate on the dusty Shore.   80
Strait to the Fort great *Ajax* turn'd his Care,
And thus bespoke his Brothers of the War:
Now valiant *Lycomede*, exert your Might,
And brave *Oïleus*, prove your Force in Fight:
To you I trust the Fortune of the Field,   85
'Till by this Arm the Foe shall be repell'd;
That done, expect me to compleat the Day:
Then, with his Sev'nfold Shield, he strode away.
With equal Steps bold *Teucer* prest the Shore,
Whose fatal Bow the strong *Pandion* bore.   90
High on the Walls appear'd the *Lycian* Pow'rs,
Like some black Tempest gath'ring round the Tow'rs:
The *Greeks* oppress'd, their utmost Force unite,
Prepar'd to labour in th'unequal Fight;
The War begins; mix'd Shouts and Groans arise;   95
Tumultuous Clamour mounts, and thickens in the Skies.
Fierce *Ajax* first th'advancing Host invades,
And sends the brave *Epicles* to the Shades,
Sarpedon's Friend; Across the Warrior's Way,

60. **War:** soldiers in battle formation.
61. **Ajaces:** followers of Ajax.
74. **Telamon:** Ajax, son of Telamon.

Rent from the Walls, a Rocky Fragment lay;   100
In modern Ages not the strongest Swain
Cou'd heave th'unwieldy Burthen from the Plain:
He poiz'd, and swung it round; then tost on high,
It flew with Force, and labour'd up the Sky;
Full on the *Lycian*'s Helmet thundring down,   105
The pondrous Ruin crush'd his batter'd Crown.
As skilful Divers from some Airy Steep
Headlong descend, and shoot into the Deep,
So falls *Epicles;* then in Groans expires,
And murm'ring from the Corps th'unwilling Soul retires.   110
     While to the Ramparts daring *Glaucus* drew,
From *Teucer's* Hand a winged Arrow flew,
The bearded Shaft the destin'd Passage found,
And on his naked Arm inflicts a Wound.
The Chief who fear'd some Foe's insulting Boast   115
Might stop the Progress of his warlike Host,
Conceal'd the Wound, and leaping from his Height,
Retir'd reluctant from th'unfinish'd Fight.
Divine *Sarpedon* with Regret beheld
Disabl'd *Glaucus* slowly quit the Field;   120
His beating Breast with gen'rous Ardour glows,
He springs to Fight, and flies upon the Foes.
Alcmaon first was doom'd his Force to feel,
Deep in his Breast he plung'd the pointed Steel,
Then from the yawning Wound with Fury tore   125
The Spear, pursu'd by gushing Streams of Gore;
Down sinks the Warrior, with a thundring Sound,
His Brazen Armour rings against the Ground.
     Swift to the Battlement the Victor flies,
Tugs with full Force, and ev'ry Nerve applies;   130
It shakes; the pondrous Stones disjoynted yield;
The rowling Ruins smoak along the Field.
A mighty Breach appears, the Walls lye bare,
And like a Deluge rushes in the War.
At once bold *Teucer* draws the twanging Bow,   135
And *Ajax* sends his Jav'lin at the Foe;
Fix'd in his Belt the feather'd Weapon stood,
And thro' his Buckler drove the trembling Wood;
But *Jove* was present in the dire Debate,
To shield his Off-spring, and avert his Fate.   140
The Prince gave back; not meditating Flight,
But urging Vengeance and severer Fight;
Then rais'd with Hope, and fir'd with Glory's Charms,
His fainting Squadrons to new Fury warms.
O where, ye *Lycians*, is the Strength you boast,   145
Your former Fame, and ancient Virtue lost?

137. his Belt: Sarpedon's.

The Breach lyes open, but your Chief in vain
Attempts alone the guarded Pass to gain:
Unite, and soon that Hostile Fleet shall fall,
The Force of pow'rful Union conquers All.   150
    This just Rebuke inflam'd the *Lycian* Crew,
They join, they thicken, and th'Assault renew;
Unmov'd, th'embody'd *Greeks* their Fury dare,
And fix'd support the Weight of all the War:
Nor cou'd the *Greeks* repell the *Lycian* Pow'rs,   155
Nor the bold *Lycians* force the *Grecian* Tow'rs.
As on the Confines of adjoyning Grounds,
Two stubborn Swains with Blows dispute their Bounds;
They tugg, they sweat; but neither gain, nor yield,
One Foot, one Inch, of the contended Field: 160
Thus obstinate to Death, they fight, they fall;
Nor these can keep, nor those can win the Wall:
Their Manly Breasts are pierc'd with many a Wound,
Loud Strokes are heard, and ratling Arms resound,
The copious Slaughter covers all the Shore,   165
And the high Ramparts drop with Human Gore.
    As when two Scales are charg'd with doubtful Loads,
From side to side the trembling Balance nods,
'Till poiz'd aloft, the resting Beam suspends
Each equal Weight, nor this, nor that descends.   170
So Conquest loth for either to declare,
Levels her Wings, and hov'ring hangs in Air.
'Till *Hector* came, to whose Superior Might
Jove ow'd the Glory of the destin'd Fight.
Fierce as a Whirlwind, up the Walls he flies,   175
And fires his Host with loud repeated Cries:
Advance ye *Trojans*, lend your valiant Hands,
Haste to the Fleet, and toss the blazing Brands!
They hear, they run, and gath'ring at his Call,
Raise scaling Engines, and ascend the Wall: 180
Around the Works a Wood of glitt'ring Spears
Shoots up, and All the rising Host appears.
A pondrous Stone bold *Hector* heav'd to throw,
Pointed above, and rough and gross below:
Nor two strong Men th'enormous Weight cou'd raise,   185
Such Men as live in these degen'rate Days.
Yet this, as easie as a Swain wou'd bear
The snowy Fleece; he tost, and shook in Air:
For *Jove* upheld, and lighten'd of its Load
Th'unwieldy Rock, the Labour of a God.   190
Thus arm'd, before the folded Gates he came,
Of massy Substance and stupendous Frame,
With Iron Bars and brazen Hinges strong,
On lofty Beams of solid Timber hung.

Then thundring thro' the Planks, with forceful Sway,   195
Drives the sharp Rock; the solid Beams give way,
The Folds are shatter'd, from the crackling Door
Leap the resounding Bars, the flying Hinges roar.
Now rushing in the furious Chief appears,
Gloomy as Night, and shakes two shining Spears;   200
A dreadful Gleam from his bright Armour came,
And from his Eye-balls flash'd the living Flame:
He moves a God, resistless in his Course,
And seems a Match for more than Mortal Force.
Then pouring after, thro' the gaping Space   205
A tide of *Trojans* flows, and fills the Place;
The *Greeks* behold, they tremble, and they fly,
The Shore is heap'd with Death, and Tumult rends the Sky.

CONNECTION OF THE FOREGOING WITH THE FOLLOWING PART

The Wall being forc'd by Hector, *an obstinate Battel was fought before the Ships, one of which was set on fire by the* Trojans. Patroclus *thereupon obtaining of* Achilles *to lead out the* Myrmidons *to the Assistance of the Greeks, made a great Slaughter of the Enemy, 'till he was oppos'd by* Sarpedon. *The Combate betwixt these Two, and the Death of the latter, with the Grief of* Jupiter *for his Son, are describ'd in the ensuing Translation, from the Sixteenth Book of the* Iliads.

WHEN now the Chief his valiant Friends beheld
    Grov'ling in Dust, and gasping on the Field,   210
    With this Reproach his flying Host he warms,
Oh Stain to Honour! oh Disgrace of Arms!
Forsake, inglorious, the contended Plain;
This Hand unaided shall the War sustain:
The Task be mine the Hero's Strength to try,   215
Who mows whole Troops, and makes whole Armies fly.
    He said, and leap'd from off his lofty Car;
Patroclus lights, and sternly waits the War.
As when two Vulturs on the Mountain's Height
Stoop with their sounding Pinions to the Fight;   220
They cuff, they tear, they raise a screaming Cry;
The Desart ecchoes, and the Rocks reply:
The Warriors thus oppos'd in Arms engage,
With equal Valour, and with equal Rage.
    Jove view'd the Combate, whose Event foreseen,   225
He thus bespoke his Sister and his Queen.

209. **the Chief:** Sarpedon.
220. **Stoop:** to plunge or swoop (used of birds of prey).   **Pinions:** wings.
226. **Sister and Queen:** Zeus married his sister Hera.

The Hour draws on; the Destinies ordain,
My God-like Son shall press the *Phrygian* Plain:
Already on the Verge of Death he stands,
His Life is ow'd to fierce *Patroclus'* Hands.   230
What Passions in a Parent's Breast debate!
Say, shall I snatch him from Impending Fate;
And send him safe to *Lycia,* distant far
From all the Dangers and the Toils of War;
Or to his Doom my bravest Off-spring yield,   235
And fatten, with Celestial Blood, the Field?
    Then thus the Goddess with the radiant Eyes:
What Words are these, O Sov'reign of the Skies?
Short is the Date prescrib'd to Mortal Man;
Shall *Jove,* for one, extend the narrow Span,   240
Whose Bounds were fix'd before his Race began?
How many Sons of Gods, foredoom'd to Death,
Before proud *Ilion* must resign their Breath!
Were thine exempt, Debate wou'd rise above,
And murm'ring Pow'rs condemn their partial *Jove.*   245
Give the bold Chief a glorious Fate in Fight;
And when th'ascending Soul has wing'd her Flight,
Let *Sleep* and *Death* convey, by thy Command,
The breathless Body to his Native Land.
His Friends and People, to his future Praise,   250
A Marble Tomb and Pyramid shall raise,
And lasting Honours to his Ashes give;
His Fame ('tis all the Dead can have!) shall live.
    She said; the Cloud-Compeller overcome,
Assents to Fate, and ratifies the Doom.   255
Then, touch'd with Grief, the weeping Heav'ns distill'd
A show'r of Blood o'er all the fatal Field.
The God, his Eyes averting from the Plain,
Laments his Son, predestin'd to be slain,
Far from the *Lycian* Shores, his happy Native Reign.   260
    Now met in Arms the Combatants appear,
Each heav'd the Shield, and pois'd the lifted Spear:
From strong *Patroclus'* Hand the Jav'lin fled,
And pass'd the Groin of valiant *Thrasymed,*
The Nerves unbrac'd no more his Bulk sustain,   265
He falls, and falling, bites the bloody Plain.
Two sounding Darts the *Lycian* Leader threw,
The first aloof with erring Fury flew,
The next more fatal pierc'd *Achilles'* Steed,
The gen'rous *Pedasus,* of *Theban* Breed;   270
Fix'd in the Shoulder's Joint, he reel'd around;
Rowl'd in the bloody Dust, and paw'd the slipp'ry Ground.
His sudden Fall the entangled Harness broke;
Each Axle groan'd; the bounding Chariot shook:

When bold *Automedon,* to disengage   275
The starting Coursers, and restrain their Rage,
Divides the Traces with his Sword, and freed
Th'incumber'd Chariot from the dying Steed:
The rest move on, obedient to the Rein;
The Car rowls slowly o'er the dusty Plain.   280
   The towring Chiefs to fiercer Fight advance,
And first *Sarpedon* tost his weighty Lance,
Which o'er the Warrior's Shoulder took its Course,
And spent, in empty Air, its dying Force.
Not so *Patroclus* never-erring Dart;   285
Aim'd at his Breast, it pierc'd the mortal Part }
Where the strong Fibres bind the solid Heart. }
Then as the stately Pine, or Poplar tall,
Hewn for the Mast of some great Admiral,
Nods, groans, and reels, 'till with a crackling Sound   290
It sinks, and spreads its Honours on the Ground;
Thus fell the King; and laid on Earth Supine,
Before his Chariot stretch'd his Form divine:
He grasp'd the Dust, distain'd with streaming Gore,
And, pale in Death, lay groaning on the Shore.   295
So lyes a Bull beneath the Lion's Paws,
While the grim Savage grinds with foamy Jaws
The trembling Limbs, and sucks the smoking Blood;
Deep Groans and hollow Roars rebellow thro' the Wood.
   Then to the Leader of the *Lycian* Band,   300
The dying Chief address'd his last Command.
Glaucus, be bold, Thy Task be first to dare
The glorious Dangers of destructive War,
To lead my Troops, to combate at their Head,
Incite the Living, and supply the Dead.   305
Tell 'em, I charg'd them with my latest Breath,
Not unreveng'd to bear *Sarpedon's* Death.
What Grief, what Shame must *Glaucus* undergo,
If these spoil'd Arms adorn a *Grecian* Foe?
Then as a Friend, and as a Warrior, fight;   310
Defend my Corps, and conquer in my Right;
That taught by great Examples, All may try
Like thee to vanquish, or like me to die.
   He ceas'd; the Fates supprest his lab'ring Breath,
And his Eyes darken'd with the Shades of Death: 315
Th'insulting Victor with Disdain bestrode
The prostrate Prince, and on his Bosom trod;

275. When: then, at that instant.
289. Admiral: an admiral's flagship.
291. Honours: foliage.
305. supply: make up for.
309. spoil'd: taken as spoils of war.

Then drew the Weapon from his panting Heart,
The reeking Fibres clinging to the Dart;
From the wide Wound gush'd out a Stream of Blood,   320
And the Soul issu'd in the Purple Flood.
  Then thus to *Phœbus*, in the Realms above,
Spoke from his Throne the Cloud-compelling *Jove:*
Descend my *Phœbus*, on the *Phrygian* Plain,
And from the Fight convey *Sarpedon* slain;   325
Then bathe his Body in the crystal Flood,
With Dust dishonour'd, and deform'd with Blood:
O'er all his Limbs *Ambrosial* Odours shed,
And with Celestial Robes adorn the mighty Dead.
Those Honours paid, his sacred Corps bequeath   330
To the soft Arms of silent *Sleep* and *Death;*
They to his Friends the mournful Charge shall bear;
His Friends a Tomb and Pyramid shall rear;
These unavailing Rites he may receive,
These, after Death, are All a God can give!   335
  Apollo bows, and from Mount *Ida*'s Height
Swift to the Field precipitates his Flight;
Thence, from the War, the breathless Hero bore,
Veil'd in a Cloud, to silver *Simois* Shore:
There bath'd his honourable Wounds, and drest   340
His Manly Members in th'Immortal Vest,
And with Perfumes of sweet *Ambrosial* Dews,
Restores his Freshness, and his Form renews.
Then *Sleep* and *Death,* two Twins of winged Race,
Of matchless Swiftness, but of silent Pace,   345
Receiv'd *Sarpedon*, at the God's Command,
And in a Moment reach'd the *Lycian* Land;
The Corps amidst his weeping Friends they laid,
Where endless Honours wait the Sacred Shade.

SAPHO TO PHAON

S AY, lovely Youth, that dost my Heart command,
  Can *Phaon*'s Eyes forget his *Sapho*'s Hand?
  Must then her Name the wretched Writer prove?
To thy Remembrance lost, as to thy Love!
Ask not the cause that I new Numbers chuse,   5
The Lute neglected, and the Lyric Muse;
Love taught my Tears in sadder Notes to flow,
And tun'd my Heart to Elegies of Woe.
I burn, I burn, as when thro' ripen'd Corn
By driving Winds the spreading Flames are born!   10
Phaon to *Ætna*'s scorching Fields retires,
While I consume with more than *Ætna*'s Fires!
No more my Soul a Charm in Musick finds,
Musick has Charms alone for peaceful Minds:
Soft Scenes of Solitude no more can please,   15
Love enters there, and I'm my own Disease:
No more the *Lesbian* Dames my Passion move,
Once the dear Objects of my guilty Love;
All other Loves are lost in only thine,
Ah Youth ungrateful to a Flame like mine!   20
Whom wou'd not all those blooming Charms surprize,
Those heav'nly Looks, and dear deluding Eyes?
The Harp and Bow wou'd you like *Phœbus* bear,
A brighter *Phœbus*, *Phaon* might appear;
Wou'd you with Ivy wreath your flowing Hair,   25
Not *Bacchus*' self with *Phaon* cou'd compare:
Yet *Phœbus* lov'd, and *Bacchus* felt the Flame,
One *Daphne* warm'd, and one the *Cretan* Dame;

SAPHO TO PHAON: First published in 1712, *Sapho to Phaon* is Pope's very free translation of Epistle XV of Ovid's *Heroides* (*Eloisa to Abelard* is Pope's original poem in the same genre). In the Latin original, the Greek poetess Sappho is writing to Phaon, her lover who has abandoned her.

5. **new Numbers:** the elegiac distichs used by Ovid, which differ from the Sapphic meter used by Sappho and named after her.

11. Phaon had fled to Sicily, where Mt. Aetna is located.

17. **Lesbian Dames:** women of the isle of Lesbos, Sappho's homeland.

26. Bacchus was reputed the most beautiful of the gods.

28. **Daphne:** a nymph beloved by Apollo, she was transformed into a laurel tree.   **Cretan Dame:** Ariadne, daughter of Minos, king of Crete. Abandoned by Theseus on the island of Naxos, she was discovered there by Bacchus.

Nymphs that in Verse no more cou'd rival me,
Than ev'n those Gods contend in Charms with thee.　　30
The Muses teach me all their softest Lays,
And the wide World resounds with *Sapho*'s Praise.
Tho' great *Alcæus* more sublimely sings,
And strikes with bolder Rage the sounding Strings,
No less Renown attends the moving Lyre,　　35
Which *Venus* tunes, and all her Loves inspire.
To me what Nature has in Charms deny'd
Is well by Wit's more lasting Flames supply'd.
Tho' short my Stature, yet my Name extends
To Heav'n it self, and Earth's remotest Ends.　　40
Brown as I am, an *Æthiopian* Dame
Inspir'd young *Perseus* with a gen'rous Flame.
Turtles and Doves of diff'ring Hues, unite,
And glossy Jett is pair'd with shining White.
If to no Charms thou wilt thy Heart resign,　　45
But such as merit, such as equal thine,
By none alas! by none thou can'st be mov'd,
Phaon alone by *Phaon* must be lov'd!
Yet once thy *Sapho* cou'd thy Cares employ,
Once in her Arms you center'd all your Joy:　　50
No Time the dear Remembrance can remove,
For oh! how vast a Memory has Love?
My Musick, then, you cou'd for ever hear,
And all my Words were Musick to your Ear.
You stop'd with Kisses my inchanting Tongue,　　55
And found my Kisses sweeter than my Song.
In all I pleas'd, but most in what was best;
And the last Joy was dearer than the rest.
Then with each Word, each Glance, each Motion fir'd,
You still enjoy'd, and yet you still desir'd,　　60
Till all dissolving in the Trance we lay,
And in tumultuous Raptures dy'd away.
The fair *Sicilians* now thy Soul inflame;
Why was I born, ye Gods, a *Lesbian* Dame?
But ah beware, *Sicilian* Nymphs! nor boast　　65
That wandring Heart which I so lately lost;
Nor be with all those tempting Words abus'd,
Those tempting Words were all to *Sapho* us'd.

---

29. **Nymphs:** Daphne was a nymph, Ariadne was not. Here, as in l. 65, the word simply describes a young and lovely woman.

33. **Alcæus:** a poet contemporary with Sappho (c. 600 B.C.), and also a native of Lesbos. Alcaic meter derives from him.

38. **Wit:** here means "genius."

41. **Æthiopian Dame:** Andromeda, daughter of Cepheus and Cassiopeia, king and queen of Ethiopia. She married Perseus, who rescued her from a sea-monster.

And you that rule *Sicilia*'s happy Plains,
Have pity, *Venus,* on your Poet's Pains!   70
Shall Fortune still in one sad Tenor run,
And still increase the Woes so soon begun?
Enur'd to Sorrow from my tender Years,
My Parent's Ashes drank my early Tears.
My Brother next, neglecting Wealth and Fame,   75
Ignobly burn'd in a destructive Flame.
An Infant Daughter late my Griefs increast,
And all a Mother's Cares distract my Breast.
Alas, what more could Fate it self impose,
But Thee, the last and greatest of my Woes?   80
No more my Robes in waving Purple flow,
Nor on my Hand the sparkling Diamonds glow,
No more my Locks in Ringlets curl'd diffuse
The costly Sweetness of *Arabian* Dews,
Nor Braids of Gold the vary'd Tresses bind,   85
That fly disorder'd with the wanton Wind:
For whom shou'd *Sapho* use such Arts as these?
He's gone, whom only she desir'd to please!
Cupid's light Darts my tender Bosom move,
Still is there cause for *Sapho* still to love: 90
So from my Birth the *Sisters* fix'd my Doom,
And gave to *Venus* all my Life to come;
Or while my Muse in melting Notes complains,
My yielding Heart keeps Measure to my Strains.
By Charms like thine which all my Soul have won,   95
Who might not — ah! who wou'd not be undone?
For those, *Aurora Cephalus* might scorn,
And with fresh Blushes paint the conscious Morn.
For those might *Cynthia* lengthen *Phaon*'s Sleep,
And bid *Endymion* nightly tend his Sheep.   100
Venus for those had rapt thee to the Skies,
But *Mars* on thee might look with *Venus*' Eyes.
O scarce a Youth, yet scarce a tender Boy!
O useful Time for Lovers to employ!
Pride of thy Age, and Glory of thy Race,   105
Come to these Arms, and melt in this Embrace!
The Vows you never will return, receive;

69–70. There was a temple dedicated to Venus on Mt. Eryx in Sicily.
75–6. Sappho's brother, Charaxus, ransomed a courtesan, Rhodopis, from Egypt.
77. Daughter: Cleis.
84. Arabian Dews: perfumes.
91. the Sisters: the fatal goddesses who controlled human destinies.
97. The hunter Cephalus, faithful husband of Procris, was loved in vain by Aurora, goddess of the morning.
98. conscious: sensible of wrong-doing.
99–100. Cynthia, goddess of the moon, loved the beautiful youth, Endymion.

And take at least the Love you will not give.
See, while I write, my Words are lost in Tears;
The less my Sense, the more my Love appears.   110
Sure 'twas not much to bid one kind Adieu,
(At least to feign was never hard to you.)
Farewel my Lesbian *Love!* you might have said,
Or coldly thus, *Farewel oh* Lesbian *Maid!*
No Tear did you, no parting Kiss receive,   115
Nor knew I then how much I was to grieve.
No Lover's Gift your *Sapho* cou'd confer,
And Wrongs and Woes were all you left with her.
No Charge I gave you, and no Charge cou'd give,
But this; *Be mindful of our Loves, and live.*   120
Now by the Nine, those Pow'rs ador'd by me,
And Love, the God that ever waits on thee,
When first I heard (from whom I hardly knew)
That you were fled, and all my Joys with you,
Like some sad Statue, speechless, pale, I stood;   125
Grief chill'd my Breast, and stop'd my freezing Blood;
No Sigh to rise, no Tear had pow'r to flow;
Fix'd in a stupid Lethargy of Woe.
But when its way th'impetuous Passion found,
I rend my Tresses, and my Breast I wound,   130
I rave, then weep, I curse, and then complain,
Now swell to Rage, now melt in Tears again.
Not fiercer Pangs distract the mournful Dame,
Whose first-born Infant feeds the Fun'ral Flame.
My scornful Brother with a Smile appears,   135
Insults my Woes, and triumphs in my Tears,
His hated Image ever haunts my Eyes,
And *why this Grief? thy Daughter lives;* he cries.
Stung with my Love, and furious with Despair,
All torn my Garments, and my Bosom bare,   140
My Woes, thy Crimes, I to the World proclaim;
Such inconsistent things are Love and Shame!
'Tis thou art all my Care and my Delight,
My daily Longing, and my Dream by Night:
O Night more pleasing than the brightest Day,   145
When Fancy gives what Absence takes away,
And drest in all its visionary Charms,
Restores my fair Deserter to my Arms!
Then round your Neck in wanton Wreaths I twine,
Then you, methinks, as fondly circle mine: 150
A thousand tender Words, I hear and speak;
A thousand melting Kisses, give, and take:
Then fiercer Joys — I blush to mention these,
Yet while I blush, confess how much they please!
But when with Day the sweet Delusions fly,   155

And all things wake to Life and Joy, but I,
As if once more forsaken, I complain,
And close my Eyes, to dream of you again.
Then frantick rise, and like some Fury rove
Thro' lonely Plains, and thro' the silent Grove,   160
As if the silent Grove, and lonely Plains
That knew my Pleasures, cou'd relieve my Pains.
I view the *Grotto*, once the Scene of Love,
The Rocks around, the hanging Roofs above,
That charm'd me more, with Native Moss o'ergrown,   165
Than *Phrygian* Marble or the *Parian* Stone.
I find the Shades that veil'd our Joys before,
But, *Phaon* gone, those Shades delight no more.
Here the prest Herbs with bending Tops betray
Where oft entwin'd in am'rous Folds we lay;   170
I kiss that Earth which once was prest by you,
And all with Tears the with'ring Herbs bedew.
For thee the fading Trees appear to mourn,
And Birds defer their Songs till thy Return:
Night shades the Groves, and all in Silence lye,   175
All, but the mournful *Philomel* and I:
With mournful *Philomel* I join my Strain,
Of *Tereus* she, of *Phaon* I complain.
    A Spring there is, whose Silver Waters show,
Clear as a Glass, the shining Sands below;   180
A flow'ry *Lotos* spreads its Arms above,
Shades all the Banks, and seems it self a Grove;
Eternal Greens the mossie Margin grace,
Watch'd by the Sylvan *Genius* of the Place.
Here as I lay, and swell'd with Tears the Flood,   185
Before my Sight a Watry Virgin stood,
She stood and cry'd, "O you that love in vain!
"Fly hence; and seek the fair *Leucadian* Main;
"There stands a Rock from whose impending Steep
"*Apollo*'s Fane surveys the rolling Deep;   190
"There injur'd Lovers, leaping from above,
"Their Flames extinguish, and forget to love.

159. Fury: i.e., one of the three Furies or Erinyes.
166. Marbles from Phrygia and the island of Paros were highly valued for statuary.
176-8. Philomela, before her transformation into a nightingale, was raped by her brother-in-law, Tereus.
181. Lotos: the jujube tree.
184. Genius of the Place: tutelary deity of a particular locale.
188-92. Leucadia, now called Leucas, is one of the Ionian islands, off the west coast of Greece. There is a promontory 2,000 feet high, on which may be seen the remains of a temple of Apollo. It was said that lovers who threw themselves from this height into the sea might be cured of their infatuation.
189. impending: hanging over.
190. Fane: temple.

"*Deucalion* once with hopeless Fury burn'd,
"In vain he lov'd, relentless *Pyrrha* scorn'd;
"But when from hence he plung'd into the Main,   195
"*Deucalion* scorn'd, and *Pyrrha* lov'd in vain.
"Haste *Sapho*, haste, from high *Leucadia* throw
"Thy wretched Weight, nor dread the Deeps below!"
She spoke, and vanish'd with the Voice — I rise,
And silent Tears fall trickling from my Eyes.   200
I go, ye Nymphs! those Rocks and Seas to prove;
How much I fear, but ah! how much I love?
I go, ye Nymphs! where furious Love inspires:
Let Female Fears submit to Female Fires!
To Rocks and Seas I fly from *Phaon's* Hate,   205
And hope from Seas and Rocks a milder Fate.
Ye gentle Gales, beneath my Body blow,
And softly lay me on the Waves below!
And thou, kind *Love*, my sinking Limbs sustain, ⎫
Spread thy soft Wings, and waft me o'er the Main, ⎬   210
Nor let a Lover's Death the guiltless Flood profane! ⎭
On *Phœbus'* Shrine my Harp I'll then bestow,
And this Inscription shall be plac'd below.
"Here She who sung, to Him that did inspire,
"*Sapho* to *Phœbus* consecrates her Lyre,   215
"What suits with *Sapho*, *Phœbus*, suits with thee;
"The Gift, the Giver, and the God agree."
    But why alas, relentless Youth! ah why
To distant Seas must tender *Sapho* fly?
Thy Charms than those may far more pow'rful be,   220
And *Phœbus'* self is less a God to me.
Ah! canst thou doom me to the Rocks and Sea,
O far more faithless and more hard than they?
Ah! canst thou rather see this tender Breast
Dash'd on these Rocks, than to thy Bosom prest?   225
This Breast which once, in vain! you lik'd so well;
Where the *Loves* play'd, and where the *Muses* dwell. —
Alas! the *Muses* now no more inspire,
Untun'd my Lute, and silent is my Lyre,
My languid Numbers have forgot to flow,   230
And Fancy sinks beneath a Weight of Woe.
Ye *Lesbian* Virgins, and ye *Lesbian* Dames,
Themes of my Verse, and Objects of my Flames,
No more your Groves with my glad Songs shall ring,
No more these Hands shall touch the trembling String: 235
My *Phaon's* fled, and I those Arts resign,

193–4. Deucalion and Pyrrha were the only survivors of a great flood sent by Zeus.
201. prove: test.
227. Loves: cupids.

(Wretch that I am, to call that *Phaon* mine!)
Return fair Youth, return, and bring along
Joy to my Soul, and Vigour to my Song:
Absent from thee, the Poet's Flame expires,   240
But ah! how fiercely burn the Lover's Fires?
Gods! can no Pray'rs, no Sighs, no Numbers move
One savage Heart, or teach it how to love?
The Winds my Pray'rs, my Sighs, my Numbers bear,
The flying Winds have lost them all in Air!   245
Oh when, alas! shall more auspicious Gales
To these fond Eyes restore thy welcome Sails?
If you return — ah why these long Delays?
Poor *Sapho* dies while careless *Phaon* stays.
O launch thy Bark, nor fear the watry Plain,   250
Venus for thee shall smooth her native Main.
O launch thy Bark, secure of prosp'rous Gales,
Cupid for thee shall spread the swelling Sails.
If you will fly — (yet ah! what Cause can be,
Too cruel Youth, that you shou'd fly from me?)   255
If not from *Phaon* I must hope for Ease,
Ah let me seek it from the raging Seas:
To raging Seas unpity'd I'll remove,
And either cease to live, or cease to love!

AN

ESSAY ON CRITICISM

——————————*Si quid novisti rectius istis,*
Candidus imperti; si non, his utere mecum.
                                        HORAT.

The Contents of the Essay on Criticism

'TIS hard to say, if greater Want of Skill
Appear in *Writing* or in *Judging* ill;
But, of the two, less dang'rous is th' Offence,
To tire our *Patience,* than mis-lead our *Sense:*
Some few in *that,* but Numbers err in *this,*   5
Ten Censure wrong for one who Writes amiss;
A *Fool* might once *himself* alone expose,
Now *One* in *Verse* makes many more in *Prose.*
   'Tis with our *Judgments* as our *Watches,* none
Go just *alike,* yet each believes his own.   10
In *Poets* as true *Genius* is but rare,
True *Taste* as seldom is the *Critick*'s Share;
Both must alike from Heav'n derive their Light,
These *born* to Judge, as well as those to Write.
Let such teach others who themselves excell,   15
And *censure freely* who have *written well.*
Authors are partial to their *Wit,* 'tis true,
But are not *Criticks* to their *Judgment* too?
   Yet if we look more closely, we shall find
Most have the *Seeds* of Judgment in their Mind;   20
Nature affords at least a *glimm'ring Light;*
The *Lines,* tho' touch'd but faintly, are drawn right.
But as the slightest Sketch, if justly trac'd,   ⎫
Is by ill *Colouring* but the more disgrac'd,   ⎬
So by *false Learning* is *good Sense* defac'd;   ⎭   25
Some are bewilder'd in the Maze of Schools,

AN ESSAY ON CRITICISM: First published anonymously on May 15, 1711, the *Essay on Criticism* was reprinted at least ten times in the next ten years. The Latin epigraph is from Horace, *Epistle* I vi 67–8: "If you know anything better than these precepts, say so frankly; if not, use these with me."

9–14. William Warburton, Pope's friend and editor, commented on these lines: "the Judgments of the multitude, like the *artificial measures of Time,* go different, and yet, each relies upon his own. But *Taste* in the Critic, is as rare as Genius in the Poet: both are derived from Heaven, and like the sun (the *natural measure of Time*) always constant and equal."

14. Compare "a poet is born, not made" (*poeta nascitur, non fit*).

17. Wit: the term has many meanings in the *Essay.* Depending on the context, "wit" may refer to a poet's genius, his art, his imagination, even his judgment or good sense.

21. Nature: another ambiguous term in the poem. Often it suggests not so much the external world, but an ordering and harmonizing principle which lies behind and sustains all things (cf. ll. 68*ff.*).

26. Schools: schools of criticism.

And some made *Coxcombs* Nature meant but *Fools*.
In search of *Wit* these lose their *common Sense*,
And then turn Criticks in their own Defence.
Each burns alike, who can, or cannot write,⁣   30
Or with a *Rival's*, or an *Eunuch's* spite.
All *Fools* have still an Itching to deride,
And fain *wou'd* be upon the *Laughing Side*:
If *Mævius* Scribble in *Apollo's* spight,
There are, who *judge* still *worse* than he can *write*.   35
    Some have at first for *Wits*, then *Poets* past,
Turn'd *Criticks* next, and prov'd plain *Fools* at last;
Some neither can for *Wits* nor *Criticks* pass,
As heavy Mules are neither *Horse* nor *Ass*.
Those half-learn'd Witlings, num'rous in our Isle,   40
As half-form'd Insects on the Banks of *Nile;*
Unfinish'd Things, one knows not what to call,
Their Generation's so *equivocal:*
To tell 'em, wou'd a *hundred Tongues* require,
Or *one vain Wit's*, that might a hundred tire.   45
    But *you* who seek to *give* and *merit* Fame,
And justly bear a Critick's noble Name,
Be sure *your self* and your own *Reach* to know,
How far your *Genius, Taste,* and *Learning* go;
Launch not beyond your Depth, but be discreet,   50
And mark *that Point* where Sense and Dulness *meet*.
    Nature to all things fix'd the Limits fit,
And wisely curb'd proud Man's pretending Wit:
As on the *Land* while *here* the *Ocean* gains,
In *other Parts* it leaves wide sandy Plains;   55
Thus in the *Soul* while *Memory* prevails,
The solid Pow'r of *Understanding* fails;
Where Beams of warm *Imagination* play,
The *Memory's* soft Figures melt away.
One *Science* only will one *Genius* fit;   60
So *vast* is Art, so *narrow* Human Wit:
Not only bounded to *peculiar Arts*,

27. **Coxcombs:** conceited pretenders to wit and judgment.
34. **Mævius:** a scribbling contemporary of Virgil and Horace who became the type of a bad poet.
41–3. The sun was thought to cause insects (a term which included frogs and snakes) to hatch from the Nile mud by equivocal (i.e., spontaneous) generation. Their generation is also called "equivocal" because they seem "half-form'd" and "unfinish'd," partly alive and partly unanimated mud.
44. **tell:** count or describe.
52–67. These lines reflect the Renaissance idea that one faculty of the mind was strengthened at the expense of another, and also emphasize that proud man must recognize his limitations.
60. **One science:** one kind of learning.
61. Cf. the first aphorism of Hippocrates: "Life is short, but art is long." "Art" in this line suggests learning in general.
62. **peculiar:** special or individual.

But oft in *those,* confin'd to *single Parts.*
Like Kings we lose the Conquests gain'd before,
By vain Ambition still to make them more: 65
Each might his *sev'ral Province* well command,
Wou'd all but *stoop* to what they *understand.*
   First follow NATURE, and your Judgment frame
By her just Standard, which is still the same:
Unerring Nature, still divinely bright,   70
One *clear, unchang'd,* and *Universal* Light,
Life, Force, and Beauty, must to all impart,
At once the *Source,* and *End,* and *Test* of *Art.*
Art from that Fund each *just Supply* provides,
Works *without Show,* and *without Pomp* presides: 75
In some fair Body thus th' informing Soul
With Spirits feeds, with Vigour fills the whole,
Each Motion guides, and ev'ry Nerve sustains;
It self unseen, but in th' *Effects,* remains.
Some, to whom Heav'n in Wit has been profuse,   80
Want as much more, to turn it to its use;
For *Wit* and *Judgment* often are at strife,
Tho' meant each other's Aid, like *Man* and *Wife.*
'Tis more to *guide* than *spur* the Muse's Steed;
Restrain his Fury, than provoke his Speed;   85
The winged Courser, like a gen'rous Horse,
Shows most true Mettle when you *check* his Course.
   Those RULES of old *discover'd,* not *devis'd,*
Are *Nature* still, but *Nature Methodiz'd;*
Nature, like *Liberty,* is but restrain'd   90
By the same Laws which first *herself* ordain'd.
   Hear how learn'd *Greece* her useful Rules indites,
When to repress, and when indulge our Flights:
High on *Parnassus'* Top her Sons she show'd,
And pointed out those arduous Paths they trod,   95
Held from afar, aloft, th' Immortal Prize,
And urg'd the rest by equal Steps to rise;
Just *Precepts* thus from great *Examples* giv'n,
She drew from *them* what they deriv'd from *Heav'n.*

68. Nature: cf. l. 21n.
69. still: always.
75. Pope here recalls the idea that "the art is to conceal the art" (*ars est celare artem*).
76. informing: animating and characterizing.
77. Spirits: the organs of the body were thought to produce certain subtle, animating "spirits" which enabled man to perform the various functions of his nature.
80–3. Cf. l. 17n.
84. Muse's Steed: Pegasus, the winged horse of poetic imagination.
86. gen'rous: spirited.
88. Rules: the body of generally accepted rules or precepts of good writing.
94. Parnassus: the mountain sacred to the Muses.

The gen'rous Critick *fann'd* the *Poet's Fire,*   100
And taught the World, *with Reason* to *Admire.*
Then Criticism the Muse's Handmaid prov'd,
To dress her Charms, and make her more belov'd;
But following Wits from that Intention stray'd;
Who cou'd not win the Mistress, woo'd the Maid;   105
Against the Poets *their own Arms* they turn'd,
Sure to hate most the Men from whom they *learn'd.*
So modern *Pothecaries,* taught the Art
By *Doctor's Bills* to play the *Doctor's Part,*
Bold in the Practice of *mistaken Rules,*   110
Prescribe, apply, and call their *Masters Fools.*
Some on the Leaves of ancient Authors prey,
Nor Time nor Moths e'er spoil'd so much as they:
Some dryly plain, without Invention's Aid,
Write dull *Receits* how Poems may be made: 115
These leave the Sense, their Learning to display,
And those explain the Meaning quite away.
　　You then whose Judgment the right Course wou'd steer,
Know well each ANCIENT's proper *Character,*
His *Fable, Subject, Scope* in ev'ry *Page,*   120
Religion, Country, Genius of his *Age:*
Without all these at once before your Eyes,
Cavil you may, but never *Criticize.*
Be *Homer's* Works your *Study,* and *Delight,*
Read them by Day, and meditate by Night,   125
Thence form your Judgment, thence your Maxims bring,
And trace the Muses *upward* to their *Spring;*
Still with *It self compar'd,* his *Text* peruse;
And let your *Comment* be the *Mantuan Muse.*
　　When first young *Maro* in his boundless Mind   130
A work t' outlast Immortal *Rome* design'd,
Perhaps he seem'd *above* the Critick's Law,
And but from *Nature's Fountains* scorn'd to draw:
But when t'examine ev'ry Part he came,

108–11. The lines refer to a quarrel between London doctors and apothecaries which developed when the latter began to write their own "bills" (pre-
scriptions) and thereby to usurp the doctor's function. The illegal practices
and high fees of the apothecaries led the College of Physicians to open a dispensary where drugs were sold at cost to the poor, and also led Dr. Samuel
Garth to write his mock-epic poem, *The Dispensary,* an attack on the apothecaries (cf. l. 619, below).
112–15. The lines attack first those editors who emend and mar poetic texts,
and second those critics who offer mechanical rules ("Receits" or recipes) for
the writing of poems.
119. Ancient: ancient writers of Greece and Rome.
120. Fable: plot.
129. Comment: commentary, gloss.　　**Mantuan Muse:** Virgil, born near
Mantua.
130. Maro: Virgil (Publius Virgilius Maro).

Nature and *Homer* were, he found, the *same:*   135
Convinc'd, amaz'd, he checks the bold Design, ⎫
And Rules as strict his labour'd Work confine, ⎬
As if the *Stagyrite* o'erlook'd each Line. ⎭
Learn hence for Ancient *Rules* a just Esteem;
To copy *Nature* is to copy *Them*.   140
   Some Beauties yet, no Precepts can declare,
For there's a *Happiness* as well as *Care*.
Musick resembles *Poetry*, in each ⎫
Are *nameless Graces* which no Methods teach, ⎬
And which a *Master-Hand* alone can reach. ⎭   145
If, where the *Rules* not far enough extend,
(Since Rules were made but to promote their End)
Some Lucky LICENCE answers to the full
Th' Intent propos'd, *that Licence* is a *Rule*.
Thus *Pegasus*, a nearer way to take,   150
May boldly deviate from the common Track.
Great Wits sometimes may *gloriously offend*,
And *rise* to *Faults* true Criticks *dare not mend;*
From *vulgar Bounds* with *brave Disorder* part,
And *snatch* a *Grace* beyond the Reach of Art,   155
Which, without passing thro' the *Judgment*, gains
The *Heart*, and all its End *at once* attains.
In *Prospects*, thus, some *Objects* please our Eyes, ⎫
Which *out of* Nature's *common Order* rise, ⎬
The shapeless *Rock*, or hanging *Precipice*. ⎭   160
But tho' the *Ancients* thus their *Rules* invade,
(As *Kings* dispense with *Laws* Themselves have made)
Moderns, beware! Or if you must offend
Against the *Precept*, ne'er transgress its *End*,
Let it be *seldom*, and *compell'd by Need*,   165
And have, at least, *Their Precedent* to plead.
The Critick else proceeds without Remorse,
Seizes your Fame, and puts his Laws in force.
   I know there are, to whose presumptuous Thoughts
Those *Freer Beauties*, ev'n in *Them*, seem Faults: 170
Some Figures *monstrous* and *mis-shap'd* appear,
Consider'd *singly*, or beheld too *near*,
Which, but *proportion'd* to their *Light*, or *Place*,
Due Distance *reconciles* to Form and Grace.
A prudent Chief not always must display   175
His Pow'rs in *equal Ranks*, and *fair Array*,
But with th' *Occasion* and the *Place* comply,

138. **Stagyrite:** Aristotle, born at Stagira in 384 B.C.
141. **declare:** make clear.
142. **Happiness:** luckiness or felicity of expression (cf. l. 148)
168. **Seizes:** in the legal sense, "to take possession of."
170. **Faults:** rhymed with *thoughts* in Pope's day.

Conceal his Force, nay seem sometimes to *Fly*.
Those oft are *Stratagems* which *Errors* seem,
Nor is it *Homer Nods*, but *We* that *Dream*.   180
    Still green with Bays each *ancient* Altar stands,
Above the reach of *Sacrilegious* Hands,
Secure from *Flames*, from *Envy's* fiercer Rage,
Destructive *War*, and all-involving *Age*.
See, from *each Clime* the Learn'd their Incense bring;   185
Hear, in *all Tongues* consenting *Pæans* ring!
In Praise so just, let ev'ry Voice be join'd,
And fill the *Gen'ral Chorus* of *Mankind!*
Hail *Bards Triumphant!* born in *happier Days;*
Immortal Heirs of *Universal* Praise!   190
Whose Honours with Increase of Ages *grow*,
As Streams roll down, *enlarging* as they flow!
Nations *unborn* your mighty Names shall sound,
And Worlds applaud that must not yet be *found!*
Oh may some Spark of *your* Cœlestial Fire   195
The last, the meanest of your Sons inspire,
(That on weak Wings, from far, pursues your Flights;
Glows while he *reads*, but *trembles* as he *writes*)
To teach vain Wits a Science *little known*,
T' *admire* Superior Sense, and *doubt* their own!   200

    OF all the Causes which conspire to blind
Man's erring Judgment, and misguide the Mind,
What the weak Head with strongest Byass rules,
Is *Pride*, the *never-failing Vice of Fools*.
Whatever Nature has in *Worth* deny'd,   205
She gives in large Recruits of *needful Pride;*
For as in *Bodies*, thus in *Souls*, we find
What wants in *Blood* and *Spirits*, swell'd with *Wind;*
Pride, where Wit fails, steps in to our Defence,
And fills up all the *mighty Void* of *Sense!*   210
If once right Reason drives *that Cloud* away,
Truth breaks upon us with *resistless Day;*
Trust not your self; but your Defects to know,
Make use of ev'ry *Friend* — and ev'ry *Foe*.

183–4. "The four great causes of the ravage amongst ancient writings are here alluded to: The destruction of the *Alexandrine* and *Palatine* libraries by fire; the fiercer rage of *Zoilus* and *Mævius* [types of bad critics and writers] and their followers against Wit; the irruption of the *Barbarians* into the empire; and the long reign of Ignorance and Superstition in the cloisters" [Warburton].
    186. consenting: harmonizing, agreeing.
    187. join'd: rhymed with *kind* in Pope's day.
    206. Recruits: supplies.
    207–10. The lines recall nature's abhorrence of a vacuum. For "Spirits," see l. 77*n*.

A *little Learning* is a dang'rous Thing;   215
Drink deep, or taste not the *Pierian* Spring:
There *shallow Draughts* intoxicate the Brain,
And drinking *largely* sobers us again.
Fir'd at first Sight with what the *Muse* imparts,
In *fearless Youth* we tempt the Heights of Arts,   220
While from the bounded *Level* of our Mind,
Short Views we take, nor see the *Lengths behind,*
But *more advanc'd*, behold with strange Surprize
New, distant Scenes of *endless* Science rise!
So pleas'd at first, the towring *Alps* we try,   225
Mount o'er the Vales, and seem to tread the Sky;
Th' Eternal Snows appear already past,
And the first *Clouds* and *Mountains* seem the last:
But *those attain'd*, we tremble to survey
The growing Labours of the lengthen'd Way,   230
Th' *increasing* Prospect *tires* our wandring Eyes,
Hills peep o'er Hills, and *Alps* on *Alps* arise!
A perfect Judge will *read* each Work of Wit
With the same Spirit that its Author *writ,*
Survey the *Whole,* nor seek slight Faults to find,   235
Where *Nature moves,* and *Rapture warms* the Mind;
Nor lose, for that malignant dull Delight,
The *gen'rous Pleasure* to be charm'd with Wit.
But in such Lays as neither *ebb,* nor *flow,*
Correctly cold, and *regularly low,*   240
That shunning Faults, one quiet *Tenour* keep;
We cannot *blame* indeed — but we may *sleep.*
In Wit, as Nature, what affects our Hearts
Is not th' Exactness of peculiar Parts;
'Tis not a *Lip,* or *Eye,* we Beauty call,   245
But the joint Force and full *Result* of *all.*
Thus when we view some well-proportion'd Dome,
(The *World's* just Wonder, and ev'n *thine* O *Rome!*)
No single Parts unequally surprize;
All comes *united* to th' admiring Eyes;   250
No monstrous Height, or Breadth, or Length appear;
The *Whole* at once is *Bold,* and *Regular.*
Whoever thinks a faultless Piece to see,
Thinks what ne'er was, nor is, nor e'er shall be.
In ev'ry Work regard the *Writer's End,*   255
Since none can compass more than they *Intend;*
And if the *Means* be just, the *Conduct* true,
Applause, in spite of trivial Faults, is due.

216. **Pierian Spring:** the Muses' fountain.
220. **tempt:** attempt.
240. **regularly low:** according to the rules (*regular*), but insipid.
247. **Dome:** any domed building, but here probably St. Peter's.

As Men of Breeding, sometimes Men of Wit,
T' avoid *great Errors*, must the *less* commit,   260
Neglect the Rules each *Verbal Critick* lays,
For *not* to know some Trifles, is a Praise.
Most Criticks, fond of some subservient Art,
Still make the *Whole* depend upon a *Part*,
They talk of *Principles*, but Notions prize,   265
And All to one lov'd Folly Sacrifice.
    Once on a time, *La Mancha*'s Knight, they say,
A certain *Bard* encountring on the Way,
Discours'd in Terms as just, with Looks as Sage,
As e'er cou'd *Dennis*, of the *Grecian* Stage;   270
Concluding all were desp'rate Sots and Fools,
Who durst depart from *Aristotle*'s Rules,
Our Author, happy in a Judge so nice,
Produc'd his Play, and beg'd the Knight's Advice,
Made him observe the *Subject* and the *Plot*,   275
The *Manners, Passions, Unities*, what not?
All which, exact to *Rule* were brought about,
Were but a *Combate in the Lists* left out.
What! Leave the Combate out? Exclaims the Knight;
Yes, or we must renounce the *Stagyrite*.   280
Not so by Heav'n (he answers in a Rage)
Knights, Squires, and Steeds, must enter on the Stage.
So vast a Throng the Stage can ne'er contain.
Then build a New, or act it in a Plain.
    Thus Criticks, of less *Judgment* than *Caprice*,   285
Curious, not *Knowing*, not *exact*, but *nice*,
Form *short Ideas;* and offend in *Arts*
(As most in *Manners*) by a *Love to Parts.*
    Some to *Conceit* alone their Taste confine,
And glitt'ring Thoughts struck out at ev'ry Line;   290
Pleas'd with a Work where nothing's just or fit;
One *glaring Chaos* and *wild Heap* of *Wit:*
Poets like Painters, thus, unskill'd to trace
The *naked Nature* and the *living Grace*,
With *Gold* and *Jewels* cover ev'ry Part,   295
And hide with *Ornaments* their *Want of Art*.

261. Verbal Critick: one who devotes himself to mere details and sacrifices the spirit to the letter of the rules.

267–84. Pope found this story about Don Quixote de la Mancha in a spurious sequel to Cervantes' work.

270. Dennis: John Dennis (1657–1734), a writer and critic much concerned with Greek drama. Though a critic of real merit, he was extremely irascible and inflexible of temperament (cf. l. 585*n*.).

273. nice: finical, fastidious.

276. Unities: the Aristotelian dramatic unity of action, and the supposed Aristotelian unities of time and place.

286. Curious: overly careful.

289. Conceit: farfetched thought or expression.

True Wit is *Nature* to Advantage drest,
What oft was *Thought,* but ne'er so well *Exprest,*
Something, whose Truth convinc'd at Sight we find,
That gives us back the Image of our Mind: 300
As Shades more sweetly recommend the Light,
So modest Plainness sets off sprightly Wit:
For *Works* may have more *Wit* than does 'em good,
As *Bodies* perish through Excess of *Blood.*
  Others for *Language* all their Care express,   305
And value *Books,* as Women *Men,* for *Dress:*
Their Praise is still — *The Stile is excellent:*
The *Sense,* they humbly take upon Content.
Words are like *Leaves;* and where they most abound,
Much *Fruit* of *Sense* beneath is rarely found.   310
False Eloquence, like the *Prismatic Glass,*
Its gawdy Colours spreads on ev'ry place;
The Face of Nature we no more Survey,
All glares *alike,* without *Distinction* gay:
But true *Expression,* like th' unchanging *Sun,* ⎫   315
Clears, and *improves* whate'er it shines upon, ⎬
It *gilds* all Objects, but it *alters* none. ⎭
Expression is the *Dress* of *Thought,* and still
Appears more *decent* as more *suitable;*
A vile Conceit in pompous Words exprest,   320
Is like a Clown in regal Purple drest;
For diff'rent *Styles* with diff'rent *Subjects* sort,
As several Garbs with Country, Town, and Court.
Some by *Old Words* to Fame have made Pretence;
Ancients in *Phrase,* meer Moderns in their *Sense!*   325
Such *labour'd Nothings,* in so *strange* a Style,
Amaze th'unlearn'd and make the Learned *Smile.*
Unlucky, as *Fungoso* in the Play, ⎫
These Sparks with aukward Vanity display ⎬
What the Fine Gentleman wore *Yesterday!* ⎭   330
And but so mimick ancient Wits at best,
As Apes our Grandsires in their *Doublets drest.*
In *Words,* as *Fashions,* the same Rule will hold;
Alike Fantastick, if *too New,* or *Old;*
Be not the *first* by whom the *New* are try'd,   335
Nor yet the *last* to lay the *Old* aside.

308. **take upon Content:** accept without question.
319. **decent:** fitting, becoming.
321. **Clown:** peasant.
322–3. The subjects appropriate to "Country, Town, and Court" are probably pastoral, satire or comedy, and epic respectively.
324–5. Pope possibly glances here at Ambrose Philips (1674–1749), who had used archaic or Spenserian dialect in his *Pastorals* and whose practice Pope satirized in *Guardian* 40.
328. **Fungoso:** a character who unsuccessfully aped the fashionable in Ben Jonson's *Every Man out of his Humour.*

But most by *Numbers* judge a Poet's Song,
And *smooth* or *rough*, with them, is *right* or *wrong*;
In the bright *Muse* tho' thousand *Charms* conspire,
Her *Voice* is all these tuneful Fools admire,   340
Who haunt *Parnassus* but to please their Ear, ⎱
Not mend their Minds; as some to *Church* repair, ⎬
Not for the *Doctrine*, but the *Musick* there. ⎰
These *Equal Syllables* alone require,
Tho' oft the Ear the *open Vowels* tire,   345
While *Expletives* their feeble Aid *do* join,
And ten low Words oft creep in one dull Line,
While they ring round the same *unvary'd Chimes*,
With sure *Returns* of still *expected Rhymes*.
Where-e'er you find *the cooling Western Breeze*,   350
In the next Line, it *whispers thro' the Trees*;
If *Chrystal Streams with pleasing Murmurs creep*,
The Reader's threaten'd (not in vain) with *Sleep*.
Then, at the *last*, and *only* Couplet fraught
With some *unmeaning* Thing they call a *Thought*,   355
A *needless Alexandrine* ends the Song,
That like a wounded Snake, drags its slow length along.
Leave such to tune their own dull Rhimes, and know
What's *roundly smooth*, or *languishingly slow*;
And praise the *Easie Vigor* of a Line,   360
Where *Denham's* Strength, and *Waller's* Sweetness join.
True Ease in Writing comes from Art, not Chance,
As those move easiest who have learn'd to dance.
'Tis not enough no Harshness gives Offence,
The *Sound* must seem an *Eccho* to the *Sense*.   365
Soft is the Strain when *Zephyr* gently blows,
And the *smooth Stream* in *smoother Numbers* flows;
But when loud Surges lash the sounding Shore,
The *hoarse, rough Verse* shou'd like the *Torrent* roar.
When *Ajax* strives, some Rock's vast Weight to throw,   370
The Line too *labours*, and the Words move *slow*;

337. **Numbers**: versification.
344. **Equal Syllables**: mechanically placed and regular accents.
345. Pope illustrates the faults he describes in this and the following lines. Open vowels occur when a word ending in a vowel is followed by one beginning with a vowel, as in *Tho' oft, the Ear*, etc.
346. **Expletives**: filler words, like *do* in this line. *Join* was pronounced to rhyme with *line*.
347. A monosyllabic line (cf. ll. 107 and 226).
357. An Alexandrine, or six-foot line. Contrast the Alexandrine at l. 373.
361. **Strength . . . Sweetness**: Sir John Denham (1615–69) and Edmund Waller (1606–87) were commonly thought to have imparted these qualities to the closed couplet.
366–83. Lines designed as illustrations of the precept that sound should echo sense in poetry.
370–1. Cf. *The Episode of Sarpedon*, ll. 97*ff.*

Not so, when swift *Camilla* scours the Plain,
Flies o'er th'unbending Corn, and skims along the Main.
Hear how *Timotheus'* vary'd Lays surprize,
And bid Alternate Passions fall and rise!   375
While, at each Change, the Son of *Lybian Jove*
Now *burns* with Glory, and then *melts* with Love;
Now his *fierce Eyes* with *sparkling Fury* glow;
Now *Sighs* steal out, and *Tears begin to flow:*
Persians and *Greeks* like *Turns of Nature* found,   380
And the *World's Victor* stood subdu'd by *Sound!*
The Pow'r of Musick all our Hearts allow;
And what *Timotheus* was, is *Dryden* now.

   Avoid *Extreams;* and shun the Fault of such,
Who still are pleas'd *too little*, or *too much*.   385
At ev'ry *Trifle* scorn to take Offence,
That always shows *Great Pride*, or *Little Sense;*
Those *Heads* as *Stomachs* are not sure the best
Which nauseate all, and nothing can digest.
Yet let not each gay *Turn* thy Rapture move,   390
For Fools *Admire*, but Men of Sense *Approve;*
As things seem *large* which we thro' *Mists* descry,
Dulness is ever apt to *Magnify*.

   Some *foreign* Writers, some our *own* despise;
The *Ancients* only, or the *Moderns* prize: 395
(Thus *Wit*, like *Faith*, by each Man is apply'd
To *one small* Sect, and All are *damn'd beside*.)
Meanly they seek the Blessing to confine,
And force *that Sun* but on a *Part* to Shine;
Which not alone the *Southern Wit* sublimes,   400
But ripens Spirits in cold *Northern Climes;*
Which from the first has shone on *Ages past*,
Enlights the *present*, and shall warm the *last:*
(Tho' *each* may feel *Increases* and *Decays*,
And see now *clearer* and now *darker Days*)   405
Regard not then if Wit be *Old* or *New*,
But blame the *False*, and value still the *True*.

   Some ne'er advance a Judgment of their own,
But *catch* the *spreading Notion* of the Town;

   372. Camilla: a warrior-maid in Virgil's *Aeneid* (see especially **Book VII**, ll. 808ff.)
   374. *See* Alexander's Feast, *or* the Power of Music; *an Ode by Mr.* Dryden.
P.   Timotheus was a Theban musician of the time of Alexander the Great.
   376. Son: When Alexander visited the oracle of Zeus Ammon in Libya, he was proclaimed son of the god.
   380. Turns of Nature: alternations of feeling.
   390. gay Turn: felicitous turn of phrase.
   398–9. Cf. Matthew 5:45: "he maketh his sun to rise on the evil and on the good, and sendeth rain on the just and on the unjust."
   400. sublimes: exalts or ripens. Pope here rejects the idea that climate imposed limitations on the minds of men.

They reason and conclude by *Precedent*,   410
And own *stale Nonsense* which they ne'er invent.
Some judge of Authors' *Names*, not *Works*, and then
Nor praise nor blame the *Writings*, but the *Men*.
Of all this *Servile Herd* the worst is He
That in *proud Dulness* joins with *Quality*,   415
A constant Critick at the Great-man's Board,
To *fetch and carry* Nonsense for my Lord.
What *woful stuff* this Madrigal wou'd be,
In some starv'd Hackny Sonneteer, or me?
But let a *Lord* once own the *happy Lines*,   420
How the *Wit brightens!* How the *Style refines!*
Before *his* sacred Name flies ev'ry Fault,
And each *exalted* Stanza *teems* with *Thought!*
   The *Vulgar* thus through *Imitation* err;
As oft the *Learn'd* by being *Singular;*   425
So much they scorn the Crowd, that if the Throng
By *Chance* go right, they *purposely* go wrong;
So Schismatics the *plain Believers* quit,
And are but damn'd for having *too much Wit*.
   Some praise at Morning what they blame at Night;   430
But always think the *last* Opinion *right*.
A Muse by these is like a Mistress us'd,
This hour she's *idoliz'd*, the next *abus'd*,
While their weak Heads, like Towns unfortify'd,
'Twixt Sense and Nonsense daily change their Side.   435
Ask them the Cause; *They're wiser still*, they say;
And still to Morrow's wiser than to Day.
We think our *Fathers* Fools, so *wise* we grow;
Our *Wiser Sons*, no doubt, will think *us* so.
Once *School-Divines* this zealous Isle o'erspread;   440
Who knew most *Sentences* was *deepest read;*
Faith, Gospel, All, seem'd made to be *disputed*,
And none had *Sense enough to be Confuted*.
Scotists and *Thomists*, now, in *Peace* remain,
Amidst their *kindred Cobwebs* in *Duck-Lane*.   445
If *Faith* it self has *diff'rent Dresses* worn,
What wonder *Modes* in *Wit* shou'd take their Turn?

415. Quality: the nobility.
419. Hackny: hireling.
440. School-Divines: medieval scholastic theologians.
441. Sentences: maxims (*sententiae*) of the great theologians.
   444. Scotists and Thomists: followers of the Franciscan Duns Scotus (from whose name the word "dunce" derives) were often in intellectual conflict with the followers of the Dominican Thomas Aquinas.
   445. kindred Cobwebs: the arguments of medieval schoolmen were frequently compared to cobwebs because they seemed to be so very fine and subtle and to be spun out of themselves.   **Duck-Lane:** A place where old and second-hand books were sold formerly, near *Smithfield*.   P

Oft, leaving what is Natural and fit,
The *current Folly* proves the *ready Wit*,
And Authors think their Reputation safe,   450
Which lives as long as *Fools* are pleas'd to *Laugh*.
   Some valuing those of their own *Side*, or *Mind*,
Still make themselves the measure of Mankind;
Fondly we think we honour Merit then,
When we but praise *Our selves* in *Other Men*.   455
Parties in *Wit* attend on those of *State*,
And publick Faction doubles private Hate.
Pride, Malice, Folly, against *Dryden* rose,
In various Shapes of *Parsons, Criticks, Beaus;*
But *Sense* surviv'd, when *merry Jests* were past;   460
For rising Merit will *buoy up* at last.
Might he return, and bless once more our Eyes,
New *Blackmores* and new *Milbourns* must arise;
Nay shou'd great *Homer* lift his awful Head,
Zoilus again would start up from the Dead.   465
Envy will *Merit* as its *Shade* pursue,
But like a Shadow, proves the *Substance* true;
For envy'd Wit, like *Sol* Eclips'd, makes known
Th' *opposing Body's* Grossness, not its *own*.
When first that Sun too powerful Beams displays,   470
It draws up Vapours which obscure its Rays;
But ev'n those Clouds at last adorn its Way,
Reflect new Glories, and augment the Day.
   Be thou the *first* true Merit to befriend;
His Praise is lost, who stays till *All* commend;   475
Short is the Date, alas, of *Modern Rhymes;*
And 'tis but just to let 'em live *betimes*.
No longer now that Golden Age appears,
When *Patriarch-Wits* surviv'd a *thousand Years;*
Now Length of *Fame* (our *second* Life) is lost,   480
And bare Threescore is all ev'n That can boast:
Our Sons their Fathers' *failing Language* see,
And such as *Chaucer* is, shall *Dryden* be.
So when the faithful *Pencil* has design'd
Some *bright Idea* of the Master's Mind,   485

454. fondly: vainly or foolishly.
456–7. I.e., writers are divided by political allegiances, Whig or Tory.
459. Parsons, Criticks, Beaus: Dryden had been attacked by the Rev. Jeremy Collier in *A Short View of the Profaneness and Immorality of the English Stage* (1698), and by the Rev. Luke Milbourne (cf. l. 463) in *Notes on Dryden's Virgil* (1698); by critics such as Sir Richard Blackmore (l. 463) in *A Satyr Against Wit* (1700); by beaus such as George Villiers, Duke of Buckingham, in *The Rehearsal* (1671).
465. Zoilus: Greek grammarian of the 3rd or 4th century B.C., famous for his carping criticisms of Homer.
482. The impermanent nature of the English language was a common complaint in Pope's day.

Where a *new World* leaps out at his command,
And ready Nature waits upon his Hand;
When the ripe Colours *soften* and *unite,*
And sweetly *melt* into just Shade and Light,
When mellowing Years their full Perfection give, 490
And each Bold Figure just begins to *Live;*
The *treach'rous Colours* the fair Art betray,
And all the bright Creation fades away!
    Unhappy *Wit*, like most mistaken Things,
Attones not for that *Envy* which it brings. 495
In *Youth* alone its empty Praise we boast,
But soon the Short-liv'd Vanity is lost!
Like some fair *Flow'r* the early *Spring* supplies,
That gaily Blooms, but ev'n in blooming *Dies.*
What is this *Wit* which must our Cares employ? 500
The *Owner's Wife*, that *other Men* enjoy,
Then most our *Trouble* still when most *admir'd,*
And still the more we *give*, the more *requir'd;*
Whose Fame with *Pains* we guard, but lose with *Ease,*
Sure *some* to *vex*, but never *all* to *please;* 505
'Tis what the *Vicious fear*, the *Virtuous shun;*
By *Fools* 'tis *hated,* and by *Knaves undone!*
    If *Wit* so much from *Ign'rance* undergo,
Ah let not *Learning* too commence its Foe!
Of old, those met *Rewards* who cou'd *excel,* 510
And such were *Prais'd* who but *endeavour'd well:*
Tho' *Triumphs* were to *Gen'rals* only due,
Crowns were reserv'd to grace the *Soldiers* too.
Now, they who reach *Parnassus'* lofty Crown,
Employ their Pains to spurn some others down; 515
And while Self-Love each jealous Writer rules,
Contending Wits become the *Sport of Fools:*
But still the *Worst* with most Regret commend,
For each *Ill Author* is as bad a *Friend.*
To what base Ends, and by what abject Ways, 520
Are Mortals urg'd thro' *Sacred Lust of Praise!*
Ah ne'er so *dire* a *Thirst of Glory* boast,
Nor in the *Critick* let the *Man* be lost!
Good-Nature and *Good-Sense* must ever join;
To Err is *Humane;* to Forgive, *Divine.* 525
    But if in Noble Minds some Dregs remain,
Not yet purg'd off, of Spleen and sow'r Disdain,
Discharge that Rage on more Provoking Crimes,

512. **Triumphs:** the magnificent ceremonies which honored Roman generals who had gained decisive victories over foreign enemies.
513. **Crowns:** at the time of a general's triumph, crowns of various kinds were awarded to soldiers who had distinguished themselves in the field.
521. **Sacred:** Latinism for *accursed.*
525: **Humane:** human.

Nor fear a Dearth in these Flagitious Times.
No Pardon vile *Obscenity* should find,   530
Tho' *Wit* and *Art* conspire to move your Mind;
But *Dulness* with *Obscenity* must prove
As Shameful sure as *Impotence* in *Love.*
In the fat Age of Pleasure, Wealth, and Ease,
Sprung the rank Weed, and thriv'd with large Increase;   535
When *Love* was all an easie Monarch's Care;
Seldom at *Council,* never in a *War:*
Jilts rul'd the State, and Statesmen *Farces* writ;
Nay *Wits* had *Pensions,* and *young Lords* had *Wit:*
The Fair sate panting at a *Courtier's Play,*   540
And not a Mask went *un-improv'd* away:
The modest Fan was lifted up no more,
And Virgins *smil'd* at what they *blush'd* before —
The following Licence of a Foreign Reign
Did all the Dregs of bold *Socinus* drain;   545
Then Unbelieving Priests reform'd the Nation,
And taught more *Pleasant* Methods of Salvation;
Where Heav'ns Free Subjects might their *Rights* dispute,
Lest God himself shou'd seem too *Absolute.*
Pulpits their *Sacred Satire* learn'd to spare,   550
And Vice *admir'd* to find a *Flatt'rer there!*
Encourag'd thus, Witt's *Titans* brav'd the Skies,
And the Press groan'd with Licenc'd *Blasphemies* —
These Monsters, Cricks! with your Darts engage,
Here point your Thunder, and exhaust your Rage!   555
Yet shun their Fault, who, *Scandalously nice,*
Will needs *mistake* an Author *into Vice;*
All seems Infected that th' Infected spy,
As all looks yellow to the Jaundic'd Eye.

LEARN then what MORALS Cricks ought to show,   560
For 'tis but *half* a *Judge's Task,* to *Know.*
'Tis not enough, Taste, Judgment, Learning, join;

534. Age: that of Charles II.

538. Jilts: Charles' mistresses.

541. Mask: a woman wearing a mask to the theater.

544. Licence: a glance at the increased religious toleration, especially towards Nonconformists, under the "Foreign Reign" of William III, a Dutchman.

545. Socinus: Laelius Socinus (1525–62) rejected the divinity of Christ and conceived the doctrines which ultimately developed into Unitarianism.

546. Unbelieving Priests: an attack on some of the more liberal divines of the 17th century.

552. Witt's Titans: the deists, who seemed to some to rebel against God in the way the Titans rebelled against Zeus.

553. Licenc'd: the Commons refused in 1695 to renew the Licensing Act, and writers were then free to publish anything they chose.

In all you speak, let Truth and Candor shine:
That not alone what to your *Sense* is due,
All may allow; but seek your *Friendship* too.   565
    Be *silent* always when you *doubt* your Sense;
And *speak*, tho' *sure*, with *seeming Diffidence*:
Some positive persisting Fops we know,
Who, if *once wrong*, will needs be *always so*;
But you, with Pleasure own your Errors past,   570
And make each Day a *Critick* on the last.
    'Tis not enough your Counsel still be *true*,
Blunt Truths more Mischief than *nice Falshoods* do;
Men must be *taught* as if you taught them *not;*
And Things *unknown* propos'd as Things *forgot:*   575
Without *Good Breeding*, *Truth* is disapprov'd;
That only makes *Superior* Sense *belov'd*.
    Be Niggards of Advice on no Pretence;
For the *worst Avarice* is that of *Sense:*
With mean Complacence ne'er betray your Trust,   580
Nor be so *Civil* as to prove *Unjust;*
Fear not the Anger of the Wise to raise;
Those best can *bear Reproof*, who *merit Praise*.
    'Twere well, might Criticks still this Freedom take;
But *Appius* reddens at each Word you speak,   585
And *stares*, *Tremendous!* with a *threatning Eye*,
Like some *fierce Tyrant* in *Old Tapestry!*
Fear most to tax an *Honourable* Fool,
Whose Right it is, *uncensur'd* to be dull;
Such without *Wit* are Poets when they please,   590
As without *Learning* they can take *Degrees*.
Leave dang'rous *Truths* to unsuccessful *Satyrs*,
And *Flattery* to fulsome *Dedicators*,
Whom, when they *Praise*, the World believes no more,
Than when they promise to give *Scribling* o'er.   595
'Tis best sometimes your Censure to restrain,

563. **Candor:** sweetness of temper.
571. **Critick:** critique, criticism.
580. **Complacence:** anxiety to please.
585. *This picture was taken to himself by* John Dennis, *a furious old Critic by profession, who, upon no other provocation, wrote against this Essay and its author, in a manner perfectly lunatic: For, as to the mention made of him in ver. 270. he took it as a Compliment, and said it was treacherously meant to cause him to overlook this Abuse of his Person.* P.   The name *Appius* recalls Dennis' tragedy, *Appius and Virginia*, which had failed on the stage in 1709. Dennis was fond of the word *tremendous*, and a *stare* was one of his notable characteristics.
588–91. Peers and other persons of "honorable" rank were admitted to unearned degrees at the universities.
593. **fulsome Dedicators:** writers whose dedications were mere servile appeals for patronage.

And *charitably* let the Dull be *vain:*
Your Silence there is better than your *Spite,*
For who can *rail* so long as they can *write?*
Still humming on, their drowzy Course they keep,   600
And *lash'd* so long, like *Tops,* are lash'd *asleep.*
False Steps but help them to renew the Race,
As after *Stumbling,* Jades will *mend* their Pace.
What Crouds of these, impenitently bold,
In *Sounds* and jingling *Syllables* grown old,   605
Still *run on* Poets in a raging Vein,
Ev'n to the Dregs and *Squeezings* of the *Brain;*
Strain out the last, dull droppings of their Sense,
And Rhyme with all the *Rage of Impotence!*
    Such shameless *Bards* we have; and yet 'tis true,   610
There are as mad, abandon'd *Criticks* too.
The Bookful Blockhead, ignorantly read,
With *Loads* of *Learned Lumber* in his Head,
With his own Tongue still edifies his Ears,
And always *List'ning to Himself* appears.   615
All Books he reads, and all he reads assails,
From *Dryden's Fables* down to *Durfey's Tales.*
With *him,* most Authors steal their Works, or buy;
Garth did not write his own *Dispensary.*
Name a new *Play,* and *he's* the Poet's *Friend,*   620
Nay show'd his Faults — but when wou'd Poets mend?
No Place so Sacred from such Fops is barr'd,
Nor is *Paul's Church* more safe than *Paul's Church-yard:*
Nay, fly to *Altars; there* they'll talk you dead;
For *Fools* rush in where *Angels* fear to tread.   625
Distrustful *Sense* with modest Caution speaks; ⎫
It still *looks home,* and *short Excursions* makes; ⎬
But *ratling Nonsense* in full *Vollies* breaks; ⎭
And never shock'd, and never turn'd aside,
Bursts out, resistless, with a thundring Tyde!   630
    But where's the Man, who Counsel *can* bestow,
Still *pleas'd to teach,* and yet not *proud to know?*
Unbiass'd, or by *Favour* or by *Spite;*
Not *dully prepossest,* nor *blindly right;*
Tho' Learn'd, well-bred; and tho' well-bred, sincere;   635
Modestly bold, and Humanly severe?
Who to a *Friend* his Faults can freely show,
And gladly praise the Merit of a *Foe?*

601. A top is said to *sleep* when it spins so fast that its motion is imperceptible.
603. mend their Pace: travel faster.
613. Lumber: junk.
619. Garth: see ll. 108–11*n.,* above, and also *Summer,* l. 9.
623. St. Paul's Cathedral was often used as a meeting-place by businessmen as well as by loiterers and gallants. Paul's Churchyard was the booksellers' quarter around the Cathedral.

Blest with a *Taste* exact, yet unconfin'd;
A *Knowledge* both of *Books* and *Humankind;*   640
Gen'rous Converse; a *Soul* exempt from *Pride;*
And *Love to Praise,* with *Reason* on his Side?
    Such once were *Criticks,* such the Happy *Few,*
Athens and *Rome* in better Ages knew.
The mighty *Stagyrite* first left the Shore,   645
Spread all his Sails, and durst the Deeps explore;
He steer'd securely, and discover'd far,
Led by the Light of the *Mæonian Star.*
Poets, a *Race* long unconfin'd and free,
Still fond and proud of *Savage Liberty,*   650
Receiv'd his Laws, and stood convinc'd 'twas fit
Who conquer'd *Nature,* shou'd preside o'er *Wit.*
    Horace still charms with graceful Negligence,
And without Method *talks* us into Sense,
Will like a *Friend* familiarly convey   655
The *truest Notions* in the *easiest way.*
He, who Supream in Judgment, as in Wit,
Might boldly censure, as he boldly writ,
Yet *judg'd* with *Coolness* tho' he sung with *Fire;*
His *Precepts* teach but what his *Works* inspire.   660
Our Criticks take a contrary Extream,
They *judge* with *Fury,* but they *write* with *Fle'me:*
Nor suffers *Horace* more in wrong *Translations*
By *Wits,* than *Criticks* in as wrong *Quotations.*
    See *Dionysius Homer's* Thoughts refine,   665
And call new Beauties forth from ev'ry Line!
    Fancy and Art in gay *Petronius* please,
The *Scholar's Learning,* with the *Courtier's Ease.*
    In grave *Quintilian's* copious Work we find
The justest *Rules,* and clearest *Method* join'd;   670
Thus *useful Arms* in Magazines we place,
All rang'd in *Order,* and dispos'd with *Grace,*
But less to please the Eye, than arm the Hand,
Still fit for *Use,* and ready at Command.
    Thee, bold *Longinus!* all the Nine inspire,   675
And bless *their Critick* with a *Poet's Fire.*

645. Stagyrite: Aristotle.
648. Mæonian Star: Homer, born in Maeonia (Lydia).
652. A tribute to Aristotle's work in science as well as to his *Poetics.*
662. Fle'me: phlegm (coldness, sluggishness).
664. than Criticks: than by critics.
665. Dionysius of Halicarnassus (c. 30 B.C.), Greek critic and rhetorician. See Pope's Preface to the *Iliad,* ll. 393–6.
667. Petronius: Petronius Arbiter (d. 66 A.D.), elegant voluptuary and writer at the court of Nero.
669. Quintilian: noted Roman rhetorician of the first century A.D.
675. Longinus: Greek critic of the first century A.D. to whom the treatise *On the Sublime* is attributed.

An ardent *Judge*, who Zealous in his Trust,
With *Warmth* gives Sentence, yet is always *Just;*
Whose *own Example* strengthens all his Laws,
And *Is himself* that great *Sublime* he draws.   680
    Thus long succeeding Criticks justly reign'd,
Licence repress'd, and *useful Laws* ordain'd;
Learning and *Rome* alike in Empire grew,
And *Arts* still *follow'd* where her Eagles *flew;*
From the same Foes, at last, both felt their Doom,   685
And the same Age saw *Learning* fall, and *Rome.*
With *Tyranny*, then *Superstition* join'd,
As that the *Body*, this enslav'd the *Mind;*
Much was *Believ'd*, but little *understood*,
And to be *dull* was constru'd to be *good;*   690
A *second* Deluge Learning thus o'er-run,
And the *Monks* finish'd what the *Goths* begun.
    At length, *Erasmus*, that *great, injur'd* Name,
(The *Glory* of the Priesthood, and the *Shame!*)
Stemm'd the *wild Torrent* of a *barb'rous Age*,   695
And drove those *Holy Vandals* off the Stage.
    But see! each *Muse*, in *Leo's* Golden Days,
Starts from her Trance, and trims her wither'd Bays!
Rome's ancient *Genius*, o'er its *Ruins* spread,
Shakes off the *Dust*, and rears his rev'rend Head!   700
Then *Sculpture* and her *Sister-Arts* revive;
Stones leap'd to *Form*, and *Rocks* began to *live;*
With *sweeter Notes* each *rising Temple* rung;
A *Raphael* painted, and a *Vida* sung!
Immortal *Vida!* on whose honour'd Brow   705
The Poet's *Bays* and Critick's *Ivy* grow:
Cremona now shall ever boast thy Name,
As next in Place to *Mantua*, next in Fame!
    But soon by Impious Arms from *Latium* chas'd,
Their *ancient Bounds* the banish'd Muses past;   710
Thence Arts o'er all the *Northern World* advance;

684. Eagles: the Eagles carried as standards by the Roman legions.
686. Rome: Pope uses an older pronunciation of *Rome*, to rhyme with *Doom.*
693–4. Pope considered Erasmus (1466–1536) the *glory* of the priesthood because of his learning, and its *shame* because of the treatment he received at its hands. See also *The First Satire of the Second Book*, ll. 63–7.
697. Leo's Golden Days: the Italian Renaissance reached its zenith under Leo X, pope from 1513 to 1521.
698. trims: restores.
704. Vida: M. Hieronymus Vida, an excellent *Latin* Poet, who writ an Art of Poetry in Verse. He flourish'd in the time of *Leo*, the Tenth.   P.
706. Critick's Ivy: Pope apparently was the first to crown a critic with ivy (traditionally associated with poets).
707–8. Vida was born in Cremona, very near to Mantua, the birthplace of Virgil.
709. Impious Arms: a reference to the Sack of Rome in 1527 by an army of the Emperor Charles V.   **Latium:** Italy.

But *Critic Learning* flourish'd most in *France.*
The *Rules,* a Nation born to serve, obeys,
And *Boileau* still in Right of *Horace* sways.
But *we,* brave *Britons, Foreign Laws* despis'd,   715
And kept *unconquer'd,* and *unciviliz'd,*
Fierce for the *Liberties of Wit, and* bold,
We still defy'd the *Romans, as of old.*
Yet *some* there were, among the *sounder Few*
Of those who *less presum'd,* and *better knew,*   720
Who durst assert the *juster Ancient Cause,*
And here *restor'd* Wit's *Fundamental Laws.*
Such was the Muse, whose Rules and Practice tell,
Nature's chief Master-piece is writing well.
Such was *Roscomon* — not more *learn'd* than *good,*   725
With Manners gen'rous as his Noble Blood;
To him the Wit of *Greece* and *Rome* was known,
And ev'ry *Author's Merit,* but his own.
Such late was *Walsh,* — the Muse's Judge and Friend,
Who justly knew to blame or to commend;   730
To Failings *mild,* but *zealous* for Desert;
The *clearest Head,* and the *sincerest Heart.*
This humble Praise, lamented *Shade!* receive,
This Praise at least a grateful Muse may give!
The Muse, whose early Voice you taught to Sing,   735
Prescrib'd her Heights, and prun'd her tender Wing,
(Her Guide now lost) no more attempts to *rise,*
But in low Numbers short Excursions tries:
Content, if hence th' Unlearn'd their Wants may view,
The Learn'd reflect on what before they knew: 740
Careless of *Censure,* nor too fond of *Fame,*
Still pleas'd to *praise,* yet not afraid to *blame,*
Averse alike to *Flatter,* or *Offend,*
Not *free* from Faults, nor yet too vain to *mend.*

713. **Nation born to serve:** it was customary for the English to sneer at the servility of the French.
714. **Boileau:** Nicolas Boileau-Despréaux (1636–1711), distinguished poet and critic, author of *L'Art Poétique.*
718. I.e., modern English writers seem to defy the precepts of classical Roman criticism in the same way their ancestors defied the ancient Roman legions who invaded Britain.
723. **the Muse:** John Sheffield, Duke of Buckingham (1648–1721), author of *An Essay upon Poetry,* from which l. 724 is taken.
725. **Roscomon:** Wentworth Dillon, fourth Earl of Roscommon (1633–85), author of *An Essay on Translated Verse.*
729. **Walsh:** William Walsh (1663–1708), minor poet who befriended the young Pope and gave him critical advice (see first note to *Winter*).   **the Muse's Judge:** the muse here and at ll. 734–5 is Pope himself.
736. **prun'd:** refers to a trimming or dressing of feathers with the beak.

MESSIAH

A SACRED ECLOGUE

In Imitation of VIRGIL'S POLLIO

ADVERTISEMENT

In reading several passages of the Prophet *Isaiah,* which foretell the coming
of Christ and the felicities attending it, I could not but observe a remarkable parity between many of the thoughts, and those in the *Pollio* of *Virgil.*
This will not seem surprizing when we reflect, that the Eclogue was taken
from a *Sybilline* prophecy on the same subject. One may judge that *Virgil*
did not copy it line by line, but selected such Ideas as best agreed with
the nature of pastoral poetry, and disposed them in that manner which
serv'd most to beautify his piece. I have endeavour'd the same in this
imitation of him, tho' without admitting any thing of my own; since it
was written with this particular view, that the reader by comparing the
several thoughts might see how far the images and descriptions of the
Prophet are superior to those of the Poet. But as I fear I have prejudiced
them by my management, I shall subjoin the passages of *Isaiah,* and those
of *Virgil,* under the same disadvantage of a literal translation.

Y<small>E</small> Nymphs of *Solyma!* begin the Song:
 To heav'nly Themes sublimer Strains belong.
 The Mossie Fountains and the Sylvan Shades,
The Dreams of *Pindus* and th'*Aonian* Maids,
Delight no more — O Thou my Voice inspire   5
Who touch'd *Isaiah*'s hallow'd Lips with Fire!
 Rapt into future Times, the Bard begun;
A *Virgin* shall conceive, a *Virgin* bear a Son!
From *Jesse*'s Root behold a Branch arise,
Whose sacred Flow'r with Fragrance fills the Skies.   10

MESSIAH: First published on May 14, 1712, in the *Spectator*, No. 378, which
prefaced the poem thus: "I Will make no Apology for entertaining the Reader
with the following Poem, which is written by a great Genius, a Friend of mine,
in the Country; who is not ashamed to employ his Wit in the Praise of his Maker."
Much of the imagery and diction of the *Messiah* derives from at least three dif-

Th' Æthereal Spirit o'er its Leaves shall move,
And on its Top descends the Mystic Dove.
Ye Heav'ns! from high the dewy Nectar pour,
And in soft Silence shed the kindly Show'r!
The Sick and Weak the healing Plant shall aid; 15
From Storms a Shelter, and from Heat a Shade.
All Crimes shall cease, and ancient Fraud shall fail;
Returning Justice lift aloft her Scale;
Peace o'er the World her Olive-Wand extend,
And white-roab'd Innocence from Heav'n descend. 20
Swift fly the Years, and rise th'expected Morn!
Oh spring to Light, Auspicious Babe, be born!
See Nature hasts her earliest Wreaths to bring,
With all the Incence of the breathing Spring:
See lofty *Lebanon* his Head advance, 25
See nodding Forests on the Mountains dance,
See spicy Clouds from lowly *Saron* rise,
And *Carmel's* flow'ry Top perfumes the Skies!
Hark! a glad Voice the lonely Desert chears:
Prepare the Way! a God, a God appears. 30
A God, a God! the vocal Hills reply,
The Rocks proclaim th'approaching Deity.
Lo Earth receives him from the bending Skies!
Sink down ye Mountains, and ye Vallies rise:

---

ferent versions of the Bible: the King James or Authorized Version, the Douai Catholic version, the Vulgate (a Latin version). The *Pollio* (of which the poem is an avowed imitation) is Virgil's fourth *Eclogue,* written about 40 B.C. to celebrate the birth of a child thought to be the son of a Roman consul, C. Asinius Pollio. Adapting a prophecy in the famed Sibylline books to his design, Virgil suggested that the birth of the infant would inaugurate a new golden age. Pope, in all editions of *Messiah,* directed his readers by means of notes to those passages in both Isaiah and the *Pollio* that were most relevant to his poem.

1. **Solyma:** latter part of the Greek name for Jerusalem.

4. **Dreams:** ancient poets were thought to receive inspired dreams by sleeping on mountains sacred to the Muses.   **Pindus:** a mountain in Thessaly regarded as a seat of the Muses.   **Aonia:** the Muses, who frequented Mt. Helicon in Aonia, were termed Aonian maidens.

5–6. See Isaiah 6:6–7.

7. **Rapt:** carried away in spirit.   **Bard:** Isaiah.

8. Compare Virgil, *Ecl.* IV 6–17, with Isaiah 7:14, 9:6–7.

9. **Jesse's Root:** see Isaiah 11:1.

12. See Isaiah 11:2, and Matthew 3:16.

13. **dewy Nectar:** Isaiah 45:8.

15–16. Isaiah 25:4.

17. **ancient Fraud:** the fraud of the serpent.

18. **Returning Justice:** see Isaiah 9:7. In classical mythology, the reappearance of Astraea, goddess of Justice, on earth was to be the first sign of the return of the golden age.

23–8. Compare Virgil, *Ecl.* IV 18–23, with Isaiah 35:1–2, 60:13.

24. **breathing:** emitting fragrance.

27. **Saron:** Sharon.

29–36. Compare Virgil, *Ecl.* IV 48–9, and *Ecl.* V 62–4, with Isaiah 40:3–4, 44:23.

With Heads declin'd, ye Cedars, Homage pay; 35
Be smooth ye Rocks, ye rapid Floods give way!
The SAVIOR comes! by ancient Bards foretold:
Hear him ye Deaf, and all ye Blind behold!
He from thick Films shall purge the visual Ray,
And on the sightless Eye-ball pour the Day. 40
'Tis he th'obstructed Paths of Sound shall clear,
And bid new Musick charm th'unfolding Ear.
The Dumb shall sing, the Lame his Crutch foregoe,
And leap exulting like the bounding Roe.
No Sigh, no Murmur the wide World shall hear, 45
From ev'ry Face he wipes off ev'ry Tear.
In adamantine Chains shall Death be bound,
And Hell's grim Tyrant feel th'eternal Wound.
As the good Shepherd tends his fleecy Care,
Seeks freshest Pasture and the purest Air, 50
Explores the lost, the wand'ring Sheep directs,
By Day o'ersees them, and by Night protects;
The tender Lambs he raises in his Arms,
Feeds from his Hand, and in his Bosom warms:
Thus shall Mankind his Guardian Care ingage, 55
The promis'd Father of the future Age.
No more shall Nation against Nation rise,
Nor ardent Warriors meet with hateful Eyes,
Nor Fields with gleaming Steel be cover'd o'er;
The Brazen Trumpets kindle Rage no more: 60
But useless Lances into Scythes shall bend,
And the broad Faulchion in a Plow-share end.
Then Palaces shall rise; the joyful Son
Shall finish what his short-liv'd Sire begun;
Their Vines a Shadow to their Race shall yield; 65
And the same Hand that sow'd, shall reap the Field.
The Swain in barren Desarts with surprize
See Lillies spring, and sudden Verdure rise;
And Starts, amidst the thirsty Wilds, to hear
New Falls of Water murm'ring in his Ear: 70
On rifted Rocks, the Dragon's late Abodes,
The green Reed trembles, and the Bulrush nods.

38–44. See Isaiah 42:18, 35:5–6.
39. visual Ray: an older theory of vision held that sight depended upon a ray of light issuing from the eye.
46. See Isaiah 25:8.
51. Explores: searches for.
53. See Isaiah 40:11.
56. promis'd Father: Isaiah 9:6.
57–62. See Isaiah 2:4.
62. Faulchion: sword.
63–6. See Isaiah, 65:21–2.
67–76. Compare Virgil, *Ecl.* IV 28–30, with Isaiah 35:1, 7; 55:13; 41:19.

Waste sandy Vallies, once perplex'd with Thorn,
The spiry Firr and shapely Box adorn;
To leaf-less Shrubs the flow'ring Palms succeed,   75
And od'rous Myrtle to the noisome Weed.
The Lambs with Wolves shall graze the verdant Mead,
And Boys in flow'ry Bands the Tyger lead;
The Steer and Lion at one Crib shall meet;
And harmless Serpents lick the Pilgrim's Feet.   80
The smiling Infant in his Hand shall take
The crested Basilisk and speckled Snake;
Pleas'd, the green Lustre of the Scales survey,
And with their forky Tongue shall innocently play.
Rise, crown'd with Light, Imperial *Salem* rise!   85
Exalt thy Tow'ry Head, and lift thy Eyes!
See, a long Race thy spatious Courts adorn;
See future Sons, and Daughters yet unborn
In crowding Ranks on ev'ry Side arise,
Demanding Life, impatient for the Skies!   90
See barb'rous Nations at thy Gates attend,
Walk in thy Light, and in thy Temple bend.
See thy bright Altars throng'd with prostrate Kings,
And heap'd with Products of *Sabæan* Springs!
For thee, *Idume's* spicy Forests blow;   95
And Seeds of Gold in *Ophyr's* Mountains glow.
See Heav'n its sparkling Portals wide display,
And break upon thee in a Flood of Day!
No more the rising *Sun* shall gild the Morn,
Nor Evening *Cynthia* fill her silver Horn,   100
But lost, dissolv'd in thy superior Rays;
One Tyde of Glory, one unclouded Blaze,
O'erflow thy Courts: The LIGHT HIMSELF shall shine
Reveal'd; and *God's* eternal Day be thine!
The Seas shall waste; the Skies in Smoke decay;   105
Rocks fall to Dust, and Mountains melt away;
But fix'd *His* Word, *His* saving Pow'r remains;
Thy *Realm* for ever lasts! thy own *Messiah* reigns!

73. **perplex'd**: entangled.
77–84. Compare Virgil, *Ecl.* IV 21–5, with Isaiah 11:6–8, 65:25.
82. **Basilisk**: a mythical reptile imaged with a crest on its head.
85. **Salem**: Jerusalem, here symbolic of the "church universal."
85–94. See Isaiah 60:1–6.
94. **Sabæan**: Saba (Sheba) was famous for its gold and incense.
95. **Idume**: Edom, to the south of Palestine.
96. **Seeds of Gold**: gold was popularly believed to ripen, plant-like, in the earth.   **Ophyr**: a region famous in antiquity for its gold.
99–104. See Isaiah 60:19–20.
100. **Cynthia**: goddess of the moon.
105–8. See Isaiah 51:6, 54:10.

EPISTLE TO MISS BLOUNT

With the Works of VOITURE

IN these gay Thoughts the Loves and Graces shine,
  And all the Writer lives in ev'ry Line;
  His easie Art may happy Nature seem,
Trifles themselves are Elegant in him.
Sure to charm all was his peculiar Fate,   5
Who without Flatt'ry pleas'd the Fair and Great;
Still with Esteem no less convers'd than read;
With Wit well-natur'd, and with Books well-bred;
His Heart, his Mistress and his Friend did share;
His Time, the Muse, the Witty, and the Fair.   10
Thus wisely careless, innocently gay,
Chearful, he play'd the Trifle, Life, away,
'Till Fate scarce felt his gentle Breath supprest,
As smiling Infants sport themselves to Rest:
Ev'n Rival Wits did *Voiture's* Death deplore,   15
And the Gay mourn'd who never mourn'd before;
The truest Hearts for *Voiture* heav'd with Sighs;
Voiture was wept by all the brightest Eyes;
The *Smiles* and *Loves* had dy'd in *Voiture's* Death,
But that for ever in his Lines they breath.   20
    Let the strict Life of graver Mortals be
A long, exact, and serious Comedy,
In ev'ry Scene some Moral let it teach,
And, if it can, at once both Please and Preach:
Let mine, an innocent gay Farce appear,   25
And more Diverting still than Regular,
Have Humour, Wit, a native Ease and Grace;

EPISTLE TO MISS BLOUNT: First published on May 20, 1712, with the title, *To a
Young Lady, with the Works of Voiture.* The poem may originally have been
written to an imaginary lady, but in 1735 Pope changed the title in compliment
to his life-long friend and favorite, Martha Blount (see first note to *Epistle to a
Lady: Of the Characters of Women*). Vincent de Voiture (1598–1648) was a
French poet much esteemed for his letters of gallantry.
    1. Loves: cupids.
    26. Regular: according to the "Rules" (see *Essay on Criticism*, l. 88n.).
    28. Time and Place: the supposed dramatic unities of time and place (see
Essay on Criticism, l. 276n.).

Tho' not too strictly bound to Time and Place:
Criticks in Wit, or Life, are hard to please,
Few write to those, and none can live to these.   30
    Too much *your Sex* is by their Forms confin'd,
Severe to all, but most to Womankind;
Custom, grown blind with Age, must be your Guide;
Your Pleasure is a Vice, but not your Pride;
By nature yielding, stubborn but for Fame;   35
Made Slaves by Honour, and made Fools by Shame.
Marriage may all those petty Tyrants chace,
But sets up One, a greater, in their Place;
Well might you wish for Change, by those accurst,
But the last Tyrant ever proves the worst.   40
Still in Constraint your suff'ring Sex remains,
Or bound in formal, or in real Chains;
Whole Years neglected for some Months ador'd,
The fawning Servant turns a haughty Lord;
Ah quit not the free Innocence of Life!   45
For the dull Glory of a virtuous Wife!
Nor let false Shows, or empty Titles please:
Aim not at Joy, but rest content with Ease.
    The Gods, to curse *Pamela* with her Pray'rs,
Gave the gilt Coach and dappled *Flanders* Mares,   50
The shining Robes, rich Jewels, Beds of State,
And to compleat her Bliss, a Fool for Mate.
She glares in *Balls*, *Front-boxes*, and the *Ring*,
A vain, unquiet, glitt'ring, wretched Thing!
Pride, Pomp, and State but reach her outward Part,   55
She sighs, and is no *Dutchess* at her Heart.
    But, Madam, if the Fates withstand, and you
Are destin'd *Hymen*'s willing Victim too,
Trust not too much your now resistless Charms,
Those, Age or Sickness, soon or late, disarms;   60
Good Humour only teaches Charms to last,
Still makes new Conquests, and maintains the past:
Love, rais'd on Beauty, will like That decay,
Our Hearts may bear its slender Chain a Day,
As flow'ry Bands in Wantonness are worn;   65
A Morning's Pleasure, and at Evening torn:
This binds in Ties more easie, yet more strong,
The willing Heart, and only holds it long.

31. Forms: prescribed conduct, the proprieties.
35. Fame: reputation.
44. Servant: lover.
49. Pamela: pronounced with the accent on the second syllable.
53. Ring: a fashionable carriage-drive in Hyde Park.
58. Hymen: god of marriage.
59–62. Cf. *The Rape of the Lock*, V 29–34.
61. Humour: habitual disposition, temperament.

Thus *Voiture's* early Care still shone the same,
And *Monthausier* was only chang'd in Name: 70
By this, ev'n now they live, ev'n now they charm,
Their Wit still sparkling and their Flames still warm.
    Now crown'd with Myrtle, on th' *Elysian* Coast,
Amid those Lovers, joys his gentle Ghost,
Pleas'd while with Smiles his happy Lines you view,   75
And finds a fairer *Ramboüillet* in you.
The brightest Eyes of *France* inspir'd his Muse,
The brightest Eyes of *Britain* now peruse,
And dead as living, 'tis our Author's Pride,
Still to charm those who charm the World beside.   80

69. **Voiture's early Care**: Madamoiselle Paulet.   P.
    70. **Monthausier**: Julie Lucine d'Angennes (1607–71), a daughter of the Marquise de Rambouillet, married the duc de Montausier.
    71. **this**: here and at l. 67, *this* refers to "Good Humour" (l. 61).
    73. **Myrtle**: emblem of love associated with Venus.
    76. **Ramboüillet**: see l. 70*n.*

WINDSOR-FOREST

TO THE RIGHT HONOURABLE

George Lord *Lansdown*

Non injussa cano: Te nostræ, Vare, Myricæ
Te Nemus omne canet; nec Phœbo gratior ulla est
Quam sibi quæ Vari præscripsit Pagina nomen.

VIRG.

THY Forests, *Windsor!* and thy green Retreats,
  At once the Monarch's and the Muse's Seats,
  Invite my Lays. Be present, Sylvan Maids!
Unlock your Springs, and open all your Shades.
Granville commands: Your Aid O Muses bring!   5
What Muse for *Granville* can refuse to sing?
  The Groves of *Eden,* vanish'd now so long,
Live in Description, and look green in Song:
These, were my Breast inspir'd with equal Flame,
Like them in Beauty, should be like in Fame.   10

WINDSOR-FOREST: With the signing of the Treaty of Utrecht on April 11, 1713, the War of the Spanish Succession came to an end, and the future greatness of Great Britain as a maritime and mercantile power was assured. *Windsor-Forest,* written in celebration of the eagerly-awaited Peace, was first published on March 7, a few weeks before the Treaty was signed, and dedicated to George Granville, Lord Lansdowne, Secretary for War under Queen Anne, and a minor poet and playwright (see *Spring,* l. 46n.). The Latin epigraph prefixed to the poem is from Virgil's *Eclogues,* VI 9–12, and reflects the fact that Pope gave his poem its final shape at the insistence of Granville: "I do not sing unbidden; of thee, Varus, our tamarisks and our groves all shall sing: no page is more pleasing to Phoebus than that which is prefixed with the name of Varus."

   1. This poem was written at two different times: the first part of it which relates to the country, in the year 1704, at the same time with the Pastorals: the latter was not added till the year 1713, in which it was publish'd. P.   See l. 290n.

   2. Monarch's: Windsor Castle, located about 20 miles west of London, was constructed on the site where King Arthur supposedly sat with his Knights of the Round Table and where William the Conqueror had built his castle. It has served as a royal residence, a burial place for many of England's monarchs, and as the meeting place of the Knights of the Garter.

   7–10. An allusion to the "Eden" created by Milton in *Paradise Lost.*

Here Hills and Vales, the Woodland and the Plain,
Here Earth and Water seem to strive again,
Not *Chaos*-like together crush'd and bruis'd,
But as the World, harmoniously confus'd:
Where Order in Variety we see,   15
And where, tho' all things differ, all agree.
Here waving Groves a checquer'd Scene display,
And part admit and part exclude the Day;
As some coy Nymph her Lover's warm Address
Nor quite indulges, nor can quite repress.   20
There, interspers'd in Lawns and opening Glades,
Thin Trees arise that shun each others Shades.
Here in full Light the russet Plains extend;
There wrapt in Clouds the blueish Hills ascend:
Ev'n the wild Heath displays her Purple Dies,   25
And 'midst the Desart fruitful Fields arise,
That crown'd with tufted Trees and springing Corn,
Like verdant Isles the sable Waste adorn.
Let *India* boast her Plants, nor envy we
The weeping Amber or the balmy Tree,   30
While by our Oaks the precious Loads are born,
And Realms commanded which those Trees adorn.
Not proud *Olympus* yields a nobler Sight,
Tho' Gods assembled grace his tow'ring Height,
Than what more humble Mountains offer here,   35
Where, in their Blessings, all those Gods appear.
See *Pan* with Flocks, with Fruits *Pomona* crown'd,
Here blushing *Flora* paints th'enamel'd Ground,
Here *Ceres'* Gifts in waving Prospect stand,
And nodding tempt the joyful Reaper's Hand,   40
Rich Industry sits smiling on the Plains,
And Peace and Plenty tell, a STUART reigns.
    Not thus the Land appear'd in Ages past,
A dreary Desart and a gloomy Waste,
To Savage Beasts and Savage Laws a Prey,   45
And Kings more furious and severe than they:
Who claim'd the Skies, dispeopled Air and Floods,

21. **Lawns:** any open space between woods.
26. **Desart:** any wild or uninhabited region.
27. **tufted:** in a small group, or clump.   **Corn:** wheat.
31. **Oaks:** the ships built of English oak which "bore" valuable spices to England and enabled her to rule over the lands whence they came.
37–9. Pan was god of flocks and pastures, Pomona was goddess of fruit trees, Flora was goddess of flowers, Ceres was goddess of grains and vegetation.
38. **enamel'd Ground:** a technical phrase from painting: metals were covered with enamel to form a "ground" or background for other colors.
42. **Stuart:** Queen Anne.
45. **Savage Laws:** *The Forest Laws.* P.   After the Norman Conquest many "forests," or royal hunting preserves, were established, and trespassers on these lands were severely punished under forest law and forest courts.
46. **Kings:** the Norman kings.

The lonely Lords of empty Wilds and Woods.
Cities laid waste, they storm'd the Dens and Caves,
(For wiser Brutes were backward to be Slaves.)   50
What could be free, when lawless Beasts obey'd,
And ev'n the Elements a Tyrant sway'd?
In vain kind Seasons swell'd the teeming Grain,
Soft Show'rs distill'd, and Suns grew warm in vain;
The Swain with Tears his frustrate Labour yields,   55
And famish'd dies amidst his ripen'd Fields.
What wonder then, a Beast or Subject slain
Were equal Crimes in a Despotick Reign;
Both doom'd alike for sportive Tyrants bled,
But while the Subject starv'd, the Beast was fed.   60
Proud *Nimrod* first the bloody Chace began,
A mighty Hunter, and his Prey was Man.
Our haughty *Norman* boasts that barb'rous Name,
And makes his trembling Slaves the Royal Game.
The Fields are ravish'd from th'industrious Swains,   65
From Men their Cities, and from Gods their Fanes:
The levell'd Towns with Weeds lie cover'd o'er,
The hollow Winds thro' naked Temples roar;
Round broken Columns clasping Ivy twin'd;
O'er Heaps of Ruin stalk'd the stately Hind;   70
The Fox obscene to gaping Tombs retires,
And savage Howlings fill the sacred Quires.
Aw'd by his Nobles, by his Commons curst,
Th' Oppressor rul'd Tyrannick where he *durst*,
Stretch'd o'er the Poor, and Church, his Iron Rod,   75
And serv'd alike his Vassals and his God.
Whom ev'n the *Saxon* spar'd, and bloody *Dane*,
The wanton Victims of his *Sport* remain.
But see the Man who spacious Regions gave
A Waste for Beasts, himself deny'd a Grave!   80
Stretch'd on the Lawn his second Hope survey,
At once the Chaser and at once the Prey.
Lo *Rufus*, tugging at the deadly Dart,

52. Elements: the places inhabited by the wild creatures.
61. Nimrod: considered the first hunter, and prototype of the despot.
65. The Fields are ravish'd: *Alluding to the destruction made in the* New Forest, *and the Tyrannies exercis'd there by* William I.   P.   The New Forest is in the very south of England, in Hampshire.
66. Fanes: temples, or churches.
71. obscene: loathesome.
72. Quires: choirs.
77. Saxon . . . Dane: earlier invaders of England.
79–80. William I's burial was delayed for a time, because of objections by the owner of the site selected for the king's grave.
81. second Hope: Richard, *second Son of* William *the* Conqueror.   P.   He was killed by a stag in the New Forest.
83. Rufus: William Rufus, third son and successor to William I, killed by an arrow while hunting in the New Forest.

Bleeds in the Forest, like a wounded Hart.
Succeeding Monarchs heard the Subjects Cries,   85
Nor saw displeas'd the peaceful Cottage rise.
Then gath'ring Flocks on unknown Mountains fed,
O'er sandy Wilds were yellow Harvests spread,
The Forests wonder'd at th'unusual Grain,
And secret Transport touch'd the conscious Swain.   90
Fair *Liberty*, *Britannia*'s Goddess, rears
Her chearful Head, and leads the golden Years.
   Ye vig'rous Swains! while Youth ferments your Blood,
And purer Spirits swell the sprightly Flood,
Now range the Hills, the gameful Woods beset,   95
Wind the shrill Horn, or spread the waving Net.
When milder Autumn Summer's Heat succeeds,
And in the new-shorn Field the Partridge feeds,
Before his Lord the ready Spaniel bounds,
Panting with Hope, he tries the furrow'd Grounds,   100
But when the tainted Gales the Game betray,
Couch'd close he lyes, and meditates the Prey;
Secure they trust th'unfaithful Field, beset,
Till hov'ring o'er 'em sweeps the swelling Net.
Thus (if small Things we may with great compare)   105
When *Albion* sends her eager Sons to War,
Some thoughtless Town, with Ease and Plenty blest,
Near, and more near, the closing Lines invest;
Sudden they seize th'amaz'd, defenceless Prize,
And high in Air *Britannia*'s Standard flies.   110
   See! from the Brake the whirring Pheasant springs,
And mounts exulting on triumphant Wings;
Short is his Joy! he feels the fiery Wound,
Flutters in Blood, and panting beats the Ground.
Ah! what avail his glossie, varying Dyes,   115
His Purple Crest, and Scarlet-circled Eyes,
The vivid Green his shining Plumes unfold;
His painted Wings, and Breast that flames with Gold?
   Nor yet, when moist *Arcturus* clouds the Sky,
The Woods and Fields their pleasing Toils deny.   120
To Plains with well-breath'd Beagles we repair,
And trace the Mazes of the circling Hare.

87. unknown Mountains: hitherto forbidden to the flocks.
90. conscious: i.e., knowing, well-aware.
93–4. The blood was thought to be permeated by certain subtle, highly-refined substances, called "spirits," which animated the body in its powers. See *Essay on Criticism*, ll. 207–10n.
96. Wind: blow.
102. meditates: observes intently.
104. Net: Once the partridges had been "set" or "pointed" by the dog, a net was spread or cast over them.
106. Albion: an old name for England.
111. Brake: thicket.
119. Arcturus: see *Autumn*, l. 72n.

(Beasts, urg'd by us, their Fellow Beasts pursue,
And learn of Man each other to undo.)
With slaught'ring Guns th'unweary'd Fowler roves,   125
When Frosts have whiten'd all the naked Groves;
Where Doves in Flocks the leafless Trees o'ershade,
And lonely Woodcocks haunt the watry Glade.
He lifts the Tube, and levels with his Eye;
Strait a short Thunder breaks the frozen Sky.   130
Oft, as in Airy Rings they skim the Heath,
The clam'rous Lapwings feel the Leaden Death:
Oft as the mounting Larks their Notes prepare,
They fall, and leave their little Lives in Air.
    In genial Spring, beneath the quiv'ring Shade   135
Where cooling Vapours breathe along the Mead,
The patient Fisher takes his silent Stand
Intent, his Angle trembling in his Hand;
With Looks unmov'd, he hopes the Scaly Breed,
And eyes the dancing Cork and bending Reed.   140
Our plenteous Streams a various Race supply;
The bright-ey'd Perch with Fins of *Tyrian* Dye,
The silver Eel, in shining Volumes roll'd,
The yellow Carp, in Scales bedrop'd with Gold,
Swift Trouts, diversify'd with Crimson Stains,   145
And Pykes, the Tyrants of the watry Plains.
    Now *Cancer* glows with *Phœbus'* fiery Car;
The Youth rush eager to the Sylvan War;
Swarm o'er the Lawns, the Forest Walks surround,
Rowze the fleet Hart, and chear the opening Hound.   150
Th'impatient Courser pants in ev'ry Vein,
And pawing, seems to beat the distant Plain,
Hills, Vales, and Floods appear already crost,
And ere he starts, a thousand Steps are lost.
See! the bold Youth strain up the threatening Steep,   155
Rush thro' the Thickets, down the Vallies sweep,
Hang o'er their Coursers Heads with eager Speed,
And Earth rolls back beneath the flying Steed.
Let old *Arcadia* boast her ample Plain,
Th' Immortal Huntress, and her Virgin Train;   160
Nor envy *Windsor!* since thy Shades have seen
As bright a Goddess, and as chast a Queen;
Whose Care, like hers, protects the Sylvan Reign,

135. **genial**: generative.
142. **Tyrian Dye**: crimson or purple.
143. **Volumes**: coils.
   147. The sun enters the zodiacal sign of Cancer (the Crab) at the summer solstice, June 22.
150. **opening**: giving tongue.
   160. **Immortal Huntress**: Diana, goddess of the woods and of the moon (and thus of the tides).
   162. **Queen**: Queen Anne, but perhaps Queen Elizabeth I also.

    The Earth's fair Light, and Empress of the Main.
      Here too, 'tis sung, of old *Diana* stray'd,   165
And *Cynthus'* Top forsook for *Windsor* Shade;
Here was she seen o'er Airy Wastes to rove,
Seek the clear Spring, or haunt the pathless Grove;
Here arm'd with Silver Bows, in early Dawn,
Her buskin'd Virgins trac'd the Dewy Lawn.   170
    Above the rest a rural Nymph was fam'd,
Thy Offspring, *Thames!* the fair *Lodona* nam'd,
(*Lodona*'s Fate, in long Oblivion cast,
The Muse shall sing, and what she sings shall last)
Scarce could the Goddess from her Nymph be known,   175
But by the Crescent and the golden Zone,
She scorn'd the Praise of Beauty, and the Care;
A Belt her Waste, a Fillet binds her Hair,
A painted Quiver on her Shoulder sounds,
And with her Dart the flying Deer she wounds.   180
It chanc'd, as eager of the Chace the Maid
Beyond the Forest's verdant Limits stray'd,
Pan saw and lov'd, and burning with Desire
Pursu'd her Flight; her Flight increas'd his Fire.
Not half so swift the trembling Doves can fly,   185
When the fierce Eagle cleaves the liquid Sky;
Not half so swiftly the fierce Eagle moves,
When thro' the Clouds he drives the trembling Doves;
As from the God she flew with furious Pace,
Or as the God, more furious urg'd the Chace.   190
Now fainting, sinking, pale, the Nymph appears;
Now close behind his sounding Steps she hears;
And now his Shadow reach'd her as she run,
(His Shadow lengthen'd by the setting Sun)
And now his shorter Breath with sultry Air   195
Pants on her Neck, and fans her parting Hair.
In vain on Father *Thames* she calls for Aid,
Nor could *Diana* help her injur'd Maid.
Faint, breathless, thus she pray'd, nor pray'd in vain;
"Ah *Cynthia!* ah — tho' banish'd from thy Train,   200
"Let me, O let me, to the Shades repair,
"My native Shades — there weep, and murmur there."
She said, and melting as in Tears she lay,
In a soft, silver Stream dissolv'd away.
The silver Stream her Virgin Coldness keeps,   205

166. Cynthus' Top: Mt. Cynthus was thought to be Diana's birthplace.
170. buskin'd: a buskin is a kind of half-boot.
172. Offspring: see l. 207n.
176. Crescent: crescent moon, emblem of Diana.   **Zone:** girdle or belt.
186. liquid: clear, transparent.
200. Cynthia: Diana.

For ever murmurs, and for ever weeps;
Still bears the Name the hapless Virgin bore,
And bathes the Forest where she rang'd before.
In her chast Current oft the Goddess laves,
And with Celestial Tears augments the Waves.   210
Oft in her Glass the musing Shepherd spies
The headlong Mountains and the downward Skies,
The watry Landskip of the pendant Woods,
And absent Trees that tremble in the Floods;
In the clear azure Gleam the Flocks are seen,   215
And floating Forests paint the Waves with Green.
Thro' the fair Scene rowl slow the lingring Streams,
Then foaming pour along, and rush into the *Thames*.
   Thou too, great Father of the *British* Floods!
With joyful Pride survey'st our lofty Woods,   220
Where tow'ring Oaks their growing Honours rear,
And future Navies on thy Shores appear.
Not *Neptune*'s self from all his Streams receives
A wealthier Tribute, than to thine he gives.
No Seas so rich, so gay no Banks appear,   225
No Lake so gentle, and no Spring so clear.
Nor *Po* so swells the fabling Poet's Lays,
While led along the Skies his Current strays,
As thine, which visits *Windsor*'s fam'd Abodes,
To grace the Mansion of our earthly Gods.   230
Nor all his Stars above a Lustre show,
Like the bright Beauties on thy Banks below;
Where *Jove*, subdu'd by mortal Passion still,
Might change *Olympus* for a nobler Hill.
   Happy the Man whom this bright Court approves,   235
His Sov'reign favours, and his Country loves;
Happy next him who to these Shades retires,
Whom Nature charms, and whom the Muse inspires,
Whom humbler Joys of home-felt Quiet please,
Successive Study, Exercise and Ease.   240
He gathers Health from Herbs the Forest yields,
And of their fragrant Physick spoils the Fields:
With Chymic Art exalts the Min'ral Pow'rs,
And draws the Aromatick Souls of Flow'rs.
Now marks the Course of rolling Orbs on high;   245
O'er figur'd Worlds now travels with his Eye.

---

207. the Name: *The River* Loddon.   P.   It is a tributary of the Thames.
221. Honours: foliage.
   227. Po: Virgil and Ovid had identified the Po with Eridanus, a constellation
with the form of a winding river.
243. exalts: old chemistry term meaning to intensify or render more powerful.
244. draws: extracts.
246. figur'd Worlds: a map or globe of the world, perhaps the Zodiac.

Of ancient Writ unlocks the learned Store,
Consults the Dead, and lives past Ages o'er.
Or wandring thoughtful in the silent Wood,
Attends the Duties of the Wise and Good,   250
T'observe a Mean, be to himself a Friend,
To follow Nature, and regard his End.
Or looks on Heav'n with more than mortal Eyes,
Bids his free Soul expatiate in the Skies,
Amid her Kindred Stars familiar roam,   255
Survey the Region, and confess her Home!
Such was the Life great *Scipio* once admir'd,
Thus *Atticus*, and *Trumbal* thus retir'd.
    Ye sacred Nine! that all my Soul possess,
Whose Raptures fire me, and whose Visions bless,   260
Bear me, oh bear me to sequester'd Scenes,
The Bow'ry Mazes and surrounding Greens;
To *Thames*'s Banks which fragrant Breezes fill,
Or where ye Muses sport on *Cooper*'s Hill.
(On *Cooper*'s Hill eternal Wreaths shall grow,   265
While lasts the Mountain, or while *Thames* shall flow)
I seem thro' consecrated Walks to rove,
I hear soft Musick dye along the Grove;
Led by the Sound I roam from Shade to Shade,
By God-like Poets Venerable made: 270
Here his first Lays Majestick *Denham* sung;
There the last Numbers flow'd from *Cowley*'s Tongue.
O early lost! what Tears the River shed
When the sad Pomp along his Banks was led?
His drooping Swans on ev'ry Note expire,   275
And on his Willows hung each Muse's Lyre.
    Since Fate relentless stop'd their Heav'nly Voice,
No more the Forests ring, or Groves rejoice;
Who now shall charm the Shades where *Cowley* strung

255. Kindred Stars: the soul was anciently believed to be of the same substance as the stars.

257–8. Scipio Africanus Major (237–183 B.C.), the conqueror of Hannibal; Titus Pomponius, or Atticus (109–32 B.C.), Roman philosopher and correspondent of Cicero; and Sir William Trumbull, Secretary of State under William III (see *Spring*, ll. 7–10n.). All three retired from public life.

264. Cooper's Hill: a mount near the Thames celebrated in Sir John Denham's *Cooper's Hill*, a mid-seventeenth-century poem of the same general kind as *Windsor-Forest.*

271. Majestick Denham: see *Essay on Criticism*, l. 361n.

272–4. *Mr.* [Abraham] Cowley *died at* Chertsey, *on the Borders of the Forest and was from thence convey'd to* Westminster. P.   Cowley died in 1667, aged 49, and his body was floated down the Thames to London. See *First Ep. of the Second Bk.*, l. 75n.

275. Swans . . . expire: swans were fabled to sing at their own death.

276. Willows: cf. Psalm 137:2.

His living Harp, and lofty *Denham* sung?   280
But hark! the Groves rejoice, the Forest rings!
Are these reviv'd? or is it *Granville* sings?
   'Tis yours, my Lord, to bless our soft Retreats,
And call the Muses to their ancient Seats,
To paint anew the flow'ry Sylvan Scenes,   285
To crown the Forests with Immortal Greens,
Make *Windsor* Hills in lofty Numbers rise,
And lift her Turrets nearer to the Skies;
To sing those Honours you deserve to wear,
And add new Lustre to her Silver *Star*.   290
   Here noble *Surrey* felt the sacred Rage,
Surrey, the *Granville* of a former Age:
Matchless his Pen, victorious was his Lance;
Bold in the Lists, and graceful in the Dance:
In the same Shades the *Cupids* tun'd his Lyre,   295
To the same Notes, of Love, and soft Desire:
Fair *Geraldine*, bright Object of his Vow,
Then fill'd the Groves, as heav'nly *Myra* now.
   Oh wou'dst thou sing what Heroes *Windsor* bore,
What Kings first breath'd upon her winding Shore,   300
Or raise old Warriors whose ador'd Remains
In weeping Vaults her hallow'd Earth contains!
With *Edward*'s Acts adorn the shining Page,
Stretch his long Triumphs down thro' ev'ry Age,
Draw Monarchs chain'd, and *Cressi*'s glorious Field,   305
The Lillies blazing on the Regal Shield.
Then, from her Roofs when *Verrio*'s Colours fall,
And leave inanimate the naked Wall;
Still in thy Song shou'd vanquish'd *France* appear,
And bleed for ever under *Britain*'s Spear.   310

289–90. The "Honours" and "Silver Star" are those of the Order of the Garter, instituted at Windsor Castle by Edward III. Granville was never admitted to the Order.

290. All the lines that follow were not added to the poem till the year 1710. P.

291. Surrey: Henry Howard, *Earl of* Surrey, *one of the first Refiners of the* English *Poetry; who flourish'd in the time of* Henry *the* VIII[th.] P.

297–8. Geraldine . . . Myra: fictitious names of the ladies to whom Surrey and Granville addressed their love poems.

299–302. Edward III and Henry VI were born at Windsor; Edward IV, Henry VIII, and Charles I were buried there.

302. weeping: alluding to the dew which forms on stone and metal in damp weather.

303–6. Edward III defeated the French at Crécy, and at one time or another held captive the kings of Scotland and France. In 1340 he assumed the title of king of France and quartered the lilies of France with the leopards of England.

307. Verrio: Antonio Verrio (1639–1707), some of whose murals adorned parts of Windsor Castle and celebrated scenes here described by Pope. Cf. *Ep. to Burlington*, l. 146n.

Let softer Strains Ill-fated *Henry* mourn,
And Palms Eternal flourish round his Urn.
Here o'er the Martyr-King the Marble weeps,
And fast beside him, once-fear'd *Edward* sleeps:
Whom not th'extended *Albion* could contain,   315
From old *Belerium* to the *Northern* Main,
The Grave unites; where ev'n the Great find Rest,
And blended lie th' Oppressor and th' Opprest!

Make sacred *Charles's* Tomb for ever known,
(Obscure the Place, and uninscrib'd the Stone)   320
Oh Fact accurst! What Tears has *Albion* shed,
Heav'ns! what new Wounds, and how her old have bled?
She saw her Sons with purple Deaths expire,
Her sacred Domes involv'd in rolling Fire,
A dreadful Series of Intestine Wars,   325
Inglorious Triumphs, and dishonest Scars.
At length great *ANNA* said — Let Discord cease!
She said, the World obey'd, and all was *Peace!*

In that blest Moment, from his Oozy Bed
Old Father *Thames* advanc'd his rev'rend Head.   330
His Tresses dropt with Dews, and o'er the Stream
His shining Horns diffus'd a golden Gleam:
Grav'd on his Urn appear'd the Moon, that guides
His swelling Waters, and alternate Tydes;
The figur'd Streams in Waves of Silver roll'd,   335
And on their Banks *Augusta* rose in Gold.
Around his Throne the Sea-born Brothers stood,
Who swell with Tributary Urns his Flood.

311–12. The pious and gentle Henry VI was murdered in the Tower of London in 1471. After his death he was revered as a saint and martyr (the "Palms Eternal" are those of martyrdom).

314. **once-fear'd Edward:** Edward, duke of York, seized the crown from Henry VI in 1461 and became Edward IV. The two kings were eventually buried, not far from one another, in St. George's chapel in Windsor Castle.

316. **Belerium:** Latin name for Land's End, in Cornwall.

319–20. Charles I was beheaded in 1649 and buried, without services, in St. George's chapel, in the same tomb as Henry VIII. He was venerated by many as a royal martyr.

321. **Fact:** crime.

323–6. The "purple Deaths" of the Great Plague of 1665, the Great Fire of London in 1666, and the civil wars and revolutions of 17th-century England were thought by some to be evidence of God's wrath at the execution of Charles I.

326. **dishonest:** shameful.

327–8. Preliminaries to the Treaty of Utrecht were signed in London in 1711 (the main treaties were signed at Utrecht in April, 1713). The War of the Spanish Succession had begun in 1701.

332–3. River gods were pictured with the head or horns of a bull to suggest their roaring or their power. An urn is also their emblem.

336. **Augusta:** Roman name for London.

337. **Sea-born Brothers:** myth held all rivers to be born of Oceanus and Tethys.

First the fam'd Authors of his ancient Name,
The winding *Isis,* and the fruitful *Tame:*   340
The *Kennet* swift, for silver Eels renown'd;
The *Loddon* slow, with verdant Alders crown'd:
Cole, whose dark Streams his flow'ry Islands lave;
And chalky *Wey,* that rolls a milky Wave:
The blue, transparent *Vandalis* appears;   345
The gulphy *Lee* his sedgy Tresses rears:
And sullen *Mole,* that hides his diving Flood;
And silent *Darent,* stain'd with *Danish* Blood.

High in the midst, upon his Urn reclin'd,
(His Sea-green Mantle waving with the Wind)   350
The God appear'd; he turn'd his azure Eyes
Where *Windsor*-Domes and pompous Turrets rise,
Then bow'd and spoke; the Winds forget to roar,
And the hush'd Waves glide softly to the Shore.

Hail Sacred *Peace!* hail long-expected Days,   355
That *Thames*'s Glory to the Stars shall raise!
Tho' *Tyber's* Streams immortal *Rome* behold,
Tho' foaming *Hermus* swells with Tydes of Gold,
From Heav'n it self tho' sev'nfold *Nilus* flows,
And Harvests on a hundred Realms bestows;   360
These now no more shall be the Muse's Themes,
Lost in my Fame, as in the Sea their Streams.
Let *Volga*'s Banks with Iron Squadrons shine,
And Groves of Lances glitter on the *Rhine,*
Let barb'rous *Ganges* arm a servile Train;   365
Be mine the Blessings of a peaceful Reign.
No more my Sons shall dye with *British* Blood
Red *Iber's* Sands, or *Ister's* foaming Flood;
Safe on my Shore each unmolested Swain
Shall tend the Flocks, or reap the bearded Grain;   370
The shady Empire shall retain no Trace
Of War or Blood, but in the Sylvan Chace,

339–40. The Thames (Tamesis) was thought to be the offspring of the Thame and the Isis.
343. **Cole:** the river Colne.
345. **Vandalis:** the Wandle.
346. **gulphy:** full of eddies and whirlpools.
347. The Mole moves underground for part of its course.
348. **Danish Blood:** the particular battle against Danish invaders alluded to here is obscure.
358. **Hermus:** a river in Asia Minor whose sands were fabled as covered with gold.
359. **Nilus:** the source of the Nile (called *sev'nfold* for its mouths) was unknown, and myth derived it from heaven.
368. **Iber:** the Ebro, in Spain, where England and her allies won a victory in 1710.   **Ister:** the Danube, where the Duke of Marlborough won his famous victory at Blenheim in 1704.

The Trumpets sleep, while chearful Horns are blown,
And Arms employ'd on Birds and Beasts alone.
Behold! th'ascending *Villa's* on my Side   375
Project long Shadows o'er the Chrystal Tyde.
Behold! *Augusta's* glitt'ring Spires increase,
And Temples rise, the beauteous Works of Peace.
I see, I see where two fair Cities bend
Their ample Bow, a new *White-Hall* ascend!   380
There mighty Nations shall inquire their Doom,
The World's great Oracle in Times to come;
There Kings shall sue, and suppliant States be seen
Once more to bend before a *British* QUEEN.

    Thy Trees, fair *Windsor!* now shall leave their Woods,   385
And half thy Forests rush into my Floods,
Bear *Britain's* Thunder, and her Cross display,
To the bright Regions of the rising Day;
Tempt Icy Seas, where scarce the Waters roll,
Where clearer Flames glow round the frozen Pole;   390
Or under Southern Skies exalt their Sails,
Led by new Stars, and born by spicy Gales!
For me the Balm shall bleed, and Amber flow,
The Coral redden, and the Ruby glow,
The Pearly Shell its lucid Globe infold,   395
And *Phœbus* warm the ripening Ore to Gold.
The Time shall come, when free as Seas or Wind
Unbounded *Thames* shall flow for all Mankind,
Whole Nations enter with each swelling Tyde,
And Seas but join the Regions they divide;   400
Earth's distant Ends our Glory shall behold,
And the new World launch forth to seek the Old.
Then Ships of uncouth Form shall stem the Tyde,
And Feather'd People crowd my wealthy Side,
And naked Youths and painted Chiefs admire   405
Our Speech, our Colour, and our strange Attire!
Oh stretch thy Reign, fair *Peace!* from Shore to Shore,
Till Conquest cease, and Slav'ry be no more:

378. Temples rise: The fifty new Churches. P. They were built at the recommendation of Queen Anne to meet the needs of London's growing population.

379. two fair Cities: London and Westminster, whose limits meet at a bend in the Thames.

380. new White-Hall: Whitehall Palace had burned down in 1698, and plans for its reconstruction were never carried out.

381–422. Throughout these lines Pope frequently echoes Isaiah, chap. 60.

384. Once more: as in the time of Elizabeth I.

387. Cross: the red cross of St. George in the Union Jack.

396. The sun, it was thought, caused gold to grow and ripen in the earth.

398. Unbounded Thames: A wish that London may be made a Free Port. P.

404. Feather'd People: four Iroquois Indian chiefs had visited England in 1710.

Till the freed *Indians* in their native Groves
Reap their own Fruits, and woo their Sable Loves,   410
Peru once more a Race of Kings behold,
And other *Mexico's* be roof'd with Gold.
Exil'd by Thee from Earth to deepest Hell,
In Brazen Bonds shall barb'rous *Discord* dwell:
Gigantick *Pride*, pale *Terror*, gloomy *Care*,   415
And mad *Ambition*, shall attend her there
There purple *Vengeance* bath'd in Gore retires,
Her Weapons blunted, and extinct her Fires:
There hateful *Envy* her own Snakes shall feel,
And *Persecution* mourn her broken Wheel: 420
There *Faction* roar, *Rebellion* bite her Chain,
And gasping Furies thirst for Blood in vain.
  Here cease thy Flight, nor with unhallow'd Lays
Touch the fair Fame of *Albion's* Golden Days.
The Thoughts of Gods let *Granville's* Verse recite,   425
And bring the Scenes of opening Fate to Light.
My humble Muse, in unambitious Strains,
Paints the green Forests and the flow'ry Plains,
Where Peace descending bids her Olives spring,
And scatters Blessings from her Dove-like Wing.   430
Ev'n I more sweetly pass my careless Days,
Pleas'd in the silent Shade with empty Praise;
Enough for me, that to the listning Swains
First in these Fields I sung the Sylvan Strains.

---

409. **freed Indians:** freed from the tyranny of Spain.
411. **Race of Kings:** the Incas.
420. **Wheel:** the torture wheel.
425. **Gods:** comparisons of royalty to gods were common. **Granville's Verse:** Granville had frequently celebrated British royalty in his poems.
434. As the close of Virgil's *Georgics* echoes the first line of his *Eclogues*, so Pope's final line here echoes the opening line of his *Pastorals* (*Spring*, l. 1).

THE

RAPE OF THE LOCK

AN HEROI-COMICAL POEM
In Five Canto's

Nolueram, Belinda, tuos, violare capillos,
Sed juvat hoc precibus me tribuisse tuis.

MARTIAL

TO MRS. ARABELLA FERMOR[1]

MADAM,

IT will be in vain to deny that I have some Regard for this Piece, since I Dedicate it to You. Yet You may bear me Witness, it was intended only to divert a few young Ladies, who have good Sense and good Humour enough, to laugh not only at their Sex's little unguarded Follies, but at their own. But as it was communicated with the Air of a Secret, it soon found its Way into the World. An imperfect Copy having been offer'd to a Bookseller, You had the Good-Nature for my Sake to consent to the Publication of one more correct: This I was forc'd to before I had executed half my Design, for the *Machinery* was entirely wanting to compleat it.

THE RAPE OF THE LOCK: Some time in 1711 a young peer, Robert Lord Petre, cut a lock from the head of Miss Arabella Fermor (probably pronounced like *farmer*), a beauteous and distant relation. A quarrel between the two prominent Roman Catholic families resulted from the incident, and Pope was asked by his friend John Caryll to write a poem that would restore good feelings. At its first publication, in 1712, *The Rape of the Lock* consisted of only two cantos (334 lines). Two years later the much expanded poem in five cantos was published: in it there appeared for the first time the supernatural "machinery" of the sylphs and gnomes, and also such episodes as Belinda's dream, the game of ombre, the Cave of Spleen. Finally, in 1717, Clarissa's speech in Canto V was introduced. The Latin epigraph is slightly altered from Martial (*Epigrams*, XII 84): "I did not wish, Belinda, to profane your locks, but it pleases me to have granted this to your prayers."

1 Mrs. Arabella Fermor: "Mrs." was used for ladies whether married or single.

The *Machinery*, Madam, is a Term invented by the Criticks, to signify that Part which the Deities, Angels, or Dæmons, are made to act in a Poem: For the ancient Poets are in one respect like many modern Ladies; Let an Action be never so trivial in it self, they always make it appear of the utmost Importance. These Machines I determin'd to raise on a very new and odd Foundation, the *Rosicrucian* Doctrine of Spirits.

I know how disagreeable it is to make use of hard Words before a Lady; but 'tis so much the Concern of a Poet to have his Works understood, and particularly by your Sex, that You must give me leave to explain two or three difficult Terms.

The *Rosicrucians* are a People I must bring You acquainted with. The best Account I know of them is in a French Book call'd *Le Comte de Gabalis*,[2] which both in its Title and Size[3] is so like a *Novel*, that many of the Fair Sex have read it for one by Mistake. According to these Gentlemen, the four Elements[4] are inhabited by Spirits, which they call *Sylphs, Gnomes, Nymphs,* and *Salamanders.* The *Gnomes,* or Dæmons of Earth, delight in Mischief; but the *Sylphs,* whose Habitation is in the Air, are the best-condition'd Creatures imaginable. For they say, any Mortals may enjoy the most intimate Familiarities with these gentle Spirits, upon a Condition very easie to all true *Adepts,* an inviolate Preservation of Chastity.

As to the following Canto's, all the Passages of them are as Fabulous, as the Vision at the Beginning, or the Transformation at the End; (except the Loss of your Hair, which I always mention with Reverence.) The Human Persons are as Fictitious as the Airy ones; and the Character of *Belinda,* as it is now manag'd, resembles You in nothing but in Beauty.

If this Poem had as many Graces as there are in Your Person, or in Your Mind, yet I could never hope it should pass thro' the World so Uncensured as You have done. But let its Fortune be what it will, mine is happy enough, to have given me this Occasion of assuring You that I am, with the truest Esteem,

> *Madam,*
> *Your Most Obedient*
> *Humble Servant.*
> A. POPE.

2 **Le Comte de Gabalis:** written by the Abbé de Montfaucon de Villars, and published in 1670. Two English translations appeared in 1680.
3 **Size:** such novels were usually published in duodecimo (about five by eight inches as a maximum).
4 **four Elements:** air, earth, water, fire.

CANTO I

W HAT dire Offence from am'rous Causes springs,
What mighty Contests rise from trivial Things,
I sing — This Verse to *Caryll*, Muse! is due;
This, ev'n *Belinda* may vouchsafe to view:
Slight is the Subject, but not so the Praise,   5
If She inspire, and He approve my Lays.
    Say what strange Motive, Goddess! cou'd compel
A well-bred *Lord* t'assault a gentle *Belle*?
Oh say what stranger Cause, yet unexplor'd,
Cou'd make a gentle *Belle* reject a *Lord*?   10
In Tasks so bold, can Little Men engage,
And in soft Bosoms dwells such mighty Rage?
    Sol thro' white Curtains shot a tim'rous Ray,
And op'd those Eyes that must eclipse the Day;
Now Lapdogs give themselves the rowzing Shake,   15
And sleepless Lovers, just at Twelve, awake:
Thrice rung the Bell, the Slipper knock'd the Ground,
And the press'd Watch return'd a silver Sound.
Belinda still her downy Pillow prest,
Her Guardian *Sylph* prolong'd the balmy Rest.   20
'Twas he had summon'd to her silent Bed
The Morning-Dream that hover'd o'er her Head.
A Youth more glitt'ring than a *Birth-night Beau*,
(That ev'n in Slumber caus'd her Cheek to glow)
Seem'd to her Ear his winning Lips to lay,   25
And thus in Whispers said, or seem'd to say.
    Fairest of Mortals, thou distinguish'd Care
Of thousand bright Inhabitants of Air!
If e'er one Vision touch'd thy infant Thought,
Of all the Nurse and all the Priest have taught,   30
Of airy Elves by Moonlight Shadows seen,
The silver Token, and the circled Green,
Or Virgins visited by Angel-Pow'rs,
With Golden Crowns and Wreaths of heav'nly Flow'rs,
Hear and believe! thy own Importance know,   35
Nor bound thy narrow Views to Things below.

    Canto I.   **17.** Ladies called their maids by ringing hand-bells, or by knocking on the floor with a high-heeled shoe.
    18. press'd Watch: watches sounded the hour and the quarters at the press of a pin.
    22. Morning-Dream: morning dreams were considered especially portentous.
    23. Birth-night Beau: splendidly dressed, as for a royal birthday celebration.
    32. silver Token: silver coins left by fairies for industrious maidservants. **circled Green:** a fairy-ring, or circular band of grass supposedly produced by fairies when dancing.

Some secret Truths from Learned Pride conceal'd,
To Maids alone and Children are reveal'd:
What tho' no Credit doubting Wits may give?
The Fair and Innocent shall still believe.   40
Know then, unnumber'd Spirits round thee fly,
The light *Militia* of the lower Sky;
These, tho' unseen, are ever on the Wing,
Hang o'er the *Box*, and hover round the *Ring*.
Think what an Equipage thou hast in Air,   45
And view with scorn *Two Pages* and a *Chair*.
As now your own, our Beings were of old,
And once inclos'd in Woman's beauteous Mold;
Thence, by a soft Transition, we repair
From earthly Vehicles to these of Air.   50
Think not, when Woman's transient Breath is fled,
That all her Vanities at once are dead:
Succeeding Vanities she still regards,
And tho' she plays no more, o'erlooks the Cards.
Her joy in gilded Chariots, when alive,   55
And Love of *Ombre*, after Death survive.
For when the Fair in all their Pride expire,
To their first Elements their Souls retire:
The Sprights of fiery Termagants in Flame
Mount up, and take a *Salamander*'s Name.   60
Soft yielding Minds to Water glide away,
And sip with *Nymphs*, their Elemental Tea.
The graver Prude sinks downward to a *Gnome*,
In search of Mischief still on Earth to roam.
The light Coquettes in *Sylphs* aloft repair,   65
And sport and flutter in the Fields of Air.
  Know farther yet; Whoever fair and chaste
Rejects Mankind, is by some *Sylph* embrac'd:
For Spirits, freed from mortal Laws, with ease
Assume what Sexes and what Shapes they please.   70
What guards the Purity of melting Maids,

44. Box: a theater box.   **Ring:** a fashionable drive in Hyde Park.
45. Equipage: a carriage with horses and footmen.
46. Chair: sedan chair.
56. Ombre: a popular card game (from Spanish *hombre:* man). See Canto
III 27*ff*.
58. first Elements: the four elements (earth, water, air, and fire) were believed to have their counterparts in the four "humours" of the human body
(melancholy, phlegm, blood, and choler). One of the elements was supposed
to dominate in each person and determine his temperament, an idea illustrated in
the next eight lines. See also the dedicatory letter to Miss Fermor, 4th paragraph, and *An Essay on Man*, Epist. II 111*ff*.
59. Sprights: spirits.
60. Salamander: salamanders were popularly believed able to live in fire.
62. Tea: pronounced *tay* in Pope's time.
63–6. See dedicatory letter to Miss Fermor, 4th paragraph.

In Courtly Balls, and Midnight Masquerades,
Safe from the treach'rous Friend, the daring Spark,
The Glance by Day, the Whisper in the Dark;
When kind Occasion prompts their warm Desires,   75
When Musick softens, and when Dancing fires?
'Tis but their *Sylph,* the wise Celestials know,
Tho' *Honour* is the Word with Men below.
    Some Nymphs there are, too conscious of their Face,
For Life predestin'd to the *Gnomes'* Embrace.   80
These swell their Prospects and exalt their Pride,
When Offers are disdain'd, and Love deny'd.
Then gay Ideas crowd the vacant Brain;
While Peers and Dukes, and all their sweeping Train,
And Garters, Stars, and Coronets appear,   85
And in soft Sounds, *Your Grace* salutes their Ear.
'Tis these that early taint the Female Soul,
Instruct the Eyes of young *Coquettes* to roll,
Teach Infant-Cheeks a bidden Blush to know,
And little Hearts to flutter at a *Beau.*   90
    Oft when the World imagine Women stray,
The *Sylphs* thro' mystick Mazes guide their Way,
Thro' all the giddy Circle they pursue,
And old Impertinence expel by new.
What tender Maid but must a Victim fall   95
To one Man's Treat, but for another's Ball?
When *Florio* speaks, what Virgin could withstand,
If gentle *Damon* did not squeeze her Hand?
With varying Vanities, from ev'ry Part,
They shift the moving Toyshop of their Heart;   100
Where Wigs with Wigs, with Sword-knots Sword-knots strive,
Beaus banish Beaus, and Coaches Coaches drive.
This erring Mortals Levity may call,
Oh blind to Truth! the *Sylphs* contrive it all.
    Of these am I, who thy Protection claim,   105
A watchful Sprite, and *Ariel* is my Name.
Late, as I rang'd the Crystal Wilds of Air,
In the clear Mirror of thy ruling *Star*
I saw, alas! some dread Event impend,
Ere to the Main this Morning Sun descend.   110
But Heav'n reveals not what, or how, or where:

73. Spark: fop, or beau.
83. Ideas: images.
85. Garters, Stars: emblems of knighthood.
86. Your Grace: form of address to a duchess.
94. Impertinence: trifle, folly.
96. Treat: feast, entertainment.
101. Sword-knots: ribbons tied to the hilt of a sword.
  108. clear Mirror: *The Language of the Platonists, the writers of the intelligible world of Spirits, etc.* P.   The language is also that of astrology.

Warn'd by thy *Sylph*, oh Pious Maid beware!
This to disclose is all thy Guardian can.
Beware of all, but most beware of Man!
    He said; when *Shock*, who thought she slept too long,   115
Leapt up, and wak'd his Mistress with his Tongue.
'Twas then *Belinda!* if Report say true,
Thy Eyes first open'd on a *Billet-doux;*
Wounds, Charms, and *Ardors,* were no sooner read,
But all the Vision vanish'd from thy Head.   120
    And now, unveil'd, the *Toilet* stands display'd,
Each Silver Vase in mystic Order laid.
First, rob'd in White, the Nymph intent adores
With Head uncover'd, the *Cosmetic* Pow'rs.
A heav'nly Image in the Glass appears,   125
To that she bends, to that her Eyes she rears;
Th'inferior Priestess, at her Altar's side,
Trembling, begins the sacred Rites of Pride.
Unnumber'd Treasures ope at once, and here
The various Off'rings of the World appear;   130
From each she nicely culls with curious Toil,
And decks the Goddess with the glitt'ring Spoil.
This Casket *India's* glowing Gems unlocks,
And all *Arabia* breathes from yonder Box.
The Tortoise here and Elephant unite,   135
Transform'd to *Combs,* the speckled and the white.
Here Files of Pins extend their shining Rows,
Puffs, Powders, Patches, Bibles, Billet-doux.
Now awful Beauty puts on all its Arms;
The Fair each moment rises in her Charms,   140
Repairs her Smiles, awakens ev'ry Grace,
And calls forth all the Wonders of her Face;
Sees by Degrees a purer Blush arise,
And keener Lightnings quicken in her Eyes.
The busy *Sylphs* surround their darling Care;   145
These set the Head, and those divide the Hair,
Some fold the Sleeve, while others plait the Gown;
And *Betty's* prais'd for Labours not her own.

---

115. Shock: the "shock" was a breed of lap-dog with exceptionally long hair, much favored by ladies of the period.

127. inferior Priestess: Belinda's maid, the "Betty" of l. 148.

131. nicely: fastidiously.   **curious:** painstaking.

138. Patches: small black beauty patches worn on the face.

139. awful: awe-inspiring.

145. *Antient Traditions of the* Rabbi's *relate, that several of the fallen Angels became amorous of Women, and particularize some; among the rest* Asael, *who lay with* Naamah, *the wife of* Noah, *or of* Ham; *and who continuing impenitent, still presides over the Women's Toilets.* Bereshi Rabbi *in* Genes. *6. 2.*   P.

CANTO II

Nᴏᴛ with more Glories, in th' Etherial Plain,
The Sun first rises o'er the purpled Main,
Than issuing forth, the Rival of his Beams
Lanch'd on the Bosom of the Silver *Thames*.
Fair Nymphs, and well-drest Youths around her shone,   5
But ev'ry Eye was fix'd on her alone.
On her white Breast a sparkling *Cross* she wore,
Which *Jews* might kiss, and Infidels adore.
Her lively Looks a sprightly Mind disclose,
Quick as her Eyes, and as unfix'd as those: 10
Favours to none, to all she Smiles extends,
Oft she rejects, but never once offends.
Bright as the Sun, her Eyes the Gazers strike,
And, like the Sun, they shine on all alike.
Yet graceful Ease, and Sweetness void of Pride,   15
Might hide her Faults, if *Belles* had Faults to hide:
If to her share some Female Errors fall,
Look on her Face, and you'll forget 'em all.
    This Nymph, to the Destruction of Mankind,
Nourish'd two Locks, which graceful hung behind   20
In equal Curls, and well conspir'd to deck
With shining Ringlets her smooth Iv'ry Neck.
Love in these Labyrinths his Slaves detains,
And mighty Hearts are held in slender Chains.
With hairy Sprindges we the Birds betray,   25
Slight Lines of Hair surprize the Finny Prey,
Fair Tresses Man's Imperial Race insnare,
And Beauty draws us with a single Hair.
    Th' Adventrous *Baron* the bright Locks admir'd,
He saw, he wish'd, and to the Prize aspir'd: 30
Resolv'd to win, he meditates the way,
By Force to ravish, or by Fraud betray;
For when Success a Lover's Toil attends,
Few ask, if Fraud or Force attain'd his Ends.
    For this, ere *Phœbus* rose, he had implor'd   35
Propitious Heav'n, and ev'ry Pow'r ador'd,
But chiefly *Love* — to *Love* an Altar built,
Of twelve vast *French* Romances, neatly gilt.
There lay three Garters, half a Pair of Gloves;
And all the Trophies of his former Loves.   40

Canto II.   **4. Lanch'd:** Belinda and her friends take a boat from one of the
London "stairs," or landings, and go up the Thames to Hampton Court Palace
(see Canto III 1–8).
    25. Sprindges: snares.

With tender *Billet-doux* he lights the Pyre,
And breathes three am'rous Sighs to raise the Fire.
Then prostrate falls, and begs with ardent Eyes
Soon to obtain, and long possess the Prize:
The Pow'rs gave Ear, and granted half his Pray'r,   45
The rest, the Winds dispers'd in empty Air.
　But now secure the painted Vessel glides,
The Sun-beams trembling on the floating Tydes,
While melting Musick steals upon the Sky,
And soften'd Sounds along the Waters die.   50
Smooth flow the Waves, the Zephyrs gently play,
Belinda smil'd, and all the World was gay.
All but the *Sylph* — With careful Thoughts opprest,
Th' impending Woe sate heavy on his Breast.
He summons strait his Denizens of Air;   55
The lucid Squadrons round the Sails repair:
Soft o'er the Shrouds Aerial Whispers breathe,
That seem'd but *Zephyrs* to the Train beneath.
Some to the Sun their Insect-Wings unfold,
Waft on the Breeze, or sink in Clouds of Gold.   60
Transparent Forms, too fine for mortal Sight,
Their fluid Bodies half dissolv'd in Light.
Loose to the Wind their airy Garments flew,
Thin glitt'ring Textures of the filmy Dew;
Dipt in the richest Tincture of the Skies,   65
Where Light disports in ever-mingling Dies,
While ev'ry Beam new transient Colours flings,
Colours that change whene'er they wave their Wings.
Amid the Circle, on the gilded Mast,
Superior by the Head, was *Ariel* plac'd;   70
His Purple Pinions opening to the Sun,
He rais'd his Azure Wand, and thus begun.
　Ye *Sylphs* and *Sylphids,* to your Chief give Ear,
Fays, Fairies, Genii, Elves, and *Dæmons* hear!
Ye know the Spheres and various Tasks assign'd,   75
By Laws Eternal, to th' Aerial Kind.
Some in the Fields of purest *Æther* play,
And bask and whiten in the Blaze of Day.

45–6. In classical epic prayers are frequently answered only in part, and the remainder abandoned to the winds.
　56. **repair:** gather.
　57. **Shrouds:** ropes.
　70. **Superior by the Head:** epic leaders were traditionally taller than their followers.
　73. **Sylphids:** young, or perhaps female, sylphs.
　74. **Genii . . . Dæmons:** guardian spirits.
　75. **Spheres:** tradition held that there were nine orders of angelic beings, and that each served to regulate one of the nine supposed heavenly spheres.
　77. **purest Æther:** the air above the moon was considered pure, and known as the ether.

Some guide the Course of wandring Orbs on high,
Or roll the Planets thro' the boundless Sky.   80
Some less refin'd, beneath the Moon's pale Light
Pursue the Stars that shoot athwart the Night,
Or suck the Mists in grosser Air below,
Or dip their Pinions in the painted Bow,
Or brew fierce Tempests on the Wintry Main,   85
Or o'er the Glebe distill the kindly Rain.
Others on Earth o'er human Race preside,
Watch all their Ways, and all their Actions guide:
Of these the Chief the Care of Nations own,
And guard with Arms Divine the *British Throne*.   90
     Our humbler Province is to tend the Fair,
Not a less pleasing, tho' less glorious Care.
To save the Powder from too rude a Gale,
Nor let th' imprison'd Essences exhale,
To draw fresh Colours from the vernal Flow'rs,   95
To steal from Rainbows ere they drop in Show'rs
A brighter Wash; to curl their waving Hairs,
Assist their Blushes, and inspire their Airs;
Nay oft, in Dreams, Invention we bestow,
To change a *Flounce*, or add a *Furbelo*.   100
     This Day, black Omens threat the brightest Fair
That e'er deserv'd a watchful Spirit's Care;
Some dire Disaster, or by Force, or Slight,
But what, or where, the Fates have wrapt in Night.
Whether the Nymph shall break *Diana*'s Law,   105
Or some frail *China* Jar receive a Flaw,
Or stain her Honour, or her new Brocade,
Forget her Pray'rs, or miss a Masquerade,
Or lose her Heart, or Necklace, at a Ball;
Or whether Heav'n has doom'd that *Shock* must fall.   110
Haste then ye Spirits! to your Charge repair;
The flutt'ring Fan be *Zephyretta's* Care;
The Drops to thee, *Brillante*, we consign;
And, *Momentilla*, let the Watch be thine;
Do thou, *Crispissa*, tend her fav'rite Lock;   115
Ariel himself shall be the Guard of *Shock*.

---

81. less refin'd: the air beneath the moon (in the sublunary world) was
thought to be more thick and dirty than that above.
   86. Glebe: cultivated ground.
   97. Wash: cosmetic lotion.
   100. Flounce: a strip of cloth, sewed on its upper edge, and left hanging
around the skirt.   Furbelo: pleated trimming for a dress or petticoat.
   103. Slight: sleight (trickery).
   105. Diana's Law: that of chastity.
   106. A crack in a glass or vase is a traditional symbol for loss of virginity.
   113. Drops: diamond earrings.
   115. Crispissa: from crisp, meaning *to curl*.

To Fifty chosen *Sylphs,* of special Note,
We trust th'important Charge, the *Petticoat:*
Oft have we known that sev'nfold Fence to fail,
Tho' stiff with Hoops, and arm'd with Ribs of Whale.   120
Form a strong Line about the Silver Bound,
And guard the wide Circumference around.
　　Whatever Spirit, careless of his Charge,
His Post neglects, or leaves the Fair at large,
Shall feel sharp Vengeance soon o'ertake his Sins,   125
Be stopt in *Vials,* or transfixt with *Pins;*
Or plung'd in Lakes of bitter *Washes* lie,
Or wedg'd whole Ages in a *Bodkin's* Eye:
Gums and *Pomatums* shall his Flight restrain,
While clog'd he beats his silken Wings in vain;   130
Or Alom-*Stypticks* with contracting Power
Shrink his thin Essence like a rivell'd Flower.
Or as *Ixion* fix'd, the Wretch shall feel
The giddy Motion of the whirling Mill,
In fumes of burning Chocolate shall glow,   135
And tremble at the Sea that froaths below!
　　He spoke; the Spirits from the Sails descend;
Some, Orb in Orb, around the Nymph extend,
Some thrid the mazy Ringlets of her Hair,
Some hang upon the Pendants of her Ear;   140
With beating Hearts the dire Event they wait,
Anxious, and trembling for the Birth of Fate.

CANTO III

C　LOSE by those Meads for ever crown'd with Flow'rs,
　　　Where *Thames* with Pride surveys his rising Tow'rs,
　　　There stands a Structure of Majestick Frame,
Which from the neighb'ring *Hampton* takes its Name.
Here *Britain's* Statesmen oft the Fall foredoom   5
Of Foreign Tyrants, and of Nymphs at home;
Here Thou, Great *Anna!* whom three Realms obey,
Dost sometimes Counsel take — and sometimes *Tea.*

126. **Vials:** small perfume bottles.
128. **Bodkin:** a blunt needle or hair ornament.
131. **Alom-Stypticks:** astringent skin medications.
132. **rivell'd:** wrinkled.
133. Ixion, a mythical king of Thessaly, attempted to seduce Juno. In punishment, he was bound to an endlessly revolving wheel in hell.
134. **Mill:** for beating chocolate.

Canto III. 3. **Structure:** Hampton Court Palace, largest of the British royal palaces, and located on the Thames about 12 miles from the heart of London.
7. **three Realms:** England, Wales, Scotland.

Hither the Heroes and the Nymphs resort,
To taste awhile the Pleasures of a Court;   10
In various Talk th' instructive hours they past,
Who gave the *Ball,* or paid the *Visit* last:
One speaks the Glory of the *British Queen,*
And one describes a charming *Indian Screen;*
A third interprets Motions, Looks, and Eyes;   15
At ev'ry Word a Reputation dies.
Snuff, or the *Fan,* supply each Pause of Chat,
With singing, laughing, ogling, and all that.
  Mean while declining from the Noon of Day,
The Sun obliquely shoots his burning Ray;   20
The hungry Judges soon the Sentence sign,
And Wretches hang that Jury-men may Dine;
The Merchant from th'*Exchange* returns in Peace,
And the long Labours of the *Toilette* cease —
Belinda now, whom Thirst of Fame invites,   25
Burns to encounter two adventrous Knights,
At *Ombre* singly to decide their Doom;
And swells her Breast with Conquests yet to come.
Strait the three Bands prepare in Arms to join,
Each Band the number of the Sacred Nine.   30
Soon as she spreads her Hand, th' Aerial Guard
Descend, and sit on each important Card:
First *Ariel* perch'd upon a *Matadore,*
Then each, according to the Rank they bore;
For *Sylphs,* yet mindful of their ancient Race,   35
Are, as when Women, wondrous fond of Place.
  Behold, four *Kings* in Majesty rever'd,
With hoary Whiskers and a forky Beard;
And four fair *Queens* whose hands sustain a Flow'r,
Th' expressive Emblem of their softer Pow'r;   40
Four *Knaves* in Garbs succinct, a trusty Band,
Caps on their heads, and Halberds in their hand;
And Particolour'd Troops, a shining Train,

  12. **Visit:** fashionable ladies, attended by servants bearing lights, paid cere-
monious visits to one another in the evenings (see ll. 167–8, below).
  23. **Exchange:** the Royal Exchange, where merchants, brokers, and bankers
met to do business.
  27. **Ombre:** Ombre (pronounced *omber*) is played by three persons with
forty cards from a full pack (the 8's, 9's, and 10's are discarded). Nine cards
are dealt to each player, and 13 cards are placed in a stock. The player who
undertakes to win the game independently, by making more tricks than either
of the other two (five to four, for example, or four to three and two), is called
the Ombre, and names the trumps.
  33. **Matadores:** the three cards of highest value. In order of strength they
are: the ace of spades, another card which varies according to trumps (the seven
if a red suit is trumps, the deuce if a black suit is trumps), and the ace of clubs.
  41. **succinct:** girded up. Pope of course describes the face cards as they
appeared in his time.

Draw forth to Combat on the Velvet Plain.
    The skilful Nymph reviews her Force with Care;   45
Let Spades be Trumps! she said, and Trumps they were.
    Now move to War her Sable *Matadores,*
In Show like Leaders of the swarthy *Moors.*
Spadillio first, unconquerable Lord!
Led off two captive Trumps, and swept the Board.   50
As many more *Manillio* forc'd to yield,
And march'd a Victor from the verdant Field.
Him *Basto* follow'd, but his Fate more hard
Gain'd but one Trump and one *Plebeian* Card.
With his broad Sabre next, a Chief in Years,   55
The hoary Majesty of *Spades* appears;
Puts forth one manly Leg, to sight reveal'd;
The rest his many-colour'd Robe conceal'd.
The Rebel-*Knave,* who dares his Prince engage,
Proves the just Victim of his Royal Rage.   60
Ev'n mighty *Pam* that Kings and Queens o'erthrew,
And mow'd down Armies in the Fights of *Lu,*
Sad Chance of War! now, destitute of Aid,
Falls undistinguish'd by the Victor *Spade!*
    Thus far both Armies to *Belinda* yield;   65
Now to the *Baron* Fate inclines the Field.
His warlike *Amazon* her Host invades,
Th' Imperial Consort of the Crown of *Spades.*
The *Club*'s black Tyrant first her Victim dy'd,
Spite of his haughty Mien, and barb'rous Pride: 70
What boots the Regal Circle on his Head,
His Giant Limbs in State unwieldy spread?
That long behind he trails his pompous Robe,
And of all Monarchs only grasps the Globe?
    The *Baron* now his *Diamonds* pours apace;   75
Th' embroider'd *King* who shows but half his Face,
And his refulgent *Queen,* with Pow'rs combin'd,
Of broken Troops an easie Conquest find.
Clubs, Diamonds, Hearts, in wild Disorder seen,
With Throngs promiscuous strow the level Green.   80
Thus when dispers'd a routed Army runs,
Of *Asia*'s Troops, and *Africk*'s Sable Sons,
With like Confusion different Nations fly,
Of various Habit and of various Dye,

    46. Cf. Genesis 1:3: "And God said, Let there be light: and there was light."
    49. Spadillio: the ace of spades.
    51. Manillio: here the deuce of spades.
    53. Basto: the ace of clubs.
    59. Rebel-Knave: the knave of spades.
    61. Pam: the knave of clubs, highest card in the game of Lu (Loo).
    74. Globe: the golden ball carried by sovereigns as an emblem of authority
(held only by the king of clubs in English packs).

The pierc'd Battalions dis-united fall,   85
In Heaps on Heaps; one Fate o'erwhelms them all.
   The *Knave* of *Diamonds* tries his wily Arts,
And wins (oh shameful Chance!) the *Queen* of *Hearts*.
At this, the Blood the Virgin's Cheek forsook,
A livid Paleness spreads o'er all her Look;   90
She sees, and trembles at th' approaching Ill,
Just in the Jaws of Ruin, and *Codille*.
And now, (as oft in some distemper'd State)
On one nice *Trick* depends the gen'ral Fate.
An *Ace* of Hearts steps forth: The *King* unseen   95
Lurk'd in her Hand, and mourn'd his captive *Queen*.
He springs to Vengeance with an eager pace,
And falls like Thunder on the prostrate *Ace*.
The Nymph exulting fills with Shouts the Sky,
The Walls, the Woods, and long Canals reply.   100
   Oh thoughtless Mortals! ever blind to Fate,
Too soon dejected, and too soon elate!
Sudden these Honours shall be snatch'd away,
And curs'd for ever this Victorious Day.
   For lo! the Board with Cups and Spoons is crown'd,   105
The Berries crackle, and the Mill turns round.
On shining Altars of *Japan* they raise
The silver Lamp; the fiery Spirits blaze.
From silver Spouts the grateful Liquors glide,
While *China*'s Earth receives the smoking Tyde.   110
At once they gratify their Scent and Taste,
And frequent Cups prolong the rich Repast.
Strait hover round the Fair her Airy Band;
Some, as she sip'd, the fuming Liquor fann'd,
Some o'er her Lap their careful Plumes display'd,   115
Trembling, and conscious of the rich Brocade.
Coffee, (which makes the Politician Wise,
And see thro' all things with his half-shut Eyes)
Sent up in Vapours to the *Baron's* Brain
New Stratagems, the radiant Lock to gain.   120
Ah cease rash Youth! desist ere 'tis too late,

   92. Codille: if the Ombre did not succeed in taking more tricks than one of his opponents, he was said to be given "codille." Belinda needs one more trick at this stage, for she and the Baron now have four apiece.
   94. nice: delicate, precise.
   95–8. When the red cards are *not* trumps, their order of strength is king, queen, knave, ace, 2, 3, 4, 5, 6, 7. Belinda's king of hearts therefore takes the Baron's ace of hearts.
   106. The berries are coffee berries, first roasted and then ground in a coffee-mill.
   107. Altars of Japan: japanned or highly varnished tables.
   109. grateful: pleasing.

Fear the just Gods, and think of *Scylla*'s Fate!
Chang'd to a Bird, and sent to flit in Air,
She dearly pays for *Nisus*' injur'd Hair!
   But when to Mischief Mortals bend their Will,   125
How soon they find fit Instruments of Ill!
Just then, *Clarissa* drew with tempting Grace
A two-edg'd Weapon from her shining Case;
So Ladies in Romance assist their Knight,
Present the Spear, and arm him for the Fight.   130
He takes the Gift with rev'rence, and extends
The little Engine on his Fingers' Ends,
This just behind *Belinda*'s Neck he spread,
As o'er the fragrant Steams she bends her Head:
Swift to the Lock a thousand Sprights repair,   135
A thousand Wings, by turns, blow back the Hair,
And thrice they twitch'd the Diamond in her Ear,
Thrice she look'd back, and thrice the Foe drew near.
Just in that instant, anxious *Ariel* sought
The close Recesses of the Virgin's Thought;   140
As on the Nosegay in her Breast reclin'd,
He watch'd th' Ideas rising in her Mind,
Sudden he view'd in spite of all her Art,
An Earthly Lover lurking at her Heart.
Amaz'd, confus'd, he found his Pow'r expir'd,   145
Resign'd to Fate, and with a Sigh retir'd.
   The Peer now spreads the glitt'ring *Forfex* wide,
T'inclose the Lock; now joins it, to divide.
Ev'n then, before the fatal Engine clos'd,
A wretched *Sylph* too fondly interpos'd;   150
Fate urg'd the Sheers, and cut the *Sylph* in twain,
(But Airy Substance soon unites again)
The meeting Points the sacred Hair dissever
From the fair Head, for ever and for ever!
   Then flash'd the living Lightning from her Eyes,   155
And Screams of Horror rend th' affrighted Skies.
Not louder Shrieks to pitying Heav'n are cast,
When Husbands or when Lap-dogs breathe their last,
Or when rich *China* Vessels, fal'n from high,

122–4. *Vide* Ovid. Metam. 8 [ll. 1–151]. P.   Scylla was the daughter of King Nisus, whose life and kingdom depended upon a purple lock growing on his head. She fell in love with King Minos of Crete, who had besieged her father's city, and to gain his favor plucked out her father's lock and carried it to him. Horrified at her treachery, Minos spurned her advances, and she was later changed by the gods into a small sea bird.
   144. **Earthly Lover:** cf. Canto I, ll. 67–8.
   147. **Forfex:** Latin for scissors.
   152. *See* Milton, *lib.* 6 [ll. 320*ff.*]. *of* Satan *cut asunder by the Angel* Michael. **P.**

In glittring Dust and painted Fragments lie!   160
  Let Wreaths of Triumph now my Temples twine,
(The Victor cry'd) the glorious Prize is mine!
While Fish in Streams, or Birds delight in Air,
Or in a Coach and Six the *British* Fair,
As long as *Atalantis* shall be read,   165
Or the small Pillow grace a Lady's Bed,
While *Visits* shall be paid on solemn Days,
When numerous Wax-lights in bright Order blaze,
While Nymphs take Treats, or Assignations give,
So long my Honour, Name, and Praise shall live!   170
  What Time wou'd spare, from Steel receives its date,
And Monuments, like Men, submit to Fate!
Steel cou'd the Labour of the Gods destroy,
And strike to Dust th' Imperial Tow'rs of *Troy;*
Steel cou'd the Works of mortal Pride confound,   175
And hew Triumphal Arches to the Ground.
What Wonder then, fair Nymph! thy Hairs shou'd feel
The conqu'ring Force of unresisted Steel?

CANTO IV

BUT anxious Cares the pensive Nymph opprest,
  And secret Passions labour'd in her Breast.
  Not youthful Kings in Battel seiz'd alive,
Not scornful Virgins who their Charms survive,
Not ardent Lovers robb'd of all their Bliss,   5
Not ancient Ladies when refus'd a Kiss,
Not Tyrants fierce that unrepenting die,
Not *Cynthia* when her *Manteau's* pinn'd awry,
E'er felt such Rage, Resentment and Despair,
As Thou, sad Virgin! for thy ravish'd Hair.   10
  For, that sad moment, when the *Sylphs* withdrew,
And *Ariel* weeping from *Belinda* flew,
Umbriel, a dusky melancholy Spright,
As ever sully'd the fair face of Light,
Down to the Central Earth, his proper Scene,   15
Repair'd to search the gloomy Cave of *Spleen.*

165. Atalantis: a scandalous chronicle of fact and fiction written by Mrs. Mary De La Riviere Manley (1672–1724).

  Canto IV. **1.** Virg. Æn. 4 [l. 1]. *At regina gravi, &c.* P.
  8. Manteau: a loose robe or cloak.
  16. Spleen: lying on the left side of the body near the stomach (see l. 24), the spleen at one time was thought to be the seat of emotions. Ultimately "the spleen" became the term, as in this episode, for a vague and fashionable malady of the idle and delicate rich.

Swift on his sooty Pinions flitts the *Gnome*,
And in a Vapour reach'd the dismal Dome.
No cheerful Breeze this sullen Region knows,
The dreaded *East* is all the Wind that blows.   20
Here, in a Grotto, sheltred close from Air,
And screen'd in Shades from Day's detested Glare,
She sighs for ever on her pensive Bed,
Pain at her Side, and *Megrim* at her Head.
Two Handmaids wait the Throne: Alike in Place,   25
But diff'ring far in Figure and in Face.
Here stood *Ill-nature* like an *ancient Maid*,
Her wrinkled Form in *Black* and *White* array'd;
With store of Pray'rs, for Mornings, Nights, and Noons,
Her Hand is fill'd; her Bosom with Lampoons.   30
There *Affectation* with a sickly Mien
Shows in her Cheek the Roses of Eighteen,
Practis'd to Lisp, and hang the Head aside,
Faints into Airs, and languishes with Pride;
On the rich Quilt sinks with becoming Woe,   35
Wrapt in a Gown, for Sickness, and for Show.
The Fair-ones feel such Maladies as these,
When each new Night-Dress gives a new Disease.
A constant *Vapour* o'er the Palace flies;
Strange Phantoms rising as the Mists arise;   40
Dreadful, as Hermit's Dreams in haunted Shades,
Or bright as Visions of expiring Maids.
Now glaring Fiends, and Snakes on rolling Spires,
Pale Spectres, gaping Tombs, and Purple Fires:
Now Lakes of liquid Gold, *Elysian* Scenes,   45
And Crystal Domes, and Angels in Machines.
Unnumber'd Throngs on ev'ry side are seen
Of Bodies chang'd to various Forms by *Spleen*.
Here living *Teapots* stand, one Arm held out,
One bent; the Handle this, and that the Spout: 50
A Pipkin there like *Homer's Tripod* walks;
Here sighs a Jar, and there a Goose-pye talks;
Men prove with Child, as pow'rful Fancy works,
And Maids turn'd Bottels, call aloud for Corks.

18. **Vapour:** a fit of spleen was often called "the vapours," and a moist climate and an east wind (see l. 20) were thought to bring on an attack.

24. **Megrim:** migraine.

35–8. Ladies frequently received "visits" (see Canto III, l. 12n.) in bed.

40–54. Splenetics commonly suffered various kinds of hallucinations.

46. **Machines:** stage machinery (but see dedicatory letter to Miss Fermor, 2nd paragraph).

51. *See* Hom. *Iliad.* 18 [ll. 439ff.], *of* Vulcan's *Walking tripods.* P.   **Pipkin:** a small earthen pot.

52. **Goose-pye:** *Alludes to a real fact, a Lady of distinction imagin'd herself in this condition.* P.

Safe past the *Gnome* thro' this fantastick Band,   55
A Branch of healing *Spleenwort* in his hand.
Then thus addrest the Pow'r — Hail wayward Queen!
Who rule the Sex to Fifty from Fifteen,
Parent of Vapors and of Female Wit,
Who give th' *Hysteric* or *Poetic* Fit,   60
On various Tempers act by various ways,
Make some take Physick, others scribble Plays;
Who cause the Proud their Visits to delay,
And send the Godly in a Pett, to pray.
A Nymph there is, that all thy Pow'r disdains,   65
And thousands more in equal Mirth maintains.
But oh! if e'er thy *Gnome* could spoil a Grace,
Or raise a Pimple on a beauteous Face,
Like Citron-Waters Matrons' Cheeks inflame,
Or change Complexions at a losing Game;   70
If e'er with airy Horns I planted Heads,
Or rumpled Petticoats, or tumbled Beds,
Or caus'd Suspicion when no Soul was rude,
Or discompos'd the Head-dress of a Prude,
Or e'er to costive Lap-Dog gave Disease,   75
Which not the Tears of brightest Eyes could ease:
Hear me, and touch *Belinda* with Chagrin;
That single Act gives half the World the Spleen.
    The Goddess with a discontented Air
Seems to reject him, tho' she grants his Pray'r.   80
A wondrous Bag with both her Hands she binds,
Like that where once *Ulysses* held the Winds;
There she collects the Force of Female Lungs,
Sighs, Sobs, and Passions, and the War of Tongues.
A Vial next she fills with fainting Fears,   85
Soft Sorrows, melting Griefs, and flowing Tears.
The *Gnome* rejoicing bears her Gifts away,
Spreads his black Wings, and slowly mounts to Day.
    Sunk in *Thalestris*' Arms the Nymph he found,
Her Eyes dejected and her Hair unbound.   90
Full o'er their Heads the swelling Bag he rent,
And all the Furies issued at the Vent.
Belinda burns with more than mortal Ire,
And fierce *Thalestris* fans the rising Fire.
O wretched Maid! she spread her Hands, and cry'd,   95
(While *Hampton*'s Ecchos, wretched Maid! reply'd)

56. Spleenwort: a fern, once believed beneficial for the spleen.
69. Citron-Waters: a liquor flavored with lemon.
71. Horns: emblem of a cuckold.
89. Thalestris: the name of a queen of the Amazons, hence suggestive of a fierce and domineering kind of woman.

Was it for this you took such constant Care
The *Bodkin, Comb,* and *Essence* to prepare;
For this your Locks in Paper-Durance bound,
For this with tort'ring Irons wreath'd around?   100
For this with Fillets strain'd your tender Head,
And bravely bore the double Loads of Lead?
Gods! shall the Ravisher display your Hair,
While the Fops envy, and the Ladies stare!
Honour forbid! at whose unrival'd Shrine   105
Ease, Pleasure, Virtue, All, our Sex resign.
Methinks already I your Tears survey,
Already hear the horrid things they say,
Already see you a degraded Toast,
And all your Honour in a Whisper lost!   110
How shall I, then, your helpless Fame defend?
'Twill then be Infamy to seem your Friend!
And shall this Prize, th' inestimable Prize,
Expos'd thro' Crystal to the gazing Eyes,
And heighten'd by the Diamond's circling Rays,   115
On that Rapacious Hand for ever blaze?
Sooner shall Grass in *Hide*-Park *Circus* grow,
And Wits take Lodgings in the Sound of *Bow;*
Sooner let Earth, Air, Sea, to *Chaos* fall,
Men, Monkies, Lap-dogs, Parrots, perish all!   120
    She said; then raging to *Sir Plume* repairs,
And bids her *Beau* demand the precious Hairs:
(*Sir Plume,* of *Amber Snuff-box* justly vain,
And the nice Conduct of a *clouded Cane*)
With earnest Eyes, and round unthinking Face,   125
He first the Snuff-box open'd, then the Case,
And thus broke out — "My Lord, why, what the Devil?
"Z—ds! damn the Lock! 'fore Gad, you must be civil!
"Plague on't! 'tis past a Jest — nay prithee, Pox!
"Give her the Hair" — he spoke, and rapp'd his Box.   130
    It grieves me much (reply'd the Peer again)
Who speaks so well shou'd ever speak in vain.
But by this Lock, this sacred Lock I swear,

---

99. Paper-Durance: curl papers, once fastened with strips of pliant lead (l. 102).
101. Fillets: bands encircling the hair.
114. Expos'd thro' Crystal: i.e., set in a ring.
117. Hide-Park Circus: carriage driving kept the "Ring" (see Canto I, l. 44n.) of Hyde Park bare of grass.
118. Sound of Bow: within sound of the bells of St. Mary-le-Bow Church (located in an unfashionable, mercantile area of London).
124. clouded: mottled.
128. Z—ds: Zounds (corrupted form of *God's wounds*).
133–6. *In allusion to* Achilles's *Oath in* Homer. *Il. i* [ll. 309ff.]   **P.**

(Which never more shall join its parted Hair,
Which never more its Honours shall renew,   135
Clipt from the lovely Head where late it grew)
That while my Nostrils draw the vital Air,
This Hand, which won it, shall for ever wear.
He spoke, and speaking, in proud Triumph spread
The long-contended Honours of her Head.   140
    But *Umbriel,* hateful *Gnome!* forbears not so;
He breaks the Vial whence the Sorrows flow.
Then see! the *Nymph* in beauteous Grief appears,
Her Eyes half-languishing, half-drown'd in Tears;
On her heav'd Bosom hung her drooping Head,   145
Which, with a Sigh, she rais'd; and thus she said.
    For ever curs'd be this detested Day,
Which snatch'd my best, my fav'rite Curl away!
Happy! ah ten times happy, had I been,
If *Hampton-Court* these Eyes had never seen!   150
Yet am not I the first mistaken Maid,
By Love of *Courts* to num'rous Ills betray'd.
Oh had I rather un-admir'd remain'd
In some lone Isle, or distant *Northern* Land;
Where the gilt *Chariot* never marks the Way,   155
Where none learn *Ombre,* none e'er taste *Bohea!*
There kept my Charms conceal'd from mortal Eye,
Like Roses that in Desarts bloom and die.
What mov'd my Mind with youthful Lords to rome?
O had I stay'd, and said my Pray'rs at home!   160
'Twas this, the Morning *Omens* seem'd to tell;
Thrice from my trembling hand the *Patch-box* fell;
The tott'ring *China* shook without a Wind,
Nay, *Poll* sate mute, and *Shock* was most Unkind!
A *Sylph* too warn'd me of the Threats of Fate,   165
In mystic Visions, now believ'd too late!
See the poor Remnants of these slighted Hairs!
My hands shall rend what ev'n thy Rapine spares:
These, in two sable Ringlets taught to break,
Once gave new Beauties to the snowie Neck.   170
The Sister-Lock now sits uncouth, alone,
And in its Fellow's Fate foresees its own;
Uncurl'd it hangs, the fatal Sheers demands;
And tempts once more thy sacrilegious Hands.
Oh hadst thou, Cruel! been content to seize   175
Hairs less in sight, or any Hairs but these!

135. Honours: beauties, graces.
    141–2. *These two lines are additional; and assign the cause of the different operation of the Passions of the two Ladies. The poem went on before without that distinction, as without any Machinery to the end of the Canto.* P.
    156. Bohea: a kind of tea.

CANTO V

S HE said: the pitying Audience melt in Tears,
But *Fate* and *Jove* had stopp'd the *Baron's* Ears.
In vain *Thalestris* with Reproach assails,
For who can move when fair *Belinda* fails?
Not half so fixt the *Trojan* cou'd remain,   5
While *Anna* begg'd and *Dido* rag'd in vain.
Then grave *Clarissa* graceful wav'd her Fan;
Silence ensu'd, and thus the Nymph began.
    Say, why are Beauties prais'd and honour'd most,
The wise Man's Passion, and the vain Man's Toast?   10
Why deck'd with all that Land and Sea afford,
Why Angels call'd, and Angel-like ador'd?
Why round our Coaches crowd the white-glov'd Beaus,
Why bows the Side-box from its inmost Rows?
How vain are all these Glories, all our Pains,   15
Unless good Sense preserve what Beauty gains:
That Men may say, when we the Front-box grace,
Behold the first in Virtue, as in Face!
Oh! if to dance all Night, and dress all Day,
Charm'd the Small-pox, or chas'd old Age away;   20
Who would not scorn what Huswife's Cares produce,
Or who would learn one earthly Thing of Use?
To patch, nay ogle, might become a Saint,
Nor could it sure be such a Sin to paint.
But since, alas! frail Beauty must decay,   25
Curl'd or uncurl'd, since Locks will turn to grey,
Since painted, or not painted, all shall fade,
And she who scorns a Man, must die a Maid;
What then remains, but well our Pow'r to use,
And keep good Humour still whate'er we lose?   30
And trust me, Dear! good Humour can prevail,
When Airs, and Flights, and Screams, and Scolding fail.
Beauties in vain their pretty Eyes may roll;
Charms strike the Sight, but Merit wins the Soul.
    So spoke the Dame, but no Applause ensu'd;   35
Belinda frown'd, *Thalestris* call'd her Prude.
To Arms, to Arms! the fierce Virago cries,

Canto V.   **5. Trojan:** Aeneas, whom Dido and her sister Anna begged to remain in Carthage (see *Aeneid*, Bk. IV).
   7. Clarissa: *A new Character introduced in the subsequent Editions, to open more clearly the* MORAL *of the Poem, in a parody of the speech of Sarpedon to Glaucus in Homer.*   P.   See *The Episode of Sarpedon*, ll. 27–52.
   35. *It is a verse frequently repeated in Homer after any speech,*
                So spoke — and all the Heroes applauded.   P.
   37. Virago: female warrior.

And swift as Lightning to the Combate flies.
All side in Parties, and begin th' Attack;
Fans clap, Silks russle, and tough Whalebones crack;   40
Heroes' and Heroins' Shouts confus'dly rise,
And base, and treble Voices strike the Skies.
No common Weapons in their Hands are found,
Like Gods they fight, nor dread a mortal Wound.
  So when bold *Homer* makes the Gods engage,   45
And heav'nly Breasts with human Passions rage;
'Gainst *Pallas, Mars; Latona, Hermes* Arms;
And all *Olympus* rings with loud Alarms.
Jove's Thunder roars, Heav'n trembles all around;
Blue *Neptune* storms, the bellowing Deeps resound;   50
Earth shakes her nodding Tow'rs, the Ground gives way;
And the pale Ghosts start at the Flash of Day!
  Triumphant *Umbriel* on a Sconce's Height
Clapt his glad Wings, and sate to view the Fight:
Propt on their Bodkin Spears, the Sprights survey   55
The growing Combat, or assist the Fray.
  While thro' the Press enrag'd *Thalestris* flies,
And scatters Deaths around from both her Eyes,
A *Beau* and *Witling* perish'd in the Throng,
One dy'd in *Metaphor,* and one in *Song.*   60
O cruel Nymph! a living Death I bear,
Cry'd *Dapperwit,* and sunk beside his Chair.
A mournful Glance Sir *Fopling* upwards cast,
Those Eyes are made so killing — was his last:
Thus on *Meander*'s flow'ry Margin lies   65
Th' expiring Swan, and as he sings he dies.
  When bold Sir *Plume* had drawn *Clarissa* down,
Chloe stept in, and kill'd him with a Frown;
She smil'd to see the doughty Hero slain,
But at her Smile, the Beau reviv'd again.   70
  Now *Jove* suspends his golden Scales in Air,
Weighs the Men's Wits against the Lady's Hair;
The doubtful Beam long nods from side to side;
At length the Wits mount up, the Hairs subside.

45. Homer *Iliad.* 20 [ll. 91*ff.*].   P.
47. **Latona:** mother of Apollo and Diana.
53. **Umbriel:** Minerva *in like manner, during the Battle of* Ulysses *with the* Suitors *in* Odyss. [XXII 261*ff.*] *perches on a beam of the roof to behold it.*   P.
Sconce: a candlestick projecting from a plate on a wall.
62–3. **Dapperwit . . . Sir Fopling:** names of social "types" in Restoration comedy.
64. *The Words in a Song in the Opera of* Camilla.   P.   The opera was the work of Marc' Antonio Buononcini.
65–6. Ovid, Ep. [*Heroides*, VII 1–2]
          Sic ubi fata vocant, udis abjectus in herbis,
              Ad vada Mæandri concinit albus olor.   P.
Meander: a winding river in Phrygia.   **Swan:** see *Windsor-Forest*, l. 275*n.*
71–4. *Vide* Homer. *Il.* 8 [ll. 87*ff.*]. & Virg. *Æn.* 12 [ll. 725*ff.*]   P.

See fierce *Belinda* on the *Baron* flies,   75
With more than usual Lightning in her Eyes;
Nor fear'd the Chief th'unequal Fight to try,
Who sought no more than on his Foe to die.
But this bold Lord, with manly Strength indu'd,
She with one Finger and a Thumb subdu'd: 80
Just where the Breath of Life his Nostrils drew,
A Charge of *Snuff* the wily Virgin threw;
The *Gnomes* direct, to ev'ry Atome just,
The pungent Grains of titillating Dust.
Sudden, with starting Tears each Eye o'erflows,   85
And the high Dome re-ecchoes to his Nose.
   Now meet thy Fate, incens'd *Belinda* cry'd,
And drew a deadly *Bodkin* from her Side.
(The same, his ancient Personage to deck,
Her great great Grandsire wore about his Neck   90
In three *Seal-Rings;* which after, melted down,
Form'd a vast *Buckle* for his Widow's Gown:
Her infant Grandame's *Whistle* next it grew,
The *Bells* she gingled, and the *Whistle* blew;
Then in a *Bodkin* grac'd her Mother's Hairs,   95
Which long she wore, and now *Belinda* wears.)
   Boast not my Fall (he cry'd) insulting Foe!
Thou by some other shalt be laid as low.
Nor think, to die dejects my lofty Mind;
All that I dread, is leaving you behind!   100
Rather than so, ah let me still survive,
And burn in *Cupid's* Flames, — but burn alive.
   Restore the Lock! she cries; and all around
Restore the Lock! the vaulted Roofs rebound.
Not fierce *Othello* in so loud a Strain   105
Roar'd for the Handkerchief that caus'd his Pain.
But see how oft Ambitious Aims are cross'd,
And Chiefs contend 'till all the Prize is lost!
The Lock, obtain'd with Guilt, and kept with Pain,
In ev'ry place is sought, but sought in vain: 110
With such a Prize no Mortal must be blest,
So Heav'n decrees! with Heav'n who can contest?
   Some thought it mounted to the Lunar Sphere,
Since all things lost on Earth, are treasur'd there.
There Heroes' Wits are kept in pondrous Vases,   115
And Beaus' in *Snuff-boxes* and *Tweezer-Cases.*
There broken Vows, and Death-bed Alms are found,
And Lovers' Hearts with Ends of Riband bound;

78. to die: here means the consummation of the sexual act.
89–96. *In Imitation of the Progress of* Agamemnon's *Scepter in* Homer, *Il.* I [Il. 129*ff.*].   P.
113–22. *Vid.* Ariosto. Canto 34. P.   Pope recalls Ariosto's *Orlando Furioso,* where Astolfo goes to the moon and there finds, among other items, Orlando's missing wits.

The Courtier's Promises, and Sick Man's Pray'rs,
The Smiles of Harlots, and the Tears of Heirs,   120
Cages for Gnats, and Chains to Yoak a Flea;
Dry'd Butterflies, and Tomes of Casuistry.
　　But trust the Muse — she saw it upward rise,
Tho' mark'd by none but quick Poetic Eyes:
(So *Rome*'s great Founder to the Heav'ns withdrew,   125
To *Proculus* alone confess'd in view.)
A sudden Star, it shot thro' liquid Air,
And drew behind a radiant *Trail of Hair*.
Not *Berenice's* Locks first rose so bright,
The Heav'ns bespangling with dishevel'd Light.   130
The *Sylphs* behold it kindling as it flies,
And pleas'd pursue its Progress thro' the Skies.
　　This the *Beau-monde* shall from the *Mall* survey,
And hail with Musick its propitious Ray.
This, the blest Lover shall for *Venus* take,   135
And send up Vows from *Rosamonda*'s Lake.
This *Partridge* soon shall view in cloudless Skies,
When next he looks thro' *Galilæo*'s Eyes;
And hence th' Egregious Wizard shall foredoom
The Fate of *Louis*, and the Fall of *Rome*.   140
　　Then cease, bright Nymph! to mourn thy ravish'd Hair
Which adds new Glory to the shining Sphere!
Not all the Tresses that fair Head can boast
Shall draw such Envy as the Lock you lost.
For, after all the Murders of your Eye,   145
When, after Millions slain, your self shall die;
When those fair Suns shall sett, as sett they must,
And all those Tresses shall be laid in Dust;
This Lock, the Muse shall consecrate to Fame,
And mid'st the Stars inscribe *Belinda*'s Name!   150

122. Casuistry: here implies specious reasoning about matters of conscience.
　　125–6. Romulus, mythical founder of Rome, disappeared from earth in the midst of a storm. A rumor that he had been translated to heaven was supposedly confirmed by Julius Proculus, a senator, who declared that Romulus had appeared to him in superhuman form.
　　127. liquid: transparent.
　　129. Berenice: when her husband, Ptolemy III, went on a military campaign, Berenice vowed her hair to Aphrodite if he returned safely. Upon his return, she placed her hair in Aphrodite's temple, but the next day it disappeared and was fabled to have been removed to heaven in the form of a constellation.
　　133. Beau-monde: high society.　　**Mall:** a walk in St. James's Park.
　　136. Rosamonda's Lake: a pond in St. James's Park considered to be a haunt of unhappy lovers. Rosamond, known as "Fair Rosamond," was mistress to Henry II, and legend held that she was murdered by his queen. See *Ep. to a Lady*, l. 92n.
　　137. John Partridge *was a ridiculous Star-gazer, who in his Almanacks every year, never fail'd to predict the downfall of the Pope, and the King of* France, *then at war with the* English.　P.
　　140. Louis: Louis XIV (see previous note).
　　142. Sphere: often pronounced "sphare" in Pope's time.

EPISTLE TO MR. JERVAS

With *Dryden's* Translation of *Fresnoy's* *Art* of *Painting*

THIS verse be thine, my friend, nor thou refuse
    This, from no venal or ungrateful Muse.
    Whether thy hand strike out some free design,
Where life awakes, and dawns at ev'ry line;
Or blend in beauteous tints the colour'd mass,   5
And from the canvas call the mimic face:
Read these instructive leaves, in which conspire
Fresnoy's close art, and *Dryden's* native fire:
And reading wish, like theirs, our fate and fame,
So mix'd our studies, and so join'd our name,   10
Like them to shine thro' long succeeding age,
So just thy skill, so regular my rage.
    Smit with the love of Sister-arts we came,
And met congenial, mingling flame with flame;
Like friendly colours found them both unite,   15
And each from each contract new strength and light.
How oft' in pleasing tasks we wear the day,
While summer suns roll unperceiv'd away?
How oft' our slowly-growing works impart,
While images reflect from art to art?   20
How oft' review; each finding like a friend
Something to blame, and something to commend?
What flatt'ring scenes our wand'ring fancy wrought,
Rome's pompous glories rising to our thought!
Together o'er the *Alps* methinks we fly,   25
Fir'd with ideas of fair *Italy*.
With thee, on *Raphael's* Monument I mourn,
Or wait inspiring dreams at *Maro's* Urn:
With thee repose, where *Tully* once was laid,

EPISTLE TO MR. JERVAS: First published on March 20, 1716. For several years
after 1712 Pope, when he was in London, resided at the house of Charles Jervas
(1675–1739), the portrait painter, and took lessons in painting from him. John
Dryden's prose translation of *De arte graphica*, a Latin poem by the French historical painter Charles Alphonse du Fresnoy (1611–65), had appeared in 1695.
    12. regular: according to the "Rules" (see l. 67, below, and *Essay on Criti-
cism*, l. 88n.).
    28. Maro: Virgil (Publius Virgilius Maro).
    29. Tully: Cicero (Marcus Tullius Cicero).

Or seek some ruin's formidable shade;   30
While fancy brings the vanish'd piles to view,
And builds imaginary *Rome* a-new.
Here thy well-study'd Marbles fix our eye;
A fading Fresco here demands a sigh:
Each heav'nly piece unweary'd we compare,   35
Match *Raphael's* grace, with thy lov'd *Guido's* air,
Caracci's strength, *Correggio's* softer line,
Paulo's free stroke, and *Titian's* warmth divine.
    How finish'd with illustrious toil appears
This small, well-polish'd gem, the work of years!   40
Yet still how faint by precept is exprest
The living image in the Painter's breast?
Thence endless streams of fair ideas flow,
Strike in the sketch, or in the picture glow;
Thence beauty, waking all her forms, supplies   45
An Angel's sweetness, or *Bridgewater's* eyes.
    Muse! at that name thy sacred sorrows shed,
Those tears eternal, that embalm the dead:
Call round her tomb each object of desire,
Each purer frame inform'd with purer fire: 50
Bid her be all that chears or softens life,
The tender sister, daughter, friend and wife;
Bid her be all that makes mankind adore;
Then view this marble, and be vain no more!
    Yet still her charms in breathing paint engage;   55
Her modest cheek shall warm a future age.
Beauty, frail flow'r that ev'ry season fears,
Blooms in thy colours for a thousand years.
Thus *Churchill's* race shall other hearts surprize,
And other Beauties envy *Worsley's* eyes,   60
Each pleasing *Blount* shall endless smiles bestow,

31. piles: buildings.
33. well-study'd Marbles: Jervas had studied in Italy.
36. Guido: Guido Reni (1575–1642), eminent Italian painter.
37. Caracci: probably Annibale Carracci (1560–1609), greatest painter of the Carracci family.   **Correggio:** Antonio Allegri da Correggio (1494–1534), eminent Italian painter.
38. Paulo: Paolo Cagliari (Paul Veronese), eminent Italian painter (1530–88).
40. work of years: *Fresnoy* employ'd about twenty years in finishing this Poem. P.
46. Bridgewater: Elizabeth, Countess of Bridgewater, one of four beautiful daughters of John Churchill, Duke of Marlborough (all four are alluded to in l. 59 as "Churchill's race").
47–54. Lady Bridgewater had died of smallpox in 1714.
60. Worsley: wife of Sir Robert Worsley.
61. Each pleasing Blount: Teresa and Martha Blount, two sisters with whom Pope was intimately acquainted (for Martha Blount, see first note to *Ep. to a Lady*).

And soft *Belinda*'s blush for ever glow.
    Oh lasting as those colours may they shine,
Free as thy stroke, yet faultless as thy line!
New graces yearly, like thy works, display;   65
Soft without weakness, without glaring gay;
Led by some rule, that guides, but not constrains;
And finish'd more thro' happiness than pains!
The kindred arts shall in their praise conspire,
One dip the pencil, and one string the lyre.   70
Yet should the Graces all thy figures place,
And breathe an air divine on ev'ry face;
Yet should the Muses bid my numbers roll,
Strong as their charms, and gentle as their soul;
With *Zeuxis' Helen* thy *Bridgewater* vie,   75
And these be sung 'till *Granville's Myra* die;
Alas! how little from the grave we claim?
Thou but preserv'st a Face and I a Name.

62. Belinda: Arabella Fermor, the inspiration for Pope's Belinda in *The Rape of the Lock.*
  68. happiness: see *Essay on Criticism,* l. 142*n.*
  71. Graces: the three Graces of classical myth.
  75. Zeuxis' Helen: a portrait of Helen was the most celebrated work of the Greek painter Zeuxis (c. 450–400 B.C.).   **thy Bridgewater:** Jervas professed to be in love with the countess.
  76. Granville's Myra: see *Windsor-Forest,* first note, and ll. 297–8*n.*

ELOISA TO ABELARD

THE ARGUMENT

Abelard and Eloisa flourish'd in the twelfth Century; they were two of the most distinguish'd persons of their age in learning and beauty, but for nothing more famous than for their unfortunate passion. After a long course of Calamities, they retired each to a several Convent, and consecrated the remainder of their days to religion. It was many years after this separation, that a letter of Abelard's to a Friend which contain'd the history of his misfortune, fell into the hands of Eloisa. This awakening all her tenderness, occasion'd those celebrated letters (out of which the following is partly extracted) which give so lively a picture of the struggles of grace and nature, virtue and passion.

IN these deep solitudes and awful cells,
   Where heav'nly-pensive, contemplation dwells,
   And ever-musing melancholy reigns;
What means this tumult in a Vestal's veins?
Why rove my thoughts beyond this last retreat?   5
Why feels my heart its long-forgotten heat?
Yet, yet I love! — From *Abelard* it came,
And *Eloisa* yet must kiss the name.
   Dear fatal name! rest ever unreveal'd,
Nor pass these lips in holy silence seal'd.   10
Hide it, my heart, within that close disguise,

ELOISA TO ABELARD: Peter Abelard (1079–1142), French philosopher and theologian, at the age of 38 fell passionately in love with his seventeen-year-old pupil, Héloïse. After the birth of a son they were married privately, but Héloïse's uncle, the canon Fulbert, nevertheless caused Abelard to be set upon by ruffians and emasculated. Héloïse entered a convent at Argenteuil, and Abelard retired to a hermitage which became a monastic school known as the Paraclete (i.e., the "Comforter," a term applied to the Holy Spirit). When Abelard became abbot of St. Gildas-de-Rhuys, he gave Paraclete to Héloïse and a sisterhood, and about this time they began their famous correspondence. The Latin texts of their letters were published in 1616, and a romanticized French version of them appeared in 1697. In 1713 John Hughes (1677–1720), a minor poet and dramatist, turned this French version into English, and Pope used this last translation as the basis of his poem, first published in the *Works* of 1717.
   4. Vestal: originally one of the virgins consecrated to Vesta, Roman goddess of the hearth and its fire.
   9. fatal: ominous (cf. l. 30).

Where, mix'd with God's, his lov'd Idea lies.
Oh write it not, my hand — The name appears
Already written — wash it out, my tears!
In vain lost *Eloisa* weeps and prays,   15
Her heart still dictates, and her hand obeys.
    Relentless walls! whose darksom round contains
Repentant sighs, and voluntary pains:
Ye rugged rocks! which holy knees have worn;
Ye grots and caverns shagg'd with horrid thorn!   20
Shrines! where their vigils pale-ey'd virgins keep,
And pitying saints, whose statues learn to weep!
Tho' cold like you, unmov'd, and silent grown,
I have not yet forgot my self to stone.
All is not Heav'n's while *Abelard* has part,   25
Still rebel nature holds out half my heart;
Nor pray'rs nor fasts its stubborn pulse restrain,
Nor tears, for ages, taught to flow in vain.
    Soon as thy letters trembling I unclose,
That well-known name awakens all my woes.   30
Oh name for ever sad! for ever dear!
Still breath'd in sighs, still usher'd with a tear.
I tremble too where-e'er my own I find,
Some dire misfortune follows close behind.
Line after line my gushing eyes o'erflow,   35
Led thro' a sad variety of woe:
Now warm in love, now with'ring in thy bloom,
Lost in a convent's solitary gloom!
There stern religion quench'd th' unwilling flame,
There dy'd the best of passions, Love and Fame.   40
    Yet write, oh write me all, that I may join
Griefs to thy griefs, and eccho sighs to thine.
Nor foes nor fortune take this pow'r away.
And is my *Abelard* less kind than they?
Tears still are mine, and those I need not spare,   45
Love but demands what else were shed in pray'r;
No happier task these faded eyes pursue,
To read and weep is all they now can do.
    Then share thy pain, allow that sad relief;
Ah more than share it! give me all thy grief.   50
Heav'n first taught letters for some wretch's aid,
Some banish'd lover, or some captive maid;
They live, they speak, they breathe what love inspires,
Warm from the soul, and faithful to its fires,

---

12. **Idea:** mental image.
20. **shagg'd:** roughened.   **horrid:** bristling.
22. **weep:** see *Windsor-Forest*, l. 302*n*.
40. **Fame:** Abelard's retirement in disgrace had defeated his professional ambitions.

The virgin's wish without her fears impart,   55
Excuse the blush, and pour out all the heart,
Speed the soft intercourse from soul to soul,
And waft a sigh from *Indus* to the *Pole*.
  Thou know'st how guiltless first I met thy flame,
When Love approach'd me under Friendship's name;
My fancy form'd thee of Angelick kind,   61
Some emanation of th' all-beauteous Mind.
Those smiling eyes, attemp'ring ev'ry ray,
Shone sweetly lambent with celestial day:
Guiltless I gaz'd; heav'n listen'd while you sung;   65
And truths divine came mended from that tongue.
From lips like those what precept fail'd to move?
Too soon they taught me 'twas no sin to love.
Back thro' the paths of pleasing sense I ran,
Nor wish'd an Angel whom I lov'd a Man.   70
Dim and remote the joys of saints I see,
Nor envy them, that heav'n I lose for thee.
  How oft', when press'd to marriage, have I said,
Curse on all laws but those which love has made!
Love, free as air, at sight of human ties,   75
Spreads his light wings, and in a moment flies.
Let wealth, let honour, wait the wedded dame,
August her deed, and sacred be her fame;
Before true passion all those views remove,
Fame, wealth, and honour! what are you to Love?   80
The jealous God, when we profane his fires,
Those restless passions in revenge inspires;
And bids them make mistaken mortals groan,
Who seek in love for ought but love alone.
Should at my feet the world's great master fall,   85
Himself, his throne, his world, I'd scorn 'em all:
Not *Cæsar's* empress wou'd I deign to prove;
No, make me mistress to the man I love;
If there be yet another name more free,
More fond than mistress, make me that to thee!   90
Oh happy state! when souls each other draw,
When love is liberty, and nature, law:

63. **attemp'ring:** softening.   **ray:** see *Messiah*, l. 39*n*.
66. *He was her Preceptor in Philosophy and Divinity.*   P.   **mended:** improved.
73. **marriage:** the historical Héloïse had been reluctant to enter into marriage because it would have damaged Abelard's career.
75–6.   *Love will not be confin'd by Maisterie:*
           When Maisterie comes, the Lord of Love anon
           Flutters his wings, and forthwith he is gone.
Chaucer [*Franklin's Tale*, ll. 36–8].   P.
85. **world's great master:** probably Alexander the Great.
87. **to prove:** to become.

All then is full, possessing, and possest,
No craving Void left aking in the breast:
Ev'n thought meets thought ere from the lips it part,   95
And each warm wish springs mutual from the heart.
This sure is bliss (if bliss on earth there be)
And once the lot of *Abelard* and me.
    Alas how chang'd! what sudden horrors rise!
A naked Lover bound and bleeding lies!   100
Where, where was *Eloise?* her voice, her hand,
Her ponyard, had oppos'd the dire command.
Barbarian stay! that bloody stroke restrain;
The crime was common, common be the pain.
I can no more; by shame, by rage supprest,   105
Let tears, and burning blushes speak the rest.
    Canst thou forget that sad, that solemn day,
When victims at yon' altar's foot we lay?
Canst thou forget what tears that moment fell,
When, warm in youth, I bade the world farewell?   110
As with cold lips I kiss'd the sacred veil,
The shrines all trembled, and the lamps grew pale:
Heav'n scarce believ'd the conquest it survey'd,
And Saints with wonder heard the vows I made.
Yet then, to those dread altars as I drew,   115
Not on the Cross my eyes were fix'd, but you;
Not grace, or zeal, love only was my call,
And if I lose thy love, I lose my all.
Come! with thy looks, thy words, relieve my woe;
Those still at least are left thee to bestow.   120
Still on that breast enamour'd let me lie,
Still drink delicious poison from thy eye,
Pant on thy lip, and to thy heart be prest;
Give all thou canst — and let me dream the rest.
Ah no! instruct me other joys to prize,   125
With other beauties charm my partial eyes,
Full in my view set all the bright abode,
And make my soul quit *Abelard* for God.
    Ah think at least thy flock deserves thy care,
Plants of thy hand, and children of thy pray'r.   130
From the false world in early youth they fled,
By thee to mountains, wilds, and deserts led.
You rais'd these hallow'd walls; the desert smil'd,
And Paradise was open'd in the Wild.
No weeping orphan saw his father's stores   135
Our shrines irradiate, or emblaze the floors;
No silver saints, by dying misers giv'n,

104. **common:** mutual.   **pain:** penalty, as well as suffering.
107–8. Abelard was present on the day when Héloïse took her religious vows.
133. *He founded the Monastery.* P.

Here brib'd the rage of ill-requited heav'n:
But such plain roofs as piety could raise,
And only vocal with the Maker's praise.   140
In these lone walls (their day's eternal bound)
These moss-grown domes with spiry turrets crown'd,
Where awful arches make a noon-day night,
And the dim windows shed a solemn light;
Thy eyes diffus'd a reconciling ray,   145
And gleams of glory brighten'd all the day.
But now no face divine contentment wears,
'Tis all blank sadness, or continual tears.
See how the force of others' pray'rs I try,
(Oh pious fraud of am'rous charity!)   150
But why should I on others' pray'rs depend?
Come thou, my father, brother, husband, friend!
Ah let thy handmaid, sister, daughter move,
And, all those tender names in one, thy love!
The darksom pines that o'er yon' rocks reclin'd   155
Wave high, and murmur to the hollow wind,
The wandring streams that shine between the hills,
The grots that eccho to the tinkling rills,
The dying gales that pant upon the trees,
The lakes that quiver to the curling breeze;   160
No more these scenes my meditation aid,
Or lull to rest the visionary maid:
But o'er the twilight groves, and dusky caves,
Long-sounding isles, and intermingled graves,
Black Melancholy sits, and round her throws   165
A death-like silence, and a dread repose:
Her gloomy presence saddens all the scene,
Shades ev'ry flow'r, and darkens ev'ry green,
Deepens the murmur of the falling floods,
And breathes a browner horror on the woods.   170
    Yet here for ever, ever must I stay;
Sad proof how well a lover can obey!
Death, only death, can break the lasting chain;
And here ev'n then, shall my cold dust remain,
Here all its frailties, all its flames resign,   175
And wait, till 'tis no sin to mix with thine.
    Ah wretch! believ'd the spouse of God in vain,
Confess'd within the slave of love and man.

142. **domes**: buildings.
152. **father**: as spiritual director.   **brother**: as fellow religious.   **friend**:
lover.
161. **meditation**: a form of spiritual exercise; deep reflection on a religious
theme.
162. **visionary**: seeing visions.
164. **isles**: aisles.
177. **spouse of God**: by her vows Eloisa had wedded herself to Christ.

Assist me heav'n! but whence arose that pray'r?
Sprung it from piety, or from despair?   180
Ev'n here, where frozen chastity retires,
Love finds an altar for forbidden fires.
I ought to grieve, but cannot what I ought;
I mourn the lover, not lament the fault;
I view my crime, but kindle at the view,   185
Repent old pleasures, and sollicit new:
Now turn'd to heav'n, I weep my past offence,
Now think of thee, and curse my innocence.
Of all affliction taught a lover yet,
'Tis sure the hardest science to forget!   190
How shall I lose the sin, yet keep the sense,
And love th' offender, yet detest th' offence?
How the dear object from the crime remove,
Or how distinguish penitence from love?
Unequal task! a passion to resign,   195
For hearts so touch'd, so pierc'd, so lost as mine.
Ere such a soul regains its peaceful state,
How often must it love, how often hate!
How often, hope, despair, resent, regret,
Conceal, disdain — do all things but forget.   200
But let heav'n seize it, all at once 'tis fir'd,
Not touch'd, but rapt; not waken'd, but inspir'd!
Oh come! oh teach me nature to subdue,
Renounce my love, my life, my self — and you.
Fill my fond heart with God alone, for he   205
Alone can rival, can succeed to thee.
     How happy is the blameless Vestal's lot!
The world forgetting, by the world forgot.
Eternal sun-shine of the spotless mind!
Each pray'r accepted, and each wish resign'd;   210
Labour and rest, that equal periods keep;
'Obedient slumbers that can wake and weep';
Desires compos'd, affections ever ev'n,
Tears that delight, and sighs that waft to heav'n.
Grace shines around her with serenest beams,   215
And whisp'ring Angels prompt her golden dreams.
For her th' unfading rose of *Eden* blooms,
And wings of Seraphs shed divine perfumes;
For her the Spouse prepares the bridal ring,
For her white virgins *Hymenæals* sing;   220

191. **sense:** sensation, but also perception.
195. **unequal:** disproportionate, excessive.
   212. *Taken from* [Richard] *Crashaw [Description of a Religious House,* l.
16]. P.
   219–20. The Spouse is Christ, whose wedding ring, conferred in the course
of their profession, is worn by certain orders of nuns (see l. 177n.). Hymenæals
are marriage songs.

To sounds of heav'nly harps, she dies away,
And melts in visions of eternal day.
    Far other dreams my erring soul employ,
Far other raptures, of unholy joy:
When at the close of each sad, sorrowing day,   225
Fancy restores what vengeance snatch'd away,
Then conscience sleeps, and leaving nature free,
All my loose soul unbounded springs to thee.
O curst, dear horrors of all-conscious night!
How glowing guilt exalts the keen delight!   230
Provoking Dæmons all restraint remove,
And stir within me ev'ry source of love.
I hear thee, view thee, gaze o'er all thy charms,
And round thy phantom glue my clasping arms.
I wake — no more I hear, no more I view,   235
The phantom flies me, as unkind as you.
I call aloud; it hears not what I say;
I stretch my empty arms; it glides away:
To dream once more I close my willing eyes;
Ye soft illusions, dear deceits, arise!   240
Alas no more! — methinks we wandring go
Thro' dreary wastes, and weep each other's woe;
Where round some mould'ring tow'r pale ivy creeps,
And low-brow'd rocks hang nodding o'er the deeps.
Sudden you mount! you becken from the skies;   245
Clouds interpose, waves roar, and winds arise.
I shriek, start up, the same sad prospect find,
And wake to all the griefs I left behind.
    For thee the fates, severely kind, ordain
A cool suspense from pleasure and from pain;   250
Thy life a long, dead calm of fix'd repose;
No pulse that riots, and no blood that glows.
Still as the sea, ere winds were taught to blow,
Or moving spirit bade the waters flow;
Soft as the slumbers of a saint forgiv'n,   255
And mild as opening gleams of promis'd heav'n.
    Come *Abelard!* for what hast thou to dread?
The torch of *Venus* burns not for the dead;
Nature stands check'd; Religion disapproves;
Ev'n thou art cold — yet *Eloisa* loves.   260
Ah hopeless, lasting flames! like those that burn
To light the dead, and warm th' unfruitful urn.
    What scenes appear where-e'er I turn my view!

226. **vengeance:** that of her uncle, the canon Fulbert (see first note, above).
230. **exalts:** intensifies.
231. **Dæmons:** demons.
254. **moving spirit:** see Genesis 1:2.
261–2. Lamps to warm the dead were burned in ancient tombs.

The dear Ideas, where I fly, pursue,
Rise in the grove, before the altar rise,   265
Stain all my soul, and wanton in my eyes!
I waste the Matin lamp in sighs for thee,
Thy image steals between my God and me,
Thy voice I seem in ev'ry hymn to hear,
With ev'ry bead I drop too soft a tear.   270
When from the Censer clouds of fragrance roll,
And swelling organs lift the rising soul;
One thought of thee puts all the pomp to flight,
Priests, Tapers, Temples, swim before my sight:
In seas of flame my plunging soul is drown'd,   275
While Altars blaze, and Angels tremble round.
   While prostrate here in humble grief I lie,
Kind, virtuous drops just gath'ring in my eye,
While praying, trembling, in the dust I roll,
And dawning grace is opening on my soul: 280
Come, if thou dar'st, all charming as thou art!
Oppose thy self to heav'n; dispute my heart;
Come, with one glance of those deluding eyes,
Blot out each bright Idea of the skies.
Take back that grace, those sorrows, and those tears,   285
Take back my fruitless penitence and pray'rs,
Snatch me, just mounting, from the blest abode,
Assist the Fiends and tear me from my God!
   No, fly me, fly me! far as Pole from Pole;
Rise *Alps* between us! and whole oceans roll!   290
Ah come not, write not, think not once of me,
Nor share one pang of all I felt for thee.
Thy oaths I quit, thy memory resign,
Forget, renounce me, hate whate'er was mine.
Fair eyes, and tempting looks (which yet I view!)   295
Long lov'd, ador'd ideas! all adieu!
O grace serene! oh virtue heav'nly fair!
Divine oblivion of low-thoughted care!
Fresh blooming hope, gay daughter of the sky!
And faith, our early immortality!   300
Enter each mild, each amicable guest;
Receive, and wrap me in eternal rest!

264. **Ideas:** images.
267. **Matin lamp:** the light used for the service sung between midnight and dawn.
268. **God:** here the Eucharist, on the altar.
269. **voice:** Abelard had an especially fine musical voice.
270. **bead:** of the rosary.
278. **Kind:** grateful.   **virtuous:** powerful.
282. **dispute:** contend for (Abelard was noted for his skill in theological disputation).
293. **quit:** absolve.

See in her Cell sad *Eloisa* spread,
Propt on some tomb, a neighbour of the dead!
In each low wind methinks a Spirit calls,   305
And more than Echoes talk along the walls.
Here, as I watch'd the dying lamps around,
From yonder shrine I heard a hollow sound.
Come, sister come! (it said, or seem'd to say)
Thy place is here, sad sister come away!   310
Once like thy self, I trembled, wept, and pray'd,
Love's victim then, tho' now a sainted maid:
But all is calm in this eternal sleep;
Here grief forgets to groan, and love to weep,
Ev'n superstition loses ev'ry fear;   315
For God, not man, absolves our frailties here.
    I come, I come! prepare your roseate bow'rs,
Celestial palms, and ever-blooming flow'rs.
Thither, where sinners may have rest, I go,
Where flames refin'd in breasts seraphic glow.   320
Thou, *Abelard!* the last sad office pay,
And smooth my passage to the realms of day:
See my lips tremble, and my eye-balls roll,
Suck my last breath, and catch my flying soul!
Ah no — in sacred vestments may'st thou stand,   325
The hallow'd taper trembling in thy hand,
Present the Cross before my lifted eye,
Teach me at once, and learn of me to die.
Ah then, thy once-lov'd *Eloisa* see!
It will be then no crime to gaze on me.   330
See from my cheek the transient roses fly!
See the last sparkle languish in my eye!
Till ev'ry motion, pulse, and breath, be o'er;
And ev'n my *Abelard* be lov'd no more.
O death all-eloquent! you only prove   335
What dust we doat on, when 'tis man we love.
    Then too, when fate shall thy fair frame destroy,
(That cause of all my guilt, and all my joy)
In trance extatic may thy pangs be drown'd,
Bright clouds descend, and Angels watch thee round,   340
From opening skies may streaming glories shine,
And Saints embrace thee with a love like mine.
    May one kind grave unite each hapless name,

320. Seraphs were traditionally conceived of as fiery beings, and associated with purification.
    321. last sad office: last rites.
    324. The soul was popularly believed to issue from the mouth at death.
    343. Abelard *and* Eloisa *were interr'd in the same grave, or in monuments adjoining, in the Monastery of the* Paraclete: *He died in the year* 1142, *she in* 1163. P.   The remains of the couple were later shifted to one sepulchre in Paris.

And graft my love immortal on thy fame.
Then, ages hence, when all my woes are o'er, 345
When this rebellious heart shall beat no more;
If ever chance two wandring lovers brings
To *Paraclete's* white walls, and silver springs,
O'er the pale marble shall they join their heads,
And drink the falling tears each other sheds, 350
Then sadly say, with mutual pity mov'd,
Oh may we never love as these have lov'd!
From the full quire when loud *Hosanna's* rise,
And swell the pomp of dreadful sacrifice,
Amid that scene, if some relenting eye 355
Glance on the stone where our cold reliques lie,
Devotion's self shall steal a thought from heav'n,
One human tear shall drop, and be forgiv'n.
And sure if fate some future Bard shall join
In sad similitude of griefs to mine, 360
Condemn'd whole years in absence to deplore,
And image charms he must behold no more,
Such if there be, who loves so long, so well;
Let him our sad, our tender story tell;
The well-sung woes will sooth my pensive ghost; 365
He best can paint 'em, who shall feel 'em most.

353. quire: choir.
354. sacrifice: the Holy Sacrifice of the Mass.
359–66. Pope at this time was passionately infatuated with Lady Mary Wortley Montagu (1689–1762), who had left England to accompany her husband on
an embassy to Turkey. The infatuation was later ended by a quarrel, and Lady
Mary, one of the most witty and talented women of the age, became a frequent
object of satire in Pope's poetry (see *Ep. to Bathurst*, l. 123n.).

ELEGY TO THE MEMORY OF
AN UNFORTUNATE LADY

WHAT beck'ning ghost, along the moonlight shade
    Invites my step, and points to yonder glade?
    'Tis she! — but why that bleeding bosom gor'd,
Why dimly gleams the visionary sword?
Oh ever beauteous, ever friendly! tell,   5
Is it, in heav'n, a crime to love too well?
To bear too tender, or too firm a heart,
To act a Lover's or a *Roman's* part?
Is there no bright reversion in the sky,
For those who greatly think, or bravely die?   10
    Why bade ye else, ye Pow'rs! her soul aspire
Above the vulgar flight of low desire?
Ambition first sprung from your blest abodes;
The glorious fault of Angels and of Gods:
Thence to their Images on earth it flows,   15
And in the breasts of Kings and Heroes glows!
Most souls, 'tis true, but peep out once an age,
Dull sullen pris'ners in the body's cage:
Dim lights of life that burn a length of years,
Useless, unseen, as lamps in sepulchres;   20
Like Eastern Kings a lazy state they keep,
And close confin'd to their own palace sleep.
    From these perhaps (ere nature bade her die)
Fate snatch'd her early to the pitying sky.
As into air the purer spirits flow,   25
And sep'rate from their kindred dregs below;
So flew the soul to its congenial place,
Nor left one virtue to redeem her Race.
    But thou, false guardian of a charge too good,
Thou, mean deserter of thy brother's blood!   30

ELEGY TO . . . AN UNFORTUNATE LADY: First published in Pope's *Works* of 1717.
The "unfortunate lady," if she had an actual existence, has not been identified.
  8. **Roman's part:** suicide.
  9. **reversion:** legal term meaning "right of future possession."
  25–6. The image is from chemistry.
  28. **Race:** family.

See on these ruby lips the trembling breath,
These cheeks, now fading at the blast of death:
Cold is that breast which warm'd the world before,
And those love-darting eyes must roll no more.
Thus, if eternal justice rules the ball,   35
Thus shall your wives, and thus your children fall:
On all the line a sudden vengeance waits,
And frequent herses shall besiege your gates.
There passengers shall stand, and pointing say,
(While the long fun'rals blacken all the way)   40
Lo these were they, whose souls the Furies steel'd,
And curs'd with hearts unknowing how to yield.
Thus unlamented pass the proud away,
The gaze of fools, and pageant of a day!
So perish all, whose breast ne'er learn'd to glow   45
For others' good, or melt at others' woe.
    What can atone (oh ever-injur'd shade!)
Thy fate unpity'd, and thy rites unpaid?
No friend's complaint, no kind domestic tear
Pleas'd thy pale ghost, or grac'd thy mournful bier;   50
By foreign hands thy dying eyes were clos'd,
By foreign hands thy decent limbs compos'd,
By foreign hands thy humble grave adorn'd,
By strangers honour'd, and by strangers mourn'd!
What tho' no friends in sable weeds appear,   55
Grieve for an hour, perhaps, then mourn a year,
And bear about the mockery of woe
To midnight dances, and the publick show?
What tho' no weeping Loves thy ashes grace,
Nor polish'd marble emulate thy face?   60
What tho' no sacred earth allow thee room,
Nor hallow'd dirge be mutter'd o'er thy tomb?
Yet shall thy grave with rising flow'rs be drest,
And the green turf lie lightly on thy breast:
There shall the morn her earliest tears bestow,   65
There the first roses of the year shall blow;
While Angels with their silver wings o'ershade
The ground, now sacred by thy reliques made.
    So peaceful rests, without a stone, a name,
What once had beauty, titles, wealth, and fame.   70

---

39. passengers: passers-by.
41. Furies: the Erinyes, avenging goddesses who brought retribution to those who violated natural pieties.
52. decent: shapely.
59. Loves: cupids.
61–2. As a suicide, the lady was not given burial in consecrated ground.
64. turf lie lightly: cf. the common Roman epitaph, *sit tibi terra levis* (may the earth lie lightly on you).
66. blow: blossom.

How lov'd, how honour'd once, avails thee not,
To whom related, or by whom begot;
A heap of dust alone remains of thee;
'Tis all thou art, and all the proud shall be!
   Poets themselves must fall, like those they sung;   75
Deaf the prais'd ear, and mute the tuneful tongue.
Ev'n he, whose soul now melts in mournful lays,
Shall shortly want the gen'rous tear he pays;
Then from his closing eyes thy form shall part,
And the last pang shall tear thee from his heart,   80
Life's idle business at one gasp be o'er,
The Muse forgot, and thou belov'd no more!

78. want: lack

TO MR. ADDISON

Occasioned by his Dialogues on Medals

SEE the wild Waste of all-devouring years!
  How Rome her own sad Sepulchre appears,
  With nodding arches, broken temples spread!
The very Tombs now vanish'd like their dead!
Imperial wonders rais'd on Nations spoil'd,   5
Where mix'd with Slaves the groaning Martyr toil'd;
Huge Theatres, that now unpeopled Woods,
Now drain'd a distant country of her Floods;
Fanes, which admiring Gods with pride survey,
Statues of Men, scarce less alive than they;   10
Some felt the silent stroke of mould'ring age,
Some hostile fury, some religious rage;
Barbarian blindness, Christian zeal conspire,
And Papal piety, and Gothic fire.
Perhaps, by its own ruins sav'd from flame,   15
Some bury'd marble half preserves a name;
That Name the learn'd with fierce disputes pursue,
And give to Titus old Vespasian's due.
   Ambition sigh'd; She found it vain to trust .
The faithless Column and the crumbling Bust;   20
Huge moles, whose shadow stretch'd from shore to shore,
Their ruins ruin'd, and their place no more!
Convinc'd, she now contracts her vast design,

TO MR. ADDISON: Possibly drafted as early as 1713, this poem was first published in 1720, the year after Joseph Addison's death. Five years before, in 1715, relations between Pope and Addison were very strained, mainly because Addison at that time entered into a design to discredit Pope's translation of the *Iliad* by sponsoring a rival translation by Thomas Tickell (see *Peri Bathous*, n. 16, p. 420.). By 1719 the two were on civil terms at least, perhaps because Pope in the interval had sent Addison an indignant letter of protest and accompanied it with a sketch of the Atticus portrait that was to appear years later in *Ep. to Arbuthnot*, ll. 193–214. The "medals" of the poem's title are antique coins.
  7–8. The woods were "unpeopled" of wild beasts, and regions drained of water, for spectacles and mock naval combats staged in Roman amphitheaters.
  9. Fanes: temples.
  18. Titus, son of Vespasian (9–79 A.D.), might be confused with his father in a half-preserved inscription, for their names (Titus Flavius Sabinus Vespasianus) were identical.
  21. moles: massive piers or breakwaters.

And all her Triumphs shrink into a Coin:
A narrow orb each crouded conquest keeps,   25
Beneath her Palm here sad Judæa weeps,
Here scantier limits the proud Arch confine,
And scarce are seen the prostrate Nile or Rhine,
A small Euphrates thro' the piece is roll'd,
And little Eagles wave their wings in gold.   30
   The Medal, faithful to its charge of fame,
Thro' climes and ages bears each form and name:
In one short view subjected to your eye
Gods, Emp'rors, Heroes, Sages, Beauties, lie.
With sharpen'd sight pale Antiquaries pore,   35
Th' inscription value, but the rust adore;
This the blue varnish, that the green endears,
The sacred rust of twice ten hundred years!
To gain Pescennius one employs his schemes,
One grasps a Cecrops in ecstatic dreams;   40
Poor Vadius, long with learned spleen devour'd,
Can taste no pleasure since his Shield was scour'd;
And Curio, restless by the Fair-one's side,
Sighs for an Otho, and neglects his bride.
   Theirs is the Vanity, the Learning thine: 45
Touch'd by thy hand, again Rome's glories shine,
Her Gods, and god-like Heroes rise to view,
And all her faded garlands bloom a-new.
Nor blush, these studies thy regard engage;
These pleas'd the Fathers of poetic rage;   50
The verse and sculpture bore an equal part,
And Art reflected images to Art.
   Oh when shall Britain, conscious of her claim,
Stand emulous of Greek and Roman fame?
In living medals see her wars enroll'd,   55
And vanquish'd realms supply recording gold?

24. Triumphs: see *Essay on Criticism*, l. 512*n.*   **Coin:** pronounced to rhyme with *design*.

25. narrow orb: perhaps a recollection of *Orbis Romanus*, a title given to their empire by the Romans.

26. Coins of Vespasian and Titus show a mourning Judea seated under a palm tree.

27. Coins of Domitian (51–96 A.D.) and Trajan (52–117 A.D.) show triumphal arches.

28–9. Prostrate river gods appear on certain coins.

30. Eagles: see *Essay on Criticism*, l. 684*n.*

35. sharpen'd: by magnifying glasses.

37. varnish: the colored coating that forms on old coins.

39. Pescennius: coins of Pescennius Niger (d. 194 A.D.) are extremely rare.

40. Cecrops: mythical first king of Athens, of whom no coins would exist.

41–3. Vadius . . . Curio: "type" names for eccentric antiquaries.

44. Otho: coins of Otho's three-month reign in 69 A.D. are very rare.

50. rage: inspiration, excitement.

Here, rising bold, the Patriot's honest face;
There Warriors frowning in historic brass:
Then future ages with delight shall see
How Plato's, Bacon's, Newton's looks agree;   60
Or in fair series laurell'd Bards be shown,
A Virgil there, and here an Addison.
Then shall thy CRAGS (and let me call him mine)
On the cast ore, another Pollio, shine;
With aspect open, shall erect his head,   65
And round the orb in lasting notes be read,
"Statesman, yet friend to Truth! of soul sincere,
"In action faithful, and in honour clear;
"Who broke no promise, serv'd no private end,
"Who gain'd no title, and who lost no friend,   70
"Ennobled by himself, by all approv'd,
"And prais'd, unenvy'd, by the Muse he lov'd."

57. **rising:** carved in relief.
63. **Crags:** James Craggs, the younger (1686–1721), in 1718 succeeded his friend Addison as Secretary of State. He and Pope esteemed one another highly, and the poet commemorated their friendship several times in his poetry (see *Sixth Ep. of the First Bk.*, l. 45; *Epil. to the Satires*, II 69).
64. **Pollio:** Asinius Pollio (76 B.C.–4 A.D.), Roman author, patron, and consul. See first note to *Messiah*.
65. **aspect:** mien, bearing.
67–72. A version of these lines was later to serve as the epitaph on Craggs' monument in Westminster Abbey.
71. **Ennobled by himself:** Craggs was of relatively humble birth.

AN

ESSAY ON MAN

OR

The First Book of Ethic Epistles

To H. St. John L. Bolingbroke

THE DESIGN

Having proposed to write some pieces on Human Life and Manners, such as (to use my lord Bacon's expression) *come home to Men's Business and Bosoms*, I thought it more satisfactory to begin with considering *Man* in the abstract, his *Nature* and his *State*: since, to prove any moral duty, to enforce any moral precept, or to examine the perfection or imperfection of any creature whatsoever, it is necessary first to know what *condition* and *relation* it is placed in, and what is the proper *end* and *purpose* of its *being*.

The science of Human Nature is, like all other sciences, reduced to a *few clear points*: There are not *many certain truths* in this world. It is therefore in the Anatomy of the Mind as in that of the Body; more good will accrue to mankind by attending to the large, open, and perceptible parts, than by studying too much such finer nerves and vessels, the conformations and uses of which will for ever escape our observation. The *disputes* are all upon these last, and, I will venture to say, they have less sharpened the *wits* than the *hearts* of men

AN ESSAY ON MAN: The four "Epistles" (or parts) of *An Essay on Man* were published successively, and anonymously, in February, March and May of 1733, and in January of 1734. As the full title and the prefatory account of its "Design" indicate, Pope at one time considered the poem to be the first or introductory "book" in a much larger work that would have contained four "books" in all. The second of these books was to consider "Knowledge and its limits"; the third, "Government; both ecclesiastical and civil"; and the fourth, "Morality, in eight or nine of the most concerning branches of it; four of which would have been the two extremes to each of the Cardinal Virtues." Although he may have composed several other poems (the *Epistles to Several Persons,* for example) with this large design vaguely in mind, so grand a scheme must ultimately have seemed impracticable, and in time Pope abandoned it.

120

against each other, and have diminished the practice, more than advanced the theory, of Morality. If I could flatter myself that this Essay has any merit, it is in steering betwixt the extremes of doctrines seemingly opposite, in passing over terms utterly unintelligible, and in forming a *temperate* yet not *inconsistent,* and a *short* yet not *imperfect* system of Ethics.

This I might have done in prose; but I chose verse, and even rhyme, for two reasons. The one will appear obvious; that principles, maxims, or precepts so written, both strike the reader more strongly at first, and are more easily retained by him afterwards: The other may seem odd, but is true, I found I could express them more *shortly* this way than in prose itself; and nothing is more certain, than that much of the *force* as well as *grace* of arguments or instructions, depends on their *conciseness.* I was unable to treat this part of my subject more in detail, without becoming dry and tedious; or more *poetically,* without sacrificing perspicuity to ornament, without wandring from the precision, or breaking the chain of reasoning: If any man can unite all these without diminution of any of them, I freely confess he will compass a thing above my capacity.

What is now published, is only to be considered as a *general Map* of MAN, marking out no more than the *greater parts,* their *extent,* their *limits,* and their *connection,* but leaving the particular to be more fully delineated in the charts which are to follow. Consequently, these Epistles in their progress (if I have health and leisure to make any progress) will be less dry, and more susceptible of poetical ornament. I am here only opening the *fountains,* and clearing the passage. To deduce the *rivers,* to follow them in their course, and to observe their effects, may be a task more agreeable.

ARGUMENT OF THE FIRST EPISTLE

Of the Nature and State of Man, with respect to the UNIVERSE. Of man *in the abstract.* — I. *That we can judge only with regard to* our own system, *being ignorant of the* relations *of systems and things,* VER. 17, &c. II. *That Man is not to be deemed* imperfect, *but a Being suited to his* place *and* rank *in the creation, agreeable to the* general Order *of things, and conformable to* Ends *and* Relations *to him unknown,* VER. 35, &c. III. *That it is partly upon his* ignorance *of future events, and partly upon the* hope *of a* future *state, that all his happiness in the present depends,* VER. 77, &c.   IV. *The* pride *of aiming at more knowledge, and pretending to more* Perfection, *the cause of Man's error and misery. The* impiety *of putting himself in the place of* God, *and judging of the fitness or unfitness, perfection or imperfection, justice or injustice of his dispensations,* VER. 113, &c.   V. *The* absurdity *of conceiting himself the* final cause *of the creation, or expecting that perfection in the* moral world, *which is not in the* natural, VER. 131, &c.   VI. *The* unreasonableness *of his complaints against* Providence, *while on the one hand he demands the Perfections of the Angels, and on the other the bodily qualifications of the Brutes; though, to possess any of the* sensitive faculties *in a higher degree, would render him miserable,* VER. 173, &c.   VII. *That throughout the whole visible world, an universal* order *and* gradation *in the sensual and mental faculties is observed, which causes a* subordination *of creature to creature, and of all creatures to Man. The gradations of* sense, instinct, thought, reflection, reason; *that Reason alone countervails all the other faculties,* VER. 207.   VIII. *How much farther this* order *and* subordination *of living creatures may extend, above and below us; were any part of which broken, not that part only, but the whole connected* creation *must be destroyed.* VER. 233.   IX. *The* extravagance, madness, *and* pride *of such a desire,* VER. 259.   X. *The consequence of all, the* absolute submission *due to Providence, both as to our* present *and* future state, VER. 281, &c. *to the end.*

EPISTLE I

Awake, my ST. JOHN! leave all meaner things
To low ambition, and the pride of Kings.
Let us (since Life can little more supply
Than just to look about us and to die)
Expatiate free o'er all this scene of Man;   5
A mighty maze! but not without a plan;
A Wild, where weeds and flow'rs promiscuous shoot,
Or Garden, tempting with forbidden fruit.
Together let us beat this ample field,
Try what the open, what the covert yield;   10
The latent tracts, the giddy heights explore
Of all who blindly creep, or sightless soar;
Eye Nature's walks, shoot Folly as it flies,
And catch the Manners living as they rise;
Laugh where we must, be candid where we can;   15
But vindicate the ways of God to Man.
    I. Say first, of God above, or Man below,

Epistle I: Of the Nature and State of Man with respect to the Universe. P.
1. St. John: Henry St. John, Viscount Bolingbroke (1678–1751), Secretary of State and, for a brief period, prime minister under Queen Anne. At the accession of George I, he fled to France to avoid prosecution on charges of high treason. Pardoned in 1723, he returned to England, resumed his early friendship with Pope, and devoted himself to political and philosophical writing. Pope also addressed the *First Ep. of the First Bk. of Horace* to Bolingbroke.
5. Expatiate: to speak at length, but also to wander.
10. covert: thicket giving shelter to game.
14. Manners: passions, habits, moral conduct.
15. candid: lenient.
17ff. *He can reason only from* Things known, *and judge only with regard to his own System.* P.

What can we reason, but from what we know?
Of Man what see we, but his station here,
From which to reason, or to which refer?   20
Thro' worlds unnumber'd tho' the God be known,
'Tis ours to trace him only in our own.
He, who thro' vast immensity can pierce,
See worlds on worlds compose one universe,
Observe how system into system runs,   25
What other planets circle other suns,
What vary'd being peoples ev'ry star,
May tell why Heav'n has made us as we are.
But of this frame the bearings, and the ties,
The strong connections, nice dependencies,   30
Gradations just, has thy pervading soul
Look'd thro'? or can a part contain the whole?
    Is the great chain, that draws all to agree,
And drawn supports, upheld by God, or thee?
    II. Presumptuous Man! the reason wouldst thou find,   35
Why form'd so weak, so little, and so blind!
First, if thou canst, the harder reason guess,
Why form'd no weaker, blinder, and no less!
Ask of thy mother earth, why oaks are made
Taller or stronger than the weeds they shade?   40
Or ask of yonder argent fields above,
Why Jove's Satellites are less than Jove?
    Of Systems possible, if 'tis confest
That Wisdom infinite must form the best,
Where all must full or not coherent be,   45
And all that rises, rise in due degree;
Then, in the scale of reas'ning life, 'tis plain
There must be, somewhere, such a rank as Man;
And all the question (wrangle e'er so long)
Is only this, if God has plac'd him wrong?   50
    Respecting Man, whatever wrong we call,
May, must be right, as relative to all.
In human works, tho' labour'd on with pain,
A thousand movements scarce one purpose gain;

25. **system:** solar system.
33. **chain:** the chain of being or scale of creation, in which all things and creatures are arranged in a hierarchical order from nothingness to God. See ll. 207–46, below.
34. **supports:** sustains.
35ff. *He is not therefore a Judge of his own perfection or imperfection, but is certainly such a Being as is suited to his* Place *and* Rank *in the Creation.* P.
42. **Jove's Satellites:** the satellites (here pronounced satéllités) of the planet Jupiter.
45. **full:** containing the maximum number of kinds of beings, all verging, from lowest to highest, upon one another and rising "in due degree" (l. 46) so as to form a "coherent" union (i.e., a chain of being with no gaps).
48. **such a rank:** one that combines a rational with an animal nature.

In God's, one single can its end produce;   55
Yet serves to second too some other use.
So Man, who here seems principal alone,
Perhaps acts second to some sphere unknown,
Touches some wheel, or verges to some goal;
'Tis but a part we see, and not a whole.   60
    When the proud steed shall know why Man restrains
His fiery course, or drives him o'er the plains;
When the dull Ox, why now he breaks the clod,
Is now a victim, and now Ægypt's God:
Then shall Man's pride and dulness comprehend   65
His actions', passions', being's, use and end;
Why doing, suff'ring, check'd, impell'd; and why
This hour a slave, the next a deity.
    Then say not Man's imperfect, Heav'n in fault;
Say rather, Man's as perfect as he ought;   70
His knowledge measur'd to his state and place,
His time a moment, and a point his space.
If to be perfect in a certain sphere,
What matter, soon or late, or here or there?
The blest today is as completely so,   75
As who began a thousand years ago.
    III. Heav'n from all creatures hides the book of Fate,
All but the page prescrib'd, their present state;
From brutes what men, from men what spirits know:
Or who could suffer Being here below?   80
The lamb thy riot dooms to bleed to-day,
Had he thy Reason, would he skip and play?
Pleas'd to the last, he crops the flow'ry food,
And licks the hand just rais'd to shed his blood.
Oh blindness to the future! kindly giv'n,   85
That each may fill the circle mark'd by Heav'n;
Who sees with equal eye, as God of all,
A hero perish, or a sparrow fall,
Atoms or systems into ruin hurl'd,
And now a bubble burst, and now a world.   90
    Hope humbly then; with trembling pinions soar;
Wait the great teacher Death, and God adore!

---

64. **Ægypt's God:** Apis, the sacred bull of Memphis, worshipped by the Egyptians as a god.

73. **in a certain sphere:** in heaven, in an afterlife.

75. **blest:** with the sight of God in heaven.

77*ff. His happiness depends on his* Ignorance *to a certain degree.*   P.

79*ff.* See this pursued in Epist. 3. Vers. 66, &c. 79, &c.   P.

81. **riot:** extravagant mode of life.

87. **equal:** impartial, but also benign.

91*ff. And on his* Hope *of a* Relation *to a future State.*   P.   This note depends on that by Pope at l. 77.

What future bliss, he gives not thee to know,
But gives that Hope to be thy blessing now.
Hope springs eternal in the human breast: 95
Man never Is, but always To be blest:
The soul, uneasy and confin'd from home,
Rests and expatiates in a life to come.

    Lo! the poor Indian, whose untutor'd mind
Sees God in clouds, or hears him in the wind;   100
His soul proud Science never taught to stray
Far as the solar walk, or milky way;
Yet simple Nature to his hope has giv'n,
Behind the cloud-topt hill, an humbler heav'n;
Some safer world in depth of woods embrac'd,   105
Some happier island in the watry waste,
Where slaves once more their native land behold,
No fiends torment, no Christians thirst for gold!
To Be, contents his natural desire,
He asks no Angel's wing, no Seraph's fire;   110
But thinks, admitted to that equal sky,
His faithful dog shall bear him company.

    IV. Go, wiser thou! and in thy scale of sense
Weigh thy Opinion against Providence;
Call Imperfection what thou fancy'st such,   115
Say, here he gives too little, there too much;
Destroy all creatures for thy sport or gust,
Yet cry, If Man's unhappy, God's unjust;
If Man alone ingross not Heav'n's high care,
Alone made perfect here, immortal there: 120
Snatch from his hand the balance and the rod,
Re-judge his justice, be the GOD of GOD!

    In Pride, in reas'ning Pride, our error lies;
All quit their sphere, and rush into the skies.
Pride still is aiming at the blest abodes,   125
Men would be Angels, Angels would be Gods.
Aspiring to be Gods, if Angels fell,
Aspiring to be Angels, Men rebel;
And who but wishes to invert the laws
Of ORDER, sins against th' Eternal Cause.   130

94. Further open'd in Epist. 2. Vers. 283. Epist. 3. Vers. 74. Epist. 4. Vers. 346, &c. P.
98. **expatiates:** roams at will.
110. **Seraph's fire:** see *Eloisa to Abelard,* l. 320*n.*
113*ff. The* Pride *of aiming at more Knowledge and Perfection, and the* Impiety *of pretending to judge of the Dispensations of Providence, the causes of his* Error *and* Misery. P.
116. **he:** God.
117. **gust:** taste.
121. **balance:** scales of justice.
124. **sphere:** place in the chain of being.

V. Ask for what end the heav'nly bodies shine,
Earth for whose use? Pride answers, " 'Tis for mine:
"For me kind Nature wakes her genial pow'r,
"Suckles each herb, and spreads out ev'ry flow'r;
"Annual for me, the grape, the rose renew   135
"The juice nectareous, and the balmy dew;
"For me, the mine a thousand treasures brings;
"For me, health gushes from a thousand springs;
"Seas roll to waft me, suns to light me rise;
"My foot-stool earth, my canopy the skies."   140
   But errs not Nature from this gracious end,
From burning suns when livid deaths descend,
When earthquakes swallow, or when tempests sweep
Towns to one grave, whole nations to the deep?
"No ('tis reply'd) the first Almighty Cause   145
"Acts not by partial, but by gen'ral laws;
"Th' exceptions few; some change since all began,
"And what created perfect?"—Why then Man?
If the great end be human Happiness,
Then Nature deviates; and can Man do less?   150
As much that end a constant course requires
Of show'rs and sun-shine, as of Man's desires;
As much eternal springs and cloudless skies,
As Men for ever temp'rate, calm, and wise.
If plagues or earthquakes break not Heav'n's design   155
Why then a Borgia, or a Catiline?
Who knows but he, whose hand the light'ning forms,
Who heaves old Ocean, and who wings the storms,
Pours fierce Ambition in a Cæsar's mind,
Or turns young Ammon loose to scourge mankind?   160
From pride, from pride, our very reas'ning springs;
Account for moral as for nat'ral things:
Why charge we Heav'n in those, in these acquit?
In both, to reason right is to submit.
   Better for Us, perhaps, it might appear,   165
Were there all harmony, all virtue here;

131ff. The Absurdity *of conceiting himself the* Final Cause *of the Creation,* *or expecting that Perfection in the* moral *world which is not in the* natural. P.

133. genial: generative.

140. canopy: covering of a throne.

142. The plague was thought caused by the sun and midsummer heats, and it left its victims a livid, or bluish, color.

147. change: deteriorations since the Fall.

156. Borgia: a member of the Italian Renaissance family notorious for its cruelty and cunning.   **Catiline:** Lucius Sergius Catiline (108–62 B.C.), the infamous conspirator who plotted with a group of assassins against the Roman republic.

160. Ammon: Alexander the Great (see *Essay on Criticism,* l. 376n.).

166. there: in "nat'ral things" (l. 162).   **here:** in the "moral" (l. 162) life of man.

That never air or ocean felt the wind;
That never passion discompos'd the mind:
But ALL subsists by elemental strife;
And Passions are the elements of Life.   170
The gen'ral ORDER, since the whole began,
Is kept in Nature, and is kept in Man.
    VI. What would this Man? Now upward will he soar,
And little less than Angel, would be more;
Now looking downwards, just as griev'd appears   175
To want the strength of bulls, the fur of bears.
Made for his use all creatures if he call,
Say what their use, had he the pow'rs of all?
Nature to these, without profusion kind,
The proper organs, proper pow'rs assign'd;   180
Each seeming want compensated of course,
Here with degrees of swiftness, there of force;
All in exact proportion to the state;
Nothing to add, and nothing to abate.
Each beast, each insect, happy in its own;   185
Is Heav'n unkind to Man, and Man alone?
Shall he alone, whom rational we call,
Be pleas'd with nothing, if not bless'd with all?
   The bliss of Man (could Pride that blessing find)
Is not to act or think beyond mankind;   190
No pow'rs of body or of soul to share,
But what his nature and his state can bear.
Why has not Man a microscopic eye?
For this plain reason, Man is not a Fly.
Say what the use, were finer optics giv'n,   195
T' inspect a mite, not comprehend the heav'n?
Or touch, if tremblingly alive all o'er,
To smart and agonize at ev'ry pore?
Or quick effluvia darting thro' the brain,
Die of a rose in aromatic pain?   200
If nature thunder'd in his op'ning ears,
And stunn'd him with the music of the spheres,
How would he wish that Heav'n had left him still
The whisp'ring Zephyr, and the purling rill?

170. See this subject extended in Epist. 2 from Vers. 100, to 122, 165, &c. P.
173*ff. The Unreasonableness of the Complaints against Providence, and that
to possess more Faculties would make us miserable.* P.
181. compensated: pronounced compénsated.   of course: naturally.
182. It is a certain Axiom in the Anatomy of Creatures, that in proportion as
they are form'd for Strength, their Swiftness is lessen'd; or as they are form'd
for Swiftness, their Strength is abated. P.
185. Vid. Epist. 3. Vers. 79, &c. and 110, &c. P.
199. effluvia: odors were thought transmitted by streams of invisible particles.
202. music: angels alone were thought able to hear the music of the spheres
(see *Rape of the Lock*, II 75n.).

Who finds not Providence all good and wise,   205
Alike in what it gives, and what denies?
    VII. Far as Creation's ample range extends,
The scale of sensual, mental pow'rs ascends:
Mark how it mounts, to Man's imperial race,
From the green myriads in the peopled grass: 210
What modes of sight betwixt each wide extreme,
The mole's dim curtain, and the lynx's beam:
Of smell, the headlong lioness between,
And hound sagacious on the tainted green:
Of hearing, from the life that fills the flood,   215
To that which warbles thro' the vernal wood:
The spider's touch, how exquisitely fine!
Feels at each thread, and lives along the line:
In the nice bee, what sense so subtly true
From pois'nous herbs extracts the healing dew: 220
How Instinct varies in the grov'ling swine,
Compar'd, half-reas'ning elephant, with thine:
'Twixt that, and Reason, what a nice barrier;
For ever sep'rate, yet for ever near!
Remembrance and Reflection how ally'd;   225
What thin partitions Sense from Thought divide:
And Middle natures, how they long to join,
Yet never pass th' insuperable line!
Without this just gradation, could they be
Subjected these to those, or all to thee?   230
The pow'rs of all subdu'd by thee alone,
Is not thy Reason all these pow'rs in one?
    VIII. See, thro' this air, this ocean, and this earth,
All matter quick, and bursting into birth.
Above, how high progressive life may go!   235
Around, how wide! how deep extend below!
Vast chain of being, which from God began,
Natures æthereal, human, angel, man,

207ff. *There is an universal* Order *and* Gradation *thro' the whole visible world, of the* sensible *and* mental *Faculties, which causes the* Subordination *of Creature to Creature, and of all Creatures to Man, whose* Reason *alone countervails all the other Faculties.* P.
    212. lynx's beam: sight was thought to depend on a ray or beam emitted from the eye, and the lynx was regarded as the creature with the keenest sight.
    213. headlong lioness: lions were thought to have a poor sense of smell.
    214. sagacious: keen-scented.
    219. nice: precise.
    223. that: instinct.   **barrier:** here accented on the last syllable.
    227. Middle natures: intermediary creatures (like frogs and bats) in the great chain of being.
    233ff. *How much farther this* Gradation *and* Subordination *may extend? were any part of which broken, the* whole connected Creation *must be destroy'd.* P.
    234. quick: alive.

Beast, bird, fish, insect! what no eye can see,
No glass can reach! from Infinite to thee, 240
From thee to Nothing!—On superior pow'rs
Were we to press, inferior might on ours:
Or in the full creation leave a void,
Where, one step broken, the great scale's destroy'd:
From Nature's chain whatever link you strike, 245
Tenth or ten thousandth, breaks the chain alike.
    And if each system in gradation roll,
Alike essential to th' amazing whole;
The least confusion but in one, not all
That system only, but the whole must fall. 250
Let Earth unbalanc'd from her orbit fly,
Planets and Suns run lawless thro' the sky,
Let ruling Angels from their spheres be hurl'd,
Being on being wreck'd, and world on world,
Heav'n's whole foundations to their centre nod, 255
And Nature tremble to the throne of God:
All this dread ORDER break — for whom? for thee?
Vile worm! — oh Madness, Pride, Impiety!
    IX. What if the foot, ordain'd the dust to tread,
Or hand to toil, aspir'd to be the head? 260
What if the head, the eye, or ear repin'd
To serve mere engines to the ruling Mind?
Just as absurd for any part to claim
To be another, in this gen'ral frame:
Just as absurd, to mourn the tasks or pains 265
The great directing MIND of ALL ordains.
    All are but parts of one stupendous whole,
Whose body Nature is, and God the soul;
That, chang'd thro' all, and yet in all the same,
Great in the earth, as in th' æthereal frame, 270
Warms in the sun, refreshes in the breeze,
Glows in the stars, and blossoms in the trees,
Lives thro' all life, extends thro' all extent,
Spreads undivided, operates unspent,
Breathes in our soul, informs our mortal part, 275
As full, as perfect, in a hair as heart;
As full, as perfect, in vile Man that mourns,
As the rapt Seraph that adores and burns;

240. **glass:** telescope or microscope.
243. **full:** see l. 45*n.*, above.
247. **system:** planetary system.
253. **ruling Angels:** see *Rape of the Lock*, II 75*n.*
258. *The Extravagance, Impiety, and Pride of such a desire.* P.
262. **engines:** agents, instruments.
265. Vid. the prosecution and application of this in Epist. 4. Ver. 162. **P.**
278. **burns:** with the fires of holy love (see *Eloisa to Abelard*, l. 320*n.*).

To him no high, no low, no great, no small;
He fills, he bounds, connects, and equals all.   280
    X. Cease then, nor ORDER Imperfection name:
Our proper bliss depends on what we blame.
Know thy own point: This kind, this due degree
Of blindness, weakness, Heav'n bestows on thee.
Submit — In this, or any other sphere,   285
Secure to be as blest as thou canst bear:
Safe in the hand of one disposing Pow'r,
Or in the natal, or the mortal hour.
All Nature is but Art, unknown to thee;
All Chance, Direction, which thou canst not see;   290
All Discord, Harmony, not understood;
All partial Evil, universal Good:
And, spite of Pride, in erring Reason's spite,
One truth is clear, "Whatever IS, is RIGHT."

ARGUMENT OF THE SECOND EPISTLE

Of the Nature and State of Man, *with respect to* Himself, *as an Individual.*
I. The *business of Man not to pry into* God, *but to study* himself. *His*
Middle Nature; *his Powers and Frailties,* VER. 1 to 18. *The Limits of his*
Capacity, VER. 19, &c. II. *The two Principles of Man,* Self-love *and*
Reason, *both necessary,* VER. 53, &c. Self-love *the stronger, and why,*
VER. 67, &c. *Their end the same,* VER. 81, &c. III. *The* PASSIONS, *and*
their use, VER. 93 to 130. *The* predominant Passion, *and its force,* VER.
131 to 160. *Its Necessity, in directing Men to different purposes,* VER.
165, &c. *Its providential Use, in fixing our Principle, and ascertaining*
our Virtue, VER. 177. IV. *Virtue and* Vice *joined in our* mixed Nature;
the limits near, yet the things separate and evident; What is the office of
Reason, VER. 203 to 216. V. *How odious* Vice *in itself, and how we de-*
ceive ourselves into it, VER. 217. VI. *That, however, the* Ends *of* Providence *and* general Good *are answered in our Passions and Imperfections,*
VER. 238, &c. *How usefully these are distributed to all* Orders *of Men,*
VER. 242. *How useful they are to* Society, VER. 249. *And to the* Individuals, VER. 261. *In every* state, *and every* age *of life,* VER. 271, &c.

280. **equals all:** makes all equal.
281*ff. The Consequence of all, the* absolute Submission *due to Providence,*
both as to our present *and* future *State.* P.
283. **kind:** natural, appropriate, but also benevolent.
285. **sphere:** here pronounced "sphare."

EPISTLE II

Know then thyself, presume not God to scan;
The proper study of Mankind is Man.
Plac'd on this isthmus of a middle state,
A being darkly wise, and rudely great:
With too much knowledge for the Sceptic side, 5
With too much weakness for the Stoic's pride,
He hangs between; in doubt to act, or rest,
In doubt to deem himself a God, or Beast;
In doubt his Mind or Body to prefer,
Born but to die, and reas'ning but to err; 10
Alike in ignorance, his reason such,
Whether he thinks too little, or too much:
Chaos of Thought and Passion, all confus'd;
Still by himself abus'd, or disabus'd;
Created half to rise, and half to fall; 15
Great lord of all things, yet a prey to all;
Sole judge of Truth, in endless Error hurl'd:
The glory, jest, and riddle of the world!
Go, wond'rous creature! mount where Science guides,
Go, measure earth, weigh air, and state the tides; 20
Instruct the planets in what orbs to run,
Correct old Time, and regulate the Sun;
Go, soar with Plato to th' empyreal sphere,
To the first good, first perfect, and first fair;
Or tread the mazy round his follow'rs trod, 25
And quitting sense call imitating God;
As Eastern priests in giddy circles run,
And turn their heads to imitate the Sun.
Go, teach Eternal Wisdom how to rule —
Then drop into thyself, and be a fool! 30
Superior beings, when of late they saw
A mortal Man unfold all Nature's law,
Admir'd such wisdom in an earthly shape,
And shew'd a Newton as we shew an Ape.
Could he, whose rules the rapid Comet bind, 35

Epistle II. *Of the* Nature *and* State *of Man as an* Individual. P.
1ff. *The business of Man not to pry into God, but to study himself. His* Middle Nature, *his* Powers, Frailties, *and the* Limits *of his* Capacity. P. scant measure.
6. **Stoic's pride:** the Stoic idea that man can free himself from passion was considered prideful.
23. **empyreal sphere:** the highest of the heavens.
26. **quitting sense:** departing not only from common sense, but also from the body (as in a trance or mystical ascent).
35. **he:** Newton.

Describe or fix one movement of his Mind?
Who saw its fires here rise, and there descend,
Explain his own beginning, or his end?
Alas what wonder! Man's superior part
Uncheck'd may rise, and climb from art to art: 40
But when his own great work is but begun,
What Reason weaves, by Passion is undone.
    Trace Science then, with Modesty thy guide;
First strip off all her equipage of Pride,
Deduct what is but Vanity, or Dress,   45
Or Learning's Luxury, or Idleness;
Or tricks to shew the stretch of human brain,
Mere curious pleasure, or ingenious pain:
Expunge the whole, or lop th'excrescent parts
Of all, our Vices have created Arts: 50
Then see how little the remaining sum,
Which serv'd the past, and must the times to come!
    II. Two Principles in human nature reign;
Self-love, to urge, and Reason, to restrain;
Nor this a good, nor that a bad we call,   55
Each works its end, to move or govern all: .
And to their proper operation still,
Ascribe all Good; to their improper, Ill.
    Self-love, the spring of motion, acts the soul;
Reason's comparing balance rules the whole.   60
Man, but for that, no action could attend,
And, but for this, were active to no end;
Fix'd like a plant on his peculiar spot,
To draw nutrition, propagate, and rot;
Or, meteor-like, flame lawless thro' the void,   65
Destroying others, by himself destroy'd.
    Most strength the moving principle requires;
Active its task, it prompts, impels, inspires.
Sedate and quiet the comparing lies,
Form'd but to check, delib'rate, and advise.   70
Self-love still stronger, as its objects nigh;
Reason's at distance, and in prospect lie:
That sees immediate good by present sense;
Reason, the future and the consequence.

44. equipage: cf. *Rape of the Lock*, I 45*n*.

53ff. *The* Two Principles *of* Man, Self-Love *and* Reason, *both necessary*, 59. *Self-Love the* stronger, *and why?*, 67. *their* End *the same*, 81.   P.

54. Self-Love: sustenance and fulfillment of self; natural and proper regard for one's own happiness.

59. acts: activates.

60. comparing balance: *comparing* suggests that *balance* refers to a set of weighing scales, but *spring* in the previous line may imply *mainspring* and thus suggest that the balance is the balance wheel of a watch.

63. peculiar: individual.

Thicker than arguments, temptations throng,   75
At best more watchful this, but that more strong.
The action of the stronger to suspend,
Reason still use, to Reason still attend:
Attention, habit and experience gains,
Each strengthens Reason, and Self-love restrains.   80
   Let subtle schoolmen teach these friends to fight,
More studious to divide than to unite,
And Grace and Virtue, Sense and Reason split,
With all the rash dexterity of Wit:
Wits, just like fools, at war about a Name,   85
Have full as oft no meaning, or the same.
Self-love and Reason to one end aspire,
Pain their aversion, Pleasure their desire;
But greedy that its object would devour,
This taste the honey, and not wound the flow'r: 90
Pleasure, or wrong or rightly understood,
Our greatest evil, or our greatest good.
   III. Modes of Self-love the Passions we may call;
'Tis real good, or seeming, moves them all;
But since not every good we can divide,   95
And Reason bids us for our own provide;
Passions, tho' selfish, if their means be fair,
List under Reason, and deserve her care;
Those, that imparted, court a nobler aim,
Exalt their kind, and take some Virtue's name.   100
   In lazy Apathy let Stoics boast
Their Virtue fix'd; 'tis fix'd as in a frost,
Contracted all, retiring to the breast;
But strength of mind is Exercise, not Rest:
The rising tempest puts in act the soul,   105
Parts it may ravage, but preserves the whole.
On life's vast ocean diversely we sail,
Reason the card, but Passion is the gale;
Nor God alone in the still calm we find,
He mounts the storm, and walks upon the wind.   110
   Passions, like Elements, tho' born to fight,

81. schoolmen: scholastic theologians.
93ff. *The* Passions, *and their Use.*   P.
95. divide: share.
98. List: enlist.
99. Those: the passions.   **that:** reason.
101. Apathy: the passionless state desired by the Stoics (see l. 6n., above).
108. card: a mariner's compass card, perhaps a mariner's chart.
   111. Elements: the four elements of the universe (earth, water, air, and fire) were thought to have their counterparts in the four "humours" of the human constitution (melancholy, phlegm, blood, and choler). The relative proportions of the "humours" in a person determined his temperament and character (see *Rape of the Lock*, I 58n.).

Yet, mix'd and soften'd, in his work unite:
These 'tis enough to temper and employ;
But what composes Man, can Man destroy?
Suffice that Reason keep to Nature's road, 115
Subject, compound them, follow her and God.
Love, Hope, and Joy, fair pleasure's smiling train,
Hate, Fear, and Grief, the family of pain;
These mix'd with art, and to due bounds confin'd,
Make and maintain the balance of the mind: 120
The lights and shades, whose well accorded strife
Gives all the strength and colour of our life.
  Pleasures are ever in our hands or eyes,
And when in act they cease, in prospect rise;
Present to grasp, and future still to find, 125
The whole employ of body and of mind.
All spread their charms, but charm not all alike;
On diff'rent senses diff'rent objects strike;
Hence diff'rent Passions more or less inflame,
As strong or weak, the organs of the frame; 130
And hence one master Passion in the breast,
Like Aaron's serpent, swallows up the rest.
  As Man, perhaps, the moment of his breath,
Receives the lurking principle of death;
The young disease, that must subdue at length, 135
Grows with his growth, and strengthens with his strength:
So, cast and mingled with his very frame,
The Mind's disease, its ruling Passion came;
Each vital humour which should feed the whole,
Soon flows to this, in body and in soul. 140
Whatever warms the heart, or fills the head,
As the mind opens, and its functions spread,
Imagination plies her dang'rous art,
And pours it all upon the peccant part.
  Nature its mother, Habit is its nurse; 145
Wit, Spirit, Faculties, but make it worse;
Reason itself but gives it edge and pow'r;
As Heav'n's blest beam turns vinegar more sowr;
We, wretched subjects tho' to lawful sway,
In this weak queen, some fav'rite still obey. 150

112. **his:** God's.
129–30. Certain passions were associated with particular organs of the body.
132. **Aaron's serpent:** Aaron cast his rod before Pharaoh, and it became a serpent. The magicians of Egypt did likewise, but Aaron's serpent devoured their serpents (see Exodus 7:10–12).
133*ff. The* Predominant Passion, *and its* Force. P.
139. **vital humour:** *humour* here seems to refer to the subtle "spirits" which were thought to permeate the vital organs of the body and to nourish man's powers (see *Essay on Criticism*, l. 77*n.*).
144. **peccant:** morbid, unhealthy.
150. **weak queen:** the reason.

Ah! if she lend not arms, as well as rules,
What can she more than tell us we are fools?
Teach us to mourn our Nature, not to mend,
A sharp accuser, but a helpless friend!
Or from a judge turn pleader, to persuade   155
The choice we make, or justify it made;
Proud of an easy conquest all along,
She but removes weak passions for the strong:
So, when small humors gather to a gout,
The doctor fancies he has driv'n them out.   160
   Yes, Nature's road must ever be prefer'd;
Reason is here no guide, but still a guard:
'Tis hers to rectify, not overthrow,
And treat this passion more as friend than foe:
A mightier Pow'r the strong direction sends,   165
And sev'ral Men impels to sev'ral ends.
Like varying winds, by other passions tost,
This drives them constant to a certain coast.
Let pow'r or knowledge, gold or glory, please,
Or (oft more strong than all) the love of ease;   170
Thro' life 'tis followed, ev'n at life's expence;
The merchant's toil, the sage's indolence,
The monk's humility, the hero's pride,
All, all alike, find Reason on their side.
   Th' Eternal Art educing good from ill,   175
Grafts on this Passion our best principle:
'Tis thus the Mercury of Man is fix'd,
Strong grows the Virtue with his nature mix'd;
The dross cements what else were too refin'd,
And in one interest body acts with mind.   180
   As fruits ungrateful to the planter's care
On savage stocks inserted learn to bear;
The surest Virtues thus from Passions shoot,
Wild Nature's vigor working at the root.
What crops of wit and honesty appear   185
From spleen, from obstinacy, hate, or fear!
See anger, zeal and fortitude supply;
Ev'n av'rice, prudence; sloth, philosophy;
Lust, thro' some certain strainers well refin'd,
Is gentle love, and charms all womankind: 190

---

159. small humors: body fluids.
161–2. The rhyming words were pronounced alike in Pope's time.
165ff. *Its* Necessity, *in directing men to different purposes.* The particular application of this to the *several Pursuits* of Men, and the *General Good* resulting thence, falls into the succeeding books. P.   **mightier Pow'r:** God.
175ff. *Its* providential Use, *in fixing our* Principle, *and ascertaining our* Virtue. P.   **Eternal Art:** Providence.
177. Mercury: elusive, capricious quality.
181. fruits: the "grafts" inserted in the stem or trunk of a wild plant (the "savage stocks" of the next line).   **ungrateful:** unresponsive.

Envy, to which th'ignoble mind's a slave,
Is emulation in the learn'd or brave:
Nor Virtue, male or female, can we name,
But what will grow on Pride, or grow on Shame.

    Thus Nature gives us (let it check our pride)   195
The virtue nearest to our vice ally'd;
Reason the byass turns to good from ill,
And Nero reigns a Titus, if he will.
The fiery soul abhor'd in Catiline,
In Decius charms, in Curtius is divine.   200
The same ambition can destroy or save,
And make a patriot as it makes a knave.

    IV. This light and darkness in our chaos join'd,
What shall divide? The God within the mind.

    Extremes in Nature equal ends produce,   205
In Man they join to some mysterious use;
Tho' each by turns the other's bound invade,
As, in some well-wrought picture, light and shade,
And oft so mix, the diff'rence is too nice
Where ends the Virtue, or begins the Vice.   210

    Fools! who from hence into the notion fall,
That Vice or Virtue there is none at all.
If white and black blend, soften, and unite
A thousand ways, is there no black or white?
Ask your own heart, and nothing is so plain;   215
'Tis to mistake them, costs the time and pain.

    V. Vice is a monster of so frightful mien,
As, to be hated, needs but to be seen;
Yet seen too oft, familiar with her face,
We first endure, then pity, then embrace.   220
But where th'Extreme of Vice, was ne'er agreed:
Ask where's the North? at York, 'tis on the Tweed;
In Scotland, at the Orcades; and there,
At Greenland, Zembla, or the Lord knows where:
No creature owns it in the first degree,   225
But thinks his neighbour farther gone than he.
Ev'n those who dwell beneath its very zone,
Or never feel the rage, or never own;

195ff. Virtue *and* Vice *join'd in our* Mixt Nature; *the Limits* near, *yet the things* separate, *and* evident. *The Office of* Reason. P.
    198. Titus: Roman emperor (79–81 A.D.) who did all he could to alleviate the distress of his people.
    199. Catiline: see Epist. I 156n., above.
    200. Decius: a Roman consul (d. 337 B.C.) who sacrificed himself for his country on the battlefield.   **Curtius:** a Roman youth celebrated for his patriotism.
    209. nice: subtle.
    217ff. Vice *odious in itself, and how we* deceive *ourselves into it.* P.
    222. Tweed: river in the south of Scotland.
    223. Orcades: the Orkney Islands, off the north coast of Scotland.
    224. Zembla: Novaya Zemlya, an arctic land off the coast of Russia.

What happier natures shrink at with affright,
The hard inhabitant contends is right.   230
    VI. Virtuous and vicious ev'ry Man must be,
Few in th'extreme, but all in the degree;
The rogue and fool by fits is fair and wise,
And ev'n the best, by fits, what they despise.
'Tis but by parts we follow good or ill,   235
For, Vice or Virtue, Self directs it still;
Each individual seeks a sev'ral goal;
But HEAV'N's great view is One, and that the Whole:
That counter-works each folly and caprice;
That disappoints th'effect of ev'ry vice: 240
That happy frailties to all ranks apply'd,
Shame to the virgin, to the matron pride,
Fear to the statesman, rashness to the chief,
To kings presumption, and to crowds belief,
That Virtue's ends from Vanity can raise,   245
Which seeks no int'rest, no reward but praise;
And build on wants, and on defects of mind,
The joy, the peace, the glory of Mankind.
    Heav'n forming each on other to depend,
A master, or a servant, or a friend,   250
Bids each on other for assistance call,
'Till one Man's weakness grows the strength of all.
Wants, frailties, passions, closer still ally
The common int'rest, or endear the tie:
To these we owe true friendship, love sincere,   255
Each home-felt joy that life inherits here:
Yet from the same we learn, in its decline,
Those joys, those loves, those int'rests to resign:
Taught half by Reason, half by mere decay,
To welcome death, and calmly pass away.   260
    Whate'er the Passion, knowledge, fame, or pelf,
Not one will change his neighbor with himself.
The learn'd is happy nature to explore,
The fool is happy that he knows no more;
The rich is happy in the plenty giv'n,   265
The poor contents him with the care of Heav'n.
See the blind beggar dance, the cripple sing,
The sot a hero, lunatic a king;
The starving chemist in his golden views
Supremely blest, the poet in his muse.   270
    See some strange comfort ev'ry state attend,

231ff. *The* Ends *of* Providence *and* General Good *answer'd in our* Passions *and* Imperfections. *How usefully these are distributed to all* Orders of men. **P.**
237. sev'ral: respective, private.
249ff. *How useful these are to* Society *in general, and to* Individuals *in particular, in every* State, 261, *and ev'ry* Age *of Life*, 271. **P.**
261. pelf: riches.
269. chemist: an alchemist (one who attempts to turn base metals into gold).

138 • *An Essay on Man*

And Pride bestow'd on all, a common friend;
See some fit Passion ev'ry age supply,
Hope travels thro', nor quits us when we die.
Behold the child, by Nature's kindly law,   275
Pleas'd with a rattle, tickled with a straw:
Some livelier play-thing gives his youth delight,
A little louder, but as empty quite:
Scarfs, garters, gold, amuse his riper stage;
And beads and pray'r-books are the toys of age: 280
Pleas'd with this bauble still, as that before;
'Till tir'd he sleeps, and Life's poor play is o'er!
Mean-while Opinion gilds with varying rays
Those painted clouds that beautify our days;
Each want of happiness by Hope supply'd,   285
And each vacuity of sense by Pride:
These build as fast as knowledge can destroy;
In Folly's cup still laughs the bubble, joy;
One prospect lost, another still we gain;
And not a vanity is giv'n in vain;   290
Ev'n mean Self-love becomes, by force divine,
The scale to measure others wants by thine.
See! and confess, one comfort still must rise,
'Tis this, Tho' Man's a fool, yet GOD IS WISE.

ARGUMENT OF THE THIRD EPISTLE

Of the Nature and State of Man, *with respect to* Society. I. THE *whole Universe one system of Society,* VER. 7, &c. *Nothing made wholly for itself, nor yet wholly for* another, VER. 27. *The happiness of* Animals mutual, VER. 49. II. Reason *or* Instinct *operate alike to the good of each Individual,* VER. 79. Reason *or* Instinct *operate also to Society, in all animals,* VER. 109. III. *How far* Society *carried by Instinct,* VER. 115. *How much farther by Reason,* VER. 131. IV. *Of that which is called the* State of Nature, VER. 147. *Reason instructed by Instinct in the invention of* Arts, VER. 171, *and in the Forms of* Society, VER. 179. V. *Origin of Political Societies,* VER. 199. *Origin of Monarchy,* VER. 209. *Patriarchal government,* VER. 215. VI. *Origin of true Religion and Government, from the same principle, of Love,* VER. 231, &c. *Origin of Superstition and Tyranny, from the same principle, of Fear,* VER. 241, &c. *The Influence*

279. **Scarfs:** the sashes of doctors of divinity.   **garter:** badge of knights of the Garter.
280. **beads:** rosaries.
291–2. See farther of the Use of this *Principle* in Man. Epist. 3. Ver. 121, 124, 134, 144, 199, &c. And Epist. 4. Ver. 358, and 368. P.

EPISTLE III

HERE then we rest: "The Universal Cause
        "Acts to one end, but acts by various laws."
        In all the madness of superfluous health,
The trim of pride, the impudence of wealth,
Let this great truth be present night and day;   5
But most be present, if we preach or pray.
      Look round our World; behold the chain of Love
Combining all below and all above.
See plastic Nature working to this end,
The single atoms each to other tend,   10
Attract, attracted to, the next in place
Form'd and impell'd its neighbour to embrace.
See Matter next, with various life endu'd,
Press to one centre still, the gen'ral Good.
See dying vegetables life sustain,   15
See life dissolving vegetate again:
All forms that perish other forms supply,
(By turns we catch the vital breath, and die)
Like bubbles on the sea of Matter born,
They rise, they break, and to that sea return.   20
Nothing is foreign: Parts relate to whole;
One all-extending, all-preserving Soul
Connects each being, greatest with the least;
Made Beast in aid of Man, and Man of Beast;
All serv'd, all serving! nothing stands alone;   25
The chain holds on, and where it ends, unknown.
      Has God, thou fool! work'd solely for thy good,
Thy joy, thy pastime, thy attire, thy food?
Who for thy table feeds the wanton fawn,
For him as kindly spread the flow'ry lawn.   30
Is it for thee the lark ascends and sings?
Joy tunes his voice, joy elevates his wings:

Epistle III. Of the Nature and State of Man with respect to Society.   P.
1ff. The whole Universe one System of Society.   P.
    7. chain of Love: the various links or orders in the chain of being were viewed as held together by love for one another.
    9. plastic: the formative power accorded to nature by God for his own purposes.
    27ff. Nothing made wholly for *Itself,* nor yet wholly for *another,* but the Happiness of all animals *mutual.*   P.

Is it for thee the linnet pours his throat?
Loves of his own and raptures swell the note:
The bounding steed you pompously bestride,   35
Shares with his lord the pleasure and the pride:
Is thine alone the seed that strews the plain?
The birds of heav'n shall vindicate their grain:
Thine the full harvest of the golden year?
Part pays, and justly, the deserving steer: 40
The hog, that plows not nor obeys thy call,
Lives on the labours of this lord of all.
    Know, Nature's children all divide her care;
The fur that warms a monarch, warm'd a bear.
While Man exclaims, "See all things for my use!"   45
"See man for mine!" replies a pamper'd goose;
And just as short of Reason he must fall,
Who thinks all made for one, not one for all.
    Grant that the pow'rful still the weak controul,
Be Man the Wit and Tyrant of the whole: 50
Nature that Tyrant checks; he only knows,
And helps, another creature's wants and woes.
Say, will the falcon, stooping from above,
Smit with her varying plumage, spare the dove?
Admires the jay the insect's gilded wings?   55
Or hears the hawk when Philomela sings?
Man cares for all: to birds he gives his woods,
To beasts his pastures, and to fish his floods;
For some his Int'rest prompts him to provide,
For more his pleasure, yet for more his pride: 60
All feed on one vain Patron, and enjoy
Th'extensive blessing of his luxury.
That very life his learned hunger craves,
He saves from famine, from the savage saves;
Nay, feasts the animal he dooms his feast,   65
And, 'till he ends the being, makes it blest;
Which sees no more the stroke, or feels the pain,
Than favour'd Man by touch etherial slain.
The creature had his feast of life before;
Thou too must perish, when thy feast is o'er!   70
    To each unthinking being, Heav'n a friend,
Gives not the useless knowledge of its end:

38. **vindicate:** claim.
50. **Wit:** sole rational animal.
53. **stooping:** swooping
56. **Philomela:** the nightingale.
61. **enjoy:** pronounced to rhyme with *die*.
64. **savage:** wild animal.
68. Several of the Ancients, and many of the Orientals since, esteem'd those who were struck by Lightning as sacred Persons, and the particular Favourites of Heaven. P.

To Man imparts it; but with such a view
As, while he dreads it, makes him hope it too:
The hour conceal'd, and so remote the fear,   75
Death still draws nearer, never seeming near.
Great standing miracle! that Heav'n assign'd
Its only thinking thing this turn of mind.
    II. Whether with Reason, or with Instinct blest,
Know, all enjoy that pow'r which suits them best;   80
To bliss alike by that direction tend,
And find the means proportion'd to their end.
    Say, where full Instinct is th'unerring guide,
What Pope or Council can they need beside?
Reason, however able, cool at best,   85
Cares not for service, or but serves when prest,
Stays 'till we call, and then not often near;
But honest Instinct comes a volunteer;
Sure never to o'er-shoot, but just to hit,
While still too wide or short is human Wit;   90
Sure by quick Nature happiness to gain,
Which heavier Reason labours at in vain.
This too serves always, Reason never long;
One must go right, the other may go wrong.
See then the acting and comparing pow'rs   95
One in their nature, which are two in ours,
And Reason raise o'er Instinct as you can,
In this 'tis God directs, in that 'tis Man.
    Who taught the nations of the field and wood
To shun their poison, and to chuse their food?   100
Prescient, the tides or tempests to withstand,
Build on the wave, or arch beneath the sand?
Who made the spider parallels design,
Sure as De-moivre, without rule or line?
Who bid the stork, Columbus-like, explore   105
Heav'ns not his own, and worlds unknown before?
Who calls the council, states the certain day,
Who forms the phalanx, and who points the way?
    III. God, in the nature of each being, founds
Its proper bliss, and sets its proper bounds: 110

79ff. *Reason* or *Instinct* alike operate for the good of each *Individual,* and operate also to Society, in *all Animals.*   P.
    84. Council: ecclesiastical assembly convened to consider matters of doctrine, discipline, and morals.
    86. prest: impressed (forced enlistment).
    95. acting and comparing pow'rs: cf. Epist. II 59–60, above.
    101. prescient: foresighted.
    102. The mythical halcyon was supposed to build its nest "on the wave"; the kingfisher (usually identified with the halcyon) builds its nest in tunnels in a bank ("beneath the sand").
    104. [Abraham] Demoivre [1667–1754], *an eminent Mathematician.*   P.

142 • *An Essay on Man*

But as he fram'd a Whole, the Whole to bless,
On mutual Wants built mutual Happiness:
So from the first eternal Order ran,
And creature link'd to creature, man to man.
Whate'er of life all-quick'ning æther keeps,   115
Or breathes thro' air, or shoòts beneath the deeps,
Or pours profuse on earth; one nature feeds
The vital flame, and swells the genial seeds.
Not Man alone, but all that roam the wood,
Or wing the sky, or roll along the flood,   120
Each loves itself, but not itself alone,
Each sex desires alike, 'till two are one.
Nor ends the pleasure with the fierce embrace;
They love themselves, a third time, in their race.
Thus beast and bird their common charge attend,   125
The mothers nurse it, and the sires defend;
The young dismiss'd to wander earth or air,
There stops the Instinct, and there ends the care;
The link dissolves, each seeks a fresh embrace,
Another love succeeds, another race.   130
A longer care Man's helpless kind demands;
That longer care contracts more lasting bands:
Reflection, Reason, still the ties improve,
At once extend the int'rest, and the love;
With choice we fix, with sympathy we burn;   135
Each Virtue in each Passion takes its turn;
And still new needs, new helps, new habits rise,
That graft benevolence on charities.
Still as one brood, and as another rose,
These nat'ral love maintain'd, habitual those: 140
The last, scarce ripen'd into perfect Man,
Saw helpless him from whom their life began:
Mem'ry and fore-cast just returns engage,
That pointed back to youth, this on to age;
While pleasure, gratitude, and hope, combin'd,   145
Still spread the int'rest, and preserv'd the kind.
    IV. Nor think, in Nature's State they blindly trod;
The state of Nature was the reign of God:
Self-love and Social at her birth began,
Union the bond of all things, and of Man.   150
Pride then was not; nor Arts, that Pride to aid;
Man walk'd with beast, joint tenant of the shade;

115*ff.* How far Society carry'd by Instinct. P.
115. æther· thought to be a fiery, generative element permeating the universe.
118. genial: generative.
131*ff.* How much farther Society is carry'd by Reason. P.
136. Cf. Epist. II 183–4, above.
146. kind: progeny, family.
147*ff.* Of the State of Nature: That it was Social. P.

The same his table, and the same his bed;
No murder cloath'd him, and no murder fed.
In the same temple, the resounding wood,   155
All vocal beings hymn'd their equal God:
The shrine with gore unstain'd, with gold undrest,
Unbrib'd, unbloody, stood the blameless priest:
Heav'n's attribute was Universal Care,
And Man's prerogative to rule, but spare.   160
Ah! how unlike the man of times to come!
Of half that live the butcher and the tomb;
Who, foe to Nature, hears the gen'ral groan,
Murders their species, and betrays his own.
But just disease to luxury succeeds,   165
And ev'ry death its own avenger breeds;
The Fury-passions from that blood began,
And turn'd on Man a fiercer savage, Man.
    See him from Nature rising slow to Art!
To copy Instinct then was Reason's part;   170
Thus then to Man the voice of Nature spake —
"Go, from the Creatures thy instructions take:
"Learn from the birds what food the thickets yield;
"Learn from the beasts the physic of the field;
"Thy arts of building from the bee receive;   175
"Learn of the mole to plow, the worm to weave;
"Learn of the little Nautilus to sail,
"Spread the thin oar, and catch the driving gale.
"Here too all forms of social union find,
"And hence let Reason, late, instruct Mankind: 180
"Here subterranean works and cities see;
"There towns aerial on the waving tree.
"Learn each small People's genius, policies,
"The Ant's republic, and the realm of Bees;
"How those in common all their wealth bestow,   185
"And Anarchy without confusion know;
"And these for ever, tho' a Monarch reign,
"Their sep'rate cells and properties maintain.
"Mark what unvary'd laws preserve each state,

168. savage: cf. l. 64*n.*, above.
169*ff. Reason* instructed by *Instinct* in the Invention of Arts, and in the Forms of *Society*. **P.**
177–8. Oppian, Halieut. Lib. I. describes this Fish in the following manner. "They swim on the surface of the Sea, on the back of their Shells, which exactly resemble the Hulk of a Ship; they raise two Feet like Masts, and extend a Membrane between which serves as a Sail; the other two Feet they employ as Oars at the side." They are usually seen in the Mediterranean. **P.**
181. works: ant-hills.
182. towns: bee-hives.
184. republic: ants were traditionally thought to live in democratic, even socialistic, societies (cf. ll. 185–6). **realm:** the proper word for a monarchal form of government (cf. l. 187).

"Laws wise as Nature, and as fix'd as Fate.   190
"In vain thy Reason finer webs shall draw,
"Entangle Justice in her net of Law,
"And right, too rigid, harden into wrong;
"Still for the strong too weak, the weak too strong.
"Yet go! and thus o'er all the creatures sway,   195
"Thus let the wiser make the rest obey,
"And for those Arts mere Instinct could afford,
"Be crown'd as Monarchs, or as Gods ador'd."
    V. Great Nature spoke; observant Men obey'd;
Cities were built, Societies were made: 200
Here rose one little state; another near
Grew by like means, and join'd, thro' love or fear.
Did here the trees with ruddier burdens bend,
And there the streams in purer rills descend?
What War could ravish, Commerce could bestow,   205
And he return'd a friend, who came a foe.
Converse and Love mankind might strongly draw,
When Love was Liberty, and Nature Law.
Thus States were form'd; the name of King unknown,
'Till common int'rest plac'd the sway in one.   210
'Twas VIRTUE ONLY (or in arts or arms,
Diffusing blessings, or averting harms)
The same which in a Sire the Sons obey'd,
A Prince the Father of a People made.
    VI. 'Till then, by Nature crown'd, each Patriarch sate,
King, priest, and parent of his growing state;   216
On him, their second Providence, they hung,
Their law his eye, their oracle his tongue.
He from the wond'ring furrow call'd the food,
Taught to command the fire, controul the flood,   220
Draw forth the monsters of th'abyss profound,
Or fetch th'aerial eagle to the ground.
'Till drooping, sick'ning, dying, they began
Whom they rever'd as God to mourn as Man:
Then, looking up from sire to sire, explor'd   225
One great first father, and that first ador'd.
Or plain tradition that this All begun,
Convey'd unbroken faith from sire to son,
The worker from the work distinct was known,
And simple Reason never sought but one: 230
Ere Wit oblique had broke that steddy light,
Man, like his Maker, saw that all was right,

199*ff*. Origine of Political Societies. P.
210*ff*. Origine of Monarchy. P.
215*ff*. [Origin] of Patriarchial Government. P.
219. wond'ring: i.e., causing wonder.
231. light: i.e., of reason.
232. like his Maker: see Genesis 1:31.

To Virtue, in the paths of Pleasure, trod,
And own'd a Father when he own'd a God.
Love all the faith, and all th'allegiance then; 235
For Nature knew no right divine in Men,
No ill could fear in God; and understood
A sov'reign being but a sov'reign good.
True faith, true policy, united ran,
That was but love of God, and this of Man. 240
Who first taught souls enslav'd, and realms undone,
Th' enormous faith of many made for one;
That proud exception to all Nature's laws,
T'invert the world, and counter-work its Cause?
Force first made Conquest, and that conquest, Law; 245
'Till Superstition taught the tyrant awe,
Then shar'd the Tyranny, then lent it aid,
And Gods of Conqu'rors, Slaves of Subjects made:
She, 'midst the light'ning's blaze, and thunder's sound,
When rock'd the mountains, and when groan'd the ground,
She taught the weak to bend, the proud to pray, 251
To Pow'r unseen, and mightier far than they:
She, from the rending earth and bursting skies,
Saw Gods descend, and fiends infernal rise:
Here fix'd the dreadful, there the blest abodes; 255
Fear made her Devils, and weak Hope her Gods;
Gods partial, changeful, passionate, unjust,
Whose attributes were Rage, Revenge, or Lust;
Such as the souls of cowards might conceive,
And, form'd like tyrants, tyrants would believe. 260
Zeal then, not charity, became the guide,
And hell was built on spite, and heav'n on pride.
Then sacred seem'd th'etherial vault no more;
Altars grew marble then, and reek'd with gore:
Then first the Flamen tasted living food; 265
Next his grim idol smear'd with human blood;
With Heav'n's own thunders shook the world below,
And play'd the God an engine on his foe.
  So drives Self-love, thro' just and thro' unjust,
To one Man's pow'r, ambition, lucre, lust: 270
The same Self-love, in all, becomes the cause
Of what restrains him, Government and Laws.
For, what one likes if others like as well,
What serves one will, when many wills rebel?
How shall he keep, what, sleeping or awake, 275

235ff. Origine of True Religion and Government from the Principle of Love: and of Superstition and Tyranny, from that of Fear. P.
242. enormous: monstrous.
246. awe: i.e., the power to inspire awe.
265. Flamen: priest.
268. engine: instrument (of revenge).
269ff. The Influence of Self-Love operating to the Social and *Public Good.* P

A weaker may surprise, a stronger take?
His safety must his liberty restrain:
All join to guard what each desires to gain.
Forc'd into virtue thus by Self-defence,
Ev'n Kings learn'd justice and benevolence: 280
Self-love forsook the path it first pursu'd,
And found the private in the public good.
 'Twas then, the studious head or gen'rous mind,
Follow'r of God or friend of human-kind,
Poet or Patriot, rose but to restore   285
The Faith and Moral, Nature gave before;
Re-lum'd her ancient light, not kindled new;
If not God's image, yet his shadow drew:
Taught Pow'r's due use to People and to Kings,
Taught nor to slack, nor strain its tender strings,   290
The less, or greater, set so justly true,
That touching one must strike the other too;
'Till jarring int'rests of themselves create
Th'according music of a well-mix'd State.
Such is the World's great harmony, that springs   295
From Order, Union, full Consent of things!
Where small and great, where weak and mighty, made
To serve, not suffer, strengthen, not invade,
More pow'rful each as needful to the rest,
And, in proportion as it blesses, blest,   300
Draw to one point, and to one centre bring
Beast, Man, or Angel, Servant, Lord, or King.
 For Forms of Government let fools contest;
Whate'er is best administer'd is best:
For Modes of Faith, let graceless zealots fight;   305
His can't be wrong whose life is in the right:
In Faith and Hope the world will disagree,
But all Mankind's concern is Charity:
All must be false that thwart this One great End,
And all of God, that bless Mankind or mend.   310
 Man, like the gen'rous vine, supported lives;
The strength he gains is from th'embrace he gives.
On their own Axis as the Planets run,
Yet make at once their circle round the Sun:
So two consistent motions act the Soul;   315
And one regards Itself, and one the Whole.
 Thus God and Nature link'd the gen'ral frame,
And bade Self-love and Social be the same.

283ff. Restoration of *True Religion* and *Government* on their first Principle.
Mixt Governments; with the various Forms of each, and the True Use of All. P.
 236. Moral: morals.
 290. strings: of a musical instrument.
 292. strike: cause to sound.
 311. gen'rous: full of spirit, fertile.
 315. act: actuate.

ARGUMENT OF THE FOURTH EPISTLE

Of the Nature and State of Man, *with respect to* Happiness. I. FALSE *Notions of Happiness, Philosophical and Popular, answered from* Ver. 19 to 76. II. *It is the End of all Men, and attainable by all,* Ver. 29. *God intends Happiness to be* equal; *and to be so, it must be* social, *since all particular Happiness depends on general, and since he governs by* general, *not* particular *Laws,* Ver. 35. *As it is necessary for* Order, *and the peace and welfare of* Society, *that* external goods *should be* unequal, *Happiness is not made to consist in these,* Ver. 49. *But, notwithstanding that inequality, the* balance *of Happiness among Mankind is kept even by* Providence, *by the two Passions of* Hope *and* Fear, Ver. 67. III. *What the Happiness of* Individuals *is, as far as is consistent with the constitution of this world; and that the* good *Man has here the advantage,* Ver. 77. *The error of imputing to* Virtue *what are only the calamities of* Nature, *or of* Fortune, Ver. 93. IV. *The folly of expecting that God should alter his general Laws in favour of particulars,* Ver. 111. V. *That we are not judges who are good; but that whoever they are, they must be happiest,* Ver. 131, &c. VI. *That* external goods *are not the proper rewards, but often inconsistent with, or destructive of Virtue,* Ver. 167. *That even these can make no Man happy without Virtue: Instanced in* Riches, Ver. 185. Honours, Ver. 193. Nobility, Ver. 205. Greatness, Ver. 217. Fame, Ver. 237. Superior Talents, Ver. 259. *With pictures of human Infelicity in Men possest of them all,* Ver. 269 &c. VII. *That* Virtue only *constitutes a Happiness, whose object is* universal, *and whose prospect* eternal, Ver. 309, &c. *That the* perfection *of Virtue and Happiness consists in a* conformity *to the* Order *of* Providence *here, and a* Resignation *to it here and hereafter,* Ver. 325, &c.

EPISTLE IV

Oʜ Happiness! our being's end and aim!
    Good, Pleasure, Ease, Content! whate'er thy name:
    That something still which prompts th'eternal sigh,
For which we bear to live, or dare to die,
Which still so near us, yet beyond us lies,   5
O'er-look'd, seen double, by the fool, and wise.
Plant of celestial seed! if dropt below,
Say, in what mortal soil thou deign'st to grow?
Fair op'ning to some Court's propitious shine,
Or deep with di'monds in the flaming mine?   10

Epistle IV. Of the Nature and State of Man, with respect to Happiness.   P.
   10. Minerals were thought to grow, plant-like, in the earth, and to be ripened by the sun's rays.

Twin'd with the wreaths Parnassian lawrels yield,
Or reap'd in iron harvests of the field?
Where grows? — where grows it not? — If vain our toil,
We ought to blame the culture, not the soil:
Fix'd to no spot is Happiness sincere,   15
'Tis no where to be found, or ev'ry where;
'Tis never to be bought, but always free,
And fled from Monarchs, St. John! dwells with thee.

    Ask of the Learn'd the way, the Learn'd are blind,
This bids to serve, and that to shun mankind;   20
Some place the bliss in action, some in ease,
Those call it Pleasure, and Contentment these;
Some sunk to Beasts, find pleasure end in pain;
Some swell'd to Gods, confess ev'n Virtue vain;
Or indolent, to each extreme they fall,   25
To trust in ev'ry thing, or doubt of all.
    Who thus define it, say they more or less
Than this, that Happiness is Happiness?

    II. Take Nature's path, and mad Opinion's leave,
All states can reach it, and all heads conceive;   30
Obvious her goods, in no extreme they dwell,
There needs but thinking right, and meaning well;
And mourn our various portions as we please,
Equal is Common Sense, and Common Ease.

    Remember, Man, "the Universal Cause   35
"Acts not by partial, but by gen'ral laws;"
And makes what Happiness we justly call
Subsist not in the good of one, but all.
There's not a blessing Individuals find,
But some way leans and hearkens to the kind.   40
No Bandit fierce, no Tyrant mad with pride,
No cavern'd Hermit, rests self-satisfy'd.
Who most to shun or hate Mankind pretend,
Seek an admirer, or would fix a friend.
Abstract what others feel, what others think,   45
All pleasures sicken, and all glories sink;
Each has his share; and who would more obtain,
Shall find, the pleasure pays not half the pain.

    Order is Heav'n's first law; and this confest,
Some are, and must be, greater than the rest,   50
More rich, more wise; but who infers from hence
That such are happier, shocks all common sense.

12. field: battlefield.
15. sincere: pure, genuine.
29*ff*. Happiness the End of all Men, and attainable by all. P.
35*ff*. God governs by *general* not *particular* Laws: intends Happiness to be
equal, and to be so, it must be *social*, since all particular Happiness *depends on
general*. P.
  49*ff*. It is necessary for Order and the common Peace, that *External Goods
be unequal*, therefore Happiness is not constituted in these. P.

Heav'n to Mankind impartial we confess,
If all are equal in their Happiness:
But mutual wants this Happiness increase,   55
All Nature's diff'rence keeps all Nature's peace.
Condition, circumstance is not the thing;
Bliss is the same in subject or in king,
In who obtain defence, or who defend,
In him who is, or him who finds a friend: 60
Heav'n breaths thro' ev'ry member of the whole
One common blessing, as one common soul.
But Fortune's gifts if each alike possest,
And each were equal, must not all contest?
If then to all Men Happiness was meant,   65
God in Externals could not place Content.

    Fortune her gifts may variously dispose,
And these be happy call'd, unhappy those;
But Heav'n's just balance equal will appear,
While those are plac'd in Hope, and these in Fear: 70
Not present good or ill, the joy or curse,
But future views of better, or of worse.

    Oh sons of earth! attempt ye still to rise,
By mountains pil'd on mountains, to the skies?
Heav'n still with laughter the vain toil surveys,   75
And buries madmen in the heaps they raise.

    III. Know, all the good that individuals find,
Or God and Nature meant to mere Mankind;
Reason's whole pleasure, all the joys of Sense,
Lie in three words, Health, Peace, and Competence.   80
But Health consists with Temperance alone,
And Peace, oh Virtue! Peace is all thy own.
The good or bad the gifts of Fortune gain,
But these less taste them, as they worse obtain.
Say, in pursuit of profit or delight,   85
Who risk the most, that take wrong means, or right?
Of Vice or Virtue, whether blest or curst,
Which meets contempt, or which compassion first?
Count all th'advantage prosp'rous Vice attains,
'Tis but what Virtue flies from and disdains: 90
And grant the bad what happiness they wou'd,
One they must want, which is, to pass for good.

    Oh blind to truth, and God's whole scheme below,
Who fancy Bliss to Vice, to Virtue Woe!

67ff. The balance of Human happiness kept equal (notwithstanding *Externals*)
by Hope and Fear. P.

73–6. The lines recall the myth of the Titans, who were buried under the
mountains they had heaped up in an attempt to invade the heavens of Zeus.

77ff. In what the Happiness of *Individuals* consists, and that the Good Man
has the advantage, even in this world. P.

80. Competence: sufficient means.

93ff. That no man is unhappy thro' Virtue. P.

Who sees and follows that great scheme the best,   95
Best knows the blessing, and will most be blest.
But fools the Good alone unhappy call,
For ills or accidents that chance to all.
See FALKLAND dies, the virtuous and the just!
See god-like TURENNE prostrate on the dust!   100
See SIDNEY bleeds amid the martial strife!
Was this their Virtue, or Contempt of Life?
Say, was it Virtue, more tho' Heav'n ne'er gave,
Lamented DIGBY! sunk thee to the grave?
Tell me, if Virtue made the Son expire,   105
Why, full of days and honour, lives the Sire?
Why drew Marseille's good bishop purer breath,
When Nature sicken'd, and each gale was death?
Or why so long (in life if long can be)
Lent Heav'n a parent to the poor and me?   110
    IV. What makes all physical or moral ill?
There deviates Nature, and here wanders Will.
God sends not ill; if rightly understood,
Or partial Ill is universal Good,
Or Change admits, or Nature lets it fall,   115
Short and but rare, 'till Man improv'd it all.
We just as wisely might of Heav'n complain,
That righteous Abel was destroy'd by Cain;
As that the virtuous son is ill at ease,
When his lewd father gave the dire disease.   120
Think we, like some weak Prince, th'Eternal Cause,
Prone for his fav'rites to reverse his laws?
    Shall burning Ætna, if a sage requires,
Forget to thunder, and recall her fires?
On air or sea new motions be imprest,   125
Oh blameless Bethel! to relieve thy breast?

99. Falkland: Lucius Cary, Viscount Falkland (1610–43), killed at Newbury in the civil wars.
100. Turenne: Henri de la Tour d'Auvergne, Vicomte de Turenne (1611–75), marshal-general of France, killed while reconnoitering at Sasbach, Germany.
101. Sidney: Sir Philip Sidney, killed at Zutphen in 1586.
103–6. Pope's friend, Robert Digby, died at the age of 40; his father, William, fifth Lord Digby, was 74 when these lines were published. See also *Epil. to the Satires*, II 241.
107. bishop: Belsunce de Castel-Moron (1671–1755), Bishop of Marseilles, devoted himself to the relief of the people of that city during the plague of 1720.
110. parent: Pope's mother had recently died, aged 91.
120. dire disease: syphilis.
123. sage: the Greek philosopher Empedocles (500–430 B.C.), reported by some to have fallen into the crater of Aetna, by others as killed during an eruption.
126. Bethel: Hugh Bethel (d. 1748), one of Pope's oldest and dearest friends, suffered from asthma (see also the first note to the *Second Sat. of the Second Bk.*).

When the loose mountain trembles from on high,
Shall gravitation cease, if you go by?
Or some old temple, nodding to its fall,
For Chartres' head reserve the hanging wall?   130
    V. But still this world (so fitted for the knave)
Contents us not. A better shall we have?
A kingdom of the Just then let it be:
But first consider how those Just agree.
The good must merit God's peculiar care;   135
But who, but God, can tell us who they are?
One thinks on Calvin Heav'n's own spirit fell,
Another deems him instrument of hell;
If Calvin feel Heav'n's blessing, or its rod,
This cries there is, and that, there is no God.   140
What shocks one part will edify the rest,
Nor with one system can they all be blest.
The very best will variously incline,
And what rewards your Virtue, punish mine.
"Whatever IS, is RIGHT." — This world, 'tis true,   145
Was made for Caesar — but for Titus too:
And which more blest? who chain'd his country, say,
Or he whose Virtue sigh'd to lose a day?
    "But sometimes Virtue starves, while Vice is fed."
What then? Is the reward of Virtue bread?   150
That, Vice may merit; 'tis the price of toil;
The knave deserves it, when he tills the soil,
The knave deserves it when he tempts the main,
Where Folly fights for kings, or dives for gain.
The good man may be weak, be indolent,   155
Nor is his claim to plenty, but content.
But grant him Riches, your demand is o'er?
"No — shall the good want Health, the good want Pow'r?"
Add Health and Pow'r, and ev'ry earthly thing;
"Why bounded Pow'r? why private? why no king?"   160
Nay, why external for internal giv'n?
Why is not Man a God, and Earth a Heav'n?
Who ask and reason thus, will scarce conceive
God gives enough, while he has more to give:
Immense that pow'r, immense were the demand;   165
Say, at what part of nature will they stand?
    VI. What nothing earthly gives, or can destroy,
The soul's calm sun-shine, and the heart-felt joy,
Is Virtue's prize: A better would you fix?
Then give Humility a coach and six,   170

130. **Chartres**: Francis Charteris (1675–1732), notorious as a colonel, card-sharp, and scoundrel (cf. *Ep. to Bathurst*, l. 20n.).
146. Titus: see Epist. II 198n., above.
169ff. That *External Goods* are not the proper rewards of *Virtue*, often in-

Justice a Conq'ror's sword, or Truth a gown,
Or Public Spirit its great cure, a Crown.
Weak, foolish man! will Heav'n reward us there
With the same trash mad mortals wish for here?
The Boy and Man an individual makes,   175
Yet sigh'st thou now for apples and for cakes?
Go, like the Indian, in another life
Expect thy dog, thy bottle, and thy wife:
As well as dream such trifles are assign'd,
As toys and empires, for a god-like mind.   180
Rewards, that either would to Virtue bring
No joy, or be destructive of the thing:
How oft by these at sixty are undone
The virtues of a saint at twenty-one!
   To whom can Riches give Repute, or Trust,   185
Content, or Pleasure, but the Good and Just?
Judges and Senates have been bought for gold,
Esteem and Love were never to be sold.
Oh fool! to think God hates the worthy mind,
The lover and the love of human-kind,   190
Whose life is healthful, and whose conscience clear;
Because he wants a thousand pounds a year.
   Honour and shame from no Condition rise;
Act well your part, there all the honour lies.
Fortune in Men has some small diff'rence made,   195
One flaunts in rags, one flutters in brocade,
The cobler apron'd, and the parson gown'd,
The friar hooded, and the monarch crown'd.
"What differ more (you cry) than crown and cowl?"
I'll tell you, friend! a Wise man and a Fool.   200
You'll find, if once the monarch acts the monk,
Or, cobler-like, the parson will be drunk,
Worth makes the man, and want of it, the fellow;
The rest is all but leather or prunella.
   Stuck o'er with titles and hung round with strings,
That thou may'st be by kings, or whores of kings.   206
Boast the pure blood of an illustrious race,

---

consistent with, or destructive of it; but that all these can make no man happy without *Virtue*. Instanced in each of them.   P.

   171. gown: emblem of academic, legal, or ecclesiastical status.

   185*ff*. 1. Riches.   P.   This note depends on the last sentence of that at l. 169, above.

   193*ff*. 2. Honours.   P.

   193. Condition: station or rank in life.

   204. leather: the cobbler's apron.   **prunella:** material of a clergyman's gown.

   205–6. 3. Titles.   P.

   205. strings: the ribbons of a knightly order (cf. ll. 277–8, below).

   207*ff*. 4. Birth.   P.

In quiet flow from Lucrece to Lucrece;
But by your father's worth if yours you rate,
Count me those only who were good and great. 210
Go! if your ancient, but ignoble blood
Has crept thro' scoundrels ever since the flood,
Go! and pretend your family is young;
Nor own, your fathers have been fools so long.
What can ennoble sots, or slaves, or cowards? 215
Alas! not all the blood of all the Howards.
    Look next on Greatness; say where Greatness lies?
"Where, but among the Heroes and the Wise?"
Heroes are much the same, the point's agreed,
From Macedonia's madman to the Swede; 220
The whole strange purpose of their lives, to find
Or make, an enemy of all mankind!
Not one looks backward, onward still he goes,
Yet ne'er looks forward farther than his nose.
No less alike the Politic and Wise, 225
All sly slow things, with circumspective eyes:
Men in their loose unguarded hours they take,
Not that themselves are wise, but others weak.
But grant that those can conquer, these can cheat,
'Tis phrase absurd to call a Villain Great: 230
Who wickedly is wise, or madly brave,
Is but the more a fool, the more a knave.
Who noble ends by noble means obtains,
Or failing, smiles in exile or in chains,
Like good Aurelius let him reign, or bleed 235
Like Socrates, that Man is great indeed.
    What's Fame? a fancy'd life in others breath,
A thing beyond us, ev'n before our death.
Just what you hear, you have, and what's unknown
The same (my Lord) if Tully's or your own. 240
All that we feel of it begins and ends
In the small circle of our foes or friends;
To all beside as much an empty shade,
An Eugene living, as a Cæsar dead,

208. **Lucrece:** a Roman matron famed for her virtue. About 507 B.C. she committed suicide after being raped by Tarquin.
216. **Howards:** the Howard family is regarded as one of the most noble and ancient in England.
217*ff.* 5. Greatness. P.
220. **Macedonia's madman:** Alexander the Great.   **Swede:** Charles XII of Sweden (1682–1718), a celebrated conqueror who was killed during a battle in Norway.
235. **Aurelius:** Marcus Aurelius Antoninus (121–80 A.D.), author of the *Meditations* and one of the noblest Roman emperors.
237*ff.* 6. Fame. P.
240. **Tully:** Cicero (Marcus Tullius Cicero).
244. **Eugene:** Prince Eugene of Savoy (1663–1736), regarded by some as the greatest general of his time.

Alike or when, or where, they shone, or shine,   245
Or on the Rubicon, or on the Rhine.
A Wit's a feather, and a Chief a rod;
An honest Man's the noblest work of God.
Fame but from death a villain's name can save,
As Justice tears his body from the grave,   250
When what t'oblivion better were resign'd,
Is hung on high, to poison half mankind.
All fame is foreign, but of true desert,
Plays round the head, but comes not to the heart:
One self-approving hour whole years out-weighs   255
Of stupid starers, and of loud huzzas;
And more true joy Marcellus exil'd feels,
Than Cæsar with a senate at his heels.
    In Parts superior what advantage lies?
Tell (for You can) what is it to be wise?   260
'Tis but to know how little can be known;
To see all others faults, and feel our own:
Condemn'd in bus'ness or in arts to drudge
Without a second, or without a judge:
Truths would you teach, or save a sinking land?   265
All fear, none aid you, and few understand.
Painful preheminence! yourself to view
Above life's weakness, and its comforts too.
    Bring then these blessings to a strict account,
Make fair deductions, see to what they mount.   270
How much of other each is sure to cost;
How each for other oft is wholly lost;
How inconsistent greater goods with these;
How sometimes life is risq'd, and always ease:
Think, and if still the things thy envy call,   275
Say, would'st thou be the Man to whom they fall?
To sigh for ribbands if thou art so silly,
Mark how they grace Lord Umbra, or Sir Billy:
Is yellow dirt the passion of thy life?
Look but on Gripus, or on Gripus' wife: 280

247. **Wit:** a "witty" writer.   **feather:** a quill pen, but also suggestive of something vain or insignificant.   **rod:** the symbolic staff of a field marshal.
250–2. Bodies of infamous men were sometimes exhumed and hung up for public display.
257. **Marcellus:** Marcus Claudius Marcellus (d. 46 B.C.), friend of Cicero, and an adherent of Pompey in the war against Caesar. After Pompey's defeat at Pharsalus, he exiled himself.
259*ff.* 7. Superior Parts. P.
260. **You:** Bolingbroke.
264. **second:** an equal, or one nearly so.
277. **ribbands:** badges of knighthood.
278. **Umbra:** Latin for *shadow,* and a name often applied to flatterers.   **Sir Billy:** any silly "Sir."
280. **Gripus:** gripulous (grasping, avaricious).

If Parts allure thee, think how Bacon shin'd,
The wisest, brightest, meanest of mankind:
Or ravish'd with the whistling of a Name,
See Cromwell, damn'd to everlasting fame!
If all, united, thy ambition call,   285
From ancient story learn to scorn them all.
There, in the rich, the honour'd, fam'd and great,
See the false scale of Happiness complete!
In hearts of Kings, or arms of Queens who lay,
How happy! those to ruin, these betray,   290
Mark by what wretched steps their glory grows,
From dirt and sea-weed as proud Venice rose;
In each how guilt and greatness equal ran,
And all that rais'd the Hero, sunk the Man.
Now Europe's laurels on their brows behold,   295
But stain'd with blood, or ill exchang'd for gold,
Then see them broke with toils, or sunk in ease,
Or infamous for plunder'd provinces.
Oh wealth ill-fated! which no act of fame
E'er taught to shine, or sanctify'd from shame!   300
What greater bliss attends their close of life?
Some greedy minion, or imperious wife,
The trophy'd arches, story'd halls invade,
And haunt their slumbers in the pompous shade.
Alas! not dazzled with their noon-tide ray,   305
Compute the morn and ev'ning to the day;
The whole amount of that enormous fame,
A Tale, that blends their glory with their shame!
   VII. Know then this truth (enough for Man to know)
"Virtue alone is Happiness below."   310
The only point where human bliss stands still,
And tastes the good without the fall to ill;
Where only Merit constant pay receives,
Is blest in what it takes, and what it gives;
The joy unequal'd, if its end it gain,   315
And if it lose, attended with no pain:
Without satiety, tho' e'er so blest,
And but more relish'd as the more distress'd:
The broadest mirth unfeeling Folly wears,
Less pleasing far than Virtue's very tears.   320
Good, from each object, from each place acquir'd,
For ever exercis'd, yet never tir'd;
Never elated, while one man's oppress'd;

282. **meanest:** Bacon pleaded guilty to charges of corruption brought against him.
288. **scale:** ladder.
309ff. That Virtue only constitutes a Happiness, whose Object is *Universal*, and whose Prospect *Eternal*. P.

Never dejected, while another's bless'd;
And where no wants, no wishes can remain,   325
Since but to wish more Virtue, is to gain.
 See! the sole bliss Heav'n could on all bestow;
Which who but feels can taste, but thinks can know:
Yet poor with fortune, and with learning blind,
The bad must miss; the good, untaught, will find;   330
Slave to no sect, who takes no private road,
But looks thro' Nature, up to Nature's God;
Pursues that Chain which links th'immense design,
Joins heav'n and earth, and mortal and divine;
Sees, that no being any bliss can know,   335
But touches some above, and some below;
Learns, from this union of the rising Whole,
The first, last purpose of the human soul;
And knows where Faith, Law, Morals, all began,
All end, in LOVE of GOD, and LOVE of MAN.   340
 For him alone, Hope leads from goal to goal,
And opens still, and opens on his soul,
'Till lengthen'd on to Faith, and unconfin'd,
It pours the bliss that fills up all the mind.
He sees, why Nature plants in Man alone   345
Hope of known bliss, and Faith in bliss unknown:
(Nature, whose dictates to no other kind
Are giv'n in vain, but what they seek they find)
Wise is her present; she connects in this
His greatest Virtue with his greatest Bliss,   350
At once his own bright prospect to be blest,
And strongest motive to assist the rest.
 Self-love thus push'd to social, to divine,
Gives thee to make thy neighbour's blessing thine.
Is this too little for the boundless heart?   355
Extend it, let thy enemies have part:
Grasp the whole worlds of Reason, Life, and Sense,
In one close system of Benevolence:
Happier as kinder, in whate'er degree,
And height of Bliss but height of Charity.   360
 God loves from Whole to Parts: but human soul
Must rise from Individual to the Whole.
Self-love but serves the virtuous mind to wake,
As the small pebble stirs the peaceful lake;
The centre mov'd, a circle strait succeeds,   365

327ff. That the *Perfection of Happiness* consists in a *Conformity* to the *Order of Providence* here, and a *Resignation* to it, here and hereafter. P.
 357. worlds: i.e., the inhabitants of the "worlds" of reason (men and angels), of sense (animals), of mere life (the creation below the animals in the chain of being).
 365. strait: straight (immediately).

Another still, and still another spreads,
Friend, parent, neighbour, first it will embrace,
His country next, and next all human race,
Wide and more wide, th'o'erflowings of the mind
Take ev'ry creature in, of ev'ry kind;   370
Earth smiles around, with boundless bounty blest,
And Heav'n beholds its image in his breast.
    Come then, my Friend, my Genius, come along,
Oh master of the poet, and the song!
And while the Muse now stoops, or now ascends,   375
To Man's low passions, or their glorious ends,
Teach me, like thee, in various nature wise,
To fall with dignity, with temper rise;
Form'd by thy converse, happily to steer
From grave to gay, from lively to severe;   380
Correct with spirit, eloquent with ease,
Intent to reason, or polite to please.
Oh! while along the stream of Time thy name
Expanded flies, and gathers all its fame,
Say, shall my little bark attendant sail,   385
Pursue the triumph, and partake the gale?
When statesmen, heroes, kings, in dust repose,
Whose sons shall blush their fathers were thy foes,
Shall then this verse to future age pretend
Thou wert my guide, philosopher, and friend?   390
That urg'd by thee, I turn'd the tuneful art
From sounds to things, from fancy to the heart;
For Wit's false mirror held up Nature's light;
Shew'd erring Pride, WHATEVER IS, IS RIGHT;
That REASON, PASSION, answer one great aim;   395
That true SELF-LOVE and SOCIAL are the same;
That VIRTUE only makes our Bliss below;
And all our Knowledge is, OURSELVES TO KNOW.

---

373. **Genius:** tutelary or guardian spirit.
375. **Muse:** Pope himself.   **stoops:** swoops (a term from falconry).
378. **to fall:** at the death of Queen Anne in 1714, Bolingbroke was prime minister, but one of the first acts of King George I was to dismiss him from office. See Epist. I 1n., above.   **temper:** calmness of mind.
389. **pretend:** profess.

EPISTLES
TO SEVERAL PERSONS

[Moral Essays]

Est brevitate opus, ut currat sententia, neu se
Impediat verbis lassis onerantibus aures:
Et sermone opus est modo tristi, sæpe jocoso,
Defendente vicem modo Rhetoris atque Poetæ,
Interdum urbani, parcentibus viribis, atque
Extenuantis eas consultò.   HOR.

EPISTLE I

To Richard Temple, Viscount Cobham

ARGUMENT OF THE FIRST EPISTLE

Of the Knowledge *and* Characters *of* Men. *That it is not sufficient for this knowledge to consider Man in the* Abstract: Books *will not serve the purpose, nor yet our own* Experience *singly,* v. 1. *General maxims, unless they be formed upon* both, *will be but notional,* v. 9. *Some* Peculiarity *in every man, characteristic to himself, yet varying from himself,* v. 15. *The*

EPISTLE TO COBHAM: Sometimes entitled "Moral Essays," Pope's *Epistles to Several Persons* were published in the following order: *To Burlington* (December, 1731), *To Bathurst* (January, 1733), *To Cobham* (January, 1734), *To a Lady* (February, 1735). When Pope brought them together in the 1735 edition of his *Works,* he arranged them in the order printed here. The Latin epigraph prefixed to these poetical epistles is from Horace, *Satires,* I x 9–14: "Brevity is necessary, so that the thought may move quickly, and not entangle itself in words that burden the wearied ears. You also need a style now grave, often playful, supporting the role now of an orator and of a poet, sometimes of an urbane talker, who curbs and deliberately weakens his force."

Sir Richard Temple, Viscount Cobham (1669–1749), was a distinguished soldier (he became a field-marshal in 1742) and Whig politician. After 1733 he was one of a group of Whigs who opposed the policies of the prime minister, Sir Robert Walpole. He rebuilt the family seat of Stowe, where Pope was a frequent visitor, and laid out its famous gardens.

further difficulty of separating and fixing this, arising from our own Passions, Fancies, Faculties, &c. v. 23. The shortness of Life, to observe in, and the uncertainty of the Principles of Action in men, to observe by, v. 29, &c. Our own Principle of action often hid from ourselves, v. 41. No judging of the Motives from the actions; the same actions proceeding from contrary Motives, and the same Motives influencing contrary actions, v. 51. Yet to form Characters, we can only take the strongest actions of a man's life, and try to make them agree: The utter uncertainty of this, from Nature itself, and from Policy, v. 71. Characters given according to the rank of men in the world, v. 87. And some reason for it, v. 93. Education alters the Nature, or at least Character of many, v. 101. Some few Characters plain, but in general confounded, dissembled, or inconsistent, v. 122. The same man utterly different in different places and seasons, v. 130. Unimaginable weaknesses in the greatest, v. 140, &c. Nothing constant and certain but God and Nature, v. 154. Actions, Passions, Opinions, Manners, Humours, or Principles all subject to change. No judging by Nature, from v. 158 to 173. It only remains to find (if we can) his RULING PASSION: *That will certainly influence all the rest, and can reconcile the seeming or real inconsistency of all his actions, v. 174. Instanced in the extraordinary character of Wharton, v. 179. A caution against mistaking second qualities for first, which will destroy all possibility of the knowledge of mankind, v. 210. Examples of the strength of the Ruling Passion, and its continuation to the last breath, v. 222, &c.*

YES, you despise the man to Books confin'd,
   Who from his study rails at human kind;
   Tho' what he learns, he speaks and may advance
Some gen'ral maxims, or be right by chance.
The coxcomb bird, so talkative and grave,   5
That from his cage cries Cuckold, Whore, and Knave,
Tho' many a passenger he rightly call,
You hold him no Philosopher at all.
   And yet the fate of all extremes is such,
Men may be read, as well as Books too much.   10
To Observations which ourselves we make,
We grow more partial for th' observer's sake;
To written Wisdom, as another's, less:
Maxims are drawn from Notions, these from Guess.
   There's some Peculiar in each leaf and grain,   15
Some unmark'd fibre, or some varying vein:
Shall only Man be taken in the gross?
Grant but as many sorts of Mind as Moss.
   That each from other differs, first confess;
Next, that he varies from himself no less: 20

7. **passenger:** passer-by.
14. **these:** the "Observations" of l. 11.
18. There are above 300 sorts of Moss observed by Naturalists. **P.**

Add Nature's, Custom's, Reason's, Passion's strife,
And all Opinion's colours cast on life.
    Yet more; the diff'rence is as great between
The optics seeing, as the objects seen.
All Manners take a tincture from our own,   25
Or come discolour'd thro' our Passions shown.
Or Fancy's beam enlarges, multiplies,
Contracts, inverts, and gives ten thousand dyes.
    Our depths who fathoms, or our shallows finds,
Quick whirls, and shifting eddies, of our minds?   30
Life's stream for Observation will not stay,
It hurries all too fast to mark their way.
In vain sedate reflections we would make,
When half our knowledge we must snatch, not take.
On human actions reason tho' you can,   35
It may be reason, but it is not man:
His Principle of action once explore,
That instant 'tis his Principle no more.
Like following life thro' creatures you dissect,
You lose it in the moment you detect.   40
    Oft in the Passions' wild rotation tost,
Our spring of action to ourselves is lost:
Tir'd, not determin'd, to the last we yield,
And what comes then is master of the field.
As the last image of the troubled heap,   45
When Sense subsides, and Fancy sports in sleep,
(Tho' past the recollection of the thought)
Becomes the stuff of which our dream is wrought:
Something as dim to our internal view,
Is thus, perhaps, the cause of most we do.   50
    In vain the Sage, with retrospective eye,
Would from th' apparent What conclude the Why,
Infer the Motive from the Deed, and show,
That what we chanc'd was what we meant to do.
Behold! If Fortune or a Mistress frowns,   55
Some plunge in bus'ness, others shave their crowns:
To ease the Soul of one oppressive weight,
This quits an Empire, that embroils a State:
The same adust complexion has impell'd
Charles to the Convent, Philip to the Field.   60

43. determin'd: decided.
46. Sense: the faculties of perception, perhaps the judgment.
56. shave their crowns: become monks.
59. adust complexion: a medical phrase of the time suggesting dryness of the body and its humours, and indicating a gloomy or melancholy temperament (cf. *Essay on Man*, II 111n.).
60. Charles: Charles V (1500–58), Emperor of Germany, resigned his crown in 1555 to retire to a Spanish monastery. Philip II (1527–98), King of Spain and the son of Charles V, inherited the morose nature of his father, waged war against France, and sent the "Invincible Armada" against England.

Not always Actions show the man: we find
Who does a kindness, is not therefore kind;
Perhaps Prosperity becalm'd his breast,
Perhaps the Wind just shifted from the east:
Not therefore humble he who seeks retreat,   65
Pride guides his steps, and bids him shun the great:
Who combats bravely is not therefore brave,
He dreads a death-bed like the meanest slave:
Who reasons wisely is not therefore wise,
His pride in Reas'ning, not in Acting lies.   70
    But grant that Actions best discover man;
Take the most strong, and sort them as you can.
The few that glare each character must mark,
You balance not the many in the dark.
What will you do with such as disagree?   75
Suppress them, half, or call them Policy?
Must then at once (the character to save)
The plain rough Hero turn a crafty Knave?
Alas! in truth the man but chang'd his mind,
Perhaps was sick, in love, or had not din'd.   80
Ask why from Britain Cæsar would retreat?
Cæsar himself might whisper he was beat.
Why risk the world's great empire for a Punk?
Cæsar perhaps might answer he was drunk.
But, sage historians! 'tis your task to prove   85
One action Conduct; one, heroic Love.
    'Tis from high Life high Characters are drawn;
A Saint in Crape is twice a Saint in Lawn;
A Judge is just, a Chanc'lor juster still;
A Gownman, learn'd; a Bishop, what you will;   90
Wise, if a Minister; but, if a King,
More wise, more learn'd, more just, more ev'rything.
Court-virtues bear, like Gems, the highest rate,
Born where Heav'n's influence scarce can penetrate:
In life's low vale, the soil the virtues like,   95
They please as Beauties, here as Wonders strike.
Tho' the same Sun with all-diffusive rays
Blush in the Rose, and in the Diamond blaze,
We prize the stronger effort of his pow'r,

64. **east:** east winds were regarded as unhealthy.
76. **Policy:** craftiness.
83. **Punk:** strumpet (presumably a reference here to Cleopatra).
86. **Conduct:** good generalship.
88. **Crape:** a thin worsted worn by the lower clergy at this time.   **Lawn:**
a fine linen used for the sleeves of a bishop.
  89. **Chanc'lor:** the Lord Chancellor, highest judicial official in England.
  90. **Gownman:** a divine, perhaps a lawyer or scholar.
  93–100. The lines recall the contemporary idea that the action of the sun
caused precious stones to grow and "ripen" in the earth.
  96. **here:** at court.

And justly set the Gem above the Flow'r.   100
   'Tis Education forms the common mind,
Just as the Twig is bent, the Tree's inclin'd.
Boastful and rough, your first son is a 'Squire;
The next a Tradesman, meek, and much a lyar;
Tom struts a Soldier, open, bold, and brave;   105
Will sneaks a Scriv'ner, an exceeding knave:
Is he a Churchman? then he's fond of pow'r: ⎫
A Quaker? sly: A Presbyterian? sow'r: ⎬
A smart Free-thinker? all things in an hour. ⎭
   True, some are open, and to all men known;   110
Others so very close, they're hid from none;
(So Darkness strikes the sense no less than Light)
Thus gracious CHANDOS is belov'd at sight,
And ev'ry child hates Shylock, tho' his soul
Still sits at squat, and peeps not from its hole.   115
   At half mankind when gen'rous Manly raves,
All know 'tis Virtue, for he thinks them knaves:
When universal homage Umbra pays,
All see 'tis Vice, and itch of vulgar praise.
When Flatt'ry glares, all hate it in a Queen.   120
While one there is who charms us with his Spleen.
   But these plain Characters we rarely find;
Tho' strong the bent, yet quick the turns of mind:
Or puzzling Contraries confound the whole,
Or Affectations quite reverse the soul.   125
Or Falshood serves the dull for poli‿y,
And in the Cunning, Truth itself's a lye:
Unthought-of Frailties cheat us in the Wise,
The Fool lies hid in inconsistencies.
   See the same man, in vigour, in the gout;   130
Alone, in company; in place, or out;
Early at Bus'ness, and at Hazard late;
Mad at a Fox-chace, wise at a Debate;
Drunk at a Borough, civil at a Ball,

106. **Scriv'ner:** a money scrivener, who loaned money on security.
107. **Churchman:** not any clergyman, but one of the Church of England, an Anglican.
109. **Free-thinker:** a name claimed by deists and atheists at this period.
113. **Chandos:** James Brydges, first Duke of Chandos (1673–1744), a Whig millionaire and M.P. His mansion at Cannons was wrongly, and maliciously, said by many at the time to have served as the model for Timon's villa in the *Ep. to Burlington,* and Pope here apparently attempts to refute such allegations.
114. **Shylock:** any extortionate usurer.
116. **gen'rous:** noble-minded.   **Manly:** type name for a plain-spoken man (and the name also of the main character in William Wycherley's play, *The Plain Dealer*).
118. **Umbra:** Latin for *shadow,* and a name often applied to flatterers.
121. **Spleen:** here suggests misanthropy.
132. **Hazard:** a game at dice.
134. **Borough:** a town, or urban constituency, that elects a member of Parliament.

Friendly at Hackney, faithless at Whitehall.   135
  Catius is ever moral, ever grave,
Thinks who endures a knave, is next a knave,
Save just at dinner — then prefers, no doubt,
A Rogue with Ven'son to a Saint without.
  Who would not praise Patritio's high desert,   140
His hand unstain'd, his uncorrupted heart,
His comprehensive head! all Int'rests weigh'd,
All Europe sav'd, yet Britain not betray'd.
He thanks you not, his pride is in Picquette,
New-market-fame, and judgment at a Bett.   145
  What made (say Montagne, or more sage Charron!)
Otho a warrior, Cromwell a buffoon?
A perjur'd Prince a leaden Saint revere,
A godless Regent tremble at a Star?
The throne a Bigot keep, a Genius quit,   150
Faithless thro' Piety, and dup'd thro' Wit?
Europe a Woman, Child, or Dotard rule,
And just her wisest monarch made a fool?
  Know, God and Nature only are the same:
In Man, the judgment shoots at flying game,   155
A bird of passage! gone as soon as found,
Now in the Moon perhaps, now under ground.
  Ask men's Opinions: Scoto now shall tell
How Trade increases, and the World goes well;
Strike off his Pension, by the setting sun,   160
And Britain, if not Europe, is undone.
  That gay Free-thinker, a fine talker once,
What turns him now a stupid silent dunce?
Some God, or Spirit he has lately found,
Or chanc'd to meet a Minister that frown'd.   165

135. Hackney: a borough of greater London and one where candidates for election to Parliament were placed in nomination.   **Whitehall:** site of government offices in London.

136. Catius: name of an epicure satirized in Horace, *Satires,* II iv.

140. Patritio: a name suggesting a noble patriot.

144. Picquette: piquet, a card-game.

145. New-market: a town noted for its horse races.

146. Charron: Pierre Charron (1531–1603), French philosopher whose principal work was entitled *Traité de la Sagesse.*

147. Otho: Marcus Salvius Otho (32–69 A.D.), Roman usurper who committed suicide after a reign of three months.

148. Louis XI of France [1423–83] wore in his Hat a leaden image of the Virgin Mary, which when he swore by, he feared to break his oath. P.   **revere:** pronounced *revar.*

149. Philip Duke of Orleans [1674–1723], Regent of France in the minority of Louis XV, superstitious in judicial [i.e., predictive] astrology, tho' an unbeliever in all religion. P.

150–1. Philip V. of Spain [1683–1746], who, after renouncing the throne for Religion, resum'd it to gratify his Queen; and Victor Amadeus II [1666–1732], King of Sardinia, who resign'd the crown, and trying to reassume it, was imprisoned till his death. P.

158. Scoto: any Scotch merchant.

Manners with Fortunes, Humours turn with Climes,
Tenets with Books, and Principles with Times.
    Judge we by Nature? Habit can efface,
Int'rest o'ercome, or Policy take place:
By Actions? those Uncertainty divides: 170
By Passions? these Dissimulation hides:
Opinions? they still take a wider range:
Find, if you can, in what you cannot change.
    Search then the Ruling Passion: There, alone,
The Wild are constant, and the Cunning known;   175
The Fool consistent, and the False sincere;
Priests, Princes, Women, no dissemblers here.
This clue once found, unravels all the rest,
The prospect clears, and Wharton stands confest.
Wharton, the scorn and wonder of our days,   180
Whose ruling Passion was the Lust of Praise;
Born with whate'er could win it from the Wise,
Women and Fools must like him or he dies;
Tho' wond'ring Senates hung on all he spoke,
The Club must hail him master of the joke.   185
Shall parts so various aim at nothing new?
He'll shine a Tully and a Wilmot too.
Then turns repentant, and his God adores
With the same spirit that he drinks and whores;
Enough if all around him but admire,   190
And now the Punk applaud, and now the Fryer.
Thus with each gift of nature and of art,
And wanting nothing but an honest heart;
Grown all to all, from no one vice exempt,
And most contemptible, to shun contempt;   195
His Passion still, to covet gen'ral praise,
His Life, to forfeit it a thousand ways;
A constant Bounty which no friend has made;
An angel Tongue, which no man can persuade;
A Fool, with more of Wit than half mankind,   200
Too quick for Thought, for Action too refin'd:
A Tyrant to the wife his heart approves;
A Rebel to the very king he loves;
He dies, sad out-cast of each church and state,

166. **Humours:** temperaments (but see *Essay on Man*, II 111n.).
169. **take place:** take precedence.
174. **Ruling Passion:** cf. *Essay on Man*, II 133ff.
178. **clue:** thread.
   179. **Wharton:** Philip, Duke of Wharton (1698–1731), an elegant and profligate peer who went to France, became a Roman Catholic, served with the Spanish against the English at the siege of Gibraltar (for which he was convicted of treason), and died in a Spanish convent.
   187. **Tully:** Cicero.   **Wilmot:** John Willmot [1647–80], Earl of Rochester, famous for his Wit and Extravagencies in the time of Charles the Second. P.

And (harder still) flagitious, yet not great!   205
Ask you why Wharton broke thro' ev'ry rule?
'Twas all for fear the Knaves should call him Fool.
    Nature well known, no prodigies remain,
Comets are regular, and Wharton plain.
    Yet, in this search, the wisest may mistake,   210
If second qualities for first they take.
When Catiline by rapine swell'd his store,
When Cæsar made a noble dame a whore,
In this the Lust, in that the Avarice
Were means, not ends; Ambition was the vice.   215
That very Cæsar, born in Scipio's days,
Had aim'd, like him, by Chastity at praise.
Lucullus, when Frugality could charm,
Had roasted turnips in the Sabin farm.
In vain th' observer eyes the builder's toil,   220
But quite mistakes the scaffold for the pile.
    In this one Passion man can strength enjoy,
As Fits give vigour, just when they destroy.
Time, that on all things lays his lenient hand,
Yet tames not this; it sticks to our last sand.   225
Consistent in our follies and our sins,
Here honest Nature ends as she begins.
    Behold a rev'rend sire, whom want of grace
Has made the father of a nameless race,
Shov'd from the wall perhaps, or rudely press'd   230
By his own son, that passes by unbless'd:
Still to his wench he crawls on knocking knees,
And envies ev'ry sparrow that he sees.
    A salmon's belly, Helluo, was thy fate:
The doctor call'd, declares all help too late.   235
Mercy! cries Helluo, mercy on my soul!

211. I.e., if what is derivative, or secondary, is mistaken for what is original, or primary.
212. **Catiline:** the infamous Roman conspirator (see *Essay on Man,* I 156*n.*).
213. **noble dame:** Servilia, mother of Brutus, became mistress to Caesar (slain by Brutus).
216. **Scipio:** the conqueror of Hannibal (cf. *Windsor-Forest,* 1. 257*n.*).
218. **Lucullus:** Lucius Licinius Lucullus (110–57 B.C.), a celebrated Roman general who lived the last part of his life in great luxury.
219. **Sabin:** a mountainous region in central Italy whose original inhabitants were noted for their simple and virtuous lives.
220. **toil:** pronounced *tile.*
221. **pile:** a large building.
224. **lenient:** softening.
225. **sand:** of an hour-glass.
230. **wall:** the inner side of the sidewalk next to the wall (the cleaner and safer side).
233. **sparrow:** an emblem of lechery.
234. **Helluo:** Latin for *glutton.*
236. **soul:** occasionally pronounced at this time to rhyme with *fowl.*

Is there no hope? Alas!—then bring the jowl.
    The frugal Crone, whom praying priests attend,
Still tries to save the hallow'd taper's end,
Collects her breath, as ebbing life retires,   240
For one puff more, and in that puff expires.
    "Odious! in woollen! 'twould a Saint provoke,
(Were the last words that poor Narcissa spoke)
"No, let a charming Chintz, and Brussels lace
"Wrap my cold limbs, and shade my lifeless face: 245
"One would not, sure, be frightful when one's dead—
"And — Betty — give this Cheek a little Red."
    Old Politicians chew on wisdom past,
And totter on in bus'ness to the last;
As weak, as earnest, and as gravely out,   250
As sober Lanesb'row dancing in the gout.
    The Courtier smooth, who forty years had shin'd
An humble servant to all human kind,
Just brought out this, when scarce his tongue could stir,
"If — where I'm going — I could serve you, Sir?"   255
    "I give and I devise, (old Euclio said,
And sigh'd) "My lands and tenements to Ned."
Your money, Sir? "My money, Sir, what all?
"Why, — if I must — (then wept) I give it Paul."
The Manor, Sir? — "The Manor! hold," he cry'd,   260
"Not that, — I cannot part with that" — and dy'd.
    And you! brave COBHAM, to the latest breath
Shall feel your ruling passion strong in death:
Such in those moments as in all the past,
"Oh, save my Country, Heav'n!" shall be your last.   265

242*ff*. This story, as well as the others, is founded on fact, tho' the author had the goodness not to mention the names. Several attribute this in particular to a very celebrated Actress, who, in detestation of the thought of being buried in woollen, gave these her last orders with her dying breath. P.   An act of Parliament (a protective measure against foreign linen) required the dead to be buried in British woolen.
    243. Narcissa: a name suggestive of self-love.
    247. Betty: type name for a lady's maid.
    248. bus'ness: affairs of state.
    251. Lanesb'row: An ancient Nobleman, who continued this practice long after his legs were disabled by the gout. Upon the death of Prince George of Denmark, he demanded an audience of the Queen, to advise her to preserve her health and dispel her grief by *Dancing*. P.   The nobleman was James Lane, second Viscount Lanesborough (1650–1724).
    256. devise: bequeath.   Euclio: name of an old miser in Plautus's play, *Aulularia*.

EPISTLE II
To a Lady

ARGUMENT

Of the Characters of *Women* (consider'd only as contradistinguished from
the other Sex.) That these are yet more inconsistent and incomprehen-
sible than those of Men, of which Instances are given even from such
Characters as are plainest, and most strongly mark'd; as in the *Affected,*
Ver.7, &c. The *Soft-natur'd.* 29. the *Cunning,* 45. the *Whimsical,* 53.
the *Wits and Refiners,* 87. the *Stupid* and *Silly,* 101. How Contrarieties
run thro' them all.

But tho' the *Particular Characters* of this Sex are more various than
those of Men, the *General Characteristick,* as to the *Ruling Passion,* is
more uniform and confin'd. In what That lies, and whence it *proceeds,*
207, &c. Men are best known in publick Life, Women in private, 199.
What are the *Aims,* and the *Fate* of the Sex, both as to *Power* and *Pleasure?*
219, 231, &c. Advice for their true Interest, 249. The Picture of an
esteemable Woman, made up of the best kind of Contrarieties, 269, &c.

> N OTHING so true as what you once let fall,
>   "Most Women have no Characters at all"
>   Matter too soft a lasting mark to bear,
> And best distinguish'd by black, brown, or fair.
>   How many pictures of one Nymph we view,   5
> All how unlike each other, all how true!
> Arcadia's Countess, here, in ermin'd pride,
> Is there, Pastora by a fountain side:
> Here Fannia, leering on her own good man,

EPISTLE TO A LADY: The lady was Martha Blount (1690–1763), a descendant
of an old Catholic family whom Pope first met about 1711. Their long and intimate friendship lasted until his death, and she is thought by some to have been
Pope's mistress. In his will, Pope left her £ 1,000, his household goods, chattels
and plate, and the residue of his estate after all legacies were paid. The *Epistle
to a Lady* throughout reflects the knowledge of painting Pope gained in lessons
taken from his friend, the portrait painter Charles Jervas (see first note to
Epistle to Mr. Jervas).

2. **Women:** That their particular Characters are not so strongly mark'd as
those of Men, seldom so fixed, and still more inconsistent with themselves.   P.

7–13. Attitudes in which several ladies affected to be drawn, and sometimes
one lady in them all. — The poet's politeness and complaisance to the sex is
observable in this instance, amongst others, that, whereas in the *Characters of
Men* [i.e. the *Ep. to Cobham*] he has sometimes made use of real names, in the
Characters of Women always fictitious.   P.

9. **Fannia:** the name of a Roman adulteress.

Is there, a naked Leda with a Swan.   10
Let then the Fair one beautifully cry,
In Magdalen's loose hair and lifted eye,
Or drest in smiles of sweet Cecilia shine,
With simp'ring Angels, Palms, and Harps divine;
Whether the Charmer sinner it, or saint it,   15
If Folly grows romantic, I must paint it.
    Come then, the colours and the ground prepare!
Dip in the Rainbow, trick her off in Air,
Chuse a firm Cloud, before it fall, and in it
Catch, ere she change, the Cynthia of this minute.   20
    Rufa, whose eye quick-glancing o'er the Park,
Attracts each light gay meteor of a Spark,
Agrees as ill with Rufa studying Locke,
As Sappho's diamonds with her dirty smock,
Or Sappho at her toilet's greasy task,   25
With Sappho fragrant at an ev'ning Mask:
So morning Insects that in muck begun,
Shine, buzz, and fly-blow in the setting-sun.
    How soft is Silia! fearful to offend,
The Frail one's advocate, the Weak one's friend: 30
To her, Calista prov'd her conduct nice,
And good Simplicius asks of her advice.

12. **Magdalen:** Mary Magdalene, who "anointed the feet of Jesus, and wiped his feet with her hair."
13. **Cecilia:** St. Cecilia, patron saint of sacred music.
16. **romantic:** extravagant.
17. **ground:** the preliminary surface laid on a canvas.
18. **trick:** sketch.
20. **Cynthia:** goddess associated with the moon (considered an emblem of female changeability).
21. Instances of contrarieties, given even from such Characters as are most strongly mark'd and seemingly therefore most consistent. As I. In the *Affected*, v. 21 &c. P.   **Rufa:** Latin for *red-haired*, considered in Pope's time a sign of wantonness.
22. **Spark:** beau or fop.
23. **Locke:** John Locke (1632–1704), English philosopher and author of the *Essay concerning Human Understanding*.
24. **Sappho:** the Greek poetess Sappho (c. 600 B.C.) was noted for erotic, even lesbian, indulgencies. Pope uses the name for any sordid poetess of dubious morals, though here and elsewhere in his poems he also probably alludes by this name to Lady Mary Wortley Montagu (1689–1762), a celebrated wit, poetess, and letter-writer, and a notorious sloven. Once on terms of intimate friendship, Pope and Lady Mary became estranged, and a bitter feud between them resulted.
28. **fly-blow:** contaminate.
29–40. II. Contrarieties in the *Soft-natured*. P.
29. **Silia:** the implication of the name is unclear, though perhaps *snub-nosed* (from Latin *silus*) is suggested. See l. 36.
31. **Calista:** Callisto was the name of a nymph made pregnant by Zeus. **nice:** modest, refined.
32. **Simplicius:** any simple-minded man.

Sudden, she storms! she raves! You tip the wink,
But spare your censure; Silia does not drink.
All eyes may see from what the change arose,   35
All eyes may see — a Pimple on her nose.
    Papillia, wedded to her doating spark,
Sighs for the shades — "How charming is a Park!"
A Park is purchas'd, but the Fair he sees
All bath'd in tears — "Oh odious, odious Trees!"   40
    Ladies, like variegated Tulips, show,
'Tis to their Changes that their charms they owe;
Their happy Spots the nice admirer take,
Fine by defect, and delicately weak.
'Twas thus Calypso once each heart alarm'd,   45
Aw'd without Virtue, without Beauty charm'd;
Her Tongue bewitch'd as odly as her Eyes,
Less Wit than Mimic, more a Wit than wise:
Strange graces still, and stranger flights she had,
Was just not ugly, and was just not mad;   50
Yet ne'er so sure our passion to create,
As when she touch'd the brink of all we hate.
    Narcissa's nature, tolerably mild,
To make a wash, would hardly stew a child,
Has ev'n been prov'd to grant a Lover's pray'r,   55
And paid a Tradesman once to make him stare,
Gave alms at Easter, in a Christian trim,
And made a Widow happy, for a whim.
Why then declare Good-nature is her scorn,
When 'tis by that alone she can be born?   60
Why pique all mortals, yet affect a name?
A fool to Pleasure, and a slave to Fame:
Now deep in Taylor and the Book of Martyrs,
Now drinking citron with his Grace and Chartres.
Now Conscience chills her, and now Passion burns;   65
And Atheism and Religion take their turns;

37. Papillia: Latin for *butterfly.*
43. nice: discriminating.
45–52. III. Contrarieties in the *Cunning* and *Artful.*   P.
45. Calypso: name of the sea-nymph who bewitched Odysseus and detained him seven years on her island.
53–68. IV. In the *Whimsical.*   P.
53. Narcissa: a name suggestive of self-love.
54. wash: a liquid cosmetic.
57. trim: mode, or fashion.
63. Taylor: the Rev. Jeremy Taylor (1613–67), author of some of the best devotional works in English.   **Book of Martyrs:** *History of the Acts and Monuments of the Church,* popularly known as *Foxe's Book of Martyrs,* by John Foxe (1516–87).
64. citron: lemon-flavored brandy.   **his Grace:** any duke.   **Chartres:** an infamous cheat, usurer, rapist, and scoundrel (see *Essay on Man,* IV 130n.).

A very Heathen in the carnal part,
Yet still a sad, good Christian at her heart.
　　See Sin in State, majestically drunk,
Proud as a Peeress, prouder as a Punk;　　　　　　　70
Chaste to her Husband, frank to all beside,
A teeming Mistress, but a barren Bride.
What then? let Blood and Body bear the fault,
Her Head's untouch'd, that noble Seat of Thought:
Such this day's doctrine — in another fit　　　　　　75
She sins with Poets thro' pure Love of Wit.
What has not fir'd her bosom or her brain?
Cæsar and Tall-boy, Charles and Charlema'ne.
As Helluo, late Dictator of the Feast,
The Nose of Hautgout, and the Tip of Taste,　　　　80
Critick'd your wine, and analyz'd your meat,
Yet on plain Pudding deign'd at-home to eat;
So Philomedé, lect'ring all mankind
On the soft Passion, and the Taste refin'd,
Th' Address, the Delicacy — stoops at once,　　　　85
And makes her hearty meal upon a Dunce.
　　Flavia's a Wit, has too much sense to Pray,
To Toast our wants and wishes, is her way;
Nor asks of God, but of her Stars to give
The mighty blessing, "while we live, to live."　　　90
Then all for Death, that Opiate of the soul!
Lucretia's dagger, Rosamonda's bowl.
Say, what can cause such impotence of mind?
A Spark too fickle, or a Spouse too kind.
Wise Wretch! with Pleasures too refin'd to please,　　95
With too much Spirit to be e'er at ease,
With too much Quickness ever to be taught,
With too much Thinking to have common Thought:
Who purchase Pain with all that Joy can give,
And die of nothing but a Rage to live.　　　　　　100

69–87. V. In the *Lewd* and *Vicious*. P.
70. Punk: strumpet.
71. frank: licentious.
73. fault: the *l* was silent in Pope's time.
78. Tall-boy: a booby character in Richard Brome's play, *The Jovial Crew* (1641), and also a term for a drinking-glass. **Charles:** typical name for a footman.
79. Helluo: Latin for *glutton*. **Feast:** pronounced to rhyme with *waist*.
80. Hautgout: high or strong flavor.
83. Philomedé: the name perhaps implies a love of the exotic.
85. Address: deportment.
87–100. VI. Contrarieties in the *Witty* and *Refin'd*. P.
87. Flavia: a blonde (from Latin *flavus*).
92. Lucretia: the Roman matron who committed suicide after she was raped by Tarquin. **Rosamonda:** Rosamond Clifford (d. 1177), mistress of King Henry II. According to legend, she was forced by Henry's queen to partake of a poisoned bowl.

Turn then from Wits; and look on Simo's Mate,
No Ass so meek, no Ass so obstinate:
Or her, that owns her Faults, but never mends,
Because she's honest, and the best of Friends:
Or her, whose life the Church and Scandal share,   105
For ever in a Passion, or a Pray'r:
Or her, who laughs at Hell, but (like her Grace)
Cries, "Ah! how charming if there's no such place!"
Or who in sweet vicissitude appears
Of Mirth and Opium, Ratafie and Tears,   110
The daily Anodyne, and nightly Draught,
To kill those foes to Fair ones, Time and Thought.
Woman and Fool are two hard things to hit,
For true No-meaning puzzles more than Wit.
But what are these to great Atossa's mind?   115
Scarce once herself, by turns all Womankind!
Who, with herself, or others, from her birth
Finds all her life one warfare upon earth:
Shines, in exposing Knaves, and painting Fools,
Yet is, whate'er she hates and ridicules.   120
No Thought advances, but her Eddy Brain
Whisks it about, and down it goes again.
Full sixty years the World has been her Trade,
The wisest Fool much Time has ever made.
From loveless youth to unrespected age,   125
No Passion gratify'd except her Rage.
So much the Fury still out-ran the Wit,
The Pleasure miss'd her, and the Scandal hit.
Who breaks with her, provokes Revenge from Hell,
But he's a bolder man who dares be well: 130
Her ev'ry turn with Violence pursu'd,
Nor more a storm her Hate than Gratitude.
To that each Passion turns, or soon or late;
Love, if it makes her yield, must make her hate:
Superiors? death! and Equals? what a curse!   135
But an Inferior not dependant? worse.
Offend her, and she knows not to forgive;
Oblige her, and she'll hate you while you live:
But die, and she'll adore you — Then the Bust
And Temple rise — then fall again to dust.   140
Last night, her Lord was all that's good and great,
A Knave this morning, and his Will a Cheat.

101. **Simo:** ape-like.
107. **her Grace:** an unspecified duchess.
110. **Opium:** used as a sedative and narcotic.   **Ratafie:** a kind of brandy.
111. **Anodyne:** an opiate or narcotic.
115. **Atossa:** name of the daughter of Cyrus the Great. She was wife to three successive Persian kings, and mother of Xerxes.
142. **Cheat:** pronounced *chate*.

Strange! by the Means defeated of the Ends,
By Spirit robb'd of Pow'r, by Warmth of Friends,
By Wealth of Follow'rs! without one distress   145
Sick of herself thro' very selfishness!
Atossa, curs'd with ev'ry granted pray'r,
Childless with all her Children, wants an Heir.
To Heirs unknown descends th' unguarded store
Or wanders, Heav'n-directed, to the Poor.   150
    Pictures like these, dear Madam, to design,
Asks no firm hand, and no unerring line;
Some wand'ring touch, or some reflected light,
Some flying stroke alone can hit 'em right:
For how should equal Colours do the knack?   155
Chameleons who can paint in white and black?
    "Yet Cloe sure was form'd without a spot — "
Nature in her then err'd not, but forgot.
"With ev'ry pleasing, ev'ry prudent part,
"Say, what can Cloe want?" — she wants a Heart.   160
She speaks, behaves, and acts just as she ought;
But never, never, reach'd one gen'rous Thought.
Virtue she finds too painful an endeavour,
Content to dwell in Decencies for ever.
So very reasonable, so unmov'd,   165
As never yet to love, or to be lov'd.
She, while her Lover pants upon her breast,
Can mark the figures on an Indian chest;
And when she sees her Friend in deep despair,
Observes how much a Chintz exceeds Mohair.   170
Forbid it Heav'n, a Favour or a Debt
She e'er should cancel — but she may forget.
Safe is your Secret still in Cloe's ear;
But none of Cloe's shall you ever hear.
Of all her Dears she never slander'd one,   175
But cares not if a thousand are undone.
Would Cloe know if you're alive or dead?
She bids her Footman put it in her head.
Cloe is prudent — would you too be wise?
Then never break your heart when Cloe dies.   180
    One certain Portrait may (I grant) be seen,
Which Heav'n has varnish'd out, and made a *Queen:*
The same for ever! and describ'd by all
With Truth and Goodness, as with Crown and Ball:

155. **equal:** flat or uniform.
157. **Cloe:** Greek for *blooming,* and a name usually given to women of beauty and simplicity.
182. **Queen:** Queen Caroline (1683–1737), wife to George II.
184. **Ball:** the golden ball or orb carried by sovereigns as an emblem of earthly authority.

Poets heap Virtues, Painters Gems at will,   185
And show their zeal, and hide their want of skill.
'Tis well — but, Artists! who can paint or write,
To draw the Naked is your true delight:
That Robe of Quality so struts and swells,
None see what Parts of Nature it conceals.   190
Th' exactest traits of Body or of Mind,
We owe to models of an humble kind.
If QUEENSBERRY to strip there's no compelling,
'Tis from a Handmaid we must take a Helen.
From Peer or Bishop 'tis no easy thing   195
To draw the man who loves his God, or King:
Alas! I copy (or my draught would fail)
From honest Mah'met, or plain Parson Hale.
    But grant, in Public Men sometimes are shown,
A Woman's seen in Private life alone: 200
Our bolder Talents in full light display'd,
Your Virtues open fairest in the shade.
Bred to disguise, in Public 'tis you hide;
There, none distinguish 'twixt your Shame or Pride,
Weakness or Delicacy; all so nice,   205
That each may seem a Virtue, or a Vice.
    In Men, we various Ruling Passions find,
In Women, two almost divide the kind;
Those, only fix'd, they first or last obey,
The Love of Pleasure, and the Love of Sway.   210
    That, Nature gives; and where the lesson taught
Is still to please, can Pleasure seem a fault?
Experience, this; by Man's oppression curst,
They seek the second not to lose the first.
    Men, some to Bus'ness, some to Pleasure take;   215
But ev'ry Woman is at heart a Rake:
Men, some to Quiet, some to public Strife;
But ev'ry Lady would be Queen for life.
    Yet mark the fate of a whole Sex of Queens!

191. **exactest:** most perfect.
193. **Queensberry:** Catherine Hyde, Duchess of Queensberry (1700–77), one
of the most beautiful women of the period.
194. **Helen:** a Helen of Troy.
198. **Mah'met:** Servant to the late king [George I], said to be the son of a
Turkish Bassa, whom he took at the siege of Buda, and constantly kept about
his person. P.   **Parson Hale:** Dr. Stephen Hales (1677–1761), clergyman,
physiologist, and friend of Pope.
205. **nice:** subtle.
207. The former part having shewn, that the *particular Characters* of Women
are more various than those of men, it is nevertheless observ'd, that the *general*
Characteristic of the sex, as to the *ruling Passion,* is more uniform.   P.
211. This is occasioned partly by their *Nature,* partly by their *Education,* and
in some degree by Necessity.   P.
219. What are the *Aims* and the *Fate* of this Sex? — I.   As to *Power.*   P.

Pow'r all their end, but Beauty all the means.   220
In Youth they conquer, with so wild a rage,
As leaves them scarce a Subject in their Age:
For foreign glory, foreign joy, they roam;
No thought of Peace or Happiness at home.
But Wisdom's Triumph is well-tim'd Retreat,   225
As hard a science to the Fair as Great!
Beauties, like Tyrants, old and friendless grown,
Yet hate to rest, and dread to be alone,
Worn out in public, weary ev'ry eye,
Nor leave one sigh behind them when they die.   230
    Pleasures the sex, as children Birds, pursue,
Still out of reach, yet never out of view,
Sure, if they catch, to spoil the Toy at most,
To covet flying, and regret when lost:
At last, to follies Youth could scarce defend,   235
'Tis half their Age's prudence to pretend;
Asham'd to own they gave delight before,
Reduc'd to feign it, when they give no more:
As Hags hold Sabbaths, less for joy than spight,
So these their merry, miserable Night;   240
Still round and round the Ghosts of Beauty glide,
And haunt the places where their Honour dy'd.
    See how the World its Veterans rewards!
A Youth of frolicks, an old Age of Cards,
Fair to no purpose, artful to no end,   245
Young without Lovers, old without a Friend,
A Fop their Passion, but their Prize a Sot,
Alive, ridiculous, and dead, forgot!
    Ah Friend! to dazzle let the Vain design,
To raise the Thought and touch the Heart, be thine!   250
That Charm shall grow, while what fatigues the Ring
Flaunts and goes down, an unregarded thing:
So when the Sun's broad beam has tir'd the sight,
All mild ascends the Moon's more sober light,
Serene in Virgin Modesty she shines,   255
And unobserv'd the glaring Orb declines.
    Oh! blest with Temper, whose unclouded ray
Can make to morrow chearful as to day;
She, who can love a Sister's charms, or hear

Decline of the aged.

231. II. As to *Pleasure.* P.
239. **Hags:** witches.   **Sabbaths:** witches' Sabbaths, or midnight assemblies where devils, sorcerers, and witches staged orgies.
241. **round and round:** the words suggest a fashionable promenade or carriage drive, like the Ring, in Hyde Park (see l. 251n., below).
249. Advice for their true Interest. P.   The "Friend" in this line is Martha Blount, of course.
251. **Ring:** a fashionable carriage-drive in Hyde Park.
257. **Temper:** serenity of mind.

Sighs for a Daughter with unwounded ear;   260
She, who ne'er answers till a Husband cools,
Or, if she rules him, never shows she rules;
Charms by accepting, by submitting sways,
Yet has her humour most, when she obeys;
Lets Fops or Fortune fly which way they will;   265
Disdains all loss of Tickets, or Codille;
Spleen, Vapours, or Small-pox, above them all,
And Mistress of herself, tho' China fall.
    And yet, believe me, good as well as ill,
Woman's at best a Contradiction still.   270
Heav'n, when it strives to polish all it can
Its last best work, but forms a softer Man;
Picks from each sex, to make its Fav'rite blest,
Your love of Pleasure, our desire of Rest.
Blends, in exception to all gen'ral rules,   275
Your Taste of Follies, with our Scorn of Fools,
Reserve with Frankness, Art with Truth ally'd,
Courage with Softness, Modesty with Pride,
Fix'd Principles, with Fancy ever new;
Shakes all together, and produces — You.   280
    Be this a Woman's Fame: with this unblest,
Toasts live a scorn, and Queens may die a jest.
This Phœbus promis'd (I forget the year)
When those blue eyes first open'd on the sphere;
Ascendant Phœbus watch'd that hour with care,   285
Averted half your Parents simple Pray'r,
And gave you Beauty, but deny'd the Pelf
Which buys your sex a Tyrant o'er itself.
The gen'rous God, who Wit and Gold refines,
And ripens Spirits as he ripens Mines,   290
Kept Dross for Duchesses, the world shall know it,
To you gave Sense, Good-humour, and a Poet.

264. **humour:** inclination.
266. **Tickets:** lottery tickets.   **Codille:** see *Rape of the Lock*, III 92*n*.
267. **Spleen, Vapours:** see *Rape of the Lock*, IV 16*n*., 18*n*.   **Small-pox:** Martha Blount's complexion, like that of many other women in the age, had been marred by small-pox.
269. The Picture of an estimable Woman, with the best kinds of contrarieties. P.
283. **the year:** born in 1690, Miss Blount was 44 when this poem was published in 1735.
285. **Ascendant:** in astrology that sign of the zodiac which rises above the horizon at one's birth is said to be *ascendant* and to have a dominant influence on one's life and fortune.
288. **Tyrant:** i.e., a husband.
289. **gen'rous God:** Phoebus Apollo who, as the god of poetry, presides over "wit," and who, as the sun, was thought to cause gold (and other precious metals) to grow and ripen in the earth.

EPISTLE III

To Allen Lord Bathurst

ARGUMENT

Of the Use *of Riches.   That it is known to few, most falling into one of the extremes,* Avarice *or* Profusion, *v. 1, &c.   The Point discuss'd, whether the invention of* Money *has been more commodious, or pernicious to Mankind, v. 21 to 78.   That Riches, either to the* Avaricious *or the* Prodigal, *cannot afford Happiness, scarcely Necessaries, v. 81 to 108.   That Avarice is an absolute Frenzy, without an End or Purpose, v. 109 &c.   Conjectures about the Motives of Avaricious men, v. 113 to 152.   That the conduct of men, with respect to Riches, can only be accounted for by the* ORDER OF PROVIDENCE, *which works the general Good out of Extremes, and brings all to its great End by perpetual Revolutions, v. 161 to 178.   How a* Miser *acts upon Principles which appear to him reasonable, v. 179.   How a* Prodigal *does the same, v. 199.   The due Medium, and true use of Riches, v. 219.   The Man of Ross, v. 250.   The fate of the* Profuse *and the* Covetous, *in two examples; both miserable in Life and in Death, v. 291, &c.   The Story of Sir* Balaam, *v. 339 to the end.*

WHO shall decide, when Doctors disagree,
    And soundest Casuists doubt, like you and me?
    You hold the word, from Jove to Momus giv'n,
That Man was made the standing jest of Heav'n;
And Gold but sent to keep the fools in play,   5
For some to heap, and some to throw away.
   But I, who think more highly of our kind,
(And surely, Heav'n and I are of a mind)
Opine, that Nature, as in duty bound,
Deep hid the shining mischief under ground: 10
But when by Man's audacious labour won,
Flam'd forth this rival to, its Sire, the Sun,

EPISTLE TO BATHURST: First published in January, 1733, with the title *Of the Use of Riches, an Epistle to the Right Honorable Allen Lord Bathurst*.
   Allen Bathurst (1684–1775), first Earl Bathurst, was a Tory statesman who became Pope's intimate and life-long friend. He had a reputation for loose morals, and in *Sober Advice From Horace*, l. 158, Pope addresses him as "Philosopher and Rake."
  1. Doctors: learned men.
  2. Casuists: experts in matters of conscience and morals.
  3. Momus: god of raillery and ridicule.
  12. Sire: the action of the sun was thought to cause gold and gems to grow and ripen in the earth.

Then careful Heav'n supply'd two sorts of Men,
To squander these, and those to hide agen.
    Like Doctors thus, when much dispute has past,   15
We find our tenets just the same at last.
Both fairly owning, Riches in effect
No grace of Heav'n or token of th' Elect;
Giv'n to the Fool, the Mad, the Vain, the Evil,
To Ward, to Waters, Chartres, and the Devil.   20
What Nature wants, commodious Gold bestows,
'Tis thus we eat the bread another sows:
But how unequal it bestows, observe,
'Tis thus we riot, while who sow it, starve.
What Nature wants (a phrase I much distrust)   25
Extends to Luxury, extends to Lust:
And if we count among the Needs of life
Another's Toil, why not another's Wife?
Useful, I grant, it serves what life requires,
But dreadful too, the dark Assassin hires: 30
Trade it may help, Society extend;
But lures the Pyrate, and corrupts the Friend:
It raises Armies in a Nation's aid,
But bribes a Senate, and the Land's betray'd.
    Oh! that such bulky Bribes as all might see,   35
Still, as of old, incumber'd Villainy!
In vain may Heroes fight, and Patriots rave;
If secret Gold saps on from knave to knave.
Could France or Rome divert our brave designs,
With all their brandies or with all their wines?   40
What could they more than Knights and Squires confound,
Or water all the Quorum ten miles round?
A Statesman's slumbers how this speech would spoil!
"Sir, Spain has sent a thousand jars of oil;
"Huge bales of British cloth blockade the door;   45
"A hundred oxen at your levee roar."
    Poor Avarice one torment more would find;
Nor could Profusion squander all in kind.
Astride his cheese Sir Morgan might we meet,

---

20. Ward: John Ward (d. 1755), an M.P. convicted of forgery and fraud, was expelled from the House of Commons and sentenced to the pillory.   **Waters:** Peter Walter, or Waters (1664–1746), an M.P. and also an unscrupulous money-lender.   **Chartres:** Francis Chartres, or Charteris (1675–1732), a notorious gambler and usurer, was twice convicted of rape.
21. commodious: serviceable.
38. saps: moves by stealthy undermining.
41. confound: intoxicate.
42. water all the Quorum: bribe the Justices of the Peace with free liquor.
46. levee: morning assembly.
49. cheese: i.e., a cargo of cheese.   **Sir Morgan:** a fictitious name, according to Pope.

And Worldly crying coals from street to street,   50
(Whom with a wig so wild, and mien so maz'd,
Pity mistakes for some poor tradesman craz'd).
Had Colepepper's whole wealth been hops and hogs,
Could he himself have sent it to the dogs?
His Grace will game: to White's a Bull be led,   55
With spurning heels and with a butting head.
To White's be carried, as to ancient games,
Fair Coursers, Vases, and alluring Dames.
Shall then Uxorio, if the stakes he sweep,
Bear home six Whores, and make his Lady weep?   60
Or soft Adonis, so perfum'd and fine,
Drive to St. James's a whole herd of swine?
Oh filthy check on all industrious skill,
To spoil the nation's last great trade, Quadrille!
      Once, we confess, beneath the Patriot's cloak,   65
From the crack'd bag the dropping Guinea spoke,
And gingling down the back-stairs, told the crew,
"Old Cato is as great a Rogue as you."
Blest paper-credit! last and best supply!
That lends Corruption lighter wings to fly!   70
Gold imp'd by thee, can compass hardest things,
Can pocket States, can fetch or carry Kings;
A single leaf shall waft an Army o'er,
Or ship off Senates to a distant Shore;

50. Some Misers of great wealth, proprietors of the coal-mines, had enter'd
at this time into an association to keep up coals to an extravagant price, whereby
the poor were reduced almost to starve, till one of them taking the advantage of
underselling the rest, defeated the design. One of these Misers was *worth ten
thousand*, another *seven thousand* a year. P.

53. Colepepper: Sir William Colepepper, Bart. [1668–1740], a person of an
ancient family, and ample fortune, without one other quality of a Gentleman,
who, after ruining himself at the Gaming-table, past the rest of his days in
sitting there to see the ruin of others, preferring to subsist upon borrowing and
begging, rather than to enter into any reputable method of life and refusing
a post in the army which was offer'd him. P.

55. his Grace: any duke.   **White's:** a gambling club.

57. ancient games: the athletic contests of ancient Greece.

59. Uxorio: any doting husband.

61. Adonis: any effeminate fop.

62. St. James's: St. James's Palace, the principal royal residence.

64. quadrille: a fashionable card-game.

65–8. This is a true story, which happened in the reign of William III, to an
unsuspected old Patriot, who coming out of the back-door from having been
closeted by the King, where he had received a large bag of Guineas, the bursting
of the bag discovered his business there. P.

68. Cato: Cato the Elder (234–149 B.C.), the Roman whose name came to
stand for incorruptible patriotism.

69. supply: succour, assistance.

71. imp'd: *to imp* is to engraft new feathers in a bird's wing to improve its
flight.

A leaf, like Sibyl's, scatter to and fro   75
Our fates and fortunes, as the winds shall blow:
Pregnant with thousands flits the Scrap unseen,
And silent sells a King, or buys a Queen.
    Since then, my Lord, on such a World we fall,
What say you? "Say? Why take it, Gold and all."   80
    What Riches give us let us then enquire:
Meat, Fire, and Cloaths. What more? Meat, Cloaths, and Fire.
Is this too little? would you more than live?
Alas! 'tis more than Turner finds they give.
Alas! 'tis more than (all his Visions past)   85
Unhappy Wharton, waking, found at last!
What can they give? to dying Hopkins Heirs;
To Chartres, Vigour; Japhet, Nose and Ears?
Can they, in gems bid pallid Hippia glow,
In Fulvia's buckle ease the throbs below,   90
Or heal, old Narses. thv obscener ail,
With all th' embroid'ry plaister'd at thy tail?
They might (were Harpax not too wise to spend)
Give Harpax self the blessing of a Friend;
Or find some Doctor that would save the life   95
Of wretched Shylock, spite of Shylock's Wife:
But thousands die, without or this or that,
Die, and endow a College, or a Cat:

75. **Sibyl:** the ancient Roman sibyl wrote her prophecies on leaves, which then were placed at the entrance of her cave; those who consulted her had to be careful less the winds dispersed them.

84. **Turner:** One [Richard Turner, d. 1733, a merchant], who, being possessed of three hundred thousand pounds, laid down his Coach, because Interest was reduced from five to four *per cent.* and then put seventy thousand into the Charitable Corporation for better interest: which sum having lost, he took it so much to heart, that he kept his chamber ever after. It is thought he would not have outliv'd it, but that he was heir to another considerable estate, which he daily expected, and that by his course of life he sav'd both cloaths and all other expences. P.

86. **Wharton:** A Nobleman of great qualities, but as unfortunate in the application of them, as if they had been vices and follies. See his Character in the first Epistle [*Ep. to Cobham*, ll. 179–209n.]. P.

87. **Hopkins:** A Citizen [John Hopkins, d. 1732], whose rapacity obtained him the name of *Vultur Hopkins*. He lived worthless, but died *worth three hundred thousand pounds.* . . . P.

88. **Vigour:** sexual vigor (Chartres was a notorious debauchee). **Japhet:** Japhet Crook [1662–1734], alias Sir *Peter Stranger*, was punished with the loss of those parts, for having forged a conveyance of an Estate to himself, upon which he took up several thousand pounds. . . . P.

89. **Hippia:** a name suggestive of hypochondria.

90. **Fulvia:** name of a licentious Roman matron.

91. **Narses:** name of a eunuch (d. 568 A.D.) who served as a private treasurer and general under the emperor Justinian I. Pope may have chosen the name merely for its sound.

93. **Harpax:** Greek for *robber.*

96. **Shylock:** any extortionate money-lender and miser.

To some, indeed, Heav'n grants the happier fate,
T' enrich a Bastard, or a Son they hate.   **100**
    Perhaps you think the Poor might have their part?
Bond damns the Poor, and hates them from his heart:
The grave Sir Gilbert holds it for a rule,
That "every man in want is knave or fool:"
"God cannot love (says Blunt, with tearless eyes)   **105**
"The wretch he starves" — and piously denies:
But the good Bishop, with a meeker air,
Admits, and leaves them, Providence's care.
    Yet, to be just to these poor men of pelf,
Each does but hate his Neighbour as himself: **110**
Damn'd to the Mines, an equal fate betides
The Slave that digs it, and the Slave that hides.
Who suffer thus, mere Charity should own,
Must act on motives pow'rful, tho' unknown:
Some War, some Plague, or Famine they foresee,   **115**
Some Revelation hid from you and me.
Why Shylock wants a meal, the cause is found,
He thinks a Loaf will rise to fifty pound.
What made Directors cheat in South-sea year?
To live on Ven'son when it sold so dear.   **120**
Ask you why Phryne the whole Auction buys?
Phryne foresees a general Excise.
Why she and Sappho raise that monstrous sum?
Alas! they fear a man will cost a plum.
    Wise Peter sees the World's respect for Gold,   **125**
And therefore hopes this Nation may be sold:
Glorious Ambition! Peter, swell thy store,

102. Bond: Denis Bond (d. 1747), an M.P., had been expelled from the House of Commons for swindling. He also engaged in schemes for profiteering off the poor.

103. Sir Gilbert: Sir Gilbert Heathcote (1651–1733), lord mayor of London and one of the founders of the Bank of England. Considered the richest commoner in England, he was famous for his parsimony.

105. Blunt: Sir John Blunt (1665–1733), a venal and unscrupulous director of the South Sea Company (a monopoly organized for trade with South America and the Pacific islands). See ll. 135–52n., below.

107. Bishop: no particular bishop seems implied.

109. pelf: riches.

119. South-sea year: the year 1720, when stock in the South Sea Company was inflated from 128 to 1,000. Wild speculation, and the stock's precipitous decline the same year, ruined thousands.

120. In the extravagance and luxury of the South-sea year, the price of a haunch of Venison was from three to five pounds.   P.

121. Phrynne: name of a celebrated Athenian courtesan who became very rich.   **general excise:** a duty charged on home goods, and in some cases on foreign products.

123. Sappho: any venal and unchaste poetess or lady-wit (but see *Ep. to a Lady*, l. 24n.).

124. plum: the sum of 100,000 pounds.

125. Peter: Peter Walter (see l. 20n.).

And be what Rome's great Didius was before.
    The Crown of Poland, venal twice an age,
To just three millions stinted modest Gage.   **130**
But nobler scenes Maria's dreams unfold,
Hereditary Realms, and worlds of Gold.
Congenial souls! whose life one Av'rice joins,
And one fate buries in th' Asturian Mines.
    Much injur'd Blunt! why bears he Britain's hate?   **135**
A wizard told him in these words our fate:
"At length Corruption, like a gen'ral flood,
"(So long by watchful Ministers withstood)
"Shall deluge all; and Av'rice creeping on,
"Spread like a low-born mist, and blot the Sun;   **140**
"Statesman and Patriot ply alike the stocks,
"Peeress and Butler share alike the Box,
"And Judges job, and Bishops bite the town,
"And mighty Dukes pack cards for half a crown.
"See Britain sunk in lucre's sordid charms,   **145**
"And France reveng'd of ANNE's and EDWARD's arms!"
No mean Court-badge, great Scriv'ner! fir'd thy brain,
Nor lordly Luxury, nor City Gain:
No, 'twas thy righteous end, asham'd to see

128. **Didius:** A Roman Lawyer, so rich as to purchase the Empire when it was set to sale upon the death of Pertinax [in 193 A.D.]. P.   Didius was murdered after a reign of only two months.

129. **Crown of Poland:** the Polish throne, which was elective, had been vacant in 1707 and 1709. The electors were the notoriously corrupt Polish nobility, who could be "bought."

130. **stinted:** fixed as his maximum price.

130–4. Joseph Gage (1678–1753) sent an emissary to Augustus, king of Poland, to offer £ 3,000,000 for his crown, which was declined. He married Lady Mary Herbert (the "Maria" of l. 131), who at one time had determined to marry no one of less rank than a sovereign prince. With the loss of their fortunes, the pair moved to Spain, where Gage obtained from the king the right to work all the gold mines (the "Asturian Mines" of l. 134) of the country.

135–52. In 1720 the South Sea Company, in return for certain concessions and interest payments, took over the national debt. Politicians of both parties, Whig and Tory, speculated in South Sea stock, and favors for the company were obtained by bribing them. Blunt, one of the company's directors (see l. 105n., above), could therefore be said (l. 152) "to buy both sides."

141. **Statesman and Patriot:** terms here used in specialized senses: "statesman" implies a member of the Walpole Government; members of the "Opposition" reserved the title of "Patriot" to themselves.

142. **Box:** in the theater.

143. **job:** use public office for personal profit.   **bite:** deceive.

144. **pack cards:** stack the deck.

146. Great victories over France had been won by the armies of the Duke of Marlborough in the reign (1702–14) of Queen Anne. In 1340 Edward III of England assumed the title of King of France (see *Windsor-Forest*, ll. 303–6n.), and in 1346 he won a great victory over the French at Crécy.

147. **Scriv'ner:** Blunt got his start as a scrivener, or money-lender.

148. **City:** The "City" is that part of old London which serves as the financial center of Britain.

Senates degen'rate, Patriots disagree,   150
And nobly wishing Party-rage to cease,
To buy both sides, and give thy Country peace.
    "All this is madness," cries a sober sage:
But who, my friend, has reason in his rage?
    "The ruling Passion, be it what it will,   155
"The ruling Passion conquers Reason still."
Less mad the wildest whimsey we can frame,
Than ev'n that Passion, if it has no Aim;
For tho' such motives Folly you may call,
The Folly's greater to have none at all.   160
    Hear then the truth: " 'Tis Heav'n each Passion sends,
"And diff'rent men directs to diff'rent ends.
"Extremes in Nature equal good produce,
"Extremes in Man concur to gen'ral use."
Ask we what makes one keep, and one bestow?   165
That Pow'r who bids the Ocean ebb and flow,
Bids seed-time, harvest, equal course maintain,
Thro' reconcil'd extremes of drought and rain,
Builds Life on Death, on Change Duration founds,
And gives th' eternal wheels to know their rounds.   170
    Riches, like insects, when conceal'd they lie,
Wait but for wings, and in their season, fly.
Who sees pale Mammon pine amidst his store,
Sees but a backward steward for the Poor;
This year a Reservoir, to keep and spare,   175
The next a Fountain, spouting thro' his Heir,
In lavish streams to quench a Country's thirst,
And men and dogs shall drink him 'till they burst.
    Old Cotta sham'd his fortune and his birth,
Yet was not Cotta void of wit or worth: 180
What tho' (the use of barb'rous spits forgot)
His kitchen vy'd in coolness with his grot?
His court with nettles, moats with cresses stor'd,
With soups unbought and sallads blest his board.
If Cotta liv'd on pulse, it was no more   185
Than Bramins, Saints, and Sages did before;
To cram the Rich was prodigal expence,
And who would take the Poor from Providence?
Like some lone Chartreux stands the good old Hall,

155–6. The quotation marks here simply reflect the contemporary practice of
signaling significant aphorisms.
161–4. Pope is quoting himself: cf. *Essay on Man*, II 165–6, 205–6.
173. Mammon: the Aramaic word for "riches," often personified as a god of
avarice.
179. Cotta: the implication of the name is uncertain.
185. pulse: peas, beans.
189. Chartreux: the mother house of the Carthusian Order (noted for the
severity of its rule) near Grenoble.

Silence without, and Fasts within the wall;   190
No rafter'd roofs with dance and tabor sound,
No noontide-bell invites the country round;
Tenants with sighs the smoakless tow'rs survey,
And turn th' unwilling steeds another way:
Benighted wanderers, the forest o'er,   195
Curse the sav'd candle, and unop'ning door;
While the gaunt mastiff growling at the gate,
Affrights the beggar whom he longs to eat.
    Not so his Son, he mark'd this oversight,
And then mistook reverse of wrong for right.   200
(For what to shun will no great knowledge need,
But what to follow, is a task indeed.)
What slaughter'd hecatombs, what floods of wine,
Fill the capacious Squire, and deep Divine!
Yet no mean motive this profusion draws,   205
His oxen perish in his country's cause;
'Tis GEORGE and LIBERTY that crowns the cup,
And Zeal for that great House which eats him up.
The woods recede around the naked seat,
The Sylvans groan — no matter — for the Fleet: 210
Next goes his Wool — to clothe our valiant bands,
Last, for his Country's love, he sells his Lands.
To town he comes, completes the nation's hope,
And heads the bold Train-bands, and burns a Pope.
And shall not Britain now reward his toils,   215
Britain, that pays her Patriots with her Spoils?
In vain at Court the Bankrupt pleads his cause,
His thankless Country leaves him to her Laws
    The Sense to value Riches, with the Art
T'enjoy them, and the Virtue to impait,   220
Not meanly, nor ambitiously pursu'd,
Not sunk by sloth, nor rais'd by servitude;
To balance Fortune by a just expence,
Join with Oeconomy, Magnificence;
With Splendor, Charity; with Plenty, Health;   225
Oh teach us, BATHURST! yet unspoil'd by wealth!
That secret rare, between th' extremes to move
Of mad Good-nature, and of mean Self-love.
    To Want or Worth well-weigh'd, be Bounty giv'n,
And ease, or emulate, the care of Heav'n,   230

191. tabor: a small drum.
198. eat: pronounced *ate*.
203. hecatombs: large public sacrifices (usually of at least 100 oxen).
208. House: the House of Hanover.
210. Sylvans: forest people or animals, perhaps woods deities.
211. bands: these are the "Train-bands" (companies of citizen-soldiers) of
l. 214.
214. burns a Pope: in effigy.

Whose measure full o'erflows on human race;
Mend Fortune's fault, and justify her grace.
Wealth in the gross is death, but life diffus'd,
As Poison heals, in just proportion us'd:
In heaps, like Ambergrise, a stink it lies,   235
But well-dispers'd, is Incense to the Skies.
    Who starves by Nobles, or with Nobles eats?
The Wretch that trusts them, and the Rogue that cheats.
Is there a Lord, who knows a cheerful noon
Without a Fiddler, Flatt'rer, or Buffoon?   240
Whose table, Wit, or modest Merit share,
Un-elbow'd by a Gamester, Pimp, or Play'r?
Who copies Your's, or OXFORD's better part,
To ease th' oppress'd, and raise the sinking heart?
Where-e'er he shines, oh Fortune, gild the scene,   245
And Angels guard him in the golden Mean!
There, English Bounty yet a-while may stand,
And Honour linger ere it leaves the land.
    But all our praises why should Lords engross?
Rise, honest Muse! and sing the MAN of ROSS: 250
Pleas'd Vaga echoes thro' her winding bounds,
And rapid Severn hoarse applause resounds.
Who hung with woods yon mountain's sultry brow?
From the dry rock who bade the waters flow?
Not to the skies in useless columns tost,   255
Or in proud falls magnificently lost,
But clear and artless, pouring thro' the plain
Health to the sick, and solace to the swain.
Whose Cause-way parts the vale with shady rows?
Whose Seats the weary Traveller repose?   260
Who taught that heav'n-directed spire to rise?
The MAN of ROSS, each lisping babe replies.
Behold the Market-place with poor o'erspread!
The MAN of ROSS divides the weekly bread:
Behold yon Alms-house, neat, but void of state,   265
Where Age and Want sit smiling at the gate:

235. Ambergrise: a wax-like substance found in sperm whales and valued for the making of perfumes.
243. Oxford: Edward Harley, Earl of Oxford [1689–1741]. The son of Robert, created Earl of Oxford and Earl Mortimer by Queen Anne. This Nobleman died regretted by all men of letters, great numbers of whom had experienc'd his benefits. He left behind him one of the most noble Libraries in Europe. P.
250. Man of Ross: The person here celebrated, who with a small Estate actually performed all these good works, and whose true name was almost lost (partly by the title of the *Man of Ross* given him by way of eminence, and partly by being buried without so much as an inscription) was called Mr. John Kyrle. He died in the year 1724, aged 90, and lies interr'd in the chancel of the church of Ross in Herefordshire. P.
251. Vaga: Latin name for the river Wye, on which the town of Ross is situated. The Severn (next line) is not far distant.

Him portion'd maids, apprentic'd orphans blest,
The young who labour, and the old who rest.
Is any sick? the MAN of Ross relieves,
Prescribes, attends, the med'cine makes, and gives.   270
Is there a variance? enter but his door,
Balk'd are the Courts, and contest is no more.
Despairing Quacks with curses fled the place,
And vile Attornies, now an useless race.
    "Thrice happy man! enabled to pursue   275
"What all so wish, but want the pow'r to do!
"Oh say, what sums that gen'rous hand supply?
"What mines, to swell that boundless charity?"
    Of Debts, and Taxes, Wife and Children clear,
This man possest — five hundred pounds a year.   28€
Blush, Grandeur, blush! proud Courts, withdraw your blaze!
Ye little Stars! hide your diminish'd rays.
"And what? no monument, inscription, stone?
"His race, his form, his name almost unknown?"
Who builds a Church to God, and not to Fame,   285
Will never mark the marble with his Name:
Go, search it there, where to be born and die,
Of rich and poor makes all the history;
Enough, that Virtue fill'd the space between;
Prov'd, by the ends of being, to have been.   290
When Hopkins dies, a thousand lights attend
The wretch, who living sav'd a candle's end:
Should'ring God's altar a vile image stands,
Belies his features, nay extends his hands;
That live-long wig which Gorgon's self might own,   295
Eternal buckle takes in Parian stone.
Behold what blessings Wealth to life can lend!
And see, what comfort it affords our end.
    In the worst inn's worst room, with mat half-hung,

267. **portion'd:** given a dowry or marriage portion.
282. **Stars:** emblems of knightly rank.
287. **there:** The Parish-register.   P.
291. **Hopkins:** see l. 87*n.*, above.
293. The poet ridicules the wretched taste of carving large periwigs on Busto's, of which there are several vile examples in the tombs at Westminster and elsewhere.   P.
295. **Gorgon:** a mythical female, with snakes for hair, whose look turned the beholder to stone.
296. **buckle:** curl.   **Parian stone:** marble from the Greek isle of Paros was much valued for statuary.
299–314. This Lord, yet more famous for his vices than his misfortunes, after having been possess'd of about 50,000 pound a year, and past thro' many of the highest posts in the kingdom, died in the year 1687, in a remote inn in Yorkshire, reduc'd to the utmost misery.   P.   Pope follows contemporary accounts of the death of George Villiers, Duke of Buckingham, though it is now known that the Duke was neither in poverty nor an inn at the time of his death.
299. **mat:** woven straw wall coverings.

The floors of plaister, and the walls of dung,   300
On once a flock-bed, but repair'd with straw,
With tape-ty'd curtains, never meant to draw,
The George and Garter dangling from that bed
Where tawdry yellow strove with dirty red,
Great Villiers lies — alas! how chang'd from him,   305
That life of pleasure, and that soul of whim!
Gallant and gay, in Cliveden's proud alcove,
The bow'r of wanton Shrewsbury and love;
Or just as gay, at Council, in a ring
Of mimick'd Statesmen, and their merry King.   310
No Wit to flatter, left of all his store!
No Fool to laugh at, which he valu'd more.
There, Victor of his health, of fortune, friends,
And fame; this lord of useless thousands ends.

    His Grace's fate sage Cutler could foresee,   315
And well (he thought) advis'd him, "Live like me."
As well his Grace reply'd, "Like you, Sir John?
"That I can do, when all I have is gone."
Resolve me, Reason, which of these is worse,
Want with a full, or with an empty purse?   320
Thy life more wretched, Cutler, was confess'd,
Arise, and tell me, was thy death more bless'd?
Cutler saw tenants break, and houses fall,
For very want; he could not build a wall.
His only daughter in a stranger's pow'r,   325
For very want; he could not pay a dow'r.
A few grey hairs his rev'rend temples crown'd,
'Twas very want that sold them for two pound.
What ev'n deny'd a cordial at his end,
Banish'd the doctor, and expell'd the friend?   330
What but a want, which you perhaps think mad,
Yet numbers feel, the want of what he had.
Cutler and Brutus, dying both exclaim,
"Virtue! and Wealth! what are ye but a name!"
    Say, for such worth are other worlds prepar'd?   335
Or are they both, in this their own reward?

301. **flock-bed:** a bed stuffed with scraps of cloth rather than feathers.
303. **George:** the image of St. George which forms part of the insignia of the Order of the Garter.
307. **Cliveden:** A delightful palace, on the banks of the Thames, built by the Duke of Buckingham. P.
308. **Shrewsbury:** The Countess of Shrewsbury, a woman abandon'd to gallantries. The Earl her husband was kill'd by the Duke of Buckingham in a duel; and it has been said, that during the combat she held the Duke's horses in the habit of a page. P.
310. **merry King:** Charles II.
315. **Cutler:** Sir John Cutler (1608–1693), a London merchant noted for his miserliness.
329. **cordial:** a heart stimulant.

A knotty point! to which we now proceed.
But you are tir'd — I'll tell a tale. Agreed.
    Where London's column, pointing at the skies
Like a tall bully, lifts the head, and lyes;   340
There dwelt a Citizen of sober fame,
A plain good man, and Balaam was his name;
Religious, punctual, frugal, and so forth;
His word would pass for more than he was worth.
One solid dish his week-day meal affords,   345
An added pudding solemniz'd the Lord's:
Constant at Church, and Change; his gains were sure,
His givings rare, save farthings to the poor.
    The Dev'l was piqu'd such saintship to behold,
And long'd to tempt him like good Job of old: 350
But Satan now is wiser than of yore,
And tempts by making rich, not making poor.
    Rouz'd by the Prince of Air, the whirlwinds sweep
The surge, and plunge his Father in the deep;
Then full against his Cornish lands they roar,   355
And two rich ship-wrecks bless the lucky shore.
    Sir Balaam now, he lives like other folks,
He takes his chirping pint, and cracks his jokes:
"Live like yourself," was soon my Lady's word;
And lo! two puddings smoak'd upon the board.   360
    Asleep and naked as an Indian lay,
An honest factor stole a Gem away:
He pledg'd it to the knight; the knight had wit,
So kept the Diamond, and the rogue was bit.
Some scruple rose, but thus he eas'd his thought,   365
"I'll now give six-pence where I gave a groat,
"Where once I went to church, I'll now go twice —
"And am so clear too of all other vice."
    The Tempter saw his time; the work he ply'd;
Stocks and Subscriptions pour on ev'ry side,   370

---

    339. London's column: The Monument, built in memory of the fire of London, with a inscription, importing that city to have been burnt by the Papists. P.
    342. Balaam: Biblical type of a man who uses religion for gain.
    347. Change: the Royal Exchange, where merchants met to transact business.
    353. Prince of Air: the air was traditionally considered the haunt of devils (see Ephesians 2:2).
    355. Cornish lands: The author has placed the scene of these shipwrecks in Cornwall, not only from their frequency on that coast, but from the inhumanity of the inhabitants to those to whom that misfortune arrives: When a ship happens to be stranded there, they have been known to bore holes in it, to prevent its getting off; to plunder, and sometimes even to massacre the people: Nor has the Parliament of England been yet able wholly to suppress these barbarities. P.
    358. chirping: merry.
    362. factor: mercantile agent.
    364. bit: cheated.
    370. Subscriptions: shares in commercial ventures.

'Till all the Dæmon makes his full descent,
In one abundant show'r of Cent. per Cent.,
Sinks deep within him, and possesses whole,
Then dubs Director, and secures his soul.

    Behold Sir Balaam, now a man of spirit,   375
Ascribes his gettings to his parts and merit,
What late he call'd a Blessing, now was Wit,
And God's good Providence, a lucky Hit,
Things change their titles, as our manners turn:
His Compting-house employ'd the Sunday-morn;   380
Seldom at Church ('twas such a busy life)
But duly sent his family and wife.
There (so the Dev'l ordain'd) one Christmas-tide
My good old Lady catch'd a cold, and dy'd.

    A Nymph of Quality admires our Knight;   385
He marries, bows at Court, and grows polite:
Leaves the dull Cits, and joins (to please the fair)
The well-bred cuckolds in St. James's air:
First, for his Son a gay Commission buys,
Who drinks, whores, fights, and in a duel dies: 390
His daughter flaunts a Viscount's tawdry wife;
She bears a Coronet and P–x for life.
In Britain's Senate he a seat obtains,
And one more Pensioner St. Stephen gains.
My Lady falls to play; so bad her chance,   395
He must repair it; takes a bribe from France;
The House impeach him; Coningsby harangues;
The Court forsake him, and Sir Balaam hangs:
Wife, son, and daughter, Satan, are thy own,
His wealth, yet dearer, forfeit to the Crown: 400
The Devil and the King divide the prize,
And sad Sir Balaam curses God and dies.

---

387. Cits: trading-class citizens who inhabited the "City," London's financial center.

388. St. James's: here the fashionable court world in general.

392. P–x: the great pox, or syphilis.

394. St. Stephen: St. Stephen's Chapel, Westminster, where the House of Commons met. Pope suggests that Sir Balaam has sold out (become a pensioner of the government).

397. Coningsby: Thomas, Earl Coningsby (1659–1729), an ardent supporter of William III and of the Hanovers. Accused by his political opponents of embezzlement and other offences, he later served on a committee appointed to investigate the Treaty of Utrecht and moved the impeachment of Robert Harley, Pope's friend who had been prime minister under Queen Anne.

EPISTLE IV
To Richard Boyle, Earl of Burlington

ARGUMENT

Of the Use *of* Riches. *The Vanity of Expence in People of Wealth and Quality. The abuse of the word* Taste, v. 13. *That the first principle and foundation, in this as in every thing else, is* Good Sense, v. 40. *The chief proof of it is to* follow Nature, *even in works of mere Luxury and Elegance. Instanced in* Architecture *and* Gardening, *where all must be adapted to the* Genius *and* Use *of the* Place, *and the Beauties not forced into it, but resulting from it,* v. 50. *How men are disappointed in their most expensive undertakings, for want of this true Foundation, without which nothing can please long, if at all; and the best* Examples *and* Rules *will but be perverted into something* burdensome *or* ridiculous, v. 65, &c. *to 98. A description of the* false Taste *of* Magnificence; *the first grand Error of which is to imagine that* Greatness *consists in the* Size *and* Dimension, *instead of the* Proportion *and* Harmony *of the* whole, v. 99, *and the second, either in joining together* Parts *incoherent, or too* minutely *resembling, or in the* Repetition *of the* same *too* frequently, v. 115, &c. *A word or two of false Taste in* Books, *in* Music, *in* Painting, *even in* Preaching *and* Prayer, *and lastly in* Entertainments, v. 133, &c. *Yet Providence is justified in giving* Wealth *to be squandered in this manner, since it is dispersed to the* Poor *and* Laborious *part of mankind,* v. 169. [*Recurring to what is laid down in the first book,* Ep. ii, *and in the Epistle preceding this,* v. 161, &c.] *What are the* proper Objects *of* Magnificence, *and a proper field for the* Expence *of* Great Men, v. 177, &c., *and finally, the* Great *and* Public Works *which become a* Prince, v. 191, *to the end.*

EPISTLE TO BURLINGTON: The full title of the first edition (December, 1731) was *An Epistle To The Right Honourable Richard Earl of Burlington. Occasion'd by his Publishing Palladio's Designs of the Baths, Arches, Theatres, &c. of Ancient Rome.* The half-title for this edition was *Of Taste, An Epistle To the Right Honourable Richard Earl of Burlington,* but in the second edition this became *Of False Taste, An Epistle* etc. When Pope collected his four Epistles together in 1735, the half-title became *Of the Use of Riches,* suggesting the poem's alliance with the *Epistle to Bathurst.*

Richard Boyle, third Earl of Burlington (1695–1753), was a friend and patron to many of the artists and writers of his time, and widely celebrated for his architectural tastes and enterprises (his beautiful edition of the works of the Italian architect Andrea Palladio, 1518–80, was published in 1730). Pope was himself widely esteemed in the period for his knowledge and skill in architecture and gardening, and he has been considered particularly influential in the movement which turned English gardens away from the highly formal and artificial mode and toward the more "natural" landscape garden.

'TIS strange, the Miser should his Cares employ,
　　To gain those Riches he can ne'er enjoy:
　　Is it less strange, the Prodigal should waste
His wealth, to purchase what he ne'er can taste?
Not for himself he sees, or hears, or eats;　　　　　　5
Artists must chuse his Pictures, Music, Meats:
He buys for Topham, Drawings and Designs,
For Pembroke Statues, dirty Gods, and Coins;
Rare monkish Manuscripts for Hearne alone,
And Books for Mead, and Butterflies for Sloane.　　10
Think we all these are for himself? no more
Than his fine Wife, alas! or finer Whore.
　　For what has Virro painted, built, and planted?
Only to show, how many Tastes he wanted.
What brought Sir Visto's ill got wealth to waste?　　15
Some Dæmon whisper'd, "Visto! have a Taste."
Heav'n visits with a Taste the wealthy fool,
And needs no Rod but Ripley with a Rule.
See! sportive fate, to punish aukward pride,
Bids Bubo build, and sends him such a Guide:　　20
A standing sermon, at each year's expense,
That never Coxcomb reach'd Magnificence!
　　You show us, Rome was glorious, not profuse,
And pompous buildings once were things of Use.
Yet shall (my Lord) your just, your noble rules　　25
Fill half the land with Imitating Fools;
Who random drawings from your sheets shall take,
And of one beauty many blunders make;

6. Artists: connoisseurs.

7. Topham: A Gentleman famous for a judicious collection of Drawings.　P.
Richard Topham (d. 1735) left his fine collection of drawings to the Eton College Library.

8. Pembroke: Thomas Herbert, eighth Earl of Pembroke (1656–1753), a Whig statesman, an enthusiastic collector, and a president of the Royal Society.
Coins: pronounced to rhyme with *lines.*

9. Hearne: Thomas Hearne (1678–1735), an eminent antiquary and collector of manuscripts.

10. Mead . . . Sloane: Two eminent Physicians; the one [Richard Mead, 1673–1754] had an excellent Library, the other [Sir Hans Sloane, 1660–1753] the finest collection in Europe of natural curiosities; both men of great learning and humanity.　P.

13. Virro: name of a rich but despicable patron in Juvenal's *Satire V.*

15. Visto: in gardening, a *vista* is a view through an avenue of trees.

16. Dæmon: spirit or genius.

18. Ripley: This man [Thomas Ripley, d. 1758] was a carpenter, employ'd by a first Minister [Sir Robert Walpole], who rais'd him to an Architect, without any genius in the art; and after some wretched proofs of his insufficiency in public Buildings, made him Comptroller of the Board of works.　P.

20. Bubo: Latin for *owl,* considered an emblem of grave stupidity in Pope's time.

23. You: The Earl of Burlington was then publishing the Designs of Inigo Jones, and the Antiquities of Rome by Palladio.　P.

Load some vain Church with old Theatric state,
Turn Arcs of triumph to a Garden-gate;   30
Reverse your Ornaments, and hang them all
On some patch'd dog-hole ek'd with ends of wall,
Then clap four slices of Pilaster on't,
That, lac'd with bits of rustic, makes a Front.
Or call the winds thro' long Arcades to roar,   35
Proud to catch cold at a Venetian door;
Conscious they act a true Palladian part,
And if they starve, they starve by rules of art.
    Oft have you hinted to your brother Peer,
A certain truth, which many buy too dear: 40
Something there is more needful than Expence,
And something previous ev'n to Taste — 'tis Sense:
Good Sense, which only is the gift of Heav'n,
And tho' no science, fairly worth the sev'n:
A Light, which in yourself you must perceive;   45
Jones and Le Nôtre have it not to give.
    To build, to plant, whatever you intend,
To rear the Column, or the Arch to bend,
To swell the Terras, or to sink the Grot;
In all, let Nature never be forgot.   50
But treat the Goddess like a modest fair,
Nor over-dress, nor leave her wholly bare;
Let not each beauty ev'ry where be spy'd,
Where half the skill is decently to hide.
He gains all points, who pleasingly confounds,   55
Surprizes, varies, and conceals the Bounds.
    Consult the Genius of the Place in all;
That tells the Waters or to rise, or fall,
Or helps th' ambitious Hill the heav'n to scale,
Or scoops in circling theatres the Vale,   60
Calls in the Country, catches opening glades,
Joins willing woods, and varies shades from shades,
Now breaks or now directs, th' intending Lines;

32. **dog-hole:** any vile dwelling.
33. **Pilaster:** a square or rectangular column engaged in a wall from which it projects with its capital and base.
34. **rustic:** artificially roughened surface.
36. **Venetian door:** A Door or Window, so called, from being much practised at Venice, by Palladio and others.   P.
37. **Palladian:** in accord with the strong classical restraint that is characteristic of Palladian architecture.
44. **sev'n:** the seven liberal arts and sciences of the medieval *Trivium* (grammar, logic, rhetoric) and *Quadrivium* (arithmetic, geometry, music, astronomy).
46. *Inigo Jones* [1573–1652], the celebrated Architect, and M. [André] *Le Nôtre* [1613–1700], the designer of the best Gardens of France.   P.
57. **Genius of the Place:** a recollection of the Roman *genius loci*, or guardian spirit of a particular locale.
63. **intending Lines:** those which guide the eye.

Paints as you plant, and, as you work, designs.
    Still follow Sense, of ev'ry Art the Soul,   65
Parts answ'ring parts shall slide into a whole,
Spontaneous beauties all around advance,
Start ev'n from Difficulty, strike from Chance;
Nature shall join you, Time shall make it grow
A Work to wonder at — perhaps a STOW.   70
    Without it, proud Versailles! thy glory falls;
And Nero's Terraces desert their walls:
The vast Parterres a thousand hands shall make,
Lo! COBHAM comes and floats them with a Lake:
Or cut wide views thro' Mountains to the Plain,   75
You'll wish your hill or shelter'd seat again.
Ev'n in an ornament its place remark,
Nor in an Hermitage set Dr. Clarke.
    Behold Villario's ten-years toil compleat;
His Quincunx darkens, his Espaliers meet,   80
The Wood supports the Plain, the parts unite,
And strength of Shade contends with strength of Light;
A waving Glow his bloomy beds display,
Blushing in bright diversities of day,
With silver-quiv'ring rills mæander'd o'er —   85
Enjoy them, you! Villario can no more;
Tir'd of the scene Parterres and Fountains yield,
He finds at last he better likes a Field.
    Thro' his young Woods how pleas'd Sabinus stray'd,
Or sat delighted in the thick'ning shade,   90
With annual joy the red'ning shoots to greet,
Or see the stretching branches long to meet!

---

    70. Stow: The seat and gardens of the Lord Viscount Cobham in Buckingham-shire.   P.   For Cobham, see first note to *Ep. to Cobham.*

    71. Versailles: the famous gardens at Versailles were laid out by Le Nôtre (l. 46).

    72. Nero's Terraces: Nero's Golden House was said to be large enough to contain fields, woods and vineyards.

    73. Parterres: a level space in a garden occupied by ornamental flower-beds.

    74. floats: floods.

    75–6. This was done in Hertfordshire, by a wealthy citizen, at the expence of above 5000 £. by which means (merely to overlook a dead plain) he let in the north-wind upon his house and parterre, which were before adorned and defended by beautiful woods.   P.

    78. Dr. S. Clarke's busto placed by the Queen in the Hermitage, while the Dr. duely frequented the Court.   P.   Samuel Clarke (1675–1729), English philosopher and divine, aroused much controversy by his unorthodox beliefs. Busts of Locke, Newton, Clarke and other English philosophers were placed by Queen Caroline in the Hermitage, an ornamental structure in Richmond Park.

    79. Villario: an adaptation of *villa.*

    80. Quincunx: five trees planted in a square (one at each corner, another in the center).   **Espaliers:** fruit trees trained upon a framework of stakes.

    89. Sabinus: the name suggests dedication to a simple country life.

His Son's fine Taste an op'ner Vista loves,
Foe to the Dryads of his Father's groves,
One boundless Green, or flourish'd Carpet views,   95
With all the mournful family of Yews;
The thriving plants ignoble broomsticks made,
Now sweep those Alleys they were born to shade.
   At Timon's Villa let us pass a day,
Where all cry out, "What sums are thrown away!"   100
So proud, so grand, of that stupendous air,
Soft and Agreeable come never there.
Greatness, with Timon, dwells in such a draught
As brings all Brobdignag before your thought.
To compass this, his building is a Town,   105
His pond an Ocean, his parterre a Down:
Who but must laugh, the Master when he sees,
A puny insect, shiv'ring at a breeze!
Lo, what huge heaps of littleness around!
The whole, a labour'd Quarry above ground.   110
Two Cupids squirt before: a Lake behind
Improves the keenness of the Northern wind.
His Gardens next your admiration call,
On ev'ry side you look, behold the Wall!
No pleasing Intricacies intervene,   115
No artful wildness to perplex the scene;
Grove nods at grove, each Alley has a brother,
And half the platform just reflects the other.
The suff'ring eye inverted Nature sees,
Trees cut to Statues, Statues thick as trees,   120
With here a Fountain, never to be play'd,
And there a Summer-house, that knows no shade;
Here Amphitrite sails thro' myrtle bow'rs;
There Gladiators fight, or die, in flow'rs;

94. **Dryads:** wood nymphs.
95. The two extremes in parterres, which are equally faulty; a *boundless Green,* large and naked as a field, or a *flourished Carpet,* where the greatness and the nobleness of the piece is lessened by being divided into too many parts, with scroll'd works and beds, of which the examples are frequent. P.
96. Touches upon the ill taste of those who are so fond of Ever-greens (particularly Yews, which are the most tonsile) as to destroy the nobler Forest-trees, to make way for such little ornaments as Pyramids of dark-green, continually repeated, not unlike a Funeral procession. P.
99. **Timon's Villa:** This description is intended to comprize the principles of a false Taste of Magnificence, and to exemplify what was said before, that nothing but Good Sense can attain it. P.
104. **Brobdignag:** book two of *Gulliver's Travels* is set in Brobdingnag, where the people and all else are on an enormous scale.
106. **Down:** an open tract of upland.
118. **platform:** a walk or terrace on top of a wall.
123. **Amphitrite:** a sea nymph, wife of Poseidon.
124. The two Statues of the *Gladiator pugnans* and *Gladiator moriens.* P.

Un-water'd see the drooping sea-horse mourn,   125
And swallows roost in Nilus' dusty Urn.
　My Lord advances with majestic mien,
Smit with the mighty pleasure, to be seen:
But soft — by regular approach — not yet —
First thro' the length of yon hot Terrace sweat,   13⁰
And when up ten steep slopes you've dragg'd your thighs,
Just at his Study-door he'll bless your eyes.
His Study! with what Authors is it stor'd?
In Books, not Authors, curious is my Lord;
To all their dated Backs he turns you round,   135
These Aldus printed, those Du Suëil has bound.
Lo some are Vellom, and the rest as good
For all his Lordship knows, but they are Wood.
For Locke or Milton 'tis in vain to look,
These shelves admit not any modern book.   ' 140
　And now the Chapel's silver bell you hear,
That summons you to all the Pride of Pray'r:
Light quirks of Musick, broken and uneven,
Make the soul dance upon a Jig to Heaven.
On painted Cielings you devoutly stare,   145
Where sprawl the Saints of Verrio or Laguerre,
On gilded clouds in fair expansion lie,
And bring all Paradise before your eye.
To rest, the Cushion and soft Dean invite,
Who never mentions Hell to ears polite.   150
　But hark! the chiming Clocks to dinner call;
A hundred footsteps scrape the marble Hall:

126. Nilus: personified god of the Nile. Urns are traditional emblems of river gods.

130. The *Approaches* and *Communications* of house with garden, or of one part with another, ill judged and inconvenient.　P.

133. The false Taste in Books; a satyr on the vanity in collecting them, more frequent in men of Fortune than the study to understand them. Many delight chiefly in the elegance of the print, or of the binding; some have carried it so far, as to cause the upper shelves to be filled with painted books of wood; others pique themselves so much upon books in a language they do not understand as to exclude the most useful in one they do.　P.

136. Aldus: Aldus Manutius (1450–1515), celebrated Venetian printer and publisher of classic texts.　**Du Suëil:** Augustin Deseuil (1673–1746), a noted Parisian bookbinder.

143. The false Taste in *Music,* improper to the subjects, as of light airs in Churches, often practised by the organists, &c.　P.

145. — And in *Painting* (from which even Italy is not free) of naked figures in Churches, &c. which has obliged some Popes to put draperies on some of those of the best masters.　P.

146. Verrio (Antonio) [1639–1707] painted many ceilings, &c. at Windsor, Hampton-court, &c. and [Louis] Laguerre [1663–1721] at Blenheim-castle, and other places.　P.

150. This is a fact; a reverend Dean preaching at Court, threatned the sinner with punishment in "a place which he thought it not decent to name in so polite an assembly."　P.

The rich Buffet well-colour'd Serpents grace,
And gaping Tritons spew to wash your face.
Is this a dinner? this a Genial room?   155
No, 'tis a Temple, and a Hecatomb.
A solemn Sacrifice, perform'd in state,
You drink by measure, and to minutes eat.
So quick retires each flying course, you'd swear
Sancho's dread Doctor and his Wand were there.   160
Between each Act the trembling salvers ring,
From soup to sweet-wine, and God bless the King.
In plenty starving, tantaliz'd in state,
And complaisantly help'd to all I hate,
Treated, caress'd, and tir'd, I take my leave,   165
Sick of his civil Pride from Morn to Eve;
I curse such lavish cost, and little skill,
And swear no Day was ever past so ill.
　　Yet hence the Poor are cloath'd, the Hungry fed;
Health to himself, and to his Infants bread   170
The Lab'rer bears: What his hard Heart denies,
His charitable Vanity supplies.
　　Another age shall see the golden Ear
Imbrown the Slope, and nod on the Parterre,
Deep Harvests bury all his pride has plann'd,   175
And laughing Ceres re-assume the land.
　　Who then shall grace, or who improve the Soil?
Who plants like BATHURST, or who builds like BOYLE.
'Tis Use alone that sanctifies Expence,
And Splendor borrows all her rays from Sense.   180
　　His Father's Acres who enjoys in peace,
Or makes his Neighbours glad, if he encrease;
Whose chearful Tenants bless their yearly toil,
Yet to their Lord owe more than to the soil;
Whose ample Lawns are not asham'd to feed   185
The milky heifer and deserving steed;

153. Taxes the incongruity of *Ornaments* (tho' sometimes practised by the
ancients) where an open mouth ejects the water into a fountain, or where the
shocking images of serpents, &c. are introduced in Grottos or Buffets.   P.
155. The proud Festivals of some men are here set forth to ridicule, where
pride destroys the ease, and formal regularity all the pleasurable enjoyment of
the entertainment.   P.
156. Hecatomb: a great public sacrifice (usually of at least 100 oxen).
160. See Don Quixote, chap. xlvii.   P.   The episode occurs in Part Two,
where a physician orders each dish set before Sancho to be taken away before
he can partake of it.
161. salvers: trays.
169. The Moral of the whole, where Providence is justified in giving Wealth
to those who squander it in this manner. A bad Taste employs more hands and
diffuses Expence more than a good one. . . .   P.
176. Ceres: Roman goddess of agriculture.
178. Bathurst: see first note to *Ep. to Bathurst.*   **Boyle:** the Earl of Burlington.

Whose rising Forests, not for pride or show,
But future Buildings, future Navies grow:
Let his plantations stretch from down to down,
First shade a Country, and then raise a Town.   190
    You too proceed! make falling Arts your care,
Erect new wonders, and the old repair,
Jones and Palladio to themselves restore,
And be whate'er Vitruvius was before:
Till Kings call forth th' Idea's of your mind,   195
Proud to accomplish what such hands design'd,
Bid Harbors open, public Ways extend,
Bid Temples, worthier of the God, ascend;
Bid the broad Arch the dang'rous Flood contain,
The Mole projected break the roaring Main;   200
Back to his bounds their subject Sea command,
And roll obedient Rivers thro' the Land;
These Honours, Peace to happy Britain brings,
These are Imperial Works, and worthy Kings.

190. **Country:** a tract or region owned by one person.
191. **You:** Boyle.
193. **Jones and Palladio:** see l. 23*n*.
194. **Vitruvius:** Marcus Vitruvius Pollio (c. 50–26 B.C.), celebrated Roman writer on architecture.
195. The poet after having touched upon the proper objects of Magnificence and Expence, in the private works of great men, comes to those great and public works which become a Prince . . . . P.
200. **Mole:** a massive pier or breakwater.

AN

EPISTLE FROM MR. POPE,
TO DR. ARBUTHNOT

Neque sermonibus Vulgi *dederis te, nec in Præmis humanis spem posueris rerum tuarum: suis te oportet illecebris* ipsa Virtus *trahat ad verum decus. Quid de te alii loquantur, ipsi videant, sed loquentur tamen.*

TULLY

ADVERTISEMENT

This Paper is a Sort of Bill of Complaint, begun many years since, and drawn up by snatches, as the several Occasions offer'd. I had no thoughts of publishing it, till it pleas'd some Persons of Rank and Fortune [the Authors of Verses to the Imitator of Horace, *and of an* Epistle to a Doctor of Divinity from a Nobleman at Hampton Court,] *to attack in a very extraordinary manner, not only my Writings (of which being publick the Publick judge) but my* Person, Morals, *and* Family, *whereof to those who know me not, a truer Information may be requisite. Being divided between the Necessity to say something of Myself, and my own Laziness to undertake so awkward a Task, I thought it the shortest way to put the last hand to this Epistle. If it have any thing pleasing, it will be That by which I am most desirous to please, the* Truth *and the* Sentiment; *and if any thing offensive, it will be only to those I am least sorry to offend, the* Vicious *or the Ungenerous.*

Many will know their own Pictures in it, there being not a Circumstance but what is true; but I have, for the most part spar'd their Names, and they may escape being laugh'd at, if they please.

EPISTLE TO DR. ARBUTHNOT: Dr. John Arbuthnot (1667–1735) was a physician to Queen Anne (cf. l. 417), a collaborator with Pope and Swift in the satiric writings which grew out of their association in the Scriblerus Club, and one of Pope's oldest and dearest friends. The poem Pope addressed to him was first published in January, 1735.

The "Persons of Rank and Fortune" whose attacks on Pope are said, in l. 4 of the poem's "Advertisement," to have prompted the publication of the *Epistle to Dr. Arbuthnot* were Lady Mary Wortley Montagu (1689–1762), a celebrated

197

*I would have some of them know, it was owing to the Request of the
learned and candid Friend to whom it is inscribed, that I make not as
free use of theirs as they have done of mine. However I shall have this
Advantage, and Honour, on my side, that whereas by their proceeding,
any Abuse may be directed at any man, no Injury can possibly be done
by mine, since a Nameless Character can never be found out, but by its
Truth and Likeness.*

SHUT, shut the door, good *John!* fatigu'd I said,
    Tye up the knocker, say I'm sick, I'm dead,
    The Dog-star rages! nay 'tis past a doubt,
All *Bedlam,* or *Parnassus,* is let out:
Fire in each eye, and Papers in each hand,   5
They rave, recite, and madden round the land.
    What Walls can guard me, or what Shades can hide?
They pierce my Thickets, thro' my Grot they glide,
By land, by water, they renew the charge,
They stop the Chariot, and they board the Barge.   10
No place is sacred, not the Church is free,
Ev'n *Sunday* shines no *Sabbath-day* to me:
Then from the *Mint* walks forth the Man of Ryme,

---

female wit and letter writer who had at one time infatuated Pope, and Lord
John Hervey (1696–1743), an effeminate, profligate courtier who became Queen
Caroline's confidant and to whom the portrait of Sporus (ll. 305–33, below)
chiefly applies. Considering themselves provoked by certain allusive couplets
Pope had written, Lady Mary and Lord Hervey joined to produce a scurrilous,
full-scale attack on the poet entitled *Verses addressed to the Imitator of Horace,*
published in March, 1733. A few months later Hervey quite on his own brought
out an equally abusive *Epistle to a Doctor of Divinity from a Nobleman at
Hampton Court.* Henceforth the two collaborators were to appear often in
Pope's verse, Lord Hervey usually under the title of *Lord Fanny,* Lady Mary at
times in her own proper name, but most often as *Sappho* (see *Ep. to a Lady,* l.
24n.).

The epigraph to the poem is from Cicero, *De Re Publica,* VI xxiii: "Do not
attend to the common talk of the mob, nor place your hope in human rewards
for your deeds; it is proper that virtue itself, by her own charms, draw you on
to true glory. Let others talk about you as they choose, for they will talk in
any case."

1. **John:** John Serle, Pope's servant and gardener.

3. **Dog-star:** Sirius, a star associated with the maddening heat (cf. l. 6) of
August, the month also when poetry recitals were held in Rome.

4. **Bedlam:** the Hospital of St. Mary of Bethlehem, London's main asylum
for the insane.   **Parnassus:** the mountain in Greece sacred to Apollo and the
muses.

8. **Grot:** beneath the London road which bisected his property at Twickenham, Pope constructed a subterranean passage and grotto which offered a vista
of his garden at one end and of the Thames at the other.

10. **Barge:** Pope sometimes journeyed by water between Twickenham and
London.

12–13. Debtors, who could not be arrested anywhere on Sundays, could find
refuge on other days in the sanctuary known as the Mint, in Southwark.

Happy! to catch me, just at Dinner-time.
   Is there a Parson, much be-mus'd in Beer,   15
A maudlin Poetess, a ryming Peer,
A Clerk, foredoom'd his Father's soul to cross,
Who pens a Stanza when he should *engross?*
Is there, who lock'd from Ink and Paper, scrawls
With desp'rate Charcoal round his darken'd walls?   20
All fly to *Twit'nam,* and in humble strain
Apply to me, to keep them mad or vain.
Arthur, whose giddy Son neglects the Laws,
Imputes to me and my damn'd works the cause:
Poor *Cornus* sees his frantic Wife elope,   25
And curses Wit, and Poetry, and *Pope.*
   Friend to my Life, (which did not you prolong,
The World had wanted many an idle Song)
What *Drop* or *Nostrum* can this Plague remove?
Or which must end me, a Fool's Wrath or Love?   30
A dire Dilemma! either way I'm sped,
If Foes, they write, if Friends, they read me dead.
Seiz'd and ty'd down to judge, how wretched I!
Who can't be silent, and who will not lye;
To laugh, were want of Goodness and of Grace,   35
And to be grave, exceeds all Pow'r of Face.
I sit with sad Civility, I read
With honest anguish, and an aking head;
And drop at last, but in unwilling ears,
This saving counsel, "Keep your Piece nine years."   40
   Nine years! cries he, who high in *Drury-lane*
Lull'd by soft Zephyrs thro' the broken Pane,
Rymes e're he wakes, and prints before *Term* ends,
Oblig'd by hunger and Request of friends:
"The Piece you think is incorrect: why take it,   45
"I'm all submission, what you'd have it, make it."
   Three things another's modest wishes bound,
My Friendship, and a Prologue, and ten Pound.

---

15. The words "Parson" and "be-mus'd in" suggest the Rev. Laurence Eusden (1688–1730), a minor poet and clergyman; he was named poet laureate in 1718, and became famous for his drunkenness.
18. engross: to write out in legal form.
23. Arthur: Arthur Moore (1666–1730), an M.P. and man of business. His "giddy Son" was James Moore Smythe (1702–34), who used some of Pope's verses without permission in a play and later joined in attacks on Pope.
25. Cornus: from Latin *cornu,* a horn (emblem of a cuckold).
29. Drop: a medicine taken in drops.   **Nostrum:** any patent medicine or remedy.
40. The same advice is given by Horace, *Ars Poetica,* ll. 386–9.
41. high: i.e., in a garret.   **Drury-lane:** a street associated not only with the theater, but with harlots and riffraff.
43. Term: legal terms during which courts were in session coincided roughly with publishing seasons.

 Pitholeon sends to me: "You know his Grace,
"I want a Patron; ask him for a Place."   50
Pitholeon libell'd me — "but here's a Letter
"Informs you Sir, 'twas when he knew no better.
"Dare you refuse him? *Curl* invites to dine,
"He'll write a *Journal,* or he'll turn *Divine.*"
 Bless me! a Packet. — " 'Tis a stranger sues,   55
"A Virgin Tragedy, an Orphan Muse."
If I dislike it, "Furies, death and rage!"
If I approve, "Commend it to the Stage."
There (thank my Stars) my whole Commission ends,
The Play'rs and I are, luckily, no friends.   60
Fir'd that the House reject him, " 'Sdeath I'll print it
"And shame the Fools — your Int'rest, Sir, with *Lintot.*"
Lintot, dull rogue! will think your price too much.
"Not Sir, if you revise it, and retouch."
All my demurrs but double his attacks,   65
At last he whispers "Do, and we go snacks."
Glad of a quarrel, strait I clap the door,
Sir, let me see your works and you no more.
 'Tis sung, when *Midas'* Ears began to spring,
(*Midas,* a sacred Person and a King)   70
His very Minister who spy'd them first,
(Some say his Queen) was forc'd to speak, or burst.
And is not mine, my Friend, a sorer case,
When ev'ry Coxcomb perks them in my face?
"Good friend forbear! you deal in dang'rous things, 75
"I'd never name Queens, Ministers, or Kings;
"Keep close to Ears, and those let Asses prick,
" 'Tis nothing" — Nothing? if they bite and kick?
Out with it, *Dunciad!* let the secret pass,
That Secret to each Fool, that he's an Ass: 80
The truth once told, (and wherefore shou'd we lie?)
The Queen of *Midas* slept, and so may I.

 49. Pitholeon: The name taken from a foolish Poet at Rhodes, who pretended much to *Greek.* . . . P.   **his Grace:** form of address proper to a duke.
 50. Place: some sinecure or other.
 53. Curl: Edmund Curll (1675–1747), an industrious but shameless and unscrupulous bookseller and publisher; he specialized in disreputable literature of all kinds, and frequently gave unauthorized publication to personal and private papers and correspondence.
 54. write a Journal: i.e., he will attack Pope in a newspaper.
 61. House: playhouse.
 62. Lintot: Bernard Lintot (1675–1736), publisher of much of Pope's early work. Lintot and Curll figure again in *Dunciad,* II 31–120.
 66. go snacks: go shares.
 69. Midas: chosen to judge a musical contest between Pan and Apollo, King Midas of Phrygia decided in favor of the former, whereupon Apollo changed the king's ears into those of an ass. In one version of the myth, Midas conceals his deformity from all but his wife, and she is unable to sleep (see ll. 81–2, below) until she whispers the secret to the waters of a lake.

You think this cruel? take it for a rule,
No creature smarts so little as a Fool.
Let Peals of Laughter, *Codrus!* round thee break,   **85**
Thou unconcern'd canst hear the mighty Crack.
Pit, Box and Gall'ry in convulsions hurl'd,
Thou stand'st unshook amidst a bursting World.
Who shames a Scribler? break one cobweb thro',
He spins the slight, self-pleasing thread anew;   **90**
Destroy his Fib, or Sophistry; in vain,
The Creature's at his dirty work again;
Thron'd in the Centre of his thin designs;
Proud of a vast Extent of flimzy lines.
Whom have I hurt? has Poet yet, or Peer,   **95**
Lost the arch'd eye-brow, or *Parnassian* sneer?
And has not *Colly* still his Lord, and Whore?
His Butchers *Henley,* his Free-masons *Moor?*
Does not one Table *Bavius* still admit? *employment of History*
Still to one Bishop *Philips* seem a Wit?   **100**
Still *Sapho* — "Hold! for God-sake — you'll offend:
"No Names — be calm — learn Prudence of a Friend:
"I too could write, and I am twice as tall,
"But Foes like these!" — One Flatt'rer's worse than all;
Of all mad Creatures, if the Learn'd are right,   **105**
It is the Slaver kills, and not the Bite.
A Fool quite angry is quite innocent;
Alas! 'tis ten times worse when they *repent.*

One dedicates, in high Heroic prose,
And ridicules beyond a hundred foes;   **110**
One from all *Grubstreet* will my fame defend,

85. Codrus: a name usually applied to wretched Roman poets who irritated people by reading their works to them.
86–8. Alluding to Horace [*Odes*, III iii 7–8]:
> Si fractus illabatur orbis,
> Impavidum ferient ruinæ.   P.
87. Pit, Box and Gall'ry: the sections of a theater.
97. Colly: Colley Cibber (1671–1757), actor, playwright and poet laureate who became the hero of the *Dunciad.*   **his Lord:** i.e., his noble patron.
98. Henley: John Henley (1692–1756), known as "Orator" Henley, an eccentric London preacher who on one occasion gave a "butchers' " sermon in which he extravagantly praised the trade.   **Moor:** James Moore Smythe (see l. 23*n.*) was a freemason.
99. Bavius: name of a stupid and malevolent poet who attacked Horace and Virgil.
100. Philips: Ambrose Philips (1670–1749), a minor poet and dramatist who in 1723 became secretary to Dr. Hugh Boulter, archbishop of Armagh. See also first note to *Guardian* No. 40, and ll. 179–80, below.
101. Sapho: see first note, above.
103. twice as tall: Pope was about four feet, six inches, tall.
106. Slaver: (1) saliva; (2) flattery or drivel.
111. Grubstreet: London habitat of needy hack writers.

And, more abusive, calls himself my friend.
This prints my Letters, that expects a Bribe,
And others roar aloud, "Subscribe, subscribe."
There are, who to my Person pay their court,   115
I cough like *Horace*, and tho' lean, am short,
Ammon's great Son one shoulder had too high,
Such *Ovid's* nose, and "Sir! you have an *Eye* —"
Go on, obliging Creatures, make me see
All that disgrac'd my Betters, met in me: 120
Say for my comfort, languishing in bed,
"Just so immortal *Maro* held his head:"
And when I die, be sure you let me know
Great *Homer* dy'd three thousand years ago.

Why did I write? what sin to me unknown   125
Dipt me in Ink, my Parents', or my own?
As yet a Child, nor yet a Fool to Fame,
I lisp'd in Numbers, for the Numbers came.
I left no Calling for this idle trade,
No Duty broke, no Father dis-obey'd.   130
The Muse but serv'd to ease some Friend, not Wife,
To help me thro' this long Disease, my Life,
To second, ARBUTHNOT! thy Art and Care,
And teach, the Being you preserv'd, to bear.

But why then publish? *Granville* the polite,   135
And knowing *Walsh*, would tell me I could write;
Well-natur'd *Garth* inflam'd with early praise,
And *Congreve* lov'd, and *Swift* endur'd my Lays;
The Courtly *Talbot, Somers, Sheffield* read,
Ev'n mitred *Rochester* would nod the head,   140

113. **Letters:** Edmund Curll (see l. 53*n*., above) had printed some of Pope's letters without permission.
114. **Subscribe:** authors sometimes asked their friends and the public to subscribe or pay in advance for copies of their works.
117. **Ammon's great Son:** Alexander the Great (see *Essay on Criticism*, l. 376*n*.). Pope himself was somewhat hunchbacked.
122. **Maro:** Virgil (Publius Virgilius Maro).
135. **Granville:** see first note to *Windsor-Forest*.
136. **Walsh:** see *Essay on Criticism*, l. 729*n*.
137. **Garth:** see *Summer*, l. 9*n*.
138. **Congreve . . . Swift:** Pope dedicated his translation of the *Iliad* to the dramatist William Congreve (1670–1729), and inscribed the *Dunciad* to Swift.
139. **Talbot, Somers, Sheffield:** Charles Talbot (1660–1718), Duke of Shrewsbury, an honored statesman under William III, Queen Anne, and George I; John Somers (1651–1716), Baron Somers, Lord Chancellor under William III; John Sheffield (1648–1721), Duke of Buckingham and Normanby, a statesman and poet (see also *Essay on Criticism*, l. 723*n*.) whose works were edited by Pope.
140. **Rochester:** Francis Atterbury (1662–1732), Bishop of Rochester, an early friend to Pope. A Jacobite sympathizer, he was banished from England in

And *St. John*'s self (great *Dryden*'s friends before)
With open arms receiv'd one Poet more.
Happy my Studies, when by these approv'd!
Happier their Author, when by these belov'd!
From these the world will judge of Men and Books,   145
Not from the *Burnets*, *Oldmixons*, and *Cooks*.
   Soft were my Numbers, who could take offence
While pure Description held the place of Sense?
Like gentle *Fanny*'s was my flow'ry Theme,
A painted Mistress, or a purling Stream.   150
Yet then did *Gildon* draw his venal quill;
I wish'd the man a dinner, and sate still:
Yet then did *Dennis* rave in furious fret;
I never answer'd, I was not in debt:
If want provok'd, or madness made them print,   155
I wag'd no war with *Bedlam* or the *Mint*.
   Did some more sober Critic come abroad?
If wrong, I smil'd; if right, I kiss'd the rod.
Pains, reading, study, are their just pretence,
And all they want is spirit, taste, and sense.   160
Comma's and points they set exactly right,
And 'twere a sin to rob them of their Mite.
Yet ne'r one sprig of Laurel grac'd these ribalds,
From slashing *Bentley* down to pidling *Tibalds*.
Each Wight who reads not, and but scans and spells,   165
Each Word-catcher that lives on syllables,
Ev'n such small Critics some regard may claim,
Preserv'd in *Milton*'s or in *Shakespear*'s name.

1723 after being found guilty of complicity in an attempt to restore the Stuart line to the throne.

141. St. John: see *Essay on Man*, I 1n.

146. Burnets, Oldmixons, and Cooks: Authors of secret and scandalous History. P.   Thomas Burnet (1694–1753), John Oldmixon (1673–1742), and Thomas Cooke (1703–56) were all minor writers who had attacked Pope in print.

149. Fanny: from Fannius, name of an inferior poet satirized by Horace. Pope probably alludes to Lord John Hervey (see first note, above).

151. Gildon: Charles Gildon (1665–1724), a mercenary writer who had abused Pope's person and family in print.

153. Dennis: see *Essay on Criticism*, l. 270n., l. 585n., and ll. 370–1, below.

163. ribalds: menials, parasites, prostitutes.

164. Bentley: Richard Bentley (1662–1742), the great classical scholar, called "slashing" because in his edition of *Paradise Lost* he arbitrarily set off in "hooks" or brackets many passages he did not think Milton could have written (see *First Ep. of the Second Bk.*, ll. 103–4, and also *Dunciad*, IV 203–74). **Tibalds:** Lewis Theobald (1688–1744) had shown the weakness of Pope's edition of Shakespeare and in consequence he preceded Colley Cibber as the first king of the dunces (see first note to the *Dunciad*). He is called "pidling" because in his own edition of Shakespeare he seemed to Pope to concentrate on pedantic details.

165. Wight: person (a term here implying some contempt).

Pretty! in Amber to observe the forms
Of hairs, or straws, or dirt, or grubs, or worms;   170
The things, we know, are neither rich nor rare,
But wonder how the Devil they got there?
    Were others angry? I excus'd them too;
Well might they rage; I gave them but their due.
A man's true merit 'tis not hard to find,   175
But each man's secret standard in his mind,
That Casting-weight Pride adds to Emptiness,
This, who can gratify? for who can *guess?*
The Bard whom pilf'red Pastorals renown,
Who turns a *Persian* Tale for half a crown,   180
Just writes to make his barrenness appear,
And strains from hard-bound brains eight lines a-year:
He, who still wanting tho' he lives on theft,
Steals much, spends little, yet has nothing left:
And he, who now to sense, now nonsense leaning,   185
Means not, but blunders round about a meaning:
And he, whose Fustian's so sublimely bad,
It is not Poetry, but Prose run mad:
All these, my modest Satire bad *translate,*
And own'd, that nine such Poets made a *Tate.*   190
How did they fume, and stamp, and roar, and chafe?
And swear, not *Addison* himself was safe.
    Peace to all such! but were there One whose fires
True Genius kindles, and fair Fame inspires,
Blest with each Talent and each Art to please,   195
And born to write, converse, and live with ease:
Shou'd such a man, too fond to rule alone,
Bear, like the *Turk,* no brother near the throne,
View him with scornful, yet with jealous eyes,
And hate for Arts that caus'd himself to rise;   200
Damn with faint praise, assent with civil leer,

179–80. Amb. Philips translated a Book called the *Persian Tales.* P. pilf'red Pastorals: in *Guardian* No. 40 Pope suggests that Philips (see l. 100n., above) in his *Fifth Pastoral* had in effect plagiarized a passage from an Italian poet.   half a crown: the ordinary fee of a prostitute.
    187. Fustian: claptrap.
    190. Tate: Nahum Tate (1652–1715), minor poet and dramatist who became poet laureate in 1692.
    193. One: Joseph Addison (1672–1719), the poet and essayist. Once on friendly terms, Pope and Addison became estranged in 1715 when Pope learned that Addison was secretly involved in attempts to discredit both him and his translation of the *Iliad* (see *Peri Bathous,* n. 16. p. 420; n. 7, p. 422). Pope responded to these attempts by composing his portrait of "Atticus" and sending a copy privately to Addison, who thereafter used him "very civilly" (the portrait was not published until after Addison's death). Years later Pope was to pay his old enemy a most generous compliment (see *Ep. to Augustus,* ll. 215–20, and also first note to *To Mr. Addison*).
    198. Turk: Turkish monarchs were proverbial for murdering off kinsmen, particularly brothers, who might become rivals to the throne.

And without sneering, teach the rest to sneer;
Willing to wound, and yet afraid to strike,
Just hint a fault, and hesitate dislike;
Alike reserv'd to blame, or to commend,   205
A tim'rous foe, and a suspicious friend,
Dreading ev'n fools, by Flatterers besieg'd,
And so obliging that he ne'er oblig'd;
Like *Cato*, give his little Senate laws,
And sit attentive to his own applause;   210
While Wits and Templers ev'ry sentence raise,
And wonder with a foolish face of praise.
Who but must laugh, if such a man there be?
Who would not weep, if *Atticus* were he?
    What tho' my Name stood rubric on the walls?   215
Or plaister'd posts, with Claps in capitals?
Or smoaking forth, a hundred Hawkers load,
On Wings of Winds came flying all abroad?
I sought no homage from the Race that write;
I kept, like *Asian* Monarchs, from their sight;   220
Poems I heeded (now be-rym'd so long)
No more than Thou, great GEORGE! a Birth-day Song.
I ne'er with Wits or Witlings past my days,
To spread about the Itch of Verse and Praise;
Nor like a Puppy daggled thro' the Town,   225
To fetch and carry Sing-song up and down;
Nor at Rehearsals sweat, and mouth'd, and cry'd,
With Handkerchief and Orange at my side:
But sick of Fops, and Poetry, and Prate,
To *Bufo* left the whole *Castalian* State.   230
    Proud, as *Apollo* on his forked hill,
Sate full-blown *Bufo*, puff'd by ev'ry quill;
Fed with soft Dedication all day long,
Horace and he went hand in hand in song.

209. **Cato:** Cato Uticensis (95–46 B.C.), Roman philosopher and patriot, about whose death Addison had written a play.   **little Senate:** Addison's literary coterie which met at Button's Coffee House.
211. **Templers:** i.e., barristers who occupied chambers in the Inner or Middle Temple (sets of buildings owned by English legal societies); they had a reputation as literary dabblers.
214. **Atticus:** Titus Pomponius (109–32 B.C.), Roman philosopher and friend to Cicero. Renowned for his generosity and love of truth, he was surnamed *Atticus* for his mastery of the Greek language.
215. **rubric:** printed in red.
216. **Claps:** placards.
217. **smoaking forth:** i.e., hot from the presses.
222. **Birth-day Song:** the poet laureate was required to compose a birthday ode for the king each year.
228. **Orange:** oranges were customarily sold in the theaters.
230. **Bufo:** Latin for *toad* (here seen as the "type" of a patron).   **Castalian:** Castalia is a spring, sacred to the muses, located below the two peaks of Parnassus (the "forked hill" of l. 231).

His Library, (where Busts of Poets dead   235
And a true *Pindar* stood without a head)
Receiv'd of Wits an undistinguish'd race,
Who first his Judgment ask'd, and then a Place:
Much they extoll'd his Pictures, much his Seat,
And flatter'd ev'ry day, and some days eat: 240
Till grown more frugal in his riper days,
He pay'd some Bards with Port, and some with Praise,
To some a dry Rehearsal was assign'd,
And others (harder still) he pay'd in kind.
Dryden alone (what wonder?) came not nigh,   245
Dryden alone escap'd this judging eye:
But still the Great have kindness in reserve,
He help'd to bury whom he help'd to starve.
    May some choice Patron bless each gray goose quill!
May ev'ry *Bavius* have his *Bufo* still!   250
So, when a Statesman wants a Day's defence,
Or Envy holds a whole Week's war with Sense,
Or simple Pride for Flatt'ry makes demands;
May Dunce by Dunce be whistled off my hands!
Blest be the *Great!* for those they take away,   255
And those they left me — For they left me GAY,
Left me to see neglected Genius bloom,
Neglected die! and tell it on his Tomb;
Of all thy blameless Life the sole Return
My Verse, and QUEENSB'RY weeping o'er thy Urn!   260
Oh let me live my own! and die so too!
("To live and die is all I have to do:")
Maintain a Poet's Dignity and Ease,
And see what friends, and read what books I please.
Above a Patron, tho' I condescend   265
Sometimes to call a Minister my Friend:
I was not born for Courts or great Affairs,
I pay my Debts, believe, and say my Pray'rs,
Can sleep without a Poem in my head,
Nor know, if *Dennis* be alive or dead.   270

236. Pindar: ridicules the affectation of Antiquaries, who frequently exhibit
the headless *Trunks* and *Terms* of Statues, for Plato, Homer, Pindar, &c. . . .   P.
239. Seat: country estate.
243. dry Rehearsal: i.e., a recitation of poetry unrewarded by a glass of wine.
244. pay'd in kind: i.e., Bufo read his own verses.
248. help'd to bury: Mr. Dryden, after having liv'd in Exigencies, had a
magnificent Funeral bestow'd upon him by the contribution of several Persons
of Quality.   P.
256. Gay: the poet John Gay (1685–1732), one of Pope's dearest friends.
Financially ruined in the "South Sea year" (see *Ep. to Bathurst,* ll. 119n.), Gay
was taken under the protection of the Duke and Duchess of Queenberry (l.
260). Pope wrote his epitaph.
262. Pope quotes l. 94 of John Denham's *Of Prudence.*
270. Dennis: see l. 153n., above.

Why am I ask'd, what next shall see the light?
Heav'ns! was I born for nothing but to write?
Has Life no Joys for me? or (to be grave)
Have I no Friend to serve, no Soul to save?
"I found him close with *Swift*" — "Indeed? no doubt"   275
(Cries prating *Balbus*) "something will come out."
'Tis all in vain, deny it as I will.
"No, such a Genius never can lye still,"
And then for mine obligingly mistakes
The first Lampoon Sir *Will.* or *Bubo* makes.   280
Poor guiltless I! and can I chuse but smile,
When ev'ry Coxcomb knows me by my *Style?*
  Curst be the Verse, how well soe'er it flow,
That tends to make one worthy Man my foe,
Give Virtue scandal, Innocence a fear,   285
Or from the soft-ey'd Virgin steal a tear!
But he, who hurts a harmless neighbour's peace,
Insults fal'n Worth, or Beauty in distress,
Who loves a Lye, lame slander helps about,
Who writes a Libel, or who copies out: 290
That Fop whose pride affects a Patron's name,
Yet absent, wounds an Author's honest fame;
Who can your Merit selfishly approve,
And show the Sense of it, without the Love;
Who has the Vanity to call you Friend,   295
Yet wants the Honour injur'd to defend;
Who tells whate'er you think, whate'er you say,
And, if he lye not, must at least betray:
Who to the *Dean* and *silver Bell* can swear,
And sees at *Cannons* what was never there: 300
Who reads but with a Lust to mis-apply,
Make Satire a Lampoon, and Fiction, Lye.
A Lash like mine no honest man shall dread,
But all such babling blockheads in his stead.
  Let *Sporus* tremble — "What? that Thing of silk,   305

276. **Balbus:** Latin for *stuttering*.
280. **Sir Will.:** any titled poetaster, but usually identified as Sir William Yonge (d. 1755), whose name became proverbial for a contemptible talker and politician.   **Bubo:** Latin for *owl*, considered an emblem of stupidity at the time. Under this name Pope sometimes alludes to George Bubb Dodington (1691–1762), a rich and corrupt politician who affected to patronize writers.
299. **Dean:** See the Epistle to the Earl of Burlington [ll. 141ff.]. P. Here and in the next line Pope refers to those who, maliciously or not, mis-applied his satire. His enemies had specifically promoted the notion that the account of Timon's Villa in the *Ep. to Burlington* was a satire directed against the Duke of Chandos and his estate, Cannons (see also *Ep. to Cobham*, l. 113n.).
305. **Sporus:** the emperor Nero caused the youth Sporus to be castrated, treated him as a woman, and married him with great ceremony. In this portrait, Pope has chiefly in view Lord John Hervey (see first note, above), noted for his effeminacy of manner and appearance.

"*Sporus*, that mere white Curd of Ass's milk?
"Satire or Sense alas! can *Sporus* feel?
"Who breaks a Butterfly upon a Wheel?"
Yet let me flap this Bug with gilded wings,
This painted Child of Dirt that stinks and stings;   310
Whose Buzz the Witty and the Fair annoys,
Yet Wit ne'er tastes, and Beauty ne'er enjoys,
So well-bred Spaniels civilly delight
In mumbling of the Game they dare not bite.
Eternal Smiles his Emptiness betray,   315
As shallow streams run dimpling all the way.
Whether in florid Impotence he speaks,
And, as the Prompter breathes, the Puppet squeaks;
Or at the Ear of *Eve*, familiar Toad,
Half Froth, half Venom, spits himself abroad,   320
In Puns, or Politicks, or Tales, or Lyes,
Or Spite, or Smut, or Rymes, or Blasphemies.
His Wit all see-saw between *that* and *this*,
Now high, now low, now Master up, now Miss,
And he himself one vile Antithesis.   325
Amphibious Thing! that acting either Part,
The trifling Head, or the corrupted Heart!
Fop at the Toilet, Flatt'rer at the Board,
Now trips a Lady, and now struts a Lord.
Eve's Tempter thus the Rabbins have exprest,   330
A Cherub's face, a Reptile all the rest;
Beauty that shocks you, Parts that none will trust,
Wit that can creep, and Pride that licks the dust.
    Not Fortune's Worshipper, nor Fashion's Fool,
Not Lucre's Madman, nor Ambition's Tool,   335
Not proud, nor servile, be one Poet's praise
That, if he pleas'd, he pleas'd by manly ways;
That Flatt'ry, ev'n to Kings, he held a shame,
And thought a Lye in Verse or Prose the same:
That not in Fancy's Maze he wander'd long,   340
But stoop'd to Truth, and moraliz'd his song:
That not for Fame, but Virtue's better end,
He stood the furious Foe, the timid Friend,
The damning Critic, half-approving Wit,
The Coxcomb hit, or fearing to be hit;   345
Laugh'd at the loss of Friends he never had,

308. **Wheel:** the torture wheel, on which criminals were "broken."
309. **Bug:** a bedbug, which has an offensive smell.
310. **painted:** Hervey painted his face.
319. In the fourth Book of Milton [l. 800], the Devil is represented in this Posture. . . . P.   **Eve:** Queen Caroline, to whose ear Hervey had frequent access.
330. **Rabbins:** rabbis.
341. **stoop'd:** swooped (as a hawk on its prey).

The dull, the proud, the wicked, and the mad;
The distant Threats of Vengeance on his head,
The Blow unfelt, the Tear he never shed;
The Tale reviv'd, the Lye so oft o'erthrown;   350
Th' imputed Trash, and Dulness not his own;
The Morals blacken'd when the Writings scape;
The libel'd Person, and the pictur'd Shape;
Abuse on all he lov'd, or lov'd him, spread,
A Friend in Exile, or a Father, dead;   355
The Whisper that to Greatness still too near,
Perhaps, yet vibrates on his SOVEREIGN's Ear —
Welcome for thee, fair Virtue! all the past:
For thee, fair Virtue! welcome ev'n the *last!*
    "But why insult the Poor, affront the Great?"   360
A Knave's a Knave, to me, in ev'ry State,
Alike my scorn, if he succeed or fail,
Sporus at Court, or *Japhet* in a Jayl,
A hireling Scribler, or a hireling Peer,
Knight of the Post corrupt, or of the Shire,   365
If on a Pillory, or near a Throne,
He gain his Prince's Ear, or lose his own.
    Yet soft by Nature, more a Dupe than Wit,
Sapho can tell you how this Man was bit:
This dreaded Sat'rist *Dennis* will confess   370
Foe to his Pride, but Friend to his Distress:
So humble, he has knock'd at *Tibbald*'s door,
Has drunk with *Cibber*, nay has rym'd for *Moor.*
Full ten years slander'd, did he once reply?
Three thousand Suns went down on *Welsted*'s Lye: 375

354. **Abuse**: Namely on the Duke of *Buckingham*, Earl of *Burlington*, Lord *Bathurst*, Lord *Bolingbroke*, Bishop *Atterbury*, Dr. *Swift*, Mr. *Gay*, Dr. *Arbuthnot*, his Friends, his Parents, and his very *Nurse* aspers'd in printed Papers by *James Moore* and *G. Ducket*, Esquires, *Welsted*, *Tho. Bentley*, and other obscure persons, &c.   P.

355. **Friend**: Atterbury (see l. 140*n.*, above).

357. **Ear**: see l. 319*n.*, above.

363. **Japhet**: Japhet Crook (1662–1734), a notorious forger who was set in the pillory, had his ears cut off (cf. l. 367) and his nose slit (see also *Ep. to Bathurst*, l. 88*n.*).

365. **Knight**: a knight of the post made a living by bearing false witness; a knight of the shire is a member of Parliament elected to represent a county.

369. **Sapho**: probably Lady Mary Wortley Montagu (see first note, above). **bit**: deceived.

370. **Dennis**: Dennis spent his last years in want, and Pope helped to organize a benefit performance at the theater for him.

372. **Tibbald**: see l. 164*n.*, above.

373. **Cibber**: see l. 97*n.*, above.   **Moor**: see l. 23*n.*, above.

374. **ten years**: It was so long, after many libels, before the Author of the *Dunciad* published that Poem, till when, he never writ a word in answer to the many Scurrilities and Falsehoods concerning him.   P.

375. **Welsted's Lye**: This Man had the Impudence to tell in print, that Mr. *P*. had occasion'd a *Lady's death*, and to *name* a person he never heard of.

To please a *Mistress,* One aspers'd his life;
He lash'd him not, but let her be his *Wife:*
Let *Budgel* charge low *Grubstreet* on his quill,
And write whate'er he pleas'd, except his *Will;*
Let the *Two Curls* of Town and Court, abuse   380
His Father, Mother, Body, Soul, and Muse.
Yet why? that Father held it for a rule
It was a Sin to call our Neighbour Fool,
That harmless Mother thought no Wife a Whore, —
Hear this! and spare his Family, *James More!*   385
Unspotted Names! and memorable long,
If there be Force in Virtue, or in Song.
    Of gentle Blood (part shed in Honour's Cause,
While yet in *Britain* Honour had Applause)
Each Parent sprung — "What Fortune, pray?" — Their own,   390

He also publish'd that he had libell'd the Duke of Chandos; with whom (it
was added) that he had liv'd in familiarity, and receiv'd from him a Present of
five hundred pounds: The Falsehood of which is known to his Grace. Mr. *P.*
never receiv'd any Present farther than the Subscription for *Homer,* from him,
or from any Great Man whatsoever. P.   Leonard Welsted (1688–1747)
was a minor writer who abused Pope in various writings (see n. to l. 354,
above).
    378. **Budgel:** Eustace Budgell (1686–1737), a miscellaneous writer who
falsely accused Pope of attacking him in the *Grub-street Journal.* Budgell was
thought guilty of forging the will (see next line) of Dr. Matthew Tindal, a
famous deist of the time.
    380. **Two Curls:** the publisher (l. 53*n.*) and Lord Hervey.
    381. In some of *Curl's* and other Pamphlets, Mr. *Pope's* Father was said to
be a Mechanic, a Hatter, a Farmer, nay a Bankrupt. But, what is stranger, a
Nobleman [Lord Hervey] (if such a Reflection can be thought to come from
a Nobleman) has dropt an Allusion to this pitiful Untruth, in his *Epistle to a
Doctor of Divinity:* And the following line,
                Hard as thy Heart, and as thy Birth Obscure,
had fallen from a like Courtly pen [see first note, above], in the *Verses to the
Imitator of Horace.* Mr. *Pope's* Father was of a Gentleman's Family in *Oxford-
shire,* the Head of which was the Earl of *Downe,* whose sole Heiress married
the Earl of Lindsey. — His Mother was the Daughter of *William Turnor,* Esq;
of *York:* She had three Brothers, one of whom was kill'd, another died in the
Service of King *Charles,* the eldest following his Fortunes, and becoming a
General Officer in *Spain,* left her what Estate remain'd after the Sequestra-
tions and Forfeitures of her Family — Mr. *Pope* died in 1717, aged 75; She in
1733, aged 93, a very few Weeks after this Poem was finished. The following
Inscription was placed by their Son on their Monument, in the Parish of
Twickenham, in Middlesex.
                                D.O.M.
                 ALEXANDRO POPE, VIRO INNOCUO,
            PROBO, PIO, QUI VIXIT ANNOS LXXV, OB. MDCCXVII.
              ET EDITHÆ CONJUGI INCULPABILI, PIENTISSIMÆ,
                 QUÆ VIXIT ANNOS XCIII, OB. MDCCXXXIII.
         PARENTIBUS BENEMERENTIBUS FILIUS FECIT, ET SIBI.   P.
    Recent investigations have shown that Pope was mistaken in some of the facts
of his ancestry.
    383. **Sin:** see Matthew 5:22.
    385. **James More:** James Moore Smythe again.
    388. **Cause:** that of Charles I.

And better got than *Bestia*'s from the Throne.
Born to no Pride, inheriting no Strife,
Nor marrying Discord in a Noble Wife,
Stranger to Civil and Religious Rage,
The good Man walk'd innoxious thro' his Age.   395
No Courts he saw, no Suits would ever try,
Nor dar'd an Oath, nor hazarded a Lye:
Un-learn'd, he knew no Schoolman's subtle Art,
No Language, but the Language of the Heart.
By Nature honest, by Experience wise,   400
Healthy by Temp'rance and by Exercise:
His Life, tho' long, to sickness past unknown,
His Death was instant, and without a groan.
Oh grant me thus to live, and thus to die!
Who sprung from Kings shall know less joy than I.   405
   O Friend! may each Domestick Bliss be thine!
Be no unpleasing Melancholy mine:
Me, let the tender Office long engage
To rock the Cradle of reposing Age,
With lenient Arts extend a Mother's breath,   410
Make Languor smile, and smooth the Bed of Death,
Explore the Thought, explain the asking Eye,
And keep a while one Parent from the Sky!
On Cares like these if Length of days attend,
May Heav'n, to bless those days, preserve my Friend,   415
Preserve him social, chearful, and serene,
And just as rich as when he serv'd a QUEEN!
Whether that Blessing be deny'd, or giv'n,
Thus far was right, the rest belongs to Heav'n.

391. Bestia: name of a corrupt Roman politician.
397. Oath . . . Lye: English Roman Catholics who refused to take various oaths were deprived of certain civil rights, and they could take the oaths only by lying or implicitly denying their faith.
398. Schoolman's subtle art: the sophistical reasoning of scholastic theologians.
410. lenient: softening.
417. Queen: Queen Anne (see first note, above).

SATIRES AND EPISTLES

OF

HORACE

IMITATED,

With Satires of Dr. *Donne*

VERSIFYED

ADVERTISEMENT

The Occasion of publishing these Imitations *was the Clamour raised on some*
of my Epistles. *An Answer from Horace was both more full, and of more*
Dignity, than any I cou'd have made in my own person; and the Example
of much greater Freedom in so eminent a Divine as Dr. Donne, *seem'd*
a proof with what Indignation and Contempt a Christian may treat Vice
or Folly, in ever so low, or ever so high, a Station. Both these Authors
were acceptable to the Princes and Ministers under whom they lived: The
Satires of Dr. Donne *I versify'd at the Desire of the Earl of* Oxford *while*
he was Lord Treasurer, and of the Duke of Shrewsbury *who had been*
Secretary of State; neither of whom look'd upon a Satire on Vicious Courts
as any Reflection on those they serv'd in. And indeed there is not in the
world a greater Error, than that which Fools are so apt to fall into, and
Knaves with good reason to incourage, the mistaking a Satyrist *for a* Libeller; *whereas to a true Satyrist nothing is so odious as a* Libeller, *for the*
same reason as to a man truly Virtuous nothing is so hateful as a Hypocrite.
— Uni aequus Virtuti atque ejus Amicis.   P.

The First Satire

OF THE

Second Book of Horace

P. THERE are (I scarce can think it, but am told)
There are to whom my Satire seems too bold,
Scarce to wise *Peter* complaisant enough,
And something said of *Chartres* much too rough.
The Lines are weak, another's pleas'd to say,   5
Lord *Fanny* spins a thousand such a Day.
Tim'rous by Nature, of the Rich in awe,
I come to Council learned in the Law.
You'll give me, like a Friend both sage and free,
Advice; and (as you use) without a Fee.   10
F. I'd write no more.
                 P. Not write? but then I *think*,
And for my Soul I cannot sleep a wink.
I nod in Company, I wake at Night,
Fools rush into my Head, and so I write.

    F. You could not do a worse thing for your Life.   15
Why, if the Nights seem tedious — take a Wife;
Or rather truly, if your Point be Rest,
Lettuce and Cowslip Wine; *Probatum est.*
But talk with *Celsus, Celsus* will advise
Hartshorn, or something that shall close your Eyes.   20
Or if you needs must write, write CÆSAR's Praise:

FIRST SATIRE OF THE SECOND BOOK: First published in 1733. In 1751 William Warburton, Pope's editor, added the sub-title: *To Mr. Fortescue.* William Fortescue (1687–1749), an M.P., became in 1741 Master of the Rolls, one of England's highest judiciary officers. Pope often went to him for legal advice, and in the poetic dialogue of this poem the lines preceded by "F." are to be assigned to him.

The "Advertisement" prefixed to the *Imitations of Horace* was first printed in the 1735 edition of Pope's *Works.* The Latin tag at the end of the "Advertisement" is translated by Pope at l. 121 of this poem.

3. **Peter:** Peter Walter, the cheat and usurer (see *Ep. to Bathurst,* l. 20n.).
4. **Chartres:** Francis Charteris, the gambler, rapist and usurer (see *Ep. to Bathurst,* l. 20n.):
6. **Fanny:** from Fannius, name of a foolish Roman poet. Pope probably alludes to Lord John Hervey (see first note to *Ep. to Dr. Arbuthnot*).
18. Lettuce was thought to inhibit sexual desire, and cowslip wine to induce sleep. *Probatum est* means "It is proved" (as a cure or remedy).
19. **Celsus:** Cornelius Celsus, a Roman medical writer of the first century A.D.
20. **Hartshorn:** ammonia, used (oddly) in sleeping potions.
21. **Cæsar:** George II, a descendant of the House of Brunswick (cf. l. 24).

You'll gain at least a *Knighthood,* or the *Bays.*

    P. What? like Sir *Richard,* rumbling, rough and fierce,
With ARMS, and GEORGE, and BRUNSWICK crowd the Verse?
Rend with tremendous Sound your ears asunder,   25
With Gun, Drum, Trumpet, Blunderbuss & Thunder?
Or nobly wild, with *Budgell's* Fire and Force,
Paint Angels trembling round his *falling Horse?*

    F. Then all your Muse's softer Art display,
Let *Carolina* smooth the tuneful Lay,   30
Lull with *Amelia's* liquid Name the Nine,
And sweetly flow through all the Royal Line.

    P. Alas! few Verses touch their nicer Ear;
They scarce can bear their *Laureate* twice a Year:
And justly CÆSAR scorns the Poet's Lays,   35
It is to *History* he trusts for Praise.

    F. Better be *Cibber,* I'll maintain it still,
Than ridicule all *Taste,* blaspheme *Quadrille,*
Abuse the City's best good Men in Metre,
And laugh at Peers that put their Trust in *Peter.*   40
Ev'n those you touch not, hate you.

                        P. What should ail 'em?

    F. A hundred smart in *Timon* and in *Balaam:*
The fewer still you name, you wound the more;
Bond is but one, but *Harpax* is a Score.

    P. Each Mortal has his Pleasure: None deny   45
Scarsdale his Bottle, *Darty* his Ham-Pye;
Ridotta sips and dances, till she see
The doubling Lustres dance as fast as she;

22. Bays: the laureateship.
23. Sir Richard: Sir Richard Blackmore (1655–1729), a physician who wrote
many tedious, bombastic epics (see *Dunciad,* II 268n.).
27. Budgell: Eustace Budgell (see *Ep. to Dr. Arbuthnot,* l. 378n.) had written a ridiculous poem in which he celebrated the fate of George II's horse, shot
from under the king at the battle of Oudenarde.
30. Carolina: Queen Caroline.
31. Amelia: third child of George and Caroline.   **the Nine:** the nine muses.
34. twice a year: the poet laureate was obliged to celebrate with odes the
New Year and the king's birthday.
37. Cibber: Colley Cibber (see *Ep. to Dr. Arbuthnot,* l. 97n.), the poet
laureate who became the hero of the *Dunciad.*
38. Quadrille: a modish card game.
39. City: London's financial and mercantile district is called the "City."
40. Peter: Peter Walter (l. 3, above).
42. Timon . . . Balaam: see *Ep. to Burlington,* ll. 99ff., and *Ep. to Bathurst,*
ll. 339ff.
44. Bond . . . Harpax: see *Ep. to Bathurst,* l. 102n., l. 93n.
46. Scarsdale: Nicholas Leke (1682–1736), fourth Earl of Scarsdale, noted
for his love of drink.   **Darty:** Charles Dartineuf (1664–1737), a noted epicure.
47. Ridotta: a giddy society woman (from Italian *ridotto:* an entertainment
of music and dancing).
48. Lustres: glass pendants attached to lights and chandeliers.

F— loves the *Senate*, *Hockley-Hole* his Brother,
Like in all else, as one Egg to another.   50
I love to pour out all myself, as plain
As downright *Shippen*, or as old *Montagne*.
In them, as certain to be lov'd as seen,
The Soul stood forth, nor kept a Thought within;
In me what Spots (for Spots I have) appear,   55
Will prove at least the Medium must be clear.
In this impartial Glass, my Muse intends
Fair to expose myself, my Foes, my Friends;
Publish the present Age, but where my Text
Is Vice too high, reserve it for the next: 60
My Foes shall wish my Life a longer date,
And ev'ry Friend the less lament my Fate.
      My Head and Heart thus flowing thro' my Quill,
Verse-man or Prose-man, term me which you will,
Papist or Protestant, or both between,   65
Like good *Erasmus* in an honest Mean,
In Moderation placing all my Glory,
While Tories call me Whig, and Whigs a Tory.
      Satire's my Weapon, but I'm too discreet
To run a Muck, and tilt at all I meet;   70
I only wear it in a Land of Hectors,
Thieves, Supercargoes, Sharpers, and Directors.
Save but our *Army!* and let Jove incrust
Swords, Pikes, and Guns, with everlasting Rust!
Peace is my dear Delight — not *Fleury's* more: 75
But touch me, and no Minister so sore.
Who-e'er offends, at some unlucky Time
Slides into Verse, and hitches in a Rhyme,
Sacred to Ridicule! his whole Life long,
And the sad Burthen of some merry Song.   80
      Slander or Poyson, dread from *Delia's* Rage,

---

49. F—: Stephen Fox (1704–76), an M.P. who became first Earl of Ilchester. His brother Henry (1705–74) also entered Parliament.   **Hockley-Hole:** a place for bear-baiting and gambling.
52. Shippen: William Shippen (1673–1743), a parliamentary leader renowned for his integrity and frankness.   **Montagne:** Pope was especially fond of the essays of the French philosopher, Michel de Montaigne (1553–92).
66. Erasmus: see *Essay on Criticism*, ll. 693–4n.
71. Hectors: bullies.
72. Supercargoes: superintendents of cargo aboard ships were notorious for their dishonesty and wealth.   **Directors:** i.e., of the South Sea Company (see *Ep. to Bathurst*, l. 105n.).
73. Army: the maintenance of a standing army was thought by some to endanger English liberties.
75. Fleury: André de Fleury (1653–1743), chief adviser to Louis XV and esteemed for his devotion to peace.
80. Burthen: refrain.
81. Delia: any vicious woman of polite society.

Hard Words or Hanging, if your Judge be *Page;*
From furious *Sappho* scarce a milder Fate,
P—x'd by her Love, or libell'd by her Hate:
Its proper Pow'r to hurt, each Creature feels,   85
Bulls aim their horns, and Asses lift their heels,
'Tis a Bear's Talent not to kick, but hug,
And no man wonders he's not stung by Pug:
So drink with *Waters,* or with *Chartres* eat,
They'll never poison you, they'll only cheat.   90
    Then learned Sir! (to cut the Matter short)
What-e'er my Fate, or well or ill at Court,
Whether old Age, with faint, but chearful Ray,
Attends to gild the Evening of my Day,
Or Death's black Wing already be display'd   95
To wrap me in the Universal Shade;
Whether the darken'd Room to muse invite,
Or whiten'd Wall provoke the Skew'r to write,
In Durance, Exile, Bedlam, or the Mint,
Like *Lee* or *Budgell,* I will Rhyme and Print.   100
    F. Alas young Man! your Days can ne'er be long,
In Flow'r of Age you perish for a Song!
Plums, and Directors, *Shylock* and his Wife,
Will club their Testers, now, to take your Life!
    P. What? arm'd for *Virtue* when I point the Pen,   105
Brand the bold Front of shameless, guilty Men,
Dash the proud Gamester in his gilded Car,
Bare the mean Heart that lurks beneath a Star;
Can there be wanting to defend Her Cause,
Lights of the Church, or Guardians of the Laws?   110
Could pension'd *Boileau* lash in honest Strain
Flatt'rers and Bigots ev'n in *Louis'* Reign?

82. **Page:** Sir Francis Page (1661–1741), a judge distinguished for his severity (see *Dunciad,* IV 29–30n.).

83. **Sappho:** see *Ep. to a Lady,* l. 24n.

84. **P–x'd:** Poxed (given syphilis).

88. **Pug:** a term for dogs, monkeys and prostitutes.

89. **Waters:** Peter Walter (l. 3, above).

97–8. The "darken'd Room" suggests a madhouse, the "whiten'd Wall" a prison.

99. **Bedlam . . . Mint:** see *Ep. to Dr. Arbuthnot,* l. 4n., ll. 12–13n.

100. **Lee:** Nathaniel Lee (1653–92), a Restoration dramatist who became insane and spent five years in Bethlehem Hospital.   **Budgell:** Budgell (l. 27n., above) was thought to have committed suicide while insane.

103. **Plums:** persons who had acquired £ 100,000 by dishonest means. **Shylock:** any unscrupulous usurer (but see *Ep. to Bathurst,* ll. 95–6).

104. **Testers:** sixpences.

106. **Brand:** criminals were branded on the forehead.

108. **Star:** emblem of knighthood.

111. **Boileau:** see *Essay on Criticism,* l. 714n. Louis XIV (see next line) appointed Boileau to the post of royal historiographer.

Could Laureate *Dryden* Pimp and Fry'r engage,
Yet neither *Charles* nor *James* be in a Rage?
And I not strip the Gilding off a Knave,   115
Un-plac'd, un-pension'd, no Man's Heir, or Slave?
I will, or perish in the gen'rous Cause.
Hear this, and tremble! you, who 'scape the Laws.
Yes, while I live, no rich or noble knave
Shall walk the World, in credit, to his grave.   120
TO VIRTUE ONLY and HER FRIENDS, A FRIEND,
The World beside may murmur, or commend.
Know, all the distant Din that World can keep
Rolls o'er my *Grotto*, and but sooths my Sleep.
There, my Retreat the best Companions grace,   125
Chiefs, out of War, and Statesmen, out of Place.
There *St. John* mingles with my friendly Bowl,
The Feast of Reason and the Flow of Soul:
And He, whose Lightning pierc'd th' *Iberian* Lines,
Now, forms my Quincunx, and now ranks my Vines,   130
Or tames the Genius of the stubborn Plain,
Almost as quickly, as he conquer'd *Spain.*

   Envy must own, I live among the Great,
No Pimp of Pleasure, and no Spy of State,
With Eyes that pry not, Tongue that ne'er repeats,   135
Fond to spread Friendships, but to cover Heats,
To help who want, to forward who excel;
This, all who know me, know; who love me, tell;
And who unknown defame me, let them be
Scriblers or Peers, alike are *Mob* to me.   140
This is my Plea, on this I rest my Cause —
What saith my Council learned in the Laws?

   F. Your Plea is good. But still I say, beware!
Laws are explain'd by Men — so have a care.
It stands on record, that in *Richard*'s Times   145
A Man was hang'd for very honest Rhymes.
Consult the Statute: *quart.* I think it is,
Edwardi Sext. or *prim. & quint. Eliz:*

113–14. Dryden was appointed laureate in 1670, under Charles II, and held the post also under James II. A Roman Catholic, he lost his appointment when the Protestant William III ascended the throne in 1688.

116. As a Roman Catholic, Pope could not occupy a government *place,* or post (see *Ep. to Dr. Arbuthnot,* l. 397n.), and he refused various pensions offered him.

124. Grotto: see *Ep. to Dr. Arbuthnot,* l. 8n.

127. St. John: Lord Bolingbroke (see *Essay on Man,* I 1n.).

129. He: *Charles Mordaunt* [1658–1735], Earl of Peterborough, who in the Year 1705 took *Barcelona,* and in the Winter following with only 280 Horse and 900 foot enterprized, and accomplished the capture of *Valentia.* P.

130. Quincunx: see *Ep. to Burlington,* l. 80n.

145. Richard: Richard III.

See *Libels, Satires* — here you have it — read.
   P. Libels and *Satires!* lawless Things indeed! 150
But grave *Epistles,* bringing Vice to light,
Such as a *King* might read, a *Bishop* write,
Such as Sir *Robert* would approve —
                    F. Indeed?
The Case is alter'd — you may then proceed.
In such a Cause the Plaintiff will be hiss'd, 155
My Lords the Judges laugh, and you're dismiss'd.

---

153. **Sir Robert:** Sir Robert Walpole, prime minister.

The Second Satire

OF THE

Second Book of Horace

PARAPHRASED

WHAT, and how great, the Virtue and the Art
  To live on little with a chearful heart,
  (A Doctrine sage, but truly none of mine)
Lets talk, my friends, but talk before we dine:
Not when a gilt Buffet's reflected pride   5
Turns you from sound Philosophy aside;
Not when from Plate to Plate your eyeballs roll,
And the brain dances to the mantling bowl.
    Hear Bethel's Sermon, one not vers'd in schools,
But strong in sense, and wise without the rules.   10
    Go work, hunt, exercise! (he thus began)
Then scorn a homely dinner, if you can.
Your wine lock'd up, your Butler stroll'd abroad,
Or fish deny'd, (the River yet un-thaw'd)
If then plain Bread and milk will do the feat,   15
The pleasure lies in *you,* and not the meat.
Preach as I please, I doubt our curious men
Will chuse a *Pheasant* still before a *Hen;*
Yet Hens of *Guinea* full as good I hold,
Except you eat the feathers, green and gold.   20
Of *Carps* and *Mullets* why prefer the *great,*
(Tho' cut in pieces e'er my Lord can eat)
Yet for *small Turbots* such esteem profess?
Because God made these large, the other less.
    Oldfield, with more than Harpy throat endu'd,   25
Cries, "Send me, Gods! a whole Hog *barbecu'd!*"
Oh blast it, South-winds! till a stench exhale,
Rank as the ripeness of a Rabbit's tail.
By what *Criterion* do ye eat, d'ye think,

SECOND SATIRE OF THE SECOND BOOK: First published in 1734. In the 1751
edition of Pope's *Works,* a sub-title was added: *To Mr. Bethel.* Hugh Bethel
(d. 1748), M.P., was one of Pope's oldest and dearest friends and an advocate
of the simple life.   8. mantling: foaming, sparkling.
    9. schools: i.e., of philosophy. *Rules* in the next line may be the rules of
right reason or of moral conduct.
    17. doubt: suspect.   curious: fastidious.
    19. Hens of Guinea: perhaps a female turkey, perhaps a guinea fowl.
    23. Turbots: flounder-like fish often weighing 30 or 40 pounds.
    25. Oldfield: a contemporary glutton about whom little is known.   Harpy:
a mythical winged monster, rapacious and filthy.
    26. barbecu'd: A *West-Indian* Term of Gluttony, a Hog roasted whole, stuff'd
with Spice, and basted with *Madera* Wine.   P.

If this is priz'd for *sweetness*, that for *stink?*   30
When the tir'd Glutton labours thro' a Treat,
He finds no relish in the sweetest Meat;
He calls for something bitter, something sour,
And the rich feast concludes extremely poor:
Cheap eggs, and herbs, and olives still we see,   35
Thus much is left of old Simplicity!
   The *Robin-red-breast* till of late had rest,
And children sacred held a *Martin*'s nest,
Till *Becca-ficos* sold so dev'lish dear
To one that was, or would have been a Peer.   40
Let me extoll a *Cat* on Oysters fed,
I'll have a Party at the *Bedford Head,*
Or ev'n to crack live *Crawfish* recommend,
I'd never doubt at Court to make a Friend.
   'Tis yet in vain, I own, to keep a pother   45
About one Vice, and fall into the other:
Between Excess and Famine lies a mean,
Plain, but not sordid, tho' not splendid, clean.
Avidien or his Wife (no matter which,
For him you'll call a dog, and her a bitch)   50
Sell their presented Partridges, and Fruits,
And humbly live on rabbits and on roots:
One half-pint bottle serves them both to dine,
And is at once their vinegar and wine.
But on some lucky day (as when they found   55
A lost Bank-bill, or heard their Son was drown'd)
At such a feast old vinegar to spare,
Is what two souls so gen'rous cannot bear;
Oyl, tho' it stink, they drop by drop impart,
But sowse the Cabbidge with a bounteous heart.   60
   He knows to live, who keeps the middle state,
And neither leans on this side, nor on that:
Nor stops, for one bad Cork, his Butler's pay,
Swears, like Albutius, a good Cook away;
Nor lets, like Nævius, ev'ry error pass,   65
The musty wine, foul cloth, or greasy glass.
   Now hear what blessings Temperance can bring:

31. **Treat:** feast.
33. **sour:** pronounced to rhyme with *poor* in Pope's time.
38. **Martin:** it was thought unlucky to kill martins.
39. **Becca-ficos:** small migratory birds considered a delicacy in Italy.
42. **Bedford Head:** A famous Eating-house.   P.
49. **Avidien:** name of the miser in the Horatian original Pope is here imitat-ing. But Pope probably glances at Edward Wortley Montagu (1681–1761), an M.P. and ambassador to Turkey famous for his avarice, and his wife, Lady Mary, frequently presented in Pope's verse as both greedy and sordid (see *Ep. to a Lady,* l. 24n., and first note to *Ep. to Dr. Arbuthnot*).
51. **presented:** given to them as presents.
64–5. **Albutius . . . Nævius:** names used at this point in the Horatian original.

(Thus said our Friend, and what he said I sing.)
First Health: The stomach (cram'd from ev'ry dish,
A Tomb of boil'd, and roast, and flesh, and fish,   70
Where Bile, and wind, and phlegm, and acid jar,
And all the Man is one intestine war)
Remembers oft the School-boy's simple fare,
The temp'rate sleeps, and spirits light as air!
    How pale, each Worshipful and rev'rend Guest   75
Rise from a Clergy, or a City, feast!
What life in all that ample Body, say,
What heav'nly Particle inspires the clay?
The Soul subsides; and wickedly inclines
To seem but mortal, ev'n in sound Divines.   80
On morning wings how active springs the Mind,
That leaves the load of yesterday behind?
How easy ev'ry labour it pursues?
How coming to the Poet ev'ry Muse?
Not but we may exceed, some Holy time,   85
Or tir'd in search of Truth, or search of Rhyme.
Ill Health some just indulgence may engage,
And more, the Sickness of long Life, Old-age:
For fainting Age what cordial drop remains,
If our intemp'rate Youth the Vessel drains?   90

    Our Fathers prais'd rank Ven'son. You suppose
Perhaps, young men! our Fathers had no nose?
Not so: a Buck was then a week's repast,
And 'twas their point, I ween, to make it last:
More pleas'd to keep it till their friends could come,   95
Than eat the sweetest by themselves at home.
Why had not I in those good times my birth,
E're Coxcomb-pyes or Coxcombs were on earth?
    Unworthy He, the voice of Fame to hear,
(That sweetest Music to an honest ear;   100
For 'faith Lord Fanny! you are in the wrong,
The World's good word is better than a Song)
Who has not learn'd, fresh Sturgeon and Ham-pye
Are no rewards for Want, and Infamy!

75. Worshipful: honorific title for magistrates, aldermen, and members of London city companies.
76. City: a feast held in the "City," that part of London within the old city walls which symbolized trade and finance.
84. coming: forward, eager.
89. cordial drop: a liquor stimulating the heart.
94. ween: think.
98. Coxcomb-pyes: presumably pies filled with crests or combs of cocks.
101. Lord Fanny: see *First Sat. of the Second Bk.*, l. 6n., and first note to *Ep. to Dr. Arbuthnot.*

When Luxury has lick'd up all thy pelf,   105
Curs'd by thy neighbours, thy Trustees, thy self,
To friends, to fortune, to mankind a shame,
Think how Posterity will treat thy name;
And buy a Rope, that future times may tell
Thou hast at least bestow'd one penny well.   110
    "Right, cries his Lordship, for a Rogue in need
"To have a Taste, is Insolence indeed:
"In me 'tis noble, suits my birth and state,
"My wealth unwieldy, and my heap too great."
Then, like the Sun, let Bounty spread her ray,   115
And shine that Superfluity away.
Oh Impudence of wealth! with all thy store,
How dar'st thou let one worthy man be poor?
Shall half the new-built Churches round thee fall?
Make Keys, build Bridges, or repair White-hall: 120
Or to thy Country let that heap be lent,
As M**o's was, but not at five *per Cent*.
    Who thinks that Fortune cannot change her mind,
Prepares a dreadful Jest for all mankind!
And who stands safest, tell me? is it he   125
That spreads and swells in puff'd Prosperity,
Or blest with little, whose preventing care
In Peace provides fit arms against a War?
    Thus Bethel spoke, who always speaks his thought,
And always thinks the very thing he ought: 130
His equal mind I copy what I can,
And as I love, would imitate the Man.
In *South-sea* days not happier, when surmis'd
The Lord of thousands, than if now *Excis'd*;
In Forest planted by a Father's hand,   135
Than in five acres now of rented land.

105. **pelf**: riches.
119. **new-built Churches**: fifty new churches had recently been built in London (see *Windsor-Forest*, l. 378n.).
120. **Keys**: quays, embankments.   **Bridges**: at this time the Thames was bridged in the London area only by London Bridge.   **White-hall**: once a royal palace, most of Whitehall had been destroyed by fire in 1698 and left in ruins (see *Windsor-Forest*, l. 380n.).
122. **M**o'**: John Churchill (1650–1722), the great Duke of Marlborough, was famous for his avarice and parsimony.
127. **preventing**: precautionary.
131. **equal**: tranquil and just.
133. **South-sea days**: see *Ep. to Bathurst*, l. 119n. Pope, along with thousands of others, had speculated in South Sea stock. When the bubble burst, he escaped in relatively good financial condition.
134. **Excis'd**: subjected to a general tax on domestic commodities.
135. **In Forest**: about 1700 Pope's father had bought a house on 14 acres of land at Binfield, in Windsor Forest, and moved his family there.
136. **five acres**: the grounds of the house Pope had leased at Twickenham in 1718.

Content with little, I can piddle here
On Broccoli and mutton, round the year;
But ancient friends, (tho' poor, or out of play)
That touch my Bell, I cannot turn away.   140
'Tis true, no Turbots dignify my boards,
But gudgeons, flounders, what my Thames affords.
To Hounslow-heath I point, and Bansted-down,
Thence comes your mutton, and these chicks my own:
From yon old wallnut-tree a show'r shall fall;   145
And grapes, long-lingring on my only wall,
And figs, from standard and Espalier join:
The dev'l is in you if you cannot dine.
Then chearful healths (your Mistress shall have place)
And, what's more rare, a Poet shall say *Grace*.   150
Fortune not much of humbling me can boast;
Tho' double-tax'd, how little have I lost?
My Life's amusements have been just the same,
Before, and after Standing Armies came.
My lands are sold, my Father's house is gone;   155
I'll hire another's, is not that my own,
And yours my friends? thro' whose free-opening gate
None comes too early, none departs too late;
(For I, who hold sage Homer's rule the best,
Welcome the coming, speed the going guest.)   160
"Pray heav'n it last! (cries Swift) as you go on;
"I wish to God this house had been your own:
"Pity! to build, without a son or wife:
"Why, you'll enjoy it only all your life." —
Well, if the Use be mine, can it concern one   165
Whether the Name belong to Pope or Vernon?
What's *Property*? dear Swift! you see it alter
From you to me, from me to Peter Walter,
Or, in a mortgage, prove a Lawyer's share,

139. **out of play:** out of office.
142. **gudgeons:** small fish related to the carp.
143. **Hounslow-heath:** a heath about 10 miles southwest of London. **Banstead-down:** near Epsom, in Surrey, and noted for sheep pasturage.
147. **standard:** a tree allowed to grow to full height.   **Espalier:** a framework upon which fruit trees are trained.
152. **double-tax'd:** after 1715 Roman Catholic estates were subjected to double taxes.
154. **Standing Armies:** standing armies were costly to maintain and considered, moreover, a threat to the liberties of the English subject.
159. **Homer's rule:** see *Odyssey*, XV 83–4, in Pope's translation.

> True friendship's laws are by this rule exprest,
> Welcome the coming, speed the parting guest.

166. **Vernon:** Thomas Vernon (d. 1726), from whom Pope had leased the property at Twickenham. At this time the property was in the name of Vernon's widow.
168. **Peter Walter:** the cheat and usurer (see *Ep. to Bathurst*, l. 20*n*.).

Or, in a jointure, vanish from the Heir,   170
Or in pure Equity (the Case not clear)
The Chanc'ry takes your rents for twenty year:
At best, it falls to some ungracious Son
Who cries, my father's damn'd, and all's my own.
Shades, that to Bacon could retreat afford,   175
Become the portion of a booby Lord;
And Hemsley once proud Buckingham's delight,
Slides to a Scriv'ner or a City Knight.
Let Lands and Houses have what Lords they will,
Let Us be fix'd, and our own Masters still.   180

170. jointure: settlement of an estate upon a wife, for the duration of her life, to take effect upon the death of her husband.

172. Chanc'ry: the Court of Chancery handled cases of equity and was notorious for the slowness of its procedures and judgments.

175–6. The estate that had been in the family of Sir Francis Bacon, near St. Albans, had by Pope's time passed into the hands of William Grimston (d. 1756), a peer frequently ridiculed for a foolish play he had written.

177. Hemsley: Helmsley, the country estate of George Villiers, Duke of Buckingham (see *Ep. to Bathurst*, ll. 299–314).

178. Scriv'ner: a money-lender.   **City Knight:** a moneyed man who had risen in the "City" (see l. 76*n.*, above) and been knighted.

The Second Satire

OF THE

First Book of Horace

THE Tribe of Templars, Play'rs, Apothecaries,
   Pimps, Poets, Wits, Lord *Fanny's*, Lady *Mary's*,
   And all the Court in Tears, and half the Town,
Lament dear charming *Oldfield*, dead and gone!
Engaging *Oldfield!* who, with Grace and Ease,   5
Could joyn the Arts, to ruin, and to please.
   Not so, who of Ten Thousand gull'd her Knight,
Then ask'd Ten Thousand for a second Night:
The Gallant too, to whom she pay'd it down,
Liv'd to refuse that Mistress half a Crown.   10
   Con. Philips cries, "A sneaking Dog I hate."
That's all three Lovers have for their Estate!
"Treat on, treat on," is her eternal Note,
And Lands and Tenements go down her Throat.
Some damn the Jade, and some the Cullies blame,   15
But not Sir *H—t*, for he does the same.
   With all a Woman's Virtues but the P—x,
Fufidia thrives in Money, Land, and Stocks:
For Int'rest, ten *per Cent.* her constant Rate is;
Her Body? hopeful Heirs may have it *gratis*.   20
She turns her very Sister to a Job,
And, in the Happy Minute, picks your Fob:
Yet starves herself, so little her own Friend,

SECOND SATIRE OF THE FIRST BOOK: First published anonymously in 1734 with
the title of *Sober Advice From Horace* and with textual notes which parodied the
editorial procedures of Richard Bentley, the great classical scholar (see *Ep. to
Dr. Arbuthnot*, 1. 164n.). In 1738 the title of the poem became *A Sermon
against Adultery, Being Sober Advice from Horace*, and later in the same year the
Bentlerian notes were dropped and the title changed to *The Second Satire of
the First Book of Horace*.

1. **Templars:** barristers, noted for literary dabbling (see *Ep. to Dr. Arbuthnot*,
l. 211n.).

2. **Lord Fanny's, Lady Mary's:** see first note to *Ep. to Dr. Arbuthnot*.

4. **Oldfield:** Anne Oldfield (1683–1730), a beautiful and talented actress
who had a reputation for amorousness.

11. **Con. Philips:** Teresia Constantia Phillips (1709–65), an avaricious courtesan.

15. **Cullies:** dupes.

16. **Sir H—t:** probably some "Sir Herbert" or other.

17. **P—x:** syphilis.

18. **Fufidia:** taken from Fufidius, name of a miser in the Horatian original.
But Pope probably has in mind Lady Mary Wortley Montagu (see the account
of Avidien and his wife in *Second Sat. of the Second Bk.*, ll. 49ff.).

21. **Job:** a profitable piece of business.

22. **Fob:** watch pocket.

And thirsts and hungers only at one End:
A Self-Tormentor, worse than (in the Play)   25
The Wretch, whose Av'rice drove his *Son* away.

　　But why all this? I'll tell ye, 'tis my Theme:
"Women and Fools are always in Extreme."
Rufa's at either end a Common-Shoar,
Sweet *Moll* and *Jack* are Civet-Cat and Boar: 30
Nothing in Nature is so lewd as *Peg*,
Yet, for the World, she would not shew her Leg!
While bashful *Jenny*, ev'n at Morning-Prayer,
Spreads her Fore-Buttocks to the Navel bare.
But diff'rent Taste in diff'rent Men prevails,   35
And one is fired by Heads, and one by Tails;
Some feel no Flames but at the *Court* or *Ball*,
And others hunt white Aprons in the Mall.
　　My Lord of *L—n*, chancing to remark
A *noted Dean* much busy'd in the Park,   40
"Proceed (he cry'd) proceed, my Reverend Brother,
"'Tis *Fornicatio simplex*, and no other:
"Better than lust for Boys, with *Pope* and *Turk*,
"Or others Spouses, like my Lord of ——."
　　May no such Praise (cries *J—s*) e'er be mine!   45
J—s, who bows at *Hi—sb—w's hoary Shrine*.
　　All you, who think the *City* ne'er can thrive,
Till ev'ry Cuckold-maker's flea'd alive;
Attend, while I their Miseries explain,
And pity Men of Pleasure still in Pain!   50
Survey the Pangs they bear, the Risques they run,

25–6. In Terence's play, *Heauton Timorumenos* ("The Self-Tormentor"),
the old man Menedemus by his harshness drives his son from home.
　29. Rufa: Latin for *red-haired*, thought a sign of wantonness.　**Common
Shoar**: common sewer.
　30. Moll and Jack: Pope perhaps alludes to Mary Lepell (1700–68), an admired court lady who married Lord John Hervey (see first note to *Ep. to Dr.
Arbuthnot*).　　Civet-Cat: a cat-like creature which secretes a substance used
in perfumery (see *Epil. to the Satires*, II 183–4).　　Boar: a boar-cat (i.e., a
tom cat).
　38. white Aprons: nursemaids.　　Mall: a fashionable promenade in St.
James's Park.
　39. My Lord of L—n: Edmund Gibson (1669–1748), Bishop of London, and
considered a shrewd and practical churchman.
　44. my Lord of ——: Lancelot Blackburne (1658–1743), Archbishop of
York, noted for his amatory alliances.
　45–6. Pope refers to a scandalous affair between Mary Hill, Viscountess Hillsborough (1684–1742), and a certain Jefferies.
　47. City: the area of London within the old walls was known as the "City"
and constituted the commercial and banking center of England. On the contemporary stage "City" merchants were typically cuckolded by young men of
more fashionable society.
　48. flea'd: flayed.

Where the most lucky are but last undone.
See wretched *Monsieur* flies to save his Throat,
And quits his Mistress, Money, Ring, and Note!
See good Sir *George* of ragged Livery stript,   55
By worthier Footmen pist upon and whipt!
Plunder'd by Thieves, or Lawyers which is worse,
One bleeds in Person, and one bleeds in Purse;
This meets a Blanket, and that meets a Cudgel —
And all applaud the Justice — All, but *Budgel*.   60
    How much more safe, dear Countrymen! his State,
Who trades in Frigates of the second Rate?
And yet some Care of S—*st* should be had,
Nothing so mean for which he can't run mad;
His Wit confirms him but a Slave the more,   65
And makes a Princess whom he found a Whore.
The Youth might save much Trouble and Expence,
Were he a Dupe of only common Sense.
But here's his point; "A Wench (he cries) for me!
"I never touch a Dame of Quality."   70
    To *Palmer's* Bed no Actress comes amiss,
He courts the whole *Personæ Dramatis:*
He too can say, "With Wives I never sin."
But Singing-Girls and Mimicks draw him in.
Sure, worthy Sir, the Diff'rence is not great,   75
With *whom* you lose your Credit and Estate?
This, or that Person, what avails to shun?
What's wrong is wrong, wherever it be done:
The Ease, Support, and Lustre of your Life,
Destroy'd alike with Strumpet, Maid, or Wife.   80
    What push'd poor *Ellis* on th' Imperial Whore?
'Twas but to be where CHARLES had been before.
The fatal Steel unjustly was apply'd,
When not his Lust offended, but his Pride:
Too hard a Penance for defeated Sin,   85
Himself shut out, and *Jacob Hall* let in.
    Suppose that honest Part that rules us all,

53. Monsieur: some French gallant or other.
54. Note: perhaps a promissory note.
60. Budgel: Eustace Budgell (see *Ep. to Dr. Arbuthnot*, l. 378*n.*).
62. Frigates: women.
63. S—st: Sallust (Crispus Sallustius), the Roman historian (86–34 B.C.), once caught in adultery. Pope may allude under this name to his friend Henry St. John, Viscount Bolingbroke (see *Essay* on *Man*, I 1*n.*).
71. Palmer: Sir Thomas Palmer (1682–1723), reputed to be a "man of pleasure."
81–6. John Ellis (1643–1738), under-secretary of state to William III, became one of the lovers of Barbara Villiers (1641–1709), Duchess of Cleveland and mistress to Charles II, and for this he apparently was emasculated. Jacob Hall (l. 86) was a famous rope-dancer whom the Duchess also took as a lover.

Should rise, and say — "Sir *Robert!* or Sir *Paul!*
"Did I demand, in my most vig'rous hour,
"A Thing descended from the Conqueror? 90
"Or when my pulse beat highest, ask for any
"Such Nicety, as Lady or Lord *Fanny?* —"
What would you answer? Could you have the Face, ⎱
When the poor Suff'rer humbly mourn'd his Case, ⎰
To cry "You weep the Favours of her GRACE?" 95
      Hath not indulgent Nature spread a Feast,
And giv'n enough for Man, enough for Beast?
But Man corrupt, perverse in all his ways,
In search of Vanities from Nature strays:
Yea, tho' the Blessing's more than he can use, 100
Shuns the permitted, the forbid pursues!
Weigh well the Cause from whence these Evils spring,
'Tis in thyself, and not in God's good Thing:
Then, lest Repentence punish such a Life,
Never, ah, never! kiss thy Neighbour's Wife. 105
      First, Silks and Diamonds veil no finer Shape,
Or plumper Thigh, than lurk in humble Crape:
And *secondly,* how innocent a *Belle*
Is she who shows what Ware she has to sell;
Not Lady-like, displays a milk-white Breast, 110
And hides in sacred Sluttishness the rest.
      Our ancient Kings (and sure those Kings were wise,
Who judg'd themselves, and saw with their own Eyes)
A War-horse never for the Service chose,
But ey'd him round, and stript off all the Cloaths; 115
For well they knew, proud Trappings serve to hide
A heavy Chest, thick Neck, or heaving Side.
But Fools are ready Chaps, agog to buy,
Let but a comely Fore-hand strike the Eye:
No Eagle sharper, every Charm to find, 120
To all defects, *Ty—y* not so blind:
Goose-rump'd, Hawk-nos'd, Swan-footed, is my Dear?
They'l praise her *Elbow, Heel,* or *Tip o' th' Ear.*
      A Lady's Face is all you see undress'd;

88. Sir Robert: Sir Robert Walpole, prime minister. He and his wife were notorious for their infidelities.   **Sir Paul:** perhaps Sir Paul Methuen (1672–1757), a contemporary statesman.

92. Lady or Lord Fanny: Pope usually alludes to the effeminate Lord Hervey under the name of "Fanny" (see first note to *Ep. to Dr. Arbuthnot* and also l. 30n., above).

95. her Grace: any duchess.

107. Crape: a thin worsted material.

118. Chaps: chapmen (customers, buyers).

121. Ty—y: perhaps James O'Hara, Baron Tyrawley (1690–1773), ambassador to Portugal, a man of indiscriminate taste, or perhaps his mother, known for her poor eyesight.

(For none but Lady M— shows the Rest)   125
But if to Charms more latent you pretend,
What Lines encompass, and what Works defend!
Dangers on Dangers! obstacles by dozens!
Spies, Guardians, Guests, old Women, Aunts, and Cozens!
Could you directly to her Person go,   130
Stays will obstruct above, and Hoops below, }
And if the Dame says yes, the Dress says no. }
Not thus at *N—dh–m*'s; your judicious Eye
May measure there the Breast, the Hip, the Thigh!
And will you run to Perils, Sword, and Law,   135
All for a Thing you ne're so much as *saw?*
    "The Hare once seiz'd the Hunter heeds no more
"The little Scut he so pursu'd before,
"Love follows flying Game (as *Sucklyn* sings)
"And 'tis for that the wanton Boy has Wings."   140
Why let him Sing — but when you're in the Wrong,
Think ye to cure the Mischief with a Song?
Has Nature set no bounds to wild Desire?
No Sense to guide, no Reason to enquire,
What solid Happiness, what empty Pride?   145
And what is best indulg'd, or best deny'd?
If neither Gems adorn, nor Silver tip
The flowing Bowl, will you not wet your Lip?
When sharp with Hunger, scorn you to be fed,
Except on *Pea-Chicks,* at the *Bedford-head?*   150
Or, when a tight, neat Girl, will serve the Turn,
In errant Pride continue stiff, and burn?
I'm a plain Man, whose Maxim is profest,
"The Thing at hand is of all Things the *best.*"
But Her who will, and then will not comply,   155
Whose Word is *If, Perhaps,* and *By-and-By,*
Z—ds! let some Eunuch or Platonic take —
So *B—t* cries, Philosopher and Rake!
Who asks no more (right reasonable Peer)
Than not to wait too long, nor pay too dear.   160
Give me a willing Nymph! 'tis all I care,
Extremely clean, and tolerably fair,

    125. Lady M—: Pope could have had any one of several ladies in mind, perhaps Lady Mary Wortley Montagu (see *Ep. to a Lady*, l. 24n., and l. 18n., above).
    131. Stays: a corset.
    133. N—dh—m: "Mother" Needham (d. 1731), owner of a notorious brothel.
    138. Scut: a hare's tail.
    139. Sucklyn: the poet, Sir John Suckling (1609–1642).
    150. Pea-Chicks: young peacocks.   **Bedford-head:** a famous London inn.
    157. Z—ds: Zounds, a contraction of "by God's wounds."
    158. B—t: Bathurst (see first note to *Ep. to Bathurst*).

> Her Shape her own, whatever Shape she have,
> And just that White and Red which Nature gave.
> Her I transported touch, transported view,   165
> And call her *Angel! Goddess! Montague!*
> No furious Husband thunders at the Door;
> No barking Dog, no Household in a Roar;
> From gleaming Swords no shrieking Women run;
> No wretched Wife cries out, *Undone! Undone!*   170
> Seiz'd in the Fact, and her Cuckold's Pow'r,
> She kneels, she weeps, and worse! resigns her Dow'r.
> Me, naked me, to Posts, to Pumps they draw,
> To Shame eternal, or eternal Law.
> Oh Love! be deep Tranquility my Luck!   175
> No Mistress *H—ysh—m* near, no Lady *B—ck!*
> For, to be taken, is the Dev'll in Hell;
> This Truth, let *L—l, J—ys, O—w* tell.

166. **Montague:** not Lady Mary Wortley Montagu, but either Elizabeth Montagu (d. 1757), wife of the third earl of Sandwich and a lady much admired by Pope, or Lady Mary Churchill, youngest daughter of the Duke of Marlborough, who became Duchess of Montagu and whose portrait Pope at one time attempted to paint.

173. **Posts:** whipping posts.   **Pumps:** a rough drenching under water pumps was a common punishment of the period.

176. A Mrs. Heysham and a Lady Buck discovered the affair between Lady Hillsborough and Jefferies (see l. 45–6n., above).

178. **L—l, J—ys, O—w:** the first two persons are Richard Liddel (d. 1746), who was forced to pay damages in a suit for adultery, and the Jefferies mentioned in ll. 45–6; the third person has not been positively identified.

The Second Epistle

OF THE

Second Book of Horace

Ludentis speciem dabit & torquebitur — HOR.

D EAR Col'nel! *Cobham's* and your Country's Friend!
    You love a Verse, take such as I can send.
    A Frenchman comes, presents you with his Boy,
Bows and begins. — "This Lad, Sir, is of Blois:
"Observe his Shape how clean! his Locks how curl'd!   5
"My only Son, I'd have him see the World:
"His French is pure; his Voice too — you shall hear —
"Sir, he's your Slave, for twenty pound a year.
"Mere Wax as yet, you fashion him with ease,
"Your Barber, Cook, Upholst'rer, what you please.   10
"A perfect Genius at an Opera-Song —
"To say too much, might do my Honour wrong:
"Take him with all his Virtues, on my word;
"His whole Ambition was to serve a Lord,
"But Sir, to you, with what wou'd I not part?   15
"Tho' faith, I fear 'twill break his Mother's heart.
"Once, (and but once) I caught him in a Lye,
"And then, unwhipp'd, he had the grace to cry:
"The Fault he has I fairly shall reveal,
"(Cou'd you o'erlook but that) — it is, to steal."   20
    If, after this, you took the graceless Lad,
Cou'd you complain, my Friend, he prov'd so bad?
Faith, in such case, if you should prosecute,
I think Sir Godfry should decide the Suit;
Who sent the Thief that stole the Cash, away,   25
And punish'd him that put it in his way.

SECOND EPISTLE OF THE SECOND BOOK: First published in 1737. The "Col'nel"
in l. 1 to whom the poem is addressed was apparently Arthur Browne (d. 1742),
who held the tenancy of Abscourt Farm (cf. ll. 232–3, below) and who presented Pope with certain ornaments, including "several Humming Birds and their
Nests," for his grotto at Twickenham.
    The Latin epigraph is from l. 124 of the Horatian original: "He will give the
appearance of playing, and yet be tortured with effort" (cf. ll. 178–9, below).
    1. Cobham: see first note to *Ep. to Cobham.*
    4. Blois: a town celebrated for the purity of French there spoken.
    24. Sir Godfry: An eminent Justice of Peace, who decided much in the
manner of Sancho Pança.   P.   The Justice was Sir Godfrey Kneller (1646–
1723), portrait painter and friend to Pope.

Consider then, and judge me in this light;
I told you when I went, I could not write;
You said the same; and are you discontent
With Laws, to which you gave your own assent?   30
Nay worse, to ask for Verse at such a time!
D'ye think me good for nothing but to rhime?

In ANNA's Wars, a Soldier poor and old,
Had dearly earn'd a little purse of Gold:
Tir'd with a tedious March, one luckless night,   35
He slept, poor Dog! and lost it, to a doit.
This put the Man in such a desp'rate Mind,
Between Revenge, and Grief, and Hunger join'd,
Against the Foe, himself, and all Mankind,
He leapt the Trenches, scal'd a Castle-Wall,   40
Tore down a Standard, took the Fort and all.
"Prodigious well!" his great Commander cry'd,
Gave him much Praise, and some Reward beside.
Next pleas'd his Excellence a Town to batter;
(Its Name I know not, and it's no great matter)   45
"Go on, my Friend (he cry'd) see yonder Walls!
"Advance and conquer! go where Glory calls!
"More Honours, more Rewards, attend the Brave" —
Don't you remember what Reply he gave?
"D'ye think me, noble Gen'ral, such a Sot?   50
"Let him take Castles who has ne'er a Groat."

Bred up at home, full early I begun
To read in Greek, the Wrath of Peleus' Son.
Besides, my Father taught me from a Lad,
The better Art to know the good from bad: 55
(And little sure imported to remove,
To hunt for Truth in *Maudlin's* learned Grove.)
But knottier Points we knew not half so well,
Depriv'd us soon of our Paternal Cell;
And certain Laws, by Suff'rers thought unjust,   60
Deny'd all Posts of Profit or of Trust:
Hopes after Hopes of pious Papists fail'd,

33. Anna's Wars: the War of the Spanish Succession (1701–14), fought in the reign of Queen Anne (the American phase of the conflict is known as "Queen Anne's War").

36. doit: a small Dutch coin, here pronounced *dite,* and equivalent to half an English farthing.

51. Groat: a coin worth about four pence.

53. Peleus' Son: Achilles.

56. imported: mattered.

57. Maudlin: Magdalen College, Oxford.

58–67. Pope alludes to various repressive measures against Roman Catholics, including laws against purchase or inheritance of land, denial of public office (see *Ep. to Dr. Arbuthnot,* l. 397*n.*), and double taxation (see *Second Sat. of the Second Bk.,* l. 152*n.*).

While mighty WILLIAM's thundering Arm prevail'd.
For Right Hereditary tax'd and fin'd,
He stuck to Poverty with Peace of Mind;   65
And me, the Muses help'd to undergo it;
Convict a Papist He, and I a Poet.
But (thanks to *Homer*) since I live and thrive,
Indebted to no Prince or Peer alive,
Sure I should want the Care of ten *Monroes*,   70
If I would scribble, rather than repose.
    Years foll'wing Years, steal something ev'ry day,
At last they steal us from our selves away;
In one our Frolicks, one Amusements end,
In one a Mistress drops, in one a Friend: 75
This subtle Thief of Life, this paltry Time,
What will it leave me, if it snatch my Rhime?
If ev'ry Wheel of that unweary'd Mill
That turn'd ten thousand Verses, now stands still.
    But after all, what wou'd you have me do?   80
When out of twenty I can please not two;
When this Heroicks only deigns to praise,
Sharp Satire that, and that Pindaric lays?
One likes the Pheasant's wing, and one the leg;
The Vulgar boil, the Learned roast an Egg;   85
Hard Task! to hit the Palate of such Guests,
When Oldfield loves, what Dartineuf detests.
    But grant I may relapse, for want of Grace,
Again to rhime, can *London* be the Place?
Who there his Muse, or Self, or Soul attends?   90
In Crouds and Courts, Law, Business, Feasts and Friends?
My Counsel sends to execute a Deed:
A Poet begs me, I will hear him read:
In Palace-Yard at Nine you'll find me there —
At Ten for certain, Sir, in Bloomsb'ry-Square —   95

63. **William:** William III, the Protestant who in 1688 ascended the throne abandoned by the Roman Catholic James II.
68. **Homer:** Pope's translations of Homer gave him financial independence.
70. **Monroes:** *Dr.* [James] Monroe [1680–1752], *Physician to Bedlam Hospital.* P.   See *Ep. to Dr. Arbuthnot*, l. 4n.
83. **Pindaric lays:** poems in the grand manner of Pindar, Greece's greatest lyric poet.
87. **Oldfield:** a contemporary glutton (see *Second Sat. of the Second Bk.*, l. 25n.).   **Dartineuf:** a noted epicure (see *First Sat. of the Second Bk.*, l. 46n.).
94–7. One's presence at the four places suggested in these four successive lines would require rapid shuttling back and forth between widely distant areas. *Palace-Yard* adjoins Westminster Hall; *Bloomsb'ry-Square*, one of the first London squares, is some distance away; *the Lords* suggests a return to Westminster Hall; *a Rehearsal* implies Drury Lane perhaps, and a return to the vicinity of Bloomsbury.

Before the Lords at Twelve my Cause comes on —
There's a Rehearsal, Sir, exact at One. —
"Oh but a Wit can study in the Streets,
"And raise his Mind above the Mob he meets."
Not quite so well however as one ought;   100
A Hackney-Coach may chance to spoil a Thought,
And then a nodding Beam, or Pig of Lead,
God knows, may hurt the very ablest Head.
Have you not seen at Guild-hall's narrow Pass,
Two Aldermen dispute it with an Ass?   105
And Peers give way, exalted as they are,
Ev'n to their own S–r–v—nce in a Carr?
Go, lofty Poet! and in such a Croud,
Sing thy sonorous Verse — but not aloud.
Alas! to Grotto's and to Groves we run,   110
To Ease and Silence, ev'ry Muse's Son:
Blackmore himself, for any grand Effort,
Would drink and doze at *Tooting* or *Earl's-Court.*
How shall I rhime in this eternal Roar?
How match the Bards whom none e'er match'd before?   115
The Man, who stretch'd in Isis' calm Retreat
To Books and Study gives sev'n years compleat,
See! strow'd with learned dust, his Night-cap on,
He walks, an Object new beneath the Sun!
The Boys flock round him, and the People stare: 120
So stiff, so mute! some Statue, you would swear,
Stept from its Pedestal to take the Air.
And here, while Town, and Court, and City roars,
With Mobs, and Duns, and Soldiers, at their doors;
Shall I, in *London,* act this idle part?   125
Composing Songs, for Fools to get by heart?
    The *Temple* late two Brother Sergeants saw,

102. **Pig of Lead:** an ingot of lead.
104. **narrow Pass:** Guildhall Alley, a passageway running back of Guildhall, the town hall of the City of London.
107. **S–r–v—nce:** Sir-reverence (i.e., human excrement).   **Carr:** at the time a word used to designate a triumphal chariot.
110. **Grotto's:** see *Ep. to Dr. Arbuthnot,* l. 8n.
112. **Blackmore:** see *First Sat. of the Second Bk.,* l. 23n.
113. **Tooting or Earl's-Court:** Two Villages within a few Miles of London.   P.
116. **Isis' calm Retreat:** Oxford University (situated on a stretch of the Thames known as the *Isis*).
117. **sev'n years:** time required for an M.A. degree.
123. **Town:** fashionable London society in general.   **Court:** the more exclusive court circle.   **City:** middle-class trading society (see *Second Sat. of the Second Bk.,* l. 76n.).
124. **Duns:** bill collectors.
127. **Temple:** name of two (the Inner and the Middle Temple) of the four sets of buildings belonging to the four Inns of Court (the legal societies of England which have the exclusive right of admitting persons to practice at the

Who deem'd each other Oracles of Law;
With equal Talents, these congenial Souls
One lull'd th' *Exchequer,* and one stunn'd the *Rolls;*   130
Each had a Gravity wou'd make you split,
And shook his head at *Murray,* as a Wit.
'Twas, "Sir your Law" — and "Sir, your Eloquence" —
"Yours *Cowper's* Manner — and yours *Talbot's* Sense."
    Thus we dispose of all poetic Merit,   135
Yours *Milton's* Genius, and mine *Homer's* Spirit.
Call *Tibbald Shakespear,* and he'll swear the Nine
Dear *Cibber!* never match'd one Ode of thine.
Lord! how we strut thro' *Merlin's* Cave, to see
No Poets there, but *Stephen,* you, and me.   140
Walk with respect behind, while we at ease
Weave Laurel Crowns, and take what Names we please.
"My dear *Tibullus!*" if that will not do,
"Let me be *Horace,* and be *Ovid* you.
"Or, I'm content, allow me *Dryden's* strains,   145
"And you shall rise up *Otway* for your pains."
Much do I suffer, much, to keep in peace
This jealous, waspish, wrong-head, rhiming Race;
And much must flatter, if the Whim should bite
To court applause by printing what I write: 150
But let the Fit pass o'er, I'm wise enough,
To stop my ears to their confounded stuff.
    In vain, bad Rhimers all mankind reject,

---

bar).   **Sergeants:** lawyers who belonged to the highest rank of barristers, and who addressed one another as "brother."
    130. Exchequer: the Court of the Exchequer, with jurisdiction over revenue matters.   **the Rolls:** the building where the records of the Court of Chancery (see *Second Sat. of the Second Bk.,* l. 172n.) were kept.
    132. Murray: William Murray, a respected and eloquent M.P. (see first note to *Sixth Ep. of the First Bk.*).
    134. Cowper: William Cowper, first Earl Cowper (1664–1723), Lord Chancellor for a period and esteemed for his eloquence.   **Talbot:** Charles Talbot, Baron Talbot (1685–1737), Lord Chancellor in 1733 and respected for his fine judgment.
    137. Tibbald: Lewis Theobald (see *Ep. to Dr. Arbuthnot,* l. 164n.).
    138. Cibber: as poet laureate, it was Colley Cibber's duty to write odes for the New Year and the monarch's birthday (see *Ep. to Dr. Arbuthnot,* l. 97n., l. 222n.).
    139. Merlin's Cave: a small cottage built by Queen Caroline in the Royal Gardens. Adorned with waxen images of Merlin and other personages, it contained a small collection of English books. Cf. *First Ep. of the Second Bk.,* l. 355n.
    140. Stephen: Stephen Duck (1705–56), an agricultural laborer whose poetry was favored by Queen Caroline and who was made Librarian and Keeper of Merlin's Cave.
    143. Tibullus: Albius Tibullus (54–19 B.C.), Latin love poet.
    146. Otway: Thomas Otway (1652–85), Restoration tragic dramatist.
    147. peace: here pronounced *pace.*

They treat themselves with most profound respect;
'Tis to small purpose that you hold your tongue,   155
Each prais'd within, is happy all day long.
But how severely with themselves proceed
The Men, who write such Verse as we can read?
Their own strict Judges, not a word they spare
That wants or Force, or Light, or Weight, or Care,   160
Howe'er unwillingly it quits its place,
Nay tho' at Court (perhaps) it may find grace:
Such they'll degrade; and sometimes, in its stead,
In downright Charity revive the dead;
Mark where a bold expressive Phrase appears,   165
Bright thro' the rubbish of some hundred years;
Command old words that long have slept, to wake,
Words, that wise *Bacon,* or brave *Raleigh* spake;
Or bid the new be *English,* Ages hence,
(For Use will father what's begot by Sense)   170
Pour the full Tide of Eloquence along,   ⎫
Serenely pure, and yet divinely strong,   ⎬
Rich with the Treasures of each foreign Tongue;   ⎭
Prune the luxuriant, the uncouth refine,
But show no mercy to an empty line;   175
Then polish all, with so much life and ease,
You think 'tis Nature, and a knack to please:
"But Ease in writing flows from Art, not Chance,
"As those move easiest who have learn'd to dance."

If such the Plague and pains to write by rule,   180
Better (say I) be pleas'd, and play the fool;
Call, if you will, bad Rhiming a disease,
It gives men happiness, or leaves them ease.
There liv'd, *in primo Georgii* (they record)
A worthy Member, no small Fool, a Lord;   185
Who, tho' the House was up, delighted sate,
Heard, noted, answer'd, as in full Debate:
In all but this, a man of sober Life,
Fond of his Friend, and civil to his Wife,
Not quite a Mad-man, tho' a Pasty fell,   190
And much too wise to walk into a Well:
Him, the damn'd Doctors and his Friends immur'd,
They bled, they cupp'd, they purg'd; in short, they cur'd:

---

168. Bacon: Sir Francis Bacon (1561–1626), whose essays were much admired by Pope.   **Raleigh:** Sir Walter Raleigh (1552–1618) had gained fame for his prose in his *History of the World.*
178–9. Cf. *Essay on Criticism,* ll. 362–3, and first note, above.
180. rule: see *Essay on Criticism,* l. 88n.
184. in primo Georgii: in the reign of George I (1714–27).
186. House was up: i.e., the House of Lords was adjourned.
190. Pasty: a meat pie.
193. cupp'd: bled by means of a cupping-glass.

Whereat the Gentleman began to stare —
My Friends? he cry'd, p—x take you for your care!   195
That from a Patriot of distinguish'd note,
Have bled and purg'd me to a simple *Vote*.
   Well, on the whole, *plain* Prose must be my fate:
Wisdom (curse on it) will come soon or late.
There is a time when Poets will grow dull: 200
I'll e'en leave Verses to the Boys at school:
To Rules of Poetry no more confin'd,
I learn to smooth and harmonize my Mind,
Teach ev'ry Thought within its bounds to roll,
And keep the equal Measure of the Soul.   205
   Soon as I enter at my Country door,
My Mind resumes the thread it dropt before;
Thoughts, which at Hyde-Park-Corner I forgot,
Meet and rejoin me, in the pensive Grott.
There all alone, and Compliments apart,   210
I ask these sober questions of my Heart.
   If, when the more you drink, the more you crave,
You tell the Doctor; when the more you have,
The more you want, why not with equal ease
Confess as well your Folly, as Disease?   215
The Heart resolves this matter in a trice,
"Men only feel the Smart, but not the Vice."
   When golden Angels cease to cure the Evil,
You give all royal Witchcraft to the Devil:
When servile Chaplains cry, that Birth and Place   220
Indue a Peer with Honour, Truth, and Grace,
Look in that Breast, most dirty Duke! be fair,
Say, can you find out one such Lodger there?
Yet still, not heeding what your Heart can teach,
You go to Church to hear these Flatt'rers preach.   225
   Indeed, could Wealth bestow or Wit or Merit,
A grain of Courage, or a spark of Spirit,
The wisest Man might blush, I must agree,
If vile Van-muck lov'd Sixpence, more than he.
   If there be truth in Law, and *Use* can give   230
A *Property*, that's yours on which you live.
Delightful *Abs-court*, if its Fields afford

195. **p—x:** pox (equivalent here to "plague take you").
206. **Country door:** at Twickenham.
208. **Hyde-Park-Corner:** on the edge of London in Pope's time.
209. **Grott:** see *Ep. to Dr. Arbuthnot*, l. 8n.
218. **the Evil:** the King's Evil, or scrofula, which the king was popularly believed to cure by his touch. The "angel" was a gold coin presented by the king to each person he "touched."
229. **Van-muck:** the name is sufficiently suggestive of a type, but Pope may have had in mind a rich merchant named Joshua Vanneck (d. 1777).
232. **Abs-court:** an estate located near Walton-on-Thames, about 15 miles southwest of London (see also first note, above).

Their Fruits to you, confesses you its Lord:
All Worldly's Hens, nay Partridge, sold to town,
His Ven'son too, a Guinea makes your own: 235
He bought at thousands, what with better wit
You purchase as you want, and bit by bit;
Now, or long since, what diff'rence will be found?
You pay a Penny, and he paid a Pound.

    Heathcote himself, and such large-acred Men,   240
Lords of fat *E'sham,* or of Lincoln Fen,
Buy every stick of Wood that lends them heat,
Buy every Pullet they afford to eat.
Yet these are Wights, who fondly call their own
Half that the Dev'l o'erlooks from Lincoln Town.   245
The Laws of God, as well as of the Land,
Abhor, a *Perpetuity* should stand:
Estates have wings, and hang in Fortune's pow'r
Loose on the point of ev'ry wav'ring Hour;
Ready, by force, or of your own accord,   250
By sale, at least by death, to change their Lord.
Man? and *for ever?* Wretch! what wou'dst thou have?
Heir urges Heir, like Wave impelling Wave:
All vast Possessions (just the same the case
Whether you call them Villa, Park, or Chace)   255
Alas, my Bathurst! what will they avail?
Join *Cotswold* Hills to *Saperton's* fair Dale,
Let rising Granaries and Temples here,
There mingled Farms and Pyramids appear,
Link Towns to Towns with Avenues of Oak,   260
Enclose whole Downs in Walls, 'tis all a joke!
Inexorable Death shall level all,
And Trees, and Stones, and Farms, and Farmer fall.

    Gold, Silver, Iv'ry, Vases sculptur'd high,
Paint, Marble, Gems, and Robes of *Persian* Dye,   265
There are who have not — and thank Heav'n there are
Who, if they have not, think not worth their care.

    Talk what you will of Taste, my Friend, you'll find,
Two of a Face, as soon as of a Mind.
Why, of two Brothers, rich and restless one   270

240. **Heathcote:** Sir Gilbert Heathcote (see *Ep. to Bathurst,* l. 103n.).
241. **E'sham:** the rich and beautiful Vale of Evesham, a Worcestershire district famed for its orchards and produce.   **Lincoln Fen:** vast drainage of the fens in Lincolnshire in the 17th century had brought extensive areas of the county under cultivation.
244. **Wights:** men.
255. **Park:** a name given at times to the tract of land surrounding a country house or mansion.   **Chace:** a tract of hunting land.
256. **Bathurst:** see first note to *Ep. to Bathurst.*
257. **Cotswold Hills:** in the west midlands of England, and famous for sheep pasturage.   **Saperton's fair dale:** at Sapperton, in Gloucestershire.
261. **Downs:** open expanses of elevated land.

Ploughs, burns, manures, and toils from Sun to Sun;
The other slights, for Women, Sports, and Wines,
All *Townshend's* Turnips, and all *Grovenor's* Mines:
Why one like *Bu*— with Pay and Scorn content,
Bows and votes on, in Court and Parliament;   275
One, driv'n by strong Benevolence of Soul,
Shall fly, like *Oglethorp*, from Pole to Pole:
Is known alone to that Directing Pow'r,
Who forms the Genius in the natal Hour;
That God of Nature, who, within us still,   280
Inclines our Action, not constrains our Will;
Various of Temper, as of Face or Frame,
Each Individual: His great End the same.
    Yes, Sir, how small soever be my heap,
A part I will enjoy, as well as keep.   285
My Heir may sigh, and think it want of Grace
A man so poor wou'd live without a *Place:*
But sure no Statute in his favour says,
How free, or frugal, I shall pass my days:
I, who at some times spend, at others spare,   290
Divided between Carlesness and Care.
'Tis one thing madly to disperse my store,
Another, not to heed to treasure more;
Glad, like a Boy, to snatch the first good day,
And pleas'd, if sordid Want be far away.   295
    What is't to me (a Passenger God wot)
Whether my Vessel be first-rate or not?
The Ship it self may make a better figure,
But I that sail, am neither less nor bigger.
I neither strut with ev'ry fav'ring breath,   300
Nor strive with all the Tempest in my teeth.
In Pow'r, Wit, Figure, Virtue, Fortune, plac'd
Behind the foremost, and before the last.
    "But why all this of Av'rice? I have none."
I wish you joy, Sir, of a Tyrant gone;   305
But does no other lord it at this hour,

273. **Townshend:** Charles, second Viscount Townshend (1674–1738), a Whig statesman who, on his retirement, conducted agricultural experiments, especially with turnips.   **Grovenor:** the Grosvenor family had long owned many coal mines in Wales.

274. **Bu—:** George Bubb Dodington, a rich but time-serving politician who dabbled in poetry and affected the role of a patron (see *Ep. to Dr. Arbuthnot*, l. 280n.).

277. **Oglethorp:** General James Edward Oglethorpe (1696–1738), philanthropist and founder of the Georgia colony.

283. **His:** God's.

287. **Place:** a government post or position.

296. **God wot:** God knows.

297. Pope was about four feet, six inches tall, of a frail constitution with a marked curvature of the spine.

As wild and mad? the Avarice of Pow'r?
Does neither Rage inflame, nor Fear appall?
Not the black Fear of Death, that saddens all?
With Terrors round can Reason hold her throne,   310
Despise the known, nor tremble at th' unknown?
Survey both Worlds, intrepid and entire,
In spight of Witches, Devils, Dreams, and Fire?
Pleas'd to look forward, pleas'd to look behind,
And count each Birth-day with a grateful mind?   315
Has Life no sourness, drawn so near its end?
Can'st thou endure a Foe, forgive a Friend?
Has Age but melted the rough parts away,
As Winter-fruits grow mild e'er they decay?
Or will you think, my Friend, your business done,   320
When, of a hundred thorns, you pull out one?
    Learn to live well, or fairly make your Will;
You've play'd, and lov'd, and eat, and drank your fill:
Walk sober off; before a sprightlier Age
Comes titt'ring on, and shoves you from the stage: 325
Leave such to trifle with more grace and ease,
Whom Folly pleases, and whose Follies please.

The First Epistle

OF THE

Second Book of Horace

IMITATED

Ne Rubeam, pingui donatus Munere! — HOR.

ADVERTISEMENT

The Reflections of Horace, and the Judgments past in his Epistle to Augustus, seem'd so seasonable to the present Times, that I could not help applying them to the use of my own Country. The Author thought them considerable enough to address them to His Prince; whom he paints with all the great and good Qualities of a Monarch, upon whom the Romans depended for the Encrease of an Absolute Empire. But to make the Poem entirely English, I was willing to add one or two of those Virtues which contribute to the Happiness of a Free People, and are more consistent with the Welfare of our Neighbours.

This epistle will show the learned World to have fallen into two mistakes; one, that Augustus was a Patron of Poets in general; whereas he not only prohibited all but the Best Writers to name him, but recommended that Care even to the Civil Magistrate: Admonebat Prætores, ne paterentur Nomen suum obsolefieri, &c. The other, that this Piece was only a general Discourse of Poetry; whereas it was an Apology for the Poets, in order to render Augustus more their Patron. Horace here pleads the Cause of his Contemporaries, first against the Taste of the Town, whose humour it was to magnify the Authors of the preceding Age; secondly against the Court and Nobility, who encouraged only the Writers for the Theatre; and lastly against the Emperor himself, who had conceived them of little use to the Government. He shews (by a view of the Progress of Learning, and the Change of Taste among the Romans) that

FIRST EPISTLE OF THE SECOND BOOK: First published in 1737. In Warburton's edition of Pope's *Works* in 1751 the sub-title, *To Augustus*, was added. The subtitle is pointedly appropriate, for King George II was christened George Augustus, and to this new "Augustus" Pope addressed the terms of a poem Horace had written to Caesar Augustus. The epigraph is from l. 267 of the original: "Lest I should blush with shame, being presented with a stupid gift" (cf. l. 414, below).

The "Neighbours" referred to at the end of the first paragraph of the "Advertisement" are the French, typically regarded by contemporary Englishmen as servile adherents of a despotic monarch (see *Essay on Criticism*, l. 713n.). The Latin quotation in the "Advertisement" is from Suetonius, *Augustus*, sect. 89: "He [Augustus] admonished the praetors not to let his name be degraded, etc."

the Introduction of the Polite Arts of Greece *had given the Writers of his Time great advantages over their Predecessors, that their* Morals *were much improved, and the Licence of those ancient Poets restrained: that* Satire *and* Comedy *were become more just and useful; that whatever extravagancies were left on the Stage, were owing to the Ill Taste of the Nobility; that Poets, under due Regulations, were in many respects useful to the* State; *and concludes, that it was upon them the Emperor himself must depend, for his Fame with Posterity.*

We may farther learn from this Epistle, that Horace made his Court to this Great Prince, by writing with a decent Freedom toward him, with a just Contempt of his low Flatterers, and with a manly Regard to his own Character.

WHILE You, great Patron of Mankind, sustain
The balanc'd World, and open all the Main;
Your Country, chief, in Arms abroad defend,
At home, with Morals, Arts, and Laws amend;
How shall the Muse, from such a Monarch, steal   5
An hour, and not defraud the Publick Weal?
   Edward and Henry, now the Boast of Fame,
And virtuous Alfred, a more sacred Name,
After a Life of gen'rous Toils endur'd,
The Gaul subdu'd, or Property secur'd,   10
Ambition humbled, mighty Cities storm'd,
Or Laws establish'd, and the World reform'd;
Clos'd their long Glories with a sigh, to find
Th' unwilling Gratitude of base mankind!
All human Virtue to its latest breath   15
Finds Envy never conquer'd, but by Death.
The great Alcides, ev'ry Labour past,
Had still this Monster to subdue at last.
Sure fate of all, beneath whose rising ray
Each Star of meaner merit fades away;   20
Oppress'd we feel the Beam directly beat,
Those Suns of Glory please not till they set.

2. balanc'd World: George II had small aptitude in foreign affairs. **open all the Main:** at this time English merchant ships were being harassed by the Spanish.
3. in Arms: George II delighted in military exploits, but during 1736 (the year this poem was written) he spent six months abroad in the "arms" of his German mistress, Amalie Sophie Wallmoden (1704–65).
4. George kept several mistresses, had little interest in the arts other than music, and was guided (if not ruled) in the administration of his country by Queen Caroline and Sir Robert Walpole, the prime minister.
7. Edward and Henry: Edward III and Henry V, both of whom won great victories over the French (the "Gaul" of l. 10).
8. Alfred: Alfred the Great (848–901), who subdued the Danes in England and consolidated and unified English monarchal government.
17. Alcides: Hercules.

To Thee, the World its present homage pays,
The Harvest early, but mature the Praise:
Great Friend of LIBERTY! in *Kings* a Name   25
Above all Greek, above all Roman Fame:
Whose Word is Truth, as sacred and rever'd,
As Heav'n's own Oracles from Altars heard.
Wonder of Kings! like whom, to mortal eyes
None e'er has risen, and none e'er shall rise.   30
    Just in one instance, be it yet confest
Your People, Sir, are partial in the rest.
Foes to all living worth except your own,
And Advocates for Folly dead and gone.
Authors, like Coins, grow dear as they grow old;   35
It is the rust we value, not the gold.
Chaucer's worst ribaldry is learn'd by rote,
And beastly Skelton Heads of Houses quote:
One likes no language but the Faery Queen;
A Scot will fight for Christ's Kirk o' the Green;   40
And each true Briton is to Ben so civil,
He swears the Muses met him at the Devil.
    Tho' justly Greece her eldest sons admires,
Why should not we be wiser than our Sires?
In ev'ry publick Virtue we excell,   45
We build, we paint, we sing, we dance as well,
And learned Athens to our Art must stoop,
Could she behold us tumbling thro' a hoop.
    If Time improve our Wit as well as Wine,
Say at what age a Poet grows divine?   50
Shall we, or shall we not, account him so,
Who dy'd, perhaps, an hundred years ago?
End all dispute; and fix the year precise
When British bards begin t'Immortalize?
    "Who lasts a Century can have no flaw,   55
"I hold that Wit a Classick, good in law."
    Suppose he wants a year, will you compound?
And shall we deem him Ancient, right and sound,
Or damn to all Eternity at once,
At ninety nine, a Modern, and a Dunce?   60
    "We shall not quarrel for a year or two;

---

38. Skelton: Poet Laureat [John Skelton, 1460–1529] to Hen. 8, a Volume
of whose Verses has been lately reprinted, consisting almost wholly of Ribaldry,
Obscenity, and Scurrilous Language.   P.   **Heads of Houses:** masters of colleges at Oxford or Cambridge.
    40. Christ's Kirk o' the Green: A Ballad made by a King of Scotland.   P.
    42. the Devil: The Devil Tavern, where Ben. Johnson held his Poetical
Club.   P.
    48. tumbling: acrobatics and pantomime appeared to be crowding serious
drama off the stage (cf. l. 309*n.*).
    57. compound: compromise.

"By Courtesy of England, he may do."
  Then, by the rule that made the Horse-tail bare,
I pluck out year by year, as hair by hair,
And melt down Ancients like a heap of snow: 65
While you, to measure merits, look in Stowe,
And estimating Authors by the year,
Bestow a Garland only on a Bier.
  Shakespear, (whom you and ev'ry Play-house bill
Style the divine, the matchless, what you will)   70
For gain, not glory, wing'd his roving flight,
And grew Immortal in his own despight.
Ben, old and poor, as little seem'd to heed
The Life to come, in ev'ry Poet's Creed.
Who now reads Cowley? if he pleases yet,   75
His moral pleases, not his pointed wit;
Forgot his Epic, nay Pindaric Art,
But still I love the language of his Heart.
  "Yet surely, surely, these were famous men!
"What Boy but hears the sayings of old Ben?   80
"In all debates where Criticks bear a part,
"Not one but nods, and talks of Johnson's Art,
"Of Shakespear's Nature, and of Cowley's Wit;
"How Beaumont's Judgment check'd what Fletcher writ;
"How Shadwell hasty, Wycherly was slow;   85
"But, for the Passions, Southern sure and Rowe.
"These, only these, support the crouded stage,
"From eldest Heywood down to Cibber's age."
  All this may be; the People's Voice is odd,

62. **Courtesy of England:** a legal concession that could be invoked in certain cases involving property settlements.

66. **Stowe:** John Stow (1525–1605), an esteemed Elizabethan chronicler and antiquary.

69. Shakespear and Ben Johnson may truly be said not much to have thought of this Immortality, the one in many pieces composed in haste for the Stage; the other in his Latter works in general, which *Dryden* call'd, his *Dotages.* P.

75. **Cowley:** Abraham Cowley's poetry was much esteemed in the latter part of the 17th century (cf. *Windsor-Forest,* ll. 272–4n.).

77. **Pindaric Art:** which has much more merit than his *Epic:* but very unlike the Character, as well as Numbers, of Pindar. P.   Cf. *Second Ep. of the Second Bk.,* l. 83n.

84. Francis Beaumont (1584–1616) and John Fletcher (1579–1625), dramatists who frequently collaborated on plays.

85. **Shadwell . . . Wycherley:** Nothing was less true than this particular: But the whole Paragraph has a mixture of Irony, and must not altogether be taken for Horace's own Judgment, only the common Chatt of the pretenders to Criticism; in some things right, in others wrong. . . . P.   Thomas Shadwell (1642–92) was a writer of Restoration comedy. For William Wycherley, see *Autumn,* l. 7n.

86. **Southern . . . Rowe:** Thomas Southerne (1659–1746), chiefly remembered for his tragedies, and Nicholas Rowe (1674–1718), Pope's friend and foremost tragic dramatist of the early 18th century.

88. **Heywood:** John Heywood (1497–1580), called "eldest" to distinguish him from the Jacobean dramatist, Thomas Heywood.   **Cibber:** the poet laureate (see *Ep. to Dr. Arbuthnot,* l. 97n., and l. 92, below).

It is, and it is not, the voice of God. 90
To Gammer Gurton if it give the bays,
And yet deny the Careless Husband praise,
Or say our fathers never broke a rule;
Why then I say, the Publick is a fool.
But let them own, that greater faults than we 95
They had, and greater Virtues, I'll agree.
Spenser himself affects the obsolete,
And Sydney's verse halts ill on Roman feet:
Milton's strong pinion now not Heav'n can bound,
Now serpent-like, in prose he sweeps the ground, 100
In Quibbles, Angel and Archangel join,
And God the Father turns a School-Divine.
Not that I'd lop the Beauties from his book,
Like slashing Bentley with his desp'rate Hook;
Or damn all Shakespear, like th' affected fool 105
At Court, who hates whate'er he read at School.
      But for the Wits of either Charles's days,
The Mob of Gentlemen who wrote with Ease;
Sprat, Carew, Sedley, and a hundred more,
(Like twinkling Stars the Miscellanies o'er) 110
One Simile, that solitary shines
In the dry Desert of a thousand lines,
Or lengthen'd Thought that gleams thro' many a page,
Has sanctify'd whole Poems for an age.
      I lose my patience, and I own it too, 115
When works are censur'd, not as bad, but new;
While if our Elders break all Reason's laws,
These fools demand not Pardon, but Applause.
      On Avon's bank, where flow'rs eternal blow,
If I but ask, if any weed can grow? 120
One Tragic sentence if I dare deride
Which Betterton's grave Action dignify'd,
Or well-mouth'd Booth with emphasis proclaims,

91. Gammer Gurton, a piece of very low humour, one of the first printed Plays in English, and therefore much valued by some Antiquaries.   P.   *Gammer Gurton's Needle*, a play of dubious authorship, was first acted in 1566.
92. Careless Husband: a very successful comedy by Cibber.
97. Spenser: Particularly in the Shepherd's Calendar, where he imitates the unequal Measures, as well as the Language, of Chaucer.   P.
98. In his *Arcadia* Sir Philip Sidney had used the quantitative forms and measures of classical meter.
102. School-Divine: a scholastic theologian.
104. slashing Bentley: see *Ep. to Dr. Arbuthnot,* l. 164n.
107. either Charles: Charles I and Charles II.
109. Thomas Sprat (1635–1713), Thomas Carew (1595–1639), and Sir Charles Sedley (1639–1701), all "wits" and minor writers of the 17th century.
110. Miscellanies: poetical anthologies of the period.
122. Betterton: Thomas Betterton (1635–1710), leading tragic actor of his time and an early friend to Pope.
123. Booth: Barton Booth (1681–1733), tragic actor famed for his graceful delivery.

(Tho' but, perhaps, a muster-roll of Names)
How will our Fathers rise up in a rage,   125
And swear, all shame is lost in George's Age!
You'd think no Fools disgrac'd the former Reign,
Did not some grave Examples yet remain,
Who scorn a Lad should teach his Father skill,
And, having once been wrong, will be so still.   130
He, who to seem more deep than you or I,
Extols old Bards, or Merlin's Prophecy,
Mistake him not; he envies, not admires,
And to debase the Sons, exalts the Sires.
Had ancient Times conspir'd to dis-allow   135
What then was new, what had been ancient now?
Or what remain'd, so worthy to be read
By learned Criticks, of the mighty Dead?
    In Days of Ease, when now the weary Sword
Was sheath'd, and *Luxury* with *Charles* restor'd;   140
In every Taste of foreign Courts improv'd,
"All, by the King's Example, liv'd and lov'd."
Then Peers grew proud in Horsemanship t' excell,
New-market's Glory rose, as Britain's fell;
The Soldier breath'd the Gallantries of France,   145
And ev'ry flow'ry Courtier writ Romance.
Then Marble soften'd into life grew warm,
And yielding Metal flow'd to human form:
Lely on animated Canvas stole
The sleepy Eye, that spoke the melting soul.   150
No wonder then, when all was Love and Sport,
The willing Muses were debauch'd at Court;
On each enervate string they taught the Note
To pant, or tremble thro' an Eunuch's throat.

124. An absurd Custom of several Actors, to pronounce with Emphasis the meer *Proper Names* of Greeks or Romans, which (as they call it) *fill the mouth* of the Player. P.

132. Merlin's Prophecy: the magician Merlin's prophecy that the Saxons would be expelled from England had been rendered in English in Aaron Thompson's translation (1718) of Geoffrey of Monmouth's *Historia Regum Britanniae.* Chapters III and IV of Book VII of Thompson's *The British History* are called "The Prophecy of Merlin."

141. foreign Courts: Pope alludes to the period of Charles II's exile in France.

142. A *Verse of the Lord* Lansdown. P.   For Lansdowne, see first note to *Windsor-Forest.*

143–6. The Duke of Newcastle's Book of Horsemanship: the Romance of *Parthenissa,* by the Earl of Orrery, and most of the French Romances translated by *Persons of Quality.* P.

144. New-market: the town, near Cambridge, famous for horse-races.

149. Lely: Sir Peter Lely (1618–80), portrait painter.

153. The Siege of Rhodes [1656] by Sir William Davenant, the first Opera sung in England. P.

154. Eunuch's throat: an allusion to the opera singers, usually imported from Italy, who had been castrated in boyhood to retain an alto or soprano voice.

But Britain, changeful as a Child at play,   155
Now calls in Princes, and now turns away.
Now Whig, now Tory, what we lov'd we hate;
Now all for Pleasure, now for Church and State;
Now for Prerogative, and now for Laws;
Effects unhappy! from a Noble Cause.   160
    Time was, a sober Englishman wou'd knock
His servants up, and rise by five a clock,
Instruct his Family in ev'ry rule,
And send his Wife to Church, his Son to school.
To worship like his Fathers was his care;   165
To teach their frugal Virtues to his Heir;
To prove, that Luxury could never hold;
And place, on good Security, his Gold.
Now Times are chang'd, and one Poetick Itch
Has seiz'd the Court and City, Poor and Rich: 170
Sons, Sires, and Grandsires, all will wear the Bays,
Our Wives read Milton, and our Daughters Plays,
To Theatres, and to Rehearsals throng,
And all our Grace at Table is a Song.
I, who so oft renounce the Muses, lye,   175
Not ——'s self e'er tells more *Fibs* than I;
When, sick of Muse, our follies we deplore,
And promise our best Friends to ryme no more;
We wake next morning in a raging Fit,
And call for Pen and Ink to show our Wit.   180
    He serv'd a 'Prenticeship, who sets up shop;
Ward try'd on Puppies, and the Poor, his Drop;
Ev'n Radcliff's Doctors travel first to France,
Nor dare to practise till they've learn'd to dance.
Who builds a Bridge that never drove a pyle?   185
(Should Ripley venture, all the World would smile)
But those who cannot write, and those who can,
All ryme, and scrawl, and scribble, to a man.
    Yet Sir, reflect, the mischief is not great;
These Madmen never hurt the Church or State: 190
Sometimes the Folly benefits mankind;
And rarely Av'rice taints the tuneful mind.

159. Prerogative: monarchical power, privilege and immunity.   **Laws:** i.e.,
constitutional laws which would protect the rights of the subject and limit the
royal prerogative.
160. Noble Cause: liberty.
170. City: see *Second Ep. of the Second Bk.*, l. 123n.
182. Ward: A famous Empirick, whose Pill and Drop had several surprizing
effects, and were one of the principal subjects of Writing and Conversation at
this time.   P.   Joshua Ward (1685–1761), was a quack patronized by the
king. See also *Ep. to Dr. Arbuthnot*, l. 29n.
183. Radcliff: John Radcliffe (1653–1714), a physician who left money for
medical fellowships which provided for study abroad.
186. Ripley: see *Ep. to Burlington*, l. 18n.

Allow him but his Play-thing of a Pen,
He ne'er rebels, or plots, like other men:
Flight of Cashiers, or Mobs, he'll never mind;   195
And knows no losses while the Muse is kind.
To cheat a Friend, or Ward, he leaves to Peter;
The good man heaps up nothing but mere metre,
Enjoys his Garden and his Book in quiet;
And then — a perfect Hermit in his Diet.   200
Of little use the Man you may suppose,
Who says in verse what others say in prose;
Yet let me show, a Poet's of some weight,
And (tho' no Soldier) useful to the State.
What will a Child learn sooner than a song?   205
What better teach a Foreigner the tongue?
What's long or short, each accent where to place,
And speak in publick with some sort of grace.
I scarce can think him such a worthless thing,
Unless he praise some monster of a King,   210
Or Virtue, or Religion turn to sport,
To please a lewd, or un-believing Court.
Unhappy Dryden! — In all Charles's days,
Roscommon only boasts unspotted Bays;
And in our own (excuse some Courtly stains)   215
No whiter page than Addison remains.
He, from the taste obscene reclaims our Youth,
And sets the Passions on the side of Truth;
Forms the soft bosom with the gentlest art,
And pours each human Virtue in the heart.   220
Let Ireland tell, how Wit upheld her cause,
Her Trade supported, and supply'd her Laws;
And leave on Swift this grateful verse ingrav'd,
The Rights a Court attack'd, a Poet sav'd.
Behold the hand that wrought a Nation's cure,   225
Stretch'd to relieve the Idiot and the Poor,
Proud Vice to brand, or injur'd Worth adorn,
And stretch the Ray to Ages yet unborn.

195. **Flight of Cashiers:** an allusion to Robert Knight (d. 1744), a cashier in the South Sea Company (see *Ep. to Bathurst,* l. 105n., l. 119n.). After the collapse of the company's stock, he was found guilty of fraud and fled to France (see also *Dunciad,* IV 561n.).

197. **Peter:** Peter Walter, the cheat and usurer (see *Ep. to Bathurst,* l. 20n.).

206–8. George II spoke English with a German accent.

212. **lewd:** an allusion to George's mistresses. **un-believing:** Queen Caroline was considered a free-thinker (see *Ep. to Cobham,* l. 109n.).

214. **Roscommon:** see *Essay on Criticism,* l. 725n.

222. **supply'd:** assisted or supplemented.

226. **the Idiot and the Poor:** A Foundation for the maintenance of Idiots, and a Fund for assisting the Poor, by lending small sums of Money on demand. P. Swift left money for the foundation of a hospital for the feeble-minded.

Not but there are, who merit other palms;
Hopkins and Sternhold glad the heart with Psalms;   230
The Boys and Girls whom Charity maintains,
Implore your help in these pathetic strains:
How could Devotion touch the country pews,
Unless the Gods bestow'd a proper Muse?
Verse chears their leisure, Verse assists their work,   235
Verse prays for Peace, or sings down Pope and Turk.
The silenc'd Preacher yields to potent strain,
And feels that grace his pray'r besought in vain,
The blessing thrills thro' all the lab'ring throng,
And Heav'n is won by violence of Song.   240
    Our rural Ancestors, with little blest,
Patient of labour when the end was rest,
Indulg'd the day that hous'd their annual grain,
With feasts, and off'rings, and a thankful strain:
The joy their wives, their sons, and servants share,   245
Ease of their toil, and part'ners of their care:
The laugh, the jest, attendants on the bowl,
Smooth'd ev'ry brow, and open'd ev'ry soul:
With growing years the pleasing Licence grew,
And Taunts alternate innocently flew.   250
But Times corrupt, and Nature, ill-inclin'd,
Produc'd the point that left a sting behind;
Till friend with friend, and families at strife,
Triumphant Malice rag'd thro' private life.
Who felt the wrong, or fear'd it, took th' alarm,   255
Appeal'd to Law, and Justice lent her arm.
At length, by wholesom dread of statutes bound,
The Poets learn'd to please, and not to wound:
Most warp'd to Flatt'ry's side; but some, more nice,
Preserv'd the freedom, and forbore the vice.   260
Hence Satire rose, that just the medium hit,
And heals with Morals what it hurts with Wit.
    We conquer'd France, but felt our captive's charms;
Her Arts victorious triumph'd o'er our Arms:
Britain to soft refinements less a foe,   265
Wit grew polite, and Numbers learn'd to flow.

230. Hopkins and Sternhold: Thomas Sternhold (d. 1549) and John Hopkins (d. 1570), joint versifiers of the Psalms whose "strains" and "song" are referred to in the succeeding lines.
231. whom Charity maintains: a great number of "charity schools," designed to give rudimentary education to the children of the poor, were founded in the late 17th and early 18th centuries.
236. Pope and Turk: alluding to a prayer in Sternhold and Hopkins: "From Turke and Pope defend us, Lord."
259. nice: precise, or subtle.

Waller was smooth; but Dryden taught to join ⎫
The varying verse, the full resounding line,   ⎬
The long majestic march, and energy divine.   ⎭
Tho' still some traces of our rustic vein   270
And splay-foot verse, remain'd, and will remain.
Late, very late, correctness grew our care,
When the tir'd nation breath'd from civil war.
Exact Racine, and Corneille's noble fire
Show'd us that France had something to admire.   275
Not but the Tragic spirit was our own,
And full in Shakespear, fair in Otway shone:
But Otway fail'd to polish or refine,
And fluent Shakespear scarce effac'd a line.
Ev'n copious Dryden, wanted, or forgot,   280
The last and greatest Art, the Art to blot.
    Some doubt, if equal pains or equal fire
The humbler Muse of Comedy require?
But in known Images of life I guess
The labour greater, as th' Indulgence less.   285
Observe how seldom ev'n the best succeed:
Tell me if Congreve's Fools are Fools indeed?
What pert low Dialogue has Farqu'ar writ!
How Van wants grace, who never wanted wit!
The stage how loosely does Astræa tread,   290
Who fairly puts all Characters to bed:
And idle Cibber, how he breaks the laws,
To make poor Pinky eat with vast applause!
But fill their purse, our Poet's work is done,
Alike to them, by Pathos or by Pun.   295
    O you! whom Vanity's light bark conveys
On Fame's mad voyage by the wind of Praise;
With what a shifting gale your course you ply;
For ever sunk too low, or born too high!

267. Mr. [Edmund] Waller about this time [1664], with the E. of Dorset, Mr. Godolphin, and others, translated the Pompey of Corneille; and the more correct French Poets began to be in reputation. P.   See *Essay on Criticism*, l. 361n.
    271. splay-foot: flat-foot, clumsy.
    274. Racine . . . Corneille: Jean Racine (1639–99), and Pierre Corneille (1606–84), the great French dramatists.
    277. Otway: see *Second Ep. of the Second Bk.*, l. 146n.
    287. Congreve: see *Ep. to Dr. Arbuthnot*, l. 138n.
    288. Farqu'ar: George Farquhar (1677–1707), comic dramatist.
    289. Van: Sir John Vanbrugh (1664–1726), comic dramatist and architect.
    290. Astræa: A Name taken by Mrs. [Aphra] Behn [1640–89], Authoress of several obscene Plays, &c. P.   Astræa was the goddess of justice (cf. "fairly" in the next line).
    292. Cibber: see l. 88n., above.   **laws:** i.e., of dramatic theory.
    293. Pinky: William Penkethman (d. 1725), a comic actor who, in one of Cibber's plays, was required to bolt down two chickens in a matter of seconds.

Who pants for glory finds but short repose,   300
A breath revives him, or a breath o'erthrows!
Farewel the stage! if just as thrives the Play,
The silly bard grows fat, or falls away.
    There still remains to mortify a Wit,
The many-headed Monster of the Pit: 305
A sense-less, worth-less, and unhonour'd crowd;
Who to disturb their betters mighty proud,
Clatt'ring their sticks, before ten lines are spoke,
Call for the Farce, the Bear, or the Black-joke.
What dear delight to Britons Farce affords!   310
Farce once the taste of Mobs, but now of Lords;
(For Taste, eternal wanderer, now flies
From heads to ears, and now from ears to eyes.)
The Play stands still; damn action and discourse,
Back fly the scenes, and enter foot and horse;   315
Pageants on pageants, in long order drawn,
Peers, Heralds, Bishops, Ermin, Gold, and Lawn;
The Champion too! and, to complete the jest,
Old Edward's Armour beams on Cibber's breast!
With laughter sure Democritus had dy'd,   320
Had he beheld an Audience gape so wide.
Let Bear or Elephant be e'er so white,
The people, sure, the people are the sight!
Ah luckless Poet! stretch thy lungs and roar,
That Bear or Elephant shall heed thee more;   325
While all its throats the Gallery extends,
And all the Thunder of the Pit ascends!
Loud as the Wolves on Orcas' stormy steep,
Howl to the roarings of the Northern deep.

---

309. Bear: a dancing bear (cf. l. 48n., above).   **Black-joke:** *The Coal Black Joke* was a popular air often used for bawdy songs.
313. I.e., from serious plays to operas, and from operas to pantomime and mere spectacle.
317. Ermin, Gold, and Lawn: *ermine* adorns the state robes of peers; *gold* may allude to the cloth and stitching of a herald's tabard, or possibly hint that heralds were sometimes bribed to fabricate genealogies (cf. *Sixth Ep. of the First Bk.*, ll. 81–2n.); *lawn* was the fabric used for the sleeves of a bishop.
318. Champion: the "champion" of the king, who at coronations rode armed into Westminster Hall and by a herald challenged anyone who would deny the king's title to the crown.
319. The Coronation of Henry the Eighth and Queen Anne Boleyn, in which the Playhouses vied with each other to represent all the pomp of a Coronation. In this noble contention, the Armour of one of the Kings of England was borrowed from the Tower, to dress the Champion. P.   **Edward:** see l. 7n., above.
320. Democritus: the celebrated Greek philosopher (460–362 B.C.) who according to tradition laughed continuously at human follies.
328. Orcas: The farthest Northern Promontory of Scotland, opposite to the Orcades. P.

Such is the shout, the long-applauding note,   330
At Quin's high plume, or Oldfield's petticoat,
Or when from Court a birth-day suit bestow'd
Sinks the lost Actor in the tawdry load.
Booth enters — hark! the Universal Peal!
"But has he spoken?" Not a syllable.   335
"What shook the stage, and made the people stare?"
Cato's long Wig, flowr'd gown, and lacquer'd chair.

    Yet lest you think I railly more than teach,
Or praise malignly Arts I cannot reach,
Let me for once presume t'instruct the times,   340
To know the Poet from the Man of Rymes:
'Tis He, who gives my breast a thousand pains,
Can make me feel each Passion that he feigns,
Inrage, compose, with more than magic Art,
With Pity, and with Terror, tear my heart;   345
And snatch me, o'er the earth, or thro' the air,
To Thebes, to Athens, when he will, and where.

    But not this part of the poetic state
Alone, deserves the favour of the Great:
Think of those Authors, Sir, who would rely   350
More on a Reader's sense, than Gazer's eye.
Or who shall wander where the Muses sing?
Who climb their Mountain, or who taste their spring?
How shall we fill a Library with Wit,
When Merlin's Cave is half unfurnish'd yet?   355

    My Liege! why Writers little claim your thought,
I guess; and, with their leave, will tell the fault:
We Poets are (upon a Poet's word)
Of all mankind, the creatures most absurd:
The season, when to come, and when to go,   360
To sing, or cease to sing, we never know;
And if we will recite nine hours in ten,
You lose your patience, just like other men.
Then too we hurt our selves, when to defend
A single verse, we quarrel with a friend;   365

    331. Quin: James Quin (1693–1766), a leading actor of the time.   **Old-**
field: see *Second Sat. of the First Bk.*, l. 4n.
    332. birth-day suit: finery worn at Court on a monarch's birthday.
    334–7. Booth (cf. l. 123n., above) played the lead in Addison's *Cato*.
    338. railly: rally, tease.
    341. Poet: as playwright or in the general sense of "maker."
    346–7. Pope here rejects the supposed Aristotelian unities of time and place.
    348. this part: i.e., the drama.
    350. Sir: George II.
    351. Cf. l. 313n.
    353. Mountain: Parnassus.   **spring:** Castalia, on Parnassus.
    355. Merlin's Cave: A building in the Royal Gardens of Richmond, where is a
small, but choice Collection of Books. P.   Cf. *Second Ep. of the Second
Bk.*, l. 139n., l. 140n.

Repeat unask'd; lament, the Wit's too fine
For vulgar eyes, and point out ev'ry line.
But most, when straining with too weak a wing,
We needs will write Epistles to the King;
And from the moment we oblige the town,   370
Expect a Place, or Pension from the Crown;
Or dubb'd Historians by express command,
T' enroll your triumphs o'er the seas and land;
Be call'd to Court, to plan some work divine,
As once for Louis, Boileau and Racine.   375

   Yet think great Sir! (so many Virtues shown)
Ah think, what Poet best may make them known?
Or chuse at least some Minister of Grace,
Fit to bestow the Laureat's weighty place.

   Charles, to late times to be transmitted fair,   380
Assign'd his figure to Bernini's care;
And great Nassau to Kneller's hand decreed
To fix him graceful on the bounding Steed:
So well in paint and stone they judg'd of merit:
But Kings in Wit may want discerning spirit.   385
The Hero William, and the Martyr Charles,
One knighted Blackmore, and one pension'd Quarles;
Which made old Ben, and surly Dennis swear,
"No Lord's anointed, but a Russian Bear."

   Not with such Majesty, such bold relief,   390
The Forms august of King, or conqu'ring Chief,
E'er swell'd on Marble; as in Verse have shin'd
(In polish'd Verse) the Manners and the Mind.
Oh! could I mount on the Mæonian wing,
Your Arms, your Actions, your Repose to sing!   395
What seas you travers'd! and what fields you fought!
Your Country's Peace, how oft, how dearly bought!
How barb'rous rage subsided at your word,
And Nations wonder'd while they dropp'd the sword!

372–5. Under Charles II the poets laureate had also been named historiographers royal. Louis XIV of France, a great patron of the arts, had appointed Racine and Boileau (see *First Sat. of the Second Bk.*, l. 111n.) as his historiographers.

378–9. Sir Robert Walpole, prime minister, had appointed Colley Cibber to the laureateship in 1730.

380–1. Giovanni Lorenzo Bernini (1598–1680), the Italian baroque sculptor, had made a bust of Charles I, the "Martyr" of l. 386.

382–3. Sir Godfrey Kneller (see *Second Ep. of the Second Bk.*, l. 24n.) painted an equestrian portrait of William III, a prince of the House of Nassau.

387. Blackmore: Sir Richard Blackmore (see *First Sat. of the Second Bk.*, l. 23n.) was knighted for services as royal physician.   **Quarles:** Francis Quarles (1592–1644), a minor poet in the time of Charles I.

388. Ben: Ben Jonson.   **Dennis:** John Dennis, the critic (see *Essay on Criticism*, l. 270n.).

394. Mæonian: Homeric (from Mæonia, birthplace of Homer).

How, when you nodded, o'er the land and deep,   400
Peace stole her wing, and wrapt the world in sleep;
Till Earth's extremes your mediation own,
And Asia's Tyrants tremble at your Throne —
But Verse alas! your Majesty disdains;
And I'm not us'd to Panegyric strains: 405
The Zeal of Fools offends at any time,
But most of all, the Zeal of Fools in ryme.
Besides, a fate attends on all I write,
That when I aim at praise, they say I bite.
A vile Encomium doubly ridicules;   410
There's nothing blackens like the ink of fools;
If true, a woful likeness, and if lyes,
"Praise undeserv'd is scandal in disguise:"
Well may he blush, who gives it, or receives;
And when I flatter, let my dirty leaves   415
(Like Journals, Odes, and such forgotten things
As Eusden, Philips, Settle, writ of Kings)
Cloath spice, line trunks, or flutt'ring in a row,
Befringe the rails of Bedlam and Sohoe.

---

413. Pope quotes from an anonymous poem, *The Celebrated Beauties* (1709).
417. Laurence Eusden (see *Ep. to Dr. Arbuthnot*, l. 15n.), a small poet who
held the laureateship from 1718 till his death in 1730; Ambrose Philips (see
Ep. to Dr. Arbuthnot, l. 100n.), known as "Namby Pamby" for the inanity of
some of his work; Elkanah Settle (1648–1724), a minor poet and dramatist who
had written flattering poems to George I.
418. Cloath spice: leaves of books and pamphlets were often used to wrap
spices and pies.
419. Befringe the rails: booksellers sometimes displayed their wares on rail-
ings in front of their shops.   **Bedlam and Sohoe:** some dealers in old books
had their shops near Bethlehem Hospital (Bedlam) and in the Soho district.

The Sixth Epistle

OF THE

First Book of Horace

Not to Admire, is all the Art I know,
"To make men happy, and to keep them so."
[Plain Truth, dear MURRAY, needs no flow'rs of speech,
So take it in the very words of *Creech*.]
  This Vault of Air, this congregated Ball,   5
Self-centred Sun, and Stars that rise and fall,
There are, my Friend! whose philosophic eyes
Look thro', and trust the Ruler with his Skies,
To him commit the hour, the day, the year,
And view this dreadful All without a fear.   10
  Admire we then what Earth's low entrails hold, ⎫
Arabian shores, or Indian seas infold?   ⎬
All the mad trade of Fools and Slaves for Gold? ⎭
Or Popularity, or Stars and Strings?
The Mob's applauses, or the gifts of Kings?   15
Say with what eyes we ought at Courts to gaze,
And pay the Great our homage of Amaze?
  If weak the pleasure that from these can spring,
The fear to want them is as weak a thing:
Whether we dread, or whether we desire,   20
In either case, believe me, we admire;
Whether we joy or grieve, the same the curse,
Surpriz'd at better, or surpriz'd at worse.
Thus good, or bad, to one extreme betray
Th' unbalanc'd Mind, and snatch the Man away;   25
For Vertue's self may too much Zeal be had;
The worst of Madmen is a Saint run mad.
  Go then, and if you can, admire the state
Of beaming diamonds, and reflected plate;
Procure a *Taste* to double the surprize,   30
And gaze on Parian Charms with learned eyes:

SIXTH EPISTLE OF THE FIRST BOOK: First published in 1738. In Warburton's 1751 edition of Pope's *Works* the sub-title, *To Mr. Murray*, was added. Famed for his eloquence and integrity, William Murray, first Earl of Mansfield (1705–93), was a lawyer, M.P., Attorney-General, and Lord Chief Justice (1756–88).
  4. **Creech:** From whose Translations of *Horace* the two first lines are taken. P.   Thomas Creech (1659–1700) was a headmaster of Sherborne School who translated the works of Lucretius and Horace.
  14. **Stars and Strings:** emblems and ribbons of knightly orders.
  31. **Parian:** white marbles from the isle of Paros were much prized.

Be struck with bright Brocade, or Tyrian Dye,
Our Birth-day Nobles splendid Livery:
If not so pleas'd, at Council-board rejoyce,
To see their Judgments hang upon thy Voice;   35
From morn to night, at Senate, Rolls, and Hall,
Plead much, read more, dine late, or not at all.
But wherefore all this labour, all this strife?
For Fame, for Riches, for a noble Wife?
Shall One whom Nature, Learning, Birth, conspir'd   40
To form, not to admire, but be admir'd,
Sigh, while his Chloë, blind to Wit and Worth,
Weds the rich Dulness of some Son of earth?
Yet Time ennobles, or degrades each Line;
It brighten'd CRAGS's, and may darken thine: 45
And what is Fame? the Meanest have their day,
The Greatest can but blaze, and pass away.
Grac'd as thou art, with all the Pow'r of Words,
So known, so honour'd, at the House of Lords;
Conspicuous Scene! another yet is nigh,   50
(More silent far) where Kings and Poets lye;
Where MURRAY (long enough his Country's pride)
Shall be no more than TULLY, or than HYDE!

    Rack'd with Sciatics, martyr'd with the Stone,
Will any mortal let himself alone?   55
See Ward by batter'd Beaus invited over,
And desp'rate Misery lays hold on Dover.
The case is easier in the Mind's disease;
There, all Men may be cur'd, whene'er they please.
Would ye be blest? despise low Joys, low Gains; ⎫   60
Disdain whatever CORNBURY disdains;   ⎬
Be Virtuous, and be happy for your pains.   ⎭

32. **Tyrian Dye:** crimson or purple (a dye of this color was anciently made at Tyre from certain molluscs).

33. **Birth-day:** alluding to finery worn at royal birthday celebrations.

34. **at Council-board:** here probably suggests the king's Privy Council.

36. **at Senate, Rolls, and Hall:** at Parliament, Court of Chancery, and High Court of Justice.

42. **Chloë:** a name, meaning "blooming," usually applied to women of beauty and simplicity. If Pope had a particular lady in mind, her identity is uncertain.

45. **Crags:** James Craggs (1686–1721), Pope's close friend who, though of humble birth, became Secretary of State in 1718.   **thine:** Murray was the son of a viscount.

50. **another:** Westminster Abbey (adjacent to the Houses of Parliament), where Murray was ultimately buried.

53. **Tully:** Cicero.   **Hyde:** Edward Hyde, first Earl of Clarendon (1608–74), Charles II's chief minister and Lord Chancellor, and author of the great *History of the Rebellion in England.*

56. **Ward:** Joshua Ward, the quack doctor (cf. *First Ep. of the Second Bk.,* l. 182n.).   **Over:** i.e., from France, where Ward had established a practice.

57. **Dover:** Thomas Dover (1660–1742), a prominent London physician.

61. **Cornbury:** Henry Hyde, Viscount Cornbury (1710–53), great-grandson to the Edward Hyde of l. 53, an M.P. for Oxford, and much esteemed for his integrity and wit.

But art thou one, whom new opinions sway,
One, who believes as Tindal leads the way,
Who Virtue and a Church alike disowns,　　　　　　65
Thinks that but words, and this but brick and stones?
Fly then, on all the wings of wild desire!
Admire whate'er the maddest can admire.
Is Wealth thy passion? Hence! from Pole to Pole,
Where winds can carry, or where waves can roll,　　70
For Indian spices, for Peruvian gold,
Prevent the greedy, and out-bid the bold:
Advance thy golden Mountain to the skies;
On the broad base of fifty thousand rise,
Add one round hundred, and (if that's not fair)　　75
Add fifty more, and bring it to a square.
For, mark th' advantage; just so many score
Will gain a Wife with half as many more,
Procure her beauty, make that beauty chaste,
And then such Friends — as cannot fail to last.　　80
A Man of wealth is dubb'd a Man of worth,
Venus shall give him Form, and Anstis Birth.
(Believe me, many a German Prince is worse,
Who proud of Pedigree, is poor of Purse)
His Wealth brave Timon gloriously confounds;　　85
Ask'd for a groat, he gives a hundred pounds;
Or if three Ladies like a luckless Play,
Takes the whole House upon the Poet's day.
Now, in such exigencies not to need,
Upon my word, you must be rich indeed;　　90
A noble superfluity it craves,
Not for your self, but for your Fools and Knaves,
Something, which for your Honour they may cheat,
And which it much becomes you to forget.
If Wealth alone then make and keep us blest,　　95
Still, still be getting, never, never rest.
But if to Pow'r and Place your Passion lye,
If in the Pomp of Life consist the Joy;
Then hire a Slave, (or if you will, a Lord)

64. Tindal: Matthew Tindal (1657–1733), a principal deistical writer of the time (see *Dunciad*, II 399–400, IV 492).
72. Prevent: outdo.
81–2. John Anstis (1669–1744), chief herald-at-arms, had genealogies and armorial bearings in his charge. Pope suggests that a man of wealth could buy himself a pedigree or knighthood.
83–4. George II kept his son, Frederick Louis, Prince of Wales, on very short allowance.
85. Timon: see *Ep. to Burlington*, ll. 99*ff*.
86. groat: a coin worth about four pence.
88. Poet's day: receipts on the third day of a play's run were for the author's benefit.
97. Place: high government position.
98. Joy: pronounced to rhyme with *high*.

To do the Honours, and to give the Word;   100
Tell at your Levee, as the Crouds approach,
To whom to nod, whom take into your Coach,
Whom honour with your hand: to make remarks,
Who rules in Cornwall, or who rules in Berks;
"This may be troublesome, is near the Chair;   105
"That makes three Members, this can chuse a May'r."
Instructed thus, you bow, embrace, protest,   ⎫
Adopt him Son, or Cozen at the least,   ⎬
Then turn about, and laugh at your own Jest.   ⎭
      Or if your life be one continu'd Treat,   110
If to live well means nothing but to eat;
Up, up! cries Gluttony, 'tis break of day,
Go drive the Deer, and drag the finny-prey;
With hounds and horns go hunt an Appetite —
So Russel did, but could not eat at night,   115
Call'd happy Dog! the Beggar at his door,
And envy'd Thirst and Hunger to the Poor.
      Or shall we ev'ry Decency confound,
Thro' Taverns, Stews, and Bagnio's take our round,
Go dine with Chartres, in each Vice out-do   120
K——l's lewd Cargo, or Ty——y's Crew,
From Latian Syrens, French Circæan Feasts,
Return well travell'd, and transform'd to Beasts,
Or for a Titled Punk, or Foreign Flame,
Renounce our Country, and degrade our Name?   125
      If, after all, we must with Wilmot own,
The Cordial Drop of Life is Love alone,

101. **Levee:** a morning reception.
104. I.e., who controls the members of Parliament from the counties of Cornwall and Berkshire.
105. **Chair:** i.e., the Speaker of the House of Commons.
106. **makes three Members:** controls or helps to elect three members of Parliament.
107. **protest:** promise.
110. **Treat:** feast.
115. **Russel:** his identity is uncertain.
119. **Stews, and Bagnio's:** brothels.
120. **Chartres:** the cheat and rapist (see *Ep. to Bathurst*, l. 20n.).
121. **K——l:** George Hay, seventh Earl of Kinnoull (d. 1758), ambassador to Turkey, and thought a vicious man.   **Ty——y:** James O'Hara, Baron Tyrawley (see *Second Sat. of the First Bk.*, l. 121n.), ambassador to Lisbon, was reported to have returned to England with three wives and fourteen children.
122. **Latian:** Italian.   **Circæan:** alluding to Circe, the sorceress in the *Odyssey* who feasted those who wandered to her isle and then transformed them into beasts.
124. **Punk:** strumpet.
126. **Wilmot:** John Wilmot, second Earl of Rochester (1647–80), the witty Restoration rake and poet.
127. **Cordial Drop:** heart-warming potion.

And Swift cry wisely, "Vive la Bagatelle!"
The Man that loves and laughs, must sure do well
Adieu — if this advice appear the worst,   130
E'en take the Counsel which I gave you first:
Or better Precepts if you can impart,
Why do, I'll follow them with all my heart.

128. **"Vive la Bagatelle!"**: "Long live trifling!"

The First Epistle

OF THE

First Book of Horace

IMITATED

S T. JOHN, whose love indulg'd my labours past
    Matures my Present, and shall bound my last!
    Why will you break the Sabbath of my days?
Now sick alike of Envy and of Praise.
Publick too long, ah let me hide my Age!   5
See modest Cibber now has left the Stage:
Our Gen'rals now, retir'd to their Estates,
Hang their old Trophies o'er the Garden gates,
In Life's cool evening satiate of applause,
Nor fond of bleeding, ev'n in BRUNSWICK'S cause.   10
    A Voice there is, that whispers in my ear,
('Tis Reason's voice, which sometimes one can hear)
"Friend Pope! be prudent, let your Muse take breath,
"And never gallop Pegasus to death;
"Lest stiff, and stately, void of fire, or force,   15
"You limp, like Blackmore, on a Lord Mayor's horse."
    Farewell then Verse, and Love, and ev'ry Toy,
The rhymes and rattles of the Man or Boy:
What right, what true, what fit, we justly call,
Let this be all my care — for this is All: 20
To lay this harvest up, and hoard with haste
What ev'ry day will want, and most, the last.
    But ask not, to what Doctors I apply?
Sworn to no Master, of no Sect am I:
As drives the storm, at any door I knock,   25

FIRST EPISTLE OF THE FIRST BOOK: First published in 1738. The sub-title, *To
L. Bolingbroke*, was added in Warburton's 1751 edition of Pope's *Works*. For
Henry St. John, Viscount Bolingbroke, see *An Essay on Man*, I 1n.
    3. Sabbath: Pope was 49 (seven times seven) at this time.
    6. Cibber: Colley Cibber (see *Ep. to Dr. Arbuthnot*, l. 97n.) had formally
announced his retirement from the stage in 1734.
    10. Brunswick's cause: i.e., George II's (but Pope also hints that, because of
George's German interests, the English had been forced to fight in foreign causes).
    16. Blackmore: The fame of this heavy Poet, however problematical else-
where, was universally received in the City of London. His versification is here
exactly described: stiff, and not strong; stately and yet dull, like the sober and
slow-paced Animal generally employed to mount the Lord Mayor: and therefore
here humorously opposed to Pegasus. P.   For Blackmore, see *First Sat. of
the Second Bk.*, l. 23n; for the "City of London," see *Second Sat. of the Second
Bk.*, l. 76n.
    23. Doctors: teachers, learned men.

And house with Montagne now, or now with Lock.
Sometimes a Patriot, active in debate,
Mix with the World, and battle for the State,
Free as young Lyttelton, her cause pursue,
Still true to Virtue, and as warm as true: 30
Sometimes, with Aristippus, or St. Paul,
Indulge my Candor, and grow all to all;
Back to my native Moderation slide,
And win my way by yielding to the tyde.
    Long, as to him who works for debt, the Day;   35
Long as the Night to her whose love's away;
Long as the Year's dull circle seems to run,
When the brisk Minor pants for twenty-one;
So slow th' unprofitable Moments roll,
That lock up all the Functions of my soul;   40
That keep me from Myself; and still delay
Life's instant business to a future day:
That task, which as we follow, or despise,
The eldest is a fool, the youngest wise;
Which done, the poorest can no wants endure,   45
And which not done, the richest must be poor.
    Late as it is, I put my self to school,
And feel some comfort, not to be a fool.
Weak tho' I am of limb, and short of sight,
Far from a Lynx, and not a Giant quite,   50
I'll do what MEAD and CHESELDEN advise,
To keep these limbs, and to preserve these eyes.
Not to go back, is somewhat to advance,
And men must walk at least before they dance.
    Say, does thy blood rebel, thy bosom move   55
With wretched Av'rice, or as wretched Love?
Know, there are Words, and Spells, which can controll

26. Montagne: see *First Sat. of the Second Bk.*, l. 52n.   **Lock:** see *Ep. to a Lady*, l. 23n.
    27. Patriot: a name adopted by those in opposition to Walpole's administration (cf. *Epil. to the Satires,* II 24n.).
    29. Lyttelton: George Lyttelton, first Baron Lyttleton (1709–73), M.P. and vigorous opponent of Walpole's government.
    31. Omnis Aristippum decuit color, & status, & res. P.   Pope cites Horace (*Ep.* I xvii 23) on the Greek hedonistic philosopher, Aristippus (*c.* 400 B.C.): "To Aristippus every condition and state and circumstance of life was fitting." **St. Paul:** see I Corinthians 9:22: "I am made all things to all men," and Philippians 4:5: "Let your moderation be known unto all men."
    32. Candor: openness of mind.
    45. endure: experience.
    50. Lynx: see *Essay on Man,* I 212n.
    51. Mead and Cheselden: Richard Mead (1673–1754), a distinguished physician, and William Cheselden (1688–1752), an esteemed surgeon.
    57–60. Pope attributes to his satire the magical power of curing diseases that was traditionally supposed to reside in spells, verbal charms, and rhymed incantations.

(Between the Fits) this Fever of the soul:
Know, there are Rhymes, which (fresh and fresh apply'd)
Will cure the arrant'st Puppy of his Pride.   60
Be furious, envious, slothful, mad or drunk,
Slave to a Wife or Vassal to a Punk,
A Switz, a High-dutch, or a Low-dutch Bear —
All that we ask is but a patient Ear.
 'Tis the first Virtue, Vices to abhor;   65
And the first Wisdom, to be Fool no more.
But to the world, no bugbear is so great,
As want of figure, and a small Estate.
To either India see the Merchant fly,
Scar'd at the spectre of pale Poverty!   70
See him, with pains of body, pangs of soul,
Burn through the Tropic, freeze beneath the Pole!
Wilt thou do nothing for a nobler end,
Nothing, to make Philosophy thy friend?
To stop thy foolish views, thy long desires,   75
And ease thy heart of all that it admires?
 Here, Wisdom calls: "Seek Virtue first! be bold!
"As Gold to Silver, Virtue is to Gold."
There, London's voice: "Get Mony, Mony still!
"And then let Virtue follow, if she will."   80
This, this the saving doctrine, preach'd to all,
From low St. James's up to high St. Paul;
From him whose quills stand quiver'd at his ear,
To him who notches Sticks at Westminster.
 BARNARD in spirit, sense, and truth abounds.   85
"Pray then what wants he?" fourscore thousand pounds,
A Pension, or such Harness for a slave
As Bug now has, and Dorimant would have.
BARNARD, thou art a *Cit*, with all thy worth;
But wretched Bug, his *Honour*, and so forth.   90

62. **Punk:** strumpet.
63. **Bear:** any boorish, unmannerly person, though Pope in this line also suggests his distaste for George II and his German ancestry.
69. **either India:** the East or West Indies.
82. **low . . . high:** low-church or high-church.
83. **quills.** quill pens, emblem of clerks.
84. **Sticks:** pieces of wood used as tallies in the Exchequer, the office charged with revenue matters. The sticks were cut in two, and each part notched to mark what was due between debtor and creditor, each of whom retained one of the parts.
85. **Barnard:** Sir John Barnard (1685–1764), M.P. for the City of London and much esteemed for his probity and modesty.
87. **Harness:** trappings of a knightly order.
88. **Bug:** nickname of Henry de Grey, Duke of Kent (1671–1740). *Bug* implied a bedbug, and de Grey was known for his "money and smell." **Dorimant:** a "type" name for a beau in Restoration comedy and poetry.
89. **Cit:** short for *citizen*, and implying a tradesman as distinguished from a gentleman (see also *Ep. to Bathurst,* l. 387n.).

Yet every child another song will sing,
"Virtue, brave boys! 'tis Virtue makes a King."
True, conscious Honour is to feel no sin,
He's arm'd without that's innocent within;
Be this thy Screen, and this thy Wall of Brass; 95
Compar'd to this, a Minister's an Ass.
    And say, to which shall our applause belong,
This new Court jargon, or the good old song?
The modern language of corrupted Peers,
Or what was spoke at Cressy and Poitiers? 100
    Who counsels best? who whispers, "Be but Great,
"With Praise or Infamy, leave that to fate:
"Get Place and Wealth, if possible, with Grace;
"If not, by any means get Wealth and Place."
For what? to have a Box where Eunuchs sing, 105
And foremost in the Circle eye a King.
Or he, who bids thee face with steddy view   ⎫
Proud Fortune, and look shallow Greatness thro': ⎬
And, while he bids thee, sets th' Example too?   ⎭
If such a Doctrine, in St. James's air, 110
Shou'd chance to make the well-drest Rabble stare;
If honest S*z take scandal at a spark,
That less admires the Palace than the Park;
Faith I shall give the answer Reynard gave,
"I cannot like, Dread Sir! your Royal Cave; 115
"Because I see by all the Tracks about,
"Full many a Beast goes in, but none comes out."
Adieu to Virtue if you're once a Slave:
Send her to Court, you send her to her Grave.
    Well, if a King's a Lion, at the least 120
The People are a many-headed Beast:
Can they direct what measures to pursue,
Who know themselves so little what to do?
Alike in nothing but one Lust of Gold,
Just half the land would buy, and half be sold: 125
Their Country's wealth our mightier Misers drain,
Or cross, to plunder Provinces, the Main:

95–6. See *Epil. to the Satires,* I 22n.
100. Great victories over the French were won by the English at Crécy (1346) and Poitiers (1356).
105. Eunuchs: see *First Ep. of the Second Bk.,* l. 154n.
106. Circle: the lowest gallery in a theater, with the most expensive seats. eye a King: George II much admired opera.
110. St. James's: St. James's Park.
112. S*z: Augustus Schutz (d. 1757), Keeper of the Privy Purse to George II. The epithet "honest" is perhaps ironic, for though Schutz had a grave exterior, he was thought to pimp for the king.   spark: beau, fop.
113. Palace: St. James's Palace.
114. the answer: the answer given by Reynard the Fox when invited into the cave of a sick lion.

The rest, some farm the Poor-box, some the Pews;
Some keep Assemblies, and wou'd keep the Stews;
Some with fat Bucks on childless Dotards fawn;   130
Some win rich Widows by their Chine and Brawn;
While with the silent growth of ten per Cent,
In Dirt and darkness hundreds stink content.
    Of all these ways, if each pursues his own,
Satire be kind, and let the wretch alone.   135
But show me one, who has it in his pow'r
To act consistent with himself an hour.
Sir Job sail'd forth, the evening bright and still,
"No place on earth (he cry'd) like Greenwich hill!"
Up starts a Palace, lo! th' obedient base   ⎫   140
Slopes at its foot, the woods its sides embrace, ⎬
The silver Thames reflects its marble face.   ⎭
Now let some whimzy, or that Dev'l within   ⎫
Which guides all those who know not what they mean   ⎬
But give the Knight (or give his Lady) spleen;   ⎭   145
"Away, away! take all your scaffolds down,
"For Snug's the word: My dear! we'll live in Town."
    At am'rous Flavio is the Stocking thrown?
That very night he longs to lye alone.
The Fool whose Wife elopes some thrice a quarter,   150
For matrimonial Solace dies a martyr.
Did ever Proteus, Merlin, any Witch,   ⎫
Transform themselves so strangely as the Rich?   ⎬
"Well, but the Poor" — the Poor have the same itch: ⎭
They change their weekly Barber, weekly News,   155
Prefer a new Japanner to their shoes,
Discharge their Garrets, move their Beds, and run
(They know not whither) in a Chaise and one;
They hire their Sculler, and when once aboard,
Grow sick, and damn the Climate — like a Lord.   160
    You laugh, half Beau half Sloven if I stand,

128. **farm:** to receive the revenues from something in return for a flat fee.
129. **Assemblies:** social gatherings.   **Stews:** brothels.
131. **Chine and Brawn:** the back and the buttock, with punning allusion to cuts of venison (cf. "Bucks" and "fawn" of previous line).
138. **Job:** the word implies a speculator in stocks, or one who uses public office for private profit.
139. **Greenwich hill:** presumably the hill in Greenwich, a few miles southeast of London, on which the Royal Observatory was founded.
145. **spleen:** see *Rape of the Lock*, IV 16n.
148. **Flavio:** some blonde youth (from Latin *flavus*).   **Stocking:** on wedding nights the bride's stocking was thrown among the guests; the person hit was supposed to be the next married.
152. **Proteus:** the sea-god who could take any shape.   **Merlin:** see *First Ep. of the Second Bk.*, l. 132n.
156. **Japanner:** a bootblack.
158. **Chaise and one:** a light carriage drawn by one horse.
159. **Sculler:** a Thames boatman.

My Wig all powder, and all snuff my Band;
You laugh, if Coat and Breeches strangely vary,
White Gloves, and Linnen worthy Lady Mary!
But when no Prelate's Lawn with Hair-shirt lin'd,   165
Is half so incoherent as my Mind,
When (each Opinion with the next at strife,
One ebb and flow of follies all my Life)
I plant, root up, I build, and then confound,
Turn round to square, and square again to round;   170
You never change one muscle of your face,
You think this Madness but a common case,
Nor once to Chanc'ry, nor to Hales apply;
Yet hang your lip, to see a Seam awry!
Careless how ill I with myself agree;   175
Kind to my dress, my figure, not to Me.
Is this my Guide, Philosopher, and Friend?
This, He who loves me, and who ought to mend?
Who ought to make me (what he can, or none,)
That Man divine whom Wisdom calls her own;   180
Great without Title, without Fortune bless'd,
Rich ev'n when plunder'd, honour'd while oppress'd,
Lov'd without youth, and follow'd without power,
At home tho' exil'd, free, tho' in the Tower.
In short, that reas'ning, high, immortal Thing,   185
Just less than Jove, and much above a King,
Nay half in Heav'n — except (what's mighty odd)
A Fit of Vapours clouds this Demi-god.

162. Band: neck-band, or collar.
164. Lady Mary: Lady Mary Wortley Montagu (see *Ep. to a Lady*, l. 24n.) was famous for her dirty and slovenly dress.
165. Lawn: fabric used for the sleeves of a bishop.
169. plant: in his garden at Twickenham.
173. Chanc'ry: the Court of Chancery had jurisdiction in cases involving lunacy.   **Hales:** Richard Hales (1670–1728), a physician, studied insanity and was famous for his kindness to lunatics; he was associated with Bethlehem Hospital (Bedlam).
177. Guide, Philosopher, and Friend: see *Essay on Man*, IV 390.
184. Tower: the Tower of London was used as a prison for political offenders.
188. Vapours: see *Rape of the Lock*, IV 18n.

THE SATIRES

OF

Dr. JOHN DONNE,

Dean of St. Paul's,

VERSIFYED

Quid vetat, ut nosmet Lucili scripta legentes
Quærere, num illius, num rerum dura negarit
Versiculos natura magis factos, & euntes
Mollius?   HOR.

The Second Satire

OF

Dr. John Donne

Yes; thank my stars! as early as I knew
 This Town, I had the sense to hate it too:
 Yet here, as ev'n in Hell, there must be still
One Giant-Vice, so excellently ill,
That all beside one pities, not abhors;   5
As who knows Sapho, smiles at other whores.
 I grant that Poetry's a crying sin;
It brought (no doubt) th' *Excise* and *Army* in:
Catch'd like the plague, or love, the Lord knows how,

SECOND SATIRE OF DR. JOHN DONNE: Originally drafted about 1713, first published in 1735. John Donne (1572–1631), metaphysical poet and Dean of St.
Paul's, wrote five "Satyres," none of which was published during his lifetime.
Of these Pope "versifyed" *Satyres II* and *IIII*, and provided for both an epigraph from Horace, *Satires*, I x 56–9: "What prevents us likewise, while reading
the work of Lucilius, from asking whether his own nature, or the difficult nature
of his material, denied him verses more polished and smooth?"
 6. Sapho: presumably Lady Mary Wortley Montagu (see *Ep. to a Lady*,
l. 24*n*.).
 8. Excise and Army: see *Second Sat. of the Second Bk.*, l. 134*n*., and *First
Sat. of the Second Bk.*, l. 73*n*.

But that the cure is starving, all allow.   10
Yet like the Papists is the Poets state,
Poor and disarm'd, and hardly worth your hate.
　　Here a lean Bard, whose wit could never give
Himself a dinner, makes an Actor live:
The Thief condemn'd, in law already dead,   15
So prompts, and saves a Rogue who cannot read.
Thus as the pipes of some carv'd Organ move,
The gilded Puppets dance and mount above,
Heav'd by the breath th' inspiring Bellows blow;
Th' inspiring Bellows lie and pant below.   20
　　One sings the Fair; but Songs no longer move,
No Rat is rhym'd to death, nor Maid to love:
In Love's, in Nature's spite, the siege they hold,
And scorn the Flesh, the Dev'l, and all but Gold.
　　These write to Lords, some mean reward to get,   25
As needy Beggars sing at doors for meat.
Those write because all write, and so have still
Excuse for writing, and for writing ill.
　　Wretched indeed! but far more wretched yet
Is he who makes his meal on others wit: 30
'Tis chang'd no doubt from what it was before,
His rank digestion makes it wit no more:
Sense, past thro' him, no longer is the same,
For food digested takes another name.
　　I pass o'er all those Confessors and Martyrs   35
Who live like S—tt—n, or who die like Chartres,
Out-cant old Esdras, or out-drink his Heir,
Out-usure Jews, or Irishmen out-swear;
Wicked as Pages, who in early years
Act Sins which Prisca's Confessor scarce hears: 40
Ev'n those I pardon, for whose sinful sake
Schoolmen new tenements in Hell must make;

10. **starving:** fasting was thought a cure for some diseases.
11–12. Roman Catholics in England at this time were double-taxed and forbidden to possess arms.
13. **Bard:** a playwright here.
15–16. In certain offenses the mere ability to read permitted one, on a first conviction, to plead an exemption from the sentence.
22. **No Rat is rhym'd:** alluding to the supposed destruction of rats by magic spells and incantations.
35. **Confessors:** those who vow their faith in the face of danger and persecution, but who do not suffer actual martyrdom. In l. 40, *Confessor* denotes a priest authorized to hear confessions.
36. **S—tt—n:** probably Richard Sutton (d. 1737), an M.P. with a reputation as a debauchee.　　**Chartres:** the cheat and rapist (see *Ep. to Bathurst,* l. 20*n.*).
37. **Esdras:** the Old Testament priest Esdras conducted public readings of the Book of the Law for seven days running. Here the name signifies any long-winded and sanctimonious hypocrite.
40. **Prisca:** any lady who is old-fashioned and severe (here hypocritically so).
42. **Schoolmen:** theologians versed in the disciplines of medieval scholasticism.

Of whose strange crimes no Canonist can tell
In what Commandment's large contents they dwell.
    One, one man only breeds my just offence;   45
Whom Crimes gave wealth, and wealth gave impudence:
Time, that at last matures a Clap to Pox,
Whose gentle progress makes a Calf an Ox,
And brings all natural events to pass,
Hath made him an Attorney of an Ass.   50
No young Divine, new-benefic'd, can be
More pert, more proud, more positive than he.
What further could I wish the Fop to do,
But turn a Wit, and scribble verses too?
Pierce the soft lab'rinth of a Lady's ear   55
With rhymes of this *per Cent.* and that *per Year?*
Or court a Wife, spread out his wily parts,
Like nets or lime-twigs, for rich Widows hearts?
Call himself Barrister to ev'ry wench,
And wooe in language of the Pleas and Bench?   60
Language, which Boreas might to Auster hold,
More rough than forty Germans when they scold.
    Curs'd be the Wretch! so venal and so vain;
Paltry and proud, as drabs in Drury-lane.
'Tis such a bounty as was never known,   65
If Peter deigns to help you to your *own:*
What thanks, what praise, if Peter but supplies!
And what a solemn face if he denies!
Grave, as when Pris'ners shake the head, and swear
'Twas only Suretyship that brought 'em there.   70
His *Office* keeps your Parchment-Fates entire,
He starves with cold to save them from the Fire;
For you, he walks the streets thro' rain or dust,
For not in Chariots Peter puts his trust;
For you he sweats and labours at the Laws,   75
Takes God to witness he affects your Cause,
And lyes to every Lord in every thing,
Like a King's Favourite — or like a King.
    These are the talents that adorn them all,

43. **Canonist:** one versed in ecclesiastical law.
47. **Clap to Pox:** gonorrhea to syphilis.
51. **new-benefic'd:** newly endowed with a church living.
58. **lime-twigs:** twigs smeared with birdlime, an adhesive substance usually made from the bark of holly trees, for catching birds.
60. **Pleas:** the Court of Common Pleas (a court for the trial of civil causes). **Bench:** the Court of King's Bench (the supreme court of common law).
61. **Boreas:** the north wind.   **Auster:** the south wind.
64. **Drury-lane:** a street frequented by prostitutes.
66. **Peter:** Peter Walter, the cheat and usurer (see *Ep. to Bathurst*, l. 20n.).
70. **Suretyship:** responsibility undertaken on behalf of another person, as for payment of a debt.
71. **Parchment-Fates:** deeds, mortgages, and so on.
76. **affects:** takes as his own.

From wicked Waters ev'n to godly —   80
Not more of Simony beneath black Gowns,
Not more of Bastardy in heirs to Crowns.
In shillings and in pence at first they deal,
And steal so little, few perceive they steal;
Till like the Sea, they compass all the land,   85
From Scots to Wight, from Mount to Dover strand.
And when rank Widows purchase luscious nights,
Or when a Duke to Jansen punts at White's,
Or City heir in mortgage melts away,
Satan himself feels far less joy than they.   90
Piecemeal they win this Acre first, then that,
Glean on, and gather up the whole Estate:
Then strongly fencing ill-got wealth by law,
Indentures, Cov'nants, Articles they draw;
Large as the Fields themselves, and larger far   95
Than Civil Codes, with all their glosses, are:
So vast, our new Divines, we must confess,
Are Fathers of the Church for writing less.
But let them write for You, each Rogue impairs
The Deeds, and dextrously omits, *ses Heires:*   100
No Commentator can more slily pass
O'er a learn'd, unintelligible place;
Or, in Quotation, shrewd Divines leave out
Those words, that would against them clear the doubt.
So Luther thought the Paternoster long,   105
When doom'd to say his Beads and Evensong:
But having cast his Cowle, and left those laws,
Adds to Christ's prayer, the *Pow'r and Glory* clause.
The Lands are bought; but where are to be found

80. **Waters:** the Peter Walter, or Waters, of l. 66n. The name intended for
the blank at the end of the line is unknown.
81. **Simony:** traffic in ecclesiastical preferment or benefices.
86. I.e., from North (Scotland) to South (the Isle of Wight), from West (St.
Michael's Mount) to East (the Dover beaches).
88. **Jansen:** Sir Henry Jansen (d. 1766), who won several thousand pounds
in one night from Wriothesley Russell, third Duke of Bedford (1708–32).
punts: bets.   **White's:** a notorious gambling house.
89. **City heir:** a London tradesman's heir.
94. **Indentures:** mutual agreements between two parties, the copies of which
are *indented* (i.e., placed together and notched along a border so that thereafter
the two edges can be shown to correspond to one another).   **Cov'nants:** legal
contracts.   **Articles:** formal agreements, or distinct clauses in a legal docu-
ment.
98. **Fathers of the Church:** early Christian writers of authority, usually those
of the first five centuries.
100. **ses Heires:** his heirs.
102. **place:** a textual crux of some kind.
106. **Beads:** the rosary.   **Evensong:** Vespers, usually celebrated just before sunset.
107. **left those laws:** those of the Roman Catholic Church.
108. **Pow'r and Glory clause:** Roman Catholics conclude the Lord's Prayer
with the clause, "But deliver us from evil."

Those ancient Woods, that shaded all the ground? 110
We see no new-built Palaces aspire,
No Kitchens emulate the Vestal Fire.
Where are those Troops of poor, that throng'd of yore
The good old Landlord's hospitable door?
Well, I could wish, that still in lordly domes 115
Some beasts were kill'd, tho' not whole hecatombs,
That both Extremes were banish'd from their walls,
Carthusian Fasts, and fulsome Bacchanals;
And all mankind might that just mean observe,
In which none e'er could surfeit, none could starve. 120
These, as good works 'tis true we all allow;
But oh! these works are not in fashion now:
Like rich old Wardrobes, things extremely rare,
Extremely fine, but what no man will wear.
    Thus much I've said, I trust without offence; 125
Let no Court-Sycophant pervert my sense,
Nor sly Informer watch these words to draw
Within the reach of Treason, or the Law.

---

   112. Vestal Fire: in the sanctuary of Vesta, Roman goddess of hearth and home, a fire burned continually, tended by virgins.
   116. hecatombs: literally, "a hundred oxen."
   118. Carthusian: the Carthusian monks were noted for the austerity of their rule and life.   **Bacchanals:** festivals of Bacchus, god of wine and fertility, were celebrated with orgiastic rites.

The Fourth Satire

OF

Dr. John Donne

W ELL, if it be my time to quit the Stage,
    Adieu to all the Follies of the Age!
    I die in Charity with Fool and Knave,
Secure of Peace at least beyond the Grave.
I've had my *Purgatory* here betimes,   5
And paid for all my Satires, all my Rhymes:
The Poet's Hell, its Tortures, Fiends and Flames,
To this were Trifles, Toys, and empty Names.
    With foolish *Pride* my Heart was never fir'd,
Nor the vain Itch *t'admire*, or *be admir'd;*   10
I hop'd for no *Commission* from his Grace;
I bought no *Benefice*, I begg'd no *Place;*
Had no *new Verses*, or *new Suit* to show;
Yet went to COURT — the Dev'l wou'd have it so.
But, as the Fool, that in reforming Days   15
Wou'd go to Mass in jest, (as Story says)
Could not but think, to pay his *Fine* was odd,
Since 'twas no form'd Design of serving God:
So was I punish'd, as if full as *proud*,
As prone to *Ill*, as negligent of *Good*,   20
As deep in *Debt*, without a thought to pay, ⎫
As *vain*, as *idle*, and as *false*, as they ⎬
Who *live* at *Court*, for going once that Way! ⎭
    Scarce was I enter'd, when behold! there came
A Thing which *Adam* had been pos'd to name;   25
Noah had refus'd it lodging in his Ark,
Where all the Race of *Reptiles* might embark:
A verier Monster than on *Africk*'s Shore
The Sun e're got, or slimy *Nilus* bore,

FOURTH SATIRE OF DR. JOHN DONNE: First published anonymously in 1733, with
the title *The Impertinent, Or a Visit to the Court.* The poem was given its present title, and acknowledged by Pope, in 1735.

  5. betimes: early.

  7. Poet's Hell: Dante's, perhaps, or Milton's.

  11. Commission: in the military.   **His Grace:** courtesy-title for any duke.

  12. Benefice: church living.   **Place:** government post.

  15–18. In 1581, under Elizabeth I, Parliament passed a law which imposed
a fine of 100 marks and a year's imprisonment on anyone attending Mass.

  25. pos'd: puzzled.   **name:** in Genesis 2:19–20, Adam is called upon to
name all the beasts of the field and fowls of the air.

  28. verier: truer.

  29. Cf. *Essay on Criticism*, ll. 41–3n.

Or *Sloane,* or *Woodward*'s wondrous Shelves contain;   30
Nay, all that lying Travellers can feign.
The Watch would hardly let him pass at noon,
At night, wou'd swear him dropt out of the moon,
One whom the mob, when next we find or make
A Popish plot, shall for a Jesuit take;   35
And the wise Justice starting from his chair
Cry, by your Priesthood tell me what you are?
    Such was the Wight: Th' apparel on his back
Tho' coarse was rev'rend, and tho' bare, was black.
The suit, if by the fashion one might guess,   40
Was velvet in the youth of good Queen *Bess,*
But mere tuff-taffety what now remained;
So Time, that changes all things, had ordain'd!
Our sons shall see it leisurely decay,
First turn plain rash, then vanish quite away.   45
    This Thing has *travell'd,* speaks each Language too,
And knows what's fit for ev'ry State to do;
Of whose best Phrase and courtly Accent join'd,
He forms one Tongue exotic and refin'd.
Talkers, I've learn'd to bear; *Motteux* I knew,   50
Henley himself I've heard, nay *Budgel* too:
The Doctor's Wormwood Style, the Hash of Tongues,
A Pedant makes; the Storm of *Gonson*'s Lungs,
The whole Artill'ry of the Terms of War,
And (all those Plagues in one) the bawling Bar;   55
These I cou'd bear; but not a Rogue so civil,
Whose Tongue can complement you to the Devil.
A Tongue that can cheat Widows, cancel Scores,
Make *Scots* speak Treason, cozen subtlest Whores,

    30. Sloane: Sir Hans Sloane, physician and naturalist (see *Ep. to Burlington,* l. 10n.).   **Woodward:** John Woodward (1665–1728), physician, geologist, and collector of fossils and antiquities.
    34. make: fabricate (here for political purposes).
    35. Popish plot: a plot fabricated in 1678, the purport of which was supposed to be the murder of Charles II, the crowning of James II, and the suppression of Protestantism in England. The supposed fact of such a Roman Catholic plot was widely believed, and many persons were falsely accused and executed.
    38. Wight: man.
    39. bare: threadbare.
    41. Bess: Elizabeth I.
    42. tuff-taffety: taffeta with the nap arranged in tufts.
    45. rash: smooth silk (i.e., the nap would be worn away).
    50. Motteux: Peter Anthony Motteux (1660–1718), dramatist and translator known for his loquacity.
    51. Henley . . . Budgell: see *Ep. to Dr. Arbuthnot,* l. 98n., l. 378n.
    52. Doctor's Wormwood Style: i.e., a scholar's bitter and scolding style.
    53. Gonson: Sir John Gonson (d. 1765), a Justice of the Peace famed for his charges to juries.
    58. Scores: debts.
    59. Scots: Scotch caution was proverbial.   **cozen:** cheat.

With Royal Favourites in Flatt'ry vie,   60
And *Oldmixon* and *Burnet* both out-lie.
  He spies me out. I whisper, gracious God!
What Sin of mine cou'd merit such a Rod?
That all the Shot of Dulness now must be
From this thy Blunderbuss discharg'd on me!   65
"Permit (he cries) no stranger to your fame
"To crave your sentiment, if —'s your name.
"What *Speech* esteem you most?" — "The *King's*," said I,
"But the best *Words?*" — "O Sir, the *Dictionary*."
"You miss my aim; I mean the most acute   70
"And perfect *Speaker?*" — "*Onslow*, past dispute."
"But Sir, of Writers?" — "*Swift*, for closer Style,
"And *Ho—y* for a Period of a Mile."
"Why yes, 'tis granted, these indeed may pass
Good common Linguists, and so *Panurge* was: 75
Nay troth, th'*Apostles*, (tho' perhaps too rough)
Had once a pretty Gift of Tongues enough.
Yet these were all *poor Gentlemen!* I dare
Affirm, 'twas *Travel* made them what they were."
  Thus others Talents having nicely shown,   80
He came by sure Transition to his own:
Till I cry'd out, "You prove yourself so able,
"Pity! you was not Druggerman at *Babel*:
"For had they found a Linguist half so good,
"I make no question but the *Tow'r* had stood."   85
  "Obliging Sir! for Courts you sure were made:
"Why then for ever buried in the shade?
"Spirits like you, believe me, shou'd be seen,
"The King would smile on you — at least the Queen?"
"Ah gentle Sir! you Courtiers so cajol us —   90
"But *Tully* has it, *Nunquam minus solus:*
"But as for *Courts*, forgive me if I say,
"No Lessons now are taught the *Spartan* way:
"Tho' in his Pictures Lust be full display'd,

61. **Oldmixon . . . Burnet:** see *Ep. to Dr. Arbuthnot*, l. 146n.
68. **The King's:** Pope glances at George II's German accent.
71. **Onslow:** Arthur Onslow (1691–1768), Speaker of the House of Commons.
72. **closer:** tighter, more concise.
73. **Ho—y:** Benjamin Hoadley (1676–1761), Bishop of Bangor (see *Dunciad,* II 400n.), wrote sentences of extreme length.
75. **Panurge:** see Rabelais, *Works,* II ix, where Panurge addresses Pantagruel in thirteen languages, three of them fictional.
77. **Gift of Tongues:** see Acts 2:1–4.
83. **Druggerman:** dragoman (an interpreter).
91. **Nunquam minus solus:** "Never less alone" — than when alone (from Cicero's *De Officiis,* III i).
93. **Spartan way:** drunkards were exhibited to Spartan youth so that they would develop an abhorrence of the vice.

"Few are the Converts *Aretine* has made;   95
"And tho' the Court show *Vice* exceeding clear,
"None shou'd, by my Advice, learn *Virtue* there."
    At this, entranc'd, he lifts his Hands and Eyes,
Squeaks like a high-stretch'd Lutestring, and replies:
"Oh 'tis the sweetest of all earthly things   100
"To gaze on Princes, and to talk of Kings!"
"Then happy Man who shows the Tombs!" said I,
"He dwells amidst the Royal Family;
"He, ev'ry Day, from *King* to *King* can walk,
"Of all our *Harries*, all our *Edwards* talk,   105
"And get by speaking Truth of Monarchs dead,
"What few can of the living, *Ease* and *Bread*."
"Lord! Sir, a meer *Mechanick!* strangely low,
"And coarse of Phrase — your *English* all are so.
"How elegant your *Frenchman?*" — "Mine, d'ye mean?   110
"I have but one, I hope the Fellow's clean."
"Oh! Sir, politely so! nay, let me dye,
"Your only wearing is your *Padua-soy*."
"Not Sir, my only — I have better still,
"And this, you see, is but my Dishabille —"   115
Wild to get loose, his Patience I provoke,
Mistake, confound, object, at all he spoke.
But as coarse Iron, sharpen'd, mangles more,
And Itch most hurts, when anger'd to a Sore;
So when you plague a Fool, 'tis still the Curse,   120
You only make the Matter worse and worse.
    He past it o'er; affects an easy Smile
At all my Peevishness, and turns his Style.
He asks, "What *News?*" I tell him of new Plays,
New Eunuchs, Harlequins, and Operas.   125
He hears; and as a Still, with Simples in it,
Between each Drop it gives, stays half a Minute;
Loth to enrich me with too quick Replies,
By little, and by little, drops his Lies.
Meer *Household Trash!* of Birth-Nights, Balls and Shows,   130

    95. **Aretine:** Pietro Aretino (1492–1557) wrote a series of sonnets for some licentious drawings.
    96. **Courts show Vice:** see *First Ep. of the Second Bk.*, l. 212n.
    102–7. The "happy Man" is the guide at Westminster Abbey.
    108. **Mechanick:** a manual laborer, or one of a vulgar occupation.
    112. **politely:** elegantly.
    113. **Padua-soy:** corded silk.
    115. **Dishabille:** careless state of dress.
    125. **Eunuchs:** see *First Ep. of the Second Bk.*, l. 154n.   **Harlequins:** mute, clownish characters of particolored costume customarily seen in pantomimes.
    126. **Simples:** plants used for medicinal purposes.
    130. **Birth-Nights:** royal birthday celebrations.   **Shows:** probably puppet-shows, or peep-shows.

More than ten *Holingsheds*, or *Halls*, or *Stows*.
When the *Queen* frown'd, or smil'd, he knows; and what
A subtle Minister may make of that?
Who sins with whom? who got his Pension *Rug*,
Or quicken'd a Reversion by a *Drug*?   135
Whose Place is *quarter'd out*, three Parts in four,
And whether to a Bishop, or a Whore?
Who, having lost his Credit, pawn'd his Rent,
Is therefore fit to have a *Government*?
Who in the *Secret*, deals in Stocks secure,   140
And cheats th'unknowing Widow, and the Poor?
Who makes a *Trust*, or *Charity*, a Job,
And gets an Act of Parliament to rob?
Why *Turnpikes* rise, and now no Cit, nor Clown
Can *gratis* see the *Country*, or the *Town*?   145
Shortly no Lad shall *chuck*, or Lady *vole*,
But some excising Courtier will have a Toll.
He tells what Strumpet Places sells for Life,
What 'Squire his Lands, what Citizen his Wife?
And last (which proves him wiser still than all)   150
What Lady's Face is not a whited Wall?
As one of *Woodward*'s Patients, sick and sore,
I puke, I nauseate, — yet he thrusts in more;
Trims *Europe*'s Balance, tops the Statesman's part,
And talks *Gazettes* and *Post-Boys* o'er by heart.   155
Like a big Wife at sight of loathsome Meat,
Ready to cast, I yawn, I sigh, and sweat:
Then as a licens'd Spy, whom nothing can
Silence, or hurt, he libels the *Great Man*;

131. Rafael Holinshed (d. 1580), Edward Hall (d. 1547), and John Stow (d. 1605), all chroniclers of English history whose accounts of great events were mingled with petty matters.
134. Rug: safe, secure.
135. Reversion: right of succession to an estate or office after the death of the holder.
136. Place: high government office.
138. Rent: income property.
139. a Government: a political position.
142. I.e., who turns a public trust or charitable organization to private gain.
144. Turnpikes: toll roads. **Cit:** tradesmen within the "City" of London were known as "Cits" or "Citizens" (see *First Ep. of the First Bk.*, l. 89n., and l. 149, below). **Clown:** peasant, country fellow.
146. chuck: i.e., pitch pennies. **vole:** try to win all tricks at cards.
147. excising: one who deducts a kind of toll or tax for services.
149. Citizen: see l. 144n., above, and *Second Sat. of the First Bk.*, l. 47n.
151. whited Wall: see Matthew 23:27. The line suggests the lady has disguised the effects of syphilis with powder, paint, and salve.
152–3. Woodward (l. 30n., above) was famous for emetics given to his patients.
156. big: pregnant.
157. cast: vomit.
159–65. The "Great Man" is Sir Robert Walpole, whose government often

Swears every *Place entail'd* for Years to come,   160
In *sure Succession* to the Day of Doom:
He names the *Price* for ev'ry *Office* paid,
And says our *Wars thrive ill,* because *delay'd;*
Nay hints, 'tis by Connivance of the Court,
That *Spain* robs on, and *Dunkirk's* still a Port.   165
Not more Amazement seiz'd on *Circe's* Guests,
To see themselves fall endlong into Beasts,
Than mine, to find a Subject staid and wise,
Already half turn'd Traytor by surprize.
I fear'd th'Infection slide from him to me,   170
As in the Pox, some give it, to get free;
And quick to swallow me, methought I saw
One of our Giant *Statutes* ope its Jaw!
In that nice Moment, as another Lye
Stood just a-tilt, the *Minister* came by.   175
Away he flies. He bows, and bows again;
And close as *Umbra* joins the dirty Train.
Not *Fannius* self more impudently near,
When half his Nose is in his Patron's Ear.
I quak'd at heart; and still afraid to see   180
All the Court fill'd with stranger things than he,
Ran out as fast, as one that pays his Bail,
And dreads more Actions, hurries from a Jail.
      Bear me, some God! oh quickly bear me hence
To wholesome Solitude, the Nurse of Sense: 185
Where Contemplation prunes her ruffled Wings,
And the free Soul looks down to pity Kings.
There sober Thought pursu'd th'amusing theme
Till Fancy colour'd it, and form'd a Dream.
A *Vision* Hermits can to Hell transport,   190
And force ev'n me to see the Damn'd at Court.
Not *Dante* dreaming all th'Infernal State,
Beheld such Scenes of *Envy, Sin,* and *Hate.*
Base Fear becomes the Guilty, not the Free;
Suits Tyrants, Plunderers, but suits not me.   195
Shall I, the Terror of this sinful Town,
Care, if a livery'd Lord or smile or frown?
Who cannot flatter, and detest who can,

---

operated by systematic bribery, whether in terms of money or government "place." Seizure of English shipping by the Spanish, and the failure of the French to carry out defortification of Dunkirk as stipulated in the Treaty of Utrecht (1712), were also causes of complaint against Walpole's administration.
   160. entail'd: settled on a certain person and his descendants.
   166–7. See *Sixth Ep. of the First Bk.,* l. 122n.
   174. nice: precise, delicate.
   177. Umbra: type-name for a flatterer (see *Essay on Man,* IV 278n.).
   178–9. Fannius: Lord John Hervey (see *Ep. to Dr. Arbuthnot,* l. 149n., 319n.).

Tremble before a *noble Serving-Man?*
O my fair Mistress, *Truth!* Shall I quit thee,   200
For huffing, braggart, puft *Nobility?*
Thou, who since Yesterday, hast roll'd o'er all
The busy, idle Blockheads of the Ball,
Hast thou, O *Sun!* beheld an emptier sort,
Than such as swell this Bladder of a Court?   205
Now pox on those who shew a *Court in Wax!*
It ought to bring all Courtiers on their backs.
Such painted Puppets, such a varnish'd Race
Of hollow Gewgaws, only Dress and Face,
Such waxen Noses, stately, staring things,   210
No wonder some Folks bow, and think them *Kings.*
    See! where the *British* Youth, engag'd no more
At *Fig's* at *White's*, with *Felons*, or a *Whore*,
Pay their last Duty to the *Court,* and come
All fresh and fragrant, to the *Drawing-Room:*   215
In Hues as gay, and Odours as divine,
As the fair Fields they sold to look so fine.
"That's *Velvet* for a *King!*" the Flattr'er swears;
'Tis true, for ten days hence 'twill be *King Lear's.*
Our Court may justly to our Stage give Rules,   220
That helps it both to *Fool's-Coats* and to *Fools.*
And why not Players strut in Courtiers Cloaths?
For these are Actors too, as well as those:
Wants reach all States; they beg but better drest,
And all is *splendid Poverty* at best.   225
    Painted for sight, and essenc'd for the smell,
Like Frigates fraught with Spice and Cochine'l,
Sail in the *Ladies:* How each Pyrate eyes
So weak a Vessel, and so rich a Prize!
Top-gallant he, and she in all her Trim,   230
He boarding her, she striking sail to him.
"*Dear Countess!* you have Charms all Hearts to hit!"
And "*sweet Sir Fopling!* you have so much wit!"
Such Wits and Beauties are not prais'd for nought,
For both the Beauty and the Wit are *bought.*   235
'Twou'd burst ev'n *Heraclitus* with the Spleen,

206. Court: A famous Show of the Court of France in Waxwork. P.
209. Gewgaws: paltry baubles.
213. *Fig's*, a Prize-fighter's Academy, where the young Nobility receiv'd instruction in those days: *White's* was a noted gaming-house. It was also customary for the nobility and gentry to visit the condemned criminals in Newgate. P.
219. I.e., the court finery will soon be given or sold to actors.
227. Cochine'l: cochineal (dye-stuff for making carmine).
233. Sir Fopling: Sir Fopling Flutter was a comic character in George Etherege's *The Man of Mode* (1676).
236-7. Heraclitus (*c.* 500 B.C.), known as "the weeping philosopher," would burst with laughter at the sight of such antic (i.e., grotesque) persons as Fopling and Courtin (some court lady or other).

278 • *Satires of Dr. John Donne*

To see those Anticks, *Fopling* and *Courtin:*
The *Presence* seems, with things so richly odd,
The Mosque of *Mahound,* or some queer *Pa-god.*
See them survey their Limbs by *Durer's* Rules,   240
Of all Beau-kind the best proportion'd Fools!
Adjust their Cloaths, and to Confession draw
Those venial sins, an Atom, or a Straw:
But oh! what Terrors must distract the Soul,
Convicted of that mortal Crime, a Hole!   245
Or should one Pound of Powder less bespread
Those Monkey-Tails that wag behind their Head!
Thus finish'd and corrected to a hair,
They march, to prate their Hour before the Fair,
So first to preach a white-glov'd Chaplain goes,   250
With Band of Lily, and with Cheek of Rose,
Sweeter than *Sharon,* in immaculate trim,
Neatness itself impertinent in him.
Let but the Ladies smile, and they are blest;
Prodigious! how the Things *Protest, Protest:*   255
Peace, Fools! or *Gonson* will for Papists seize you,
If once he catch you at your *Jesu! Jesu!*
        Nature made ev'ry Fop to plague his Brother,
Just as one Beauty mortifies another.
But here's the *Captain,* that will plague them both,   260
Whose Air cries Arm! whose very Look's an Oath:
Tho' his Soul's Bullet, and his Body Buff!
Damn him, he's honest, Sir, — and that's enuff.
He spits fore-right; his haughty Chest before,
Like batt'ring Rams, beats open ev'ry Door;   265
And with a Face as red, and as awry,
As *Herod's* Hang-dogs in old Tapestry,
Scarecrow to Boys, the breeding Woman's curse;
Has yet a strange Ambition to *look worse:*
Confounds the Civil, keeps the Rude in awe,   270
Jests like a licens'd Fool, commands like Law.
Frighted, I quit the Room, but leave it so,

238. **Presence:** the royal presence-chamber.
239. **Mahoud:** Mohammed, at one time thought to be worshipped as a god.
Pa-god: an idol temple.
240. **Durer:** Albrecht Dürer (1471–1528), German painter who wrote a
Treatise on Human Proportion.
251. **Band:** collar.
252. **Sharon:** cf. Song of Solomon 2:1 ("rose of Sharon").
255. **Protest:** avow, call God to witness.
256. **Gonson:** see l. 53*n.,* above.
262. **Buff:** a stout leather.
267. **Hang-dogs:** the ruffians who executed Christ.
268. **curse:** alludes to the old superstition that a frightening experience could
"mark" an unborn child.
271. **licens'd Fool:** a privileged court fool or jester.

As Men from Jayls to Execution go;
For hung with *Deadly Sins* I see the Wall,
And lin'd with *Giants*, deadlier than 'em all: 275
Each Man an *Ascapart*, of Strength to toss
For Quoits, both *Temple-Bar* and *Charing-Cross*.
Scar'd at the grizly Forms, I sweat, I fly,
And shake all o'er, like a discover'd Spy.
Courts are too much for Wits so weak as mine;   280
Charge them with Heav'n's Artill'ry, bold *Divine!*
From such alone the Great Rebukes endure,
Whose *Satyr's sacred*, and whose Rage *secure*.
'Tis mine to wash a few slight Stains; but theirs
To deluge Sin, and drown a Court in Tears.   285
Howe'er, what's now *Apocrypha*, my Wit,
In time to come, may pass for *Holy Writ*.

FINIS

274. The Room hung with old Tapestry, representing the *Seven Deadly Sins.*
P.   The tapestries were in the anteroom to the Presence Chamber at Hampton
Court.
275. Giants: the royal guards were men of large size.
276. Ascapart: A Giant famous in Romances.   P.
277. Temple-Bar: a stone arch or gateway which spanned Fleet Street at the
city limit of London.   Charing-Cross: the cross which Edward I had erected
in memory of his queen, in Westminster.
286. Apocrypha: writings of doubtful authority.

EPILOGUE

TO THE SATIRES

Written in 1738

Dialogue I

Fr.

NOT twice a twelvemonth you appear in Print,
    And when it comes, the Court see nothing in't.
    You grow *correct* that once with Rapture writ,
And are, besides, too *Moral* for a Wit.
Decay of Parts, alas! we all must feel —   5
Why now, this moment, don't I see you steal?
'Tis all from *Horace: Horace* long before ye
Said, "Tories call'd him Whig, and Whigs a Tory;"
And taught his Romans, in much better metre,
"To laugh at Fools who put their trust in *Peter*."   10
    But *Horace*, Sir, was delicate, was nice;
Bubo observes, he lash'd no sort of *Vice:*
Horace would say, *Sir Billy serv'd the Crown*,
Blunt *could do Bus'ness*, H—ggins *knew the Town*,

EPILOGUE TO THE SATIRES. DIALOGUE I: First published in May, 1738, with the title *One Thousand Seven Hundred and Thirty Eight, A Dialogue Something like Horace*, and with the dialogue distributed between speakers labeled "A" and "B." Later in the same year the identification of the speakers was changed to "Fr." ("Friend") and "P." ("Pope" or the "Poet"). In 1740 this and the following poetic dialogue were subsumed under the title of *Epilogue to the Satires.*

  1–2. These two lines are from Horace [*Sat.* II iii 1–4]; and the only lines that are so in the whole Poem; being meant to give a handle to that which follows in the character of an impertinent Censurer, *'Tis all from Horace; etc.* P.

  8. Cf. *First Sat. of the Second Bk.*, l. 68.

  10. Ibid., l. 40. For Peter Walter, see *Ep. to Bathurst*, l. 20n.

  11. nice: tactful, delicate.

  12. Bubo: Some guilty person very fond of making such an observation. P. Under the name of *Bubo* (see *Ep. to Burlington*, l. 20n.) Pope sometimes refers to George Bubb Dodington (see *Second Ep. of the Second Bk.*, l. 274n.).

  13. Sir Billy: Sir William Yonge, a time-serving politician (see *Ep. to Dr. Arbuthnot*, l. 280n.).

  14. Blunt: Sir John Blunt, an unscrupulous businessman (see *Ep. to Bathurst*, l. 105n.).   H—ggins: Formerly Jaylor of the Fleet Prison [John Huggins, d. 1745], enriched himself by many exactions, for which he was tried and expelled. P.

In *Sappho* touch the *Failing of the Sex,* 15
In rev'rend Bishops note some *small Neglects,*
And own, the *Spaniard* did a *waggish thing,*
Who cropt our Ears, and sent them to the King.
His sly, polite, insinuating stile
Could please at Court, and make Augustus smile: 20
An artful Manager, that crept between
His Friend and Shame, and was a kind of *Screen.*
But 'faith your very Friends will soon be sore;
Patriots there are, who wish you'd jest no more —
And where's the Glory? 'twill be only thought 25
The Great man never offer'd you a Groat.
Go see Sir Robert —

         P. See Sir Robert! — hum —
And never laugh — for all my life to come?
Seen him I have, but in his happier hour
Of Social Pleasure, ill-exchang'd for Pow'r; 30
Seen him, uncumber'd with the Venal tribe,
Smile without Art, and win without a Bribe.
Would he oblige me? let me only find,
He does not think me what he thinks mankind.
Come, come, at all I laugh He laughs, no doubt, 35
The only diff'rence is, I dare laugh out.

     F. Why yes: with *Scripture* still you may be free;
A Horse-laugh, if you please, at *Honesty;*
A Joke on Jekyl, or some odd *Old Whig,*

15. **Sappho:** Lady Mary Wortley Montague (see *Ep. to a Lady,* l. 24n., and first note to *Ep. to Dr. Arbuthnot*).
18. **cropt our Ears:** Said to be executed by the Captain of a Spanish ship on Jenkins a Captain of an English one. He cut off his ears, and bid him carry them to the King his master. P. This outrage, along with other actions against English merchant ships, brought on war with Spain (the "War of Jenkins's Ear").
20. **Augustus:** Caesar Augustus, the patron of Horace and Virgil, though Pope glances at George Augustus (see first note to *First Ep. of the Second Bk.*).
22. **Screen:** A metaphor peculiarly appropriated to a certain person in power. P. The "certain person" was Sir Robert Walpole, prime minister (alluded to in ll. 26ff.), who "screened" his friends and political allies from parliamentary investigations.
24. **Patriots:** This appellation was generally given to those in opposition to the Court. Though some of them (which our author hints at) had views too mean and interested to deserve that name. P.
26. **The Great man:** A phrase, by common use, appropriated to the first minister. P. **Groat:** a coin worth about four pence.
34. Pope refers to an axiom attributed to Walpole: "All men have their price."
39. **Jekyl:** Sir Joseph Jekyl [1663–1738], Master of the Rolls, a true Whig in his principles, and a man of the utmost probity. He sometimes voted against the Court, which drew upon him the laugh here described of One [Walpole] who bestowed it equally upon Religion and Honesty. He died a few months after the publication of this poem. P.

Who never chang'd his Principle, or Wig: 40
A Patriot is a Fool in ev'ry age,
Whom all Lord Chamberlains allow the Stage:
These nothing hurts; they keep their Fashion still,
And wear their strange old Virtue as they will.

If any ask you, "Who's the Man, so near   45
"His Prince, that writes in Verse, and has his Ear?"
Why answer Lyttelton, and I'll engage
The worthy Youth shall ne'er be in a rage:
But were his Verses vile, his Whisper base,
You'd quickly find him in Lord *Fanny's* case.   50
Sejanus, Wolsey, hurt not honest Fleury,
But well may put some Statesmen in a fury.

Laugh then at any, but at Fools or Foes;
These you but anger, and you mend not those:
Laugh at your Friends, and if your Friends are sore,   55
So much the better, you may laugh the more.
To Vice and Folly to confine the jest,
Sets half the World, God knows, against the rest;
Did not the Sneer of more impartial men
At Sense and Virtue, balance all agen.   60
Judicious Wits spread wide the Ridicule,
And charitably comfort Knave and Fool.

P. Dear Sir, forgive the Prejudice of Youth:
Adieu Distinction, Satire, Warmth, and Truth!
Come harmless *Characters* that no one hit,   65
Come *Henley's* Oratory, *Osborn's* Wit!
The Honey dropping from *Favonio's* tongue,

40. Wig: Jekyll wore the old-fashioned full-bottomed wig.
42. Lord Chamberlains: the Playhouse Act of 1737 provided that no play could be acted without the approval of the Lord Chamberlain (see *Dialogue II,* ll. 1–3n.).
47. Lyttelton: George Lyttelton, Secretary to the Prince of Wales, distinguished both for his writings and speeches in the spirit of Liberty.   P.   Pope's compliment gains force when it is understood that Frederick Louis, Prince of Wales, had come to an open breach with his father, George II, and that in 1737 Queen Caroline had died unreconciled to her son. For Lyttleton, see *First Ep. of the First Bk.,* l. 29n.
50. Fanny: Lord John Hervey (see *Ep. to Dr. Arbuthnot,* first note and also l. 149n., ll. 305ff.).
51. Sejanus, Wolsey: The one the wicked minister of Tiberius; the other of Henry VIII. The writers against the Court usually bestowed these and other odious names on the Minister, without distinction, and in the most injurious manner. See *Dial.* II 137.   P.
66. Henley . . . Osborn: See them in their places in the *Dunciad* [III 199, and II 312].   P.
67. Favonio: the "favoring one," implying a flatterer.

The Flow'rs of *Bubo,* and the Flow of *Y—ng!*
The gracious Dew of Pulpit Eloquence;
And all the well-whipt Cream of Courtly Sense,   70
That first was *H—vy's, F—*'s next, and then
The *S—te's,* and then *H—vy's* once agen.
O come, that easy *Ciceronian* stile,
So *Latin,* yet so *English* all the while,
As, tho' the Pride of *Middleton* and *Bland,*   75
All Boys may read, and Girls may understand!
Then might I sing without the least Offence,
And all I sung should be the *Nation's Sense:*
Or teach the melancholy Muse to mourn,
Hang the sad Verse on CAROLINA's Urn,   80
And hail her passage to the Realms of Rest,
All Parts perform'd, and *all* her Children blest!
So — Satire is no more — I feel it die —
No *Gazeteer* more innocent than I!
And let, a God's-name, ev'ry Fool and Knave   85
Be grac'd thro' Life, and flatter'd in his Grave.

    F. Why so? if Satire know its Time and Place,
You still may lash the Greatest — in Disgrace:
For Merit will by turns forsake them all;
Would you know when? exactly when they fall.   90
But let all Satire in all Changes spare
Immortal *S—k,* and grave *De—re!*

68. Bubo . . . Y—ng: cf. l. 12*n.*, l. 13*n.*, above.
69ff. Alludes to some court sermons, and florid panegyrical speeches; particularly one very full of puerilities and flatteries; which afterwards got into an address in the same pretty style; and was lastly serv'd up in an Epitaph, between Latin and English, published by its author. P.   Pope refers to a speech of condolence to George II on the death of Queen Caroline, originally composed, he says, by *Lord John Hervey,* delivered as his own by *Henry Fox* (see *First Sat. of the Second Bk.,* l. 49*n.*), adopted by the *Senate* (i.e., Parliament), and later used again by *Hervey* in a Latin epitaph written for the Queen.
75. Middleton and Bland: Pope suggests that these two celebrated Latinists (Conyers Middleton, 1683–1750, who wrote a life of Cicero, and Henry Bland, d. 1746, a headmaster of Eton) wrote, or helped to write, Hervey's Latin epitaph on the Queen.
78. Nation's Sense: i.e., the official governmental view.
80. Carolina: Queen consort to George II. She died in 1737. Her death gave occasion, as is observed above, to many indiscreet and mean performances unworthy of her memory, whose last moments manifested the utmost courage and resolution. P.   The last part of Pope's note is ironic: ll. 81–2 allude to reports that the Queen refused the last sacrament and also refused to be reconciled to her son, the Prince of Wales.   **hang the sad Verse:** mourning verses were sometimes pinned to the palls of coffins.
84. Gazeteer: a journalist hired by the government.
92. S—k . . . De—re: a title given *that* Lord [Charles Douglas, Earl of Selkirk, 1663–1739] by King James II. He was of the Bedchamber to King William; he was so to King George I. He was so to King George II. *This* Lord [John West, Earl De La Warr, 1693–1766] was very skilful in all the forms of the House, in which he discharged himself with great gravity. P.

Silent and soft, as Saints remove to Heav'n,
All Tyes dissolv'd, and ev'ry Sin forgiv'n,
These, may some gentle, ministerial Wing   95
Receive, and place for ever near a King!
There, where no Passion, Pride, or Shame transport,
Lull'd with the sweet *Nepenthe* of a Court;
There, where no Father's, Brother's, Friend's Disgrace
Once break their Rest, or stir them from their Place;   100
But past the Sense of human Miseries,
All Tears are wip'd for ever from all Eyes;
No Cheek is known to blush, no Heart to throb,
Save when they lose a Question, or a Job.

P. Good Heav'n forbid, that I shou'd blast their Glory,
Who know how like Whig-Ministers to Tory,   106
And when three Sov'reigns dy'd, could scarce be vext,
Consid'ring what a Gracious Prince was next.
Have I in silent wonder seen such things
As Pride in Slaves, and Avarice in Kings,   110
And at a Peer, or Peeress shall I fret,
Who starves a Sister, or forswears a Debt?
Virtue, I grant you, is an empty boast;
But shall the Dignity of *Vice* be lost?
Ye Gods! shall *Cibber's* Son, without rebuke   115
Swear like a Lord? or a *Rich* out-whore a Duke?
A Fav'rite's *Porter* with his Master vie,
Be brib'd as often, and as often lie?
Shall *Ward* draw Contracts with a Statesman's skill?
Or *Japhet* pocket, like his Grace, a Will?   120
Is it for *Bond* or *Peter* (paltry Things!)
To pay their Debts or keep their Faith like Kings?
If *Blount* dispatch'd himself, he play'd the man,

98. Nepenthe: a drug supposed to cause forgetfulness.
100. Place: government post.
102. Cf. *Messiah,* l. 46n.
104. Question: a parliamentary proposal.   **Job:** a public trust turned to private gain.
107–8. George II was the fourth sovereign under whom Pope had lived.
115–16. Cibber's Son . . . Rich: Two Players [Theophilus Cibber and John Rich]; look for them in the *Dunciad* [III 139n., 255–63n.].   P.
119. Ward: John Ward, the forger (see *Ep. to Bathurst,* l. 20n.).
120. Japhet: Japhet Crook, another forger (see *Ep. to Dr. Arbuthnot,* l. 363n.).   **his Grace:** any duke.
121. Bond or Peter: the swindlers Denis Bond and Peter Walter (see *Ep. to Bathurst,* l. 102n., l. 20n.).
123. Blount: Author of an impious and foolish Book called The Oracles of Reason, who being in love with a near kinswoman of his, and rejected, gave himself a stab in the arm, as pretending to kill himself, of the consequence of which he really died. P.   Charles Blount (1654–93) was a deist, and *The Oracles of Reason* contains a number of free-thinking essays.

And so may'st Thou, Illustrious *Passeran!*
But shall a *Printer,* weary of his life,   125
Learn from their Books to hang himself and Wife?
This, this, my friend, I cannot, must not bear;
Vice thus abus'd, demands a Nation's care;
This calls the Church to deprecate our Sin,
And hurls the Thunder of the Laws on *Gin.*   130

    Let modest *Foster,* if he will, excell
Ten Metropolitans in preaching well;
A simple Quaker, or a Quaker's Wife,
Out-do *Landaffe,* in Doctrine — yea, in Life;
Let humble ALLEN, with an aukward Shame,   135
Do good by stealth, and blush to find it Fame.
Virtue may chuse the high or low Degree,
'Tis just alike to Virtue, and to me;
Dwell in a Monk, or light upon a King,
She's still the same, belov'd, contented thing.   140
Vice is undone, if she forgets her Birth,
And stoops from Angels to the Dregs of Earth:
But 'tis the *Fall* degrades her to a Whore;
Let *Greatness* own her, and she's mean no more:
Her Birth, her Beauty, Crowds and Courts confess,   145
Chaste Matrons praise her, and grave Bishops bless:
In golden Chains the willing World she draws,
And hers the Gospel is, and hers the Laws:
Mounts the Tribunal, lifts her scarlet head,
And sees pale Virtue carted in her stead!   150
Lo! at the Wheels of her Triumphal Car,

124. Passeran: Author of another, called a Philosophical Discourse on Death. P.   Alberto Radicati, Count of Passerano (1698–1737), Italian deist who argued that suicide is not evil, and who had fled to England to avoid persecution.
125–6. A Fact that happened in London a few years past. The unhappy man left behind him a paper justifying his action by the reasonings of some of these authors. P.
130. Gin: A spirituous liquor, the exorbitant use of which had almost destroyed the lowest rank of the People till it was restrained by an act of Parliament in 1736. P.
131. Foster: James Foster (1697–1753), Anabaptist minister esteemed for his sermons.
132. Metropolitans: archbishops.
134. Landaffe: A poor Bishoprick in Wales, as poorly supplied. P.   The Bishop of Llandaff was John Harris (1680–1738), who had once attempted to ridicule both Swift and Pope.
135. Allen: Ralph Allen (1694–1764), Pope's wealthy and extremely charitable friend.
142. Angels: alluding, in part at least, to Satan and the rebel angels who fell with him.
144. mean: ignoble, base.
150. carted: prostitutes were punished by being exhibited in carts drawn through the streets.
151. Car: chariot.

Old *England*'s Genius, rough with many a Scar,
Dragg'd in the Dust! his Arms hang idly round,
His Flag inverted trails along the ground!
Our Youth, all liv'ry'd o'er with foreign Gold,   155
Before her dance; behind her crawl the Old!
See thronging Millions to the Pagod run,
And offer Country, Parent, Wife, or Son!
Hear her black Trumpet thro' the Land proclaim,
That "Not to be corrupted is the Shame."   160
In Soldier, Churchman, Patriot, Man in Pow'r,
'Tis Av'rice all, Ambition is no more!
See, all our Nobles begging to be Slaves!
See, all our Fools aspiring to be Knaves!
The Wit of Cheats, the Courage of a Whore,   165
Are what ten thousand envy and adore.
All, all look up, with reverential Awe,
On Crimes that scape, or triumph o'er the Law:
While Truth, Worth, Wisdom, daily they decry —
"Nothing is Sacred now but Villany."   170

    Yet may this Verse (if such a Verse remain)
Show there was one who held it in disdain.

152. **Genius:** distinctive character or spirit.
157. **Pagod:** idol.

Dialogue II

Fr.

Tis all a Libel — *Paxton* (Sir) will say.
   P. Not yet, my Friend! to-morow 'faith it may; }
   And for that very cause I print to day.
How shou'd I fret, to mangle ev'ry line,
In rev'rence to the Sins of *Thirty-nine!*   5
Vice with such Giant-strides comes on amain,
Invention strives to be before in vain;
Feign what I will, and paint it e'er so strong,
Some rising Genius sins up to my Song.
   F. Yet none but you by Name the Guilty lash;   10

EPILOGUE TO THE SATIRES. DIALOGUE II: First published in July, 1738, with the title *One Thousand Seven Hundred and Thirty Eight, Dialogue II*, and with the dialogue spoken by "A" and "B." In 1740 the present title was given the poem and the speakers altered to "Fr." and "P."
1–3. Nicholas Paxton (d. 1744) was hired by the Walpole administration to report printed slurs upon the court and government. Pope here attacks what he felt to be increasing restraints upon English liberties (see l. 255*n.*, below, and *Dialogue I*, l. 42*n.*).
7. **Invention:** Poetic imagination.

Ev'n *Guthry* saves half *Newgate* by a Dash.
Spare then the Person, and expose the Vice.
   P. How Sir! not damn the Sharper, but the Dice?
Come on then Satire! gen'ral, unconfin'd,
Spread thy broad wing, and sowze on all the Kind.   15
Ye Statesmen, Priests, of one Religion all!
Ye Tradesmen vile, in Army, Court, or Hall!
Ye Rev'rend Atheists! — *F.* Scandal! name them, Who?
   P. Why that's the thing you bid me not to do.
Who starv'd a Sister, who forswore a Debt,   20
I never nam'd — the Town's enquiring yet.
The pois'ning Dame — *Fr.* You mean — *P.* I don't. — *Fr.* You do.
   P. See! now I keep the Secret, and not you.
The bribing Statesman — *Fr.* Hold! too high you go.
   P. The brib'd Elector — *Fr.* There you stoop too low.   25
   P. I fain wou'd please you, if I knew with what:
Tell me, which Knave is lawful Game, which not?
Must great Offenders, once escap'd the Crown,
Like Royal Harts, be never more run down?
Admit your Law to spare the Knight requires;   30
As Beasts of Nature may we hunt the Squires?
Suppose I censure — you know what I mean —
To save a Bishop, may I name a Dean?
   Fr. A Dean, Sir? no: his Fortune is not made,
You hurt a man that's rising in the Trade.   35
   P. If not the Tradesman who set up to day,
Much less the 'Prentice who to morrow may.
Down, down, proud Satire! tho' a Realm be spoil'd,
Arraign no mightier Thief than wretched *Wild*,
Or if a Court or Country's made a Job,   40
Go drench a Pick-pocket, and join the Mob.
   But Sir, I beg you, for the Love of Vice!
The matter's weighty, pray consider twice:
Have you less Pity for the needy Cheat,
The poor and friendless Villain, than the Great?   45

   11. Guthry: The Ordinary [i.e., prison chaplain] of *Newgate*, who publishes the Memoirs of the Malefactors, and is often prevailed upon to be so tender of their reputation, as to set down no more than the initials of their name. P.   **15. sowze:** swoop.
   17. Court: Court of St. James.   **Hall:** i.e., of justice.
   20–1. See *Dialogue I*, l. 112.
   25. Elector: one qualified to vote in the election of members of Parliament.
   29. Royal Harts: a stag over six years is a *hart;* if hunted by a monarch he is a *hart royal;* if he has escaped the pursuit of a king or queen he is termed a *hart royal proclaimed,* and proclamation issued that none should harm him.
   31. Squires: the English rank of gentry next in dignity below a knight.
   39. Wild: Jonathan Wild [d. 1725], a famous Thief, and Thief-Impeacher, who was at last caught in his own train and hanged. P.
   40. made a Job: exploited for private gain.
   41. drench: under a pump or in a trough.

Alas! the small Discredit of a Bribe
Scarce hurts the Lawyer, but undoes the Scribe.
Then better sure it Charity becomes
To tax Directors, who (thank God) have Plums;
Still better, Ministers; or if the thing   50
May pinch ev'n there — why lay it on a King.
    Fr. Stop! stop!
                P. Must Satire, then, nor *rise*, nor *fall?*
Speak out, and bid me blame no Rogues at all.
    Fr. Yes, strike that *Wild*, I'll justify the blow.
    P. Strike? why the man was hang'd ten years ago: 55
Who now that obsolete Example fears?
Ev'n *Peter* trembles only for his Ears.
    Fr. What always *Peter?* *Peter* thinks you mad,
You make men desp'rate if they once are bad:
Else might he take to Virtue some years hence —   60
    P. As S—*k*, if he lives, will love the Prince.
    Fr. Strange spleen to S—*k!*
                P. Do I wrong the Man?
God knows, I praise a Courtier where I can.
When I confess, there *is* who feels for Fame,
And melts to Goodness, need I Scarbrow name?   65
Pleas'd let me own, in *Esher's* peaceful Grove
(Where *Kent* and Nature vye for Pelham's Love)
The Scene, the Master, opening to my view,
I sit and dream I see my Crags anew!
    Ev'n in a Bishop I can spy Desert;   70
Secker is decent, *Rundel* has a Heart,
Manners with Candour are to *Benson* giv'n,

49. Directors: see *First Sat. of the Second Bk.*, l. 72n.   **Plums:** a plum was
£ 100,000 (usually gained dishonestly).
    57. Peter had, the year before this, narrowly escaped the Pillory for forgery;
and got off with a severe rebuke only from the bench.   P.   Peter is Peter
Walter (see *Ep. to Bathurst*, l. 20n.).
    61. S—k: see *Dialogue I*, l. 92n., where Selkirk's sycophancy to successive
monarchs is noted.   **Prince:** Frederick Louis, Prince of Wales, at this time
bitterly estranged from George II.
    65. Scarbrow: Earl of [Richard Lumley, 1688–1740]; and Knight of the
Garter, whose personal attachments to the king appeared from his steddy adherence to the royal interest, after his resignation of his great employment of
Master of the Horse; and whose known honour and virtue made him esteemed
by all parties.   P.
    66–9. The House and Gardens of *Esher* in *Surrey*, belonging to the Honour-
able Mr. [Henry] Pelham [1695–1754], Brother of the Duke of Newcastle. The
author could not have given a more amiable idea of his Character than in comparing him to Mr. Craggs.   P.   Pelham was a Whig supporter of Walpole
who became head of the government after 1746. His estate was designed by
William Kent (1685–1748), the esteemed architect and landscape gardener. For
Craggs, see *Sixth Ep. of the First Bk.*, l. 45n.
    71. Secker: Thomas Secker (1693–1768), Archbishop of Canterbury.   **de-
cent:** modest and moderate.   **Rundel:** Thomas Rundle (1688–1743), Bishop
of Derry.
    72. Benson: Martin Benson (1689–1752), Bishop of Gloucester.

To *Berkley,* ev'ry Virtue under Heav'n.
  But does the Court a worthy Man remove?
That instant, I declare, he has my Love: 75
I shun his Zenith, court his mild Decline;
Thus SOMMERS once, and HALIFAX were mine.
Oft in the clear, still Mirrour of Retreat,
I study'd SHREWSBURY, the wise and great:
CARLETON's calm Sense, and STANHOPE's noble Flame,
Compar'd, and knew their gen'rous End the same: 81
How pleasing ATTERBURY's softer hour!
How shin'd the Soul, unconquer'd in the Tow'r!
How can I PULT'NEY, CHESTERFIELD forget,
While *Roman* Spirit charms, and *Attic* Wit: 85
ARGYLE, the State's whole Thunder born to wield,
And shake alike the Senate and the Field:
Or WYNDHAM, just to Freedom and the Throne,
The Master of our Passions, and his own.
Names, which I long have lov'd, nor lov'd in vain,   90
Rank'd with their Friends, not number'd with their Train;
And if yet higher the proud List should end,
Still let me say! No Follower, but a Friend.

  Yet think not Friendship only prompts my Lays;
I follow *Virtue,* where she shines, I praise,   95

73. Berkley: George Berkeley (1685–1753), distinguished philosopher and Bishop of Cloyne.

77. Sommers: John Lord Sommers [see *Ep. to Dr. Arbuthnot,* l. 139n.] died in 1716. He had been Lord Keeper in the reign of William III, who took from him the seals in 1700. The author had the honour of knowing him in 1706. A faithful, able, and incorrupt minister; who, to the qualities of a consummate statesman, added those of a man of Learning and Politeness. P. **Halifax:** A peer [Charles Montagu, first Earl of Halifax, 1661–1715], no less distinguished by his love of letters than his abilities in Parliament. He was disgraced in 1710, on the Change of Q. Anne's ministry. P.

79. Shrewsbury: Charles Talbot, Duke of Shrewsbury [see *Second Ep. of the Second Bk.,* l. 134n.], had been Secretary of state, Embassador in France, Lord Lieutenant of Ireland, Lord Chamberlain, and Lord Treasurer. He several times quitted his employments, and was often recalled. He died in 1718. P.

80. Carleton: Hen. Boyle [d. 1725], Lord Carleton (nephew of the famous Robert Boyle) who was Secretary of state under William III and President of the Council under Q. Anne. P. **Stanhope:** James Earl Stanhope [1673–1721]. A Nobleman of equal courage, spirit, and learning. General in Spain, and Secretary of state. P.

82. Atterbury: Francis Atterbury, Bishop of Rochester, Pope's friend who was imprisoned in the Tower, found guilty of treason, and exiled to France (see *Ep. to Dr. Arbuthnot,* l. 140n.).

84. Pult'ney: William Pulteney (1686–1764), statesman and opponent of Walpole. **Chesterfield:** Philip Dormer Stanhope, fourth Earl of Chesterfield (1694–1773), statesman, opponent of Walpole, and author of the famed *Letters . . . to his Son.*

86. Argyle: John Campbell, second Duke of Argyle (1678–1743), brigadier-general and statesman.

88. Sir William Wyndham [1687–1740], Chancellor of the Exchequer under Queen Anne, made early a considerable figure; but since a much greater both by his ability and eloquence, joined with the utmost judgment and temper. P.

Point she to Priest or Elder, Whig or Tory,
Or round a Quaker's Beaver cast a Glory.
I never (to my sorrow I declare)
Din'd with the MAN of Ross, or my LORD MAY'R.
Some, in their choice of Friends (nay, look not grave)   100
Have still a secret Byass to a Knave:
To find an honest man, I beat about,
And love him, court him, praise him, in or out.
  Fr. Then why so few commended?

                             P. Not so fierce;
Find you the Virtue, and I'll find the Verse.   105
But random Praise — the Task can ne'er be done,
Each Mother asks it for her Booby Son,
Each Widow asks it for the Best of Men,
For him she weeps, and him she weds agen.
Praise cannot stoop, like Satire, to the Ground;   110
The Number may be hang'd, but not be crown'd.
Enough for half the Greatest of these days
To 'scape my Censure, not expect my Praise:
Are they not rich? what more can they pretend?
Dare they to hope a Poet for their Friend?   115
What RICHELIEU wanted, LOUIS scarce could gain,
And what young AMMON wish'd, but wish'd in vain.
No Pow'r the Muse's Friendship can command;
No Pow'r, when Virtue claims it, can withstand:
To *Cato*, *Virgil* pay'd one honest line;   120
O let my Country's Friends illumin mine!
— What are you thinking? *Fr.* Faith, the thought's no Sin,
I think your Friends are out, and would be in.
  P. If merely to come in, Sir, they go out,
The way they take is strangely round about.   125
  Fr. They too may be corrupted, you'll allow?
  P. I only call those Knaves who are so now.
Is that too little? Come then, I'll comply —
Spirit of *Arnall!* aid me while I lye.

97. Beaver: beaver hat.
99. Man of Ross: John Kyrle, the philanthropist (see *Ep. to Bathurst*, l. 250n.).   **Lord May'r:** Sir John Barnard. P.   See *First Ep. of the First Bk.*, l. 85n.
110. stoop: swoop (a term from falconry).
111. Number: the multitude.
116. Richelieu: Cardinal Richelieu (1585–1642), minister of state to Louis XIII.   **Louis:** Louis XIV (1638–1715), who patronized the French poet Nicolas Boileau (cf. l. 231n., below).
117. Ammon: Alexander the Great, who claimed descent from Jupiter Ammon, was supposed to have wished for another Homer to celebrate his exploits.
120. Patronized by the first of the Roman emperors, Augustus Caesar, Virgil yet dared in the *Aeneid* (VIII 670) to praise Cato Uticensis (95–46 B.C.), the patriot who had struggled valiantly for republican ideals.
129. Arnall: William Arnall (1700–41), a hireling political journalist.

Cobham's a Coward, Polwarth is a Slave, 130
And Lyttleton a dark, designing Knave,
St. John has ever been a wealthy Fool —
But let me add, Sir Robert's mighty dull,
Has never made a Friend in private life,
And was, besides, a Tyrant to his Wife. 135
    But pray, when others praise him, do I blame?
Call *Verres, Wolsey,* any odious name?
Why rail they then, if but a Wreath of mine
Oh All-accomplish'd St. John! deck thy Shrine?
    What? shall each spur-gall'd Hackney of the Day, 140
When *Paxton* gives him double Pots and Pay,
Or each new-pension'd Sycophant, pretend
To break my Windows, if I treat a Friend;
Then wisely plead, to me they meant no hurt,
But 'twas my Guest at whom they threw the dirt? 145
Sure, if I spare the Minister, no rules
Of Honour bind me, not to maul his Tools;
Sure, if they cannot cut, it may be said
His Saws are toothless, and his Hatchets Lead.
    It anger'd Turenne, once upon a day, 150
To see a Footman kick'd that took his pay:
But when he heard th' Affront the Fellow gave,
Knew one a Man of Honour, one a Knave;
The prudent Gen'ral turn'd it to a jest,
And begg'd, he'd take the pains to kick the rest. 155
Which not at present having time to do —
    Fr. Hold Sir! for God's-sake, where's th' Affront to you?
Against your worship when had S—k writ?
Or *P—ge* pour'd forth the Torrent of his Wit?
Or grant, the Bard whose Distich all commend, 160

130. Cobham: see first note to *Ep. to Cobham.* **Polwarth:** The Hon. Hugh Hume [1708–94], Son of Alexander Earl of Marchmont, Grandson of Patric Earl of Marchmont, and distinguished, like them, in the cause of Liberty. P.
131. Lyttleton: see *First Ep. of the First Bk.*, l. 29n.
132. St. John: see *Essay on Man,* I 1n.
133. Sir Robert: Walpole, the prime minister.
135. Tyrant: Walpole ignored his wife's infidelities.
136. him: Walpole.
137. Verres: Caius Verres (112–42 B.C.), a cruel and extortionate Roman governor of Sicily. **Wolsey:** Cardinal Thomas Wolsey (1475–1530); see *Dialogue I,* l. 51n.
140. Hackney: hack writer.
141. Paxton: see ll. 1–3n., above. **double Pots:** double tankards of ale or some other liquor.
142. pretend: attempt.
150. Turenne: Henri de la Tour d'Auvergne, Vicomte de Turenne (1611–75), a famous marshal of France.
158. S—k: see l. 61n., above.
159. P—ge: Sir Francis Page, the judge (see *First Sat. of the Second Bk.,* l. 82n.).

[*In Pow'r a Servant, out of Pow'r a Friend.*]
To *W—le* guilty of some venial Sin,
What's that to you, who ne'er was out nor in?
    The Priest whose Flattery be-dropt the Crown,
How hurt he you? he only stain'd the Gown.   165
And how did, pray, the Florid Youth offend,
Whose Speech you took, and gave it to a Friend?
    P. Faith it imports not much from whom it came ⎫
Whoever borrow'd, could not be to blame,   ⎬
Since the whole House did afterwards the same: ⎭   170
Let Courtly Wits to Wits afford supply,
As Hog to Hog in Huts of *Westphaly;*
If one, thro' Nature's Bounty or his Lord's,
Has what the frugal, dirty soil affords,
From him the next receives it, thick or thin,   175
As pure a Mess almost as it came in;
The blessed Benefit, not there confin'd,
Drops to the third who nuzzles close behind;
From tail to mouth, they feed, and they carouse;
The last, full fairly gives it to the *House.*   180
    Fr. This filthy Simile, this beastly Line,
Quite turns my Stomach — *P.* So does Flatt'ry mine;
And all your Courtly Civet-Cats can vent,
Perfume to you, to me is Excrement.
    But hear me further. — *Japhet,* 'tis agreed,   185
Writ not, and *Chartres* scarce could write or read,
In all the Courts of *Pindus* guiltless quite;
But Pens can forge, my Friend, that cannot write.
And must no Egg in *Japhet's* Face be thrown,
Because the Deed he forg'd was not my own?   190
Must never Patriot then declaim at Gin,
Unless, good man! he has been fairly in?
No zealous Pastor blame a failing Spouse,
Without a staring Reason on his Brows?
And each Blasphemer quite escape the Rod,   195
Because the insult's not on Man, but God?
    Ask you what Provocation I have had?

161. A verse take out of a poem to Sir R. W. P. The poem was written
by Bubb Dodington (see *Second Ep. of the Second Bk.,* l. 274n.).
    164. Spoken not of any particular priest, but of many priests. P.
    166. This seems to allude to a complaint made v. 71 of the preceding Dia-
logue. P. The "Florid Youth" is Henry Fox (see *Dialogue I,* l. 69n.).
    170. House: House of Commons.
    172. Westphaly: Westphalia, a Prussian province famous for its hams.
    183. Civet-Cats: see *Second Sat. of the First Bk.,* l. 30n.
    185. Japhet: Japhet Crook, the forger (see *Ep. to Bathurst,* l. 88n.).
    186. Chartres: the cheat and rapist (see *Ep. to Bathurst,* l. 20n.).
    189. Egg: eggs were thrown at those in the pillory.
    191. Patriot: see *Dialogue I,* l. 24n.
    192. in: in office.
    194. Brows: alluding to the horns of a cuckold.

The strong Antipathy of Good to Bad.
When Truth or Virtue an Affront endures,
Th' Affront is mine, my Friend, and should be yours.   200
Mine, as a Foe profess'd to false Pretence,
Who think a Coxcomb's Honour like his Sense;
Mine, as a Friend to ev'ry worthy mind;
And mine as Man, who feel for all mankind.
   Fr. You're strangely proud.

                            P. So proud, I am no Slave: ⎫   205
So impudent, I own myself no Knave: ⎬
So odd, my Country's Ruin makes me grave. ⎭
Yes, I am proud; I must be proud to see
Men not afraid of God, afraid of me:
Safe from the Bar, the Pulpit, and the Throne,   210
Yet touch'd and sham'd by *Ridicule* alone.
   O sacred Weapon! left for Truth's defence,
Sole Dread of Folly, Vice, and Insolence!
To all but Heav'n-directed hands deny'd,
The Muse may give thee, but the Gods must guide.   215
Rev'rent I touch thee! but with honest zeal;
To rowze the Watchmen of the Publick Weal,
To Virtue's Work provoke the tardy Hall,
And goad the Prelate slumb'ring in his Stall.
   Ye tinsel Insects! whom a Court maintains,   220
That counts your Beauties only by your Stains,
Spin all your Cobwebs o'er the Eye of Day!
The Muse's wing shall brush you all away:
All his Grace preaches, all his Lordship sings,
All that makes Saints of Queens, and Gods of Kings,   225
All, all but Truth, drops dead-born from the Press,
Like the last Gazette, or the last Address.
   When black Ambition stains a Publick Cause,
A Monarch's sword when mad Vain-glory draws,
Not *Waller's* Wreath can hide the Nation's Scar,   230

   204. From Terence: "Homo sum: humani nihil a me alienum puto." **P.**
See *Heauton Timorumenos,* l. 77: "I am a man, and think nothing human is
alien to me."
   218. Hall: Westminster Hall, once the seat of the High Court of Justice (see
l. 17, above).
   219. Stall: ecclesiastical seat of office (though "goad" suggests punning
allusion to an ox's "stall").
   222. Cobwebs: Weak and slight sophistry against virtue and honour. Thin
colours over vice, as unable to hide the light of Truth, as cobwebs to shade the
sun. **P.**
   224. his Grace: here a courtesy-title for any archbishop.   **Lordship:** courtesy-title for a lord (other than a duke) or a judge.
   227. Gazette: official government journal.   **Address:** a formal reply from
the Lords or Commons to a monarch's speech on the opening of Parliament.
   228–9. The case of Cromwell in the civil war of England; and (v. 229) of
Louis XIV in his conquest of the Low Countries. **P.**
   230. Pope refers to a poem by Edmund Waller (see *Essay on Criticism,* l.
361*n.*) which mourned the death of Oliver Cromwell.

Nor *Boileau* turn the Feather to a Star.

   Not so, when diadem'd with Rays divine,
Touch'd with the Flame that breaks from Virtue's Shrine,
Her Priestess Muse forbids the Good to dye,
And ope's the Temple of Eternity;   235
There other *Trophies* deck the truly Brave,
Than such as *Anstis* casts into the Grave;
Far other *Stars* than * and ** wear,
And may descend to *Mordington* from *Stair*:
Such as on Hough's unsully'd Mitre shine,   240
Or beam, good Digby! from a Heart like thine.
Let Envy howl while Heav'n's whole Chorus sings,
And bark at Honour not confer'd by Kings;
Let Flatt'ry sickening see the Incense rise,
Sweet to the World, and grateful to the Skies: 245
Truth guards the Poet, sanctifies the line,
And makes Immortal, Verse as mean as mine.
   Yes, the last Pen for Freedom let me draw,
When Truth stands trembling on the edge of Law:
Here, Last of *Britons!* let your Names be read;   250
Are none, none living? let me praise the Dead,
And for that Cause which made your Fathers shine,
Fall, by the Votes of their degen'rate Line!
   Fr. Alas! alas! pray end what you began,
And write next winter more *Essays on Man.*   255

    231. Feather: in one of his poems Boileau suggests that the white plume of his master Louis XIV would be as a star portending disaster to his enemies.
    237. Anstis: The chief Herald at Arms. It is the custom, at the funeral of great peers, to cast into the grave the broken staves and ensigns of honour. P. For Anstis, see *Sixth Ep. of the First Bk.,* ll. 81–2*n.*
    238. *Stars* are here emblematic of knightly orders. The blanks in the line are probably designed for *George* (the king) and *Frederick* (the Prince of Wales).
    239. Mordington: Lord Mordington is known only by the fact that his wife ran a gambling house. **Stair:** John Dalrymple, Earl of Stair [1673–1747], Knight of the Thistle; served in all the wars under the Duke of Marlborough; and afterwards as Embassador in France. P.
    240–1. Dr. John Hough [1651–1743], Bishop of Worcester, and the Lord Digby. The one [Hough] an assertor of the Church of England in opposition to the false measures of King James II. The other as firmly attached to the cause of that King. Both acting out of principle, and equally men of honour and virtue. P.   William Digby (1662–1752), M.P., was father of Pope's friend, Robert Digby (see *Essay on Man,* IV 103–6*n.*).
    249. See above, ll. 1–3*n.*
    252. Cause: liberty.
    255. This was the last poem of the kind printed by our author, with a resolution to publish no more; but to enter thus, in the most plain and solemn manner he could, a sort of PROTEST against that insuperable corruption and depravity of manners, which he had been so unhappy as to live to see. Could he have hoped to have amended any, he had continued those attacks; but bad men were grown so shameless and powerful, that Ridicule was become as unsafe as it was ineffectual. The Poem raised him, as he knew it would, some enemies; but he had reason to be satisfied with the approbation of good men, and the testimony of his own conscience. P.

THE

DUNCIAD

IN FOUR BOOKS

Printed according to the complete Copy
found in the Year 1742

WITH THE
PROLEGOMENA OF SCRIBLERUS,
AND NOTES VARIORUM
To which are added,
SEVERAL NOTES now first publish'd, the HYPERCRITICS OF
ARISTARCHUS, and his *Dissertation* on the HERO of the POEM

Tandem Phœbus *adest, morsusque inferre parantem
Congelat, et patulos, ut erant, indurat hiatus.*

OVID.

THE DUNCIAD, IN FOUR BOOKS: The *Dunciad*, in three books, was first published, anonymously, in May, 1728. In this version the king of the dunces was Lewis Theobald (see *Ep. to Dr. Arbuthnot*, l. 164n.), a minor poet and playwright who had embarrassed Pope by publishing in 1726 a volume entitled *Shakespeare Restored: Or, a Specimen of the Many Errors, As Well Committed, as Unamended, by Mr. Pope in his Late Edition of this Poet* (see first note to Pope's *Preface to Shakespeare*). In 1729 Pope re-issued the *Dunciad* in a "Variorum" edition: many of the blank spaces in the original text were filled in with proper names, and the poem was provided with an extensive prose apparatus ("*Proeme, Prolegomena, Testimonia Scriptorum, Index Authorum,* and *Notes Variorum*"). Many of these additions to the poem professed themselves as the work of the fictional pedant and blockhead, Martinus Scriblerus.

In 1742, fourteen years after the poem first appeared, Pope suddenly published a fourth book of the *Dunciad* in which Theobald was not even mentioned. Then, after revising all four books, he published (in October, 1743) the final version of his poem, *The Dunciad, in Four Books*, in which Colley Cibber (the actor and playwright who had become George II's poet laureate) replaced Theobald as king of the dunces.

The Latin epigraph is part of a three-line passage in Ovid's *Metamorphoses*, XI 58–60: "But Phoebus comes to his aid, and checks the monster, ready for the devouring grasp; whose expanded jaws, transformed to stone, stand hardened in a ghastly grin."

BY AUTHORITY

BY virtue of the Authority in Us vested by the Act for subjecting Poets to the power of a Licenser, we have revised this Piece; where finding the style and appellation of KING to have been given to a certain Pretender, Pseudo-Poet, or Phantom, of the name of TIBBALD; and apprehending the same may be deemed in some sort a Reflection on Majesty, or at least an insult on that Legal Authority which has bestowed on another person the Crown of Poesy: We have ordered the said Pretender, Pseudo-Poet, or Phantom, utterly to vanish, and evaporate out of this work: And do declare the said Throne of Poesy from henceforth to be abdicated and vacant, unless duly and lawfully supplied by the LAUREATE himself. And it is hereby enacted, that no other person do presume to fill the same.

ƆC. Ch.

BY AUTHORITY: This mock proclamation first appeared in 1743. The signature, a monogram of two C's back to back, recalls a monogram of King Charles II, and the "Ch." seems designed to recall the Lord Chamberlain, one of whose duties was to grant licenses for literary productions (see *Epil. to the Satires, Dial. I* 42n.).

A *Letter to the Publisher,*

OCCASIONED BY THE FIRST CORRECT
EDITION OF THE DUNCIAD

I T is with pleasure I hear, that you have procured a correct copy of the DUNCIAD, which the many surreptitious ones have rendered so necessary; and it is yet with more, that I am informed it will be attended with a COMMENTARY: A Work so requisite, that I cannot think the Author himself would have omitted it, had he approved of the first appearance of this Poem.[1]

Such *Notes* as have occurred to me I herewith send you: You will oblige me by inserting them amongst those which are, or will be, transmitted to you by others; since not only the Author's friends, but even strangers, appear engaged by humanity, to take some care of an Orphan of so much genius and spirit, which its parent seems to have abandoned from the very beginning, and suffered to step into the world naked, unguarded, and unattended.

It was upon reading some of the abusive papers[2] lately published, that my great regard to a Person, whose Friendship I esteem as one of the chief honours of my life, and a much greater respect to Truth, than to him or any man living, engaged me in enquiries, of which the inclosed *Notes* are the fruit.

I perceived, that most of these Authors had been (doubtless very wisely) the first aggressors. They had tried, 'till they were weary, what was to be got by railing at each other: Nobody was either concerned or surprised, if this or that scribler was proved a dunce. But every one was curious to read what could be said to prove Mr. POPE one, and was ready to pay something for such a discovery: A stratagem, which would they fairly own, it might not only reconcile them to me, but screen them from the resentment of their lawful Superiors, whom they daily abuse, only (as I charitably hope) to get that *by* them, which they cannot get *from* them.

I found this was not all: Ill success in that had transported them to Personal abuse, either of himself, or (what I think he could less forgive) of his Friends. They had called Men of virtue and honour bad Men, long before he had either leisure or inclination to call them bad Writers: And some had been such old offenders, that he had quite for-

---

A LETTER: First printed in 1729, and revised for the final version of the poem in 1743. Though signed by Pope's friend William Cleland (d. 1741), it is generally thought that the letter was written by Pope himself.

1 Pope pretended that the first, 1728, edition of the poem was published without his consent.

2 **abusive papers:** attacks on Pope by the Dunces.

gotten their persons as well as their slanders, 'till they were pleased to revive them.

Now what had Mr. POPE done before, to incense them? He had published those works which are in the hands of everybody, in which not the least mention[3] is made of any of them. And what has he done since? He has laughed, and written the DUNCIAD. What has that said of them? A very serious truth, which the public had said before, that they were dull: And what it had no sooner said, but they themselves were at great pains to procure or even purchase room in the prints, to testify under their hands to the truth of it.

I should still have been silent, if either I had seen any inclination in my friend to be serious with such accusers, or if they had only meddled with his Writings; since whoever publishes, puts himself on his trial by his Country. But when his Moral character was attacked, and in a manner from which neither truth nor virtue can secure the most innocent, in a manner, which, though it annihilates the credit of the accusation with the just and impartial, yet aggravates very much the guilt of the accusers; I mean by Authors *without names:* then I thought, since the danger was common to all, the concern ought to be so; and that it was an act of justice to detect the Authors, not only on this account, but as many of them are the same who for several years past have made free with the greatest names in Church and State, exposed to the world the private misfortunes of Families, abused all, even to Women, and whose prostituted papers (for one or other Party, in the unhappy divisions of their Country) have insulted the Fallen, the Friendless, the Exil'd, and the Dead.

Besides this, which I take to be a public concern, I have already confessed I had a private one. I am one of that number who have long loved and esteemed Mr. POPE; and had often declared it was not his capacity or writings (which we ever thought the least valuable part of his character) but the honest, open, and beneficent man, that we most esteemed, and loved in him. Now, if what these people say were believed, I must appear to all my friends either a fool, or a knave; either imposed on myself, or imposing on them; so that I am as much interested in the confutation of these calumnies, as he is himself.

I am no Author, and consequently not to be suspected either of jealousy or resentment against any of the Men, of whom scarce one is known to me by sight; and as for their Writings, I have sought them (on this one occasion) in vain, in the closets and libraries of all my acquaintance. I had still been in the dark, if a Gentleman had not procured me (I suppose from some of themselves, for they are generally much more dangerous friends than enemies) the passages I send you. I solemnly protest I have added nothing to the malice or absurdity

---

[3] **not the least mention:** an inaccurate statement.

of them; which it behoves me to declare, since the vouchers themselves will be so soon and so irrecoverably lost. You may in some measure prevent it, by preserving at least their Titles,[4] and discovering (as far as you can depend on the truth of your information) the Names of the concealed authors.

The first objection I have heard made to the Poem is, that the persons are too *obscure* for satyr. The persons themselves, rather than allow the objection, would forgive the satyr; and if one could be tempted to afford it a serious answer, were not all assassinates, popular insurrections, the insolence of the rabble without doors, and of domestics within, most wrongfully chastised, if the Meanness of offenders indemnified them from punishment? On the contrary, Obscurity renders them more dangerous, as less thought of: Law can pronounce judgment only on open facts; Morality alone can pass censure on intentions of mischief; so that for secret calumny, or the arrow flying in the dark, there is no public punishment left, but what a good Writer inflicts.

The next objection is, that these sort of authors are *poor*. That might be pleaded as an excuse at the Old Baily,[5] for lesser crimes than Defamation, (for 'tis the case of almost all who are tried there) but sure it can be none: For who will pretend that the robbing another of his Reputation supplies the want of it in himself? I question not but such authors are poor, and heartily wish the objection were removed by any honest livelihood. But Poverty is here the accident, not the subject: He who describes Malice and Villany to be pale and meagre, expresses not the least anger against Paleness or Leanness, but against Malice and Villany. The Apothecary in Romeo and Juliet is poor; but is he therefore justified in vending poison? Not but Poverty itself becomes a just subject of satyr, when it is the consequence of vice, prodigality, or neglect of one's lawful calling; for then it increases the public burden, fills the streets and highways with Robbers, and the garrets with Clippers, Coiners,[6] and Weekly Journalists.

But admitting that two or three of these offend less in their morals, than in their writings; must Poverty make nonsense sacred? If so, the fame of bad authors would be much better consulted than that of all the good ones in the world; and not one of an hundred had ever been called by his right name.

They mistake the whole matter: It is not charity to encourage them in the way they follow, but to get them out of it; for men are not bunglers because they are poor, but they are poor because they are bunglers.

[4] **Titles:** a list of published attacks on Pope was given in an appendix to the *Dunciad*.

[5] **Old Baily:** the seat of the Central Criminal Court in London.

[6] **Clippers, Coiners:** "Clippers" were those who pared the edges of coins (the clippings were then melted down and sold). "Coiners" were counterfeiters.

Is it not pleasant enough, to hear our authors crying out on the one hand, as if their persons and characters were too sacred for Satyr; and the public objecting on the other, that they are too mean even for Ridicule? But whether Bread or Fame be their end, it must be allowed, our author, by and in this Poem, has mercifully given them a little of both.

There are two or three, who by their rank and fortune have no benefit from the former objections, supposing them good, and these I was sorry to see in such company. But if, without any provocation, two or three Gentlemen will fall upon one, in an affair wherein his interest and reputation are equally embarked; they cannot certainly, after they have been content to print themselves his enemies, complain of being put into the number of them.

Others, I am told, pretend to have been once his Friends. Surely they are their enemies who say so, since nothing can be more odious than to treat a friend as they have done. But of this I cannot persuade myself, when I consider the constant and eternal aversion of all bad writers to a good one.

Such as claim a merit from being his Admirers I would gladly ask, if it lays him under a personal obligation? At that rate he would be the most obliged humble servant in the world. I dare swear for these in particular, he never desired them to be his admirers, nor promised in return to be theirs: That had truly been a sign he was of their acquaintance; but would not the malicious world have suspected such an approbation of some motive worse than ignorance, in the author of the Essay on Criticism? Be it as it will, the reasons of their Admiration and of his Contempt are equally subsisting,[7] for his works and theirs are the very same that they were.

One, therefore, of their assertions I believe may be true, "That he has a contempt for their writings." And there is another, which would probably be sooner allowed by himself than by any good judge beside, "That his own have found too much success with the public." But as it cannot consist with his modesty to claim this as a justice, it lies not on him, but entirely on the public, to defend its own judgment.

There remains what in my opinion might seem a better plea for these people, than any they have made use of. If Obscurity or Poverty were to exempt a man from satyr, much more should Folly or Dulness, which are still more involuntary; nay, as much so as personal Deformity. But even this will not help them: Deformity becomes an object of Ridicule when a man sets up for being handsome; and so must Dulness when he sets up for a Wit. They are not ridiculed because Ridicule in itself is, or ought to be, a pleasure; but because it is just to undeceive and vindicate the honest and unpretending part

---

[7] **subsisting**: "substantial," or perhaps "of lasting duration."

of mankind from imposition, because particular interest ought to yield to general, and a great number who are not naturally Fools, ought never to be made so, in complaisance to a few who are. Accordingly we find that in all ages, all vain pretenders, were they ever so poor or ever so dull, have been constantly the topics of the most candid satyrists, from the Codrus of Juvenal to the Damon of Boileau.[8]

Having mentioned Boileau, the greatest Poet and most judicious Critic of his age and country, admirable for his Talents, and yet perhaps more admirable for his Judgment in the proper application of them; I cannot help remarking the resemblance betwixt him and our author, in Qualities, Fame, and Fortune; in the distinctions shewn them by their Superiors, in the general esteem of their Equals, and in their extended reputation amongst Foreigners; in the latter of which ours has met with the better fate, as he has had for his Translators persons of the most eminent rank and abilities in their respective nations. But the resemblance holds in nothing more, than in their being equally abused by the ignorant pretenders to Poetry of their times; of which not the least memory will remain but in their own Writings, and in the Notes made upon them. What Boileau has done in almost all his poems, our author has only in this: I dare answer for him he will do it in no more; and on this principle, of attacking few but who had slandered him, he could not have done it at all, had he been confined from censuring obscure and worthless persons, for scarce any other were his enemies. However, as the parity is so remarkable, I hope it will continue to the last; and if ever he shall give us an edition of this Poem himself, I may see some of them treated as gently, on their repentance or better merit, as Perrault and Quinault[9] were at last by Boileau.

In one point I must be allowed to think the character of our English Poet the more amiable. He has not been a follower of Fortune or Success; he has lived with the Great without flattery; been a friend to Men in power, without pensions, from whom, as he asked, so he received no favour, but what was done Him in his Friends. As his Satyrs were the more just for being delayed, so were his Panegyrics; bestowed only on such persons as he had familiarly known, only for such virtues as he had long observed in them, and only at such times as others cease to praise, if not begin to calumniate them, I mean when out of power or out of fashion.[10] A satyr, therefore, on writers so notorious for the

---

[8] **Codrus:** a poverty-stricken poet who appears in Juvenal's *Satire III*, ll. 205*ff.*
Damon: the poet and chief speaker in Boileau's *Satire I.*

[9] **Perrault . . . Quinault:** Charles Perrault (1628–1703), French poet and critic, and Philippe Quinault (1635–88), French dramatist.

[10] **power . . . fashion:** As Mr. *Wycherley* [see *Autumn,* l. 7*n.*], at the time the Town declaim'd against his Book of Poems: Mr. *Walsh* [see *Essay on Criticism,* l. 729*n.*], after his death: Sir *William Trumbull* [see *Spring,* ll. 7–10*n.*], when he had resign'd the Office of Secretary of State; Lord *Bolingbroke* [see *Essay*

contrary practice, became no man so well as himself; as none, it is plain, was so little in their friendships, or so much in that of those whom they had most abused, namely the Greatest and Best of all Parties. Let me add a further reason, that, though engaged in their Friendships, he never espoused their Animosities; and can almost singly challenge this honour, not to have written a line of any man, which, through Guilt, through Shame, or through Fear, through variety of Fortune, or change of Interests, he was ever unwilling to own.

I shall conclude with remarking what a pleasure it must be to every reader of Humanity, to see all along, that our Author in his very laughter is not indulging his own ill-nature, but only punishing that of others. As to his Poem, those alone are capable of doing it justice, who, to use the words of a great writer, know how hard it is (with regard both to his subject and his manner) VETUSTIS DARE NOVITATEM, OBSOLETIS NITOREM, OBSCURIS LUCEM, FASTIDITIS GRATIAM.[11] I am

Your most humble servant,

St. James's
Dec. 22, 1728

WILLIAM CLELAND.

---

on Man, I 1*n*.] at his leaving *England* after the Queen's [Queen Anne] death: Lord *Oxford* [see *Ep. to Bathurst,* l. 243*n*.] in his last decline of Life: Mr. Secretary *Craggs* [see *Sixth Ep. of the First Bk.,* l. 45*n*.] at the end of the South-Sea Year [see *Ep. to Bathurst,* l. 119*n*.], and after his death: Others, only in *Epitaphs.* P.

11 From the Preface to Pliny's *Natural History:* "to give freshness to what is old, splendor to what is shabby, brightness to what is dark, charm to what is disdained."

Martinus Scriblerus

OF THE POEM

THIS poem, as it celebrateth the most grave and ancient of things, Chaos, Night, and Dulness; so is it of the most grave and ancient kind. Homer (saith Aristotle) was the first who gave the *Form*, and (saith Horace) who adapted the *Measure*, to heroic poesy. But even before this, may be rationally presumed from what the Ancients have left written, was a piece by Homer[1] composed, of like nature and matter with this of our poet. For of Epic sort it appeareth to have been, yet of matter surely not unpleasant, witness what is reported of it by the learned archbishop Eustathius,[2] in Odyss. x. And accordingly Aristotle, in his Poetic, chap. iv. doth further set forth, that as the Iliad and Odyssey gave example to Tragedy, so did this poem to Comedy its first idea.

From these authors also it should seem, that the Hero, or chief personage of it was no less *obscure*, and his understanding and sentiments no less quaint and strange (if indeed not more so) than any of the actors of our poem. MARGITES was the name of this personage, whom Antiquity recordeth to have been *Dunce the first;* and surely from what we hear of him, not unworthy to be the root of so spreading a tree, and so numerous a posterity. The poem therefore celebrating him was properly and absolutely a *Dunciad;* which though now unhappily lost, yet is its nature sufficiently known by the infallible tokens aforesaid. And thus it doth appear, that the first Dunciad was the first Epic poem, written by Homer himself, and anterior even to the Iliad or Odyssey.

Now, forasmuch as our poet had translated those two famous works of Homer which are yet left, he did conceive it in some sort his duty to imitate that also which was lost: And was therefore induced to bestow on it the same form which Homer's is reported to have had, namely that of Epic poem; with a title also framed after the ancient Greek manner, to wit, that of *Dunciad.*

MARTINUS SCRIBLERUS: the learnedly obtuse Martinus Scriblerus is a fictional pedant and blockhead whose personality was created by a group which consisted of Pope, Swift, Gay, Arbuthnot, Lord Oxford, Bolingbroke, and Thomas Parnell (1679–1718). Dedicated to the ridicule of literary folly and false learning, the group became known as the Scriblerus Club and met irregularly for only a short time in 1714. But though events, mainly political, were to disband the circle after only a short period, the Club seems to have been the stimulus for a number of works, including Swift's *Gulliver's Travels* and Pope's *Dunciad* and *Peri Bathous,* that were to appear in much later years.

[1] **a piece by Homer:** *Margites,* a lost satire on a blockhead of antiquity which is sometimes attributed to Homer.

[2] **Eustathius:** Archbishop of Thessalonica (died about 1200) who wrote a voluminous commentary on the *Iliad* and the *Odyssey.*

Wonderful it is, that so few of the moderns have been stimulated to attempt some Dunciad! since, in the opinion of the multitude, it might cost less pain and oil than an imitation of the greater Epic. But possible it is also, that, on due reflection, the maker might find it easier to paint a Charlemagne, a Brute,[3] or a Godfrey,[4] with just pomp and dignity heroic, than a Margites, a Codrus, or a Fleckno.[5]

We shall next declare the occasion and the cause which moved our poet to this particular work. He lived in those days, when (after Providence had permitted the invention of Printing as a scourge for the sins of the learned) Paper also became so cheap, and Printers so numerous, that a deluge of Authors covered the land: Whereby not only the peace of the honest unwriting subject was daily molested, but unmerciful demands were made of his applause, yea of his money, by such as would neither earn the one, nor deserve the other. At the same time, the licence of the Press was such, that it grew dangerous to refuse them either; for they would forthwith publish slanders unpunished, the authors being anonymous, and skulking under the wings of Publishers, a set of men who never scrupled to vend either Calumny or Blasphemy, as long as the Town would call for it.

Now our author, living in those times, did conceive it an endeavour well worthy an honest Satyrist, to dissuade the dull, and punish the wicked, *the only way that was left*. In that public-spirited view he laid the plan of this Poem, as the greatest service he was capable (without much hurt, or being slain) to render his dear country. First, taking things from their original, he considereth the Causes creative of such Authors, namely *Dulness* and *Poverty;* the one born with them, the other contracted by neglect of their proper talents, through self-conceit of greater abilities. This truth he wrappeth in an *Allegory* (as the construction of Epic poesy requireth) and feigns that one of these Goddesses had taken up her abode with the other, and that they jointly inspired all such writers and such works. He proceedeth to shew the *qualities* they bestow on these authors, and the *effects* they produce: then the *materials,* or *stock,* with which they furnish them; and (above all) that *self-opinion* which causeth it to seem to themselves vastly greater than it is, and is the prime motive of their setting up in this sad and sorry merchandice. The great power of these Goddesses acting in alliance (whereof as the one is the mother of Industry, so is the other of Plodding) was to be exemplified in some *one, great* and *remarkable Action:* And none could be more so than that which our poet hath chosen, *viz.* the restoration of the reign of Chaos and

[3] **Brute:** Brute, or Brutus, a great-grandson of Aeneas, was considered the legendary founder of the British race.
[4] **Godfrey:** Godfrey of Bouillon (1061–1100), leader of the first crusade and liberator of Jerusalem. He is the hero of Torquato Tasso's epic, *Jerusalem Delivered* (1581).
[5] **Codrus:** see "A Letter to the Publisher," n. 8.   **Fleckno:** Richard Flecknoe (d. 1678), a minor poet who is the ruling dunce in Dryden's *MacFlecknoe*.

Night, by the ministry of Dulness their daughter, in the removal of her imperial seat from the City to the polite World;[6] as the Action of the Æneid is the restoration of the empire of Troy, by the removal of the race from thence to Latium.[7] But as Homer singing only the *Wrath* of Achilles, yet includes in his poem the whole history of the Trojan war; in like manner our author hath drawn into this *single Action* the whole history of Dulness and her children.

A *Person* must next be fixed upon to support this Action. This *Phantom* in the poet's mind must have a *Name:* He finds it to be ——;[8] and he becomes of course the Hero of the poem.

The *Fable*[9] being thus, according to the best example, one and entire, as contained in the Proposition;[10] the *Machinery* is a continued chain of Allegories, setting forth the whole Power, Ministry, and Empire of Dulness, extended through her subordinate instruments, in all her various operations.

This is branched into *Episodes,* each of which hath its Moral apart, though all conducive to the main end. The Crowd assembled in the second book, demonstrates the design to be more extensive than to bad poets only, and that we may expect other Episodes of the Patrons, Encouragers, or Paymasters of such authors, as occasion shall bring them forth. And the third book, if well considered, seemeth to embrace the whole World. Each of the Games relateth to some or other vile class of writers: The first concerneth the Plagiary, to whom he giveth the name of More;[11] the second the libellous Novellist, whom he styleth Eliza;[12] the third, the flattering Dedicator; the fourth, the bawling Critic, or noisy Poet; the fifth, the dark and dirty Party-writer; and so of the rest; assigning to each some *proper name* or other, such as he could find.

As for the *Characters,* the public hath already acknowledged how justly they are drawn: The manners are so depicted, and the sentiments so peculiar to those to whom applied, that surely to transfer them to any other or wiser personages, would be exceeding difficult: And certain it is that every person concerned, being consulted apart, hath readily owned the resemblance of every portrait, his own excepted. So Mr. Cibber calls them, "a parcel of *poor wretches,* so many *silly flies:*

---

[6] **the City to the polite World:** the "City" is that part of London within the old city walls; it was associated with trade, finance, and the middle classes. The "polite World" stands for the court and aristocratic world of the City of Westminster, immediately west of the City of London.

[7] **Latium:** Italy.

[8] ——: Colley Cibber.

[9] **Fable:** the plot, or story.

[10] **Proposition:** statement of the theme or subject (see *Dunciad,* I 1–3). **Machinery:** see *Rape of the Lock,* dedicatory letter.

[11] **More:** James Moore Smythe (see *Dunciad,* II 35*ff.*, and *Ep. to Dr. Arbuthnot,* l. 23*n.*).

[12] **Eliza:** Eliza Haywood (1693–1756), a writer of scandalous memoirs (see *Dunciad,* II 157*n.*).

but adds, our Author's Wit is remarkably more bare and barren, when-ever it would fall foul on *Cibber*, than upon any other Person what-ever."[13]

The *Descriptions* are singular, the *Comparisons* very quaint, the *Narration* various, yet of one colour: The purity and chastity of *Diction* is so preserved, that in the places most suspicious, not the *words* but only the *images* have been censured, and yet are those images no other than have been sanctified by ancient and classical Authority, (though, as was the manner of those good times, not so curiously wrapped up) yea, and commented upon by most grave Doctors, and approved Critics.

As it beareth the name of *Epic*, it is thereby subjected to such severe indispensable rules as are laid on all Neoterics,[14] a strict imitation of the Ancients; insomuch that any deviation, accompanied with what-ever poetic beauties, hath always been censured by the sound Critic. How exact that Imitation hath been in this piece, appeareth not only by its general structure, but by particular allusions infinite, many whereof have escaped both the commentator and poet himself; yea divers by his exceeding diligence are so altered and interwoven with the rest, that several have already been, and more will be, by the ignorant abused, as altogether and originally his own.

In a word, the whole poem proveth itself to be the work of our Author, when his faculties were in full vigour and perfection; at that exact time when years have ripened the Judgment, without diminish-ing the Imagination: which, by good Critics, is held to be punctually at *forty*.[15] For, at that season it was that Virgil finished his Georgics; and Sir Richard Blackmore[16] at the like age composing his Arthurs, declared the same to be the very *Acme* and pitch of life for Epic poesy: Though since he hath altered it to *sixty*, the year in which he published his Alfred. True it is, that the talents for *Criticism*, namely smartness, quick censure, vivacity of remark, certainty of asseveration, indeed all but acerbity, seem rather the gifts of Youth than of riper Age: But it is far otherwise in *Poetry*; witness the works of Mr. Rymer[17] and Mr. Dennis,[18] who beginning with Criticism, became afterwards such Poets as no age hath paralleled. With good reason therefore did our author chuse to write his Essay on that subject at twenty, and reserve for his maturer years this great and wonderful work of the Dunciad.

13 Cibber's Letter to Mr. P. pag. 9, 12, 41.   P.

14 Neoterics: i.e., modern writers.

15 forty: Pope was born in May, 1688; the *Dunciad* was first published in May, 1728.

16 Blackmore: the author of many tedious epics, among them *Prince Arthur* (1695) and *King Arthur* (1697). See *First Sat. of the Second Bk.*, l. 23n., and *Dunciad*, II 268n.

17 Rymer: Thomas Rymer (1641–1713), famous for his inflexible dramatic criticism, was an inconsequential poet.

18 Dennis: known chiefly for his literary criticism, John Dennis was an un-distinguished poet and playwright (see *Essay on Criticism*, l. 270n.).

BOOK THE FIRST

ARGUMENT

The Proposition, the Invocation, and the Inscription. Then the Original of the great Empire of Dulness, *and cause of the continuance thereof. The College of the* Goddess *in the City, with her private Academy for Poets in particular; the Governors of it, and the four Cardinal Virtues. Then the Poem hastes into the midst of things, presenting her, on the evening of a Lord Mayor's day, revolving the long succession of her Sons, and the glories past and to come. She fixes her eye on Bays to be the Instrument of that great Event which is the Subject of the Poem. He is described pensive among his Books, giving up the Cause, and apprehending the Period of her Empire: After debating whether to betake himself to the Church, or to Gaming, or to Party-writing, he raises an Altar of proper books, and (making first his solemn prayer and declaration) purposes thereon to sacrifice all his unsuccessful writings. As the pile is kindled, the Goddess beholding the flame from her seat, flies and puts it out by casting upon it the poem of* Thulé. *She forthwith reveals herself to him, transports him to her Temple, unfolds her Arts, and initiates him into her Mysteries; then announcing the death of* Eusden *the Poet Laureate, anoints him, carries him to Court, and proclaims him Successor.*

THE Mighty Mother, and her Son who brings
The Smithfield Muses to the ear of Kings,
I sing. Say you, her instruments the Great!
Call'd to this work by Dulness, Jove, and Fate;
You by whose care, in vain decry'd and curst,   5
Still Dunce the second reigns like Dunce the first;
Say how the Goddess bade Britannia sleep,

BOOK THE FIRST. **1.** The Reader ought here to be cautioned, that the *Mother* [the goddess Dulness], and not the *Son* [Colley Cibber], is the principal Agent of this Poem: The latter of them is only chosen as her Collegue (as was anciently the custom in Rome before some great Expedition), the main action of the Poem being by no means the Coronation of the Laureate, which is performed in the very first book, but the Restoration of the Empire of Dulness in Britain, which is not accomplished 'till the last. W.   Notes signed "W." are by Pope's literary executor and editor, William Warburton.

2. Smithfield Muses: Smithfield is the place where Bartholomew Fair was kept, whose shews, machines, and dramatical entertainments, formerly agreeable only to the taste of the Rabble, were, by the Hero of this poem and others of equal genius, brought to the Theatres of Covent-garden, Lincolns-inn-fields, and the Hay-market, to be the reigning pleasures of the Court and Town. This happened in the Reigns of King George I, and II. See Book 3.   P.

3. the Great: the king and nobility.

6. Pope alludes not only to Cibber, who had succeeded Laurence Eusden (see *Ep. to Dr. Arbuthnot,* l. 15n., and l. 104, below) to the laureateship, but to King George II, who had succeeded George I shortly before the *Dunciad* was first published.

And pour'd her Spirit o'er the land and deep.
   In eldest time, e'er mortals writ or read,
E'er Pallas issu'd from the Thund'rer's head,   10
Dulness o'er all possess'd her ancient right,
Daughter of Chaos and eternal Night:
Fate in their dotage this fair Ideot gave,
Gross as her sire, and as her mother grave,
Laborious, heavy, busy, bold, and blind,   15
She rul'd in native Anarchy, the mind.
   Still her old Empire to restore she tries,
For, born a Goddess, Dulness never dies.
   O Thou! whatever title please thine ear,
Dean, Drapier, Bickerstaff, or Gulliver!   20
Whether thou chuse Cervantes' serious air,
Or laugh and shake in Rab'lais' easy chair,
Or praise the Court, or magnify Mankind,
Or thy griev'd Country's copper chains unbind;
From thy Bœotia tho' her Pow'r retires,   25
Mourn not, my SWIFT, at ought our Realm acquires,
Here pleas'd behold her mighty wings out-spread
To hatch a new Saturnian age of Lead.
   Close to those walls where Folly holds her throne,
And laughs to think Monroe would take her down,   30
Where o'er the gates, by his fam'd father's hand
Great Cibber's brazen, brainless brothers stand;
One Cell there is, conceal'd from vulgar eye,
The Cave of Poverty and Poetry.
Keen, hollow winds howl thro' the bleak recess,   35
Emblem of Music caus'd by Emptiness.
Hence Bards, like Proteus long in vain ty'd down,
Escape in Monsters, and amaze the town.
Hence Miscellanies spring, the weekly boast

   10. Pallas: the goddess of wisdom, who issued from the head of Jove.
   17. This Restoration makes the Completion of the Poem. *Vide* Book 4. P.
   19. Thou: Jonathan Swift, to whom Pope dedicated this poem, was Dean of St. Patrick's Cathedral, Dublin. He was author of the *Drapier's Letters*, written to protest a patent granted for a new copper coinage in Ireland (see l. 24), and also wrote under the name of Isaac Bickerstaff.
   23. *Ironicè*, alluding to Gulliver's representations of both. . . . P.
   25. Bœotia: a district of ancient Greece noted for the moistness of its climate and the stupidity of its people. In Pope's time the name was commonly applied to Ireland.
   28. Saturnian: The ancient Golden Age is by Poets styled *Saturnian;* but in the Chemical language *Saturn* is lead. . . . P.
   29–30. The allusion is to Bethlehem Hospital (Bedlam), for the insane, where Dr. James Monro (1680–1752) was physician.
   31–2. Mr. Caius-Gabriel Cibber, father of the Poet Laureate. The two Statues of the Lunatics over the gates of Bedlam-hospital were done by him, and (as the son justly says of them), are no ill monuments of his fame as an Artist. P.
   37. Proteus: the sea-god who, when seized, would change his shape.
   38. Monsters: i.e., monstrous, unnatural writings.
   39. Miscellanies: poetry anthologies.

Of Curl's chaste press, and Lintot's rubric post: 40
Hence hymning Tyburn's elegiac lines,
Hence Journals, Medleys, Merc'ries, Magazines:
Sepulchral Lyes, our holy walls to grace,
And New-year Odes, and all the Grub-street race.

   In clouded Majesty here Dulness shone;   45
Four guardian Virtues, round, support her throne:
Fierce champion Fortitude, that knows no fears
Of hisses, blows, or want, or loss of ears:
Calm Temperance, whose blessings those partake
Who hunger, and who thirst for scribling sake: 50
Prudence, whose glass presents th' approaching jayl:
Poetic Justice, with her lifted scale,
Where, in nice balance, truth with gold she weighs,
And solid pudding against empty praise.

   Here she beholds the Chaos dark and deep,   55
Where nameless Somethings in their causes sleep,
'Till genial Jacob, or a warm Third day,
Call forth each mass, a Poem, or a Play:
How hints, like spawn, scarce quick in embryo lie,
How new-born nonsense first is taught to cry,   60
Maggots half-form'd in rhyme exactly meet,
And learn to crawl upon poetic feet.
Here one poor word an hundred clenches makes,

---

   40. Two Booksellers [Edmund Curll and Bernard Lintot], of whom see Book 2. The former was fined by the Court of King's Bench for publishing obscene books; the latter usually adorned his shop with titles in red letters. P.

   41. It is an ancient English custom for the Malefactors to sing a Psalm at their execution at Tyburn; and no less customary to print Elegies on their deaths, at the same time, or before. P.

   42. Newspapers and other publications used the words "Journal," "Medley," "Mercury," in their titles.

   43. Is a just satyr on the Flatteries and Falsehoods admitted to be inscribed on the walls of Churches, in Epitaphs. P.

   44. Odes: the poet laureate had the duty of writing odes for the New Year and for the monarch's birthday. **Grub-street:** a London street associated with hack writers.

   48. loss of ears: certain crimes were punished by cropping or cutting off the offender's ears.

   50. Cf. Matthew 5:6: "Blessed are they which do hunger and thirst after righteousness. . . ."

   51. glass: Prudence was often portrayed as gazing through a perspective, or spy-glass.

   57. genial Jacob: Jacob Tonson (1656–1736), a leading publisher (the epithet "genial" implies powers of "generation"). **Third day:** receipts at the third performance of a play went to the author.

   59. quick: alive.

   61. Maggots: a pun: (1) worms, or grubs; (2) perverse fancies.

   63. It may not be amiss to give an instance or two of these operations of *Dulness* out of the Works of her Sons, celebrated in the Poem. A great Critic [John Dennis] formerly held these clenches [i.e., puns] in such abhorrence, that he declared "he that would pun would pick a pocket." Yet Mr. *Dennis*'s works afford us notable examples in this kind: "*Alexander Pope* hath sent abroad into the world as many *Bulls* as his namesake Pope *Alexander* — Let us take the

And ductile dulness now meanders takes;
There motley Images her fancy strike,   65
Figures ill pair'd, and Similies unlike.
She sees a Mob of Metaphors advance,
Pleas'd with the madness of the mazy dance:
How Tragedy and Comedy embrace;
How Farce and Epic get a jumbled race;   70
How Time himself stands still at her command,
Realms shift their place, and Ocean turns to land.
Here gay Description Ægypt glads with show'rs,
Or gives to Zembla fruits, to Barca flow'rs;
Glitt'ring with ice here hoary hills are seen,   75
There painted vallies of eternal green,
In cold December fragrant chaplets blow,
And heavy harvests nod beneath the snow.
    All these, and more, the cloud-compelling Queen
Beholds thro' fogs, that magnify the scene.   80
She, tinsel'd o'er in robes of varying hues,
With self-applause her wild creation views;
Sees momentary monsters rise and fall,
And with her own fools-colours gilds them all.
    'Twas on the day, when * * rich and grave,   85
Like Cimon, triumph'd both on land and wave:
(Pomps without guilt, of bloodless swords and maces,
Glad chains, warm furs, broad banners, and broad faces)
Now Night descending, the proud scene was o'er,
But liv'd, in Settle's numbers, one day more.   90

---

initial and final letters of his Name, *viz. A. P*—*E*, and they give you the idea
of an *Ape.* — *Pope* comes from the Latin word *Popa*, which signifies a little
Wart; or from *Poppysma*, because he was continually *popping* out squibs of wit,
or rather *Popysmata*, or *Popisms.*" Dennis on *Hom.* [i.e., Pope's Homer] and
Daily Journal, June 11, 1728.   P.
    73–8. These six verses represent the Inconsistencies in the descriptions of
poets, who heap together all glittering and gawdy images, though incompatible
in one season, or in one scene. — See the Guardian, No. 40, parag. 6. See also
[Laurence] *Eusden's* whole works, if to be found. . . .   Scribl.
    74. Zembla: see *Essay on Man*, II 224n.   Barca: in Libya.
    85–6. The Procession of a Lord Mayor [from the City of London to West-
minster to receive the royal assent to his election] is made partly by land, and
partly by water. — Cimon, the famous Athenian General, obtained a victory by
sea. and another by land, on the same day, over the Persians and Barbarians. P.
In early editions of the poem, the blank space was filled with "Thorold" (Sir
George Thorold, Lord Mayor in 1720).
    88. Glad chains: The Ignorance of these Moderns! This was altered in one
edition to *Gold chains*, shewing more regard to the metal of which the chains
of Aldermen are made, than to the beauty of the Latinism and Græcism, nay of
figurative speech itself: *Lætas segetes*, glad, for making glad, &c.   Scribl.
    90. Settle [see *First Ep. of the Second Bk.*, l. 417n.] was poet to the City of
London. His office was to compose yearly panegyrics upon the Lord Mayors, and
verses to be spoken in the Pageants: But that part of the shows being at length
frugally abolished, the employment of City-poet ceased; so that upon Settle's
demise there was no successor to the place.   P.

Now May'rs and Shrieves all hush'd and satiate lay,
Yet eat, in dreams, the custard of the day;
While pensive Poets painful vigils keep,
Sleepless themselves, to give their readers sleep.
Much to the mindful Queen the feast recalls   95
What City Swans once sung within the walls;
Much she revolves their arts, their ancient praise,
And sure succession down from Heywood's days.
She saw, with joy, the line immortal run,
Each sire imprest and glaring in his son: 100
So watchful Bruin forms, with plastic care,
Each growing lump, and brings it to a Bear.
She saw old Pryn in restless Daniel shine,
And Eusden eke out Blackmore's endless line;
She saw slow Philips creep like Tate's poor page,   105
And all the mighty Mad in Dennis rage.

91. **Shrieves:** sheriffs.
96. **walls:** of the City of London.
98. *John Heywood* [see *First Ep. of the Second Bk.*, l. 88n.], whose Interludes were printed in the time of Henry VIII.   P.
101–2. An old notion held that bear cubs were born shapeless, and had to be licked into form.
103. **Pryn:** William Prynne (1600–69) was sent to the pillory and had his ears cut off for writing his *Histriomastix*.   **Daniel:** Daniel Defoe (1660–1731) was pilloried for his *Shortest Way with the Dissenters*.
104. **Eusden:** the Rev. Laurence Eusden (see *Ep. to Dr. Arbuthnot*, l. 15n.). **Blackmore:** see *First Sat. of the Second Bk.*, l. 23n., and *Dunciad*, II 268n.
105. **Philips . . . Tate:** Ambrose Philips and Nahum Tate (see *Ep. to Dr. Arbuthnot*, l. 100n., l. 190n.
106. Mr. Theobald, in the Censor, vol. ii, No. 33, calls Mr. Dennis by the name of Furius. "The modern Furius is to be looked upon as more an object of pity, than of that which he daily provokes, laughter and contempt. Did we really know how much this *poor* man (*I wish that reflection on* poverty *had been spared*) suffers by being contradicted, or, which is the same thing in effect, by hearing another praised; we should, in compassion, sometimes attend to him with a silent nod, and let him go away with the triumphs of his ill nature. . . ." Indeed his pieces against our poet are somewhat of an angry character, and as they are now scarce extant, a taste of his style may be satisfactory to the curious. "A young, squab, short gentleman, whose outward form, though it should be that of downright monkey, would not differ so much from human shape as his unthinking immaterial part does from human understanding. — He is as stupid and venomous as a hunch-back'd toad. . . ." Reflect. on the Essay on Criticism, p. 26, 29, 30.
It would be unjust not to add his reasons for this Fury, they are so strong and so coercive: "I regard him [Pope] . . . as an *Enemy*, not so much to me, as to my King, to my Country, to my Religion, and to that Liberty which has been the sole felicity of my life. A vagary of Fortune, who is sometimes pleased to be frolicksome, and the epidemic *Madness of the times* have given him *Reputation,* and Reputation (as Hobbes says) is *Power,* and *that has made him dangerous.* Therefore I look on it as my duty to *King George,* whose faithful subject I am; to my *Country,* of which I have appeared a constant lover; to the *Laws,* under whose protection I have so long lived; and to the *Liberty* of my *Country,* more dear to me than life, of which I have now for forty years been a constant asserter, &c., I look upon it as my duty, I say, to do — *you shall see what* — to pull the lion's skin from this little Ass, which popular error has

In each she marks her Image full exprest,
But chief in BAⅎ's monster-breeding breast;
Bays, form'd by nature, Stage and Town to bless,
And act, and be, a Coxcomb with success.   110
Dulness with transport eyes the lively Dunce,
Remembring she herself was Pertness once.
Now (shame to Fortune!) an ill Run at Play
Blank'd his bold visage, and a thin Third day:
Swearing and supperless the Hero sate,   115
Blasphem'd his Gods, the Dice, and damn'd his Fate.
Then gnaw'd his pen, then dash'd it on the ground,
Sinking from thought to thought, a vast profound!
Plung'd for his sense, but found no bottom there,
Yet wrote and flounder'd on, in mere despair.   120
Round him much Embryo, much Abortion lay,
Much future Ode, and abdicated Play;
Nonsense precipitate, like running Lead,
That slip'd thro' Cracks and Zig-zags of the Head;
All that on Folly Frenzy could beget,   125
Fruits of dull Heat, and Sooterkins of Wit.
Next, o'er his Books his eyes began to roll,
In pleasing memory of all he stole,
How here he sipp'd, how there he plunder'd snug
And suck'd all o'er, like an industrious Bug.   130
Here lay poor Fletcher's half-eat scenes, and here
The Frippery of crucify'd Moliere;
There hapless Shakespear, yet of Tibbald sore,
Wish'd he had blotted for himself before.

thrown round him; and to shew that this Author, who has been lately so much
in vogue, has neither sense in his thoughts, nor English in his expressions."
Dennis Rem. on Hom. Pref. p. 2, 91, &c . . .   P.
   108. **Bays:** Cibber, so-called because as poet laureate he ostensibly has won
the poet's crown of bay leaves.
   113. **at Play:** at dice.
   122. **abdicated:** abandoned.
   126. **Sooterkins:** Dutch women, by sitting over their stoves, were jokingly
said to produce a small creature about the size of a rat, called a sooterkin.
   128. **stole:** i.e., "borrowed" or adapted plots of older dramatists for his own
use.
   131. **Fletcher:** the playwright John Fletcher (1579–1625).
   132. **Frippery:** "When I fitted up an old play, it was as a good housewife
will mend old linnen, when she has not better employment." [Cibber's] Life,
p. 217, octavo.   P.
   133. This Tibbald, or Theobald, published an edition of Shakespear, of which
he was so proud himself as to say, in one of Mist's Journals, June 8, "That to
expose any Errors in it was impracticable." And in another, April, 27, "That
whatever care might for the future be taken by any other Editor, he would still
give above five hundred Emendations, that *shall* escape them all."   P.
   134. It was a ridiculous praise which the Players gave to Shakespear, "that
he never blotted a line." Ben Johnson honestly wished he had blotted a thousand;
and Shakespear would certainly have wished the same, if he had lived to see
those alterations in his works, which, not the Actors only (and especially the

The rest on Out-side merit but presume, 135
Or serve (like other Fools) to fill a room;
Such with their shelves as due proportion hold,
Or their fond Parents drest in red and gold;
Or where the pictures for the page attone,
And Quarles is sav'd by Beauties not his own. 140
Here swells the shelf with Ogilby the great;
There, stamp'd with arms, Newcastle shines complete:
Here all his suff'ring brotherhood retire,
And 'scape the martyrdom of jakes and fire:
A Gothic Library! of Greece and Rome 145
Well purg'd, and worthy Settle, Banks, and Broome.
  But, high above, more solid Learning shone,
The Classics of an Age that heard of none;
There Caxton slept, with Wynkyn at his side,

---

daring Hero of this poem) have made on the *Stage,* but the presumptuous Critics of our days in their *Editions.* P.

135ff. This Library is divided into three parts; the first consists of those authors from whom he stole and whose works he mangled; the second, of such as fitted the shelves [l. 137], or were gilded for shew [ll. 135, 138], or adorned with pictures [ll. 139–40]; the third class our author calls solid learning, old bodies of Divinity, old Commentaries, old English Printers, or old English Translations; all very voluminous, and fit to erect altars to Dulness.   P.

140. **Quarles:** Francis Quarles (1592–1644), religious poet whose work was lavishly illustrated.

141. "John Ogilby [1600–76] was one, who, from a late initiation into literature, made such a progress as might well style him the prodigy of his time! sending into the world so many *large Volumes!* His translations of Homer and Virgil *done to the life,* and *with such excellent sculptures!* And (what added great grace to his works) "he printed them all on *special good paper,* and in a *very good letter.*" Winstanly, Lives of Poets.   P.

142. "The *Duchess of Newcastle* [Margaret Cavendish, 1624–74] was one who busied herself in the ravishing delights of Poetry; leaving to posterity in print three *ample Volumes* of her studious endeavors." Winstanly, ibid. Langbaine reckons up *eight* Folios of her Grace's; which were usually adorned with gilded covers, and had her coat of arms upon them.   P.

144. **jakes:** privy.

145. **Gothic:** here means "barbarous."   **Rome:** at this time often pronounced to rhyme with "room."

146. The Poet has mentioned these three authors in particular, as they are parallel to our Hero in his three capacities: 1. Settle [see l. 90n., above], was his Brother Laureate; only indeed upon half-pay, for the City instead of the Court; but equally famous for unintelligible flights in his poems on public occasions, such as Shows, Birthdays, &c. 2. Banks [John Banks, *fl.* 1696] was his Rival in *Tragedy* (tho' more successful in one of his Tragedies, the *Earl of Essex,* which is yet alive: *Anna Boleyn,* the *Queen of Scots,* and *Cyrus the Great,* are dead and gone). These he drest in a sort of *Beggars Velvet,* or a happy mixture of the *thick Fustian* and *thin Prosaic:* exactly imitated [by Cibber] in *Perolla and Isidora, Cæsar in Ægypt,* and the *Heroic Daughter.* 3. Broome [Richard Brome, d. 1652] was a serving-man of Ben Johnson, who once picked up a *Comedy* from his Betters, or from some cast scenes of his Master, not entirely contemptible.   P.

149. **Caxton:** A Printer [William Caxton, 1422–91] in the time of Ed. IV, Rich. III, and Hen. VII; Wynkyn de Word [d. 1534], his successor, in that of Hen. VII and VIII. The former translated into prose Virgil's Æneis, as a his-

One clasp'd in wood, and one in strong cow-hide;   150
There, sav'd by spice, like Mummies, many a year,
Dry Bodies of Divinity appear:
De Lyra there a dreadful front extends,
And here the groaning shelves Philemon bends.
    Of these twelve volumes, twelve of amplest size,   155
Redeem'd from tapers and defrauded pies,
Inspir'd he seizes: These an altar raise:
An hecatomb of pure, unsully'd lays
That altar crowns: A folio Common-place
Founds the whole pile, of all his works the base: 160
Quartos, octavos, shape the less'ning pyre;
A twisted Birth-day Ode completes the spire.
    Then he: "Great Tamer of all human art!
First in my care, and ever at my heart;
Dulness! whose good old cause I yet defend,   165
With whom my Muse began, with whom shall end;
E'er since Sir Fopling's Periwig was Praise,
To the last honours of the Butt and Bays:
O thou! of Bus'ness the directing soul!
To this our head like byass to the bowl,   170
Which, as more pond'rous, made its aim more true,
Obliquely wadling to the mark in view:
O! ever gracious to perplex'd mankind,
Still spread a healing mist before the mind;
And lest we err by Wit's wild dancing light,   175
Secure us kindly in our native night.
Or, if to Wit a coxcomb make pretence,

---

tory; of which he speaks, in his Proeme, in a very singular manner, as of a book hardly known. P.
    153. De Lyra: Nicholas de Lyra (d. 1340), author of several volumes of Biblical commentary.
    154. *Philemon Holland* [d. 1637], Doctor in Physic. He translated *so many books,* that a man would think he had done *nothing else; insomuch that he might be called Translator general of his age.* The books alone of his turning into English are sufficient to make a *Country Gentleman* a *complete Library. Winstanl.* P.
    156. Leaves of old books were used to light candles and to wrap spices and pies.
    158. hecatomb: a large sacrifice.   unsully'd: untouched (i.e., unread).
    159. folio Common-place: a large scrapbook of ideas and literary passages, some perhaps his own, some copied from other writers.
    162. See l. 44n., above.
    167. The first visible cause of the passion of the Town for our Hero, was a fair flaxen full-bottomed Periwig, which, he tells us, he wore in his first play of the *Fool in fashion* [i.e., *Love's Last Shift,* 1696]. . . . This remarkable Periwig usually made its entrance upon the stage in a sedan, brought in by two chairmen, with infinite approbation of the audience. P.
    168. Butt and Bays: the cask of sack given to the laureate each year, and his crown of bay leaves.
    169. Bus'ness: stage business.
    175. Wit: here the poetic imagination.

Guard the sure barrier between that and Sense;
Or quite unravel all the reas'ning thread,
And hang some curious cobweb in its stead!   180
As, forc'd from wind-guns, lead itself can fly,
And pond'rous slugs cut swiftly thro the sky;
As clocks to weight their nimble motion owe,
The wheels above urg'd by the load below:
Me Emptiness, and Dulness could inspire,   185
And were my Elasticity, and Fire.
Some Dæmon stole my pen (forgive th' offence)
And once betray'd me into common sense:
Else all my Prose and Verse were much the same;
This, prose on stilts; that, poetry fall'n lame.   190
Did on the stage my Fops appear confin'd?
My Life gave ampler lessons to mankind.
Did the dead Letter unsuccessful prove?
The brisk Example never fail'd to move.
Yet sure had Heav'n decreed to save the State,   195
Heav'n had decreed these works a longer date.
Could Troy be sav'd by any single hand,
This grey-goose weapon must have made her stand.
What can I now? my Fletcher cast aside,
Take up the Bible, once my better guide?   200
Or tread the path by vent'rous Heroes trod,
This Box my Thunder, this right hand my God?
Or chair'd at White's amidst the Doctors sit,
Teach Oaths to Gamesters, and to Nobles Wit?
Or bidst thou rather Party to embrace?   205
(A friend to Party thou, and all her race;
'Tis the same rope at different ends they twist;
To Dulness Ridpath is as dear as Mist.)

181. wind-guns: guns using compressed air.
187. Dæmon: guardian spirit, or genius.
188. once: in his play *The Careless Husband* (cf. *First Ep. of the Second Bk.*, l. 92n.).
197. Troy: see "Martinus Scriblerus of the Poem," 6th paragraph and n. 6.
198. grey-goose weapon: his quill pen.
199. my Fletcher: A familiar manner of speaking, used by modern Critics, of a favourite author. Bays might as justly speak thus of Fletcher [see l. 131n., above], as a French Wit did of Tully [Marcus Tullius Cicero], seeing his works in a library, "Ah! mon cher Ciceron! je le connois bien; c'est le même que Marc Tulle." But he had a better title to call Fletcher *his own*, having made so free with him. P.
200. Take up the Bible: When, according to his Father's intention, he had been a *Clergyman,* or (as he thinks himself) a *Bishop* of the Church of England. . . . P.
202. Box: dice box.
203. White's: a notorious gambling club.   Doctors: (1) learned men (here those learned in gambling); (2) a cant word for loaded dice.
205. Party: political party, either Whig or Tory.
208. George Ridpath [d. 1726], author of a Whig paper, called the Flying post; Nathaniel Mist [d. 1737], of a famous Tory Journal. P.

Shall I, like Curtius, desp'rate in my zeal,
O'er head and ears plunge for the Commonweal?   210
Or rob Rome's ancient geese of all their glories,
And cackling save the Monarchy of Tories?
Hold — to the Minister I more incline;
To serve his cause, O Queen! is serving thine.
And see! thy very Gazetteers give o'er,   215
Ev'n Ralph repents, and Henly writes no more.
What then remains? Ourself. Still, still remain
Cibberian forehead, and Cibberian brain.
This brazen Brightness, to the 'Squire so dear;
This polish'd Hardness, that reflects the Peer;   220
This arch Absurd, that wit and fool delights;
This Mess, toss'd up of Hockley-hole and White's;
Where Dukes and Butchers join to wreathe my crown,
At once the Bear and Fiddle of the town.
"O born in sin, and forth in folly brought!   225
Works damn'd, or to be damn'd! (your father's fault)
Go, purify'd by flames ascend the sky,
My better and more christian progeny!
Unstain'd, untouch'd, and yet in maiden sheets;
While all your smutty sisters walk the streets.   230

209. Curtius: when a wide gap opened in the forum at Rome, the youth Curtius, fully armed and mounted, leaped into it as a human sacrifice, and the gap immediately closed.
211. geese: when the Gauls besieged Rome in 390 B.C., the Romans were warned of their approach by the cackling of the geese on the Capitol.
213. Minister: the Whig prime minister, Sir Robert Walpole.
215. Gazetteers: hireling writers for the government.
216. Ralph: James Ralph (1705–62), poet and journalist. See *Dunciad*, III 165–6*n.*, below.   **Henley:** John Henley (see *Ep. to Dr. Arbuthnot*, l. 98*n.*, and *Dunciad*, II 2, 370; III, 199).
218. Cibberian forehead: So indeed all the MSS. read; but I make no scruple to pronounce them all wrong, the Laureate being elsewhere celebrated by our Poet [see *First Ep. of the First Bk.*, l. 6] for his great *Modesty — modest Cibber* — Read, therefore, at my peril, *Cerberean forehead.* This is perfectly classical, and, what is more, *Homerical;* the *Dog* was the ancient, as the *Bitch* is the modern, symbol of Impudence. . . . But as to the latter part of this verse, *Cibberian brain*, that is certainly the genuine reading. Bentl.   P.   Pope in this and other notes parodies the style of the great classical scholar, Richard Bentley (see *Ep. to Dr. Arbuthnot*, l. 164*n.*, and *Dunciad*, IV 203–74).
222. Hockley-hole: a site in London famous for disreputable gatherings, bear-baitings, dog-fights, etc.   **White's:** see l. 203*n.*, above.
224. Bear: the person baited (as in bear-baiting).   **Fiddle:** jester.
225. This is a tender and passionate Apostrophe to his own works, which he is going to sacrifice, agreeable to the nature of man in great affliction; and reflecting like a parent on the many miserable fates to which they would otherwise be subject.   P.
228. "It may be observable, that my muse and my spouse were equally prolific; that the one was seldom the mother of a Child, but in the same year the other made me the father of a Play. I think we had a dozen of each sort between us; of both which kinds some *died* in their *Infancy.*" &c. Life of C.C., p. 217.   P.
229. Unstain'd: see l. 158*n.*, above.

Ye shall not beg, like gratis-given Bland,
Sent with a Pass, and vagrant thro' the land;
Not sail, with Ward, to Ape-and-monkey climes,
Where vile Mundungus trucks for viler rhymes;
Not sulphur-tipt, emblaze an Ale-house fire; 235
Not wrap up Oranges, to pelt your sire!
O! pass more innocent, in infant state,
To the mild Limbo of our Father Tate:
Or peaceably forgot, at once be blest
In Shadwell's bosom with eternal Rest! 240
Soon to that mass of Nonsense to return,
Where things destroy'd are swept to things unborn."
     With that, a Tear (portentous sign of Grace!)
Stole from the Master of the sev'nfold Face:
And thrice he lifted high the Birth-day brand, 245
And thrice he dropt it from his quiv'ring hand;
Then lights the structure, with averted eyes:
The rowling smokes involve the sacrifice.
The op'ning clouds disclose each work by turns,
Now flames the Cid, and now Perolla burns; 250
Great Cæsar roars, and hisses in the fires;
King John in silence modestly expires:
No merit now the dear Nonjuror claims,
Moliere's old stubble in a moment flames.
Tears gush'd again, as from pale Priam's eyes 255

231–2. It was a practice so to give the Daily Gazetteer and ministerial pamphlets (in which this B. [Henry Bland, d. 1746] was a writer) and to send them *Post-free* to all the Towns in the kingdom. P.

233–4. "Edward Ward [1667–1731], a very voluminous Poet in Hudibrastic verse, but best known by the London Spy, in prose. He has of late years kept a public house in the City (but in a genteel way) and with his wit, humour, and good liquor (ale) afforded his guests a pleasurable entertainment, especially those of the high-church party." Jacob, Lives of Poets, vol. ii, p. 225. Great numbers of his works were yearly sold into the Plantations. . . . P. **Mundungus:** bad-smelling tobacco. **trucks:** barters, pays.

236. Oranges: sold at the theaters, and sometimes thrown at the actors.

238–40. Tate . . . Shadwell: Two of his predecessors in the Laurel. P. For Nahum Tate, see *Ep. to Dr. Arbuthnot*, l. 190n. For Thomas Shadwell, the heir to the throne of Dulness in Dryden's *MacFlecknoe*, see *First Ep. of the Second Bk.*, l. 85n.

240. bosom: cf. "Abraham's bosom," in Luke 16:22.

244. sev'nfold Face: the Greek warrior Ajax possessed a "sevenfold shield" (i.e., of seven thicknesses of bull's hide).

250–2. the Cid: Cibber's *Ximena* (1712), a play based on Corneille's *Le Cid*. **Perolla:** his *Perolla and Izadora* (1705). **Great Cæsar:** his *Cæsar in Egypt* (1724). **King John:** his *Papal Tyranny*, adapted from Shakespeare's *King John;* after rehearsals for this play, Cibber decided against having it performed.

253–4. the dear Nonjuror: A Comedy threshed out of Moliere's Tartuffe, and so much the Translator's favourite, that he assures us all our author's dislike to it could only arise from *disaffection to the Government.* . . . P. *The Nonjuror* attacked Catholics and nonjurors (i.e., those who refused to take certain oaths of allegiance).

255. Priam: father of Aeneas.

When the last blaze sent Ilion to the skies.
    Rowz'd by the light, old Dulness heav'd the head;
Then snatch'd a sheet of Thulè from her bed,
Sudden she flies, and whelms it o'er the pyre;
Down sink the flames, and with a hiss expire.   260
    Her ample presence fills up all the place;
A veil of fogs dilates her awful face:
Great in her charms! as when on Shrieves and May'rs
She looks, and breathes herself into their airs.
She bids him wait her to her sacred Dome: 265
Well pleas'd he enter'd, and confess'd his home.
So Spirits ending their terrestrial race,
Ascend, and recognize their Native Place.
This the Great Mother dearer held than all
The clubs of Quidnuncs, or her own Guild-hall: 270
Here stood her Opium, here she nurs'd her Owls,
And here she plann'd th' Imperial seat of Fools.
    Here to her Chosen all her works she shews;
Prose swell'd to verse, verse loit'ring into prose:
How random thoughts now meaning chance to find,   275
Now leave all memory of sense behind:
How Prologues into Prefaces decay,
And these to Notes are fritter'd quite away:
How Index-learning turns no student pale,
Yet holds the eel of science by the tail: 280
How, with less reading than makes felons scape,
Less human genius than God gives an ape,
Small thanks to France, and none to Rome or Greece,
A past, vamp'd, future, old, reviv'd, new piece,
'Twixt Plautus, Fletcher, Shakespear, and Corneille,   285

256. Ilion: Troy (see l. 197n., above). In the immediately preceding lines, Pope parodies *Aeneid*, II 310–12.
258. Thulè: An unfinished poem of that name, of which one sheet was printed many years ago, by Amb. Philips, a northern author [see *Ep. to Dr. Arbuthnot*, l. 100n.]. It is an usual method of putting out a fire, to cast wet sheets upon it. Some critics have been of opinion that this sheet was of the nature of the Asbestos, which cannot be consumed by fire: But I rather think it an allegorical allusion to the coldness and heaviness of the writing. P.   *Thule* is the classical name for the most northerly land in the world.
269–70. Great Mother: *Magna mater* [a Roman earth goddess], here applied to *Dulness*. The *Quidnuncs*, a name given to the ancient members of certain political clubs, who were constantly enquiring *quid nunc?* what news? P. **Guild-hall:** the town hall of the City of London.
271. Opium: considered both an intoxicant and a stupefying agent at the time. Shadwell (see ll. 238–40n.) was a noted opium addict.   **Owls:** often used as a symbol of grave stupidity in the period.
279–80. In *A Tale of a Tub* Swift describes contemporary short-cuts to learning; one way of reading books is "to get a thorough insight into the index, by which the whole book is governed and turned, like fishes by the tail."
281. reading ... felons: see *Second Sat. of Dr. Donne*, ll. 15–16n.
284. vamp'd: patched.

Can make a Cibber, Tibbald, or Ozell.
   The Goddess then, o'er his anointed head,
With mystic words, the sacred Opium shed.
And lo! her bird, (a monster of a fowl,
Something betwixt a Heideggre and owl,)   290
Perch'd on his crown. "All hail! and hail again,
My son! the promis'd land expects thy reign.
Know, Eusden thirsts no more for sack or praise;
He sleeps among the dull of ancient days;
Safe, where no Critics damn, no duns molest,   295
Where wretched Withers, Ward, and Gildon rest,
And high-born Howard, more majestic sire,
With Fool of Quality compleats the quire.
Thou Cibber! thou, his Laurel shalt support,
Folly, my son, has still a Friend at Court.   300
Lift up your gates, ye Princes, see him come!
Sound, sound ye Viols, be the Cat-call dumb!
Bring, bring the madding Bay, the drunken Vine;
The creeping, dirty, courtly Ivy join.
And thou! his Aid de camp, lead on my sons,   305
Light-arm'd with Points, Antitheses, and Puns.
Let Bawdry, Bilingsgate, my daughters dear,
Support his front, and Oaths bring up the rear:
And under his, and under Archer's wing,

286. Ozell: John Ozell (d. 1743), a minor poet and indefatigable translator of classical and foreign works.
289–92. Cf. Matthew 3:16–17.
290. Heideggre: John James Heidegger (1659–1749), a Swiss theatrical promoter who was by many considered the ugliest man of his day.
293. Eusden: see l. 104*n.*, above.
295. duns: bill collectors, creditors.
296. Withers: George Withers (1588–1667), poet and hymn writer, and a political and religious pamphleteer.   **Ward:** see ll. 233–4*n.*, above.   **Gildon:** Charles Gildon (see *Ep. to Dr. Arbuthnot*, l. 151*n.*).
297. Howard: Edward Howard (*fl.* 1669), a dramatist much satirized by the Restoration wits, son of Thomas Howard, first Earl of Berkshire.
298. Fool of Quality: Lord John Hervey (see first note to *Ep. to Dr. Arbuthnot*) had died in August, 1743.   **quire:** choir.
299. his: Eusden's.
301. Lift up your Gates: see Psalms 24:7.
304. Ivy: associated, like the bay, with the poet's crown.
305. Aid de camp: apparently Lord Hervey (Pope seems to have overlooked the contradiction of l. 298, where Hervey has been transported to some kind of celestial "quire").
306. Points: witty turns of phrase.
307. Bilingsgate: foul language (a fish market near Billingsgate, in London, had become notorious for the coarse language there used).
309–10. When the Statute against Gaming was drawn up, it was represented, that the King, by ancient custom, plays at Hazard one night [Twelfth Night] in the year; and therefore a clause was inserted, with an exception as to that particular. Under this pretence, the Groom-porter [Thomas Archer, d. 1743] had a Room appropriated to Gaming all the summer the Court was at Kensington, which his Majesty accidentally being acquainted of, with a just indignation pro-

Gaming and Grub-street skulk behind the King.   310
    "O! when shall rise a Monarch all our own,
And I, a Nursing-mother, rock the throne,
'Twixt Prince and People close the Curtain draw,
Shade him from Light, and cover him from Law;
Fatten the Courtier, starve the learned band,   315
And suckle Armies, and dry-nurse the land:
'Till Senates nod to Lullabies divine,
And all be sleep, as at an Ode of thine."

    She ceas'd. Then swells the Chapel-royal throat:
"God save king Cibber!" mounts in ev'ry note.   320
Familiar White's, "God save king Colley!" cries;
"God save king Colley!" Drury-lane replies:
To Needham's quick the voice triumphal rode,
But pious Needham dropt the name of God;
Back to the Devil the last echoes roll,   325
And "Coll!" each Butcher roars at Hockley-hole.
    So when Jove's block descended from on high
(As sings thy great forefather Ogilby)
Loud thunder to its bottom shook the bog,
And the hoarse nation croak'd, "God save King Log!"

hibited. It is reported, the same practice is yet continued wherever the Court resides, and the Hazard Table there open to all the professed Gamesters in town. . . . P.

316. suckle Armies: alluding to maintenance of a large standing army at home (see *First Sat. of the Second Bk.*, l. 73n.) and to treaties by which England was obliged to subsidize the armies of Denmark and Hanover.

319. Chapel-royal: The Voices and Instruments used in the service of the Chapel-royal being also employed in the performance of the Birth-day and New-year Odes. P.

322. Drury Lane, site of Drury-lane Theater (of which Cibber was a manager), was also a haunt of prostitutes.

323. Needham: A Matron ["Mother" Needham, d. 1731, was a procuress] of great fame, and very religious in her way; whose constant prayer it was, that she might "get enough by her profession to leave it off in time, and make her peace with God." But her fate was not so happy; for being convicted, and set in the pillory, she was (to the lasting shame of all her great Friends and Votaries) so ill used by the populace, that it put an end to her days. P.

325. Devil: The Devil Tavern in Fleet-street, where these Odes are usually rehearsed before they are performed at Court. P.

326. Hockley-hole: see l. 222n., above.

328. Ogilby: See Ogilby's Æsop's Fables, where, in the story of the Frogs and their King, this excellent hemistic is to be found. P.   In the fable, the frogs implored Jove to send them a king, so he threw a log down among them. For Ogilby, see l. 141n., above.

BOOK THE SECOND

ARGUMENT

The King being proclaimed, the solemnity is graced with public Games and sports of various kinds; not instituted by the Hero, as by Æneas in Virgil, but for greater honour by the Goddess in person (in like manner as the games Pythia, Isthmia, &c. were anciently said to be ordained by the Gods, and as Thetis herself appearing, according to Homer, Odyss. 24. proposed the prizes in honour of her son Achilles.) Hither flock the Poets and Critics, attended as is but just, with their Patrons and Booksellers. The Goddess is first pleased, for her disport, to propose games to the Booksellers, and setteth up the Phantom of a Poet, which they contend to overtake. The Races described, with their divers accidents. Next, the game for a Poetess. Then follow the Exercises for the Poets, of tickling, vociferating, diving: The first holds forth the arts and practices of Dedicators, the second of Disputants and fustian Poets, the third of profound, dark, and dirty Party-writers. Lastly, for the Critics, the Goddess proposes (with great propriety) an Exercise, not of their parts, but their patience, in hearing the works of two voluminous Authors, one in verse, and the other in prose, deliberately read, without sleeping: The various effects of which, with the several degrees and manners of their operation, are here set forth; 'till the whole number, not of Critics only, but of spectators, actors, and all present, fall fast asleep; which naturally and necessarily ends the games.

H IGH on a gorgeous seat, that far out-shone
Henley's gilt tub, or Fleckno's Irish throne,
Or that where on her Curls the Public pours,

BOOK THE SECOND. 1. Parody of Milton, book 2 [*Par. Lost,* II 1–5]. P.

2. **Henley's gilt tub:** The pulpit of a Dissenter is usually called a Tub; but that of Mr. Orator Henley [see *Ep. to Dr. Arbuthnot,* l. 98n.] was covered with velvet, and adorned with gold. He had also a fair altar, and over it is this extraordinary inscription, *The Primitive Eucharist.* See the history of this person, book 3 [l. 199n.]. P.   **Fleckno's Irish throne:** Richard Fleckno [d. 1678] was an Irish priest, but had laid aside (as himself expressed it) the mechanic part of priesthood. He printed some plays, poems, letters, and travels. I doubt not our author took occasion to mention him in respect to the Poem of Mr. Dryden, to .which this bears some resemblance. . . . P.   See *Dunciad,* I 238–40n., above.

3. **Curls:** Edmund Curl [see *Ep. to Dr. Arbuthnot,* l. 53n.] stood in the pillory at Charing-cross, in March, 1727–8.

Mr. Curl loudly complained of this note, as an untruth; protesting "that he stood in the pillory, not in March, but in February." And of another on ver. 152, saying, "he was not tossed in a *Blanket,* but a *Rug.*" Curliad, duodecimo, 1729, p. 19, 25. Much in the same manner Mr. Cibber remonstrated that his Brothers at Bedlam, mentioned Book i [l. 32] were not *Brazen,* but *Blocks;* yet our author let it pass unaltered, as a trifle, that no way lessened the Relationship. P.

All-bounteous, fragrant Grains and Golden show'rs,
Great Cibber sate: The proud Parnassian sneer,   5
The conscious simper, and the jealous leer,
Mix on his look: All eyes direct their rays
On him, and crowds turn Coxcombs as they gaze.
His Peers shine round him with reflected grace,
New edge their dulness, and new bronze their face.   10
So from the Sun's broad beam, in shallow urns
Heav'ns twinkling Sparks draw light, and point their horns.
    Not with more glee, by hands Pontific crown'd,
With scarlet hats wide-waving circled round,
Rome in her Capitol saw Querno sit,   15
Thron'd on sev'n hills, the Antichrist of wit.
    And now the Queen, to glad her sons, proclaims
By herald Hawkers, high heroic Games.
They summon all her Race: an endless band
Pours forth, and leaves unpeopled half the land.   20
A motley mixture! in long wigs, in bags,
In silks, in crapes, in Garters, and in rags,
From drawing rooms, from colleges, from garrets,
On horse, on foot, in hacks, and gilded chariots:
All who true Dunces in her cause appear'd,   25
And all who knew those Dunces to reward.
    Amid that area wide they took their stand,
Where the tall may-pole once o'er-look'd the Strand;
But now (so ANNE and Piety ordain)
A Church collects the saints of Drury-lane.   30

    4. Grains and Golden show'rs: used malt grains and rotten eggs.
    5. Parnassian: the Greek mountain Parnassus was sacred to Apollo and the muses.
    7. rays: see *Messiah*, l. 39n.
    14. scarlet hats: those of Roman Catholic cardinals.
    15. Camillo Querno was of Apulia, who hearing the great Encouragement which Leo X gave to poets, travelled to Rome with a harp in his hand, and sung to it twenty thousand verses of a poem called Alexias. He was introduced *as a Buffoon* to Leo, and promoted to the honour of the *Laurel;* a jest which the court of Rome and the Pope himself entered into so far, as to cause him to ride on an elephant to the Capitol, and to hold a solemn festival on his coronation; at which it is recorded the Poet himself was so transported as to *weep for joy.* He was ever after a constant frequenter of the Pope's table, drank abundantly, and poured forth verses without number. . . . P.
    16. sev'n hills: the seven hills of Rome.
    18. Hawkers: peddlers.
    21. bags: small silk pouches used to contain the back-hair of wigs.
    22. Rich dunces would wear *silk; crape* would be worn by those of lesser means (or perhaps by the clergy). *Garters* suggests those belonging to the knightly Order of the Garter.
    24. hacks: hackney carriages.
    27–30. St. Mary le Strand Church, one of fifty new churches built according to an act passed under Queen Anne, stood on the site in the Strand where a may-pole (a symbol of heathenism to many) had once stood. The area represents a kind of border line between the City of London and the City of Westminster (see "Martinus Scriblerus of the Poem," n. 6.). The "saints of Drury-lane" are the prostitutes who frequented the area.

With Authors, Stationers obey'd the call,
(The field of glory is a field for all.)
Glory, and gain, th'industrious tribe provoke;
And gentle Dulness ever loves a joke.
A Poet's form she plac'd before their eyes,   35
And bade the nimblest racer seize the prize;
No meagre, muse-rid mope, adust and thin,
In a dun night-gown of his own loose skin;
But such a bulk as no twelve bards could raise,
Twelve starv'ling bards of these degen'rate days.   40
All as a partridge plump, full-fed, and fair,
She form'd this image of well-body'd air;
With pert flat eyes she window'd well its head;
A brain of feathers, and a heart of lead;
And empty words she gave, and sounding strain,   45
But senseless, lifeless! idol void and vain!
Never was dash'd out, at one lucky hit,
A fool, so just a copy of a wit;
So like, that critics said, and courtiers swore,
A Wit it was, and call'd the phantom More.   50
    All gaze with ardour: Some a poet's name,
Others a sword-knot and lac'd suit inflame.
But lofty Lintot in the circle rose:
"This prize is mine; who tempt it are my foes;
With me began this genius, and shall end."   55
He spoke: and who with Lintot shall contend?
    Fear held them mute. Alone, untaught to fear,
Stood dauntless Curl; "Behold that rival here!
"The race by vigour, not by vaunts is won;
"So take the hindmost, Hell." — He said, and run.   60
Swift as a bard the bailiff leaves behind,
He left huge Lintot, and out-strip'd the wind.
As when a dab-chick waddles thro' the copse

31. **Stationers:** booksellers.
37. **adust:** sallow of face, and gloomy of temperament.
39–40. Pope alludes to the old idea that man has degenerated in size and strength since the old heroic days.
41. **partridge:** considered a stupid bird at the time.
43. **flat:** dull.
50. **More:** James Moore Smythe (see *Ep. to Dr. Arbuthnot*, l. 23n.).
52. **sword knot:** an ornamental ribbon for a sword.
53. **lofty Lintot:** We enter here upon the episode of the Booksellers: Persons, whose names being more known and famous in the learned world than those of the Authors in this poem, do therefore need less explanation. The action of Mr. Lintot [see *Ep. to Dr. Arbuthnot*, l. 62n.] here imitates that of Dares in Virgil [*Aen.*, V 381ff.], rising just in this manner to lay hold on a *Bull*. . . . P.
61. Something like this is in Homer, *Il.* X. ver. 220, of Diomed. Two different manners of the same author in his similes are also imitated in the two following; the first, of the Bailiff, is short, unadorned, and (as the Critics well know) from *familiar life*; the second, of the Water-fowl, more extended, picturesque, and from *rural life* . . . P.
63. **dab-chick:** a bird related to the coots.

On feet and wings, and flies, and wades, and hops;
So lab'ring on, with shoulders, hands, and head,   65
Wide as a wind-mill all his figures spread,
With arms expanded Bernard rows his state,
And left-legg'd Jacob seems to emulate.
Full in the middle way there stood a lake,
Which Curl's Corinna chanc'd that morn to make: 70
(Such was her wont, at early dawn to drop
Her evening cates before his neighbour's shop,)
Here fortun'd Curl to slide; loud shout the band,
And Bernard! Bernard! rings thro' all the Strand.
Obscene with filth the miscreant lies bewray'd,   75
Fal'n in the plash his wickedness had laid:
Then first (if Poets aught of truth declare)
The caitiff Vaticide conceiv'd a pray'r.
    Hear Jove! whose name my bards and I adore,
As much at least as any God's, or more;   80
And him and his, if more devotion warms,
Down with the Bible, up with the Pope's Arms.
    A place there is, betwixt earth, air, and seas,
Where, from Ambrosia, Jove retires for ease.
There in his seat two spacious vents appear,   85
On this he sits, to that he leans his ear,

64–5. Pope refers the reader to *Paradise Lost*, II 947–50.
67. Bernard: Bernard Lintot.
68. Jacob: Jacob Tonson, another bookseller (see *Dunciad*, I 57n.), was famous for his clumsiness of foot.
70. Curl's Corinna: This name, it seems, was taken by one Mrs. T— [Elizabeth Thomas, d. 1731, mistress to Henry Cromwell, one of Pope's friends], who procured some private letters of Mr. Pope's, while almost a boy, to Mr. Cromwell, and sold them without the consent of either of those Gentlemen to Curl, who printed them in 12mo, 1727. . . . P.
72. cates: dainty foods.   **shop:** Curll's.
75. Though this incident may seem too low and base for the dignity of an Epic poem, the learned very well know it to be but a copy of Homer and Virgil; . . . though our poet (in compliance to modern nicety) has remarkably enriched and coloured his language, as well as raised the versification, in this Episode, and in the following one of Eliza. Mr. Dryden in *Mack-Fleckno*, has not scrupled to mention the *Morning Toast* at which the fishes bite in the Thames, *Pissing Alley, Reliques of the Bum, &c.*, but our author is more grave, and (as a fine writer says of Virgil in his Georgics) *tosses about his* Dung *with an air of Majesty*. If we consider that the exercises of his *Authors* could with justice be no higher than *tickling, chattering, braying,* or *diving,* it was no easy matter to invent such games as were proportioned to the meaner degree of *Booksellers.* In Homer and Virgil, Ajax and Nisus, the persons drawn in this plight are *Heroes;* whereas here they are such with whom it had been great impropriety to have joined any but vile ideas; besides the natural connection there is between Libellers and common Nusances. Nevertheless I have heard our author own, that this part of his Poem was (as it frequently happens) what cost him most trouble and pleased him least; but that he hoped it was excusable, since levelled at such as understand no delicate satyr. . . . P.
78. caitiff: despicable.   **Vaticide:** a "poet-murderer." The term could be applied to Curll because of the starvation wages he paid his hack writers, or because he printed mangled editions of literary works.
82. The Bible, Curl's sign; the Cross-keys, Lintot's.   P.

And hears the various vows of fond mankind:
Some beg an eastern, some a western wind,
All vain petitions, mounting to the sky,
With reams abundant this abode supply,   90
Amus'd he reads, and then returns the bills
Sign'd with that Ichor which from Gods distils.
   In office here fair Cloacina stands,
And ministers to Jove with purest hands.
Forth from the heap she pick'd her Vot'ry's pray'r,   95
And plac'd it next him, a distinction rare!
Oft had the Goddess heard her servant's call,
From her black grottos near the Temple-wall,
List'ning delighted to the jest unclean
Of link-boys vile, and watermen obscene;   100
Where as he fish'd her nether realms for Wit,
She oft had favour'd him, and favours yet.
Renew'd by ordure's sympathetic force,
As oil'd with magic juices for the course,
Vig'rous he rises; from th' effluvia strong   105
Imbibes new life, and scours and stinks along;
Re-passes Lintot, vindicates the race,
Nor heeds the brown dishonours of his face.
   And now the victor stretch'd his eager hand
Where the tall Nothing stood, or seem'd to stand;   110
A shapeless shade, it melted from his sight,
Like forms in clouds, or visions of the night.
To seize his papers, Curl, was next thy care;
His papers light, fly diverse, tost in air;
Songs, sonnets, epigrams the winds uplift,   115
And whisk 'em back to Evans, Young, and Swift.
Th' embroider'd suit at least he deem'd his prey;
That suit an unpay'd taylor snatch'd away.
No rag, no scrap, of all the beau, or wit,
That once so flutter'd, and that once so writ.   120
   Heav'n rings with laughter: of the laughter vain,

92. **Ichor:** an ethereal body-fluid of the heathen gods.
93. **Cloacina:** The Roman Goddess of the common-sewers.   P.
95. **Vot'ry:** votary (devotee).
98. **black grottos:** coal wharves along the Thames in the London district known as The Temple.
100. **link-boys:** boys who carried *links*, or torches.   **watermen:** Thames boatmen who had craft for hire.
101. **fish'd her nether realms:** searched her sewers for papers deposited there by writers.
103. **sympathetic:** kindred, congenial.
104. **magic juices:** Alluding to the opinion that there are ointments used by witches to enable them to fly in the air, &c.   P.
107. **vindicates:** claims victory in the race.
116. **Evans, Young, and Swift:** Some of those persons whose writings, epigrams, or jests he [the phantom, James Moore Smythe] had owned.   P.   Abel Evans (1679–1737) was a clergyman and minor poet.   Edward Young (1683–1765) was a wit, poet, and clergyman.

Dulness, good Queen, repeats the jest again.
Three wicked imps, of her own Grubstreet choir,
She deck'd like Congreve, Addison, and Prior;
Mears, Warner, Wilkins run: delusive thought!   125
Breval, Bond, Besaleel, the varlets caught.
Curl stretches after Gay, but Gay is gone,
He grasps an empty Joseph for a John:
So Proteus, hunted in a nobler shape,
Became, when seiz'd, a puppy, or an ape.   130
    To him the Goddess: "Son! thy grief lay down,
And turn this whole illusion on the town:
As the sage dame, experienc'd in her trade,
By names of Toasts retails each batter'd jade;
(Whence hapless Monsieur much complains at Paris   135
Of wrongs from Duchesses and Lady Maries;)
Be thine, my stationer! this magic gift;
Cook shall be Prior, and Concanen, Swift:
So shall each hostile name become our own,

123. **Grubstreet:** see *Dunciad*, I 44n.
124. **Congreve, Addison, and Prior:** These authors being such whose names will reach posterity, we shall not give any account of them, but proceed to those [1. 126] of whom it is necessary.—Besaleel Morris [d. 1749] was author of some satyrs on the translators of Homer, with many other things printed in newspapers. — "[William] Bond [d. 1735] writ a satyr against Mr. P—. Capt. [John] Breval [d. 1738] was author of The Confederates, an ingenious dramatic performance to expose Mr. P., Mr. Gay, Dr. Arb. and some ladies of quality," says Curl. . . . P.
125. **Mears, Warner, Wilkins:** Booksellers, and Printers of much anonymous stuff. P.
128. Joseph Gay, a fictitious name put by Curl before several pamphlets, which made them pass with many for Mr. [John] Gay's. P.   A "Joseph" was also a term for a long cloak.
129. **Proteus:** see *Dunciad*, I 37n.
132. It was a common practice of this bookseller to publish vile pieces of obscure hands under the names of eminent authors. P.
133. **sage dame:** i.e., a procuress.
134. **jade:** prostitute.
135–6. The "hapless Monsieur" is any Frenchman, and the "Duchesses and Lady Maries" are high-priced prostitutes who have assumed the names of titled English ladies to further their trade. At the same time, Pope glances at Lady Mary Wortley Montagu (see first note to *Ep. to Dr. Arbuthnot*) and her relationship with one M. Remond.
138. **Cook shall be Prior:** The man here specified [Thomas Cooke, 1703–56] writ a thing called The Battle of Poets, in which Philips and Welsted were the Heroes, and Swift and Pope utterly routed. He also published some malevolent things in the British, London, and Daily Journals; and at the same time wrote letters to Mr. Pope, protesting his innocence. His chief work was a translation of Hesiod, to which Theobald writ notes and half-notes, which he carefully owned. P.   **and Concanen, Swift:** In the first edition of this poem there were only asterisks in this place, but the names [of Cooke, and of Matthew Concanen, 1701–49] were since inserted, merely to fill up the verse, and give ease to the ear of the reader. P.   **Prior:** Matthew Prior (1664–1721), wit, diplomat and poet, and associate of Swift and Lord Bolingbroke (see also l. 124, above).

And we too boast our Garth and Addison."   **140**
    With that she gave him (piteous of his case,
Yet smiling at his rueful length of face)
A shaggy Tap'stry, worthy to be spread
On Codrus' old, or Dunton's modern bed;
Instructive work! whose wry-mouth'd portraiture   **145**
Display'd the fates her confessors endure.
Earless on high, stood unabash'd De Foe,
And Tutchin flagrant from the scourge below.
There Ridpath, Roper, cudgell'd might ye view,
The very worsted still look'd black and blue.   **150**
Himself among the story'd chiefs he spies,
As from the blanket high in air he flies,

140. Garth: see *Summer,* l. 9n.

142. rueful length of face: "The decrepid person or figure of a man are no reflections upon his *Genius:* An honest mind will love and esteem a *man of worth,* though he be deformed or poor. Yet the author of the Dunciad hath libelled a person for his *rueful length of face!*" Mist's Journal, June 8. This *Genius* and *man of worth,* whom an honest mind should *love,* is Mr. Curl. True it is, he stood in the Pillory, an incident which will lengthen the face of any man tho' it were ever so comely, therefore is no reflection on the natural beauty of Mr. Curl. But as to reflections on any man's face, or figure, Mr. [John] Dennis saith excellently; "Natural deformity comes not by our fault; 'tis often occasioned by calamities and diseases, which a man can no more help than a monster can his deformity. There is no one misfortune, and no one disease, but what all the rest of mankind are subject to. — But the deformity of this *Author* [Pope] is visible, present, lasting, unalterable, and peculiar to himself. 'Tis the mark of God and Nature upon him, to give us warning that we should hold no society with him, as a creature not of our original, nor of our species: and they who have refused to take this warning which God and nature have given them, and have in spite of it by a senseless presumption ventured to be familiar with him, have severely suffered, &c. 'Tis certain his original is not from Adam, but from the Devil," &c. Dennis, Charact. of Mr. P., octavo, 1716. P.

144. Of Codrus the poet's bed, see Juvenal, describing his *poverty* very copiously, Sat. iii, ver. 202, &c. . . . John Dunton [1659–1733] was a broken bookseller and abusive scribler; he writ Neck or Nothing, a violent satyr on some ministers of state; a libel on the Duke of Devonshire and the Bishop of Peterborough, &c. P.

146. confessors: see *Second Sat. of Dr. Donne,* l. 35n.

147. Daniel Defoe was pilloried, but did not have his ears clipped.

148. John Tutchin [d. 1707], author of some vile verses, and of a weekly paper called the Observator: He was sentenced to be whipped through several towns in the west of England, upon which he petitioned King James II to be hanged. When that prince died in exile, he wrote an invective against his memory, occasioned by some humane elegies on his death. He lived to the time of Queen Anne. P.

149. Ridpath, Roper: Authors [George Ridpath, d. 1726, and Abel Roper, d. 1726] of the Flying-post and Post-boy, two scandalous papers on different [i.e., Whig and Tory] sides, for which they equally and alternately deserved to be cudgelled, and were so. P.

151–6. The history of Curl's being tossed in a blanket, and whipped by the scholars of Westminster, is well known. Of his purging and vomiting, see a full and true Account of a horrid Revenge on the body of Edm. Curl, &c., in Swift and Pope's Miscell. P.

"And oh! (he cry'd) what street, what lane but knows,
Our purgings, pumpings, blankettings, and blows?
In ev'ry loom our labours shall be seen,   155
And the fresh vomit run for ever green!"
    See in the circle next, Eliza plac'd,
Two babes of love close clinging to her waist;
Fair as before her works she stands confess'd,
In flow'rs and pearls by bounteous Kirkall dress'd.   160
The Goddess then: "Who best can send on high
"The salient spout, far-streaming to the sky;
"His be yon Juno of majestic size,
"With cow-like udders, and with ox-like eyes.
"This China Jordan let the chief o'ercome   165
"Replenish, not ingloriously, at home."
Osborne and Curl accept the glorious strife,
(Tho' this his Son dissuades, and that his Wife.)
One on his manly confidence relies,
One on his vigour and superior size.   170
First Osborne lean'd against his letter'd post;
It rose, and labour'd to a curve at most.
So Jove's bright bow displays its wat'ry round,
(Sure sign, that no spectator shall be drown'd)
A second effort brought but new disgrace,   175
The wild Meander wash'd the Artist's face:
Thus the small jett, which hasty hands unlock,
Spirts in the gard'ner's eyes who turns the cock.
Not so from shameless Curl; impetuous spread

155. **labours:** sufferings.
157. In this game is exposed, in the most contemptuous manner, the profligate licentiousness of those shameless scriblers (for the most part of that Sex, which ought least to be capable of such malice or impudence) who in libellous Memoirs and Novels, reveal the faults or misfortunes of both sexes, to the ruin of public fame, or disturbance of private happiness. Our good poet (by the whole cast of his work being obliged not to take off the Irony) where he could not shew his indignation, hath shewn his contempt, as much as possible; having here drawn as vile a picture as could be represented in the colours of Epic poesy. Scribl.
    Eliza Haywood; this woman [d. 1756] was authoress of those most scandalous books called the Court of Carimania, and the New Utopia . . . P.
160. *Kirkall* [Elisha Kirkall, d. 1742], the name of an Engraver. Some of this Lady's works were printed in four volumes in 12mo, with her picture thus dressed up before them. P.
165. **China Jordan:** In the games of Homer, Il. XXIII, there are set together, as prizes, a Lady and a Kettle, as in this place Mrs. Haywood and a Jordan. But there the preference in value is given to the Kettle, at which Mad. Dacier [a French literary critic] is justly displeased. Mrs. H. is here treated with distinction, and acknowledged to be the more valuable of the two. P.
167. **Osborne:** Thomas Osborne (d. 1767), a shameless, disreputable bookseller.
168. **this:** Curll.   **that:** Osborne.
171. **letter'd post:** books were advertised on sheets fastened to posts.

The stream, and smoking flourish'd o'er his head.   180
So (fam'd like thee for turbulence and horns)
Eridanus his humble fountain scorns;
Thro' half the heav'ns he pours th' exalted urn;
His rapid waters in their passage burn.
    Swift as it mounts, all follow with their eyes: 185
Still happy Impudence obtains the prize.
Thou triumph'st, Victor of the high-wrought day,
And the pleas'd dame, soft-smiling, lead'st away.
Osborne, thro' perfect modesty o'ercome,
Crown'd with the Jordan, walks contented home.   190
    But now for Authors nobler palms remain;
Room for my Lord! three jockeys in his train;
Six huntsmen with a shout precede his chair:
He grins, and looks broad nonsense with a stare.
His Honour's meaning Dulness thus exprest,   195
"He wins this Patron, who can tickle best."
    He chinks his purse, and takes his seat of state:
With ready quills the Dedicators wait;
Now at his head the dextrous task commence,
And, instant, fancy feels th' imputed sense;   200
Now gentle touches wanton o'er his face,
He struts Adonis, and affects grimace:
Rolli the feather to his ear conveys,
Then his nice taste directs our Operas:
Bentley his mouth with classic flatt'ry opes,   205
And the puff'd orator bursts out in tropes.
But Welsted most the Poet's healing balm
Strives to extract from his soft, giving palm;
Unlucky Welsted! thy unfeeling master,
The more thou ticklest, gripes his fist the faster.   210
    While thus each hand promotes the pleasing pain,
And quick sensations skip from vein to vein;

181. **horns:** emblem of both river gods and cuckolds.
182. **Eridanus:** The Poets fabled of this river Eridanus, that it flowed through the skies. P.   See *Windsor-Forest*, l. 227n.
183. **urn:** see *Windsor-Forest*, ll. 332–3n.
196. **tickle:** to "tickle with a feather" (cf. the quills of l. 198) meant to flatter.
203. *Paolo Antonio Rolli* [1687–1767], an Italian Poet, and writer of many Operas in that language, which, partly by the help of his genius, prevailed in England near twenty years. He taught Italian to some fine Gentlemen, who affected to direct the Operas. P.
205. Not spoken of the famous Dr. Richard Bentley [see *Ep. to Dr. Arbuthnot*, l. 164n.] but of one Thom. Bentley [d. 1742], a small critic, who aped his uncle [Richard] in a *little Horace*. . . . P.
206. **tropes:** figures of speech.
207. **Welsted:** Leonard Welsted (see *Ep. to Dr. Arbuthnot*, l. 375n., and *Dunciad*, III 169–72).

A youth unknown to Phœbus, in despair,
Puts his last refuge all in heav'n and pray'r.
What force have pious vows! The Queen of Love   215
His sister sends, her vot'ress, from above.
As taught by Venus, Paris learnt the art
To touch Achilles' only tender part;
Secure, thro' her, the noble prize to carry,
He marches off, his Grace's Secretary.   220
   "Now turn to diff'rent sports (the Goddess cries)
And learn, my sons, the wond'rous pow'r of Noise.
To move, to raise, to ravish ev'ry heart,
With Shakespear's nature, or with Johnson's art,
Let others aim: 'Tis yours to shake the soul   225
With Thunder rumbling from the mustard bowl,
With horns and trumpets now to madness swell,
Now sink in sorrows with a tolling bell;
Such happy arts attention can command,
When fancy flags, and sense is at a stand.   230
Improve we these, Three Cat-calls be the bribe
Of him, whose chatt'ring shames the Monkey tribe:
And his this Drum, whose hoarse heroic base
Drowns the loud clarion of the braying Ass."
   Now thousand tongues are heard in one loud din: 235
The Monkey-mimics rush discordant in;
'Twas chatt'ring, grinning, mouthing, jabb'ring all,
And Noise and Norton, Brangling and Breval,
Dennis and Dissonance, and captious Art,

---

213. A youth unknown: The satyr of this Episode being levelled at the base flatteries of authors to worthless wealth or greatness, concludes here with an excellent lesson to such men: That altho' their pens and praises were as exquisite as they conceit of themselves, yet (even in their own mercenary views) a creature unlettered, who serveth the passions, or pimpeth to the pleasures, of such vain, braggart, puft Nobility, shall with those patrons be much more inward, and of them much higher rewarded.   Scribl.

215. Queen of love: Venus.

217–8. Paris is supposed to have slain Achilles by hitting him in the heel with an arrow.

226. The old way of making Thunder and Mustard [i.e., by pounding in a wooden bowl] were the same, but since, it is more advantageously performed by troughs of wood with stops in them. Whether Mr. Dennis was the inventor of that improvement, I know not; but it is certain, that being once at a Tragedy of a new author, he fell into a great passion at hearing some, and cried, " 'Sdeath! that is *my* Thunder."   P.

228. tolling bell: A mechanical help [as at stage funerals] to the Pathetic, not unuseful to the modern writers of Tragedy.   P.

231. Cat-calls: Certain musical instruments used by one sort of Critics to confound the Poets of the Theatre.   P.

238. Norton: Benjamin Norton Defoe, son of Daniel Defoe, was a journalist in government pay.   **Breval:** see l. 124 *n.*, l. 126, above.

239. captious: carping.

And Snip-snap short, and Interruption smart,   240
And Demonstration thin, and Theses thick,
And Major, Minor, and Conclusion quick.
"Hold (cry'd the Queen) a Cat-call each shall win;
Equal your merits! equal is your din!
But that this well-disputed game may end,   245
Sound forth my Brayers, and the welkin rend."
    As when the long-ear'd milky mothers wait
At some sick miser's triple-bolted gate,
For their defrauded, absent foals they make
A moan so loud, that all the guild awake;   250
Sore sighs Sir Gilbert, starting at the bray,
From dreams of millions, and three groats to pay.
So swells each wind-pipe; Ass intones to Ass,
Harmonic twang! of leather, horn, and brass;
Such as from lab'ring lungs th' Enthusiast blows,   255
High Sound, attemp'red to the vocal nose;
Or such as bellow from the deep Divine;
There Webster! peal'd thy voice, and Whitfield! thine.
But far o'er all, sonorous Blackmore's strain;
Walls, steeples, skies, bray back to him again.   260
In Tot'nam fields, the brethren, with amaze,
Prick all their ears up, and forget to graze;
Long Chanc'ry-lane retentive rolls the sound,
And courts to courts return it round and round;
Thames wafts it thence to Rufus' roaring hall,   265

240. **Snip-snap:** sharp repartee.
241. **Demonstration . . . Theses:** terms from logic.
242. **Major, Minor, and Conclusion:** the three propositions of a syllogism.
246. **welkin:** sky.
247. **As when the, &c.:** A Simile with a long tail, in the manner of Homer. P. The "milky mothers" are asses, whose milk was considered to have tonic qualities.
250. **guild:** Pope compares a herd of asses to one of the merchant guilds of London.
251. **Sir Gilbert:** Sir Gilbert Heathcote (see *Ep. to Bathurst*, l. 103n.).
255. **Enthusiast:** a fanatical preacher, especially one of a dissenting sect. Dissenting preaching was also often characterized as having a nasal quality (see next line).
258. **Webster . . . Whitfield:** The one [Dr. William Webster, 1689–1758] the writer of a News-paper called the Weekly Miscellany, the other [George Whitfield, 1714–70, a famous Methodist preacher] a Field-preacher. . . . P.
259. The poet here celebrated, Sir R. B. [Richard Blackmore; see l. 268n., below, and *First Sat. of the Second Bk.*, l. 23n.], delighted much in the word *bray*, which he endeavoured to ennoble by applying it to the sound of *Armour, War, &c.* In imitation of him, and strengthened by his authority, our author has here admitted it into Heroic Poetry. P.
261. **Tot'nam fields:** Tottenham Fields, an open region in upper Westminster.
263. **Chanc'ry-lane:** The place where the offices of Chancery are kept. The long detention of Clients in that Court, and the difficulty of getting out, is humourously allegorized in these lines. P.
265. **Rufus' roaring hall:** Westminster Hall, the principal seat of justice, was originally built by King William Rufus (William II).

332 • *The Dunciad*

And Hungerford re-echoes bawl for bawl.
All hail him victor in both gifts of song,
Who sings so loudly, and who sings so long.
  This labour past, by Bridewell all descend,
(As morning pray'r, and flagellation end)   270
To where Fleet-ditch with disemboguing streams
Rolls the large tribute of dead dogs to Thames,
The King of dykes! than whom no sluice of mud
With deeper sable blots the silver flood.
"Here strip, my children! here at once leap in,   275
"Here prove who best can dash thro' thick and thin,
"And who the most in love of dirt excel,
"Or dark dexterity of groping well,
"Who flings most filth, and wide pollutes around
"The stream, be his the Weekly Journals bound,   280
"A pig of lead to him who dives the best;
"A peck of coals a-piece shall glad the rest."

  266. Hungerford: Hungerford Market.
  268. A just character of Sir Richard Blackmore knight, who (as Mr. Dryden expresseth it)
               Writ to the rumbling of his coach's wheels,
and whose indefatigable Muse produced no less than six Epic poems: Prince and King Arthur, twenty books; Eliza, ten; Alfred, twelve; the Redeemer, six; besides Job, in folio; the whole Book of Psalms; the Creation, seven books; Nature of Man, three books; and many more. 'Tis in this sense he is styled afterwards the *everlasting Blackmore* [see l. 302, below]. Notwithstanding all which, Mr. Gildon [see *Ep. to Dr. Arbuthnot*, l. 151*n.*, and *Dunciad*, I 296] seems assured, that "this admirable author did not think himself upon the *same foot* with *Homer.*" Comp. Art of Poetry, vol. i, p. 108. . . . P.
  269*ff.* It is between eleven and twelve in the morning, after church services, that the criminals are whipt in Bridewell. — This is to mark punctually the *time* of the day: Homer does it by the circumstance of the Judges rising from court, or of the Labourer's dinner; our author by one very proper both to the *Persons* and *Scene* of his poem, which we may remember commenced in the evening of the Lord-Mayor's day: The first book passed in that *night*; the next *morning* the games begin in the Strand, thence along Fleet-street (places inhabited by Booksellers), then they proceed by Bridewell toward Fleet-ditch, and lastly thro' Ludgate to the City and the Temple of the Goddess. P.
  271. disemboguing: outpouring.   **273. dykes:** ditches.
  276–8. The three chief qualifications of Party-writers; to stick at nothing, to delight in flinging dirt, and to slander in the dark by guess. P.
  280. Weekly Journals: Papers of news and scandal intermixed, on different sides and parties, and frequently shifting from one side to the other, called the London Journal, British Journal, Daily Journal, *&c.*, the concealed writers of which for some time were [John] Oldmixon, [Edward] Roome, [William] Arnall, [Matthew] Concanen, and others; persons never seen by our author. P.
  281. pig: ingot.
  282. Our indulgent Poet, whenever he has spoken of any dirty or low work, constantly puts us in mind of the *Poverty* of the offenders, as the only extenuation of such practices. Let any one but remark, when a Thief, a Pick-pocket, an Highwayman, or a Knight of the post [a professional perjurer] are spoken of, how much our hate to these characters is lessened, if they add a *needy* Thief, a *poor* Pick-pocket, an *hungry* Highwayman, a *starving* Knight of the post, *&c.* P.

In naked majesty Oldmixon stands,
And Milo-like surveys his arms and hands;
Then sighing, thus, "And am I now three-score?   285
"Ah why, ye Gods! should two and two make four?"
He said, and clim'd a stranded lighter's height,
Shot to the black abyss, and plung'd down-right.
The Senior's judgment all the crowd admire,
Who but to sink the deeper, rose the higher.   290
   Next Smedley div'd; slow circles dimpled o'er
The quaking mud, that clos'd, and op'd no more.
All look, all sigh, and call on Smedley lost;
Smedley in vain resounds thro' all the coast.
   Then * essay'd; scarce vanish'd out of sight,   295
He buoys up instant, and returns to light:
He bears no token of the sabler streams,
And mounts far off among the Swans of Thames.
   True to the bottom, see Concanen creep,
A cold, long-winded, native of the deep: 300
If perseverance gain the Diver's prize,
Not everlasting Blackmore this denies:
No noise, no stir, no motion can'st thou make,
Th' unconscious stream sleeps o'er thee like a lake.
   Next plung'd a feeble, but a desp'rate pack,   305
With each a sickly brother at his back:
Sons of a Day! just buoyant on the flood,

283. Mr. John Oldmixon [see l. 280*n.*, above, and *Ep. to Dr. Arbuthnot*, l. 146 *n.*], next to Mr. Dennis, the most ancient Critic of our Nation. . . . He was all his life a virulent Party-writer for hire, and received his reward in a small place, which he enjoyed to his death. He is here likened to Milo, in allusion to that verse of Ovid [*Metamorphoses*, XV 229–31] . . . either with regard to his Age, or because he was undone by trying to pull to pieces an Oak that was too strong for him. . . . P.   Milo, a celebrated athlete of Crotona, in his old age tried to rend a tree asunder, but was trapped in the cleft and eaten by wild beasts.

287. lighter: barge (here stranded at low tide).

291. The person [Jonathan Smedley, b. 1671] here mentioned, an Irishman, was author and publisher of many scurrilous pieces, a weekly Whitehall Journal, in the year 1722, in the name of Sir James Baker; and particularly whole volumes of Billingsgate against Dr. Swift and Mr. Pope, called Gulliveriana and Alexandriana, printed in octavo, 1728. P.   For more on Smedley, who was also a clergyman, see l. 326*n.*

295. Then * essay'd: A Gentleman of genius and spirit, who was secretly dipt in some papers of this kind, on whom our Poet bestows a panegyric instead of a satyr, as deserving to be better employed than in Party-quarrels and personal invectives. P.   The blank was undoubtedly designed originally for Aaron Hill (d. 1750), a minor poet and essayist who prevailed upon Pope to remove his name from the poem.

299. Concanen: Matthew Concanen, a hireling political writer (see l. 138*n.*, above).

305–7. These were daily Papers, a number of which, to lessen the expence, were printed one on the back of another. P.

Then number'd with the puppies in the mud.
Ask ye their names? I could as soon disclose
The names of these blind puppies as of those.   310
Fast by, like Niobe (her children gone)
Sits Mother Osborne, stupify'd to stone!
And Monumental Brass this record bears,
"These are, — ah no! these were, the Gazetteers!"
Not so bold Arnall; with a weight of skull,   315
Furious he dives, precipitately dull.
Whirlpools and storms his circling arm invest,
With all the might of gravitation blest.
No crab more active in the dirty dance,
Downward to climb, and backward to advance.   320
He brings up half the bottom on his head,
And loudly claims the Journals and the Lead.
  The plunging Prelate, and his pond'rous Grace,
With holy envy gave one Layman place.
When lo! a burst of thunder shook the flood.   325
Slow rose a form, in majesty of Mud;
Shaking the horrors of his sable brows,
And each ferocious feature grim with ooze.
Greater he looks, and more than mortal stares:
Then thus the wonders of the deep declares.   330
  First he relates, how sinking to the chin,

311. **Niobe:** See the story in Ovid, Met. [VI 165*ff*.], where the miserable Petrefaction of this old Lady is pathetically described. P.   Niobe, mother of seven sons and seven daughters, boasted that her children excelled Apollo and Diana, children of Latona. For her pride, her children were killed by Apollo and Diana, and she in her grief was turned to stone.

312. **Mother Osborne:** A name assumed by the eldest and gravest of these writers, who at last being ashamed of his Pupils, gave his paper over, and in his age remained silent. P.   He was James Pitt (1679–1763), and given the epithet "Mother" because of the heaviness of his style.

314. **Gazetteers:** We ought not to suppress that a modern Critic here taxeth the Poet with an Anachronism, affirming these Gazetteers not to have lived within the time of his poem, and challenging us to produce any such paper of that date. But we may with equal assurance assert, these Gazetteers not to have lived since, and challenge all the learned world to produce one such paper at this day. Surely therefore, where the point is so obscure, our author ought not to be censured rashly. Scribl.

315. William Arnall [d. 1736], bred an Attorney, was a perfect Genius in this sort of work. He began under twenty with furious Party-papers; then succeeded Concanen in the British Journal. At the first publication of the Dunciad, he prevailed on the Author not to give him his due place in it, by a letter professing his detestation of such practices as his Predecessor's. But since, by the most unexampled insolence, and personal abuse of several great men, the Poet's particular friends, he most amply deserved a niche in the Temple of Infamy. . . . P.

323. **Prelate . . . Grace:** two clergymen not positively identified.

326. **a form:** presumably that of Jonathan Smedley, who had disappeared into the mud, ll. 291–4. As a clergyman (he was Dean of Clogher) who was a hireling writer for Walpole, he would fit the details of ll. 347–58, below.

Smit with his mien, the Mud-nymphs suck'd him in:
How young Lutetia, softer than the down,
Nigrina black, and Merdamante brown,
Vy'd for his love in jetty bow'rs below,   335
As Hylas fair was ravish'd long ago.
Then sung, how shown him by the Nut-brown maids
A branch of Styx here rises from the Shades,
That tinctur'd as it runs with Lethe's streams,
And wafting Vapours from the Land of dreams,   340
(As under seas Alphæus' secret sluice
Bears Pisa's off'rings to his Arethuse)
Pours into Thames: and hence the mingled wave
Intoxicates the pert, and lulls the grave:
Here brisker vapours o'er the Temple creep,   345
There, all from Paul's to Aldgate drink and sleep.
    Thence to the banks where rev'rend Bards repose,
They led him soft; each rev'rend Bard arose;
And Milbourn chief, deputed by the rest,
Gave him the cassock, surcingle, and vest.   350
"Receive (he said) these robes which once were mine,
"Dulness is sacred in a sound divine."
    He ceas'd, and spread the robe; the crowd confess
The rev'rend Flamen in his lengthen'd dress.
Around him wide a sable Army stand,   355

333. Lutetia: Latin name for ancient Paris, thought to refer to its dirty or muddy site. *Lutum* is Latin for mud, filth, scum.
    334. Nigrina: from *niger* (black, sable).   **Merdamante:** *merda* means dung; *amante* means loving.
    336. Hylas: a beautiful Greek youth drawn down by nymphs while drinking at a spring.
    339–40. *Lethe* and the *Land of Dreams* allegorically represent the *Stupefaction* and *visionary Madness* of Poets, equally dull and extravagant. . . . P. The waters of Lethe, a river in Hades, were supposed to cause forgetfulness.
    341–2. The river Alpheus (on whose banks the ancient Greek city of Pisa once stood) was fabled to pass unmixed through the sea and to rise in the fountain of Arethusa at Syracuse, near Sicily (an allegory of the ardent love of the river-god Alpheus for the nymph Arethusa). Objects thrown into the river at Pisa were thought to appear eventually in the fountain.
    345. the Temple: the district of London near the Thames and Fleet Ditch where the English legal societies were established (see l. 98*n.*, above).
    346. from Paul's to Aldgate: from St. Paul's Cathedral, near the western boundary of the City, to the principal east gate of the City. See "Martinus Scriblerus of the Poem," n. 6.
    347. rev'rend Bards: presumably bards who were also clergymen.
    349. Milbourn: Luke Milbourn [1649–1720], a Clergyman, the fairest of Critics; who, when he wrote against Mr. Dryden's Virgil, did him justice in printing at the same time his own translations of him, which were intolerable. . . . P.
    350. surcingle: a girdle or belt which confines a clergyman's cassock, or frock.
    354. Flamen: priest.
    355. Around him wide: It is to be hoped that the satyr in these lines will be understood in the confined sense in which the Author meant it, of such only of

A low-born, cell-bred, selfish, servile band,
Prompt or to guard or stab, to saint or damn,
Heav'n's Swiss, who fight for any God, or Man.
    Thro' Lud's fam'd gates, along the well-known Fleet
Rolls the black troop, and overshades the street,   360
'Till show'rs of Sermons, Characters, Essays,
In circling fleeces whiten all the ways:
So clouds replenish'd from some bog below,
Mount in dark volumes, and descend in snow.
Here stopt the Goddess; and in pomp proclaims   365
A gentler exercise to close the games.
    "Ye Critics! in whose heads, as equal scales,
"I weigh what author's heaviness prevails;
"Which most conduce to sooth the soul in slumbers,
"My H—ley's periods, or my Blackmore's numbers;   370
"Attend the trial we propose to make:
"If there be man, who o'er such works can wake,
"Sleep's all-subduing charms who dares defy,
"And boasts Ulysses' ear with Argus' eye;
"To him we grant our amplest pow'rs to sit   375
"Judge of all present, past, and future wit;
"To cavil, censure, dictate, right or wrong,
"Full and eternal privilege of tongue."
    Three College Sophs, and three pert Templars came,
The same their talents, and their tastes the same;   380
Each prompt to query, answer, and debate,
And smit with love of Poesy and Prate.
The pond'rous books two gentle readers bring;
The heroes sit, the vulgar form a ring;
The clam'rous crowd is hush'd with mugs of Mum,   385
'Till all tun'd equal, send a gen'ral hum.
Then mount the Clerks, and in one lazy tone
Thro' the long, heavy, painful page drawl on;

---

the Clergy, who, tho' solemnly engaged in the service of Religion, dedicate
themselves for venal and corrupt ends to that of Ministers or Factions. . . . P.
    356. cell-bred: bred in the cells of a religious house or seminary.
    358. Heav'n's Swiss: religious mercenaries.
    359. Lud's fam'd gates: one of the principal gates in the western wall of the
City, traditionally associated with King Lud, a mythical king of Britain.   Fleet:
Fleet street.
    361. Characters: literary sketches of human types.
    370. H—ley: "Orator" Henley (see l. 2n., above).
    374. Ulysses' ear: alluding to the story of Ulysses and the Sirens.   Argus'
eye: Argus was a legendary monster having eyes all over his body, only two of
which were asleep at a time (see also *Dunciad*, IV 637–8).
    379. Templars: barristers having chambers in The Temple (see l. 345n.,
above, and also *Ep. to Dr. Arbuthnot*, l. 211n.).
    385. Mum: a kind of beer.
    388. "All these lines very well imitate the slow drowziness with which they
proceed. It is impossible to any one, who has a poetical ear, to read them with-

Soft creeping, words on words, the sense compose,
At ev'ry line they stretch, they yawn, they doze.   390
As to soft gales top-heavy pines bow low
Their heads, and lift them as they cease to blow:
Thus oft they rear, and oft the head decline,
As breathe, or pause, by fits, the airs divine.
And now to this side, now to that they nod,   395
As verse, or prose, infuse the drowzy God.
Thrice Budgel aim'd to speak, but thrice supprest
By potent Arthur, knock'd his chin and breast.
Toland and Tindal, prompt at priests to jeer,
Yet silent bow'd to Christ's No kingdom here.   400
Who sate the nearest, by the words o'ercome,
Slept first; the distant nodded to the hum.
Then down are roll'd the books; stretch'd o'er 'em lies
Each gentle clerk, and mutt'ring seals his eyes.
As what a Dutchman plumps into the lakes,   405
One circle first, and then a second makes;
What Dulness dropt among her sons imprest
Like motion from one circle to the rest;
So from the mid-most the nutation spreads
Round and more round, o'er all the sea of heads.   410
At last Centlivre felt her voice to fail,
Motteux himself unfinish'd left his tale,
Boyer the State, and Law the Stage gave o'er,

---

out perceiving the heaviness that lags in the verse, to imitate the action it describes. The simile of the Pines is very just and well adapted to the subject;" says an Enemy, in his Essay on the Dunciad, p. 21.   P.

396. drowzy God: Sleep.

397. Budgel: Eustace Budgell (see *Ep. to Dr. Arbuthnot,* l. 378n.).

398. Arthur: either of Blackmore's two epics, *Prince Arthur* (1695) or *King Arthur* (1697).

399. Toland and Tindal: Two persons, not so happy as to be obscure, who writ against the Religion of their Country.   P.   John Toland (1670–1722) was a noted deistical writer. For Matthew Tindal, another deist, see *Sixth Ep. of the First Bk.,* l. 64n.

400. Christ's No Kingdom here: an allusion to a famous sermon, "The Nature of the Kingdom or Church of Christ," by Benjamin Hoadley, Bishop of Bangor (see *Fourth Sat. of Dr. Donne,* l. 73n.). The sermon, which denied the existence of a visible church of Christ, gave rise to the "Bangorian controversy."

409. nutation: nodding of the head.

410. sea of heads: *A waving sea of heads was round me spread,*
                        And still fresh streams the gazing deluge fed.
                        Blackmore. Job.   P.

411. Mrs. Susanna Centlivre [d. 1723], wife to Mr. Centlivre, Yeoman of the Mouth to his Majesty. She writ many Plays, and a Song (says Mr. Jacob, vol. i, p. 32) before she was seven years old. She also writ a Ballad against Mr. Pope's Homer, before he begun it.   P.

412. Motteux: the dramatist Pierre Motteux (see *Fourth Sat. of Dr. Donne,* l. 50n.).

413. A. Boyer [1667–1729], a voluminous compiler of Annals, Political Collections, &c. — William Law, A.M. [1686–1761], wrote with great zeal against

Morgan and Mandevil could prate no more;
Norton, from Daniel and Ostrœa sprung,   415
Bless'd with his father's front, and mother's tongue,
Hung silent down his never-blushing head;
And all was hush'd, as Folly's self lay dead.
    Thus the soft gifts of Sleep conclude the day,
And stretch'd on bulks, as usual, Poets lay.   420
Why should I sing what bards the nightly Muse
Did slumb'ring visit, and convey to stews;
Who prouder march'd, with magistrates in state,
To some fam'd round-house, ever open gate!
How Henley lay inspir'd beside a sink,   425
And to mere mortals seem'd a Priest in drink:
While others, timely, to the neighb'ring Fleet
(Haunt of the Muses) made their safe retreat.

---

the Stage; Mr. Dennis answered with as great: Their books were printed in
1726. . . . P.
    414. Morgan: A writer [Thomas Morgan, a deist, d. 1743] against Religion,
distinguished no otherwise from the rabble of his tribe than by the pompousness
of his Title; for having stolen his Morality from Tindal [see l. 399n., above],
and his Philosophy from Spinoza, he calls himself, by the courtesy of England,
a *Moral Philosopher.* P.
    Mandevil: This writer [Bernard Mandeville, 1670–1733], who prided him-
self as much in the reputation of an *Immoral Philosopher,* was author of a
famous book called the Fable of the Bees; which may seem written to prove,
that Moral Virtue is the invention of knaves, and Christian Virtue the imposition of fools; and that Vice is necessary, and alone sufficient to render Society
flourishing and happy. P.
    415. Norton: see l. 238n., above.   **Ostrœa:** Pope suggests that Norton
Defoe's mother was an "oyster-wench"; such women were noted for their coarse-
ness of speech (see next line).
    416. front: (1) forehead; (2) impudence.
    420. bulks: the stalls in front of shops.
    422. stews: brothels.
    424. round-house: jail.
    425. sink: cesspool, or sewer.
    426. This line presents us with an excellent moral, that we are never to pass
judgment merely by *appearances;* a lesson to all men who may happen to see a
reverend Person in the like situation, not to determine too rashly: since not only
the Poets frequently describe a Bard inspired in this posture, (*On Cam's fair
bank, where Chaucer lay inspir'd,* and the like) but an eminent Casuist tells us,
that "if a Priest be seen in any indecent action, we ought to account it a de-
ception of sight, or illusion of the Devil, who sometimes takes upon him the
shape of holy men on purpose to cause scandal." Scribl.
    427. Fleet: A prison for insolvent Debtors on the bank of the Ditch. P.

BOOK THE THIRD

ARGUMENT

After the other persons are disposed in their proper places of rest, the Goddess transports the King to her Temple, and there lays him to slumber with his head on her lap; a position of marvellous virtue, which causes all the Visions of wild enthusiasts, projectors, politicians, inamoratos, castle-builders, chemists, and poets. He is immediately carried on the wings of Fancy, and led by a mad Poetical Sibyl, to the Elysian shade; where, on the banks of Lethe, the souls of the dull are dipped by Bavius, before their entrance into this world. There is met by the ghost of Settle, and by him made acquainted with the wonders of the place, and with those which he himself is destined to perform. He takes him to a Mount of Vision, from whence he shews him the past triumphs of the Empire of Dulness, then the present, and lastly the future: how small a part of the world was ever conquered by Science, how soon those conquests were stopped, and those very nations again reduced to her dominion. Then distinguishing the Island of Great-Britain, shews by what aids, by what persons, and by what degrees it shall be brought to her Empire. Some of the persons he causes to pass in review before his eyes, describing each by his proper figure, character, and qualifications. On a sudden the Scene shifts, and a vast number of miracles and prodigies appear, utterly surprising and unknown to the King himself, 'till they are explained to be the wonders of his own reign now commencing. On this Subject Settle breaks into a congratulation, yet not unmixed with concern, that his own times were but the types of these. He prophesies how first the nation shall be over-run with Farces, Operas, and Shows; how the throne of Dulness shall be advanced over the Theatres, and set up even at Court; then how her Sons shall preside in the seats of Arts and Sciences: giving a glimpse, or Pisgah-sight of the future Fulness of her Glory, the accomplishment whereof is the subject of the fourth and last book.

B<small>UT</small> in her Temple's last recess inclos'd
　On Dulness' lap th' Anointed head repos'd.
　Him close she curtains round with Vapours blue,
And soft besprinkles with Cimmerian dew.
Then raptures high the seat of Sense o'erflow,　　　　5
Which only heads refin'd from Reason know.

<small>BOOK THE THIRD.</small> **4. Cimmerian dew:** the gloomy mist of Cimmeria, a remote and mythical realm whose people were supposed to dwell in perpetual darkness.
5–6. Hereby is intimated that the following Vision is no more than the chimera of the dreamer's brain, and not a real or intended satyr on the present Age, doubtless more learned, more enlightened, and more abounding with great

Hence, from the straw where Bedlam's Prophet nods,
He hears loud Oracles, and talks with Gods:
Hence the Fool's Paradise, the Statesman's Scheme,
The air-built Castle, and the golden Dream,   10
The Maid's romantic wish, the Chemist's flame,
And Poet's vision of eternal Fame.
   And now, on Fancy's easy wing convey'd,
The King descending, views th' Elysian Shade.
A slip-shod Sibyl led his steps along,   15
In lofty madness meditating song;
Her tresses staring from Poetic dreams,
And never wash'd, but in Castalia's streams.
Taylor, their better Charon, lends an oar,
(Once swan of Thames, tho' now he sings no more.)   20
Benlowes, propitious still to blockheads, bows;
And Shadwell nods the Poppy on his brows.
Here, in a dusky vale where Lethe rolls,
Old Bavius sits, to dip poetic souls,
And blunt the sense, and fit it for a skull   25
Of solid proof, impenetrably dull:
Instant, when dipt, away they wing their flight,

Genius's in Divinity, Politics, and whatever arts and sciences, than all the preceding. For fear of any such mistake of our Poet's honest meaning, he hath
again at the end of the Vision repeated this monition, saying that it all past
through the *Ivory gate,* which (according to the Ancients) denoteth Falsity.
Scribl.

   How much the good Scriblerus was mistaken, may be seen from the Fourth
book, which, it is plain from hence, he had never seen.   Bent.

   7. **Bedlam:** the Hospital of St. Mary of Bethlehem, London's asylum for the
insane.

   11. **Chemist's flame:** an allusion to the attempts by alchemists to turn base
metals into gold (the "golden Dream" of l. 10).

   14. Pope here begins a parody of the conventional epic descent to an under-
world, more particularly that of Virgil, *Aeneid,* Book VI.

   18. **Castalia:** the spring, sacred to the muses, on the lower slopes of Mt.
Parnassus.

   19. **Taylor:** John Taylor the Water-Poet, an honest man, who owns he
learned not so much as the Accidence [i.e., grammatical inflections]: A rare
example of modesty in a Poet! He wrote fourscore books in the reign of James I
and Charles I and afterwards (like Edward Ward) kept an Alehouse in Long-
Acre. He died in 1654.   P.

   21. **Benlowes:** A country gentleman [Edward Benlowes, 1602–76], famous
for his own bad Poetry, and for patronizing bad Poets, as may be seen from
many Dedications of Quarles and others to him. Some of these anagram'd his
name, *Benlowes* into *Benevolus:* to verify which, he spent his whole estate upon
them.   P.

   22. Shadwell [see *Dunciad,* I 238–40*n.*, 270*n.*] took Opium for many years,
and died of too large a dose, in the year 1692.   P.

   24. Bavius was an ancient Poet, celebrated by Virgil for the like cause as
Bays by our author, though not in so Christian-like a manner: For heathenishly
it is declared by Virgil of Bavius, that he ought to be *hated* and *detested* for
his evil works; *Qui Bavium non* odit; whereas we have often had occasion to
observe our Poet's *Good nature* and *Mercifulness* thro' the whole course of this
Poem.   Scribl.

Where Brown and Mears unbar the gates of Light,
Demand new bodies, and in Calf's array,
Rush to the world, impatient for the day.   30
Millions and millions on these banks he views,
Thick as the stars of night, or morning dews,
As thick as bees o'er vernal blossoms fly,
As thick as eggs at Ward in Pillory.

    Wond'ring he gaz'd: When lo! a Sage appears,   35
By his broad shoulders known, and length of ears,
Known by the band and suit which Settle wore
(His only suit) for twice three years before:
All as the vest, appear'd the wearer's frame,
Old in new state, another yet the same.   40
Bland and familiar as in life, begun
Thus the great Father to the greater Son.
    "Oh born to see what none can see awake!
Behold the wonders of th' oblivious Lake.
Thou, yet unborn, hast touch'd this sacred shore;   45
The hand of Bavius drench'd thee o'er and o'er.
But blind to former as to future fate,
What mortal knows his pre-existent state?
Who knows how long thy transmigrating soul
Might from Bœotian to Bœotian roll?   50
How many Dutchmen she vouchsaf'd to thrid?

28. Brown and Mears: Booksellers, Printers for any body. — The allegory of the souls of the dull coming forth in the form of books, dressed in calf's leather, and being let abroad in vast numbers by Booksellers, is sufficiently intelligible. P.

34. Ward: John Ward of Hackney Esq. Member of Parliament, being convicted of forgery, was first expelled the House, and then sentenced to the Pillory on the 17th of February, 1727. . . . P. See *Ep. to Bathurst*, l. 20*n.*

36. length of ears: This is a *sophisticated* reading. I think I may venture to affirm all the Copyists are mistaken here: I believe I may say the same of the Critics; Dennis, Oldmixon, Welsted have passed it in silence. I have also stumbled at it, and wondered how an error so manifest could escape such accurate persons. I dare assert it proceeded originally from the inadvertency of some Transcriber, whose head run on the *Pillory,* mentioned two lines before; it is therefore amazing that Mr. Curl himself should over-look it! Yet that *Scholiast* takes not the least notice hereof. That the learned Mist also read it thus, is plain from his ranging this passage among those in which our author was blamed for *personal Satyr* on a *Man's face* (whereof doubtless he might take the *ear* to be a part;) so likewise Concanen, Ralph, the Flying Post, and all the herd of Commentators. — *Tota armenta sequuntur.*

    A very little sagacity (which all these Gentlemen therefore wanted) will restore us to the true sense of the Poet, thus,

        By his broad shoulders known, and length of years.

See how easy a change; of one single letter! That Mr. Settle [see *Dunciad,* I 90*n.*] was old, is most certain; but he was (happily) a stranger to the *Pillory.* This note partly Mr. Theobald's, partly Scribl. P.

37. Settle: Elkanah Settle was once a Writer in vogue, as well as Cibber, both for Dramatic Poetry and Politics. . . . P. The "band" of this line is a collar.

50. Bœotian: see *Dunciad,* I 25*n.*

51. Dutchmen: considered heavy and dull of mind.

How many stages thro' old Monks she rid?
And all who since, in mild benighted days,
Mix'd the Owl's ivy with the Poet's bays?
As man's Mæanders to the vital spring   55
Roll all their tides, then back their circles bring;
Or whirligigs, twirl'd round by skilful swain,
Suck the thread in, then yield it out again:
All nonsense thus, of old or modern date,
Shall in thee centre, from thee circulate.   60
For this, our Queen unfolds to vision true
Thy mental eye, for thou hast much to view:
Old scenes of glory, times long cast behind
Shall, first recall'd, rush forward to thy mind:
Then stretch thy sight o'er all her rising reign,   65
And let the past and future fire thy brain.

"Ascend this hill, whose cloudy point commands
Her boundless empire over seas and lands.
See, round the Poles where keener spangles shine,
Where spices smoke beneath the burning Line,   70
(Earth's wide extremes) her sable flag display'd,
And all the nations cover'd in her shade!

"Far eastward cast thine eye, from whence the Sun
And orient Science their bright course begun:
One god-like Monarch all that pride confounds,   75
He, whose long wall the wand'ring Tartar bounds;
Heav'ns! what a pile! whole ages perish there,

52. **Monks:** Pope's attitude toward monkish learning is suggested by *An Essay on Criticism*, ll. 687–92.

54. **Owl's ivy:** ivy was sometimes used as the emblem for learned men or critics, but here the owl (a bird used as the sign of grave and pompous stupidity) qualifies the emblem.

61–2. This has a resemblance to that passage in Milton, book xi [ll. 411–14], where the Angel

> To nobler sights from Adam's eye remov'd
> The film; then purg'd with Euphrasie and Rue
> The visual nerve — For he had much to see.

There is a general allusion in what follows to that whole Episode. P.

67. The scenes of this vision are remarkable for the order of their appearance. First, from ver. 67 to 73, those places of the globe are shewn where Science *never* rose; then from ver. 73 to 83, those where she was destroyed by *Tyranny;* from ver. 85 to 95, by inundations of *Barbarians;* from ver. 96 to 106, by *Superstition*. Then Rome, the Mistress of Arts, described in her degeneracy; and lastly Britain, the scene of the action of the poem; which furnishes the occasion of drawing out the Progeny of Dulness in review. P.

69. **Poles:** Almost the whole Southern and Northern Continent wrapt in ignorance. P.

70. **Line:** the equator.

73. Our author favours the opinion that all Sciences came from the Eastern nations. P.

74. **Science:** learning in general.

75. **Monarch:** Chi Ho-am-ti, Emperor of China, the same who built the great wall between China and Tartary, destroyed all the books and learned men of that empire. P.

And one bright blaze turns Learning into air.
   "Thence to the south extend thy gladden'd eyes;
There rival flames with equal glory rise,   80
From shelves to shelves see greedy Vulcan roll,
And lick up all their Physic of the Soul.
   "How little, mark! that portion of the ball,
Where, faint at best, the beams of Science fall:
Soon as they dawn, from Hyperborean skies   85
Embody'd dark, what clouds of Vandals rise!
Lo! where Mæotis sleeps, and hardly flows
The freezing Tanais thro' a waste of snows,
The North by myriads pours her mighty sons,
Great nurse of Goths, of Alans, and of Huns!   90
See Alaric's stern port! the martial frame
Of Genseric! and Attila's dread name!
See the bold Ostrogoths on Latium fall;
See the fierce Visigoths on Spain and Gaul!
See, where the morning gilds the palmy shore   95
(The soil that arts and infant letters bore)
His conqu'ring tribes th' Arabian prophet draws,
And saving Ignorance enthrones by Laws.
See Christians, Jews, one heavy sabbath keep,
And all the western world believe and sleep.   100
   "Lo! Rome herself, proud mistress now no more
Of arts, but thund'ring against heathen lore;
Her grey-hair'd Synods damning books unread,
And Bacon trembling for his brazen head.
Padua, with sighs, beholds her Livy burn,   105

81–2. The Caliph, Omar I, having conquered Ægypt, caused his General to burn the Ptolmæan library, on the gates of which was this inscription, ΨΥΧΗΣ ἰΑΤΡΕΙΟΝ, the Physic of the Soul. P.
85. Hyperborean: i.e., northern. Here and in the next few lines, Pope recalls the ancient belief that the extreme north was a region of darkness and devils.
87. Mæotis: ancient name for the Sea of Azov.
88. Tanais: the river Don, which flows into the Sea of Azov.
90. Alans: a nomadic tribe, from southern Russia, which united with the Huns.
91. Alaric: first Gothic conqueror of Rome, in 410.
92. Genseric: king of the Vandals who sacked Rome in 455.   Attila: king of the Huns (d. 453).
93. Ostrogoths: East Goths.   Latium: Italy.
94. Visigoths: West Goths.
96. The soil: Phoenicia, Syria, &c., where Letters are said to have been invented. In these countries Mahomet began his conquests. P.
101. Rome: i.e., the Papacy.
103. Synods: ecclesiastical councils.
104. Bacon: Roger Bacon (1214–94), the medieval philosopher who was supposed to have made a bronze head that could speak. Since Friar Bacon incurred the displeasure of his Franciscan superiors, and was forced to give up writing for a time, Pope may suggest that Bacon's own head was too "brazen" for the "grey-hair'd Synods" at Rome.
105. The Roman historian Livy (d. 17 A.D.) was born at Patavium, now Padua.

And ev'n th' Antipodes Vigilius mourn.
See, the Cirque falls, th' unpillar'd Temple nods,
Streets pav'd with Heroes, Tyber choak'd with Gods:
'Till Peter's keys some christ'ned Jove adorn,
And Pan to Moses lends his pagan horn;   110
See graceless Venus to a Virgin turn'd,
Or Phidias broken, and Apelles burn'd.
    "Behold yon' Isle, by Palmers, Pilgrims trod,
Men bearded, bald, cowl'd, uncowl'd, shod, unshod,
Peel'd, patch'd, and pyebald, linsey-wolsey brothers,   115
Grave Mummers! sleeveless some, and shirtless others.
That once was Britain — Happy! had she seen
No fiercer sons, had Easter never been.
In peace, great Goddess, ever be ador'd;
How keen the war, if Dulness draw the sword!   120
Thus visit not thy own! on this blest age
Oh spread thy Influence, but restrain thy Rage.
    "And see, my son! the hour is on its way,
That lifts our Goddess to imperial sway;
This fav'rite Isle, long sever'd from her reign,   125
Dove-like, she gathers to her wings again.
Now look thro' Fate! behold the scene she draws!
What aids, what armies to assert her cause!
See all her progeny, illustrious sight!

106. **Vigilius:** Saint Virgilius (d. 785), a Bishop of Salzburg, was severely criticized for expressing a belief in the existence of the Antipodes (i.e., dwellers on the opposite side of the earth).
107. **Cirque:** the Coliseum at Rome.
108. After the government of Rome devolved to the Popes, their zeal was for some time exerted in demolishing the heathen Temples and Statues, so that the Goths scarce destroyed more monuments of Antiquity out of rage, than these out of devotion. At length they spared some of the Temples, by converting them to Churches; and some of the Statues, by modifying them into images of Saints. In much later times, it was thought necessary to change the statues of Apollo and Pallas, on the tomb of Sannazarius [Italian poet, 1458–1530], into David and Judith; the Lyre easily became a Harp, and the Gorgon's head turned to that of Holofernes. P.
109. **Peter's keys:** the symbol of papal power and jurisdiction (see Matthew 16:19). Cf. *Dunciad,* II 82n.
110. **Moses . . . horn:** an error in translation led to the medieval belief that Moses had descended from Mt. Sinai with horns (rather than rays) on his head.
112. **Phidias:** greatest of ancient Greek sculptors.   **Apelles:** greatest painter of antiquity.
113. **Palmers:** those pilgrims who had visited the Holy Land and wore crossed palm leaves in token of the event.
115. **linsey-wolsey:** material woven of a mixture of wool and flax; hence, "neither one thing nor the other."
116. **Mummers:** actors, buffoons.
117–18: Wars in England anciently about the right time of celebrating Easter. P.
126. This is fulfilled in the fourth book. P.
127. **scene she draws:** as when a stage-curtain is drawn.

Behold, and count them, as they rise to light.   130
As Berecynthia, while her offspring vye
In homage to the Mother of the sky,
Surveys around her, in the blest abode,
An hundred sons, and ev'ry son a God:
Not with less glory mighty Dulness crown'd,   135
Shall take thro' Grub-street her triumphant round;
And her Parnassus glancing o'er at once,
Behold an hundred sons, and each a Dunce.
   "Mark first that Youth who takes the foremost place,
And thrusts his person full into your face.   140
With all thy Father's virtues blest, be born!
And a new Cibber shall the stage adorn.
   "A second see, by meeker manners known,
And modest as the maid that sips alone;
From the strong fate of drams if thou get free,   145
Another Durfey, Ward! shall sing in thee.
Thee shall each ale-house, thee each gill-house mourn,
And answ'ring gin-shops sowrer sighs return.
   "Jacob, the scourge of Grammar, mark with awe,
Nor less revere him, blunderbuss of Law.   150
Lo P—p—le's brow, tremendous to the town,
Horneck's fierce eye, and Roome's funereal Frown.

131–4. Berecynthia, an appellation of Cybele, the *Magna Mater* (see *Dunciad*,
I 269–70*n*.) of the gods. She is described by Virgil (*Aeneid*, VI 784*ff*.) as em-
bracing a "hundred" of her offspring.
   139. that Youth: Theophilus Cibber (1703–58) followed his father on the
stage.
   143–8. See *Dunciad*, I 233–4*n*., where Edward Ward is described as a tavern-
keeper. Thomas Durfey (1653–1723), poet and dramatist, wrote many extremely popular drinking songs.
   147. gill-house: wine shop.
   149–50. Jacob: "This *Gentleman* is son of a *considerable Maltster* of Romsey
in Southamptonshire, and bred to the Law under a *very eminent Attorney:* Who,
between his *more laborious* studies, has *diverted* himself with Poetry. He is a
great admirer of Poets and their works, which has occasion'd him to try his
genius that way. — He has writ in prose the *Lives* of the *Poets*, *Essays*, and a
great many Law-Books, *The Accomplish'd Conveyancer*, *Modern Justice*, &c."
Giles Jacob [1686–1744] of himself, *Lives* of Poets, vol. I. He very grossly, and
unprovok'd, abused in that book the Author's Friend, Mr. *Gay*. P.
   151. P—p—le: William Popple (1701–64), who became Governor of Ber-
muda. See next note.
   152. These two were virulent Party-writers, worthily coupled together, and
one would think prophetically, since, after the publishing of this piece, the
former dying, the latter succeeded him in *Honour* and Employment. The first
was Philip Horneck [d. 1728], Author of a Billingsgate paper call'd The High
German Doctor. Edward Roome [d. 1729] was son of an Undertaker for
Funerals in Fleetstreet, and writ some of the papers call'd Pasquin, where by
malicious Innuendos he endeavoured to represent our Author guilty of malevolent
practices with a great man [Bishop Francis Atterbury; see *Ep. to Dr. Arbuthnot*,
l. 140*n*.] then under prosecution of Parliament. P[opp]le was the author of some
vile Plays and Pamphlets. He published abuses on our author in a Paper called
the Prompter. P.

Lo sneering Goode, half malice, and half whim,
A Fiend in glee, ridiculously grim.
Each Cygnet sweet of Bath and Tunbridge race,   155
Whose tuneful whistling makes the waters pass:
Each Songster, Riddler, ev'ry nameless name,
All crowd, who foremost shall be damn'd to Fame.
Some strain in rhyme; the Muses, on their racks,
Scream like the winding of ten thousand jacks: 160
Some free from rhyme or reason, rule or check,
Break Priscian's head, and Pegasus's neck;
Down, down they larum, with impetuous whirl,
The Pindars, and the Miltons of a Curl.

    "Silence, ye Wolves! while Ralph to Cynthia howls,   165
And makes Night hideous — Answer him, ye Owls!

    "Sense, speech, and measure, living tongues and dead,
Let all give way — and Morris may be read.

    "Flow Welsted, flow! like thine inspirer, Beer,
Tho' stale, not ripe; tho' thin, yet never clear;   170
So sweetly mawkish, and so smoothly dull;
Heady, not strong; o'erflowing, tho' not full.

    "Ah Dennis! Gildon ah! what ill-starr'd rage
Divides a friendship long confirm'd by age?
Blockheads with reason wicked wits abhor,   175
But fool with fool is barb'rous civil war.
Embrace, embrace my sons! be foes no more!

153. Goode: An ill-natur'd Critic [Barnham Goode, 1674–1739], who writ
a Satyr on our Author, call'd *The mock Æsop,* and many anonymous Libels in
News-papers for hire.   P.
155–6. There were several successions of these sort of minor poets, at Tunbridge, Bath [fashionable spas], &c., singing the praise of the Annuals [i.e.,
young women] flourishing for that season: whose names indeed would be nameless, and therefore the Poet slurs them over with others in general.   P.   A
cygnet is a young swan.
160. jacks: probably refers to the contrivance used for turning the spit in
roasting meat; it was wound up like a clock, and very noisy.
162. Break Priscian's head: i.e., violate the rules of grammar. Priscian
(*c.* 500) was a celebrated Roman grammarian.
163. larum: sound loudly.
165–6. James Ralph [see *Dunciad,* I 216*n.*], a name inserted after the first
editions, not known to our author till he writ a swearing-piece called *Sawney,*
very abusive of Dr. Swift, Mr. Gay, and himself. These lines allude to a
thing of his, intitled, *Night,* a poem. . . .   P.
168. Morris: *Besaleel,* see Book 2 [l. 124*n.,* l. 126].   P.
169. Welsted: see *Ep. to Dr. Arbuthnot,* l. 375*n.,* and *Dunciad,* II 207.
169–72. Parody on Denham, *Cooper's Hill* [ll. 189–92].

> *O could I flow like thee, and make thy stream*
> *My great example, as it is my theme:*
> *Tho' deep, yet clear; tho' gentle, yet not dull;*
> *Strong without rage; without o'erflowing, full.*   P.

173. Dennis: John Dennis (see *Dunciad,* I 63 *n.*).   **Gildon:** Charles Gildon
(see *Ep. to Dr. Arbuthnot,* l. 151*n.,* and *Dunciad,* I 296). Nothing is known
of a quarrel between these two critics.
175. wits: men of intelligence and imagination.

Nor glad vile Poets with true Critic's gore.
   "Behold yon Pair, in strict embraces join'd;
How like in manners, and how like in mind!   180
Equal in wit, and equally polite,
Shall this a Pasquin, that a Grumbler write;
Like are their merits, like rewards they share,
That shines a consul, this Commissioner."
   "But who is he, in closet close y-pent,   185
Of sober face, with learned dust besprent?"
"Right well mine eyes arede the myster wight,
On parchment scraps y-fed, and Wormius hight.
To future ages may thy dulness last,
As thou preserv'st the dulness of the past!   190
   "There, dim in clouds, the poring Scholiasts mark,
Wits, who like owls, see only in the dark,
A Lumberhouse of books in ev'ry head,
For ever reading, never to be read!
   "But, where each Science lifts its modern type,   195
Hist'ry her Pot, Divinity his Pipe,
While proud Philosophy repines to show,
Dishonest sight! his breeches rent below;
Imbrown'd with native bronze, lo! Henley stands,
Tuning his voice, and balancing his hands.   200
How fluent nonsense trickles from his tongue!
How sweet the periods, neither said, nor sung!

179–84. One of these [Sir Thomas Burnet, 1694–1753, at one time British
Consul at Lisbon] was Author of a weekly paper call'd *The Grumbler,* as the
other [George Duckett, 1684–1732, who became an excise commissioner] was
concerned in another call'd *Pasquin,* in which Mr. *Pope* was abused with the
Duke of *Buckingham* and Bishop of *Rochester.* They also joined in a piece
against his first undertaking to translate the *Iliad,* intitled *Homerides,* by Sir
Iliad Doggrel, printed 1715. . . .   P.

184. Consul . . . Commissioner: Such places were given at this time to such
sort of Writers.   P.

187. myster wight: Uncouth mortal.   P.   Pope mistakes the meaning of
the archaic phrase; it suggests rather a craftsman, a man having a certain occu-
pation.

188. Wormius: Let not this name, purely fictitious, be conceited to mean the
learned *Olaus Wormius* [a Danish physician and antiquary, 1588–1654]; much
less (as it was unwarrantably foisted into the surreptitious editions) our own
Antiquary Mr. *Thomas Hearne* [1678–1735], who had no way aggrieved our
Poet, but on the contrary published many curious tracts which he hath to his
great contentment perused.

Most rightly are *ancient Words* here employed, in speaking of such who so
greatly delight in the same. . . .   P.   **hight:** named.

191. Scholiasts: textual commentators.

193. Lumberhouse: storehouse for junk or unused furniture.

195. type: emblem, or allegorical figure.

196. Pot: ale tankard.

199. Henley: J. Henley the Orator [see *Dunciad,* II 2n., 370]; he preach^d
on the Sundays upon Theological matters, and on the Wednesdays upon all other
sciences. Each auditor paid one shilling. He declaimed some years against the
greatest persons, and occasionally did our Author that honour. . . .   P.

Still break the benches, Henley! with thy strain,
While Sherlock, Hare, and Gibson preach in vain.
Oh great Restorer of the good old Stage,   205
Preacher at once, and Zany of thy age!
Oh worthy thou of Ægypt's wise abodes,
A decent priest, where monkeys were the gods!
But fate with butchers plac'd thy priestly stall,
Meek modern faith to murder, hack, and mawl;   210
And bade thee live, to crown Britannia's praise,
In Toland's, Tindal's, and in Woolston's days.
    "Yet oh, my sons! a father's words attend:
(So may the fates preserve the ears you lend)
'Tis yours, a Bacon or a Locke to blame,   215
A Newton's genius, or a Milton's flame:
But oh! with One, immortal one dispense,
The source of Newton's Light, of Bacon's Sense!
Content, each Emanation of his fires
That beams on earth, each Virtue he inspires,   220
Each Art he prompts, each Charm he can create,
Whate'er he gives, are giv'n for you to hate.
Persist, by all divine in Man unaw'd,
But, 'Learn, ye DUNCES! not to scorn your GOD.' "
    Thus he, for then a ray of Reason stole   225
Half thro' the solid darkness of his soul;
But soon the cloud return'd — and thus the Sire:
"See now, what Dulness and her sons admire!
See what the charms, that smite the simple heart
Not touch'd by Nature, and not reach'd by Art."   230
    His never-blushing head he turn'd aside,
(Not half so pleas'd when Goodman prophesy'd)
And look'd, and saw a sable Sorc'rer rise,

203. break the benches: bring down the house.
204. Sherlock, Hare, and Gibson: Bishops of Salisbury, Chichester, and London. P.
206. Zany: buffoon.
209. butchers: see *Ep. to Dr. Arbuthnot*, l. 98n.
212. Of *Toland* and *Tindal*, see book 2 [l. 399n.]. Tho. Woolston [1670–1733] was an impious madman, who wrote in a most insolent style against the Miracles of the Gospel, in the years 1726, 1727, &c. P.
215. Bacon: Francis Bacon.
231. he: Cibber.
232. Mr. Cibber tells us, in his Life, p. 149, that Goodman [Cardell Goodman, 1649–99, actor, rake, and gamester] being at the rehearsal of a play, in which he had a part, clapped him on the shoulder, and cried, "If he does not make a good actor, I'll be d——d. — And (says Mr. Cibber) I make it a question, whether Alexander himself, or Charles the twelfth of Sweden, when at the head of their first victorious armies, could feel a greater transport in their bosoms than I did in mine." P.
233. sable Sorc'rer: Dr. Faustus, the subject of a sett of Farces, which lasted in vogue two or three seasons, in which both Playhouses strove to outdo each other for some years. All the extravagancies in the sixteen lines following were

Swift to whose hand a winged volume flies:
All sudden, Gorgons hiss, and Dragons glare,   235
And ten-horn'd fiends and Giants rush to war.
Hell rises, Heav'n descends, and dance on Earth:
Gods, imps, and monsters, music, rage, and mirth,
A fire, a jigg, a battle, and a ball,
'Till one wide conflagration swallows all.   240
    Thence a new world to Nature's laws unknown,
Breaks out refulgent, with a heav'n its own:
Another Cynthia her new journey runs,
And other planets circle other suns.
The forests dance, the rivers upward rise,   245
Whales sport in woods, and dolphins in the skies;
And last, to give the whole creation grace,
Lo! one vast Egg produces human race.
    Joy fills his soul, joy innocent of thought;
"What pow'r, he cries, what pow'r these wonders wrought?"   250
"Son; what thou seek'st is in thee! Look, and find
Each Monster meets his likeness in thy mind.
Yet would'st thou more? In yonder cloud behold,
Whose sarsenet skirts are edg'd with flamy gold,
A matchless Youth! his nod these worlds controuls,   255
Wings the red lightning, and the thunder rolls.
Angel of Dulness, sent to scatter round
Her magic charms o'er all unclassic ground:
Yon stars, yon suns, he rears at pleasure higher,
Illumes their light, and sets their flames on fire.   260
Immortal Rich! how calm he sits at ease
'Mid snows of paper, and fierce hail of pease;
And proud his Mistress' orders to perform,
Rides in the whirlwind, and directs the storm.
    "But lo! to dark encounter in mid air   265
New wizards rise; I see my Cibber there!
Booth in his cloudy tabernacle shrin'd,
On grinning dragons thou shalt mount the wind.

---

introduced on the Stage, and frequented by persons of the first quality in England, to the twentieth and thirtieth time. P.
  235. Gorgons: mythical sisters with snaky hair.
  237. This monstrous absurdity was actually represented in Tibbald's Rape of Proserpine. P.
  243. Cynthia: moon goddess.
  248. In another of these Farces Harlequin is hatched upon the stage, out of a large Egg. P.   **254. sarsenet:** a soft silk.
  255–63. Mr. John Rich [1682–1761], Master of the Theatre Royal in Covent-garden, was the first that excelled this way. P.
  266–7. *Booth* [Barton Booth; see *First Ep. of the Second Bk.*, l. 123n.] and *Cibber* were joint managers of the Theatre in Drury-lane. P.
  268. On grinning dragons: In his Letter to Mr. P., Mr. C[ibber] solemnly declares this not to be *literally* true. We hope therefore the reader will understand it *allegorically* only. P.

Dire is the conflict, dismal is the din,
Here shouts all Drury, there all Lincoln's-inn;   270
Contending Theatres our empire raise,
Alike their labours, and alike their praise.
   "And are these wonders, Son, to thee unknown?
Unknown to thee? These wonders are thy own.
These Fate reserv'd to grace thy reign divine,   275
Foreseen by me, but ah! with-held from mine.
In Lud's old walls tho' long I rul'd, renown'd
Far as loud Bow's stupendous bells resound;
Tho' my own Aldermen confer'd the bays,
To me committing their eternal praise,   280
Their full-fed Heroes, their pacific May'rs,
Their annual trophies, and their monthly wars:
Tho' long my Party built on me their hopes,
For writing Pamphlets, and for roasting Popes;
Yet lo! in me what authors have to brag on!   285
Reduc'd at last to hiss in my own dragon.
Avert it Heav'n! that thou, my Cibber, e'er
Should'st wag a serpent-tail in Smithfield fair!
Like the vile straw that's blown about the streets,
The needy Poet sticks to all he meets,   290
Coach'd, carted, trod upon, now loose, now fast,
And carry'd off in some Dog's tail at last.
Happier thy fortunes! like a rolling stone,
Thy giddy dulness still shall lumber on,
Safe in its heaviness, shall never stray,   295
But lick up ev'ry blockhead in the way.
Thee shall the Patriot, thee the Courtier taste,

276. **Foreseen by me:** as City Poet Settle had created pageantry for the Lord Mayor's Day celebrations, so his work could be regarded as anticipating the theatrical extravagancies just described.

277. **Lud's old walls:** see *Dunciad*, II 35*n*.

278. **Bow's:** the bells of St. Mary-le-Bow Church. The area within the sound of these celebrated bells was thought to coincide with the limits of the "City" of London.

282. *Annual trophies*, on the Lord-mayor's day; and *monthly wars* [i.e., military exercises by the City Trainbands] in the Artillery-ground. P.

283–6. Settle, like most Party-writers, was very uncertain in his political principles. He was employed to hold the pen in the *Character* of a *popish successor*, but afterwards printed his *Narrative* on the other side. He had managed the ceremony of a famous Pope-burning on Nov. 17, 1680, then became a trooper in King James's army, at Hounslow-heath. After the Revolution he kept a booth at Bartholomew-fair, where, in the droll called *St. George for England*, he acted in his old age in a Dragon of green leather of his own invention; he was at last taken into the Charter-house, and there died, aged sixty years. P.

288. **Smithfield:** see *Dunciad*, I 2*n*.

291. **coach'd:** furnished with a coach.   **carted:** carried in a cart through the streets, as a punishment (usually of prostitutes).

297. **Patriot . . . Courtier:** It stood in the first edition with blanks, * * * and * * *. Concanen was sure "they must needs mean no body but *King GEORGE* and *Queen CAROLINE;* and said he would insist it was so, 'till the poet cleared

And ev'ry year be duller than the last.
'Till rais'd from booths, to Theatre, to Court,
Her seat imperial Dulness shall transport.　　　　300
Already Opera prepares the way,
The sure fore-runner of her gentle sway:
Let her thy heart, next Drabs and Dice, engage,
The third mad passion of thy doting age.
Teach thou the warb'ling Polypheme to roar,　　　305
And scream thyself as none e'er scream'd before!
To aid our cause, if Heav'n thou can'st not bend,
Hell thou shalt move; for Faustus is our friend:
Pluto with Cato thou for this shalt join,
And link the Mourning Bride to Proserpine.　　　310
Grubstreet! thy fall should men and Gods conspire,
Thy stage shall stand, ensure it but from Fire.
Another Æschylus appears! prepare
For new abortions, all ye pregnant fair!
In flames, like Semele's, be brought to bed,　　　315
While op'ning Hell spouts wild-fire at your head.
　　"Now Bavius take the poppy from thy brow,
And place it here! here all ye Heroes bow!
This, this is he, foretold by ancient rhymes:

---

himself by filling up the blanks otherwise, agreeably to the context, and consistent with his *allegiance*." Pref. to a Collection of verses, essays, letters, &c.
against Mr. P., printed for A. Moor, p. 6. P.　　The note enables Pope to
make it clear that he *was* glancing at royalty. For the precise implications of
the word "Patriot," see *Epil. to the Satires*, I 24n.

299. booths: stalls at a fair.

301. Opera: Italian opera, partly because of its emphasis on spectacle, partly
because it seemed to offer sound without sense, was considered by many in
Pope's time to be a degenerate art form. See *Dunciad*, IV 45n.

303. Drabs: harlots.

305. Polypheme: He [Cibber] translated the Italian Opera of Polifemo; but
unfortunately lost the whole jest of the story [i.e., the story of Ulysses and the
Cyclops]. . . . P.

308–10. Faustus . . . Pluto . . . Proserpine: Names of miserable Farces
which it was the custom to act at the end of the best Tragedies [i.e., such as
Addison's *Cato*, l. 309, and Congreve's *The Mourning Bride*, l. 310], to spoil
the digestion of the audience. P.

312. Fire: In the farce of Proserpine a corn-field was set on fire: whereupon
the other playhouse had a barn burnt down for the recreation of the spectators.
They also rival'd each other in showing the burnings of hell-fire, in Dr.
Faustus. P.

313–4. It is reported of Æschylus, that when his tragedy of the Furies was
acted, the audience were so terrified that the children fell into fits, and the big-
bellied women miscarried. P.

315. Semele: Beloved by Jupiter, Semele entreated him to come to her bed
in his full majesty. Though reluctant to do so, the god came to her attended
by his thunderbolts and lightning, and she was instantly consumed with fire. Her
unborn child, Bacchus, was saved from the flames.

317. Bavius: see l. 24n., above. Because of the poppy mentioned in this line,
Pope may be alluding to Shadwell under the title of Bavius (see l. 22n., above).

Th' Augustus born to bring Saturnian times.   320
Signs following signs lead on the mighty year!
See! the dull stars roll round and re-appear.
See, see, our own true Phœbus wears the bays!
Our Midas sits Lord Chancellor of Plays!
On Poets' Tombs see Benson's titles writ!   325
Lo! Ambrose Philips is prefer'd for Wit!
See under Ripley rise a new White-hall,
While Jones' and Boyle's united labours fall:
While Wren with sorrow to the grave descends,
Gay dies unpension'd with a hundred friends,   330
Hibernian Politics, O Swift! thy fate;
And Pope's, ten years to comment and translate.
    "Proceed, great days! 'till Learning fly the shore,

320. *Saturnian* here relates to the age of *Lead*, mentioned Book I, ver. 28. P.

324. **Midas:** King Midas imprudently judged Pan to be superior to Apollo in singing and playing the flute; in punishment he was given the ears of an ass to show his stupidity.   **sits Lord Chancellor:** no play could be acted without the approval of the Lord Chancellor [see *Epil. to the Satires*, I 42n.]. As laureate, and as one of the managers of Drury Lane Theater, Cibber could be regarded as almost having the powers of a Lord Chancellor.

325. **Benson's titles:** William Benson (1682–1754) succeeded Sir Christopher Wren as Surveyor-General, but was removed from office for incompetency. In 1737 he erected a monument to Milton in Westminster Abbey. See *Dunciad*, IV 110n.

326. **Ambrose Philips:** see *Ep. to Dr. Arbuthnot*, l. 100n.

327. **Ripley:** Thomas Ripley (see *Ep. to Burlington*, l. 18n.).

328. **Jones' and Boyle's:** At the time when this poem was written, the banquetting-house of White-hall, the church and piazza of Covent-garden, and the palace and chapel of Somerset-house, the works of the famous Inigo Jones [1575–1652], had been for many years so neglected, as to be in danger of ruin. The portico of Covent-garden church had been just then restor'd and beautified at the expence of the Earl of Burlington [Richard Boyle: see first note to *Ep. to Burlington*]; who, at the same time, by his publication of the designs of that great Master and Palladio, as well as by many noble buildings of his own, revived the true taste of Architecture in this Kingdom. P.

329. **Wren:** Christopher Wren (1632–1723), the celebrated architect. During his last years he was subjected to repeated annoyances.

330. Pope's friend John Gay (see *Ep. to Dr. Arbuthnot*, l. 256n.) was offered a small sinecure by Queen Caroline, but he declined it.

331. **Hibernian:** Irish.

332. The author here plainly laments that he was so long employed in translating and commentary. He began the Iliad in 1713, and finished it in 1719. The Edition of Shakespear (which he undertook merely because no body else would) took up nearly two years more in the drudgery of comparing impressions, rectifying the Scenary, &c., and the Translation of half the Odyssey employed him from that time to 1725. P.

333. It may perhaps seem incredible, that so great a Revolution in Learning as is here prophesied, should be brought about by such *weak Instruments* as have been (hitherto) described in our poem: But do not thou, gentle reader, rest too secure in thy contempt of these Instruments. Remember what the Dutch stories somewhere relate, that a great part of their Provinces was once overflowed, by a small opening made in one of their dykes by a single *Water-Rat*.

    However, that such is not seriously the judgment of our Poet, but that he conceiveth better hopes from the Diligence of our Schools, from the Regularity of our Universities, the Discernment of our Great men, the Accomplishments of

'Till Birch shall blush with noble blood no more,
'Till Thames see Eaton's sons for ever play,   335
'Till Westminster's whole year be holiday,
'Till Isis' Elders reel, their pupils' sport,
And Alma mater lie dissolv'd in Port!"
    "Enough, enough!" the raptur'd Monarch cries;
And thro' the Iv'ry Gate the Vision flies.   340

---

our Nobility, the Encouragement of our Patrons, and the Genius of our Writers
in all kinds (notwithstanding some few exceptions in each) may plainly be seen
from his conclusion; where causing all this vision to pass through the Ivory Gate,
he expressly, in the language of Poesy, declares all such imaginations to be
wild, ungrounded, and fictitious.   Scribl.   But see that part of the note to
ll. 5–6, above, attributed to "Bent." [i.e., Richard Bentley].
    336. **Westminster:** Westminster School.
    337. **Isis' Elders:** Oxford dons.
    338. **Port:** port wine (cf. *Dunciad*, IV 201–2n.).

BOOK THE FOURTH

ARGUMENT

The Poet being, in this Book, to declare the Completion *of the* Prophecies *mention'd at the end of the former, makes a new* Invocation; *as the greater Poets are wont, when some high and worthy matter is to be sung. He shews the Goddess coming in her Majesty, to destroy* Order *and* Science, *and to substitute the* Kingdom *of the* Dull *upon earth. How she leads captive the* Sciences, *and silenceth the* Muses; *and what they be who succeed in their stead. All her* Children, *by a wonderful attraction, are drawn about her; and bear along with them divers others, who promote her* Empire *by* connivance, *weak resistance, or discouragement of Arts; such as* Half-wits, *tasteless* Admirers, *vain* Pretenders, *the* Flatterers *of* Dunces, *or the* Patrons *of them. All these crowd round her; one of them offering to approach her, is driven back by a* Rival, *but she commends and encourages both. The first who speak in form are the* Genius's *of the* Schools, *who assure her of their care to advance her* Cause, *by confining* Youth *to* Words, *and keeping them out of the way of real* Knowledge. *Their Address, and her gracious Answer; with her Charge to them and the* Universities. *The* Universities *appear by their proper Deputies, and assure her that the same method is observ'd in the progress of* Education: *The speech of* Aristarchus *on this subject. They are driven off by a band of young* Gentlemen *return'd from* Travel *with their* Tutors; *one of whom delivers to the Goddess, in a polite oration, an account of the whole Conduct and Fruits of their* Travels: *presenting to her at the same time a young* Nobleman *perfectly accomplished. She receives him graciously, and indues him with the happy quality of* Want of Shame. *She sees loitering about her a number of* Indolent Persons *abandoning all business and duty, and dying with laziness: To these approaches the Antiquary* Annius, *intreating her to make them* Virtuosos, *and assign them over to him: But* Mummius, *another Antiquary, complaining of his fraudulent proceeding, she finds a method to reconcile their difference. Then enter a Troop of people fantastically adorn'd, offering her strange and exotic presents: Amongst them, one stands forth and demands justice on another, who had deprived him of one of the greatest* Curiosities *in nature: but he justifies himself so well, that the Goddess gives them both her approbation. She recommends to them to find proper employment for the* Indolents *beforementioned, in the study of* Butterflies, Shells, Birds-nests, Moss, *&c. but with particular caution, not to proceed beyond* Trifles, *to any useful or extensive views of* Nature, *or of the* Author *of* Nature. *Against the last of these apprehensions, she is secured by a hearty Address from the* Minute Philosophers *and* Freethinkers, *one of whom speaks in the name of the rest. The* Youth *thus instructed and principled, are delivered to her in a body, by the hands of* Silenus; *and then admitted to taste the* Cup *of the* Magus *her High Priest, which causes a total oblivion of all*

*Obligations, divine, civil, moral, or rational. To these her Adepts she
sends Priests, Attendants, and Comforters, of various kinds; confers on
them Orders and Degrees; and then dismissing them with a speech, con-
firming to each his Privileges and telling what she expects from each,
concludes with a Yawn of extraordinary virtue: The Progress and Effects
whereof on all Orders of men, and the Consummation of all, in the Restoration of Night and Chaos, conclude the Poem.*

Y ET, yet a moment, one dim Ray of Light
   Indulge, dread Chaos, and eternal Night!
   Of darkness visible so much be lent,
As half to shew, half veil the deep Intent.
Ye Pow'rs! whose Mysteries restor'd I sing,   5
To whom Time bears me on his rapid wing,
Suspend a while your Force inertly strong,
Then take at once the Poet and the Song.
   Now flam'd the Dog-star's unpropitious ray,
Smote ev'ry Brain, and wither'd ev'ry Bay;   10
Sick was the Sun, the Owl forsook his bow'r,
The moon-struck Prophet felt the madding hour:
Then rose the Seed of Chaos, and of Night,
To blot out Order, and extinguish Light,
Of dull and venal a new World to mold,   15
And bring Saturnian days of Lead and Gold.
   She mounts the Throne: her head a Cloud conceal'd,
In broad Effulgence all below reveal'd,
('Tis thus aspiring Dulness ever shines)
Soft on her lap her Laureat son reclines.   20

BOOK THE FOURTH. **2. Chaos . . . Night:** Invoked, as the Restoration of their
Empire is the Action of the Poem. P.
   3. darkness visible: from Milton, *Paradise Lost,* I 63.
   4. half: This is a great propriety, for a dull Poet can never express himself
otherwise than by *halves,* or imperfectly. Scribl.
   I understand it very differently; the Author in this work had indeed a *deep
Intent;* there were in it *Mysteries . . .* which he durst not fully reveal, and
doubtless in divers verses (according to *Milton*) — *more is meant than meets
the ear.* Bentl.
   7. Force inertly strong: Alluding to the *Vis inertiæ of Matter,* which, tho' it
really be no Power, is yet the Foundation of all the Qualities and Attributes of
that sluggish Substance. P.
   9. Dog-star: see *Ep. to Dr. Arbuthnot,* l. 3n.
   15. new World: In allusion to the Epicurean opinion, that from the dissolu-
tion of the natural World into Night and Chaos, a new one should arise; this the
Poet alluding to, in the Production of a new moral World, makes it partake of
its original Principles. P.
   16. Lead and Gold: i.e., dull and venal. P.
   18. all below reveal'd: Vet. Adag [i.e., old adage]. 𝕿𝖍𝖊 𝖍𝖎𝖌𝖍𝖊𝖗 𝖞𝖔𝖚 𝖈𝖑𝖎𝖒𝖇,
𝖙𝖍𝖊 𝖒𝖔𝖗𝖊 𝖞𝖔𝖚 𝖘𝖍𝖊𝖜 𝖞𝖔𝖚𝖗 𝕬 —. Verified in no instance more than in Dulness
aspiring. Emblematized also by an Ape climbing and exposing his posteriors.
Scribl.

Beneath her foot-stool, *Science* groans in Chains,
And *Wit* dreads Exile, Penalties and Pains.
There foam'd rebellious *Logic*, gagg'd and bound,
There, stript, fair *Rhet'ric* languish'd on the ground;
His blunted Arms by *Sophistry* are born,   25
And shameless *Billingsgate* her Robes adorn.
Morality, by her false Guardians drawn,
Chicane in Furs, and *Casuistry* in Lawn,
Gasps, as they straiten at each end the cord,
And dies, when Dulness gives her Page the word.   30
Mad *Mathesis* alone was unconfin'd,
Too mad for mere material chains to bind,
Now to pure Space lifts her extatic stare,
Now running round the Circle, finds it square.
But held in ten-fold bonds the *Muses* lie,   35
Watch'd both by Envy's and by Flatt'ry's eye:
There to her heart sad Tragedy addrest
The dagger wont to pierce the Tyrant's breast;
But sober History restrain'd her rage,
And promis'd Vengeance on a barb'rous age.   40
There sunk Thalia, nerveless, cold, and dead,
Had not her Sister Satyr held her head:
Nor cou'd'st thou, CHESTERFIELD! a tear refuse,
Thou wept'st, and with thee wept each gentle Muse.
    When lo! a Harlot form soft sliding by,   45

21. Science: learning in general.
22. Wit: imagination, intelligence.
26. Billingsgate: see *Dunciad*, I 307n.
28. Chicane in Furs: legal trickery by judges, who wear ermine robes. **Casuistry in Lawn:** sophistry on the part of bishops, whose sleeves are made of fine linen.
29–30. Page: There was a Judge [Sir Francis Page; see *First Sat. of the Second Bk.*, l. 82n.] of this name, always ready to hang any man, of which he was suffered to give a hundred miserable examples during a long life, even to his dotage. . . . P.
31. Mad Mathesis: Alluding to the strange Conclusions some Mathematicians have deduced from their principles concerning the *real Quantity of Matter*, the *Reality of Space, &c.* P.
36. One of the misfortunes falling on Authors, from the *Act* for subjecting *Plays* to the power of a *Licenser* [see *Epil. to the Satires*, I 42n.], being the false representations to which they were expos'd, from such as either gratify'd their Envy to Merit, or made their Court to Greatness, by perverting general Reflections against Vice into Libels on particular Persons. P.
38. wont: accustomed.
41. Thalia: the muse of Comedy.
43. Chesterfield: This Noble Person [Philip Stanhope, fourth Earl of Chesterfield; see *Epil. to the Satires*, II 84n.] in the year 1737, when the [Licensing] Act aforesaid was brought into the House of Lords, opposed it in an excellent speech. . . . P.
45. Harlot form: The Attitude given to this Phantom represents the nature and genius of the *Italian* Opera; its affected airs, its effeminate sounds, and the practice of patching up these Operas with favourite Songs, incoherently put together. These things were supported by the subscriptions of the Nobility. This

With mincing step, small voice, and languid eye;
Foreign her air, her robe's discordant pride
In patch-work flutt'ring, and her head aside:
By singing Peers up-held on either hand,
She tripp'd and laugh'd, too pretty much to stand;   50
Cast on the prostrate Nine a scornful look,
Then thus in quaint Recitativo spoke.
    "O *Cara! Cara!* silence all that train:
Joy to great Chaos! let Division reign:
Chromatic tortures soon shall drive them hence,   55
Break all their nerves, and fritter all their sense:
One Trill shall harmonize joy, grief, and rage,
Wake the dull Church, and lull the ranting Stage;
To the same notes thy sons shall hum, or snore,
And all thy yawning daughters cry, *encore*.   60
Another Phœbus, thy own Phœbus, reigns,
Joys in my jiggs, and dances in my chains.
But soon, ah soon Rebellion will commence,
If Music meanly borrows aid from Sense:
Strong in new Arms, lo! Giant Handel stands,   65
Like bold Briareus, with a hundred hands;
To stir, to rouze, to shake the Soul he comes,
And Jove's own Thunders follow Mars's Drums.
Arrest him, Empress; or you sleep no more" —
She heard, and drove him to th' Hibernian shore.   70
    And now had Fame's posterior Trumpet blown,
And all the Nations summon'd to the Throne.
The young, the old, who feel her inward sway,
One instinct seizes, and transports away.

---

circumstance that Opera should prepare for the opening of the grand Sessions,
was prophesied of in Book 3, ver. 301.   P.
    52. Recitativo: a style of musical declamation, intermediary between singing
and ordinary speech.
    53. train: the nine muses of l. 51.
    54. let Division reign: Alluding to the false taste of playing tricks in Music
with numberless divisions [i.e., a series of notes sung in one breath to a single
syllable], to the neglect of that harmony which conforms to the Sense, and
applies to the Passions. Mr. *Handel* [see ll. 65–70] had introduced a great
numbers of Hands, and more variety of Instruments into the Orchestra, and employed even Drums and Cannon to make a fuller Chorus; which prov'd so
much too manly for the fine Gentlemen of his age, that he was obliged to remove his Music into Ireland. After which they were reduced, for want of Composers, to practice the patch-work above mentioned.   P.
    55. Chromatic tortures: That species of the ancient music called the *Chro-
matic* was a variation and embellishment, in odd irregularities, of the *Diatonic*
kind. They say it was invented about the time of *Alexander,* and that the *Spar-
tans* forbad the use of it, as languid and effeminate.   P.
    65. Handel: Pope wrote the book for Handel's first oratorio, *Esther* (see also
l. 54*n.*, above).
    66. Briareus: a mythical giant having 50 heads and 100 hands.
    70. Hibernian shore: Ireland (see l. 54*n.*).

None need a guide, by sure Attraction led,   75
And strong impulsive gravity of Head:
None want a place, for all their Centre found,
Hung to the Goddess, and coher'd around.
Not closer, orb in orb, conglob'd are seen
The buzzing Bees about their dusky Queen.   80
    The gath'ring number, as it moves along,
Involves a vast involuntary throng,
Who gently drawn, and struggling less and less,
Roll in her Vortex, and her pow'r confess.
Not those alone who passive own her laws,   85
But who, weak rebels, more advance her cause.
Whate'er of dunce in College or in Town
Sneers at another, in toupee or gown;
Whate'er of mungril no one class admits,
A wit with dunces, and a dunce with wits.   90
    Nor absent they, no members of her state,
Who pay her homage in her sons, the Great;
Who false to Phœbus, bow the knee to Baal;
Or impious, preach his Word without a call.
Patrons, who sneak from living worth to dead,   95
With-hold the pension, and set up the head;
Or vest dull Flatt'ry in the sacred Gown;
Or give from fool to fool the Laurel crown.
And (last and worst) with all the cant of wit,
Without the soul, the Muse's Hypocrit.   100
    There march'd the bard and blockhead, side by side,
Who rhym'd for hire, and patroniz'd for pride.
Narcissus, prais'd with all a Parson's pow'r,
Look'd a white lilly sunk beneath a show'r.
There mov'd Montalto with superior air;   105
His stretch'd-out arm display'd a Volume fair;
Courtiers and Patriots in two ranks divide,

88. in toupee: fops.   **gown:** scholars.
92. the Great: see *Dunciad*, I 3n.
93. Baal: a false god (the Baals were a multitude of local deities in the area of Palestine and Syria).
96. set up the head: commission the bust of a dead poet.
97. I.e., bestow a rich benefice on an ecclesiastical flatterer.
98. Laurel crown: the laureateship (Cibber had succeeded Laurence Eusden to the post).
100. Muse's Hypocrit: He who thinks the only end of poetry is to amuse, and the only business of the poet to be witty; and consequently who cultivates only such trifling talents in himself, and encourages only such in others. P.
103–4. Narcissus: Lord John Hervey (see first note to *Ep. to Dr. Arbuthnot*), who was very vain, had a white face, and was "showered" with praise by Dr. Conyers Middleton (see *Epil. to the Satires*, I 75n.), a theologian who dedicated his *Life of Cicero* to Hervey.
105. Montalto: An eminent person [Sir Thomas Hanmer, 1677–1746], speaker of the House of Commons], who was about to publish a very pompous Edition of a great Author [Shakespeare], *at his own expence.* P.

Thro' both he pass'd, and bow'd from side to side:
But as in graceful act, with awful eye
Compos'd he stood, bold Benson thrust him by: 110
On two unequal crutches propt he came,
Milton's on this, on that one Johnston's name.
The decent Knight retir'd with sober rage,
Withdrew his hand, and clos'd the pompous page.
[But (happy for him as the times went then)   115
Appear'd Apollo's May'r and Aldermen,
On whom three hundred gold-capt youths await,
To lug the pond'rous volume off in state.]
When Dulness, smiling — "Thus revive the Wits!
But murder first, and mince them all to bits;   120
As erst Medea (cruel, so to save!)
A new Edition of old Æson gave,
Let standard-Authors, thus, like trophies born,
Appear more glorious as more hack'd and torn,
And you, my Critics! in the chequer'd shade,   125
Admire new light thro' holes yourselves have made.

"Leave not a foot of verse, a foot of stone,
A Page, a Grave, that they can call their own;
But spread, my sons, your glory thin or thick,
On passive paper, or on solid brick.   130
So by each Bard an Alderman shall sit,
A heavy Lord shall hang at ev'ry Wit,
And while on Fame's triumphal Car they ride,
Some Slave of mine be pinion'd to their side."
    Now crowds on crowds around the Goddess press,   135

110. **Benson:** This man endeavoured to raise himself to Fame by erecting monuments, striking coins, setting up heads, and procuring translations, of *Milton;* and afterwards by a great passion for *Arthur Johnston,* a Scotch physician's Version of the Psalms, of which he printed many fine Editions. See more of him, Book 3, ver. 325. P.

113. **decent Knight:** Sir Thomas Hanmer.

115–18. The Clarendon Press at Oxford University had agreed to publish Hanmer's edition of Shakespeare. "Apollo's May'r" apparently refers to the Vice-Chancellor of the University; the "Aldermen" are heads of the colleges; the "gold-capt" youths are gentlemen-commoners (i.e., students who paid higher fees and were given special academic dress and privileges).

119. The Goddess applauds the practice of tacking the obscure names of Persons not eminent in any branch of learning, to those of the most distinguished Writers; either by printing *Editions* of their works with impertinent alterations of their Text, as in the former instances [i.e., of Hanmer], or by setting up *Monuments* disgraced with their own vile names and inscriptions, as in the latter [of Benson]. P.

121–2. Medea restored the aged Aeson, father of Jason, to youth and vigor by cutting his throat so that his old blood might run out and by refilling his veins with a magic brew.

133. **Car:** ceremonial chariot.

134. **Slave . . . pinioned:** Roman generals who were awarded a "triumph" entered the city of Rome in an imposing ceremonial parade and accompanied by their fettered captives.

Each eager to present the first Address.
Dunce scorning Dunce beholds the next advance,
But Fop shews Fop superior complaisance.
When lo! a Spectre rose, whose index-hand
Held forth the Virtue of the dreadful wand;   140
His beaver'd brow a birchen garland wears,
Dropping with Infant's blood, and Mother's tears.
O'er ev'ry vein a shudd'ring horror runs;
Eton and Winton shake thro' all their Sons.
All Flesh is humbled, Westminster's bold race   145
Shrink, and confess the Genius of the place:
The pale Boy-Senator yet tingling stands,
And holds his breeches close with both his hands.
    Then thus. "Since Man from beast by Words is known,
Words are Man's province, Words we teach alone.   150
When Reason doubtful, like the Samian letter,
Points him two ways, the narrower is the better.
Plac'd at the door of Learning, youth to guide,
We never suffer it to stand too wide.
To ask, to guess, to know, as they commence,   155
As fancy opens the quick springs of Sense,
We ply the Memory, we load the brain,
Bind rebel Wit, and double chain on chain,
Confine the thought, to exercise the breath;
And keep them in the pale of Words till death.   160
Whate'er the talents, or howe'er design'd,
We hang one jingling padlock on the mind:
A Poet the first day, he dips his quill;
And what the last? a very Poet still.
Pity! the charm works only in our wall,   165

136. **Address:** petition.
139. **a Spectre:** the ghost of Dr. Richard Busby (1605–95), a famous head-master of Westminster School.
140. **dreadful wand:** A Cane usually born by Schoolmasters, which drives the poor Souls about like the wand of Mercury [the caduceus, with which Mercury was supposed to control the souls of the dead].   Scribl.
141. **beaver'd brow:** he wore a beaver hat.
144–5. **Eton, Winton, and Westminster:** English public schools ("Winton" is Winchester College).
146. **Genius of the place:** tutelary spirit or guardian (Latin: *genius loci*).
147. **Boy-Senator:** a youthful Member of Parliament.
151. **Samian letter:** The letter Y, used by Pythagoras [of Samos] as an emblem of the different roads of Virtue and Vice. . . .   P.
159. **exercise the breath:** By obliging them to get the classic poets by heart, which furnishes them with endless matter for Conversation, and Verbal amusement for their whole lives.   P.
160. **pale:** enclosure.
162. **jingling padlock:** For youth being used like Pack-horses and beaten on under a heavy load of Words, lest they should tire, their instructors contrive to make the Words jingle in rhyme or metre.   P.

Lost, lost too soon in yonder House or Hall.
There truant WYNDHAM ev'ry Muse gave o'er,
There TALBOT sunk, and was a Wit no more!
How sweet an Ovid, MURRAY was our boast!
How many Martials were in PULT'NEY lost!   170
Else sure some Bard, to our eternal praise,
In twice ten thousand rhyming nights and days,
Had reach'd the Work, the All that mortal can;
And South beheld that Master-piece of Man."
    "Oh (cry'd the Goddess) for some pedant Reign!   175
Some gentle JAMES, to bless the land again;
To stick the Doctor's Chair into the Throne,
Give law to Words, or war with Words alone,
Senates and Courts with Greek and Latin rule,
And turn the Council to a Grammar School!   180
For sure, if Dulness sees a grateful Day,
'Tis in the shade of Arbitrary Sway.
O! if my sons may learn one earthly thing,
Teach but that one, sufficient for a King;
That which my Priests, and mine alone, maintain,   185
Which as it dies, or lives, we fall, or reign:
May you, may Cam, and Isis preach it long!
'The RIGHT DIVINE of Kings to govern wrong.' "
    Prompt at the call, around the Goddess roll
Broad hats, and hoods, and caps, a sable shoal: 190
Thick and more thick the black blockade extends,

166. House or Hall: Westminster hall [site of the law courts] and the House of Commons.   P.
167. Wyndham: Sir William Wyndham, at one time Chancellor of the Exchequer (see *Epil. to the Satires,* II 88n.).
168. Talbot: Charles Talbot, Duke of Shrewsbury (see *Epil. to the Satires,* II 79n.).
169. Murray: William Murray, who became Lord Chief Justice (see first note to *Sixth Ep. of the First Bk.*).
170. Pult'ney: William Pulteney (see *Epil. to the Satires,* II 84n.). Martial (40–102 A.D.) was a Latin epigrammatist.
174. that Master-piece: viz. an Epigram. The famous Dr. [Robert] South [English divine; d. 1716] declared a perfect Epigram to be as difficult a performance as an Epic Poem. And the Critics say, "an Epic Poem is the greatest work human nature is capable of."   P.
176. James: Wilson [Arthur Wilson, in his *History of Great Britain,* 1653] tells us that this King, *James* the first, took upon himself to teach the Latin tongue to Car, Earl of Somerset; and that Gondomar the Spanish Ambassador wou'd speak false Latin to him, on purpose to give him the pleasure of correcting it, whereby he wrought himself into his good graces.
This great Prince was the first who assumed the title of *Sacred Majesty,* which his loyal Clergy transfer'd from *God* to *Him.* . . .   P.
180. Council: the king's Privy Council.
187. Cam: Cambridge University, situated on the River Cam.   **Isis: Ox**-ford University, situated on the River Isis.
190. shoal: school.

A hundred head of Aristotle's friends.
Nor wert thou, Isis! wanting to the day,
[Tho' Christ-church long kept prudishly away.]
Each staunch Polemic, stubborn as a rock,   195
Each fierce Logician, still expelling Locke,
Came whip and spur, and dash'd thro' thin and thick
On German Crouzaz, and Dutch Burgersdyck.
As many quit the streams that murm'ring fall
To lull the sons of Marg'ret and Clare-hall,   200
Where Bentley late tempestuous wont to sport
In troubled waters, but now sleeps in Port.
Before them march'd that awful Aristarch;
Plow'd was his front with many a deep Remark:
His Hat, which never vail'd to human pride,   205

192. Aristotle: The Philosophy of *Aristotle* had suffered a long disgrace in this learned University [Oxford]: being first expelled by the *Cartesian,* which, in its turn, gave place to the *Newtonian.* But it had all this while some faithful followers in secret, who never bowed the knee to *Baal,* nor acknowledged any strange God in Philosophy. These, on this new appearance of the Goddess, come out like Confessors, and make an open profession of the ancient faith in the *ipse dixit* ["he himself has said"] of their Master.   Scribl.

194. This line is doubtless spurious, and foisted in by the impertinence of the Editor; and accordingly we have put it between Hooks. For I affirm this College came as early as any other, by its *proper Deputies;* nor did any College pay homage to Dulness in its *whole body.*   Bentl.   The brackets about the line, and the note, parody Bentley's editorial procedures in his edition of *Paradise Lost* (see *Ep. to Dr. Arbuthnot,* l. 164n.).

195. Polemic: controversialist.

196. In the year 1703 there was a meeting of the heads of the University of Oxford to censure Mr. Locke's Essay on Human Understanding, and to forbid the reading it. See his Letters in the last Edit.   P.

198. German Crouzaz: Jean Pierre de Crousaz (1663–1748), Swiss philosopher and mathematician who attacked Pope's *Essay on Man* after reading it in a French translation.   **Dutch Burgersdyck:** Francis Burgersdyck (1590–1629), a professor of philosophy at Leyden.

199–200. The River Cam, running by the walls of these Colleges, which are particularly famous for their skill in Disputation.   P.

201. Bentley: Richard Bentley, the great classical scholar (see l. 194n., above).

202. sleeps in Port: viz. "now retired into harbour, after the tempests that had long agitated his society." So *Scriblerus.* But the learned *Scipio Maffei* understands it of a certain Wine called *Port,* from *Oporto,* a city of Portugal, of which this Professor invited him to drink abundantly. Scip. Maff. *de Compotationibus Academicis.*   P.   Scipio Maffei (d. 1755), an Italian scholar who held a doctorate from Oxford, may have visited Bentley at Cambridge (see l. 206n.), but the work attributed to him in the note is entirely fictional.

203. Aristarch: i.e., Bentley. See also l. 210n., below.

204. deep Remark: alludes to Bentley's critical remarks, or glosses, on classical texts, or perhaps to the contemporary habit of beginning the title of a scholarly work with the words "Some Remarks on. . . ." Cf. also *Paradise Lost,* I 599–601; II 301–3.

205–8. The Hat-worship, as the Quakers call it, is an abomination to that sect: yet, where it is necessary to pay that respect to man (as in the Courts of Justice and Houses of Parliament) they have, to avoid offence, and yet not violate their conscience, permitted other people to uncover them.   P.

Walker with rev'rence took, and lay'd aside.
Low bow'd the rest: He, kingly, did but nod;
So upright Quakers please both Man and God.
"Mistress! dismiss that rabble from your throne:
Avaunt — is Aristarchus yet unknown?   210
Thy mighty Scholiast, whose unweary'd pains
Made Horace dull, and humbled Milton's strains.
Turn what they will to Verse, their toil is vain,
Critics like me shall make it Prose again.
Roman and Greek Grammarians! know your Better: 215
Author of something yet more great than Letter;
While tow'ring o'er your Alphabet, like Saul,
Stands our Digamma, and o'er-tops them all.
'Tis true, on Words is still our whole debate,
Disputes of *Me* or *Te*, of *aut* or *at*,   220
To sound or sink in *cano*, O or A,
Or give up Cicero to C or K.
Let Freind affect to speak as Terence spoke,
And Alsop never but like Horace joke:
For me, what Virgil, Pliny may deny,   225
Manilius or Solinus shall supply:
For Attic Phrase in Plato let them seek,
I poach in Suidas for unlicens'd Greek.

206. Walker: Bentley was Master of Trinity College, Cambridge. Dr. Richard Walker (1679–1764) was his Vice-Master.
210. Aristarchus: A famous Commentator [Aristarchus of Samothrace, d. 150 B.C.], and Corrector of Homer, whose name has been frequently used to signify a complete Critic. . . . Scribl.   **211. Scholiast:** textual commentator.
212. humbled Milton's strains: see *Ep. to Dr. Arbuthnot*, l. 164n.
216–18. Alludes to the boasted restoration of the Æolic Digamma, in his long projected Edition of Homer. He calls it *something more than Letter*, from the enormous figure it would make among the other letters, being one Gamma set upon the shoulders of another. P.   **Saul:** see I Samuel 9:2, where Saul is said to be taller than any of the Israelites.
220. It was a serious dispute, about which the learned were much divided, and some treatises written: Had it been about *Meum* or *Tuum* it could not be more contested, than whether at the end of the first Ode of Horace, to read, Me *doctarum hederæ præmia frontium*, or, Te *doctarum hederæ* —. P.
222. Grammatical disputes about the manner of pronouncing Cicero's name [i.e., whether Cicero or Kikero]. . . . P.
223–4. Dr. Robert Freind [1667–1751], master of Westminster-school, and canon of Christ-church. — Dr. Anthony Alsop [classical scholar and poet, d. 1726], a happy imitator of the Horatian style. P.
225–6. Some Critics having had it in their choice to comment either on Virgil or Manilius, Pliny or Solinus, have chosen the worse author, the more freely to display their critical capacity. P.   Bentley had published an edition of Manilius, a Latin mathematician and writer of the first century B.C. who composed a poetical treatise on astronomy. Caius Julius Solinus was a Latin grammarian of the third century A.D. whose *Polyhistor* is little more than a compilation of historical and geographical information.
227. Attic: pure or classical Greek.
228–31. Suidas, Gellius Stobæus: The first [*fl.* 1100 A.D.] a Dictionary-writer, a collector of impertinent facts and barbarous words; the second [Aulus Gellius,

In ancient Sense if any needs will deal,
Be sure I give them Fragments, not a Meal;   230
What Gellius or Strobæus hash'd before,
Or chew'd by blind old Scholiasts o'er and o'er.
The critic Eye, that microscope of Wit,
Sees hairs and pores, examines bit by bit:
How parts relate to parts, or they to whole,   235
The body's harmony, the beaming soul,
Are things which Kuster, Burman, Wasse shall see,
When Man's whole frame is obvious to a *Flea*.
    "Ah, think not, Mistress! more true Dulness lies
In Folly's Cap, than Wisdom's grave disguise.   240
Like buoys, that never sink into the flood,
On Learning's surface we but lie and nod.
Thine is the genuine head of many a house,
And much Divinity without a Noûs.
Nor could a BARROW work on ev'ry block,   245
Nor has one ATTERBURY spoil'd the flock.
See! still thy own, the heavy Canon roll,
And Metaphysic smokes involve the Pole.
For thee we dim the eyes, and stuff the head

---

d. 180 A.D., a Roman writer and grammarian] a minute Critic; the third [Joannes Stobaeus, *c.* 400 A.D., a Greek compiler of extracts from many ancient authors] an author, who gave his Common-place book to the public, where we happen to find much Mince-meat of old books. P.

232. chew'd: These taking the same things eternally from the mouth of one another. P.

237. Kuster: Ludolph Kuster (1670–1716), German classical scholar who edited Suidas.   Burman: Peter Burmann (1688–1741), Dutch classical scholar.   Wasse: Joseph Wasse (1672–1738), English classical scholar, editor of Sallust.

243. house: a college in a university.

244. Noûs: A word much affected by the learned Aristarchus [i.e., Bentley] in common conversation, to signify *Genius* or natural *acumen.* But this passage has a farther view: Noûs was the Platonic term for *Mind,* or the *first Cause,* and that system of Divinity is here hinted at which terminates in blind Nature without a Noûs: such as the Poet afterwards [see ll. 487–92, below] describes. . . . P.

245–6. Isaac Barrow [1630–77], Master of Trinity, Francis Atterbury [see *Ep. to Dr. Arbuthnot,* l. 140*n.*], Dean of Christ-Church, both great Genius's and eloquent Preachers; one more conversant in the sublime Geometry, the other in classical Learning; but who equally made it their care to advance the polite Arts in their several societies. P.   For "block" (l. 245), see l. 270*n.*

247–8. Canon here, if spoken of *Artillery,* is in the plural number; if of the *Canons of the House* [a canon is a clergyman residing within the precincts of a cathedral or collegiate church who orders his life by the "canons" or rules of the church; here perhaps Pope refers to a canon at Oxford's Christ Church College, which contains the cathedral of Oxford within its walls and is also known as "the House"], in the singular, and meant only of *one:* in which case I suspect the *Pole* to be a false reading, and that it should be the *Poll,* or *Head* of that Canon. It may be objected, that this is a mere *Paranomasia* or *Pun.* But what of that? Is any figure of Speech more apposite to our gentle Goddess, or more frequently used by her, and her Children, especially of the University? . . . . Scribl.   "Pole" in l. 248 probably means the "sky," or "heaven."

With all such reading as was never read: 250
For thee explain a thing till all men doubt it,
And write about it, Goddess, and about it:
So spins the silk-worm small its slender store,
And labours till it clouds itself all o'er.
    "What tho' we let some better sort of fool   255
Thrid ev'ry science, run thro' ev'ry school?
Never by tumbler thro' the hoops was shown
Such skill in passing all, and touching none.
He may indeed (if sober all this time)
Plague with Dispute, or persecute with Rhyme.   260
We only furnish what he cannot use,
Or wed to what he must divorce, a Muse:
Full in the midst of Euclid dip at once,
And petrify a Genius to a Dunce:
Or set on Metaphysic ground to prance,   265
Show all his paces, not a step advance.
With the same Cement, ever sure to bind,
We bring to one dead level ev'ry mind.
Then take him to devellop, if you can,
And hew the Block off, and get out the Man.   270
But wherefore waste I words? I see advance
Whore, Pupil, and lac'd Governor from France.
Walker! our hat" — nor more he deign'd to say,
But, stern as Ajax' spectre, strode away.
    In flow'd at once a gay embroider'd race,   275
And titt'ring push'd the Pedants off the place:
Some would have spoken, but the voice was drown'd
By the French horn, or by the op'ning hound.
The first came forwards, with as easy mien,
As if he saw St. James's and the Queen.   280
When thus th' attendant Orator begun.
"Receive, great Empress! thy accomplish'd Son:
Thine from the birth, and sacred from the rod,
A dauntless infant! never scar'd with God.
The Sire saw, one by one, his Virtues wake: 285
The Mother begg'd the blessing of a Rake.

261–4. Those who have no Genius, employ'd in works of imagination; those who have, in abstract sciences. P.

270. A notion of Aristotle, that there was originally in every block of marble, a Statue, which would appear on the removal of the superfluous parts. P.

272. Governor: tutor and traveling companion.

274. Ajax: See Homer, Odyss. XI, where the Ghost of Ajax turns sullenly from Ulysses. A passage extremely admired by Longinus. P.

275–336. Here occurs Pope's account of a "Grand Tour" of the Continent, usually taken after graduation from a university, and commonly considered a necessary "finishing" of a young gentleman's education.

278. op'ning: giving tongue.

281. attendant Orator: the "Governor", or cicerone, of l. 272.

283. sacred: protected.

Thou gav'st that Ripeness, which so soon began,
And ceas'd so soon, he ne'er was Boy, nor Man.
Thro' School and College, thy kind cloud o'ercast,
Safe and unseen the young Æneas past: 290
Thence bursting glorious, all at once let down,
Stunn'd with his giddy Larum half the town.
Intrepid then, o'er seas and lands he flew:
Europe he saw, and Europe saw him too.
There all thy gifts and graces we display,   295
Thou, only thou, directing all our way!
To where the Seine, obsequious as she runs,
Pours at great Bourbon's feet her silken sons;
Or Tyber, now no longer Roman, rolls,
Vain of Italian Arts, Italian Souls: 300
To happy Convents, bosom'd deep in vines,
Where slumber Abbots, purple as their wines:
To Isles of fragrance, lilly-silver'd vales,
Diffusing languor in the panting gales:
To lands of singing, or of dancing slaves,   305
Love-whisp'ring woods, and lute-resounding waves.
But chief her shrine where naked Venus keeps,
And Cupids ride the Lyon of the Deeps;
Where, eas'd of Fleets, the Adriatic main
Wafts the smooth Eunuch and enamour'd swain.   310
Led by my hand, he saunter'd Europe round,
And gather'd ev'ry Vice on Christian ground;
Saw ev'ry Court, heard ev'ry King declare
His royal Sense, of Op'ra's or the Fair;
The Stews and Palace equally explor'd,   315
Intrigu'd with glory, and with spirit whor'd;
Try'd all *hors-d'œuvres*, all *liqueurs* defin'd,
Judicious drank, and greatly-daring din'd,
Dropt the dull lumber of the Latin store,
Spoil'd his own language, and acquir'd no more;   320
All Classic learning lost on Classic ground;
And last turn'd *Air*, the Echo of a Sound!
See now, half-cur'd, and perfectly well-bred,

289–90. In the *Aeneid*, I 411–14, Venus wraps Aeneas and his companions
in a thick cloud that they may enter Carthage safe and unseen.
298. great Bourbon's feet: those of Louis XV.
303. lilly-silver'd vales: Tuberoses.   P.
307–10. The winged Lyon, the Arms of Venice. This Republic heretofore
the most considerable in Europe, for her Naval Force and the extent of her Commerce; now illustrious for her *Carnivals*.   P.   Venice at this time had the
reputation of being the brothel of Europe.
310. Eunuch: see *First Ep. of the Second Bk.*, l. 154n.
315. Stews: brothels.
316. intrigu'd: carried on love affairs, perhaps meddled in state affairs.
319. Latin store: classical learning.
322. turn'd Air: i.e., his learning diminished to knowledge of operatic *arias*.

With nothing but a Solo in his head;
As much Estate, and Principle, and Wit,   325
As Jansen, Fleetwood, Cibber shall think fit;
Stol'n from a Duel, follow'd by a Nun,
And, if a Borough chuse him, not undone;
See, to my country happy I restore
This glorious Youth, and add one Venus more.   330
Her too receive (for her my soul adores)
So may the sons of sons of sons of whores,
Prop thine, O Empress! like each neighbour Throne,
And make a long Posterity thy own."
    Pleas'd, she accepts the Hero, and the Dame,   335
Wraps in her Veil, and frees from sense of Shame.
    Then look'd, and saw a lazy, lolling sort,
Unseen at Church, at Senate, or at Court,
Of ever-listless Loit'rers, that attend
No cause, no Trust, no Duty, and no Friend.   340
Thee too, my Paridel! she mark'd thee there,
Stretch'd on the rack of a too easy chair,
And heard thy everlasting yawn confess
The Pains and Penalties of Idleness.
She pity'd! but her Pity only shed   345
Benigner influence on thy nodding head.
    But Annius, crafty Seer, with ebon wand,
And well dissembled em'rald on his hand,
False as his Gems, and canker'd as his Coins,
Came, cramm'd with capon, from where Pollio dines.   350
Soft, as the wily Fox is seen to creep,
Where bask on sunny banks the simple sheep,
Walk round and round, now prying here, now there;
So he; but pious, whisper'd first his pray'r.
    "Grant, gracious Goddess! grant me still to cheat,   355

324. With nothing but a *Solo?* Why, if it be a *Solo,* how should there be any thing else? Palpable Tautology! Read boldly an *Opera,* which is enough of conscience for such a head as has lost all its Latin.   Bentl.
326. Sir Henry Jansen (see *Second Sat. of Dr. Donne,* l. 88n.), Charles Fleetwood (d. 1747), a manager of Drury Lane Theater, and Cibber were all notorious gamblers.
328. chuse him: i.e., elect him to Parliament, and thus make him immune from arrest for debt.
330. one Venus more: the nun who had become the youth's mistress.
341. Paridel: The Poet seems to speak of this young gentleman with great affection. The name is taken from Spenser, who gives it to a *wandering 'Squire,* that travell'd about for the same reason, for which many young Squires are now fond of travelling, and especially to *Paris.* P.
347. Annius: The name taken from Annius [1432–1502] the Monk of Viterbo, famous for many Impositions and Forgeries of ancient manuscripts and inscriptions, which he was prompted to by mere Vanity, but our Annius had a more substantial motive. P.
349. canker'd: corrupt, tarnished.
350. Pollio: a name suggestive of any rich patron of the arts.

O may thy cloud still cover the deceit!
Thy choicer mists on this assembly shed,
But pour them thickest on the noble head.
So shall each youth, assisted by our eyes,
See other Cæsars, other Homers rise;   360
Thro' twilight ages hunt th' Athenian fowl,
Which Chalcis Gods, and mortals call an Owl,
Now see an Attys, now a Cecrops clear,
Nay, Mahomet! the Pigeon at thine ear;
Be rich in ancient brass, tho' not in gold,   365
And keep his Lares, tho' his house be sold;
To headless Phœbe his fair bride postpone,
Honour a Syrian Prince above his own;
Lord of an Otho, if I vouch it true;
Blest in one Niger, till he knows of two."   370
    Mummius o'erheard him; Mummius, Fool-renown'd,
Who like his Cheops stinks above the ground,
Fierce as a startled Adder, swell'd, and said,
Rattling an ancient Sistrum at his head.
    "Speak'st thou of Syrian Princes? Traitor base!   375

360. **other Cæsars, other Homers:** i.e., counterfeit ancient coinage embossed with these heads.
361–2. **th' Athenian fowl:** The Owl stamp'd on the reverse of the ancient money of Athens.
                  Which Chalcis *Gods, and Mortals call an* Owl,
is the verse by which [Thomas] Hobbes renders that of Homer [*Iliad*, XIV 291]. ... P.   Chalcis is Greek for "a bird of prey."
363. **Attys . . . Cecrops:** The first Kings of Athens, of whom it is hard to suppose any Coins are extant; but not so improbable as what follows, that there should be any of Mahomet, who forbad all Images. Nevertheless one of these Annius's made a counterfeit one, now in the collection of a learned Nobleman. P.   Cf. *To Mr. Addison*, l. 40n.
364. **the Pigeon:** Mahomet trained a white pigeon to take grains from his ear, and persuaded his followers that the bird was the angel Gabriel delivering messages from God. See also previous note.
366. **Lares:** Roman deities of the home and family.
367. I.e., neglect his bride for a headless statue of Phoebe, the goddess of chastity.
369–70. **Otho . . . Niger:** Roman emperors who ruled for a very short time and whose coins are therefore extremely rare. See *To Mr. Addison*, l. 39n., l. 44n.
371. **Mummius:** some foolish collector of mummies and other Egyptian antiquities.
372. **Cheops:** a false mummy of the Egyptian King Cheops.
374. **Sistrum:** a kind of rattle used in Egyptian religious rites.
375–86. The strange story following which may be taken for a fiction of the Poet, is justified by a true relation in Spon's Voyages. Vaillant (who wrote the History of the Syrian Kings as it is to be found on medals) coming from the Levant, where he had been collecting various Coins, and being pursued by a Corsaire of Sallee, swallowed down twenty gold medals. A sudden Bourasque [a squall] freed him from the Rover, and he got to land with them in his belly. On his road to Avignon he met two Physicians, of whom he demanded assistance. One advis'd Purgations, the other Vomits. In this uncertainty, he took neither, but pursued his way to Lyons, where he found his ancient friend, the famous Physician and Antiquary Dufour, to whom he related his adventure. Dufour first

Mine, Goddess! mine is all the horned race.
True, he had wit, to make their value rise;
From foolish Greeks to steal them, was as wise;
More glorious yet, from barb'rous hands to keep,
When Sallee Rovers chac'd him on the deep.   380
Then taught by Hermes, and divinely bold,
Down his own throat he risqu'd the Grecian gold;
Receiv'd each Demi-God, with pious care,
Deep in his Entrails — I rever'd them there,
I bought them, shrouded in that living shrine,   385
And, at their second birth, they issue mine."
    "Witness great Ammon! by whose horns I swore,
(Reply'd soft Annius) this our paunch before
Still bears them, faithful; and that thus I eat,
Is to refund the Medals with the meat.   390
To prove me, Goddess! clear of all design,
Bid me with Pollio sup, as well as dine:
There all the Learn'd shall at the labour stand,
And Douglas lend his soft, obstetric hand."
    The Goddess smiling seem'd to give consent;   395
So back to Pollio, hand in hand, they went.
    Then thick as Locusts black'ning all the ground,
A tribe, with weeds and shells fantastic crown'd,
Each with some wond'rous gift approach'd the Pow'r,
A Nest, a Toad, a Fungus, or a Flow'r.   400
But far the foremost, two, with earnest zeal,
And aspect ardent to the Throne appeal.
    The first thus open'd: "Hear thy suppliant's call,

---

ask'd him *whether the Medals were of the higher Empire?* He assur'd him they
were. Dufour was ravish'd with the hope of possessing such a treasure, he bar-
gain'd with him on the spot for the most curious of them, and was to recover
them at his own expence.   P.

376. horned race: see l. 387*n*.

380. Sallee Rovers: Moorish pirates.

381. Hermes: god of thieves and travelers.

383. Demi-God: They are called Θεῖοι on their Coins.   P.

387. Ammon: Jupiter Ammon is call'd to witness, as the father of Alexander
[see *Essay on Criticism*, l. 376*n*.], to whom those Kings succeeded in the division
of the Macedonian Empire, and whose *Horns* they wore on their Medals.   P.
Ammon was typically represented in the shape of a ram with enormous curving
horns.

389. thus I eat: see l. 350.

394. Douglas: A Physician [James Douglas, 1675–1742, a famous obste-
trician] of great Learning and no less Taste; above all curious in what related
to *Horace*, of whom he collected every Edition, Translation, and Comment, to
the number of several hundred volumes.   P.

397. Thick as Locusts: The similitude of *Locusts* does not refer more to the
numbers than to the qualities of the Virtuosi [i.e., experimental "scientists" of
the period; many were amateurish dabblers]: who not only devour and lay
waste every tree, shrub, and green leaf in their *Course*, i.e. of experiments; but
suffer neither a moss nor fungus to escape untouched.   Scribl.

Great Queen, and common Mother of us all!
Fair from its humble bed I rear'd this Flow'r,   405
Suckled, and chear'd, with air, and sun, and show'r,
Soft on the paper ruff its leaves I spread,
Bright with the gilded button tipt its head,
Then thron'd in glass, and nam'd it CAROLINE:
Each Maid cry'd, charming! and each Youth, divine!
Did Nature's pencil ever blend such rays,   411
Such vary'd light in one promiscuous blaze?
Now prostrate! dead! behold that Caroline:
No Maid cries, charming! and no Youth, divine!
And lo the wretch! whose vile, whose insect lust   415
Lay'd this gay daughter of the Spring in dust.
Oh punish him, or to th' Elysian shades
Dismiss my soul, where no Carnation fades."
    He ceas'd, and wept. With innocence of mien,
Th' Accus'd stood forth, and thus address'd the Queen.
    "Of all th' enamel'd race, whose silv'ry wing   421
Waves to the tepid Zephyrs of the spring,
Or swims along the fluid atmosphere,
Once brightest shin'd this child of Heat and Air.
I saw, and started from its vernal bow'r   425
The rising game, and chac'd from flow'r to flow'r.
It fled, I follow'd; now in hope, now pain;
It stopt, I stopt; it mov'd, I mov'd again.
At last it fix'd, 'twas on what plant it pleas'd,
And where it fix'd, the beauteous bird I seiz'd: 430
Rose or Carnation was below my care;
I meddle, Goddess! only in my sphere.
I tell the naked fact without disguise,
And, to excuse it, need but shew the prize;
Whose spoils this paper offers to your eye,   435
Fair ev'n in death! this peerless *Butterfly*."
    "My sons! (she answer'd) both have done your parts:
Live happy both, and long promote our arts.
But hear a Mother, when she recommends
To your fraternal care, our sleeping friends.   440

407. leaves: petals.
408. button: perhaps the seed-vessels of the flower.
409. nam'd it Caroline: It is a compliment which the Florists usually pay to
Princes and great persons, to give their names to the most curious [i.e., choice or
rare] Flowers of their raising: Some have been very jealous of vindicating this
honour, but none more than that ambitious Gardiner at Hammersmith, who
caused his Favourite to be painted on his Sign, with this inscription. *This is* My
Queen Caroline. P.
421. enamel'd race: butterflies.
427–9. Pope refers the reader to *Paradise Lost*, IV 462–5.
430. bird: the butterfly.
435. paper: the paper on which the butterfly is mounted.
440. our sleeping friends: of whom see [ll. 337–46] above. P.

The common Soul, of Heav'n's more frugal make,
Serves but to keep fools pert, and knaves awake:
A drowzy Watchman, that just gives a knock,
And breaks our rest, to tell us what's a clock.
Yet by some object ev'ry brain is stirr'd;   445
The dull may waken to a Humming-bird;
The most recluse, discreetly open'd, find
Congenial matter in the Cockle-kind;
The mind, in Metaphysics at a loss,
May wander in a wilderness of Moss;   450
The head that turns at super-lunar things,
Poiz'd with a tail, may steer on Wilkins' wings.
   "O! would the Sons of Men once think their Eyes
And Reason giv'n them but to study *Flies!*
See Nature in some partial narrow shape,   455
And let the Author of the Whole escape:
Learn but to trifle; or, who most observe,
To wonder at their Maker, not to serve."
   "Be that my task (replies a gloomy Clerk,
Sworn foe to Myst'ry, yet divinely dark;   460
Whose pious hope aspires to see the day
When Moral Evidence shall quite decay,
And damns implicit faith, and holy lies,
Prompt to impose, and fond to dogmatize:)
Let others creep by timid steps, and slow,   465
On plain Experience lay foundations low,
By common sense to common knowledge bred,
And last, to Nature's Cause thro' Nature led.
All-seeing in thy mists, we want no guide,
Mother of Arrogance, and Source of Pride!   470
We nobly take the high Priori Road,

450. **wilderness of Moss:** Of which the Naturalists count I can't tell how many hundred species. P.
452. **Wilkins' wings:** One of the first Projectors [i.e., promoters of scientific projects] of the Royal Society, who, among many enlarged and useful notions, entertain'd the extravagant hope of a possibility to fly to the Moon; which has put some volatile Genius's upon making wings for that purpose. P.   Bishop John Wilkins (1614–72), first secretary of the Royal Society, and author of *The Discovery of a World in the Moone.*
459. **Clerk:** a clergyman, but here one of a deistical bent.
460. **Myst'ry:** Christian revelation.
463. **implicit faith:** acceptance of all that the church teaches without definite knowledge of what its doctrines are.
471. **high Priori Road:** Those who, from the effects in this Visible world, deduce the Eternal Power and Godhead of the First Cause, tho' they cannot attain to an adequate idea of the Deity, yet discover so much of him, as enables them to see the End of their Creation, and the Means of their Happiness: whereas they who take this high Priori [a pun on *a priori*] Road (such as Hobbs, Spinoza, Des Cartes, and some better Reasoners) for one that goes right, ten lose themselves in Mists, or ramble after Visions which deprive them of all sight of their End, and mislead them in the choice of wrong means. P.

And reason downward, till we doubt of God:
Make Nature still incroach upon his plan;
And shove him off as far as e'er we can:
Thrust some Mechanic Cause into his place;   475
Or bind in Matter, or diffuse in Space.
Or, at one bound o'er-leaping all his laws,
Make God Man's Image, Man the final Cause,
Find Virtue local, all Relation scorn,
See all in *Self*, and but for self be born: 480
Of nought so certain as our *Reason* still,
Of nought so doubtful as of *Soul* and *Will*.
Oh hide the God still more! and make us see
Such as Lucretius drew, a God like Thee:
Wrapt up in Self, a God without a Thought,   485
Regardless of our merit or default.
Or that bright Image to our fancy draw,
Which Theocles in raptur'd vision saw,
While thro' Poetic scenes the Genius roves,
Or wanders wild in Academic Groves;   490
That Nature our Society adores,
Where Tindal dictates, and Silenus snores."

    Rous'd at his name, up rose the bowzy Sire,
And shook from out his Pipe the seeds of fire;
Then snapt his box, and strok'd his belly down: 495

473–4. This relates to such as being ashamed to assert a mere Mechanic Cause, and yet unwilling to forsake it intirely, have had recourse to a certain *Plastic Nature, Elastic Fluid, Subtile Matter, &c.* P.

475–6. The first of these Follies is that of Des Cartes, the second of Hobbs, the third of some succeeding Philosophers. P.

477. Cf. *Paradise Lost*, IV 181.

478. final Cause: the ultimate end or purpose of the creation.

479. local: variable according to time and place.　　all Relation scorn: i.e., be so totally self-centered (see next line) as to scorn all relations with other men and with God.

481–2. Reason: Of which we have most cause to be diffident. P.　　Soul and Will: Two things the most self-evident, the Existence of our Soul, and the Freedom of our Will. P.

484. Lucretius: the Epicurean poet and philosopher (d. 55 B.C.) who portrayed the gods as being totally indifferent to man's lot.

487. bright Image: *Bright Image* was the Title given by the later Platonists to that Idea of *Nature*, which they had form'd in their fancy, so bright, that they call'd it . . . the *Self-seen Image*, i.e. seen by its own light. P.　　See l. 244*n.*, above.

488–90. Theocles, the chief speaker in the Earl of Shaftesbury's *The Moralists, a Philosophical Rhapsody*, invokes a "Nature" that seems to have usurped the Christian God's creative and providential powers.

492. Tindal: Matthew Tindal, the deist (see *Sixth Ep. of the First Bk.*, l. 64*n.*, and *Dunciad*, II 399*n.*).　　Silenus: Silenus [an old and drunken demi-god] was an Epicurean Philosopher, as appears from Virgil, Eclog. 6, where he sings the Principles of that Philosophy in his drink. P.

493. bowzy Sire: the boozy Silenus.

494. seeds of fire: The Epicurean language, *Semina rerum*, or Atoms. Virg. Eclog. 6 [31*ff*.]. . . . P.　　495. box: presumably a snuff-box.

Rosy and rev'rend, tho' without a Gown.
Bland and familiar to the throne he came,
Led up the Youth, and call'd the Goddess *Dame*.
Then thus. "From Priest-craft happily set free,
Lo! ev'ry finish'd Son returns to thee: 500
First slave to Words, then vassal to a Name,
Then dupe to Party; child and man the same;
Bounded by Nature, narrow'd still by Art,
A trifling head, and a contracted heart.
Thus bred, thus taught, how many have I seen,   505
Smiling on all, and smil'd on by a Queen.
Mark'd out for Honours, honour'd for their Birth,
To thee the most rebellious things on earth:
Now to thy gentle shadow all are shrunk,
All melted down, in Pension, or in Punk!   510
So K * so B * * sneak'd into the grave,
A Monarch's half, and half a Harlot's slave.
Poor W * * nipt in Folly's broadest bloom,
Who praises now? his Chaplain on his Tomb.
Then take them all, oh take them to thy breast!   515
Thy *Magus*, Goddess! shall perform the rest."
    With that, a WIZARD OLD his *Cup* extends;
Which whoso tastes, forgets his former friends,
Sire, Ancestors, Himself. One casts his eyes
Up to a *Star*, and like Endymion dies: 520
A *Feather* shooting from another's head,

496. Gown: i.e., a clergyman's gown.
498. Youth: here in the plural sense.
501ff. A Recapitulation of the whole Course of Modern Education describ'd in this book, which confines Youth to the study of *Words* only in Schools, subjects them to the authority of *Systems* in the Universities, and deludes them with the names of *Party-distinctions* in the World. All equally concurring to narrow the Understanding, and establish Slavery and Error in Literature, Philosophy, and Politics. The whole finished in modern Free-thinking; the completion of whatever is vain, wrong, and destructive to the happiness of mankind, as it establishes *Self-love* for the sole Principle of Action. P.
506. Queen: Pope glances at Queen Caroline.
510. in Pension, or in Punk: corrupted by government pay, or by whores.
511. So K * so B * * : the blanks perhaps refer to Henry de Grey, Duke of Kent (see *First Ep. of the First Bk.*, l. 88n.) and to James, third Earl of Berkeley (d. 1736). Pope may imply in the next line that they owed their government posts to a royal mistress with whom they had to share their profits.
513. Poor W * * : some young and dissolute youth who has not been positively identified.   **516. Magus:** magician.
517. Cup: The *Cup* of *Self-Love*, which causes a total oblivion of the obligations of Friendship, or Honour, and of the Service of God or our Country; all sacrificed to Vain-glory, Court-worship, or yet meaner considerations of Lucre and brutal Pleasures. From ver. 520 to 528. P.
520. Star: emblem of a knightly order.   **Endymion:** the Endymion of classical myth died for love of the moon; this new Endymion "dies" (i.e., forsakes his principles) for love of a knighthood.
521. Feather: the feather worn in the cap of a Knight of the Garter.

Extracts his brain, and Principle is fled,
Lost is his God, his Country, ev'ry thing;
And nothing left but Homage to a King!
The vulgar herd turn off to roll with Hogs,   525
To run with Horses, or to hunt with Dogs;
But, sad example! never to escape
Their Infamy, still keep the human shape.

But she, good Goddess, sent to ev'ry child
Firm Impudence, or Stupefaction mild;   530
And strait succeeded, leaving shame no room,
Cibberian forehead, or Cimmerian gloom.

Kind Self-conceit to some her glass applies,
Which no one looks in with another's eyes:
But as the Flatt'rer or Dependant paint,   535
Beholds himself a Patriot, Chief, or Saint.

On others int'rest her gay liv'ry flings,
Int'rest, that waves on Party-colour'd wings:
Turn'd to the Sun, she casts a thousand dyes,
And, as she turns, the colours fall or rise.   540

Others the Syren Sisters warble round,
And empty heads console with empty sound.
No more, alas! the voice of Fame they hear,
The balm of Dulness trickling in their ear.
Great C * *, H * *, P * *, R * *, K *,   545
Why all your Toils? your Sons have learn'd to sing.
How quick Ambition hastes to ridicule!
The Sire is made a Peer, the Son a Fool.

On some, a Priest succinct in amice white
Attends; all flesh is nothing in his sight!   550
Beeves, at his touch, at once to jelly turn,
And the huge Boar is shrunk into an Urn:
The board with specious miracles he loads,
Turns Hares to Larks, and Pigeons into Toads.
Another (for in all what one can shine?)   555
Explains the *Seve* and *Verdeur* of the Vine.
What cannot copious Sacrifice attone?

525–8. The Effects of the Magus's Cup are just contrary to that of Circe. Hers took away the shape, and left the human mind: This takes away the mind, and leaves the human shape. P.

532. Cibberian: see *Dunciad*, I 218n.   Cimmerian: see *Dunciad*, III 4n.

538. Party-colour'd: Pope puns on the word "party."

541. Syren Sisters: the operatic muses or singers.

545. The blanks may possibly be intended for Cowper, Harcourt, Parker, Raymond, King, all men who attained to the peerage by their own efforts (their "Toils" of l. 546). Their offspring patronized the opera and were, on the whole, undistinguished.

549. Priest succinct in amice white: a chef engirdled in a piece of white linen comparable to an item of clerical dress.

556. Seve and Verdeur: *Sève* signifies the strength of flavor proper to wine, *verdeur* the tartness.

Thy Treufles, Perigord! thy Hams, Bayonne!
With French Libation, and Italian Strain,
Wash Bladen white, and expiate Hays's stain.   560
Knight lifts the head, for what are crowds undone
To three essential Partriges in one?
Gone ev'ry blush, and silent all reproach,
Contending Princes mount them in their Coach.
   Next bidding all draw near on bended knees,   565
The Queen confers her *Titles* and *Degrees*.
Her children first of more distinguish'd sort,
Who study Shakespeare at the Inns of Court,
Impale a Glow-worm, or Vertù profess,
Shine in the dignity of F. R. S.   570
Some, deep Free-Masons, join the silent race
Worthy to fill Pythagoras's place:
Some Botanists, or Florists at the least,
Or issue Members of an Annual feast.
Nor past the meanest unregarded, one   575
Rose a Gregorian, one a Gormogon.
The last, not least in honour or applause,

558. Perigord: a French province.   **Bayonne:** a town of France.

560–61. Names of Gamesters. Bladen is a black man. Robert Knight [see *First Ep. of the Second Bk.*, l. 195n.], Cashier of the South-sea Company, who fled from England in 1720, (afterwards pardoned in 1742.) — These lived with the utmost magnificence at Paris, and kept open Tables frequented by persons of the first Quality of England, and even by Princes of the Blood of France. P. Bladen was probably Thomas Bladen (the word "black" was often used to describe a person with a dark complexion or black hair). Hays is unknown.

561. crowds undone: the thousands who were ruined in the collapse of South Sea Company stock (see *Ep. to Bathurst*, l. 119n.).

562. three essential Partriges in one: i.e., two dissolved into Quintessence to make sauce for the third. The honour of this invention belongs to France, yet has it been excell'd by our native luxury, an hundred squab Turkeys being not unfrequently deposited in one Pye in the Bishopric of Durham: to which our Author alludes in ver. 594 of this work. P.

564. them: Bladen, Hays, and Knight.

568. Who . . . Court: lawyers and law students who neglect their careers because of literary dabblings (the Inns of Court are the four sets of buildings in London belonging to the four legal societies of England: the Inner Temple, the Middle Temple, Lincoln's Inn, and Gray's Inn). See *Ep. to Dr. Arbuthnot*, l. 211n.

569. Vertù: artistic taste.

570. F.R.S.: Fellow of the Royal Society.

571–2. The Poet all along expresses a very particular concern for this silent Race [see ll. 437–52]: He has here provided, that in case they will not waken or open (as was before proposed) to a *Humming-Bird* or *Cockle*, yet at worst they may be made Free-Masons; where *Taciturnity* is the *only* essential Qualification, as it was the chief of the disciples of Pythagoras. P.   The Greek philosopher Pythagoras (582–507 B.C.) would not permit his students to speak in his presence until they had been his auditors for several years.

574. Annual feast: yearly banquet of some society or other.

576. Gregorian . . . Gormogon: A sort of Lay-brothers, *Slips* [cuttings] from the Root of the Free-Masons. P.   These organizations were founded as burlesque imitations of the Freemasons.

Isis and Cam made Doctors of her Laws.
   Then blessing all, "Go Children of my care!
To Practice now from Theory repair.   580
All my commands are easy, short, and full:
My Sons! be proud, be selfish, and be dull.
Guard my Prerogative, assert my Throne:
This Nod confirms each Privilege your own.
The Cap and Switch be sacred to his Grace;   585
With Staff and Pumps the Marquis lead the Race;
From Stage to Stage the licens'd Earl may run,
Pair'd with his Fellow-Charioteer the Sun;
The learned Baron Butterflies design,
Or draw to silk Arachne's subtile line;   590
The Judge to dance his brother Sergeant call;
The Senator at Cricket urge the Ball;
The Bishop stow (Pontific Luxury!)
An hundred Souls of Turkeys in a pye;
The sturdy Squire to Gallic masters stoop,   595
And drown his Lands and Manors in a Soupe.
Others import yet nobler arts from France,
Teach Kings to fiddle, and make Senates dance.
Perhaps more high some daring son may soar,
Proud to my list to add one Monarch more;   600
And nobly conscious, Princes are but things
Born for First Ministers, as Slaves for Kings,
Tyrant supreme! shall three Estates command,
And MAKE ONE MIGHTY DUNCIAD OF THE LAND!"
   More she had spoke, but yawn'd — All Nature nods:

578. **Isis and Cam:** Oxford and Cambridge.   **her:** Dulness's.
585. **Cap and Switch:** of a jockey.   **his Grace:** a duke.
586. **Staff and Pumps:** running-footmen, who ran alongside their master's coach, carried a long staff and wore a kind of shoe without heels. Young gentlemen at this time had made a fad of dressing like grooms, footmen, etc.
587. I.e., the earl delights in driving his own stagecoach. He is "licens'd" (i.e., privileged) because of his rank, or because he has actually taken out the licence which had to be purchased by the owner of a stagecoach.
589. **design:** sketch.
590. This is one of the most ingenious employments assign'd, and therefore recommended only to Peers of Learning. Of weaving Stockings of the Webs of Spiders, see the Phil[osophical] Trans[actions]. P.   Arachne means *spider*.
591. Alluding perhaps to that ancient and solemn *Dance* intitled *A Call of Sergeants*. P.   A *sergeant* was a member of a superior order of barristers from which the Common Law judges were chosen; they were "called" to the order in a special rite, which Pope refers to as a "dance," and henceforth termed "brother" by the judges.
593–4. The Bishop was William Talbot (1659–1731), Bishop of Durham. Pope's note to l. 562, above, describes his love of turkey pie.
599. **some daring son:** alluding to Sir Robert Walpole, who was First Minister (cf. l. 602) from 1721 to 1742, and who had been in effect the ruler of England during that period.
602. **First Ministers:** prime ministers.
603. **three Estates:** the Lords Spiritual, the Lords Temporal, the Commons.

What Mortal can resist the Yawn of Gods? 606
Churches and Chapels instantly it reach'd;
(St. James's first, for leaden Gilbert preach'd)
Then catch'd the Schools; the Hall scarce kept awake;
The Convocation gap'd, but could not speak: 610
Lost was the Nation's Sense, nor could be found,
While the long solemn Unison went round:
Wide, and more wide, it spread o'er all the realm;
Ev'n Palinurus nodded at the Helm:
The Vapour mild o'er each Committee crept; 615
Unfinish'd Treaties in each Office slept;
And Chiefless Armies doz'd out the Campaign;
And Navies yawn'd for Orders on the Main.
O Muse! relate (for you can tell alone,
Wits have short Memories, and Dunces none) 620
Relate, who first, who last resign'd to rest;
Whose Heads she partly, whose completely blest;
What Charms could Faction, what Ambition lull,
The Venal quiet, and intrance the Dull;
'Till drown'd was Sense, and Shame, and Right, and
Wrong — 625
O sing, and hush the Nations with thy song!

❀   ❀   ❀   ❀   ❀   ❀

In vain, in vain, — the all-composing Hour
Resistless falls: The Muse obeys the Pow'r.
She comes! she comes! the sable Throne behold
Of *Night* Primæval, and of *Chaos* old! 630
Before her, *Fancy's* gilded clouds decay,
And all its varying Rain-bows die away.
Wit shoots in vain its momentary fires,
The meteor drops, and in a flash expires.
As one by one, at dread Medea's strain, 635
The sick'ning stars fade off th' ethereal plain;

608. **leaden:** An Epithet from the *Age* she had just then restored, according to that sublime custom of the Easterns, in calling new-born Princes after some great and recent event. Scribl.   **Gilbert:** Dr. John Gilbert (1693–1761), who became Archbishop of York.
609. **Schools:** Eton, Westminster, etc.   **Hall:** Westminster Hall, site of the law courts.
610. **Convocation:** the House of Convocation, an assembly of clergymen, was debarred from transacting ecclesiastical business at this period.
611. **Nation's Sense:** the majority view of the House of Commons was frequently termed the "Sense of the Nation."
612. **Unison:** single unvaried sound.
614. **Palinurus:** the pilot of Aeneas's ship who went to sleep and fell into the sea. Pope here alludes to Walpole, pilot of the ship of state.
633. **Wit:** imagination, intelligence.
635–6. The enchantress Medea (see ll. 121–2n., above) had the power to cause eclipses and to call down the constellations.

As Argus' eyes by Hermes' wand opprest,
Clos'd one by one to everlasting rest;
Thus at her felt approach, and secret might,
Art after *Art* goes out, and all is Night.   640
See skulking *Truth* to her old Cavern fled,
Mountains of Casuistry heap'd o'er her head!
Philosophy, that lean'd on Heav'n before,
Shrinks to her second cause, and is no more.
Physic of *Metaphysic* begs defence,   645
And *Metaphysic* calls for aid on *Sense!*
See *Mystery* to *Mathematics* fly!
In vain! they gaze, turn giddy, rave, and die.
Religion blushing veils her sacred fires,
And unawares *Morality* expires.   650
Nor *public* Flame, nor *private,* dares to shine;
Nor *human* Spark is left, nor Glimpse *divine!*
Lo! thy dread Empire, Chaos! is restor'd;
Light dies before thy uncreating word;
Thy hand, great Anarch! lets the curtain fall;   655
And Universal Darkness buries All.

637–8. Hermes, or Mercury, slew Argus, the monster with 100 eyes (see *Dunciad,* II 374n.). Hermes' wand is the caduceus.

642. Casuistry: specious reasoning about law and morals.

644. second cause: God is the First Cause in theological reckoning; a second cause is a cause caused by something else, a cause through which God works.

645. Physic: natural science.

647. Mystery: Christian divine revelation.

654. uncreating word: in contradistinction to the Logos, the creating Word of God.

THE GUARDIAN

No. 40

MONDAY, APRIL 27, 1713

Compulerantque Greges Corydon & Thyrsis in unum.
Ex illo Corydon, Corydon est tempore nobis.

I DESIGNED to have troubled the Reader with no farther Discourses of *Pastorals*, but being informed that I am taxed of Partiality in not mentioning an Author,[1] whose Eclogues are published in the same Volume[2] with Mr. *Philips*'s; I shall employ this Paper in Observations upon him, written in the free Spirit of Criticism, and without Apprehension of offending that Gentleman,[3] whose Character it is, that he takes the greatest Care of his Works before they are published, and has the least Concern for them afterwards.

I have laid it down as the first Rule of Pastoral, that its Idea should be taken from the Manners of the *Golden Age*, and the Moral form'd upon the Representation of Innocence; 'tis therefore plain that any Deviations from that Design degrade a Poem from being true Pastoral. In this View it will appear that *Virgil* can only have two of his Eclogues allowed to be such: His First and Ninth must be rejected,

GUARDIAN NO. 40: Early in 1713 Thomas Tickell (1685–1740), a minor poet and essayist (see *Peri Bathous*, n. 16, p. 420), wrote a series of five *Guardian* papers in which he lavishly praised the pastoral poems of Ambrose Philips (see *Ep. to Arbuthnot*, l. 100n.), and at the same time pointedly ignored the pastorals written by Pope which had originally appeared in the same miscellany volume with those of Philips. Pope then wrote and submitted, anonymously, a sixth paper, No. 40, which professed to be by the author of the earlier papers but which now ironically juxtaposed the pastorals of Philips with his own work.

The Latin epigraph is from Virgil's *Eclogue VII*, ll. 2, 70: "Corydon and Thyrsis had driven their flocks together. . . . From that day, it is Corydon, Corydon with us."

[1] an Author: Pope himself.

[2] same Volume: Philips's pastorals had appeared at the beginning, and Pope's at the end, of a volume entitled *Poetical Miscellanies, The Sixth Part*, in 1709.

[3] Gentleman: Pope again.

because they describe the Ravages of Armies, and Oppressions of the Innocent; *Corydon's* Criminal[4] Passion for *Alexis* throws out the Second; the Calumny and Railing in the Third are not proper to that State of Concord; the Eighth represents unlawful Ways of procuring Love by Inchantments, and introduces a Shepherd whom an inviting Precipice tempts to Self-Murder. As to the Fourth, Sixth, and Tenth, they are given up by *Heinsius, Salmasius, Rapin,*[5] and the Criticks in general. They likewise observe that but eleven of all the *Idyllia* of *Theocritus*[6] are to be admitted as Pastorals; and even out of that Number the greater Part will be excluded for one or other of the Reasons abovementioned. So that when I remark'd in a former Paper,[7] that *Virgil's* Eclogues, taken all together, are rather *Select Poems* than *Pastorals;* I might have said the same thing, with no less Truth, of *Theocritus.* The Reason of this I take to be yet unobserved by the Criticks, *viz. They never meant them all for Pastorals.* Which it is plain *Philips* hath done, and in that Particular excelled both *Theocritus* and *Virgil.*

As Simplicity is the distinguishing Characteristick of Pastoral, *Virgil* hath been thought guilty of too Courtly a Stile; his Language is perfectly pure, and he often forgets he is among Peasants. I have frequently wonder'd that since he was so conversant in the Writings of *Ennius,*[8] he had not imitated the Rusticity of the *Doric,*[9] as well, by the help of the old obsolete *Roman* Language, as *Philips* hath by the antiquated *English:* For Example, might he not have said *Quoi* instead of *Cui; Quoijum* for *Cujum; volt* for *vult,* &c. as well as our Modern hath *Welladay* for *Alas, Whilome* for *of Old, make mock* for *deride,* and *witless Younglings* for *simple Lambs,* &c. by which Means he had attained as much of the Air of *Theocritus,* as *Philips* hath of *Spencer.*

Mr. *Pope* hath fallen in to the same Error with *Virgil.* His Clowns[10] do not converse in all the Simplicity proper to the Country: His Names are borrow'd from *Theocritus* and *Virgil,* which are improper to the Scene of his Pastorals. He introduces *Daphnis, Alexis* and *Thyrsis* on *British* Plains, as *Virgil* had done before him on the *Mantuan;*[11] whereas *Philips,* who hath the strictest Regard to Propriety,

4 **Criminal:** i.e., homosexual.

5 **Heinsius:** Daniel Heinsius (1580–1655), esteemed Dutch classical scholar and critic.   **Salmasius:** Claudius Salmasius (1588–1653), celebrated French scholar.   **Rapin:** René Rapin (1621–87), French critic and poet.

6 **Theocritus:** Greek pastoral poet of the third century B.C.

7 **former Paper:** *Guardian* No. 28 (Pope of course still speaks in the guise of Tickell).

8 **Ennius:** celebrated Roman poet (239–169 B.C.) noted for the vigor of his style.

9 **Doric:** the Doric dialect.

10 **Clowns:** peasants, rustic fellows.

11 **Mantuan:** Virgil was born at Mantua.

makes choice of Names peculiar[12] to the Country, and more agreeable to a Reader of Delicacy; such as *Hobbinol, Lobbin, Cuddy,* and *Colin Clout.*

So easie as Pastoral Writing may seem, (in the Simplicity we have described it) yet it requires *great Reading*, both of the *Ancients* and *Moderns*, to be a Master of it. *Philips* hath given us manifest Proofs of his Knowledge of Books;[13] it must be confessed his Competitor hath imitated some single Thoughts of the Ancients well enough, if we consider he had not the Happiness of an University Education;[14] but he hath dispersed them, here and there, without that Order and Method which Mr. *Philips* observes, whose whole third Pastoral is an Instance how well he hath studied the fifth of *Virgil*, and how judiciously reduced *Virgil's* Thoughts to the Standard of Pastoral; as his Contention of *Colin Clout* and the *Nightingale* shows with what Exactness he hath imitated *Strada.*

When I remarked it as a principal Fault to introduce Fruits and Flowers of a Foreign Growth, in Descriptions where the Scene lies in our Country, I did not design that Observation should extend also to Animals, or the Sensitive Life;[15] for *Philips* hath with great Judgement described *Wolves*[16] in *England* in his first Pastoral. Nor would I have a Poet slavishly confine himself (as Mr. *Pope* hath done) to one particular Season of the Year, one certain time of the Day, and one unbroken Scene in each Eclogue. 'Tis plain *Spencer* neglected this Pedantry, who in his Pastoral of *November* mentions the mournful Song of the Nightingale:

Sad Philomel[17] *her Song in Tears doth steep.*

And Mr. *Philips,* by a Poetical Creation, hath raised up finer Beds of Flowers than the most industrious Gardiner; his Roses, Lillies and Daffadils blow in the same Season.

But the better to discover the Merits of our two Contemporary Pastoral Writers, I shall endeavour to draw a Parallel of them, by setting several of their particular Thoughts in the same light, whereby it will be obvious how much *Philips* hath the Advantage. With what Simplicity he introduces two Shepherds singing alternately.

[12] **peculiar:** characteristic, distinctive.

[13] In this passage Pope in effect charges Philips with plagiarizing some verses by Famianus Strada (1572–1649), an Italian priest, scholar and poet (see also *Ep. to Dr. Arbuthnot*, ll. 179–80*n*.).

[14] **University Education:** as a Catholic, Pope was barred from attending Oxford or Cambridge.

[15] **Sensitive Life:** the life of animals as distinct from that of plants.

[16] **Wolves:** wolves had apparently become extinct in England by the end of the 15th century.

[17] **Philomel:** i.e., mythical name for the nightingale; a migratory bird, it would not appear in England in November.

Hobb.[18]   *Come,* Rosalind, *O come, for without thee*
What Pleasure can the Country have for me:
Come, Rosalind, *O Come; my brindled Kine,*[19]
My snowy Sheep, my Farm, and all is thine.

Lanq.[1]   *Come,* Rosalind, *O come; here shady Bowers,*
Here are cool Fountains, and here springing Flow'rs.
Come, Rosalind; *Here ever let us stay,*
And sweetly wast, our live-long Time away.

Our other Pastoral Writer, in expressing the same Thought, deviates into downright Poetry.

Streph.[2]   *In Spring the Fields, in Autumn Hills I love,*
At Morn the Plains, at Noon the shady Grove,
But Delia *always; forc'd from* Delia's *Sight,*
Nor Plains at Morn, nor Groves at Noon delight.

Daph.[3]   Sylvia's *like Autumn ripe, yet mild as* May,
More bright than Noon, yet fresh as early Day;
Ev'n Spring displeases, when she shines not here.
But blest with her, 'tis Spring throughout the Year.

In the first of these Authors, two Shepherds thus innocently describe the Behaviour of their Mistresses.

Hobb.   *As Marian bath'd, by chance I passed by,*
She blush'd, and at me cast a side-long Eye:
Then swift beneath the Crystal Wave she try'd
Her beauteous Form, but all in vain, to hide.

Lanq.   *As I to cool me bath'd one sultry Day,*
Fond Lydia *lurking in the Sedges lay.*
The Wanton laugh'd, and seem'd in Haste to fly;
Yet often stopp'd, and often turn'd her Eye.

The other Modern (who it must be confessed hath a knack of Versifying) hath it as follows.[4]

Streph.   *Me gentle* Delia *beckons from the Plain,*
Then, hid in Shades, eludes her eager Swain;
But feigns a Laugh, to see me search around,
And by that Laugh the willing Fair is found.

18 **Hobb.**: Hobbinol.
19 **Kine:** cows.

1 **Lanq.**: Lanquet.
2 **Streph.**: Strephon. See Pope's *Spring,* ll. 77–84.
3 **Daph.**: Daphnis.
4 The passage is from Pope's *Spring,* ll. 53–60.

Daph. *The sprightly Sylvia trips along the Green,*
She runs, but hopes she does not run unseen;
While a kind Glance at her Pursuer flyes,
How much at Variance are her Feet and Eyes!

There is nothing the Writers of this kind of Poetry are fonder of, than Descriptions of Pastoral Presents. *Philips* says thus of a Sheep-hook.

Of Season'd Elm; where Studs of Brass appear,
To speak the Giver's Name, the Month and Year.
The Hook of polish'd Steel, the Handle turn'd,
And richly by the Graver's Skill adorn'd.

The other of a Bowl embossed with Figures.[5]

———— where wanton Ivy twines,
And swelling Clusters bend the curling Vines;
Four Figures rising from the Work appear,
The various Seasons of the rolling Year;
And what is That which binds the radiant Sky,
Where twelve bright Signs in beauteous Order lie.

The Simplicity of the Swain in this Place, who forgets the Name of the *Zodiack,* is no ill Imitation of *Virgil;* but how much more plainly and unaffectedly would *Philips* have dressed this Thought in his *Doric?*[6]

And what That hight, which girds the Welkin sheen,[7]
Where twelve gay Signs in meet[8] *array are seen.*

If the Reader would indulge his Curiosity any farther in the Comparison of Particulars, he may read the first Pastoral of *Philips* with the second of his Contemporary, and the fourth and sixth of the former, with the fourth and first of the latter; where several Parallel Places will occur to every one.

Having now shown some Parts, in which these two Writers may be compared, it is a Justice I owe to Mr. *Philips,* to discover those in which no Man can compare with him. First, That *beautiful Rusticity,* of which I shall only produce two Instances, out of a hundred not yet quoted.

O woful Day! O Day of Woe, quoth he,
And woful I, who live the Day to see!

That Simplicity of Diction, the Melancholy Flowing of the Numbers, the Solemnity of the Sound, and the easie Turn[9] of the Words, in this *Dirge* (to make use of our Author's Expression) are extreamly Elegant.

[5] From Pope's *Spring,* ll. 35–40.
[6] Doric: *Doric* is often synonymous with *rustic, uncouth.*
[7] hight: called.   Welkin: sky.   sheen: bright.
[8] meet: fitting, proper.
[9] Turn: repetition of the same or similar words.

In another of his Pastorals, a Shepherd utters a *Dirge* not much inferior to the former, in the following Lines.

> *Ah me the while! ah me! the luckless Day,*
> *Ah luckless Lad! the rather might I say;*
> *Ah silly*[10] *I! more silly than my Sheep,*
> *Which on the flowry Plains I once did keep.*

How he still Charms the Ear with these artful Repetitions of the Epithets;[11] and how significant is the last Verse! I defy the most common Reader to repeat them, without feeling some Motions of Compassion.

In the next Place I shall rank his *Proverbs,* in which I formerly observed he excells: For Example,

> *A rolling Stone is ever bare of Moss;*
> *And, to their Cost, green Years old Proverbs cross.*

> —— *He that late lyes down, as late will rise,*
> *And, Sluggard-like, till Noon-day snoaring lyes.*

> *Against* Ill-Luck *all cunning Fore-sight fails;*
> *Whether we sleep or wake it nought avails.*

> —— *Nor fear, from* upright *Sentence,* Wrong.

Lastly, His *Elegant Dialect,* which alone might prove him the eldest Born of *Spencer,* and our only true *Arcadian;*[12] I should think it proper for the several Writers of Pastoral, to confine themselves to their several *Counties. Spencer* seems to have been of this Opinion: for he hath laid the Scene of one of his Pastorals in *Wales,* where with all the Simplicity natural to that Part of our Island, one Shepherd bids the other *Good-morrow* in an unusual and elegant Manner.[13]

> Diggon Davy, *I bid hur God-day:*
> *Or* Diggon *hur is, or I mis-say.*[14]

Diggon answers,

> *Hur was hur while it was Day-light;*
> *But now hur is a most wretched Wight,* &c.[15]

10 **silly:** Philips of course invokes the more archaic meanings of the word (*helpless, pitiful, simple*), while Pope counts on the reader taking it in its more modern sense of *fatuous, foolish.*

11 **Epithets:** adjectives.

12 **Arcadian:** Arcadia was the region of Greece associated with pastoral life and poetry.

13 Pope quotes from Spenser's *Shepheardes Calendar,* "September," ll. 1–4.

14 In these lines "hur" signifies *you.*

15 In these lines "hur" signifies *I.*

But the most beautiful Example of this kind that I ever met with, is in a very valuable Piece, which I chanced to find among some old Manuscripts, entituled, *A Pastoral Ballad;* which I think, for its Nature and Simplicity, may (notwithstanding the Modesty of the Title) be allowed a Perfect Pastoral: It is composed in the *Somersetshire* Dialect, and the Names such as are proper to the Country People. It may be observed, as a further Beauty of this Pastoral, the Words *Nymph, Dryad, Naiad, Fawn, Cupid,* or *Satyr,* are not once mentioned through the whole. I shall make no Apology for Inserting some few Lines of this excellent Piece. *Cicily* breaks thus into the Subject, as she is going a Milking;

Cicily.　*Rager go vetch tha Kee, or else tha Zun,*
　　　　Will quite be go, be vore c'have half a don.[16]

Roger.　*Thou shouldst not ax ma tweece, but I've a be*
　　　　To dreave our Bull to Bull tha Parson's Kee.[17]

It is to be observed, that this whole Dialogue is formed upon the Passion of Jealousie; and his mentioning the Parson's Kine naturally revives the Jealousie of the Shepherdess *Cicily,* which she expresses as follows:

Cicily.　*Ah Rager, Rager, chez*[18] *was zore avraid*
　　　　Ween in yond Vield you kiss'd tha Parsons Maid:
　　　　Is this the Love that once to me you zed,
　　　　When from tha Wake[19] *thou brought'st me Gingerbread?*

Roger.　Cicily *thou charg'st me false, — I'll zwear to thee,*
　　　　Tha Parson's Maid is still a Maid for me.

In which Answer of his are express'd at once that *Spirit of Religion,* and that *Innocence of the Golden Age,* so necessary to be observed by all Writers of Pastoral.

At the Conclusion of this Piece, the Author reconciles the Lovers, and ends the Eclogue the most Simply in the World.

　　　　So Rager *parted vor to vetch tha Kee,*
　　　　And vor her Bucket in went Cicily.

I am loath to show my Fondness for Antiquity so far as to prefer this Ancient *British* Author to our present *English* Writers of Pastoral; but

16 "Roger, go fetch the cow, or else the sun,
　　Will quite be gone, before I have half done."
17 "Thou shouldst not ask me twice, but I have been
　　To drive our bull to bull the parson's cow."
18 **chez**: "I was," making "was" in the line a redundant word.
19 **Wake**: probably a parish festival of some kind.

I cannot avoid making this obvious Remark, that both *Spencer* and *Philips* have hit into the same Road with this old *West Country* Bard of ours.

After all that hath been said, I hope none can think it any Injustice to Mr. *Pope*, that I forbore to mention him as a Pastoral Writer; since upon the whole, he is of the same Class with *Moschus* and *Bion*,[20] whom we have excluded that Rank; and of whose Eclogues, as well as some of *Virgil's*, it may be said, that according to the Description we have given of this sort of Poetry, they are by no means *Pastorals*, but *something Better*.

[20] **Moschus and Bion:** celebrated Greek bucolic poets of the second century B.C.

MARTINUS SCRIBLERUS

ΠΕΡΙ ΒΑΘΟΤΣ

OR

Of the Art of Sinking in Poetry

WRITTEN IN THE YEAR 1727

CONTENTS

CHAP. I

IT hath been long (my dear Countrymen) the Subject of my Concern and Surprize, that whereas numberless Poets, Criticks and Orators have compiled and digested the Art of *Ancient Poesie,* there hath not arisen among us one Person so publick spirited, as to perform the like for the *Modern.* Altho' it is universally known, that our every-way-industrious Moderns, both in the Weight of their *Writings,* and in the Velocity of their *Judgments,* do so infinitely excel the said Ancients.

NEVERTHELESS, too true it is, that while a plain and direct Road is pav'd to their ὕψος, or *sublime;* no Track has been yet chalk'd out, to arrive at our βα'θος, or *profound.* The *Latins,* as they came between the *Greeks* and Us, make use of the Word *Altitudo,* which implies equally *Height* and *Depth.* Wherefore considering with no small Grief, how many promising Genius's of this Age are wandering (as I may say) in the dark without a Guide, I have undertaken this arduous but necessary Task, to lead them as it were by the hand, and step by step, the gentle down-hill way to the *Bathos;* the Bottom, the End, the Central Point, the *non plus ultra*[1] of true Modern Poesie!

WHEN I consider (my dear Countrymen) the Extent, Fertility, and Populousness of our *Lowlands* of *Parnassus,* the flourishing State of our Trade, and the Plenty of our Manufacture; there are two Reflections which administer great Occasion of Surprize; the one, that all Dignities and Honours should be bestow'd upon the exceeding few meager Inhabitants of the Top of the Mountain; the other, that our own Nation should have arriv'd to that Pitch of Greatness it now possesses, without any regular *System of Laws.*[2] As to the first, it is with great Pleasure I have observ'd of late the gradual Decay of Delicacy and Refinement among Mankind, who are become too reasonable to require that we should labour with infinite Pains to come up

PERI BATHOUS: First published on March 8, 1728, only two months before the first appearance of the *Dunciad. Peri Bathous* is generally ascribed to Pope, though it is also understood that he probably received aid and encouragement in the work from fellow members of the Scriblerus Club, particularly from Swift and Dr. Arbuthnot. A satire on the false taste, bad writing, and commercial values which seemed to characterize much contemporary literature, the work pretends to come from the hand of a bookish numskull, Martinus Scriblerus, whose fictive personality was the joint creation of members of the Scriblerus Club (see the first note to that section of the *Dunciad* entitled "Martinus Scriblerus of the Poem"). As his title suggests, Pope modeled his work on *Peri Hupsous* (i.e., *On the Sublime*), a treatise generally attributed to the third-century Greek critic, Longinus. *Bathos* can mean either *height* or *depth,* and Pope ironically exploits the ambiguities inherent in this term as well as in such a word as *profound.* He was also the first in English to use the word *bathos* to suggest a ludicrous descent from the elevated to the low or commonplace.

[1] non plus ultra: uttermost point.
[2] Laws: rules of art.

to the Taste of those Mountaineers, when they without any, may condescend to ours. But as we have now an *unquestionable Majority* on our side, I doubt not but we shall shortly be able to level the *Highlanders*, and procure a farther Vent for our own Product, which is already so much relish'd, encourag'd, and rewarded, by the Nobility and Gentry of *Great Britain*.

THEREFORE to supply our former Defect, I purpose to collect the scatter'd Rules of our Art into regular Institutes,[3] from the Example and Practice of the deep Genius's of our Nation; imitating herein my Predecessors, the Master of *Alexander*,[4] and the Secretary of the renown'd *Zenobia*:[5] And in this my Undertaking I am the more animated, as I expect more Success than has attended even those great Criticks, since their Laws (tho' they might be good) have ever been slackly executed, and their Precepts (however strict) obey'd only by Fits, and by a very small Number.

AT the same time I intend to do justice upon our Neighbours, Inhabitants of the *upper Parnassus;* who taking advantage of the rising Ground, are perpetually throwing down Rubbish, Dirt, and Stones upon us, never suffering us to live in Peace: These Men, while they enjoy the Chrystal Stream of *Helicon*,[6] envy us our common Water, which (thank our Stars) tho' it is somewhat muddy, flows in much greater abundance. Nor is this the greatest injustice that we have to complain of; for tho' it is evident that we never made the least *Attempt* or *Inrode* into *their* Territories, but lived contented in our Native Fens;[7] they have often, not only committed *Petty Larcenys* upon our Borders, but driven the Country, and carried off at once *whole Cartloads* of our *Manufacture;* to reclaim some of which stolen Goods is part of the Design of this Treatise.

FOR we shall see in the course of this Work, that our greatest Adversaries have sometimes descended towards us; and doubtless might now and then have arrived at the *Bathos* itself, had it not been for that mistaken Opinion they all entertained, that the *Rules* of the *Antients* were *equally necessary* to the *Moderns,* than which there cannot be a more grievous Error, as will be amply proved in the following Discourse.

AND indeed when any of these have gone so far, as by the light of their own Genius to attempt upon *new Models*, it is wonderful to observe, how nearly they have approach'd Us in those particular Pieces; tho' in their others they differ'd *toto cœlo*[8] from us.

---

3 **Institutes:** collections of precepts or principles.
4 **Master of Alexander:** Aristotle, tutor to Alexander the Great.
5 **Secretary . . . Zenobia:** Longinus was secretary to Zenobia, a celebrated queen of Palmyra.
6 **Helicon:** the Greek mountain supposed the residence of Apollo and the Muses, and the site of Hippocrene, the spring thought to inspire poets.
7 **Fens:** muddy marshlands.
8 **toto cœlo:** by the whole extent of the heavens (i.e., poles apart).

CHAP. II

That the Bathos, *or Profund, is the natural Taste of Man, and in particular, of the present Age.*

THE Taste of the *Bathos* is implanted by Nature itself in the Soul of Man; 'till perverted by Custom or Example he is taught, or rather compell'd, to relish the *Sublime.* Accordingly, we see the unprejudiced Minds of Children delight only in such Productions, and in such Images, as our true modern Writers set before them. I have observ'd how fast the general Taste is returning to this first Simplicity and Innocence; and if the Intent of all Poetry be to divert and instruct, certainly that Kind which diverts and instructs the greatest Number, is to be preferr'd. Let us look round among the Admirers of Poetry, we shall find those who have a Taste of the *Sublime* to be very few, but the *Profound* strikes universally, and is adapted to every Capacity. 'Tis a fruitless Undertaking to write for Men of a nice and foppish *Gusto,*[9] whom, after all, it is almost impossible to please; and 'tis still more Chimerical[10] to write for *Posterity,* of whose Taste we cannot make any Judgment, and whose Applause we can never enjoy. It must be confess'd, our wiser Authors have a present End,

Et prodesse volunt, & delectare Poetæ:[11]

Their true Design is *Profit* or *Gain;* in order to acquire which, 'tis necessary to procure Applause, by administring *Pleasure* to the Reader: From whence it follows demonstrably, that their Productions must be suited to the *present Taste;* and I cannot but congratulate our Age on this peculiar Felicity, that tho' we have made indeed great Progress in all other Branches of Luxury, we are not yet debauch'd with any *high relish* in Poetry, but are in this one Taste, less *nice* than our Ancestors. If an Art is to be estimated by its Success, I appeal to Experience, whether there have not been, in proportion to their Number, as many starving good Poets, as bad ones?

NEVERTHELESS, in making *Gain* the principal End of our Art, far be it from me to exclude any great *Genius's* of *Rank* or *Fortune* from diverting themselves this way. They ought to be praised no less than those Princes, who pass their vacant Hours in some ingenious Mechanical or Manual Art: And to such as these, it would be Ingratitude not to own, that our Art has been often infinitely indebted.

---

[9] **nice:** fastidious, delicate.   **Gusto:** taste.
[10] **Chimerical:** visionary, fantastic.
[11] "Poets wish to profit and to please." Scriblerus misquotes slightly, and bends to his own purposes, l. 333 of Horace's *Ars Poetica.*

CHAP. III

The Necessity of the Bathos, *Physically consider'd.*

FARTHERMORE, it were great Cruelty and Injustice, if all such Authors as cannot write in the other Way, were prohibited from writing at all. Against this, I draw an Argument from what seems to me an undoubted Physical Maxim, That Poetry is a *natural* or *morbid*[12] *Secretion from the Brain.* As I would not suddenly stop a Cold in the Head, or dry up my Neighbour's Issue,[13] I would as little hinder him from necessary Writing. It may be affirm'd with great truth, that there is hardly any human Creature past Childhood, but at one time or other has had some Poetical Evacuation, and no question was much the better for it in his Health; so true is the Saying, *Nascimur Poetæ:*[14] Therefore is the Desire of Writing properly term'd *Pruritus,*[15] the *Titillation of the Generative Faculty of the Brain;* and the Person is said to *conceive;* Now such as conceive must *bring forth.* I have known a Man thoughtful, melancholy, and raving for divers days, who forthwith grew wonderfully easy, lightsome and cheerful, upon a Discharge of the peccant Humour,[16] in exceeding purulent[17] Metre. Nor can I question, but abundance of untimely Deaths are occasion'd for want of this laudable Vent of unruly Passions; yea, perhaps, in poor Wretches, (which is very lamentable) for meer Want of Pen, Ink, and Paper! From hence it follows, that a Suppression of the very worst Poetry is of dangerous consequence to the State: We find by Experience, that the same Humours which vent themselves in Summer in *Ballads* and *Sonnets,* are condens'd by the Winter's Cold into *Pamphlets* and *Speeches* for and against the *Ministry:* Nay I know not, but many times a Piece of Poetry may be the most innocent Composition of a *Minister himself.*

It is therefore manifest that *Mediocrity* ought to be allow'd, yea indulg'd, to the good Subjects of *England.* Nor can I conceive how the World has swallow'd the contrary as a Maxim, upon the single Authority of that *Horace?*[18] Why should the *Golden Mean,* and Quintessence

---

[12] **morbid:** unwholesome.
[13] **issue:** any bodily discharge or flux.
[14] **Nascimur Poetæ:** poets are born (not made).
[15] **Pruritus:** itching.
[16] **peccant:** unhealthy, sinning.   **Humour:** a term alluding to the fluids of the body, the relative proportions of which were traditionally thought to influence a person's character or disposition (see *Rape of the Lock,* I 58n.).
[17] **purulent:** full of pus.
[18] **Horace:**   —— *Mediocribus esse poetis*
           Non dii, non homines, &c. Hor.   P.
Horace (*Ars Poetica,* ll. 372–3) says that neither gods nor men nor booksellers ever pardoned mediocrity in poets.

of all Virtues, be deem'd so offensive in this Art? Or *Coolness* or *Mediocrity* be so amiable a Quality in a Man, and so detestable in a Poet?

However, far be it from me to compare these Writers with those *Great Spirits*, who are born with a *Vivacité de pesanteur*, or (as an *English* Author[19] calls it) an *Alacrity of sinking*; and who by *Strength of Nature* alone can excell. All I mean is to evince the *Necessity* of Rules to these lesser Genius's, as well as the *Usefulness* of them to the Greater.

[19] **English Author:** Shakespeare, *Merry Wives of Windsor,* III v 13.

CHAP. IV

That there is an Art of the Bathos, *or* Profund.

WE come now to prove, that there is an *Art of Sinking* in Poetry. Is there not an Architecture of Vaults and Cellars, as well as of lofty Domes and Pyramids? Is there not as much Skill and Labour in making *Dykes*,[1] as in raising *Mounts*? Is there not an Art of *Diving* as well as of *Flying*? And will any sober Practitioner affirm, That a diving Engine[2] is not of singular Use in making him long-winded, assisting his Sight, and furnishing him with other ingenious means of keeping under Water?

IF we search the Authors of Antiquity, we shall find as few to have been distinguish'd in the *true Profund*, as in the *true Sublime*. And the very same thing (as it appears from *Longinus*) had been imagin'd of that, as now of this; namely, that it was entirely the Gift of Nature. I grant, that to excel in the *Bathos* a Genius is requisite; yet the Rules of Art must be allow'd so far useful, as to add Weight, or as I may say, hang on Lead, to facilitate and enforce our Descent, to guide us to the most advantageous Declivities, and habituate our Imagination to a Depth of thinking. Many there are that can fall, but few can arrive at the Felicity of falling gracefully; much more for a Man who is amongst the lowest of the Creation at the very bottom of the Atmosphere, to descend *beneath himself,* is not so easy a Task unless he calls in Art to his Assistance. It is with the *Bathos* as with small Beer,[3] which is indeed vapid and insipid, if left at large and let abroad; but being by our Rules confin'd, and well stopt, nothing grows so frothy, pert and bouncing.

THE *Sublime* of Nature is the Sky, the Sun, Moon, Stars, &c. The *Profund* of Nature is Gold, Pearls, precious Stones, and the Treasures of the Deep, which are inestimable as unknown. But all that lies between these, as Corn, Flowers, Fruits, Animals, and Things for the meer Use of Man, are of mean price,[4] and so common as not to be greatly esteem'd by the Curious:[5] It being certain, that any thing, of which we know the true Use, cannot be Invaluable: Which affords a Solution, why *common* Sense hath either been totally despis'd, or held in small Repute, by the greatest modern Criticks and Authors.

---

1 **Dykes:** ditches.
2 **diving Engine:** a diving bell (in use in England for at least a century).
3 **small Beer:** (1) weak beer; (2) trifles.
4 **mean price:** low or inferior value.
5 **Curious:** those considered connoisseurs.

CHAP. V

Of the true Genius for the Profund, *and by what it is constituted.*

A ND I will venture to lay it down, as the first Maxim and Corner-Stone of this our Art, That whoever would excell therein must studiously avoid, detest, and turn his Head from all the Ideas, Ways, and Workings of that pestilent Foe to Wit and Destroyer of fine Figures, which is known by the Name of *Common Sense.* His Business must be to contract the true *Gout de travers;*[6] and to acquire a most *happy, uncommon, unaccountable Way of Thinking.*

HE is to consider himself as a *Grotesque* Painter, whose Works would be spoil'd by an Imitation of Nature, or Uniformity of Design. He is to mingle Bits of the most various, or discordant kinds, Landscape, History, Portraits, Animals, and connect them with a great deal of *Flourishing,* by *Heads* or *Tails,* as it shall please his Imagination, and contribute to his principal End, which is to glare by strong Oppositions of Colours, and surprize by Contrariety of Images.

Serpentes avibus geminentur, tigribus agni.[7]

His Design ought to be like a Labyrinth, out of which no body can get clear but himself. And since the great Art of all Poetry is to mix Truth with Fiction, in order to join the Credible with the Surprizing; our Author shall produce the *Credible,* by painting Nature in her *lowest Simplicity;* and the *Surprizing,* by contradicting *Common Opinion.* In the very *Manners*[8] he will affect the Marvellous; he will draw *Achilles* with the Patience of *Job;* a Prince talking like a Jack-pudding;[9] a Maid of Honour selling *Bargains;*[10] a Footman speaking like a Philosopher; and a fine Gentleman like a Scholar. Whoever is conversant in *modern Plays,* may make a most noble Collection of this kind, and at the same time, form a compleat Body of *Modern Ethicks and Morality.*

NOTHING seem'd more plain to our great Authors, than that the World had long been weary of natural Things. How much the contrary are form'd to please, is evident from the universal Applause daily given to the admirable Entertainments of *Harlequins* and *Magicians* on our Stage.[11] When an Audience behold a Coach turn'd into a Wheel-bar-

---

[6] **Gout de travers:** perverse taste.
[7] "Serpents couple with birds, lambs with tigers" — Horace, *Ars Poetica,* l. 13.
[8] **Manners:** social conduct, ethical deportment.
[9] **Jack-pudding:** buffoon.
[10] **selling Bargains:** engaging in bawdy repartee.
[11] **Harlequins:** see *Fourth Sat. of Dr. Donne,* l. 125n.   **Magicians on our Stage:** see *Dunciad,* III 233*ff.*

row, a Conjurer into an Old Woman, or a Man's Head where his Heels should be; how are they struck with Transport and Delight? Which can only be imputed to this Cause, that each Object is chang'd into That which hath been suggested to them by their own low Ideas before.

HE ought therefore to render himself Master of this happy and anti-natural way of thinking to such a degree, as to be able, on the appearance of any Object, to furnish his Imagination with Ideas infinitely below it. And his Eyes should be like unto the wrong end of a Perspective Glass,[12] by which all the Objects of Nature are lessen'd.

FOR example, when a true Genius looks upon the *Sky*, he immediately catches the Idea of a Piece of *Blue Lutestring*,[13] or a *Child's Mantle*.

> *The Skies, whose spreading Volumes scarce have room,*
> *Spun thin, and wove in Nature's finest Loom,*
> *The* new-born *World in* their soft Lap *embrac'd,*
> *And all around their* starry Mantle *cast.*[14]

IF he looks upon a *Tempest*, he shall have an Image of a tumbled Bed, and describe a succeeding Calm in this manner,

> *The Ocean joy'd to see the Tempest fled,*
> New lays *his Waves and* smooths his ruffled Bed.[15]

THE *Triumphs* and *Acclamations* of the *Angels*, at the Creation of the Universe, present to his Imagination the *Rejoicings of the Lord Mayor's Day;*[16] and he beholds those glorious Beings celebrating the Creator, by Huzzaing, making Illuminations, and flinging Squibbs, Crackers and Sky-rockets.

> *Glorious* Illuminations, *made on high*
> *By all the Stars and Planets of the Sky,*
> *In* just Degrees, *and* shining Order *plac'd,*
> *Spectators charm'd, and the* blest Dwelling *grac'd.*
> *Thro' all th' enlighten'd Air swift* Fireworks *flew,*
> *Which with repeated* Shouts *glad Cherubs* threw.
> *Comets* ascended with their sweeping Train,
> *Then fell in* starry Showers *and* glittering Rain.
> *In Air ten thousand Meteors* blazing hung,
> *Which from th' Eternal* Battlements *were* flung.[17]

12 **Perspective Glass:** spy-glass.
13 **Lutestring:** a kind of glossy silk fabric.
14 *Prince Arthur*, pp. 41, 42.
  N.B. In order to do justice to these great Poets, our Citations are taken from the best, the last, and most correct Editions of their Works. That which we use of Prince *Arthur*, is in *duodecimo*, 1714. The fourth Edition, *revised*. P. *Prince Arthur* was the first of the many epics written by Sir Richard Blackmore (see *Dunciad*, II 268n.).   15 P. 14 [of *Prince Arthur*].   P.
16 **Lord Mayor's Day:** see *Dunciad*, I 85–6n.   17 P. 50.   P.

IF a Man who is violently fond of *Wit*, will sacrifice to that Passion his Friend or his God; would it not be a shame, if he who is smit with the Love of the *Bathos* should not sacrifice to it all other transitory Regards? You shall hear a zealous Protestant Deacon invoke a Saint, and modestly beseech her to do more for us than Providence.

> *Look down, blest Saint, with Pity then look down,*
> *Shed on this Land thy kinder Influence,*
> *And guide us through the Mists of Providence,*
> *In which we stray.* ———— 18

Neither will he, if a goodly Simile come in his way, scruple to affirm himself an Eye-witness of things never yet beheld by Man, or never in Existence; as thus,

> *Thus have I seen, in* Araby *the blest,*
> A Phœnix *couch'd upon her Fun'ral Nest.* 19

BUT to convince you, that nothing is so great which a marvellous Genius, prompted by this laudable Zeal, is not able to lessen; hear how the most Sublime of all Beings is represented in the following Images.

First he is a PAINTER.

> *Sometimes the Lord of Nature in the Air,*
> Spreads forth *his Clouds, his* sable Canvass *where*
> *His* Pencil, dipt *in heavenly* Colour *bright*,
> Paints *his fair Rain-bow, charming to the Sight.* 1

Now he is a CHYMIST.

> *Th'* Almighty Chymist *does his Work prepare*,
> *Pours down his* Waters *on the thirsty Plain*,
> Digests 2 *his Lightning, and* distills *his Rain.* 3

Now he is a WRESTLER.

> *Me in his* griping Arms *th' Eternal took,*
> *And with such* mighty Force *my* Body shook,
> *That the* strong Grasp *my Members* sorely bruis'd,
> Broke *all* my Bones, *and all my* Sinews loos'd. 4

18 A. Philips on the Death of Queen Mary. P. For Ambrose Philips, see *Ep. to Dr. Arbuthnot*, l. 100n.

19 Anon. P. The phoenix was a bird fabled to live 500 years, then to be consumed in fire by its own act, and finally to arise in youthful freshness from its own ashes.

1 *Blackm., Job.* opt. edit. [i.e., best edition], *duod.* 1716, pag. 172. P.

2 **Digests:** melts or softens by heat and moisture (in chemical terminology).

3 *Black.*, Ps[alm]. 104, p. 263. P. Blackmore's volume entitled *A Paraphrase on the Book of Job* contained translations of certain psalms and also of passages from other books of the Bible.

4 Pag. 75 [of *Job*]. P.

Now a Recruiting Officer.

For Clouds the Sun-Beams levy fresh Supplies,
And raise Recruits *of Vapours, which arise,*
Drawn *from the Seas, to* muster *in the Skies.*[5]

Now a peaceable Guarantee.

In Leagues *of* Peace *the* Neighbours *did agree,*
And to maintain them, God was Guarantee.[6]

Then he is an Attorney.

Job, *as a vile Offender, God* indites,
And terrible Decrees against me writes. —
God will not be my Advocate,
My Cause *to* manage, *or* debate.[7]

In the following Lines he is a Gold-beater.

Who the rich Metal beats, *and then, with Care,*
Unfolds *the* Golden Leaves, *to* gild *the Fields of Air.*[8]

Then a Fuller.[9]

—— *th' exhaling Reeks that secret rise,*
Born on rebounding Sun-beams thro' the Skies;
Are thicken'd, wrought, *and* whiten'd, *'till they grow*
A Heavenly Fleece. ——[10]

A Mercer,[11] or Packer.

Didst thou one End *of Air's wide* Curtain *hold,*
And help the Bales *of* Æther *to* unfold;
Say, which cerulian[12] Pile *was by thy Hand* unroll'd?[13]

A Butler.

He measures all the Drops *with* wondrous Skill,
Which the black Clouds, *his floating Bottles, fill.*[14]

And a Baker.

God in the Wilderness his Table spread,
And in his Airy Ovens bak'd their Bread.[15]

[5] Pag. 170. P.
[6] Pag. 70. P.
[7] Pag. 61. P.
[8] Pag. 181. P.
[9] **Fuller:** one who cleans and thickens cloth by treading or beating it.
[10] Pag. 180. P.
[11] **Mercer:** a dealer in fabrics.
[12] **cerulian:** sky-blue.
[13] Pag. 174. P.
[14] Page 131. P.
[15] *Black.,* Song of Moses, p. 218. P.

CHAP. VI

Of the several Kinds of Genius's in the Profund,
and the Marks and Characters of each.

I DOUBT not but the Reader, by this *Cloud* of Examples, begins to be convinc'd of the Truth of our Assertion, that the *Bathos* is an *Art;* and that the Genius of no Mortal whatever, following the meer Ideas of Nature, and unassisted with an habitual, nay laborious Peculiarity of thinking, could arrive at Images so wonderfully low and unaccountable. The great Author,[16] from whose Treasury we have drawn all these Instances (the Father of the *Bathos,* and indeed the *Homer* of it) has like that immortal *Greek,* confin'd his Labours to the greater Poetry,[17] and thereby left room for others to acquire a due share of Praise in inferiour kinds. Many Painters who could never hit a Nose or an Eye, have with Felicity copied a Small-Pox, or been admirable at a Toad or a Red-Herring.[18] And seldom are we without *Genius's* for *Still Life,* which they can work up and stiffen with incredible Accuracy.

AN universal Genius rises not in an Age; but when he rises, Armies rise in him! he pours forth five or six Epick Poems[19] with greater Facility, than five or six Pages can be produc'd by an elaborate and servile copyer after Nature or the Ancients. It is affirm'd by *Quintilian,*[1] that the same Genius which made *Germanicus*[2] so great a General, would with equal Application have made him an excellent Heroic Poet. In like manner, reasoning from the Affinity there appears between Arts and Sciences, I doubt not but an active Catcher of Butterflies, a careful and fanciful Pattern-drawer, an industrious Collector of Shells, a laborious and tuneful Bagpiper, or a diligent Breeder of tame Rabbits, might severally excel in their respective parts of the *Bathos.*

I SHALL range these confin'd and less copious Genius's under proper Classes, and (the better to give their Pictures to the Reader) under the Names of Animals of some sort or other; whereby he will be enabled, at the first sight of such as shall daily come forth, to know to what *Kind* to refer, and with what *Authors* to compare them.

1. THE *Flying Fishes;* these are Writers who now and then *rise* upon

---

16 **great Author:** Blackmore.
17 **greater Poetry:** epic poetry.
18 **Red-Herring:** a herring dried and smoked so as to turn red.
19 **five or six Epick Poems:** see *Dunciad,* II 268n.
1 **Quintilian:** the Latin rhetorician (see *Essay on Criticism,* l. 669n.).
2 **Germanicus:** Germanicus Julius Caesar (d. 19 A.D.), a celebrated and beloved Roman general.

their *Fins*, and fly out of the *Profund;* but their Wings are soon *dry*, and they drop down to the *Bottom.* G.S. A.H. C.G.[3]

2. THE *Swallows* are Authors that are eternally *skimming* and *fluttering* up and down, but all their Agility is employ'd to *catch Flies.* L.T. W.P. Lord H.

3. THE *Ostridges* are such whose Heaviness rarely permits them to raise themselves from the Ground; their Wings are of no use to lift them up, and their Motion is between *flying* and *walking;* but then they *run* very fast. D.F. L.E. The Hon. E.H.

4. THE *Parrots* are they that repeat *another's Words,* in such a *hoarse, odd* Voice, as makes them seem *their own.* W.B. W.H. C.C. The Reverend D.D.

5. THE *Didappers*[4] are Authors that keep themselves long *out of sight,* under water, and *come up* now and then where you *least expected* them. L.W. G.D. Esq; The Hon. Sir W.Y.

6. THE *Porpoises* are unweildly and big; they put all their Numbers into a great *Turmoil* and *Tempest,* but whenever they appear in *plain Light,* (which is seldom) they are only *shapeless* and *ugly Monsters.* J.D. C.G. J.O.

7. THE *Frogs* are such as can neither *walk* nor *fly,* but can *leap* and *bound* to admiration: They live generally in the *Bottom of a Ditch,* and make a *great Noise* whenever they thrust their *Heads above Water.* E.W. J.M. Esq; T.D. Gent.

8. THE *Eels* are obscure Authors, that wrap themselves up in their *own Mud,* but are mighty *nimble* and *pert.* L.W. L.T. P.M. General C.

9. THE *Tortoises* are *slow* and *chill,* and like *Pastoral* Writers delight much in *Gardens:* they have for the most part a *fine embroider'd Shell,* and underneath it, a *heavy Lump.* A.P. W.B. L.E. The Rt. Hon. E. of S.

THESE are the chief Characteristicks of the *Bathos,* and in each of these kinds we have the comfort to be bless'd with sundry and manifold choice Spirits in this our Island.

---

[3] G.S. A.H. C.G.: In a note to the *Dunciad* Pope refers to this chapter of *Peri Bathous* and says: "the Species of bad Writers were rang'd in Classes, and initial Letters of Names prefix'd, for the most part at random. But such was the number of Poets eminent in that Art [of sinking], that some one or other took every Letter to himself." No attempt will be made here to decipher the initials, for it seems impossible to do so with any certainty (though of course any student of Pope's poetry will be able to make some shrewd guesses). And in any event, as Pope said of the names to be found in the *Dunciad,* the reader should not be "too much troubled or anxious, if he cannot decipher them; since when he shall have found them out, he will probably know no more of the Persons than before."

[4] **Didappers:** small diving ducks.

CHAP. VII

Of the Profund, *when it consists in the Thought.*

WE have already laid down the Principles upon which our Author is to proceed, and the Manner of forming his Thought by familiarizing his Mind to the lowest Objects; to which it may be added, that *vulgar Conversation* will greatly contribute. There is no Question but the *Garret* or the *Printer's Boy* may often be discern'd in the Compositions made in such Scenes, and Company; and much of Mr. *Curl*[5] himself has been insensibly infused into the Works of his learned Writers.

THE Physician, by the Study and Inspection of Urine and Ordure, approves[6] himself in the Science; and in like sort should our Author accustom and exercise his Imagination upon the Dregs of Nature.

THIS will render his Thoughts truly and fundamentally Low, and carry him many fathoms beyond Mediocrity. For, certain it is, (tho' some lukewarm Heads imagine they may be safe by temporizing between the Extreams) that where there is not a Triticalness[7] or Mediocrity in the *Thought*, it can never be sunk into the genuine and perfect *Bathos*, by the most elaborate low *Expression:* It can, at most, be only carefully obscured, or metaphorically debased. But 'tis the *Thought* alone that strikes, and gives the whole that Spirit, which we admire and stare at. For instance, in that ingenious Piece on a Lady's drinking the *Bath*-Waters.

> She drinks! She drinks! Behold the matchless Dame!
> To her 'tis Water, but to us 'tis Flame:
> Thus Fire is Water, Water Fire, by turns,
> And the same Stream at once both cools and burns.[8]

WHAT can be more easy and unaffected than the *Diction* of these Verses? 'Tis the Turn of *Thought* alone, and the Variety of Imagination, that charm and surprize us. And when the same Lady goes into the Bath, the Thought (as in justness it ought) goes still deeper.

> Venus *beheld her, 'midst her Crowd of Slaves,*
> *And thought* Herself *just risen from the Waves.*[9]

How much out of the way of common Sense is this Reflection of *Venus,* not knowing herself from the Lady?

[5] **Curl:** the notorious piratical bookseller, Edmund Curll (see *Ep. to Dr. Arbuthnot,* l. 53*n.*).
[6] **approves:** tests.
[7] **Triticalness:** a word combining the implications of *trite* and *critical.*
[8] Anon. P.   [9] Idem. P.

OF the same nature is that noble Mistake of a frightened Stag in **a** full Chace, who (saith the Poet)

> *Hears his own Feet, and thinks they sound like more;*
> *And fears the hind Feet will o'ertake the fore.*[10]

So astonishing as these are, they yield to the following, which is *Profundity* itself,

> *None but* Himself *can be his* Parallel.[11]

unless it may seem borrow'd from the Thought of that *Master of a Show* in *Smithfield*,[12] who writ in large Letters, over the Picture of his Elephant,

> *This is the greatest Elephant in the World, except* Himself.

HOWEVER our next Instance is certainly an Original: Speaking of a beautiful Infant,

> *So fair thou art, that if great* Cupid *be*
> *A Child, as Poets say, sure* thou art He.
> *Fair* Venus *would mistake thee for her own,*
> *Did not thy Eyes proclaim thee* not her Son.
> *There all the Lightnings of thy* Mother's *shine,*
> *And with a fatal Brightness* kill *in* thine.[13]

FIRST he is *Cupid,* then he is not *Cupid;* first *Venus* would mistake him, then she would not mistake him; next his Eyes are his Mother's; and lastly they are not his Mother's but his own.

ANOTHER Author, describing a Poet that shines forth amidst a Circle of Criticks,

> *Thus* Phœbus *thro' the Zodiack takes his way,*
> *And amid* Monsters *rises into Day.*[14]

WHAT a Peculiarity is here of Invention? The Author's Pencil, like the Wand of *Circe*,[15] turns all into *Monsters* at a Stroke. A great Genius takes things in the Lump, without stopping at minute Considerations: In vain might the Ram, the Bull, the Goat, the Lion, the Crab, the Scorpion, the Fishes, all stand in his way, as mere natural Animals:

---

[10] The lines have not been identified.
[11] Theobald, *Double Falsehood.* P.   For Theobald, see *Ep. to Dr. Arbuthnot*, l. 164n., and first note to the *Dunciad*.
[12] Smithfield: see *Dunciad*, I 2n.
[13] The lines are from *On the Birthday of Mr. Robert Trefusis*, by the Rev. William Broome (1689–1745), one of Pope's collaborators in the translation of the *Odyssey*.
[14] The lines are from Broome's *Epistle to My Friend Mr. Elijah Fenton.*
[15] Circe: see *Dunciad*, IV 525–8n.

much more might it be pleaded that a pair of Scales, an old Man, and two innocent Children, were no Monsters: There were only the Centaur and the Maid that could be esteem'd out of Nature. But what of that? with a Boldness peculiar to these daring Genius's, what he found not Monsters, he made so.

CHAP. VIII

Of the Profund *consisting in the Circumstances,*[16] *and of Amplification and Periphrase in general.*

WHAT in a great measure distinguishes other Writers from ours, is their chusing and separating such Circumstances in a Description as ennoble or elevate the Subject.

THE Circumstances which are most natural are obvious, therefore not astonishing or peculiar. But those that are far-fetch'd, or unexpected, or hardly compatible, will surprize prodigiously. These therefore we must principally hunt out; but above all, preserve a laudable *Prolixity;*[17] presenting the Whole and every Side at once of the Image to view. For Choice and Distinction are not only a Curb to the Spirit, and limit the Descriptive Faculty, but also lessen the Book, which is frequently of the worst consequence of all to our Author.[18]

WHEN *Job* says in short, *He wash'd his Feet in Butter,* (a Circumstance some Poets would have soften'd, or past over) now hear how this Butter is spread out by the Great Genius.

> *With Teats distended with their milky Store,*
> *Such num'rous lowing Herds, before my Door,*
> *Their painful Burden to unload did meet,*
> *That we with Butter might have wash'd our Feet.*[19]

How cautious! and particular! He had (says our Author) so many Herds, which Herds thriv'd so well, and thriving so well, gave so much Milk, and that Milk produc'd so much Butter, that if he *did not,* he *might* have wash'd his Feet in it.

THE ensuing Description of Hell is no less remarkable in the Circumstances.

> *In flaming Heaps the raging Ocean rolls,*
> *Whose livid Waves involve despairing Souls;*
> *The liquid Burnings dreadful Colours shew,*
> *Some deeply red, and others faintly blue.*[1]

COULD the most minute *Dutch* Painters[2] have been more exact? How inimitably circumstantial is this also of a War-Horse!

---

16 **Circumstances:** particulars, details.
17 **Prolixity:** here suggests a tedious abundance of detail.
18 The size of the book frequently determined the size of the author's profit.
19 *Blackm., Job,* p. 133.   P.
1 *Pr. Arth.,* p. 89.   P.
2 **Dutch Painters:** noted for their attention to detail.

His Eye-Balls burn, he wounds the smoking Plain,
And knots of scarlet Ribbond deck his Mane.[3]

Of certain Cudgel-Players:

They brandish high in Air their threatening Staves,
Their Hands a woven Guard of Ozier[4] *saves,*
In which, they fix their hazel weapon's end.[5]

Who would not think the Poet had past his whole Life at Wakes[6] in such laudable Diversions? since he teaches us how to hold, nay how to make a Cudgel!

Periphrase is another great Aid to *Prolixity;* being a diffus'd circumlocutory Manner of expressing a known Idea, which should be so misteriously couch'd, as to give the Reader the Pleasure of guessing what it is that the Author can possibly mean; and a strange Surprize when he finds it.

The Poet I last mention'd is incomparable in this Figure.

A waving Sea of Heads was round me spread,
And still fresh Streams the gazing Deluge fed.[7]

Here is a waving Sea of Heads, which by a fresh Stream of Heads, grows to be a gazing Deluge of Heads. You come at last to find it means a *great Crowd.*

How pretty and how genteel is the following.

Nature's Confectioner, ———
Whose Suckets are moist Alchimy:
The Still of his refining Mold,
Minting the Garden into Gold.[8]

What is this, but a *Bee* gathering Honey?

Little Syren of the Stage
Empty warbler, breathing Lyre,
Wanton Gale of fond desire,
Tuneful mischief, vocal Spell —.[9]

Who would think this was only a poor Gentlewoman that sung finely?

We may define *Amplification* to be making the most of a *Thought;* it is the spinning Wheel of the *Bathos,* which draws out and spreads it in

[3] Anon. P.

[4] **Ozier:** osier, a kind of willow whose pliable twigs could be used for various woven products.

[5] Pr. *Arth.,* p. 197. P.

[6] **Wakes:** celebrations on feast-days of patron saints; village sports were often a feature of these festivals.

[7] *Job,* p. 78. P.

[8] *Cleveland.* P.   The lines are from *Fuscara,* by John Cleveland (1613–58).

[9] Ph. to C——. P.   The reference is to Ambrose Philips's poem, *To Signora Cuzzoni.*

the finest Thread. There are Amplifiers who can extend half a dozen thin Thoughts over a whole Folio;[10] but for which, the Tale of many a vast Romance, and the Substance of many a fair Volume might be reduced into the size of a *Primmer.*

In the Book of *Job,* are these Words, *Hast thou commanded the Morning, and caused the Day Spring to know his Place?* How is this extended by the most celebrated Amplifier of our Age?

> *Canst thou set forth th' etherial* Mines on high,
> *Which the refulgent* Ore *of Light supply?*
> *Is the Celestial* Furnace *to thee known,*
> *In which I* melt *the golden* Metal *down?*
> *Treasures, from whence I* deal *out Light as fast,*
> *As all my Stars and* lavish Suns *can* waste.[11]

The same Author hath amplified a Passage in the 104th Psalm; *He looks on the Earth, and it trembles. He touches the Hills, and they smoke.*

> *The Hills* forget they're fix'd, *and in their Fright,*
> Cast off their Weight, *and* ease *themselves for flight:*
> *The Woods, with Terror* wing'd, out-fly *the Wind,*
> *And leave the* heavy, panting *Hills behind.*[12]

You here see the Hills not only trembling, but shaking off their Woods from their Backs, to run the faster: After this you are presented with a Foot Race of Mountains and Woods, where the Woods distance the Mountains, that like corpulent pursy[13] Fellows, come puffing and panting a vast way behind them.

---

10 **Folio:** a book of the largest size.
11 *Job,* p. 180.   P.
12 P. 267.   P.
13 pursy: shortwinded.

CHAP. IX

Of Imitation, and the manner of Imitating.

THAT the true Authors of the *Profund* are to imitate diligently the Examples in their own Way, is not to be question'd, and that divers have by this Means attain'd to a Depth whereunto their own Weight could never have carried them, is evident by sundry Instances. Who sees not that *DeFoe*[14] was the Poetical Son of *Withers, Tate* of *Ogilby, E. Ward* of *John Taylor,*[15] and *E——n*[16] of *Blackmore?* Therefore when we sit down to write, let us bring some great Author to our Mind, and ask our selves this Question; How would Sir *Richard* have said this? Do I express myself as simply as *Amb. Philips?* Or flow my Numbers with the quiet thoughtlessness of Mr. *Welsted?*[17]

BUT it may seem somewhat strange to assert, that our Proficient should also read the Works of those famous Poets who have excell'd in the Sublime: Yet is not this a Paradox? As *Virgil* is said to have read *Ennius,*[18] out of his Dunghill to draw Gold; so may our Author read *Shakespear, Milton,* and *Dryden,* for the contrary End, to bury their Gold in his own Dunghill. A true Genius, when he find any thing lofty or shining in them, will have the Skill to bring it down, take off the Gloss, or quite discharge the Colour, by some ingenious Circumstance, or Periphrase, some Addition, or Diminution, or by some of those Figures the use of which we shall shew in our next Chapter.

THE Book of *Job* is acknowledg'd to be infinitely sublime, and yet has not the Father of the *Bathos*[19] reduc'd it in every Page? Is there a Passage in all *Virgil* more painted up and labour'd[1] than the Description of *Ætna* in the Third *Æneid.*

> — *Horrificis juxta tonat Ætna ruinis,*
> *Interdumque atram prorumpit ad æthera nubem,*
> *Turbine fumantem piceo, & candente favilla,*
> *Attollitque globos flammarum, & sidera lambit.*
> *Interdum scopulos avulsaque viscera montis*
> *Erigit eructans, liquefactaque saxa sub auras*
> *Cum genitu glomerat, fundoque exæstuat imo.*[2]

14 **DeFoe:** see *Dunciad,* I 103n.
15 **Withers:** George Withers (see *Dunciad,* I 296n.). **Tate:** Nahum Tate (see *Ep. to Dr. Arbuthnot,* l. 190n.). **Ogilby:** John Ogilby (see *Dunciad,* I 141n.). **Ward:** Edward Ward (see *Dunciad,* I 233–4n.). For John Taylor, see *Dunciad,* III 19n.
16 **E——n:** Laurence Eusden (see *Ep. to Dr. Arbuthnot,* l. 15n.).
17 **Welsted:** Leonard Welsted (see *Ep. to Dr. Arbuthnot,* l. 375n.).
18 **Ennius:** known as the "father of Roman poetry," Ennius (239–169 B.C.) was an influence on Virgil. 19 **Father of the Bathos:** Blackmore.
1 **labour'd:** highly wrought. 2 *Aeneid,* III 571–7.

(I beg Pardon of the gentle *English* Reader, and such of our Writers as understand not *Latin*) Lo! how this is taken down by our *British* Poet, by the single happy Thought of throwing the Mountain into a Fit of *Cholic.*

> Ætna, *and all the burning Mountains, find*
> *Their kindled Stores with* inbred *Storms of* Wind
> Blown up *to Rage, and* roaring out, *complain,*
> As torn *with* inward Gripes, *and* torturing Pain:
> Lab'ring, they *cast* their dreadful Vomit *round,*
> And with their *melted Bowels, spread* the Ground.[3]

HORACE,[4] in search of the *Sublime,* struck his Head against the Stars; but *Empedocles,*[5] to fathom the *Profund,* threw himself into *Ætna:* And who but would imagine our excellent Modern had also been there, from this Description?

IMITATION is of two Sorts; the First is when we force to our own Purposes the Thoughts of others; The Second consists in copying the Imperfections, or Blemishes of celebrated Authors. I have seen a Play professedly writ in the Stile of *Shakespear,* wherein the Resemblance lay in one single Line,

> *And so good Morrow t'ye, good Master Lieutenant.*[6]

And sundry Poems in Imitation of *Milton,* where with the utmost Exactness, and not so much as one Exception, nevertheless was constantly *nathless,* embroider'd was *broider'd,* Hermits were *Eremites,* disdain'd was *'sdeign'd,* shady *umbrageous,* Enterprize *Emprize,* Pagan *Paynim,* Pinions *Pennons,* sweet *dulcet,* Orchards *Orchats,* Bridgework *Pontifical;* nay, her was *hir,* and their was *thir* thro' the whole Poem. And in very Deed, there is no other Way by which the true modern Poet could read to any purpose the Works of such Men as *Milton* and *Shakespear.*

IT may be expected, that like other Criticks, I should next speak of the PASSIONS: But as the main End and principal Effect of the *Bathos* is to produce *Tranquillity of Mind,* (and sure it is a better Design to promote Sleep than Madness) we have little to say on this Subject. Nor will the short Bounds of this Discourse allow us to treat at large of the *Emollients*[7] and *Opiats* of *Poesy,* of the *Cool,* and the Manner of producing it, or of the *Methods* us'd by our Authors in *managing* the *Passions.* I shall but transiently remark, that nothing contributes

---

[3] *Pr. Arth.,* Pag. 75.   P.

[4] **Horace:** *Sublimi feriam sidera vertice.*   P.   See *Carmina,* I i 36.

[5] Empedocles (493–433 B.C.), Greek poet, philosopher, and statesman, reportedly threw himself into the crater of Aetna so that his prophecy as to the time of his death would be fulfilled.

[6] The line is from *Lady Jane Gray,* by Nicholas Rowe (1674–1718).

[7] **Emollients:** softeners.

so much to the *Cool,* as the Use of *Wit*[8] in expressing Passion: The true Genius rarely fails of *Points,*[9] *Conceits,* and proper *Similes* on such Occasions: This we may term the *Pathetic epigrammatical,* in which even Puns are made use of with good Success. Hereby our best Authors have avoided throwing themselves or their Readers into any indecent Transports.

But as it is sometimes needful to excite the Passions of our Antagonist in the Polemic way, the true Students in the *Low* have constantly taken their Methods from *Low*-Life, where they observ'd, that to move *Anger,* use is made of *scolding* and *railing;* to move *Love,* of *Bawdry;* to beget *Favour* and Friendship, of gross *Flattery;* and to produce *Fear,* of calumniating an Adversary with *Crimes* obnoxious to the *State.* As for *Shame,* it is a silly Passion, of which as our Authors are incapable themselves, so they would not produce it in others.

[8] Wit: here means mere ingenuity.
[9] Points: ingenious turns of thought.

CHAP. X

Of Tropes[10] *and* Figures: *and first of the variegating, confounding, and reversing* Figures.

BUT we proceed to the *Figures*. We cannot too earnestly recommend to our Authors the Study of the *Abuse of Speech*. They ought to lay it down as a Principle, to say nothing in the usual way, but (if possible) in the direct contrary. Therefore the Figures must be so turn'd, as to manifest that intricate and wonderful *Cast of Head*, which distinguishes all Writers of this Kind; or (as I may say) to refer[11] exactly the *Mold* in which they were form'd, in all its *Inequalities, Cavities, Obliquities,* odd *Crannies,* and *Distortions.*

IT would be endless, nay impossible to enumerate all *such Figures;* but we shall content ourselves to range the Principal which most powerfully contribute to the *Bathos,* under three Classes.

> I. THE Variegating, Confounding, or Reversing *Tropes* and *Figures.*
>
> II. THE Magnifying, and
>
> III. THE Diminishing.

WE cannot avoid giving to these the *Greek* or *Roman* Names; but in Tenderness to our Countrymen and fellow Writers, many of whom, however exquisite,[12] are wholly ignorant of those Languages, we have also explain'd them in our Mother Tongue.

I. OF the First Sort, nothing so much conduces to the *Bathos,* as the

CATACHRESIS.[13]

A Master of this will say,

> *Mow* the Beard,
> *Shave* the Grass,
> *Pin* the Plank,
> *Nail* my Sleeve.

From whence results the same kind of Pleasure to the Mind, as to the Eye when we behold *Harlequin* trimming himself with a Hatchet, hewing down a Tree with a Rasor, making his Tea in a Cauldron, and

10 **Tropes:** figures of speech.
11 **refer:** reflect.
12 **exquisite:** accomplished.
13 **Catachresis:** improper use of words.

brewing his Ale in a Tea-pot, to the incredible Satisfaction of the *British* Spectator. Another Source of the *Bathos* is:

The METONYMY,

the Inversion of Causes for Effects, of Inventors for Inventions, &c.

> *Lac'd in her* Cosins *new appear'd the Bride,*
> *A* Bubble-boy *and* Tompion *at her Side,*
> *And with an Air divine her* Colmar *ply'd.*
> *Then oh! she cries, what Slaves I round me see?*
> *Here a bright* Redcoat, *there a smart* Toupee.[14]

The SYNECHDOCHE.

Which consists, in the Use of a *Part* for the *Whole;* you may call a young Woman sometimes Pretty-*face* and Pigs-*eyes*,[15] and sometimes Snotty-*nose* and Draggle-*tail*. Or of *Accidents* for *Persons;* as a Lawyer is call'd *Split-cause*, a Taylor *Prick-louse*, &c. Or of things belonging to a Man, for the Man himself; as a *Sword*-man, a *Gown*-man, a *T–m–T––d–man;* a *White-Staff*, a *Turn-key*, &c.[16]

The APOSIOPESIS.[17]

An excellent Figure for the Ignorant, as, *What shall I say?* when one has nothing to say; or *I can no more*, when one really can no more: Expressions which the gentle Reader is so good, as never to take in earnest.

The METAPHOR.

The first Rule is to draw it from the lowest things, which is a certain way to sink the highest; as when you speak of the Thunder of Heaven, say,

> *The* Lords above *are* angry *and* talk big.[18]

[14] One of Pope's early editors, Joseph Warton, said that "These five lines . . . are quoted from his own youthful poems, as indeed are most of those marked *Anonymous*."

The words *Cosins, Bubble-boy, Tompion, Colmar* and *Toupee* are explained thus by Pope: "*Stays, Tweezer-case, Watch, Fan,* and a sort of *Perriwig:* All Words in use this present Year 1727." Cosins is known to have been a corset-maker, and Thomas Tompion was a famous watchmaker.

[15] **Pigs-eyes:** *pigsney* (literally, *pig's* plus *eye*) was an archaic word meaning *dear,* or *darling.*

[16] **Gown-man:** a lawyer, clergyman or scholar.   **T–m–T––d––man:** a Tom Turdman, or "night man," one employed to empty cesspools during the night. **White-Staff:** the white rod carried as a symbol of office by the lord high treasurer and certain other officials.   **Turn-key:** jailer.

[17] **Aposiopesis:** a sudden halt or silence in speech (a stratagem used for rhetorical effect).

[18] Pope notes that the line comes from *The Rival Queens,* by Nathaniel Lee (1649–92).

IF you would describe a rich Man refunding his Treasures, express it thus,

> *Tho' he (as said) may Riches gorge, the Spoil*
> *Painful in massy Vomit shall recoil.*
> *Soon shall he perish with a swift Decay,*
> *Like his own Ordure, cast with Scorn away.*[19]

THE Second, that whenever you *start* a Metaphor, you must be sure to *Run it down,* and pursue it as far as it can go. If you get the Scent of a State Negotiation, follow it in this manner.

> *The Stones and all the Elements with thee*
> *Shall ratify a strict Confederacy;*
> *Wild Beasts their savage Temper shall forget,*
> *And for a firm Alliance with thee treat;*
> *The finny Tyrant of the spacious Seas*
> *Shall send a scaly Embassy for Peace:*
> *His plighted Faith the Crocodile shall keep,*
> *And seeing thee, for Joy sincerely weep.*[1]

OR if you represent the Creator denouncing War against the Wicked, be sure not to omit one Circumstance usual in proclaiming and levying War.

> *Envoys and Agents, who by my Command*
> *Reside in Palestina's Land,*
> *To whom Commissions I have given,*
> *To manage there the Interests of Heaven.*
> *Ye holy Heralds who proclaim*
> *Or War or Peace, in mine your Master's Name:*
> *Ye Pioneers of Heaven, prepare a Road,*
> *Make it plain, direct and broad; —*
> *For I in person will my People head;*
> *— For the divine Deliverer*
> *Will on his March in Majesty appear,*
> *And needs the Aid of no Confederate Pow'r.*[2]

UNDER the Article of the Confounding, we rank

1. The MIXTURE OF FIGURES,

which raises so many Images, as to give you no Image at all. But its principal Beauty is when it gives an Idea just opposite to what it seem'd meant to describe. Thus an ingenious Artist painting the

[19] *Black.*, Job, p. 91, 93.   P.
[1] *Job,* p. 22.   P.
[2] *Blackm.*, Isaiah, chap. 40.   P.

Spring, talks of a *Snow* of *Blossoms,* and thereby raises an unexpected Picture of *Winter.* Of this Sort is the following:

> *The gaping Clouds pour Lakes of Sulphur down,*
> *Whose livid flashes sickning Sunbeams drown.*[3]

WHAT a noble Confusion? Clouds, Lakes, Brimstone, Flames, Sunbeams, gaping, pouring, sickning, drowning! all in two Lines.

2. The JARGON,

> *Thy Head shall rise, tho' buried in the Dust,*
> *And 'midst the Clouds his glittering Turrets thrust.*[4]

Quære, what are the glittering Turrets of a Man's Head?

> *Upon the* Shore, *as* frequent *as the* Sand,
> *To meet the Prince, the glad* Dimetians *stand.*[5]

Quære, where these *Dimetians* stood? and of what Size they were? Add also to the *Jargon* such as the following.

> Destruction's *Empire shall no longer* last,
> *And* Desolation *lye for ever* waste.[6]

> *Here* Niobe, *sad Mother, makes her moan,*
> *And seems converted to a* Stone in Stone.[7]

BUT for Variegation, nothing is more useful than

3. The PARANOMASIA, or PUN,

where a Word, like the *Tongue* of a *Jackdaw,* speaks twice as much by being split: As this of Mr. *Dennis.*[8]

> *Bullets that wound, like Parthians,*[9] *as they fly;*[10]

or this excellent one of Mr. *Welsted,*

> —— *Behold the Virgin lye*
> *Naked, and only* cover'd *by the Sky.*[11]

---

[3] Pr. *Arthur,* p. 73. P.
[4] *Job,* p. 107. P.
[5] Pr. *Arthur,* p. 157. P.
[6] *Job,* p. 89. P.
[7] T. Cook, *Poems.* P. For Thomas Cooke, see *Dunciad,* II 138*n.* Niobe: see *Dunciad,* II 311*n.*
[8] Dennis: the critic, John Dennis (see *Essay on Criticism,* l. 270*n.*).
[9] Parthians: the warriors of Parthia fought with bows on horseback, and their horses were turned as if in flight after the discharge of their arrows.
[10] [Dennis] *Poems,* 1693, p. 13. P.
[11] Welsted, *Poems, Acon.* and *Lavin.* P.

To which thou may'st add,

> *To see her Beauties no Man needs to stoop,*
> *She has the whole Horizon for her Hoop.*[12]

4. The ANTITHESIS, or SEE-SAW,

whereby Contraries and Oppositions are ballanc'd in such a way, as to cause a Reader to remain suspended between them, to his exceeding Delight and Recreation. Such are these, on a Lady who made herself appear out of size, by hiding a young Princess under her Cloaths.

> *While the kind Nymph changing her faultless Shape*
> *Becomes* unhandsome, handsomely *to scape.* [13]

On the Maids of Honour in Mourning:

> *Sadly they charm, and dismally they please.*[14]

> —— *His Eyes so bright*
> Let in *the Object; and* let out *the Light.*[15]

> *The Gods look* pale *to see us look so* red.[16]

> —— *The Fairies and their Queen*
> In Mantles blue *came tripping o'er the* Green.[17]

> *All Nature felt a reverential Shock,*
> *The Sea* stood still *to see the Mountains* rock.[18]

---

[12] Pope did not identify the lines. He may have made them up.
[13] Waller. P.   For Edmund Waller, see *Essay on Criticism,* l. 361n.
[14] Steel on Queen Mary. P.   Steel is Sir Richard Steele (1672–1729), the essayist and playwright.
[15] Quarles. P.   For Francis Quarles, see *Dunciad,* I 140n.
[16] From Nathaniel Lee's *Sophonisba* (cf. n. 18, p. 411, above).
[17] From Ambrose Philips' *Pastorals* (see first note to *Guardian* No. 40).
[18] *Black.,* Job, p. 176. P.

CHAP. XI

The Figures continued: Of the Magnifying and diminishing Figures.

A GENUINE Writer of the Profund will take Care never to *magnify* any Object without *clouding* it at the same time; His Thought will appear in a true *Mist*, and very unlike what it is in Nature. It must always be remember'd that *Darkness* is an essential Quality of the *Profund*, or if there chance to be a Glimmering, it must be as *Milton* expresses it,

> *No Light, but rather Darkness visible.*

The chief Figure of this sort is,

1. The HYPERBOLE, or *Impossible*,

For Instance, of a Lion;

> *He roar'd so loud, and look'd so wondrous grim,*
> *His very Shadow durst not follow him.*[19]

Of a Lady at Dinner.

> *The silver Whiteness that adorns thy Neck,*
> *Sullies the Plate, and makes the Napkin black.*[1]

Of the same.

> —— *Th' obscureness of her Birth*
> *Cannot eclipse the Lustre of her Eyes,*
> *Which make her all one Light.*[2]

Of a Bull-baiting.

> *Up to the Stars the sprawling Mastives fly,*
> *And add new Monsters to the frighted Sky.*[3]

Of a Scene of Misery.

> *Behold a Scene of Misery and Woe!*
> *Here Argus' soon might weep himself quite blind,*

[19] Vet. Aut. P.   The *vetus autor* ("old author") has not been identified.
[1] Unidentified.
[2] Theob., *Double Falsehood.* P.   The heading preceding these lines may suggest that Theobald also wrote the verses immediately above them.
[3] Blackm. P.

> *Ev'n tho' he had* Briareus' *hundred Hands*
> *To wipe those hundred Eyes* ——4

And that modest Request of two absent Lovers,

> *Ye Gods! annihilate but* Space *and* Time,
> *And make two Lovers happy.* ——5

2. The PERIPHRASIS, which the Moderns call the *Circumbendibus*,6 whereof we have given Examples in the ninth Chapter, and shall again in the twelfth.

To the same Class of the *Magnifying* may be referr'd the following, which are so excellently Modern, that we have yet no Name for them. In describing a Country Prospect

> *I'd call them Mountains, but can't call them so,*
> *For fear to wrong them with a Name too low;*
> *While the fair Vales beneath so humbly lie,*
> *That even humble seems a Term too high.*7

III. THE third Class remains, of the *Diminishing* Figures: And 1. The ANTICLIMAX, where the second Line drops quite short of the first, than which nothing creates greater Surprize.

On the Extent of the *British* Arms.

> *Under the Tropicks is our Language spoke,*
> *And* Part of Flanders *hath received our Yoke.*8

On a Warrior.

> *And thou* Dalhoussy *the great God of War,*
> *Lieutenant Colonel to the Earl of Mar.*9

On the Valour of the *English.*

> *Nor* Art *nor* Nature *has the force*
> *To stop its steddy course,*
> *Nor* Alps *nor* Pyrenæns *keep it out,*
> *Nor fortify'd Redoubt.*10

AT other times this Figure operates in a larger Extent; and when the gentle Reader is in Expectation of some great Image, he either finds it surprizingly *imperfect,* or is presented with something *low,* or quite *ridiculous.* A Surprize resembling that of a curious Person in a

4 Anon.   P.   For Argus and Briareus, see *Dunciad,* II 374*n.;* IV 66*n.*
5 Unidentified.
6 **Circumbendibus:** roundabout.
7 Anon.   P.
8 Wall. [i.e., Edmund Waller].   P.
9 Anon.   P.
10 Denn. on Namur.   P.   The lines actually appear in Dennis's *A Pindarick Ode on the King.*

Cabinet[11] of antique Statues, who beholds on the Pedestal the Names of *Homer*, or *Cato;* but looking up, finds *Homer* without a Head, and nothing to be seen of *Cato* but his privy Member. Such are these Lines on a *Leviathan* at Sea.

> *His Motion works, and beats the oozy Mud,*
> *And with its Slime incorporates the Flood,*
> *'Till all th' encumber'd, thick, fermenting Stream*
> *Does like* one Pot of boiling Ointment seem.
> *Where'er he swims, he leaves along the Lake*
> *Such frothy Furrows, such a foamy Track,*
> *That all the Waters of the Deep appear*
> Hoary — *with* Age, *or* grey *with sudden* Fear.[12]

BUT perhaps even these are excell'd by the ensuing.

> *Now the resisted Flames and fiery Store,* ⎫
> *By Winds assaulted, in wide Forges roar,* ⎬
> *And raging Seas flow down of melted Oar.* ⎭
> *Sometimes they hear* long Iron Bars remov'd,
> *And* to *and* fro *huge* Heaps of Cynders shov'd.[13]

2. The VULGAR

Is also a Species of the *Diminishing;* By this a Spear flying in the Air is compar'd to a Boy whistling as he goes on an Errand.

> *The mighty* Stuffa *threw a massy Spear,*
> *Which, with its* Errand pleas'd, *sung thro' the Air.*[14]

A Man raging with Grief to a Mastiff Dog.

> *I cannot stifle this gigantic Woe,*
> *Nor on my raging Grief a* Muzzle *throw.*[15]

And Clouds big with Water to a Woman in great Necessity.

> Distended *with the* Waters *in 'em pent,*
> *The Clouds* hang deep *in Air, but* hang unrent.[16]

3. The INFANTINE.

THIS is when a Poet grows so very simple, as to think and talk like a Child. I shall take my Examples from the greatest Master[17] in this way. Hear how he fondles, like a meer Stammerer.

---

[11] **Cabinet:** a room devoted to display of works of art.
[12] *Black.,* Job, p. 197.   P.
[13] Pr. *Arthur,* p. 157.   P.
[14] Pr. Arthur.   P.   The lines are from *King Arthur.*
[15] *Job,* p. 41.   P.
[16] One of Pope's editors, Mrs. Edna L. Steeves, identified the lines as coming from Blackmore's *Job (The Art of Sinking in Poetry,* a critical edition, by Edna Leake Steeves, King's Crown Press, New York. 1952).
[17] **greatest Master:** Ambrose Philips.

> Little Charm *of placid Mien*,
> Miniature *of Beauty's Queen*,
> *Hither* British *Muse* of mine,
> *Hither, all ye* Græcian Nine,
> *With the lovely Graces* Three,
> *And your* pretty Nurseling *see*.

> *When the Meadows next are seen,*
> *Sweet Enamel, white and green.*
> *When again the Lambkins Play,*
> Pretty Sportlings *full of* May.

> *Then the Neck so white and round,*
> (Little Neck *with Brilliants bound*.)
> *And thy* Gentleness *of Mind*,
> (Gentle *from a* gentle *Kind*) &c.
> Happy *thrice, and* thrice agen,
> Happiest *he of* happy Men, &c.[18]

and the rest of those excellent *Lullabies* of his Composition.
How prettily he asks the Sheep to teach him to bleat?

> *Teach me to grieve with bleating Moan, my Sheep*.[19]

Hear how a Babe would reason on his Nurse's Death:

> *That ever she* could *dye! Oh most* unkind!
> *To die, and leave poor* Colinet *behind?*
> *And yet, — Why blame I her? ——*[1]

WITH no less Simplicity does he suppose that Shepherdesses tear
their Hair and beat their Breasts, at their own Deaths:

> *Ye brighter Maids, faint Emblems of my Fair,*
> *With Looks cast down, and with dishevel'd Hair,*
> *In bitter Anguish beat your Breasts, and moan*
> *Her Death untimely, as it were your own.*[2]

4. The INANITY, or NOTHINGNESS.

OF this the same Author furnishes us with most beautiful Instances·

> *Ah silly I, more silly than my Sheep,*
> (*Which on the flow'ry Plain I once did keep.*)[3]

[18] *A. Phil.* on Miss *C——*.   P.
[19] *Phil., Past[orals]*.   P.
[1] *Phil., Past.*   P.
[2] *Ibid.*   P.
[3] *Phil., Past.*   P.

> To the grave Senate she could Counsel give,
> (Which with Astonishment they did receive.)[4]

> He whom loud Cannon could not terrify,
> Falls (from the Grandeur of his Majesty.)[5]

> Happy, merry as a King,
> Sipping *Dew, you* sip, *and sing.*[6]

> The Noise *returning with returning* Light,

What did it?

> — Dispers'd the Silence, and dispell'd the Night.[7]

You easily perceive the Nothingness of every second Verse.

> The Glories of proud London to survey,
> The Sun himself shall rise — by break of Day.[8]

5. The EXPLETIVE,[9]

admirably exemplified in the Epithets of many Authors.

> Th' umbrageous Shadow, and the verdant Green,
> The running Current, and odorous Fragrance,
> Chear my lone Solitude with joyous Gladness.[10]

Or in pretty drawling words like these,

> All Men his Tomb, all Men his Sons adore,
> And his Sons' Sons, till there shall be no more.[11]

> The rising Sun our Grief did see,
>   The setting Sun did see the same,
> While wretched we remembred thee,
>   O Sion, Sion, lovely Name.[12]

6. The MACROLOGY and PLEONASM,[13]

are as generally coupled, as a lean Rabbit with a fat one; nor is it a wonder, the Superfluity of Words and Vacuity of Sense, being just the

[4] *Phil.* on Q. *Mary.* P.
[5] *Ibid.* P.
[6] T. Cook, on a Grasshopper. P.
[7] *Anon.* P.
[8] *Autor Vet.* P.
[9] **Expletive:** a word used merely to fill out a line of verse.
[10] Pope himself may have composed these lines for the occasion.
[11] T. *Cook,* Poems. P.
[12] *Ibid.* P.
[13] **Macrology and Pleonasm:** terms denoting redundancy of speech.

same thing. I am pleas'd to see one[14] of our greatest Adversaries employ this Figure.

> *The Growth of Meadows, and the Pride of Fields.*
> *The Food of Armies and Support of Wars.*
> *Refuse of Swords, and Gleanings of a Fight.*
> *Lessen his Numbers, and contract his Host.*
> *Where'er his Friends retire, or Foes succeed.*
> *Cover'd with Tempests, and in Oceans drown'd.*

Of all which the Perfection is

The TAUTOLOGY.[15]

> *Break thro' the Billows, and — divide the Main.*[16]
> *In smoother Numbers, and — in softer Verse.*
> *Divide — and part — the sever'd World — in two.*[17]

WITH ten thousand others equally musical, and plentifully flowing thro' most of our celebrated modern Poems.

---

[14] **one:** Joseph Addison, from whose poem, *The Campaign,* the six verses in the text are taken.

[15] **Tautology:** repetition of same or synonymous words.

[16] Mrs. Steeves (see n. 16, p. 417, above) identified the line as from a poem by Thomas Tickell (see first note to *Guardian* No. 40), a friend of Addison and the author of a translation of Book One of the *Iliad* designed to rival or over-shadow Pope's translation of the same poem. Pope obviously suspected that Addison had a hand in Tickell's translation (see n. 7, p. 422, below), and in consequence composed the portrait of Atticus in the *Ep. to Dr. Arbuthnot.*

[17] For these verses Pope refers the reader to poems, almost certainly by Addison, printed in Jacob Tonson's *Miscellany,* vols. IV and VI (for Tonson, see *Dunciad,* I 57*n.*).

CHAP. XII

Of Expression, *and the several Sorts of* Style *of the present Age.*

THE *Expression* is adequate, when it is proportionably low to the Profundity of the Thought. It must not be always *Grammatical,* lest it appear pedantic and ungentlemanly; nor too *clear,* for fear it becomes vulgar; for Obscurity bestows a Cast of the Wonderful, and throws an oracular Dignity upon a Piece which hath no meaning.

FOR example, sometimes use the wrong Number; *The Sword and Pestilence at once* devours, instead of *devour.* Sometimes the wrong Case; *And who more fit to sooth the God than* thee, instead of *thou:* And rather than say, *Thetis*[18] *saw Achilles* weep, she *heard* him weep.[19]

WE must be exceeding careful in two things; first, in the *Choice* of *low Words;* secondly, in the *sober* and *orderly* way of *ranging* them. Many of our Poets are naturally bless'd with this Talent, insomuch that they are in the Circumstance of that honest Citizen,[1] who had made *Prose* all his Life without knowing it. Let Verses run in this manner, just to be a Vehicle to the Words. (I take them from my last cited Author, who tho' otherwise by no means of our Rank, seem'd once in his Life to have a mind to be simple.)

> *If not, a Prize I will my self decree,*
> *From him, or him, or else perhaps from thee.*[2]

> ——— *full of Days was he;*
> *Two Ages past, he liv'd the third to see.*[3]

> *The King of forty Kings, and honour'd more*
> *By mighty* Jove *than e'er was King before.*[4]

> *That I may know, if thou my Prayer deny,*
> *The most despis'd of all the Gods am I.*[5]

> *Then let my Mother once be rul'd by me,*
> *Tho' much more wise than I pretend to be.*[6]

---

[18] **Thetis:** the sea nymph who was mother to Achilles.

[19] For the examples in this paragraph Pope refers the reader to *"Ti. Hom., Il. I"* (i.e., Tickell's translation of Homer's *Iliad,* Bk. I).

[1] **honest Citizen:** Monsieur Jourdain in Molière's *Le Bourgeois Gentilhomme.*

[2] *Ti., Hom., Il.* I, p. 11. P.

[3] *Idem.* p. 17. P.

[4] P. 19. P.

[5] P. 34. P.

[6] P. 38. P.

Or these of the same hand.[7]

I leave the Arts of Poetry and Verse
To them that practice them with more success:
Of greater Truths I now prepare to tell,
And so at once, dear Friend and Muse, farewel.

Sometimes a single *Word* will vulgarize a poetical Idea; as where a Ship set on fire owes all the Spirit of the *Bathos* to one choice Word that ends the Line.

And his scorch'd Ribs the hot Contagion fry'd.[8]

And in that Description of a World in Ruins.

Should the whole Frame of Nature round him break,
He unconcern'd would hear the mighty Crack.[9]

So also in these:

Beasts tame and savage to the River's Brink
Come from the Fields and wild Abodes — to drink.[10]

FREQUENTLY two or three Words will do it effectually.

He from the Clouds does the sweet Liquor squeeze,
That chears the Forest and the Garden Trees.[11]

IT is also useful to employ *Technical Terms*, which estrange your Stile from the great and general Ideas of Nature: And the higher your Subject is, the lower should you search into Mechanicks for your Expression. If you describe the Garment of an Angel, say that his *Linnen* was *finely spun,* and *bleach'd on the happy Plains.*[12] Call an Army of Angels, *Angelic Cuirassiers,*[13] and if you have Occasion to mention a Number of Misfortunes, stile them

Fresh Troops *of Pains, and* regimented W*oes.*[14]

STILE is divided by the Rhetoricians into the Proper and the Figured.[15] Of the Figur'd we have already treated, and the Proper is what our Authors have nothing to do with. Of Stiles we shall mention only

---

[7] **the same hand:** the verses which follow this line are from Addison's *An Account of the Greatest English Poets,* and so Pope seems to assert his belief that Addison had a hand in Tickell's translation of the *Iliad,* Bk. I.

[8] Pr. *Arthur,* p. 151.

[9] *Tons.* Misc., vol. 6, 119.   P.   The lines are from Addison's translation of "Horace, Ode III, Book III."

[10] *Job,* p. 262.   P.

[11] *Id.,* Job, p. 264.   P.

[12] **Linnen . . . Plains:** Pr. *Arth.,* p. 19.   P.

[13] **Angelic Cuirassiers:** *Ibid.* p. 239.   P.   Cuirassiers are horsemen wearing close-fitting body armor.

[14] *Job,* p. 86.   P.

[15] **the Proper and the Figured:** the literal and the metaphorical.

the Principal, which owe to the *Moderns* either their *chief Improvement,* or entire *Invention.*

1. The FLORID Stile,

Than which none is more proper to the *Bathos,* as Flowers which are the *Lowest* of Vegetables are most *Gaudy,* and do many times grow in great Plenty at the bottom of *Ponds* and *Ditches.*

A fine Writer[16] in this kind presents you with the following Posie:

> *The Groves appear all drest with Wreaths of Flowers,*
> *And from their Leaves drop aromatic Showers,*
> *Whose fragrant Heads in mystic Twines above,*
> *Exchang'd their Sweets, and mix'd with thousand Kisses,*
> *As if the willing Branches strove*
> *To beautify and shade the Grove.* ——

(Which indeed most Branches do.) But this is still excell'd by our Laureat.[17]

> *Branches in Branches twin'd compose the Grove,*
> *And shoot and spread, and blossom into Love.*
> *The trembling Palms their mutual Vows repeat,*
> *And bending Poplars bending Poplars meet.*
> *The distant Plantanes seem to press more nigh,*
> *And to the sighing Alders, Alders sigh.*

Hear also our *Homer.*[18]

> *His* Robe of State *is form'd of Light refin'd,*
> *An endless* Train *of Lustre spreads behind.*
> *His Throne's of bright* compacted Glory *made,*
> *With* Pearl *celestial, and with* Gems *inlaid:*
> *Whence* Floods *of Joy, and* Seas *of Splendor flow,*
> *On all th' Angelic gazing Throng below.*

2. The PERT Stile.

This does in as peculiar a manner become the low in Wit, as a Pert Air does the low in Stature. Mr. *Thomas Brown,* the Author of the *London Spy,*[19] and all the *Spies* and *Trips*[1] in general, are herein to be diligently study'd: In Verse, Mr. *Cibber's*[2] *Prologues.*

---

16 **fine Writer:** Aphra Behn (see *First Ep. of the Second Bk.,* l. 290n.).
17 **our Laureat:** Laurence Eusden (see *Ep. to Dr. Arbuthnot,* l. 15n.).
18 **our Homer:** Blackmore.
19 **Thomas Brown:** a hack writer and translator (1663–1704) who wrote sketches of contemporary London life.   **London Spy:** a periodical publication by Edward Ward (see n. 15, p. 407, above) devoted to sketches of the London scene.
1 **Trips:** a typical word (as was "Spy") in the titles of accounts of journeys or excursions (e.g., Ward's *A Trip to Jamaica,* etc.).
2 **Cibber:** see first note to the *Dunciad.*

BUT the Beauty and Energy of it is never so conspicuous, as when it is employ'd in *Modernizing* and *Adapting* to the *Taste of the Times* the Works of the Antients. This we rightly phrase *Doing* them *into English,* and *making* them *English;* two Expressions of great Propriety, the one denoting our *Neglect* of the *Manner how,* the other the *Force* and *Compulsion* with which, it is brought about. It is by Virtue of this Stile that *Tacitus*[3] talks like a *Coffee-House Politician, Josephus* like the *British Gazeteer,*[4] *Tully* is as short and smart as *Seneca* or *Mr. Asgill,*[5] *Marcus Aurelius* is excellent at *Snipsnap,*[6] and honest *Thomas a Kempis*[7] as *Prim* and *Polite* as any Preacher at Court.

3. The ALAMODE Stile,

Which is fine by being *new,* and has this Happiness attending it, that it is as durable and extensive as the Poem itself. Take some Examples of it, in the Description of the Sun in a Mourning Coach upon the Death of Q. *Mary.*

> *See* Phœbus *now, as once for* Phæton,
> *Has* mask'd *his Face; and put* deep Mourning *on;*
> *Dark Clouds his* sable Chariot *do surround,*
> *And the* dull Steeds stalk o'er *the* melancholy Round.[8]

Of Prince *Arthur's* Soldiers drinking.

> *While rich* Burgundian *Wine, and bright* Champaign,
> *Chase from their Minds the Terrors of the Main.*[9]

(Whence we also learn, that *Burgundy* and *Champaign* make a Man on Shore despise a Storm at Sea.)

Of the Almighty encamping his Regiments.

> —— *He sunk a vast capacious deep,*
> *Where he his* liquid Regiments *does keep:*
> *Thither the Waves* file off, *and make their way,*
> *To form the mighty* Body *of the Sea:*
> *Where they incamp, and in their Station stand,*
> *Entrench'd in* Works *of Rock, and* Lines *of Sand.*[10]

3 **Tacitus:** celebrated Roman historian (55–120 A.D.).
4 **Josephus:** Jewish historian and soldier (37–100 A.D.), much admired for his bold yet exact style.   **Gazeteer:** see *Dunciad,* II 314n.; *Epil. to the Satires,* I 84n.
5 **Tully:** Cicero.   **Seneca:** Roman philosopher and rhetorician (d. 65 A.D.), noted for his epigrammatic style.   **Asgill:** John Asgill (1659–1738), M.P. and pamphleteer who employed an abrupt, pert style.
6 **Marcus Aurelius:** Roman emperor and philosopher (121–80 A.D.), author of the famous *Meditations.*   **Snipsnap:** smart repartee.
7 **Thomas a Kempis:** German devotional writer (1379–1471), author of the *Imitation of Christ.*
8 *A. Phil*[ips].   P.
9 Pr. *Ar.,* p. 16.   P.
10 *Blackm.,* Ps. 104, p. 261.   P.

Of two Armies on the Point of engaging.

Yon' Armies are the Cards which both must play;
At least come off a Saver[11] *if you may:*
Throw boldly *at the* Sum *the Gods have* set;
These on your Side will all their Fortunes bet.[12]

All perfectly agreeable to the present Customs and best Fashions of our Metropolis.

But the principal Branch of the *Alamode* is the Prurient,[13] a Stile greatly advanc'd and honour'd of late by the practise of Persons of the *first Quality*, and by the encouragement of the *Ladies* not unsuccessfully introduc'd even into the *Drawing-Room*. Indeed its *incredible Progress* and *Conquests* may be compar'd to those of the great *Sesostris*,[14] and are every where known by the *same Marks*, the Images of the Genital Parts of Men or Women. It consists wholly of Metaphors drawn from two most fruitful Sources or Springs, the very *Bathos* of the human Body, that is to say * * * and * * * * * * * * * * * * * * * *Hiatus Magnus lachrymabilis*.[15] *. And *selling of Bargains*,[16] and *double Entendre*, and Κιββέρισμος, and Ὀλδφιέλδισμος,[17] all derived from the said Sources.

4. The Finical Stile, which consists of the most curious,[18] affected. mincing Metaphors, and partakes of the *alamode*.

As this, of a Brook dry'd by the Sun.

Won *by the Summer's* importuning *Ray*.
Th' eloping Stream did from her Channel stray.
And with enticing *Sun-beams* stole away.[19]

Of an easy Death.

When watchful Death shall on his Harvest look,
And see thee ripe with Age, invite *the Hook;*
He'll gently *cut thy* bending *Stalk, and thee*
Lay kindly *in the* Grave, *his* Granary.[1]

---

[11] **Saver:** one who wins as much as he loses, or one who hedges his bets.
[12] Lee, *Sophon.* P.   See n. 16, p. 414, above.
[13] **Prurient:** lewd.
[14] **Sesostris:** a mythical Egyptian king supposed to have made great conquests in Africa and Asia.
[15] **Hiatus Magnus lachrymabilis:** a large, lamentable gap (in the manuscript).
[16] **selling of Bargains:** bawdy repartee.
[17] Κιββέρισμος, and Ὀλδφιέλδισμος: Cibberism and Oldfieldism. Anne Oldfield (see *Second Sat. of the First Bk.*, l. 4n.) and Cibber both won great applause acting comic parts with some degree of bawdiness.
[18] **curious:** dainty.
[19] Blackm., *Job*, p. 26.   P.
[1] *Ibid.* p. 23.   P.

Of Trees in a Storm.

Oaks whose extended Arms the Winds defy,
The Tempest sees their Strength and sighs, and passes by.[2]

Of Water simmering over the Fire.

The sparkling Flames raise Water to a Smile,
Yet the pleas'd Liquor pines, and lessens all the while.[3]

5. LASTLY, I shall place the CUMBROUS, which moves heavily under a Load of Metaphors, and draws after it a long Train of Words.

AND the BUSKIN,[4] or *Stately,* frequently and with great Felicity mix'd with the Former. For as the first is the proper Engine to depress what is High, so is the second to raise what is Base and Low to a ridiculous Visibility: When both these can be done at once, then is the *Bathos* in Perfection; as when a Man is set with his Head downward, and his Breech upright, his Degradation is compleat: One End of him is as high as ever, only that End is the wrong one. Will not every true Lover of the *Profund* be delighted to behold the most vulgar and low Actions of Life exalted in the following Manner?

Who knocks at the Door?

For whom thus rudely pleads my loud-tongu'd Gate,
That he may enter? ——[5]

See who is there?

Advance the fringed Curtains of thy Eyes,
And tell me who comes yonder. ——[6]

Shut the Door.

The wooden Guardian of our Privacy
Quick on its Axle turn. ——

Bring my Cloaths.

Bring me what Nature, Taylor to the Bear,
To Man himself deny'd: She gave me Cold,
But would not give me Cloaths. ——

[2] Denn[is]. P.
[3] *Anon.* in *Tonson's* Misc. Part 6, p. 234. P.
[4] **Buskin:** lofty (the term derives from the high, thick-soled boots, called *buskins,* worn by actors in ancient Greek tragedy).
[5] Unidentified.
[6] Pope seems to be misquoting Shakespeare, *Tempest,* I ii 408–9.

Light the Fire.

Bring forth some Remnant of Promethean[7] *Theft,*
Quick to expand th' inclement Air congeal'd
By Boreas's *rude Breath.* ——

Snuff the Candle.

Yon Luminary Amputation needs,
Thus shall you save its half-extinguish'd Life.[8]

Open the Letter

Wax! render up thy Trust. ——[9]

Uncork the Bottle, and chip the Bread

Apply thine Engine to the spungy Door,
Set Bacchus *from his glassy Prison free,*
And strip white Ceres *of her nut-brown Coat.*[10]

[7] Promethean: the Titan Prometheus stole fire from heaven to give to man.
[8] The four passages have not been identified.
[9] *Theob.*, Double Falsehood. P.
[10] Unidentified. Bacchus is the god of wine, and Ceres the goddess of wheat and vegetation.

CHAP. XIII[11]

A Project for the Advancement of the Bathos.

Tʜᴜs have I (my dear Countrymen) with incredible Pains and Diligence, discover'd the hidden Sources of the *Bathos*, or as I may say broke open the Abysses of this *Great Deep*. And having now establish'd the good and wholesome *Laws*, what remains but that all true Moderns with their utmost Might do proceed to put the same in execution? In order whereto, I think I shall in the second place highly deserve of my Country, by proposing such a *Scheme*, as may facilitate this great End.

As our Number is confessedly far superior to that of the Enemy, there seems nothing wanting but Unanimity among our selves. It is therefore humbly offer'd, that all and every Individual of the *Bathos* do enter into a firm *Association*, and incorporate into *one Regular Body*, whereof every Member, even the meanest, will some way contribute to the Support of the whole; in like manner as the weakest Reeds when join'd in one Bundle, become infrangible. To which end our Art ought to be put upon the same foot with other Arts of this Age. The vast Improvement of modern Manufactures ariseth from their being divided into several Branches, and parcel'd out to several *Trades:* For instance, in *Clock-making*, one Artist makes the Balance, another the Spring, another the Crown-Wheels,[12] a fourth the Case, and the principal Workman puts all together; To this Œconomy[13] we owe the Perfection of our modern Watches; and doubtless we also might that of our modern Poetry and Rhetoric, were the several Parts branched out in the like manner.

Nothing is more evident than that divers Persons, no other way remarkable, have each a strong Disposition to the Formation of some particular Trope or Figure. *Aristotle* saith, that the *Hyperbole* is an Ornament fit for *young Men of Quality;* accordingly we find in those Gentlemen a wonderful Propensity toward it, which is marvellously improv'd by *travelling*.[14] *Soldiers* also and *Seamen* are very happy in the same Figure. The *Periphrasis* or *Circumlocution* is the peculiar Talent of *Country Farmers*, the Proverb and Apologue[15] of *Old Men* at their Clubs, the *Ellipsis* or Speech by half-words of *Ministers* and *Politicians*,

---

[11] **Chap. XIII:** This chapter in the first edition of *Peri Bathous* was preceded by the word "APPENDIX," suggesting that the work as originally conceived ended with Chapter XII, and that the last four chapters are to be regarded as accessory rather than integral.

[12] **Crown-Wheels:** gears with teeth set at right angles to their planes.

[13] **Œconomy:** orderly management.

[14] **travelling:** see the episode of the Grand Tour, *Dunciad*, IV 275ff.

[15] **Apologue:** moral fable.

the *Aposiopesis*[16] of *Courtiers,* the *Litotes*[17] or Diminution of *Ladies,* *Whisperers* and *Backbiters;* and the *Anadyplosis*[18] of Common *Cryers* and *Hawkers,* who by redoubling the same Words, persuade People to buy their Oysters, green Hastings,[19] or new Ballads. *Epithets* may be found in great plenty at *Billinsgate,*[1] *Sarcasm* and *Irony* learn'd upon the *Water,*[2] and the *Epiphonema* or *Exclamation* frequently from the *Beargarden,*[3] and as frequently from the *Hear him*[4] of the House of Commons.

Now each man applying his whole Time and Genius upon his particular Figure, would doubtless attain to Perfection; and when each became incorporated and sworn into the Society, (as hath been propos'd) a Poet or Orator would have no more to do, but to send to the particular Traders in each Kind; to the *Metaphorist* for his *Allegories,* to the *Simile-maker* for his *Comparisons,* to the *Ironist* for his *Sarcasmes,* to the *Apothegmatist* for his *Sentences,*[5] &c. whereby a *Dedication* or *Speech* would be compos'd in a Moment, the superior Artist having nothing to do but to put together all the Materials.

I THEREFORE propose that there be contrived with all convenient Dispatch, at the publick Expence, a *Rhetorical Chest of Drawers,* consisting of three Stories, the highest for the *Deliberative,* the middle for the *Demonstrative,* and the lowest for the *Judicial.*[6] These shall be divided into *Loci* or *Places,*[7] being Repositories for Matter and Argument in the several Kinds of Oration or Writing; and every Drawer shall again be sub-divided into Cells, resembling those of Cabinets for Rarities. The Apartment for *Peace* or *War,* and that of the *Liberty* of the *Press,* may in a very few Days be fill'd with several Arguments *perfectly new;* and the *Vituperative Partition* will as easily be replenish'd with a most choice Collection, entirely of the Growth and Manufacture of the present Age. Every Composer will soon be taught the Use of this Cabinet, and how to manage all the Registers[8] of it, which will be drawn out much in the Manner of those in an Organ.

[16] **Aposiopesis:** see n. 17, p. 411, above.

[17] **Litotes:** a figure of speech in which an affirmative is expressed by the negative of the contrary (e.g., she has a nose of no mean proportion).

[18] **Anadyplosis:** beginning a sentence or clause with the concluding or prominent word of the preceding sentence.

[19] **green Hastings:** early fruits or vegetables.

[1] **Billinsgate:** see *Dunciad,* I 307*n.*

[2] **upon the Water:** i.e., from the boatmen who transported passengers to and fro on the Thames.

[3] **Beargarden:** any place for the baiting of bears.

[4] **Hear him:** the old form of "hear! hear!"

[5] **Apothegmatist:** maker of maxims.   **Sentences:** pithy sayings.

[6] Traditionally, there were three species of rhetoric: (1) the *deliberative,* or political, consisting of speeches about courses of action to be followed; (2) the *demonstrative,* or epideictic, consisting mainly of declamatory or panegyrical speeches; (3) the *judicial,* or forensic, speeches on legal questions of fact.

[7] **Loci or Places:** topics.

[8] **Registers:** contrivances which control sets of organ-pipes.

THE Keys of it must be kept in honest Hands, by some *Reverend Prelate*, or *Valiant Officer*, of unquestion'd Loyalty and Affection to every present Establishment in *Church* and *State;* which will sufficiently guard against any Mischief which might otherwise be apprehended from it.

AND being lodg'd in such Hands, it may be at discretion *let out* by the *Day,* to several great Orators in both Houses;[9] from whence it is to be hop'd much *Profit* and *Gain* will also accrue to our Society.

9 **Houses:** of Parliament.

CHAP. XIV

How to make Dedications, Panegyricks *or* Satyrs, *and of the* Colours[10] *of Honourable and Dishonourable.*

Now of what Necessity the foregoing Project may prove, will appear from this single Consideration, that nothing is of equal consequence to the Success of our Works, as *Speed* and *Dispatch.* Great pity it is, that solid Brains are not, like other solid Bodies, constantly endow'd with a *Velocity* in sinking, proportion'd to their *Heaviness:* For it is with the *Flowers*[11] of the *Bathos* as with those of Nature, which if the careful Gardener brings not hastily to the Market in the *Morning,* must unprofitably perish and wither before *Night.* And of all our Productions none is so short-liv'd as the *Dedication* and *Panegyric,* which are often but the *Praise of a Day,* and become by the next, utterly useless, improper, indecent and false. This is the more to be lamented, inasmuch as these two are the Sorts whereon in a manner depends that *Profit,* which must still be remember'd to be the main end of *our Writers* and *Speakers.*

WE shall therefore employ this Chapter in shewing the *quickest* Method of composing them; after which we will teach a *short Way* to *Epick Poetry.* And these being confessedly the Works of most Importance and Difficulty, it is presum'd we may leave the rest to each Author's own Learning or Practice.

FIRST of *Panegyrick:* Every Man is *honourable,* who is so by *Law, Custom* or *Title;* The Publick are better Judges of what is honourable, than private Men. The Virtues of great Men, like those of Plants, are *inherent* in them whether they are *exerted* or not; and the more strongly inherent the less they are exerted; as a Man is the more rich the less he spends.

ALL great Ministers, without either private or œconomical[12] Virtue, are virtuous by their *Posts;* liberal and generous upon the *Publick Money,* provident upon *Publick Supplies,* just by paying *Publick Interest,* couragious and magnanimous by the *Fleets* and *Armies,* magnificent upon the *Publick Expences,* and prudent by *Publick Success.* They have by their *Office,* a Right to a share of the *Publick Stock* of Virtues; besides they are by *Prescription immemorial* invested in all the celebrated Virtues of their *Predecessors* in the same *Stations,* especially those of their own *Ancestors.*

As to what are commonly call'd the *Colours* of *Honourable* and *Dishonourable,* they are various in different Countries: In this they are

10 **Colours:** rhetorical modes or embellishments
11 **Flowers:** rhetorical embellishments.
12 **œconomical:** public or social.

Blue, Green and *Red.*[13] But forasmuch as the Duty we owe to the Publick doth often require that we should put some things in a strong Light, and throw a Shade over others, I shall explain the Method of turning a vicious Man into a Hero.

THE first and chief Rule is *the Golden Rule* of *Transformation,* which consists in converting Vices into their *bordering* Virtues. A man who is a Spendthrift and will not pay a just debt, may have his Injustice *transform'd* into Liberality; Cowardice may be metamorphos'd into Prudence; Intemperance into good Nature and good Fellowship, Corruption into Patriotism, and Lewdness into Tenderness and Facility.[14]

THE Second is the *Rule of Contraries:* It is certain the less a Man is endu'd with any Virtue, the more need he has to have it plentifully bestow'd, especially those good Qualities of which the World generally believes he hath none at all: For who will thank a Man for giving him that which he *has?*

THE Reverse of these Precepts will serve for *Satire,* wherein we are ever to remark, that whoso loseth his Place, or becomes out of Favour with the Government, hath forfeited his Share in *Publick Praise* and *Honour.* Therefore the truly-publick-spirited Writer ought in Duty to strip him whom the Government has stripp'd: Which is the real *poetical Justice* of this Age. For a full Collection of Topics and Epithets to be used in the Praise and Dispraise of Ministerial and Unministerial Persons, I refer to our *Rhetorical Cabinet;* concluding with an earnest Exhortation to all my Brethren, to observe the Precepts here laid down; the Neglect of which hath cost some of them their *Ears*[15] in a *Pillory.*

13 **Blue, Green and Red:** here these "colours" are symbolic of the three principal knightly orders: blue for the Order of the Garter, red for the Order of the Bath, green for the Order of the Thistle.

14 **Facility:** affability, pliancy.

15 **Ears:** persons sentenced to the pillory sometimes had their ears cropped also.

CHAP. XV[16]

A *Receipt to make an* Epic Poem.

AN Epic Poem, the Criticks agree, is the greatest Work Human Nature is capable of. They have already laid down many mechanical Rules for Compositions of this Sort, but at the same time they cut off almost all Undertakers from the Possibility of ever performing them; for the first Qualification they unanimously require in a Poet, is a *Genius*. I shall here endeavour (for the Benefit of my Countrymen) to make it manifest, that Epick Poems may be made *without a Genius*, nay without Learning or much Reading. This must necessarily be of great Use to all those who confess they never *Read,* and of whom the World is convinc'd they never *Learn*. *Moliere*[17] observes of making a Dinner, that any Man can do it *with Money,* and if a profess'd Cook cannot do it *without* he has his Art for nothing; the same may be said of making a Poem, 'tis easily brought about by him that *has* a Genius, but the Skill lies in doing it without one. In pursuance of this End, I shall present the Reader with a plain and certain *Recipe,* by which any Author in the *Bathos* may be qualified for this grand Performance.

For the *Fable*.[18]

TAKE out of any old Poem, History-book, Romance, or Legend, (for Instance *Geffry of Monmouth* or *Don Belianis of Greece*)[19] those Parts of Story which afford most Scope for *long Descriptions:* Put these Pieces together, and throw all the Adventures you fancy into *one Tale*. Then take a Hero, whom you may chuse for the Sound of his Name, and put him into the midst of these Adventures: There let him *work,*[1] for twelve Books; at the end of which you may take him out, ready prepared to *conquer* or to *marry;* it being necessary that the Conclusion of an Epick Poem be *fortunate.*

To make an Episode.

TAKE any remaining Adventure of your former Collection, in which you could no way involve your Hero; or any unfortunate Accident that

---

[16] **Chap. XV:** The substance of this chapter had earlier been published as *Guardian* No. 78.

[17] **Moliere observes:** in *L'Avare,* III i.

[18] **Fable:** plot or story.

[19] **Geffry of Monmouth:** Welsh chronicler (1100–54) and an important source of literary theme and plot. **Don Belianis of Greece:** a chivalric romance, first published, in Spanish, in 1547.

[1] **work:** (1) struggle; (2) ferment, as a yeast.

was too good to be thrown away; and it will be of Use, apply'd to any other Person; who may be lost and *evaporate* in the Course of the Work, without the least Damage to the Composition.

For the Moral and Allegory.

THESE you may extract out of the Fable afterwards, at your leisure: Be sure you *strain* them sufficiently.

For the Manners.[2]

FOR those of the *Hero*, take all the best Qualities you can find in the most celebrated Heroes of Antiquity; if they will not be reduced to a *Consistency*, lay 'em *all on a Heap* upon him. But be sure they are Qualities which your *Patron* would be thought to have; and to prevent any Mistake which the World may be subject to, select from the Alphabet those Capital Letters that compose his Name, and set them at the Head of a Dedication before your Poem. However, do not absolutely observe the exact Quantity of these Virtues, it not being determin'd whether or no it be necessary for the Hero of a Poem to be an *honest Man*. For the *Under-Characters*, gather them from *Homer* and *Virgil*, and change the Names as occasion serves.

For the Machines.[3]

TAKE of *Deities*, Male and Female, as many as you can use. Separate them into two equal Parts, and keep *Jupiter* in the middle. Let *Juno* put him in a Ferment, and *Venus* mollify him. Remember on all occasions to make use of Volatile *Mercury*. If you have need of Devils, draw them out of *Milton's Paradise*, and extract your *Spirits* from *Tasso*.[4] The Use of these Machines is evident; since no Epick Poem can possibly subsist without them, the wisest way is to reserve them for your greatest Necessities. When you cannot extricate your Hero by any human means, or your self by your own Wit, seek Relief from Heaven, and the Gods will do your business very readily. This is according to the direct Prescription of *Horace* in his Art of Poetry.

Nec Deus intersit, nisi dignus vindice Nodus Inciderit. ———[5]

That is to say, *A Poet should never call upon the Gods for their Assistance, but when he is in great Perplexity.*

---

2 **Manners:** character traits.
3 **Machines:** see *Rape of the Lock*, dedicatory letter.
4 **Tasso:** Torquato Tasso (1544–95), Italian poet, author of *Jerusalem Delivered*.
5 Ll. 191–2.

For the Descriptions.

FOR a *Tempest*. Take *Eurus, Zephyr, Auster* and *Boreas*,[6] and cast them together in one Verse: Add to these of Rain, Lightning and Thunder (the loudest you can) *quantum sufficit*.[7] Mix your Clouds and Billows well together 'till they foam, and thicken your Description here and there with a Quicksand. Brew your Tempest well in your Head, before you set it a blowing.

FOR a *Battle*. Pick a large Quantity of Images and Descriptions from *Homer's* Iliads, with a Spice or two of *Virgil*, and if there remain any Overplus, you may lay them by for a *Skirmish*. Season it well with *Similes*, and it will make an *Excellent Battle*.

FOR a *Burning Town*. If such a Description be necessary, (because it is certain there is one in *Virgil*,) Old *Troy* is ready burnt to your Hands. But if you fear that would be thought borrow'd, A Chapter or two of the Theory of the *Conflagration*,[8] well circumstanced, and done into Verse, will be a good *Succedaneum*.[9]

As for *Similes* and *Metaphors*, they may be found all over the Creation; the most ignorant may *gather* them, but the Difficulty is in *applying* them. For this advise with your *Bookseller*.[10]

---

[6] **Eurus, Zephyr, Auster and Boreas:** the southeast, west, south and north winds.

[7] **quantum sufficit:** as much as suffices.

[8] **Theory of the Conflagration:** in his *Sacred Theory of the Earth,* Thomas Burnet (1635–1715) had argued, often with extremely vivid terminology, the theory that the earth would ultimately be destroyed by fire.

[9] **Succedaneum:** substitute.

[10] **Bookseller:** in Pope's time often equivalent to a publisher.

CHAP. XVI

A *Project for the Advancement of the* Stage.

IT may be thought that we should not wholly omit the *Drama*, which makes so great and so lucrative a Part of Poetry. But this Province is so well taken care of, by the present *Managers* of the Theatre, that it is perfectly needless to suggest to them any other Methods than they have already practis'd for the Advancement of the *Bathos*.

HERE therefore, in the name of all our Brethren, let me return our sincere and humble Thanks to the Most August Mr. *Barton Booth*,[11] the Most Serene Mr. *Robert Wilks*,[12] and the Most Undaunted Mr. *Colley Cibber;* of whom, let it be known *when the People of this Age shall be Ancestors*, and to all *the Succession of our Successors*, that to this present day they continue to *Out-do* even their *own Out-doings:*[13] And when the inevitable Hand of sweeping *Time* shall have brush'd off all the Works of *To-day*, may this Testimony of a *Co-temporary Critick* to their Fame, be extended as far as *To-morrow!*

YET, if to so wise an Administration it be possible any thing can be added, it is that more ample and comprehensive Scheme which Mr. *Dennis* and Mr. *Gildon*,[14] (the two greatest Criticks and Reformers then living) made publick[15] in the Year 1720. in a Project sign'd with their Names, and dated the 2d of *February*. I cannot better conclude than by presenting the Reader with the Substance of it.

1. IT is propos'd that the two *Theatres*[16] be incorporated into one Company; that the *Royal Academy of Musick* be added to them as an *Orchestra;* and that Mr. *Figg* with his Prize-fighters, and *Violante* with the Rope-dancers, be admitted in Partnership.[17]

2. THAT a spacious Building be erected at the Publick Expence, capable of containing at least ten thousand Spectators, which is become absolutely necessary by the great addition of Children and Nurses to the Audience, since the new Entertainments.[18] That there be a Stage as large[19] as the *Athenian*, which was near ninety thousand Geometrical Paces square, and separate Divisions for the two *Houses* of *Parlia-*

---

11 **Barton Booth:** see *Dunciad*, III 266–7n.

12 **Wilks:** Robert Wilks (1665–1732), noted actor, and associated with Booth and Cibber in the management of Drury Lane Theater.

13 **their own Out-doings:** see *Dunciad*, III 231ff.

14 **Gildon:** Charles Gildon (see *Ep. to Dr. Arbuthnot*, l. 151n.).

15 **made publick:** the treatise or project, if it actually existed, has not come down to us.

16 **two Theatres:** Drury Lane and Lincoln's Inn Fields.

17 **Figg:** James Figg (d. 1734), a noted pugilist.   **Violante:** Madame Violante was a famous Italian acrobat and rope-dancer.

18 **new Entertainments:** i.e., farce and pantomime.

19 **Stage as large:** this passage should be compared with *Essay on Criticism*, ll. 276–84.

ment, my *Lords* the *Judges,* the honourable the *Directors* of the *Academy,* and the *Court of Aldermen,* who shall all have their Places frank.[1]

3. If *Westminster Hall*[2] be not allotted to this Service, (which by reason of its Proximity to the two Chambers of Parliament above mention'd, seems not altogether improper;) it is left to the Wisdom of the Nation whether *Somerset House*[3] may not be demolish'd, and a *Theatre* built upon that Site, which lies convenient to receive Spectators from the County of *Surrey,* who may be wafted thither by Water-Carriage, esteem'd by all Projectors[4] the cheapest whatsoever. To this may be added, that the River *Thames* may in the readiest manner convey those eminent Personages from Courts beyond the Seas, who may be drawn either by Curiosity to behold some of our most celebrated Pieces, or by Affection to see their Countrymen the Harlequins and Eunuchs;[5] Of which convenient notice may be given for two or three Months before, in the Publick Prints.

4. That the *Theatre* abovesaid be environ'd with a fair Quadrangle of Buildings, fitted for the Accommodation of decay'd *Criticks* and *Poets;* out of whom *Six* of the most Aged (their Age to be computed from the Year wherein their first Work was publish'd) shall be elected to manage the Affairs of the Society, provided nevertheless that the *Laureat* for the time being, may be always one. The Head or President over all, (to prevent Disputes, but too frequent among the Learned) shall be the *most ancient Poet* and *Critick* to be found in the whole Island.

5. The *Male-Players* are to be lodg'd in the Garrets of the said Quadrangle, and to attend the Persons of the *Poets,* dwelling under them, by brushing their Apparel, drawing on their Shoes, and the like. The *Actresses* are to make their Beds, and wash their Linnen.

6. A Large Room shall be set apart for a *Library,* to consist of all the modern Dramatick Poems, and all the Criticisms extant. In the midst of this Room shall be a round Table for the *Council of* Six to sit and deliberate on the Merits of *Plays.* The *Majority* shall determine the Dispute; and if it should happen that *three* and *three* should be of each Side, the President shall have a *casting Voice,*[6] unless where the Contention may run so high as to require a Decision by *Single Combat.*

7. It may be convenient to place the *Council of* Six in some conspicuous Situation in the Theatre, where after the manner usually practised by Composers in Musick, they may give *Signs* (before settled and agreed upon) of Dislike or Approbation. In consequence of these Signs the whole Audience shall be requir'd to *clap* or *hiss,* that the Town may learn certainly when and how far they ought to be pleas'd.

8. It is submitted whether it would not be proper to distinguish the

1 frank: free of charge.   2 **Westminster Hall:** see *Dunciad,* II 265*n.*
3 **Somerset House:** a palace in the Strand belonging to the crown.
4 **Projectors:** schemers or planners of public works.
5 **Eunuchs:** the castrati (male opera singers) were usually Italian.
6 **casting Voice:** deciding vote.

Council of Six by some particular Habit or Gown of an honourable Shape and Colour, to which may be added a square Cap and a white Wand.

9. That to prevent unmarried Actresses making away with their Infants, a competent Provision be allow'd for the Nurture of them, who shall for that reason be deem'd the *Children of the Society;* and that they may be educated according to the Genius of their Parents, the said Actresses shall declare upon Oath (as far as their Memory will allow) the true Names and Qualities of their several Fathers. A private Gentleman's Son shall at the Publick Expence be brought up a Page to attend the *Council of* Six. A more ample Provision shall be made for the Son of a *Poet;* and a greater still for the Son of a *Critick.*

10. If it be discover'd that any Actress is got with Child, during the Interludes of any Play, wherein she hath a part, it shall be reckon'd a neglect of her Business, and she shall *forfeit* accordingly. If any Actor for the future shall commit *Murder,* except upon the Stage, he shall be left to the Laws of the Land; the like is to be understood of *Robbery* and *Theft.* In all other Cases, particularly in those for *Debt,* it is propos'd that this, like the other Courts of *Whitehall* and *St. James's,* may be held a *Place of Priviledge.*[7] And whereas it has been found, that an Obligation to satisfy *paultry Creditors* has been a Discouragement to *Men of Letters,* if any Person of Quality or others shall send for any *Poet* or *Critick* of this Society to any remote Quarter of the Town, the said *Poet* or *Critick* shall freely pass and repass without being liable to an *Arrest.*

11. The fore-mention'd Scheme in its several Regulations may be supported by Profits arising from every third Night[8] throughout the Year. And as it would be hard to suppose that so many Persons could live without any Food (tho' from the former Course of their Lives, a *very little* will be deem'd sufficient) the Masters of Calculation will, we believe, agree, that out of those Profits, the said Persons might be subsisted in a sober and decent manner. We will venture to affirm further, that not only the proper Magazines of Thunder and Lightning, but *Paint, Diet-Drinks, Spitting-Pots,* and all other *Necessaries* of *Life,* may in like manner fairly be provided for.

12. If some of the Articles may at first view seem liable to Objections, particularly those that give so vast a Power to the *Council of* Six (which is indeed larger than any intrusted to the Great Officers of State) this may be obviated, by swearing those *Six* Persons of his Majesty's Privy Council, and obliging them to pass every thing of Moment *previously* at that most honourable Board.

Vale & Fruere,[9]

MAR. SCRIB.

7 **Place of Priviledge:** a place of immunity from arrest.
8 **third Night:** see *Dunciad,* I 57n.
9 **Vale & Fruere:** roughly, "Farewell, and enjoy yourself."

PREFACE

THE ILIAD

HOMER is universally allow'd to have had the greatest Invention[1] of any Writer whatever. The Praise of Judgment *Virgil* has justly contested with him, and others may have their Pretensions as to particular Excellencies; but his Invention remains yet unrival'd. Nor is it a Wonder if he has ever been acknowledg'd the greatest of Poets, who most excell'd in That which is the very Foundation of Poetry. It is the Invention that in different degrees distinguishes all great Genius's: The utmost Stretch of human Study, Learning, and Industry, which masters every thing besides, can never attain to this. It furnishes Art with all her Materials, and without it Judgment itself can at best but *steal wisely:* For Art is only like a prudent Steward that lives on managing the Riches of Nature. Whatever Praises may be given to Works of Judgment, there is not even a single Beauty in them but is owing to the Invention: As in the most regular Gardens, however Art may carry the greatest Appearance, there is not a Plant or Flower but is the Gift of Nature. The first can only reduce the Beauties of the latter into a more obvious Figure, which the common Eye may better take in, and is therefore more entertain'd with. And perhaps the reason why most Criticks are inclin'd to prefer a judicious and methodical Genius to a great and fruitful one, is, because they find it easier for themselves to pursue their Observations through an uniform and bounded Walk of Art, than to comprehend the vast and various Extent of Nature.

Our Author's Work is a wild Paradise, where if we cannot see all the Beauties so distinctly as in an order'd Garden, it is only because the Number of them is infinitely greater. 'Tis like a copious Nursery which contains the Seeds and first Productions of every kind, out of which those who follow'd him have but selected some particular Plants, each according to his Fancy, to cultivate and beautify. If some things are too luxuriant, it is owing to the Richness of the Soil; and if others are

PREFACE TO THE ILIAD: First published June 6, 1715, in the first volume of Pope's translation of the *Iliad*. The other five volumes of the translation appeared during the years between 1716 and 1720.

1 **Invention:** neo-classical term for what today would be called "creativity" or "imagination."

not arriv'd to Perfection or Maturity, it is only because they are over-run and opprest by those of a stronger Nature.

It is to the Strength of this amazing Invention we are to attribute that unequal'd Fire and Rapture, which is so forcible in *Homer,* that no Man of a true Poetical Spirit is Master of himself while he reads him. What he writes is of the most animated Nature imaginable; every thing moves, every thing lives, and is put in Action. If a Council be call'd, or a Battle fought, you are not coldly inform'd of what was said or done as from a third Person; the Reader is hurry'd out of himself by the Force of the Poet's Imagination, and turns in one place to a Hearer, in another to a Spectator. The Course of his Verses resembles that of the Army he describes,

οι δ' ἄρ ἴσαν, ὡσεί τε πυρὶ χθὼν πᾶσα νέμοιτο. [2]

They pour along like a Fire that sweeps the whole Earth before it. 'Tis however remarkable that his Fancy, which is every where vigorous, is not discover'd immediately at the beginning of his Poem in its fullest Splendor: It grows in the Progress both upon himself and others, and becomes on Fire like a Chariot-Wheel, by its own Rapidity. Exact Disposition, just Thought, correct Elocution, polish'd Numbers, may have been found in a thousand; but this Poetical *Fire,* this *Vivida vis animi,*[3] in a very few. Even in Works where all those are imperfect or neglected, this can over-power Criticism, and make us admire even while we dis-approve. Nay, where this appears, tho' attended with Absurdities, it brightens all the Rubbish about it, 'till we see nothing but its own Splendor. This *Fire* is discern'd in *Virgil,* but discern'd as through a Glass, reflected, and more shining than warm, but every where equal and constant: In *Lucan* and *Statius,*[4] it bursts out in sudden, short, and interrupted Flashes: In *Milton,* it glows like a Furnace kept up to an uncommon Fierceness by the Force of Art: In *Shakespear,* it strikes before we are aware, like an accidental Fire from Heaven: But in *Homer,* and in him only, it burns every where clearly, and every where irresistibly.

I shall here endeavour to show, how this vast *Invention* exerts itself in a manner superior to that of any Poet, thro' all the main constituent Parts of his Work, as it is the great and peculiar Characteristick which distinguishes him from all other Authors.

This strong and ruling Faculty was like a powerful Planet, which in the Violence of its Course, drew all things within its *Vortex.* It seem'd not enough to have taken in the whole Circle of Arts, and the whole Compass of Nature; all the inward Passions and Affections of Mankind

---

2 *Iliad,* II 780.

3 Vivida vis animi: lively force of mind (from Lucretius, *De Rerum Natura,* I 72).

4 Lucan: Marcus Annaeus Lucanus (39–65 A.D.), Roman epic poet, author of the *Pharsalia.* Statius: Publius Papinius Statius (45–96 A.D.), Roman poet; part of his epic *Thebais* was translated by Pope as a youth.

to supply his Characters, and all the outward Forms and Images of Things for his Descriptions; but wanting yet an ampler Sphere to expatiate in, he open'd a new and boundless Walk for his Imagination, and created a World for himself in the Invention of *Fable*. That which *Aristotle* calls the *Soul of Poetry,* was first breath'd into it by *Homer*. I shall begin with considering him in this Part, as it is naturally the first, and I speak of it both as it means the Design of a Poem, and as it is taken for Fiction.

Fable may be divided into the *Probable,* the *Allegorical,* and the *Marvelous.* The *Probable Fable* is the Recital of such Actions as tho' they did not happen, yet might, in the common course of Nature: Or of such as tho' they did, become Fables by the additional Episodes and manner of telling them. Of this sort is the main Story of an Epic Poem, *the Return of* Ulysses, *the Settlement of the* Trojans *in* Italy, or the like. That of the *Iliad* is *the Anger of* Achilles, the most short and single Subject that ever was chosen by any Poet. Yet this he has supplied with a vaster Variety of Incidents and Events, and crouded with a greater Number of Councils, Speeches, Battles, and Episodes of all kinds, than are to be found even in those Poems whose Schemes are of the utmost Latitude and Irregularity. The Action is hurry'd on with the most vehement Spirit, and its whole Duration employs not so much as fifty Days. *Virgil,* for want of so warm a Genius, aided himself by taking in a more extensive Subject, as well as a greater Length of Time, and contracting the Design of both *Homer's* Poems into one, which is yet but a fourth part as large as his. The other Epic Poets have us'd the same Practice, but generally carry'd it so far as to superinduce a Multiplicity of Fables, destroy the Unity of Action, and lose their Readers in an unreasonable Length of Time. Nor is it only in the main Design that they have been unable to add to his Invention, but they have follow'd him in every Episode and Part of Story. If he has given a regular *Catalogue* of an *Army,* they all draw up their Forces in the same Order. If he has funeral Games for *Patroclus,*[5] *Virgil* has the same for *Anchises,*[6] and *Statius* (rather than omit them) destroys the Unity of his Action for those of *Archemorus.*[7] If *Ulysses* visit the Shades, the *Æneas* of *Virgil* and *Scipio* of *Silius*[8] are sent after him. If he be detain'd from his Return by the Allurements of *Calypso,*[9] so is *Æneas* by *Dido,*[10] and *Rinaldo* by *Armida.*[11] If *Achilles* be absent from the Army on the Score of a Quarrel thro' half the Poem, *Rinaldo*

[5] **Patroclus:** the friend who donned Achilles' armor and was slain by Hector.
[6] **Anchises:** father of Aeneas.
[7] **Archemorus:** infant son of King Lycurgus of Nemea. Killed by a serpent, the Nemean Games were founded in his memory.
[8] **Silius:** Silius Italicus (26–101 A.D.), author of *Punica,* an epic poem whose hero is Scipio Africanus.
[9] **Calypso:** the sea-nymph who detained Ulysses on her island for seven years.
[10] **Dido:** queen of Carthage.
[11] **Rinaldo by Armida:** Rinaldo, one of the heroes in Torquato Tasso's *Jerusalem Delivered,* falls in love with Armida, a beautiful sorceress.

442 • *Preface to the Iliad*

must absent himself just as long, on the like account. If he gives his Heroe a Suit of celestial Armour, *Virgil* and *Tasso* make the same Present to theirs. *Virgil* has not only observ'd this close Imitation of *Homer*, but where he had not led the way, supply'd the Want from other *Greek* Authors. Thus the Story of *Sinon*[12] and the *Taking of Troy* was copied (says *Macrobius*[13]) almost word for word from *Pisander*,[14] as the Loves of *Dido* and *Æneas* are taken from those of *Medæa* and *Jason* in *Apollonius*,[15] and several others in the same manner.

To proceed to the *Allegorical Fable:* If we reflect upon those innumerable Knowledges, those Secrets of Nature and Physical Philosophy[16] which *Homer* is generally suppos'd to have wrapt up in his *Allegories*, what a new and ample Scene of Wonder may this Consideration afford us? How fertile will that Imagination appear, which was able to cloath all the Properties of Elements, the Qualifications of the Mind, the Virtues and Vices, in Forms and Persons; and to introduce them into Actions agreeable to the Nature of the Things they shadow'd? This is a Field in which no succeeding Poets could dispute with *Homer;* and whatever Commendations have been allow'd them on this Head, are by no means for their Invention in having enlarg'd his Circle, but for their Judgment in having contracted it. For when the Mode of Learning chang'd in following Ages, and Science[17] was deliver'd in a plainer manner, it then became as reasonable in the more modern Poets to lay it aside, as it was in *Homer* to make use of it. And perhaps it was no unhappy Circumstance for *Virgil*, that there was not in his Time that Demand upon him of so great an Invention, as might be capable of furnishing all those Allegorical Parts of a Poem.

The *Marvelous Fable* includes whatever is supernatural, and especially the Machines[18] of the Gods. If *Homer* was not the first who introduc'd the Deities (as *Herodotus*[19] imagines) into the Religion of *Greece*, he seems the first who brought them into a System of *Machinery* for Poetry, and such an one as makes its greatest Importance and Dignity. For we find those Authors who have been offended at the literal Notion of the Gods, constantly laying their Accusation against *Homer* as the undoubted Inventor of them. But whatever cause there might be to blame his *Machines* in a Philosophical or Religious View, they are so perfect in the Poetick, that Mankind have

12 **Sinon:** the Greek spy whose guile persuaded the Trojans to admit the wooden horse within their walls (see *Aeneid*, II 57ff.).
13 **Macrobius:** Latin grammarian and antiquary (d. 415 A.D.).
14 **Pisander:** Peisander of Rhodes (*c.* 650 B.C.) wrote an epic on the exploits of Hercules.
15 **Apollonius:** Apollonius Rhodius, of the third century B.C., wrote an epic entitled *Argonautica*.
16 **Physical Philosophy:** natural knowledge, now called *science*.
17 **Science:** knowledge in general.
18 **Machines:** supernatural agencies (see *Rape of the Lock*, dedicatory epistle).
19 **Herodotus:** celebrated Greek historian (485–425 B.C.).

been ever since contented to follow them: None have been able to en-
large the Sphere of Poetry beyond the Limits he has set: Every Attempt of this Nature has prov'd unsuccessful; and after all the various
Changes of Times and Religions, his Gods continue to this Day the
Gods of Poetry.

We come now to the *Characters* of his Persons, and here we shall
find no Author has ever drawn so many with so visible and surprizing
a Variety, or given us such lively and affecting Impressions of them.
Every one has something so singularly his own, that no Painter could
have distinguish'd them more by their Features, than the Poet has by
their Manners.[1] Nothing can be more exact than the Distinctions he
has observ'd in the different degrees of Virtues and Vices. The single
Quality of *Courage* is wonderfully diversify'd in the several Characters
of the *Iliad*. That of *Achilles* is furious and intractable; that of *Dio-
mede* forward, yet list'ning to Advice and subject to Command: We
see in *Ajax* an heavy and self-considering Valour, in *Hector* an active
and vigilant one: The Courage of *Agamemnon* is inspirited by Love of
Empire and Ambition, that of *Menelaus* mix'd with Softness and Tenderness for his People: We find in *Idomeneus* a plain direct Soldier, in
Sarpedon a gallant and generous one. Nor is this judicious and astonishing Diversity to be found only in the principal Quality which constitutes the Main of each Character, but even in the Under-parts of it,
to which he takes care to give a Tincture of that principal one. For
Example, the main Characters of *Ulysses* and *Nestor* consist in *Wisdom*, and they are distinct in this; the Wisdom of one is *artificial* and
various,[2] of the other *natural, open,* and *regular*. But they have, besides, Characters of *Courage;* and this Quality also takes a different
Turn in each from the difference of his Prudence: For one in the War
depends still upon *Caution*, the other upon *Experience*. It would be
endless to produce Instances of these Kinds. The Characters of *Virgil*
are far from striking us in this open manner; they lie in a great degree
hidden and undistinguish'd, and where they are mark'd most evidently,
affect us not in proportion to those of *Homer*. His Characters of Valour
are much alike; even that of *Turnus* seems no way peculiar but as it is
in a superior degree; and we see nothing that differences the Courage
of *Mnestheus* from that of *Sergesthus, Cloanthus,* or the rest. In like
manner it may be remark'd of *Statius's* Heroes, that an Air of Impetuosity runs thro' them all; the same horrid[3] and savage Courage appears
in his *Capaneus, Tydeus, Hippomedon,* &c. They have a Parity of
Character which makes them seem Brothers of one Family. I believe
when the Reader is led into this Track of Reflection, if he will pursue

---

[1] **Manners:** characters, or distinctive varieties of disposition (see the first and
third sentences of the following paragraph).
[2] **artificial and various:** artful and many-sided.
[3] **horrid:** rude or rough.

it through the *Epic* and *Tragic* Writers, he will be convinced how infinitely superior in this Point the Invention of *Homer* was to that of all others.

The *Speeches* are to be consider'd as they flow from the Characters, being perfect or defective as they agree or disagree with the Manners of those who utter them. As there is more variety of Characters[4] in the *Iliad,* so there is of Speeches, than in any other Poem. *Every thing in it has Manners* (as *Aristotle* expresses it) that is, every thing is acted or spoken. It is hardly credible in a Work of such length, how small a Number of Lines are employ'd in Narration. In *Virgil* the Dramatic Part is less in proportion to the Narrative; and the Speeches often consist of general Reflections or Thoughts, which might be equally just in any Person's Mouth upon the same Occasion. As many of his Persons have no apparent Characters, so many of his Speeches escape being apply'd and judg'd by the Rule of Propriety.[5] We oftner think of the Author himself when we read *Virgil,* than when we are engag'd in *Homer:* All which are the Effects of a colder Invention, that interests us less in the Action describ'd: *Homer* makes us Hearers, and *Virgil* leaves us Readers.

If in the next place we take a View of the *Sentiments,*[6] the same presiding Faculty is eminent in the Sublimity and Spirit of his Thoughts. *Longinus*[7] has given his Opinion, that it was in this Part *Homer* principally excell'd. What were alone sufficient to prove the Grandeur and Excellence of his Sentiments in general, is that they have so remarkable a Parity with those of the Scripture: *Duport,* in his *Gnomologia Homerica,*[8] has collected innumerable Instances of this sort. And it is with Justice an excellent modern Writer allows, that if *Virgil* has not so many Thoughts that are low and vulgar, he has not so many that are sublime and noble; and that the *Roman* Author seldom rises into very astonishing Sentiments where he is not fired by the *Iliad.*

If we observe his *Descriptions, Images,* and *Similes,* we shall find the Invention still predominant. To what else can we ascribe that vast Comprehension of Images of every sort, where we see each Circumstance and Individual of Nature summon'd together by the Extent and Fecundity of his Imagination; to which all things, in their various Views, presented themselves in an Instant, and had their Impressions taken off to Perfection at a Heat? Nay, he not only gives us the full Prospects of Things, but several unexpected Peculiarities and Side-Views, unobserv'd by any Painter but *Homer.* Nothing is so surprizing

---

4 **Characters:** individuating characteristics.

5 **Propriety:** suitability, appropriateness.

6 **Sentiments:** moral or striking thoughts and aphorisms.

7 **Longinus:** see *Peri Hupsous,* sec. IX (and first note to Pope's *Peri Bathous*).

8 **Duport:** James Duport (1606–79), professor of Greek and chaplain to Charles II.   **Gnomologia:** suggests aphorisms and striking thoughts.

as the Descriptions of his Battels, which take up no less than half the *Iliad*, and are supply'd with so vast a Variety of Incidents, that no one bears a Likeness to another; such different Kinds of Deaths, that no two Heroes are wounded in the same manner; and such a Profusion of noble Ideas, that every Battel rises above the last in Greatness, Horror, and Confusion. It is certain there is not near that Number of Images and Descriptions in any Epic Poet; tho' every one has assisted himself with a great Quantity out of him: And it is evident of *Virgil* especially, that he has scarce any Comparisons which are not drawn from his Master.

If we descend from hence to the *Expression*, we see the bright Imagination of *Homer* shining out in the most enliven'd Forms of it. We acknowledge him the Father of Poetical Diction, the first who taught that *Language of the Gods* to Men. His Expression is like the colouring of some great Masters, which discovers itself to be laid on boldly, and executed with Rapidity. It is indeed the strongest and most glowing imaginable, and touch'd with the greatest Spirit. *Aristotle* had reason to say, He was the only Poet who had found out *Living Words;* there are in him more daring Figures and Metaphors than in any good Author whatever. An Arrow is *impatient* to be on the Wing, a Weapon *thirsts* to drink the Blood of an Enemy, and the like. Yet his Expression is never too big for the Sense, but justly great in proportion to it: 'Tis the Sentiment that swells and fills out the Diction, which rises with it, and forms itself about it. For in the same degree that a *Thought* is warmer, an *Expression* will be brighter; and as That is more strong, This will become more perspicuous: Like Glass in the Furnace which grows to a greater Magnitude, and refines to a greater Clearness, only as the *Breath* within is more powerful, and the *Heat* more intense.

To throw his Language more out of Prose, *Homer* seems to have affected the *Compound-Epithets*. This was a sort of Composition peculiarly proper to Poetry, not only as it heighten'd the *Diction*, but as it assisted and fill'd the *Numbers*[9] with greater Sound and Pomp, and likewise conduced in some measure to thicken the *Images*. On this last Consideration I cannot but attribute these to the Fruitfulness of his Invention, since (as he has manag'd them) they are a sort of supernumerary[10] Pictures of the Persons or Things they are join'd to. We see the Motion of *Hector's* Plumes in the Epithet Κορυθαίολος,[11] the Landscape of Mount *Neritus* in that of Εἰνοσίφυλλος,[12] and so of others; which particular Images could not have been insisted upon so long as to express them in a Description (tho' but of a single Line) without

9 **Numbers:** metrical measures or feet.
10 **supernumerary:** superfluous.
11 Κορυθαίολος: with glancing helm.
12 Εἰνοσίφυλλος: with shaking foliage.

diverting the Reader too much from the principal Action or Figure. As a Metaphor is a short Simile, one of these Epithets is a short Description.

Lastly, if we consider his *Versification,* we shall be sensible what a Share of Praise is due to his Invention in that also. He was not satisfy'd with his Language as he found it settled in any one Part of *Greece,* but search'd thro' its differing *Dialects* with this particular View, to beautify and perfect his Numbers: He consider'd these as they had a greater Mixture of Vowels or Consonants, and accordingly employ'd them as the Verse requir'd either a greater Smoothness or Strength. What he most affected was the *Ionic,* which has a peculiar Sweetness from its never using Contractions, and from its Custom of resolving the Diphthongs into two Syllables; so as to make the Words open themselves with a more spreading and sonorous Fluency. With this he mingled the *Attic* Contractions, the broader *Doric,* and the feebler *Æolic,* which often rejects its Aspirate, or takes off its Accent; and compleated this Variety by altering some Letters with the License of Poetry. Thus his Measures, instead of being Fetters to his Sense, were always in readiness to run along with the Warmth of his Rapture; and even to give a farther Representation of his Notions, in the Correspondence of their Sounds to what they signify'd. Out of all these he has deriv'd that Harmony, which makes us confess he had not only the richest Head, but the finest Ear in the World. This is so great a Truth, that whoever will but consult the Tune of his Verses even without understanding them (with the same sort of Diligence as we daily see practis'd in the Case of *Italian Opera's*[13]) will find more Sweetness, Variety, and Majesty of Sound, than in any other Language or Poetry. The Beauty of his Numbers is allow'd by the Criticks to be copied but faintly by *Virgil* himself, tho' they are so just to ascribe it to the Nature of the *Latine* Tongue. Indeed the *Greek* has some Advantages both from the natural *Sound* of its *Words,* and the Turn and *Cadence* of its *Verse,* which agree with the Genius of no other Language. *Virgil* was very sensible of this, and used the utmost Diligence in working up a more intractable Language to whatsoever Graces it was capable of, and in particular never fail'd to bring the Sound of his Line to a beautiful Agreement with its Sense. If the *Grecian* Poet has not been so frequently celebrated on this Account as the *Roman,* the only reason is, that fewer Criticks have understood one Language than the other. *Dionysius* of *Halicarnassus*[14] has pointed out many of our Author's Beauties in this kind, in his Treatise of the *Composition of Words,* and others will be taken notice of in the Course

[13] **Italian Opera's**: see *Dunciad,* IV 45n.
[14] **Dionysius of Halicarnassus**: Greek critic and rhetorician of the first century B.C.

of the Notes.[15] It suffices at present to observe of his Numbers, that they flow with so much ease, as to make one imagine *Homer* had no other care than to transcribe as fast as the *Muses* dictated; and at the same time with so much Force and inspiriting Vigour, that they awaken and raise us like the Sound of a Trumpet. They roll along as a plentiful River, always in motion, and always full; while we are borne away by a Tide of Verse, the most rapid, and yet the most smooth imaginable.

Thus on whatever side we contemplate *Homer,* what principally strikes us is his *Invention.* It is that which forms the Character of each Part of his Work; and accordingly we find it to have made his Fable more *extensive* and *copious* than any other, his Manners more *lively* and *strongly marked,* his Speeches more *affecting* and *transported,* his Sentiments more *warm* and *sublime,* his Images and Descriptions more *full* and *animated,* his Expression more *rais'd* and *daring,* and his Numbers more *rapid* and *various.* I hope in what has been said of *Virgil* with regard to any of these Heads, I have no way derogated from his Character. Nothing is more absurd or endless, than the common Method of comparing eminent Writers by an Opposition of particular Passages in them, and forming a Judgment from thence of their Merit upon the whole. We ought to have a certain Knowledge of the principal Character and distinguishing Excellence of each: It is in *that* we are to consider him, and in proportion to his Degree in *that* we are to admire him. No Author or Man ever excell'd all the World in more than one Faculty, and as *Homer* has done this in Invention, *Virgil* has in Judgment. Not that we are to think *Homer* wanted Judgment, because *Virgil* had it in a more eminent degree; or that *Virgil* wanted Invention, because *Homer* possest a larger share of it: Each of these great Authors had more of both than perhaps any Man besides, and are only said to have less in Comparison with one another. *Homer* was the greater Genius, *Virgil* the better Artist. In one we most admire the *Man,* in the other the *Work.* *Homer* hurries and transports us with a commanding Impetuosity, *Virgil* leads us with an attractive Majesty: *Homer* scatters with a generous Profusion, *Virgil* bestows with a careful Magnificence: *Homer* like the *Nile,* pours out his Riches with a sudden Overflow; *Virgil* like a River in its Banks, with a gentle and constant Stream. When we behold their Battels, methinks the two Poets resemble the Heroes they celebrate: *Homer,* boundless and irresistible as *Achilles,* bears all before him, and shines more and more as the Tumult increases; *Virgil* calmly daring like *Æneas,* appears undisturb'd in the midst of the Action, disposes all about him, and conquers with Tranquillity: And when we look upon their Machines, *Homer* seems like his own *Jupiter* in his Terrors, shaking *Olympus,* scattering the Lightnings, and firing the Heavens; *Virgil* like the same

15 Notes: Pope's own notes to his translation.

Power in his Benevolence, counselling with the Gods, laying Plans for Empires, and regularly ordering his whole Creation.

But after all, it is with great Parts as with great Virtues, they naturally border on some Imperfection; and it is often hard to distinguish exactly where the Virtue ends, or the Fault begins. As Prudence may sometimes sink to Suspicion, so may a great Judgment decline to Coldness; and as Magnanimity may run up to Profusion or Extravagance, so may a great Invention to Redundancy or Wildness. If we look upon *Homer* in this View, we shall perceive the chief *Objections* against him to proceed from so noble a Cause as the Excess of this Faculty.

Among these we may reckon some of his *Marvellous Fictions,* upon which so much Criticism has been spent as surpassing all the Bounds of Probability. Perhaps it may be with great and superior Souls as with gigantick Bodies, which exerting themselves with unusual Strength, exceed what is commonly thought the due Proportion of Parts, to become Miracles in the whole; and like the old Heroes of that Make, commit something near Extravagance amidst a Series of glorious and inimitable Performances. Thus *Homer* has his *speaking Horses,* and *Virgil* his *Myrtles distilling Blood,*[16] without so much as contriving the easy Intervention of a Deity to save the Probability.

It is owing to the same vast Invention that his *Similes* have been thought too exuberant and full of Circumstances. The Force of this Faculty is seen in nothing more, than its Inability to confine itself to that single Circumstance upon which the Comparison is grounded: It runs out into Embellishments of additional Images, which however are so manag'd as not to overpower the main one. His Similes are like Pictures, where the principal Figure has not only its proportion given agreeable to the Original, but is also set off with occasional[17] Ornaments and Prospects. The same will account for his manner of heaping a Number of Comparisons together in one Breath, when his Fancy suggested to him at once so many various and correspondent Images. The Reader will easily extend this Observation to more Objections of the same kind.

If there are others which seem rather to charge him with a Defect or Narrowness of Genius, than an Excess of it; those seeming Defects will be found upon Examination to proceed wholly from the Nature of the Times he liv'd in. Such are his *grosser Representations* of the *Gods,* and the vicious and *imperfect Manners* of his *Heroes,* which will be treated of in the following *Essay:*[18] But I must here speak a word of the latter, as it is a Point generally carried into Extreams both by the Censurers and Defenders of *Homer.* It must be a strange Partiality to

[16] speaking Horses: see *Iliad,* Bk. XIX (ll. 446ff. in Pope's translation). Myrtles distilling Blood: see *Aeneid,* III 22ff.

[17] occasional: i.e., appropriate to the occasion.

[18] Following Essay: this Preface was followed by "An Essay on the Life, Writings, and Learning of Homer."

Antiquity to think with Madam *Dacier*,[19] "that those Times and Manners are so much the more excellent, as they are more contrary to ours."
Who can be so prejudiced in their Favour as to magnify the Felicity
of those Ages, when a Spirit of Revenge and Cruelty reign'd thro' the
World, when no Mercy was shown but for the sake of Lucre, when
the greatest Princes were put to the Sword, and their Wives and
Daughters made Slaves and Concubines? On the other side I would
not be so delicate as those modern Cricks, who are shock'd at the
servile Offices and *mean Employments* in which we sometimes see the
Heroes of *Homer* engag'd. There is a Pleasure in taking a view of that
Simplicity in Opposition to the Luxury of succeeding Ages; in beholding Monarchs without their Guards, Princes tending their Flocks, and
Princesses drawing Water from the Springs. When we read *Homer,*
we ought to reflect that we are reading the most ancient Author in the
Heathen World; and those who consider him in this Light, will double
their Pleasure in the Perusal of him. Let them think they are growing
acquainted with Nations and People that are now no more; that they
are stepping almost three thousand Years backward into the remotest
Antiquity, and entertaining themselves with a clear and surprizing
Vision of Things no where else to be found, and the only authentick
Picture of that ancient World. By this means alone their greatest
Obstacles will vanish; and what usually creates their Dislike, will
become a Satisfaction.

This Consideration may farther serve to answer for the constant Use
of the same *Epithets* to his Gods and Heroes, such as the *far-darting
Phœbus,* the *blue-ey'd Pallas,* the *swift-footed Achilles,* &c. which some
have censured as impertinent and tediously repeated. Those of the
Gods depended upon the Powers and Offices then believ'd to belong to
them, and had contracted a Weight and Veneration from the Rites
and solemn Devotions in which they were us'd: They were a sort of
Attributes that it was a Matter of Religion to salute them with on all
Occasions, and an Irreverence to omit. As for the Epithets of great
Men, Mons. *Boileau*[1] is of Opinion; that they were in the Nature of
Sir-Names, and repeated as such; for the *Greeks* having no Names
deriv'd from their Fathers, were oblig'd when they mention'd any one
to add some other Distinction; either naming his Parents expressly, or
his Place of Birth, Profession, or the like: As *Alexander*[2] Son of *Philip,
Herodotus* of *Halicarnassus,*[3] *Diogenes* the *Cynic, &c. Homer* therefore complying with the Custom of his Countrey, us'd such distinctive
Additions as better agreed with Poetry. And indeed we have some-

[19] **Madam Dacier:** Anne Dacier (1654–1720), celebrated French critic and
scholar, wife of André Dacier, also an eminent critic.
[1] **Boileau:** see *Essay on Criticism*, l. 714n.
[2] **Alexander:** Alexander the Great.
[3] **Herodotus of Halicarnassus:** the celebrated 5th century Greek historian.
Diogenes the Cynic: celebrated Cynic philosopher (d. 323 B.C.).

thing parallel to these in modern Times, such as the Names of *Harold Harefoot, Edmund Ironside, Edward Long-shanks, Edward* the *black Prince, &c.*[4] If yet this be thought to account better for the Propriety than for the Repetition, I shall add a farther Conjecture. *Hesiod*[5] dividing the World into its Ages, has plac'd a fourth Age between the Brazen and the Iron one, of *Heroes distinct from other Men, a divine Race, who fought at* Thebes *and* Troy, *are called Demi-Gods, and live by the Care of* Jupiter *in the Islands of the Blessed.* Now among the divine Honours which were paid them, they might have this also in common with the Gods, not to be mention'd without the Solemnity of an Epithet, and such as might be acceptable to them by its celebrating their Families, Actions, or Qualities.

What other Cavils have been rais'd against *Homer* are such as hardly deserve a Reply, but will yet be taken notice of as they occur in the Course of the Work. Many have been occasion'd by an injudicious Endeavour to exalt *Virgil;* which is much the same, as if one should think to praise the Superstructure by undermining the Foundation: One would imagine by the whole Course of their Parallels, that these Criticks never so much as heard of *Homer's* having written first; a Consideration which whoever compares these two Poets ought to have always in his Eye. Some accuse him for the same things which they overlook or praise in the other; as when they prefer the Fable and Moral of the *Æneis* to those of the *Iliad,* for the same Reasons which might set the *Odysses* above the *Æneis:* as that the Heroe is a wiser Man; and the Action of the one more beneficial to his Countrey than that of the other: Or else they blame him for not doing what he never design'd; as because *Achilles* is not as good and perfect a Prince as *Æneas,* when the very Moral of his Poem requir'd a contrary Character. It is thus that *Rapin*[6] judges in his Comparison of *Homer* and *Virgil.* Others select those particular Passages of *Homer* which are not so labour'd[7] as some that *Virgil* drew out of them: This is the whole Management of *Scaliger*[8] in his *Poetices.* Others quarrel with what they take for low and mean Expressions, sometimes thro' a false Delicacy and Refinement, oftner from an Ignorance of the Graces of the Original; and then triumph in the Aukwardness of their own Translations. This is the Conduct of *Perault* in his *Parallels.*[9] Lastly, there

---

[4] **Harold Harefoot:** Harold I, King of England (d. 1040). **Edmund Ironside:** Eadmund II, King of England (d. 1016). **Edward Long-shanks:** Edward I, King of England (d. 1307). **Edward the black Prince:** son of Edward III and renowned for his military exploits (d. 1376).

[5] **Hesiod:** Greek poet of the 8th century B.C.

[6] **Rapin:** see *Guardian* No. 40, n. 5, p. 380.

[7] **labour'd:** carefully wrought.

[8] **Scaliger:** Julius Caesar Scaliger (1484–1558), Italian scholar and critic, author of *Poetices Libri septem.*

[9] **Perault:** Charles Perrault (1628–1703), French author who wrote *Parallèle des anciens et des modernes.*

are others, who pretending to a fairer Proceeding, distinguish between the personal Merit of *Homer*, and that of his *Work*; but when they come to assign the Causes of the great Reputation of the *Iliad*, they found it upon the Ignorance of his Times, and the Prejudice of those that followed. And in pursuance of this Principle, they make those Accidents (such as the Contention of the Cities,[10] &c.) to be the Causes of his Fame, which were in Reality the Consequences of his Merit. The same might as well be said of *Virgil*, or any great Author, whose general Character will infallibly raise many casual Additions to their Reputation. This is the Method of Mons. *de la Motte*;[11] who yet confesses upon the whole, that in whatever Age *Homer* had liv'd he must have been the greatest Poet of his Nation, and that he may be said in this Sense to be the Master even of those who surpass'd him.

In all these Objections we see nothing that contradicts his Title to the Honour of the chief *Invention;* and as long as this (which is indeed the Characteristic of Poetry itself) remains unequal'd by his Followers, he still continues superior to them. A cooler Judgment may commit fewer Faults, and be more approv'd in the Eyes of *One Sort* of Criticks: but that Warmth of Fancy will carry the loudest and most universal Applauses which holds the Heart of a Reader under the strongest Enchantment. *Homer* not only appears the Inventor of Poetry, but excells all the Inventors of other Arts in this, that he has swallow'd up the Honour of those who succeeded him. What he has done admitted no Encrease, it only left room for Contraction or Regulation. He shew'd all the Stretch of Fancy at once; and if he has fail'd in some of his Flights, it was but because he attempted every thing. A Work of this kind seems like a mighty Tree which rises from the most vigorous Seed, is improv'd with Industry, flourishes, and produces the finest Fruit; Nature and Art have conspir'd to raise it; Pleasure and Profit join'd to make it valuable: and they who find the justest Faults, have only said, that a few Branches (which run luxuriant thro' a Richness of Nature) might be lopp'd into Form to give it a more regular Appearance.

Having now spoken of the Beauties and Defects of the Original, it remains to treat of the Translation, with the same View to the chief Characteristic.[12] As far as that is seen in the main Parts of the Poem, such as the *Fable, Manners,* and *Sentiments,* no Translator can prejudice it but by wilful Omissions or Contractions. As it also breaks out in every particular *Image, Description,* and *Simile;* whoever lessens or

10 **Contention of the Cities:** seven cities contended for the honor of being Homer's birthplace.
11 **de la Motte:** Antoine Houdart de la Motte (1672–1731), French critic and dramatist who translated the *Iliad.*
12 **chief Characteristic:** i.e., "invention."

too much softens those, takes off from this chief Character. It is the first grand Duty of an Interpreter to give his Author entire and un-maim'd; and for the rest, the *Diction* and *Versification* only are his proper Province; since these must be his own, but the others he is to take as he finds them.

It should then be consider'd what Methods may afford some Equiva-lent in our Language for the Graces of these in the *Greek*. It is certain no literal Translation can be just to an excellent Original in a superior Language: but it is a great Mistake to imagine (as many have done) that a rash Paraphrase can make amends for this general Defect; which is no less in danger to lose the Spirit of an Ancient, by deviating into the modern Manners of Expression. If there be sometimes a *Darkness,* there is often a *Light* in Antiquity, which nothing better preserves than a Version almost literal. I know no Liberties one ought to take, but those which are necessary for transfusing the Spirit of the Original, and supporting the Poetical Style of the Translation: and I will venture to say, there have not been more Men misled in former times by a servile dull Adherence to the Letter, than have been deluded in ours by a chimerical insolent Hope of raising and improving their Author. It is not to be doubted that the *Fire* of the Poem is what a Translator should principally regard, as it is most likely to expire in his managing: However it is his safest way to be content with preserving this to his utmost in the Whole, without endeavouring to be more than he finds his Author is, in any particular Place. 'Tis a great Secret in Writing to know when to be plain, and when poetical and figurative; and it is what *Homer* will teach us if we will but follow modestly in his Foot-steps. Where his Diction is bold and lofty, let us raise ours as high as we can; but where his is plain and humble, we ought not to be deterr'd from imitating him by the fear of incurring the Censure of a meer *English* Critick. Nothing that belongs to *Homer* seems to have been more commonly mistaken than the just Pitch of his Style: Some of his Translators having swell'd into Fustian in a proud Confidence of the *Sublime;* others sunk into Flatness, in a cold and timorous Notion of *Simplicity.* Methinks I see these different Followers of *Homer,* some sweating and straining after him by violent Leaps and Bounds, (the certain Signs of false Mettle) others slowly and servilely creeping in his Train, while the Poet himself is all the time proceeding with an unaffected and equal[13] Majesty before them. However of the two Extreams one could sooner pardon Frenzy than Frigidity: No Author is to be envy'd for such Commendations as he may gain by that Char-acter of Style, which his Friends must agree together to call *Simplicity,* and the rest of the World call *Dulness.* There is a *graceful* and *dig-nify'd* Simplicity, as well as a *bald* and *sordid* one, which differ as much from each other as the Air of a *plain* Man from that of a *Sloven:*

---

13 **equal:** constant, unruffled.

'Tis one thing to be tricked up, and another not to be dress'd at all. Simplicity is the Mean between Ostentation and Rusticity.

This pure and noble Simplicity is no where in such Perfection as in the *Scripture* and our Author. One may affirm with all respect to the inspired Writings, that the *Divine Spirit* made use of no other Words but what were intelligible and common to Men at that Time, and in that Part of the World; and as *Homer* is the Author nearest to those, his Style must of course bear a greater Resemblance to the sacred Books than that of any other Writer. This Consideration (together with what has been observ'd of the Parity of some of his Thoughts) may methinks induce a Translator on the one hand to give into several of those general Phrases and Manners of Expression, which have attain'd a Veneration even in our Language from their use in the *Old Testament;* as on the other, to avoid those which have been appropriated to the Divinity, and in a manner consign'd to Mystery[14] and Religion.

For a farther Preservation of this Air of Simplicity, a particular Care should be taken to express with all Plainness those *Moral Sentences* and *Proverbial Speeches* which are so numerous in this Poet. They have something Venerable, and as I may say *Oracular,* in that unadorn'd Gravity and Shortness with which they are deliver'd: a Grace which would be utterly lost by endeavouring to give them what we call a more ingenious (that is a more modern) Turn in the Paraphrase.

Perhaps the Mixture of some *Græcisms* and old Words after the manner of *Milton,* if done without too much Affectation, might not have an ill Effect in a Version of this particular Work, which most of any other seems to require a venerable *Antique* Cast. But certainly the use of *modern Terms* of *War* and *Government,* such as *Platoon, Campagne, Junto,* or the like (which some of his Translators have fallen into) cannot be allowable; those only excepted, without which it is impossible to treat the Subjects in any living Language.

There are two Peculiarities in *Homer's* Diction that are a sort of *Marks* or *Moles,* by which every common Eye distinguishes him at first sight: Those who are not his greatest Admirers look upon them as Defects, and those who are seem pleased with them as Beauties. I speak of his *Compound-Epithets* and of his *Repetitions.* Many of the former cannot be done literally into *English* without destroying the Purity of our Language. I believe such should be retain'd as slide easily of themselves into an *English-Compound,* without Violence to the Ear or to the receiv'd Rules of Composition; as well as those which have receiv'd a Sanction from the Authority of our best Poets, and are become familiar thro' their use of them; such as the *Cloud-compelling Jove, &c.* As for the rest, whenever any can be as fully and significantly exprest in a single word as in a compounded one, the Course to be taken is obvious. Some that cannot be so turn'd as to preserve their full

14 **Mystery:** Christian revelation.

Image by one or two Words, may have Justice done them by Circumlocution; as the Epithet Εἰνοσίφυλλος, to a Mountain would appear little or ridiculous translated literally *Leaf-shaking*, but affords a majestic Idea in the *Periphrasis: The lofty Mountain shakes his waving Woods*. Others that admit of differing Significations, may receive an Advantage by a judicious Variation according to the Occasions on which they are introduc'd. For Example, the Epithet of *Apollo*, ἐκηβόλος, or *far-shooting*, is capable of two Explications; one literal in respect of the Darts and Bow, the Ensigns of that God, the other allegorical with regard to the Rays of the Sun: Therefore in such Places where *Apollo* is represented as a God in Person, I would use the former Interpretation, and where the Effects of the Sun are describ'd, I would make choice of the latter. Upon the whole, it will be necessary to avoid that perpetual Repetition of the same Epithets which we find in *Homer*, and which, tho' it might be accommodated (as has been already shewn) to the Ear of those Times, is by no means so to ours: But one may wait for Opportunities of placing them, where they derive an additional Beauty from the Occasions on which they are employed; and in doing this properly, a Translator may at once shew his Fancy and his Judgment.

As for *Homer's Repetitions;* we may divide them into three sorts; of whole Narrations and Speeches, of single Sentences, and of one Verse or Hemistich. I hope it is not impossible to have such a Regard to these, as neither to lose so known a Mark of the Author on the one hand, nor to offend the Reader too much on the other. The Repetition is not ungraceful in those Speeches where the Dignity of the Speaker renders it a sort of Insolence to alter his Words; as in the Messages from Gods to Men, or from higher Powers to Inferiors in Concerns of State, or where the Ceremonial of Religion seems to require it, in the solemn Forms of Prayers, Oaths, or the like. In other Cases, I believe the best Rule is to be guided by the Nearness, or Distance, at which the Repetitions are plac'd in the Original: When they follow too close one may vary the Expression, but it is a Question whether a profess'd Translator be authorized to omit any: If they be tedious, the Author is to answer for it.

It only remains to speak of the *Versification*. *Homer* (as has been said) is perpetually applying the Sound to the Sense, and varying it on every new Subject. This is indeed one of the most exquisite Beauties of Poetry, and attainable by very few: I know only of *Homer* eminent for it in the *Greek*, and *Virgil* in *Latine*. I am sensible it is what may sometimes happen by Chance, when a Writer is warm, and fully possest of his Image: however it may be reasonably believed they design'd this, in whose Verse it so manifestly appears in a superior degree to all others. Few Readers have the Ear to be Judges of it, but those who have will see I have endeavour'd at this Beauty.

Upon the whole, I must confess my self utterly incapable of doing Justice to *Homer*. I attempt him in no other Hope but that which one may entertain without much Vanity, of giving a more tolerable Copy of him than any entire Translation in Verse has yet done. We have only those of *Chapman, Hobbes,* and *Ogilby*.[15] *Chapman* has taken the Advantage of an immeasurable Length of Verse, notwithstanding which there is scarce any Paraphrase more loose and rambling than his. He has frequent Interpolations of four or six Lines, and I remember one in the thirteenth Book of the *Odysses, ver.* 312, where he has spun twenty Verses out of two. He is often mistaken in so bold a manner, that one might think he deviated on purpose, if he did not in other Places of his Notes insist so much upon Verbal Trifles. He appears to have had a strong Affection of extracting new Meanings out of his Author, insomuch as to promise in his Rhyming Preface, a Poem of the Mysteries he had revealed in *Homer;* and perhaps he endeavoured to strain the obvious Sense to this End. His Expression is involved in Fustian, a Fault for which he was remarkable in his Original Writings, as in the Tragedy of *Bussy d'Amboise,* &c. In a word, the Nature of the Man may account for his whole Performance; for he appears from his Preface and Remarks to have been of an arrogant Turn, and an Enthusiast[16] in Poetry. His own Boast of having finish'd half the *Iliad* in less than fifteen Weeks, shews with what Negligence his Version was performed. But that which is to be allowed him, and which very much contributed to cover his Defects, is a daring fiery Spirit that animates his Translation, which is something like what one might imagine *Homer* himself would have writ before he arriv'd to Years of Discretion. *Hobbes* has given us a correct Explanation of the Sense in general, but for Particulars and Circumstances he continually lopps them, and often omits the most beautiful. As for its being esteem'd a close Translation, I doubt not many have been led into that Error by the Shortness of it, which proceeds not from his following the Original Line by Line, but from the Contractions above-mentioned. He sometimes omits whole Similes and Sentences, and is now and then guilty of Mistakes which no Writer of his Learning could have fallen into, but thro' Carelessness. His Poetry, as well as *Ogilby*'s, is too mean for Criticism.

It is a great Loss to the Poetical World that Mr. *Dryden* did not live to translate the *Iliad*. He has left us only the first Book and a small Part of the sixth; in which if he has in some Places not truly interpreted

---

[15] **Chapman:** George Chapman (1559–1634), poet and dramatist, used a fourteen-syllable line in his translation of the *Iliad*. **Hobbes:** Thomas Hobbes (1588–1679), the philosopher. **Ogilby:** see *Dunciad,* I 141*n*.

[16] **Enthusiast:** one whose judgment seems subordinate to his ardent interest in a subject (cf. the sentence above, in this same paragraph: "He appears to have had a strong affection . . .").

the Sense, or preserved the Antiquities,[17] it ought to be excused on account of the Haste he was obliged to write in. He seems to have had too much Regard to *Chapman*, whose Words he sometimes copies, and has unhappily follow'd him in Passages where he wanders from the Original. However had he translated the whole Work, I would no more have attempted *Homer* after him than *Virgil*, his Version of whom (notwithstanding some human Errors) is the most noble and spirited Translation I know in any Language. But the Fate of great Genius's is like that of great Ministers, tho' they are confessedly the first in the Commonwealth of Letters, they must be envy'd and calumniated only for being at the Head of it.

That which in my Opinion ought to be the Endeavour of any one who translates *Homer*, is above all things to keep alive that Spirit and Fire which makes his chief Character. In particular Places, where the Sense can bear any Doubt, to follow the strongest and most Poetical, as most agreeing with that Character. To copy him in all the Variations of his Style, and the different Modulations of his Numbers. To preserve in the more active or descriptive Parts, a Warmth and Elevation; in the more sedate or narrative, a Plainness and Solemnity; in the Speeches a Fulness and Perspicuity; in the Sentences[18] a Shortness and Gravity. Not to neglect even the little Figures and Turns[19] on the Words, nor sometimes the very Cast of the Periods.[1] Neither to omit or confound any Rites or Customs of Antiquity. Perhaps too he ought to include the whole in a shorter Compass, than has hitherto been done by any Translator who has tolerably preserved either the Sense or Poetry. What I would farther recommend to him, is to study his Author rather from his own Text than from any Commentaries, how learned soever, or whatever Figure they make in the Estimation of the World. To consider him attentively in Comparison with *Virgil* above all the Ancients, and with *Milton* above all the Moderns. Next these the Archbishop of *Cambray*'s[2] *Telemachus* may give him the truest Idea of the Spirit and Turn of our Author, and *Bossu*'s[3] admirable Treatise of the Epic Poem the justest Notion of his Design and Conduct. But after all, with whatever Judgment and Study a Man may proceed, or with whatever Happiness[4] he may perform such a Work; he must hope to please but a few, those only who have at once a Taste

[17] **Antiquities:** matters, or customs, of ancient times.
[18] **Sentences:** sententious or aphoristic utterances.
[19] **Figures:** figures of speech and thought.   **Turns:** see *Guardian* No. 40, n. 9, p. 383.
[1] **Periods:** complete sentences.
[2] **Archbishop of Cambray:** François de Salignac de la Mothe Fénelon (1651–1715), French prelate and author of *Les Aventures de Télémaque*.
[3] **Bossu:** René Le Bossu (1631–80), French critic, published his *Traité du poème épique* in 1675.
[4] **Happiness:** luckiness.

of Poetry, and competent Learning. For to satisfy such as want either, is not in the Nature of this Undertaking; since a meer Modern Wit can like nothing that is not *Modern*, and a Pedant nothing that is not *Greek*.

What I have done is submitted to the Publick, from whose Opinions I am prepared to learn; tho' I fear no Judges so little as our best Poets, who are most sensible of the Weight of this Task. As for the worst, whatever they shall please to say, they may give me some Concern as they are unhappy Men, but none as they are malignant Writers. I was guided in this Translation by Judgments very different from theirs, and by Persons for whom they can have no Kindness, if an old Observation be true, that the strongest Antipathy in the World is that of Fools to Men of Wit. Mr. *Addison*[5] was the first whose Advice determin'd me to undertake this Task, who was pleas'd to write to me upon that Occasion in such Terms as I cannot repeat without Vanity. I was obliged to Sir *Richard Steele* for a very early Recommendation of my Undertaking to the Publick. Dr. *Swift* promoted my Interest with that Warmth with which he always serves his Friend. The Humanity and Frankness of Sir *Samuel Garth*[6] are what I never knew wanting on any Occasion. I must also acknowledge with infinite Pleasure the many friendly Offices as well as sincere Criticisms of Mr. *Congreve*,[7] who had led me the way in translating some Parts of *Homer*, as I wish for the sake of the World he had prevented[8] me in the rest. I must add the Names of Mr. *Rowe* and Dr. *Parnell*,[9] tho' I shall take a farther Opportunity of doing Justice to the last, whose Good-nature (to give it a great Panegyrick) is no less extensive than his Learning. The Favour of these Gentlemen is not entirely undeserved by one who bears them so true an Affection. But what can I say of the Honour so many of the *Great* have done me, while the *First Names* of the Age appear as my Subscribers,[10] and the most distinguish'd Patrons and Ornaments of Learning as my chief Encouragers. Among these it is a particular Pleasure to me to find, that my highest Obligations are to such who have done most Honour to the Name of Poet: That his Grace the *Duke* of *Buckingham* was not displeas'd I should undertake the Author to whom he has given (in his excellent *Essay*) the finest Praise he ever yet receiv'd.

[5] **Addison . . . Advice:** Pope also believed, however, that Addison had conspired in a translation of the *Iliad* designed to rival and discredit his own (see *Peri Bathous*, n. 16, p. 420).   [6] **Garth:** see *Summer*, l. 9n.

[7] **Congreve:** when the last volume of his *Iliad* appeared in 1720, Pope dedicated the whole work to the dramatist William Congreve.

[8] **prevented:** anticipated.

[9] **Rowe:** see *First Ep. of the Second Bk.*, l. 86n.   **Parnell:** Thomas Parnell (1679–1718), poet and clergyman, and member of the Scriblerus Club.

[10] **Subscribers:** the first volume of Pope's *Iliad* listed 575 subscribers to the edition. See also *Ep. to Dr. Arbuthnot*, l. 114n.

Read Homer once, *and you can read no more;*
For all things else appear so mean and poor,
Verse will seem Prose: yet often *on him look,*
And you will hardly need another Book.[11]

That the Earl of *Halifax*[12] was one of the first to favour me, of whom it is hard to say whether the Advancement of the Polite Arts is more owing to his Generosity or his Example. That such a Genius as my Lord *Bolingbroke,*[13] not more distinguished in the great Scenes of Business than in all the useful and entertaining Parts of Learning, has not refus'd to be the Critick of these Sheets, and the Patron of their Writer. And that so excellent an Imitator of *Homer* as the noble Author[14] of the Tragedy of *Heroic Love,* has continu'd his Partiality to me from my writing Pastorals to my attempting the *Iliad.* I cannot deny my self the Pride of confessing, that I have had the Advantage not only of their Advice for the Conduct in general, but their Correction of several Particulars of this Translation.

I could say a great deal of the Pleasure of being distinguish'd by the *Earl* of *Carnarvon,*[15] but it is almost absurd to particularize any one generous Action in a Person whose whole Life is a continued Series of them. The Right Honourable Mr. *Stanhope,*[16] the present Secretary of State, will pardon my Desire of having it known that he was pleas'd to promote this Affair. The particular Zeal of Mr. *Harcourt*[17] (the Son of the late Lord Chancellor) gave me a Proof how much I am honour'd in a Share of his Friendship. I must attribute to the same Motive that of several others of my Friends, to whom all Acknowledgments are render'd unnecessary by the Privileges of a familiar Correspondence: And I am satisfy'd I can no way better oblige Men of their Turn, than by my Silence.

In short, I have found more Patrons than ever *Homer* wanted. He would have thought himself happy to have met the same Favour at *Athens,* that has been shewn me by its learned Rival, the University of *Oxford.*[18] If my Author had the *Wits* of After-Ages for his Defenders, his Translator has had the *Beauties*[19] of the present for his

[11] Pope quotes from *An Essay upon Poetry,* by John Sheffield, Duke of Buckingham (see *Essay on Criticism,* l. 723n.).

[12] Halifax: Charles, first Earl of Halifax (1661–1715). See *Epil. to the Satires,* II 77n.

[13] Bolingbroke: see *Essay on Man,* I 1n.

[14] noble Author: George Granville, Lord Lansdowne (see first note to *Windsor-Forest*).

[15] Earl of Carnarvon: James Brydges, later first Duke of Chandos (see *Ep. to Cobham,* l. 113n.).

[16] Stanhope: James, first Earl Stanhope (see *Epil. to the Satires,* II 80n.).

[17] Harcourt: Simon Harcourt (1684–1720), M.P., was very zealous in getting subscriptions for Pope's *Iliad.*

[18] Oxford: ten of the colleges at Oxford subscribed to Pope's translation.

[19] Beauties: the names of 47 ladies appear among the subscribers.

Advocates; a Pleasure too great to be changed for any Fame in Reversion.[20] And I can hardly envy him those pompous Honours he receiv'd after Death, when I reflect on the Enjoyment of so many agreeable Obligations, and easy Friendships which make the Satisfaction of Life. This Distinction is the more to be acknowledg'd, as it is shewn to one whose Pen has never gratify'd the Prejudices of particular *Parties,* or the Vanities of particular *Men.*[21] Whatever the Success may prove, I shall never repent of an Undertaking in which I have experienc'd the Candour and Friendship of so many Persons of Merit; and in which I hope to pass some of those Years of Youth that are generally lost in a Circle of Follies, after a manner neither wholly unuseful to others, nor disagreeable to my self.

[20] **Reversion:** the right or expectation of receiving something in the future.
[21] **Parties:** political parties.   **particular Men:** patrons.

PREFACE

TO THE

WORKS OF SHAKESPEAR

I T is not my design to enter into a Criticism upon this Author; tho' to do it effectually and not superficially, would be the best occasion that any just Writer could take, to form the judgment and taste of our nation. For of all *English* Poets *Shakespear* must be confessed to be the fairest and fullest subject for Criticism, and to afford the most numerous, as well as most conspicuous instances, both of Beauties and Faults of all sorts. But this far exceeds the bounds of a Preface, the business of which is only to give an account of the fate of his Works, and the disadvantages under which they have been transmitted to us. We shall hereby extenuate many faults which are his, and clear him from the imputation of many which are not: A design, which tho' it can be no guide to future Criticks to do him justice in one way, will at least be sufficient to prevent their doing him an injustice in the other.

I cannot however but mention some of his principal and character-istic Excellencies, for which (notwithstanding his defects) he is justly and universally elevated above all other Dramatic Writers. Not that this is the proper place of praising him, but because I would not omit any occasion of doing it.

If ever any Author deserved the name of an *Original*, it was *Shake-spear*. *Homer* himself drew not his art so immediately from the foun-tains of Nature, it proceeded thro' *Ægyptian* strainers and channels, and came to him not without some tincture of the learning, or some cast of the models, of those before him. The Poetry of *Shakespear* was Inspiration indeed: he is not so much an Imitator, as an Instrument, of Nature; and 'tis not so just to say that he speaks from her, as that she speaks thro' him.

His *Characters* are so much Nature her self, that 'tis a sort of injury to call them by so distant a name as Copies of her. Those of other

PREFACE TO THE WORKS OF SHAKESPEAR: First published on March 12, 1725. In the very next year Lewis Theobald published his *Shakespeare Restored*, in which Pope's deficiencies as an editor of Shakespeare were thoroughly exposed. Two years later, in 1728, Pope retaliated by crowning Theobald as King of the Dunces (see first note to the *Dunciad*).

Poets have a constant resemblance, which shews that they receiv'd them from one another, and were but multiplyers of the same image: each picture like a mock-rainbow is but the reflexion of a reflexion. But every single character in *Shakespear* is as much an Individual, as those in Life itself; it is as impossible to find any two alike; and such as from their relation or affinity in any respect appear most to be Twins, will upon comparison be found remarkably distinct. To this life and variety of Character, we must add the wonderful Preservation of it; which is such throughout his plays, that had all the Speeches been printed without the very names of the Persons, I believe one might have apply'd them with certainty to every speaker.

The *Power* over our *Passions* was never possess'd in a more eminent degree, or display'd in so different instances. Yet all along, there is seen no labour, no pains to raise them; no preparation to guide our guess to the effect, or be perceiv'd to lead toward it: But the heart swells, and the tears burst out, just at the proper places: We are surpriz'd, the moment we weep; and yet upon reflection find the passion so just, that we shou'd be surpriz'd if we had not wept, and wept at that very moment.

How astonishing is it again, that the passions directly opposite to these, Laughter and Spleen, are no less at his command! that he is not more a master of the *Great*, than of the *Ridiculous* in human nature; of our noblest tendernesses, than of our vainest foibles; of our strongest emotions, than of our idlest sensations!

Nor does he only excell in the Passions: In the coolness of Reflection and Reasoning he is full as admirable. His *Sentiments* are not only in general the most pertinent and judicious upon every subject; but by a talent very peculiar, something between Penetration and Felicity, he hits upon that particular point on which the bent of each argument turns, or the force of each motive depends. This is perfectly amazing, from a man of no education or experience in those great and publick scenes of life which are usually the subject of his thoughts: So that he seems to have known the world by Intuition, to have look'd thro' humane[1] nature at one glance, and to be the only Author that gives ground for a very new opinion, That the Philosopher and even the Man of the world, may be *Born*, as well as the Poet.

It must be own'd that with all these great excellencies, he has almost as great defects; and that as he has certainly written better, so he has perhaps written worse, than any other. But I think I can in some measure account for these defects, from several causes and accidents; without which it is hard to imagine that so large and so enlighten'd a mind could ever have been susceptible of them. That all these Contingencies should unite to his disadvantage seems to me almost as

---

1 **humane:** human.

singularly unlucky, as that so many various (nay contrary) Talents should meet in one man, was happy[2] and extraordinary.

It must be allowed that Stage-Poetry of all other, is more particularly levell'd to please the *Populace,* and its success more immediately depending upon the *Common Suffrage.* One cannot therefore wonder, if *Shakespear* having at his first appearance no other aim in his writings than to procure a subsistence, directed his endeavours solely to hit the taste and humour that then prevailed. The Audience was generally composed of the meaner sort of people; and therefore the Images of Life were to be drawn from those of their own rank: accordingly we find, that not our Author's only but almost all the old Comedies have their Scene among *Tradesmen* and *Mechanicks:*[3] And even their Historical Plays strictly follow the common *Old Stories* or *Vulgar Traditions* of that kind of people. In Tragedy, nothing was so sure to *Surprize* and cause *Admiration,* as the most strange, unexpected, and consequently most unnatural, Events and Incidents; the most exaggerated Thoughts; the most verbose and bombast Expression; the most pompous Rhymes, and thundering Versification. In Comedy, nothing was so sure to *please,* as mean buffoonry, vile ribaldry, and unmannerly jests of fools and clowns.[4] Yet even in these, our Author's Wit buoys up and is born above his subject: his Genius in those low parts is like some Prince of a Romance in the disguise of a Shepherd or Peasant; a certain Greatness and Spirit now and then break out, which manifest his higher extraction and qualities.

It may be added, that not only the common Audience had no notion of the rules of writing, but few even of the better sort piqu'd themselves upon any great degree of knowledge or nicety[5] that way; till *Ben Johnson* getting possession of the Stage, brought critical learning into vogue: And that this was not done without difficulty, may appear from those frequent lessons (and indeed almost Declamations) which he was forced to prefix to his first plays, and put into the mouth of his Actors, the *Grex,*[6] *Chorus,* &c. to remove the prejudices, and inform the judgment of his hearers. Till then, our Authors had no thoughts of writing on the model of the Ancients: their Tragedies were only Histories in Dialogue; and their Comedies follow'd the thread of any Novel[7] as they found it, no less implicitly than if it had been true History.

To judge therefore of *Shakespear* by *Aristotle's* rules, is like trying a man by the Laws of one Country, who acted under those of another. He writ to the *People;* and writ at first without patronage from the

2 **happy:** lucky, fortunate.
3 **Mechanicks:** workmen of a low social class.
4 **clowns:** countrymen, peasants.
5 **nicety:** delicacy, discrimination.
6 **Grex:** company or troupe of actors.
7 **Novel:** a tale or story like those to be found in Boccaccio's *Decameron.*

better sort, and therefore without aims of pleasing them: without assistance or advice from the Learned, as without the advantage of education or acquaintance among them: without that knowledge of the best models, the Ancients, to inspire him with an emulation of them; in a word, without any views of Reputation, and of what Poets are pleas'd to call Immortality: Some or all of which have encourag'd the vanity, or animated the ambition, of other writers.

Yet it must be observ'd, that when his performances had merited the protection of his Prince, and when the encouragement of the Court had succeeded to that of the Town; the works of his riper years are manifestly raised above those of his former. The Dates of his plays sufficiently evidence that his productions improved, in proportion to the respect he had for his auditors. And I make no doubt this observation would be found true in every instance, were but Editions extant from which we might learn the exact time when every piece was composed, and whether writ for the Town, or the Court.

Another Cause (and no less strong than the former) may be deduced from our Author's being a *Player*, and forming himself first upon the judgments of that body of men whereof he was a member. They have ever had a Standard to themselves, upon other principles than those of *Aristotle*. As they live by the Majority, they know no rule but that of pleasing the present humour, and complying with the wit in fashion; a consideration which brings all their judgment to a short point. Players are just such judges of what is *right*, as Taylors are of what is *graceful*. And in this view it will be but fair to allow, that most of our Author's faults are less to be ascribed to his wrong judgment as a Poet, than to his right judgment as a Player.

By these men it was thought a praise to *Shakespear*, that he scarce ever *blotted a line*. This they industriously propagated, as appears from what we are told by *Ben Johnson* in his *Discoveries*,[8] and from the preface of *Heminges* and *Condell*[9] to the first folio Edition. But in reality (however it has prevailed) there never was a more groundless report, or to the contrary of which there are more undeniable evidences. As, the Comedy of the *Merry Wives* of *Windsor*, which he entirely new writ; the *History of* Henry *the 6th*, which was first published under the Title of the *Contention of* York *and* Lancaster; and that of *Henry the 5th*, extreamly improved; that of *Hamlet* enlarged to

8 In *Timber, or Discoveries,* Ben Jonson says "I remember the players have often mentioned it as an honour to Shakespeare that in his writing, whatsoever he penned, he never blotted ou'. [a] line. My answer hath been, 'Would he had blotted a thousand': which they thought a malevolent speech."

9 **preface of Heminges and Condell:** John Heminge (d. 1630) and Henry Condell (d. 1627), the two actors who published the first collected edition of Shakespeare's plays (the First Folio of 1623), stated in their preface: "And what he thought, he uttered with that easiness, that we have scarce received from him a blot in his papers." See *Dunciad,* I 134n.

almost as much again as at first, and many others. I believe the common opinion of his want of Learning proceeded from no better ground. This too might be thought a Praise by some; and to this his Errors have as injudiciously been ascribed by others. For 'tis certain, were it true, it could concern but a small part of them; the most are such as are not properly Defects, but Superfœtations:[10] and arise not from want of learning or reading, but from want of thinking or judging: or rather (to be more just to our Author) from a compliance to those wants in others. As to a wrong choice of the subject, a wrong conduct of the incidents, false thoughts, forc'd expressions, &c. if these are not to be ascrib'd to the foresaid accidental reasons, they must be charg'd upon the Poet himself, and there is no help for it. But I think the two Disadvantages which I have mentioned (to be obliged to please the lowest of people, and to keep the worst of company) if the consideration be extended as far as it reasonably may, will appear sufficient to mis-lead and depress the greatest Genius upon the earth. Nay the more modesty with which such a one in endued, the more he is in danger of submitting and conforming to others, against his own better judgment.

But as to his *Want of Learning*, it may be necessary to say something more: There is certainly a vast difference between *Learning* and *Languages*. How far he was ignorant of the latter, I cannot determine; but 'tis plain he had much Reading at least, if they will not call it Learning. Nor is it any great matter, if a man has Knowledge, whether he has it from one language or from another. Nothing is more evident than that he had a taste of natural Philosophy,[11] Mechanicks,[12] ancient and modern History, Poetical learning and Mythology: We find him very knowing in the customs, rites, and manners of Antiquity. In *Coriolanus* and *Julius Cæsar*, not only the Spirit, but Manners, of the *Romans* are exactly drawn; and still a nicer distinction is shown, between the manners of the *Romans* in the time of the former, and of the latter. His reading in the ancient Historians is no less conspicuous, in many references to particular passages: and the speeches copy'd from *Plutarch*[13] in *Coriolanus* may, I think, as well be made an instance of his learning, as those copy'd from *Cicero* in *Catiline*, of *Ben Johnson*'s. The manners of other nations in general, the *Egyptians, Venetians, French*, &c. are drawn with equal propriety. Whatever object of nature, or branch of science, he either speaks of or describes; it is always with competent, if not extensive knowledge: his descriptions are still exact; all his metaphors appropriated,[14] and remarkably drawn from

---

10 **Superfœtations:** excesses.
11 **natural Philosophy:** the study of nature, now usually called *science*.
12 **Mechanicks:** the science which treats of the action of forces on bodies.
13 **Plutarch:** the celebrated Greek biographer and moralist (d. 120 A.D.).
14 **appropriated:** specially suited.

the true nature and inherent qualities of each subject. When he treats of Ethic or Politic,[15] we may constantly observe a wonderful justness of distinction, as well as extent of comprehension. No one is more a master of the Poetical story,[16] or has more frequent allusions to the various parts of it: Mr. *Waller*[17] (who has been celebrated for this last particular) has not shown more learning this way than *Shakespear.* We have Translations from *Ovid*[18] published in his name, among those Poems which pass for his, and for some of which we have undoubted authority, (being published by himself, and dedicated to his noble Patron the Earl of *Southampton:*) He appears also to have been conversant in *Plautus,*[19] from whom he has taken the plot of one of his plays:[1] he follows the *Greek* Authors, and particularly *Dares Phrygius,*[2] in another: (altho' I will not pretend to say in what language he read them.) The modern *Italian* writers of Novels[3] he was manifestly acquainted with; and we may conclude him to be no less conversant with the Ancients of his own country, from the use he has made of *Chaucer* in *Troilus* and *Cressida,* and in the *Two Noble Kinsmen,* if that Play be his, as there goes a Tradition it was, (and indeed it has little resemblance of *Fletcher,*[4] and more of our Author than some of those which have been received as genuine.)

I am inclined to think, this opinion proceeded originally from the zeal of the Partizans of our Author and *Ben Johnson;* as they endeavoured to exalt the one at the expence of the other. It is ever the nature of Parties to be in extremes; and nothing is so probable, as that because *Ben Johnson* had much the most learning, it was said on the one hand that *Shakespear* had none at all; and because *Shakespear* had much the most wit and fancy, it was retorted on the other, that *Johnson* wanted both. Because *Shakespear* borrowed nothing, it was said that *Ben Johnson* borrowed every thing. Because *Johnson* did not write extempore, he was reproached with being a year about every piece; and because *Shakespear* wrote with ease and rapidity, they cryed, he never once made a blot. Nay the spirit of opposition ran so high, that whatever those of the one side objected to the other, was taken at the rebound, and turned into Praises; as injudiciously, as their antagonists before had made them Objections.

[15] **Ethic or Politic:** ethics or politics.
[16] **Poetical story:** myth, legend, perhaps history also.
[17] **Waller:** see *Essay on Criticism,* l. 361n.
[18] **Translations from Ovid:** *Venus and Adonis* and *The Rape of Lucrece.*
[19] **Plautus:** see *Autumn,* ll. 7–8n.
[1] **one of his plays:** probably *The Comedy of Errors.*
[2] **Dares Phrygius:** supposed author of an ancient Greek history (not extant) of the Trojan War. A Latin work, of a much later period, was long regarded as a translation of Dares.
[3] **Novels:** see above, n. 7, p. 462.
[4] **Fletcher:** see *Dunciad,* I 131n.

Poets are always afraid of Envy; but sure they have as much reason to be afraid of Admiration. They are the *Scylla* and *Charybdis*[5] of Authors; those who escape one, often fall by the other. *Pessimum genus inimicorum Laudantes,*[6] says *Tacitus:* and *Virgil* desires to wear a charm against those who praise a Poet without rule or reason.

> — *Si ultra placitum laudarit, baccare frontem*
> *Cingito, ne Vati noceat* —[7]

But however this contention might be carried on by the Partizans on either side, I cannot help thinking these two great Poets were good friends, and lived on amicable terms and in offices of society with each other. It is an acknowledged fact, that *Ben Johnson* was introduced upon the Stage, and his first works encouraged, by *Shakespear.* And after his death, that Author writes *To the memory of his beloved Mr. William Shakespear,* which shows as if the friendship had continued thro' life. I cannot for my own part find any thing *Invidious* or *Sparing* in those verses, but wonder Mr. *Dryden*[8] was of that opinion. He exalts him not only above all his Contemporaries, but above *Chaucer* and *Spenser,* whom he will not allow to be great enough to be rank'd with him; and challenges the names of *Sophocles, Euripides,* and *Æschylus,* nay all *Greece* and *Rome* at once, to equal him. And (which is very particular) expresly vindicates him from the imputation of wanting *Art,* not enduring that all his excellencies shou'd be attributed to *Nature.* It is remarkable too, that the praise he gives him in his *Discoveries* seems to proceed from a *personal kindness;* he tells us that he lov'd the man, as well as honoured his memory; celebrates the honesty, openness, and frankness of his temper; and only distinguishes, as he reasonably ought, between the real merit of the Author, and the silly and derogatory applauses of the Players. *Ben Johnson* might indeed be sparing in his Commendations (tho' certainly he is not so in this instance) partly from his own nature, and partly from judgment. For men of judgment think they do any man more service in praising him justly, than lavishly. I say, I would fain believe they were Friends, tho' the violence and ill-breeding of their Followers and Flatterers were enough to give rise to the contrary report. I would hope that it may be with *Parties,* both in Wit and State, as with those Monsters described

---

[5] **Scylla and Charybdis:** Scylla is traditionally a rock on the Italian coast opposite a whirlpool called Charybdis off the Sicilian coast. In mythology, each is personified as a female monster.

[6] "Those worst of enemies, flatterers" (Tacitus, *Agricola,* sec. 41).

[7] "If he should praise immoderately, encircle the brow with foxglove, lest the poet be harmed" (Virgil, *Eclogues,* VII 27–8).

[8] **Dryden:** in *A Discourse Concerning the Original and Progress of Satire,* Dryden terms Jonson's verses to the memory of Shakespeare "an insolent, sparing, and invidious panegyric."

by the Poets; and that their *Heads* at least may have something humane, tho' their *Bodies* and *Tails* are wild beasts and serpents.

As I believe that what I have mentioned gave rise to the opinion of *Shakespear*'s want of learning; so what has continued it down to us may have been the many blunders and illiteracies of the first Publishers of his works. In these Editions their ignorance shines almost in every page; nothing is more common than *Actus tertia. Exit Omnes. Enter three Witches solus.* Their *French* is as bad as their *Latin,* both in construction and spelling: Their very *Welsh* is false. Nothing is more likely than that those palpable blunders of *Hector*'s quoting *Aristotle,*[9] with others of that gross kind, sprung from the same root. It not being at all credible that these could be the errors of any man who had the least tincture of a School, or the least conversation with such as had. *Ben Johnson* (whom they will not think partial to him) allows him at least to have had *some Latin;* which is utterly inconsistent with mistakes like these. Nay the constant blunders in proper names of persons and places, are such as must have proceeded from a man, who had not so much as read any history, in any language: so could not be *Shakespear*'s.

I shall now lay before the reader some of those almost innumerable Errors, which have risen from one source, the ignorance of the Players, both as his actors, and as his editors. When the nature and kinds of these are enumerated and considered, I dare to say that not *Shakespear* only, but *Aristotle* or *Cicero,* had their works undergone the same fate, might have appear'd to want sense as well as learning.

It is not certain that any one of his Plays was published by himself. During the time of his employment in the Theatre, several of his pieces were printed separately in Quarto. What makes me think that most of these were not publish'd by him, is the excessive carelessness of the press: every page is so scandalously false spelled, and almost all the learned or unusual words so intolerably mangled, that it's plain there either was no Corrector to the press at all, or one totally illiterate. If any were supervised by himself, I should fancy the two parts of *Henry the 4th,* and *Midsummer-Night's Dream* might have been so: because I find no other printed with any exactness; and (contrary to the rest) there is very little variation in all the subsequent editions of them. There are extant two Prefaces, to the first quarto edition of *Troilus* and *Cressida* in 1609, and to that of *Othello;* by which it appears, that the first was publish'd without his knowledge or consent, and even before it was acted, so late as seven or eight years before he died: and that the latter was not printed till after his death. The whole number of genuine plays which we have been able to find printed in his life-time, amounts but to eleven.[10] And of some of these, we meet with two or

9 **quoting Aristotle:** see *Troilus and Cressida,* II ii 165*ff.*
10 **eleven:** Pope was mistaken; there were more.

more editions by different printers, each of which has whole heaps of trash different from the other: which I should fancy was occasion'd, by their being taken from different copies, belonging to different Play-houses.

The folio edition (in which all the plays we now receive as his, were first collected) was published by two Players, *Heming* and *Condell*, in 1623, seven years after his decease. They declare, that all the other editions were stolen and surreptitious, and affirm theirs to be purged from the errors of the former. This is true as to the literal errors, and no other; for in all respects else it is far worse than the Quarto's:

First, because the additions of trifling and bombast passages are in this edition far more numerous. For whatever had been added, since those Quarto's, by the actors, or had stolen from their mouths into the written parts, were from thence conveyed into the printed text, and all stand charged upon the Author. He himself complained of this usage in *Hamlet,* where he wishes that *those who play the Clowns*[11] *wou'd speak no more than is set down for them.* (Act. 3. Sc. 4.) But as a proof that he could not escape it, in the old editions of *Romeo* and *Juliet* there is no hint of a great number of the mean conceits[12] and ribaldries now to be found there. In others, the low scenes of Mobs, Plebeians and Clowns, are vastly shorter than at present: And I have seen one in particular (which seems to have belonged to the playhouse, by having the parts divided with lines, and the Actors' names in the margin) where several of those very passages were added in a written hand, which are since to be found in the folio.

In the next place, a number of beautiful passages which are extant in the first single editions, are omitted in this: as it seems, without any other reason, than their willingness to shorten some scenes: These men (as it was said of *Procrustes*[13]) either lopping, or stretching an Author, to make him just fit for their Stage.

This edition is said to be printed from the *Original Copies;* I believe they meant those which had lain ever since the Author's days in the playhouse, and had from time to time been cut, or added to, arbitrarily. It appears that this edition, as well as the Quarto's, was printed (at least partly) from no better copies than the *Prompter's Book,* or *Piece-meal Parts* written out for the use of the actors: For in some places their very names[14] are thro' carelessness set down instead of the *Per-sonæ Dramatis:* And in others the notes of direction to the *Property-*

[11] Clowns: see above, n. 4, p. 462.

[12] conceits: see *Essay on Criticism,* l. 289n.

[13] Procrustes: a legendary Greek outlaw who tied travellers on a bed. If their length exceeded that of the bed their legs were cut off to fit it; if they were short, they were stretched on a rack to fit it.

[14] names: Much ado about nothing. Act 2. *Enter Prince* Leonato, Claudio, *and* Jack Wilson, *instead of* Balthasar. *And in Act* 4. Cowley, and Kemp, *con-stantly thro' a whole Scene.* Edit. Fol. of 1623, and 1632. P.

men for their *Moveables,* and to the *Players* for their *Entries,*[15] are inserted into the Text, thro' the ignorance of the Transcribers.

The Plays not having been before so much as distinguish'd by *Acts* and *Scenes,* they are in this edition divided according as they play'd them; often where there is no pause in the action, or where they thought fit to make a breach in it, for the sake of Musick, Masques, or Monsters.[16]

Sometimes the scenes are transposed and shuffled backward and forward; a thing which could no otherwise happen, but by their being taken from separate and piece-meal-written parts.

Many verses are omitted intirely, and others transposed; from whence invincible obscurities have arisen, past the guess of any Commentator to clear up, but just where the accidental glympse of an old edition enlightens us.

Some Characters were confounded and mix'd, or two put into one, for want of a competent number of actors. Thus in the Quarto edition of *Midsummer-Night's Dream,* Act. 5. *Shakespear* introduces a kind of Master of the Revels called *Philostratus:* all whose part is given to another character (that of *Ægeus*) in the subsequent editions: So also in *Hamlet* and *King Lear.* This too makes it probable that the Prompter's Books were what they call'd the Original Copies.

From liberties of this kind, many speeches also were put into the mouths of wrong persons, where the Author now seems chargeable with making them speak out of character: Or sometimes perhaps for no better reason, than that a governing Player, to have the mouthing of some favourite speech himself, would snatch it from the unworthy lips of an Underling.

Prose from verse they did not know, and they accordingly printed one for the other throughout the volume.

Having been forced to say so much of the Players, I think I ought in justice to remark, that the Judgment, as well as Condition, of that class of people was then far inferior to what it is in our days. As then the best Playhouses were Inns and Taverns (the *Globe,* the *Hope,* the *Red Bull,* the *Fortune,* &c.) so the top of the profession were then meer Players, not Gentlemen of the stage: They were led into the Buttery[17] by the Steward, not plac'd at the Lord's table, or Lady's toilette:[18] and consequently were intirely depriv'd of those advantages they now enjoy, in the familiar conversation of our Nobility, and an intimacy (not to say dearness) with people of the first condition.

---

[15] **Entries:** *Such as,*
   — My Queen is murder'd! *Ring the little Bell* —
   — His nose grew as sharp as a pen, and *a table of Green-field's* &c.   P.
[16] **Musick, Masques, or Monsters:** interludes of some kind or other. *Monsters* could refer to showings of marvels or prodigies, perhaps to mere spectacles.
[17] **Buttery:** store-room for food and drink.
[18] **toilette:** 18th-century ladies frequently received visitors while dressing.

From what has been said, there can be no question but had *Shakespear* published his works himself (especially in his latter time, and after his retreat from the stage) we should not only be certain which are genuine; but should find in those that are, the errors lessened by some thousands. If I may judge from all the distinguishing marks of his style, and his manner of thinking and writing, I make no doubt to declare that those wretched plays, *Pericles, Locrine, Sir John Oldcastle, Yorkshire Tragedy, Lord Cromwell, The Puritan,* and *London Prodigal,*[19] cannot be admitted as his. And I should conjecture of some of the others, (particularly *Love's Labour Lost, The Winter's Tale,* and *Titus Andronicus*) that only some characters, single scenes, or perhaps a few particular passages, were of his hand. It is very probable what occasion'd some Plays to be supposed *Shakespear*'s was only this; that they were pieces produced by unknown authors, or fitted up for the Theatre while it was under his administration: and no owner claiming them, they were adjudged to him, as they give Strays[1] to the Lord of the Manor. A mistake, which (one may also observe) it was not for the interest of the House to remove. Yet the Players themselves, *Hemings* and *Condell,* afterwards did *Shakespear* the justice to reject those eight[2] plays in their edition; tho' they were then printed in his name, in every body's hands, and acted with some applause; (as we learn from what *Ben Johnson* says of *Pericles* in his Ode on the *New Inn.*) That *Titus Andronicus* is one of this class I am the rather induced to believe, by finding the same Author openly express his contempt of it in the *Induction* to *Bartholomew-Fair,* in the year 1614, when *Shakespear* was yet living. And there is no better authority for these latter sort, than for the former, which were equally published in his life-time.

If we give into this opinion, how many low and vicious parts and passages might no longer reflect upon this great Genius, but appear unworthily charged upon him? And even in those which are really his, how many faults may have been unjustly laid to his account from arbitrary Additions, Expunctions, Transpositions of scenes and lines, confusion of Characters and Persons, wrong application of Speeches, corruptions of innumerable Passages by the Ignorance, and wrong Corrections of 'em again by the Impertinence, of his first Editors? From one or other of these considerations, I am verily perswaded, that the greatest and the grossest part of what are thought his errors would vanish, and leave his character in a light very different from that disadvantageous one, in which it now appears to us.

This is the state in which *Shakespear*'s writings lye at present; for since the above-mentioned Folio Edition, all the rest have implicitly followed it, without having recourse to any of the former, or ever mak-

---

19 Of these plays only *Pericles* is thought to be, in part, by Shakespeare.

1 Strays: stray cattle.

2 eight: only seven are listed above, in the second sentence of this paragraph.

ing the comparison between them. It is impossible to repair the Injuries already done him; too much time has elaps'd, and the materials are too few. In what I have done I have rather given a proof of my willingness and desire, than of my ability, to do him justice. I have discharg'd the dull duty of an Editor, to my best judgment, with more labour than I expect thanks, with a religious abhorrence of all Innovation, and without any indulgence to my private sense or conjecture. The method taken in this Edition will show it self. The various Readings are fairly put in the margin, so that every one may compare 'em; and those I have prefer'd into the Text are constantly *ex fide Codicum*,[3] upon authority. The Alterations or Additions which *Shakespear* himself made, are taken notice of as they occur. Some suspected passages which are excessively bad, (and which seem Interpolations by being so inserted that one can intirely omit them without any chasm, or deficience in the context) are degraded to the bottom of the page; with an Asterisk referring to the places of their insertion. The Scenes are mark'd so distinctly that every removal of place is specify'd; which is more necessary in this Author than any other, since he shifts them more frequently: and sometimes without attending to this particular, the reader would have met with obscurities. The more obsolete or unusual words are explained. Some of the most shining passages are distinguish'd by comma's in the margin; and where the beauty lay not in particulars but in the whole, a star is prefix'd to the scene. This seems to me a shorter and less ostentatious method of performing the better half of Criticism[4] (namely the pointing out an Author's excellencies) than to fill a whole paper with citations of fine passages, with *general Applauses*, or *empty Exclamations* at the tail of them. There is also sub-join'd a Catalogue of those first Editions by which the greater part of the various readings and of the corrected passages are authorised, (most of which are such as carry their own evidence along with them.) These Editions now hold the place of Originals, and are the only materials left to repair the deficiencies or restore the corrupted sense of the Author: I can only wish that a greater number of them (if a greater were ever published) may yet be found, by a search more successful than mine, for the better accomplishment of this end.

I will conclude by saying of *Shakespear*, that with all his faults, and with all the irregularity of his *Drama*, one may look upon his works, in comparison of those that are more finish'd and regular, as upon an ancient majestick piece of *Gothick* Architecture, compar'd with a neat Modern building: The latter is more elegant and glaring,[5] but the former is more strong and more solemn. It must be allow'd, that in one

3 **ex fide Codicum:** according to textual authority.
4 **better half of Criticism:** the other half of criticism was considered to be the pointing out of faults (see the second sentence of the Preface).
5 **glaring:** bright, conspicuous.

of these there are materials enough to make many of the other. It has much the greater variety, and much the nobler apartments; tho' we are often conducted to them by dark, odd, and uncouth passages. Nor does the Whole fail to strike us with greater reverence, tho' many of the Parts are childish, ill-plac'd, and unequal to its grandeur.